CLUSTERS, NETWORKS AND INNOVATION

Clusters, Networks and Innovation

BRESCHI AND MALERBA

OXFORD

UNIVERSITY PRESS

Great Clarendon Street, Oxford OX2 6DP

Oxford University Press is a department of the University of Oxford.
It furthers the University's objective of excellence in research, scholarship,
and education by publishing worldwide in

Oxford New York

Auckland Cape Town Dar es Salaam Hong Kong Karachi
Kuala Lumpur Madrid Melbourne Mexico City Nairobi
New Delhi Shanghai Taipei Toronto

With offices in

Argentina Austria Brazil Chile Czech Republic France Greece
Guatemala Hungary Italy Japan Poland Portugal Singapore
South Korea Switzerland Thailand Turkey Ukraine Vietnam

Oxford is a registered trade mark of Oxford University Press
in the UK and in certain other countries

Published in the United States
by Oxford University Press Inc., New York

© Oxford University Press 2005

The moral rights of the authors have been asserted
Database right Oxford University Press (maker)

First published 2005
First published in paperback 2007

British Library Cataloguing in Publication Data

Data available

Library of Congress Cataloging in Publication Data

Data available

Typeset by SPI Publisher Services, Pondicherry, India
Printed in Great Britain
on acid-free paper by
Biddles Ltd, King's Lynn, Norfolk

ISBN 978–0–19–927555–7 (Hbk.)   978–0–19–927556–4 (Pbk.)

1 3 5 7 9 10 8 6 4 2

Acknowledgements

We would like to thank: David Musson (Oxford University Press) for his support at an early stage of this project; Matthew Derbyshire, Jenni Craig, and Colin Owens for their patience and help throughout the production process. We also wish to express our gratitude to Adriana Mongelli for her invaluable work as editorial secretary of the journal *Industrial and Corporate Change*.

In addition we would like to thank *The Journal of Economic Gergraphy* and *Industrial and Corporate Change* for their kind permission to reprint the following articles in original or revised form:

Newly revised versions of papers originally published in *Industrial and Corporate Change*, © Oxford University Press: Chapters 3, 6, and 14.

Papers originally published in *Industrial and Corporate Change*, © Oxford University Press: Chapters 4, 5, 7, and 8.

Papers originally published in *The Journal of Economic Geography*, © Oxford University Press: Chapters 11, 13, and 15.

Contents

Part II

Part IV

Part V

Notes on Contributors

James D. Adams

James D. Adams is Professor of Economics at Rensselaer Polytechnic Institute, Troy, NY. In addition he is a research associate of the National Bureau of Economic Research in Cambridge, Massachusetts. Prior to joining Rensselaer he was Professor of Economics at the University of Florida. He has also held visiting appointments at the US Bureau of Labor Statistics, the US Bureau of the Census, and the George J. Stigler Center for the Study of the Economy and the State at the University of Chicago. He recently served on the Telecommunications R&D Board of the National Academy of Sciences, Washington, DC and currently advises the Advanced Technology Program of the US National Institute of Standards and Technology on issues of data quality and policy evaluation. He received a BA in economics from the University of New Mexico in 1967 and a PhD in economics from the University of Chicago in 1976.

Dr. Adams has published many articles on the economics of technical change, with emphasis on the causes and consequences of industrial and academic research and development, as well as numerous articles in the fields of labor and public economics. His current research focuses on the limits of the firm in research and development, the measurement of scientific influence, the identification of alternative channels of knowledge externalities in the economy, the structure and meaning of scientific teams and collaborations, the speed of diffusion of scientific research, the interaction between investment in industrial research and development and investment in physical capital, and the determinants of research and teaching productivity in academia.

Giulio Bottazzi

Giulio Bottazzi is Associate Professor of Economic Policy and Director of the Center for the Analysis of Financial Markets at Sant'Anna School for Advanced Studies, Pisa. He is the author of several paperspublished in international and Italian journals. His research interests range from industrial dynamics to experimental economics, encompassing theoretical and empirical aspects of market interactions, applied econometrics and game theory. He holds a Laurea degree from ParmaUniversity and a PhD from Milano University.

Stefano Breschi

Stefano Breschi PhD is Associate Professor of Industrial Economics and Deputy Director of the Centre for Innovation and Internationalisation

Processes (CESPRI), Bocconi University, Milan, Italy. His main research interests are in the economics of technical change, industrial dynamics, social networks, economic geography and regional economics. He participated in several national as well as international research projects and his academic research has been published in *Economic Journal, Research Policy, Industrial and Corporate Change, Annales d'Economie et Statistique, Regional Studies, Economics of Innovation and New Technology, Papers in Regional Science, Revue d'Economie Industrielle, International Journal of Technology Management*.

Timothy Bresnahan

Timothy Bresnahan is Landau Professor of Technology and the Economy at Stanford University. He is Director of the Center for Research in Employment and Economic Growth in SIEPR. Previously, he has served as Chief Economist of the Antitrust Division of the US Department of Justice and head of the Information Technology in Use research program and of the Stanford Computer Industry Project. His research interests lie in the economics of industry, especially of high-technology industry. Recently, he has been writing on the competition and the structure of the computer and software industries, on the impact of information technology on labor demand and income distribution, and on the implications of entrepreneurship in high tech industries for growth and change. His recent writings on these and other subjects and further contact information can be found at http://www.stanford.edu/tbres/

Philip Cooke

Philip Cooke is University Research Professor and founding Director (1993) of the Centre for Advanced Studies, University of Wales, Cardiff. His research interests lie in studies of Economics of Biotechnology (partner in ESRC CESAGen Research Centre), Regional Innovation Systems, Knowledge Economies, and Policy Actions for Business Clusters and Networks. He co-edited a book entitled 'Regional Innovation Systems' in 1998, a fully revised 2nd edition of which was published in 2004. He co-authored a book on network governance, called 'The Associational Economy', also published in 1998, and is co-author of 'The Governance of Innovation in Europe' published in 2000. His authored book 'Knowledge Economies: Clusters, Learning and Cooperative Advantage' was published by Routledge in 2002. In 2004 he co-edited 'Regional Economies as Knowledge Laboratories' (Edward Elgar). Prof. Cooke was adviser to Lord Sainsbury's Biotechnology Clusters mission in 1999 and subsequently UK government Cluster Policy, and Innovation Review adviser. He has been EU adviser on Regional Foresight, Universities & Regional Development, and in 2004–5 chaired the EU committee on 'Constructing Regional Advantage'. He is OECD adviser on Knowledge Economies, and UNIDO adviser on Innovation Systems. In addition to the books, he is author of more than 100 research and scholarly articles in leading journals. He is also Editor of 'European Planning Studies' a bi-monthly journal devoted to European urban and regional governance, innovation and development issues. In 2003 he was elected *Academician* of the UK Academy of Social Sciences (AcSS). In 2004 he was made Distinguished Research Fellow (PRIME) of the University of Ottawa Management School.

Robin Cowan

Robin Cowan is Professor of Economics of Technical Change within the MERIT research institute and the department of General Economics at the University of Maastricht. He received his Bachelor's degree from Queen's University in Canada, and his PhD from Stanford University in the US. He was an assistant professor at New York University and the University of Western Ontario before moving the the University of Maastricht. His research on the networks initially involved examination of the relationship between network structure and performance, but has recently expanded to include models of network formation. The tools he employs include both simulation and analytical modelling. His earlier research has been broader than network economics, and involved the study of the economics of technology more generally, including network externalities and externalities of adoption; path dependence and technological lock-in; technology competitions and standardization; the economics of knowledge; consumption dynamics.

Giovanni Dosi

Giovanni Dosi is Professor of Economics at the Sant'Anna School of Advanced Studies in Pisa, where he also coordinates the Doctoral Program in Economics and Management and leads the Laboratory of Economics and Management (LEM).

His major research areas include economics of innovation and technological change, industrial organisation and industrial dynamics, theory of the firm and corporate governance, economic growth and development.

Professor Dosi is Co-Director of the task force in Industrial Policy, Initiative for Policy Dialogue (Joseph Stiglitz chairman), Columbia University, New York; Editor for Continental Europe of *Industrial and Corporate Change*; Research consultant for, among others, OECD, Brazilian Ministry of Planning, UNCTAD, French Ministry of Research, Italian Ministry of Research, EU Commission, Bank of Italy, and Honorary Research Professor at the University of Sussex. He is author and editor of several works in the areas of Economics of Innovation, Industrial Economics, Evolutionary Theory, Organizational Studies. A selection of his works has been published in *Innovation, Organization and Economic Dynamics. Selected Essays*, Cheltenham, Edward Elgar, 2000.

Giorgio Fagiolo

Giorgio Fagiolo is Assistant Professor in Economics at the Department of Economics of the University of Verona (Italy). He holds a BA in Statistics from the University of Rome "La Sapienza" and a PhD in Economics from the European University Institute (Florence, Italy). His main research interests are: models of social interactions with endogenous network formation; agent-based models of industrial- and market-dynamics; spatial agglomeration and industrial concentration. His academic research has been published in the *Journal of Economics Dynamics and Control, Computational Economics, Industrial and Corporate Change, Structural Change and Economic Dynamics, Mathematical Population Studies, Advances in Complex Systems*, as well as in several edited books.

Maryann P. Feldman

Maryann Feldman is Jeffery S. Skoll Chair in Technical Innovation and Entrepreneurship; and Professor of Business Economics at the Rotman School of Management, University of Toronto. She holds a MS and PhD from Carnegie Mellon University. Her research and teaching interests focus on the areas of innovation, the commercialization of research and the factors that promote technological change and economic growth. A large part of Dr. Feldman's work concerns the geography of innovation - investigating the reasons why innovation clusters spatially and the mechanisms that support and sustain industrial clusters. She is the author of over fifty academic articles that have been published in the *American Economic Review, the Review of Economics and Statistics, Management Science, Industrial and Corporate Change and Minerva*.

Alfonso Gambardella

Alfonso Gambardella (PhD, Stanford 1991) is Professor of Management at the Università Commerciale "Luigi Bocconi", Milan, Italy. His research interests are in the economics and management of technology and innovation. He published on the major international journals in this field, and participated in several international research projects. He published books with MIT Press, Cambridge University Press, and Oxford University Press. Among the others, his 2001 book, *Markets for Technology* (with Ashish Arora and Andrea Fosfuri) is widely cited. He has also taught courses on the economics of technology at the Department of Economics of Stanford University. His website is at www.alfonsogambardella.it

Jinn-Yuh Hsu

Dr. Jinn-yuh Hsu is currently an associate professor in Geography at National Taiwan University. He received his PhD degree from the University of California at Berkeley. He is an economic geographer who specializes in high-technology industries and regional development in late-industrializing countries, particularly Taiwan. He has focused his research on the Hsinchu Science-based Industrial Park since he started his dissertation writing in 1995. Dr. Hsu has published a series of papers (both in Chinese and English) on the labor market, technology learning, industrial organization and dynamic institutionalism of the Hsinchu Region and its connection with Silicon Valley. Currently he is doing a new research project to study the research and development activities of the Taiwanese information and communication technology firms in the triangle connection among Silicon Valley, Hsinchu and Shanghai.

Steven Klepper

Steven Klepper is the Arthur Arton Professor of Economics and Social Science at Carnegie Mellon University. He received his BA, MA, and PhD in economics from Cornell University, the latter in 1975. Before coming to Carnegie Mellon University in 1980, he was an assistant professor of economics at the State University of New York at Buffalo. Klepper's research has examined the evolution of new industries, looking at how the market and geographic structure of new industries evolve, how specific companies come to dominate markets, and how innovation influences and is influenced by the evolution of industry market and geographic structure. Klepper also has developed statistical diagnostics to calibrate the sensitivity of inferences in empirical analyses to errors of measurement that have been used in economics, criminology, and environmental studies. His research has been published in the leading journals in economics and management, including the *American Economic Review*, the *Journal of Political Economy*, *Econometrica*, and *Management Science*.

Mark H. Lazerson

Mark H. Lazerson is professor of Economic Sociology in the Faculty of Economics and Business of the Catholic University of Portugal in Oporto. He holds advanced degrees in sociology from the University of Wisconsin-Madison and in law from the NYU School of Law and has served as a consultant on industrial and economic development to both the ILO and the OECD. He is currently researching the formation of alliances and joint ventures among family-owned firms in Italy. He has published articles in *American Sociological Review*, *Administrative Science Quarterly*, *Journal of Industrial and Corporate Change* and several Italian journals.

Giovanni Lorenzoni

Giovanni Lorenzoni is a professor of Strategic Management in the Faculty of Economics at the University of Bologna and President of Alma Web, a graduate school of business. He has been a visiting scholar at Stanford and

NYU Schools of Business and visiting professor at Texas A & M. He has published widely in Italian and English on clusters and networks, business models of new firms, development of entrepreneurial skills, inter-firm agreements and relationships, and knowledge formation within and among companies. His most recent articles can be found in the *Journal of Industrial and Corporate Change*, *California Management Review*, and *Strategic Management Journal*.

Francesco Lissoni

Francesco Lissoni is Associate Professor of Applied Economics at the University of Brescia, deputy director of CESPRI-Bocconi University (Milan), and managing director of ESSID, the European Summer School of Industrial Dynamics. He holds a PhD from the University of Manchester. His research activity covers the economics of innovation adoption, technology transfer, and the geography of knowledge diffusion, and it has been mainly published on Research Policy, Economics of Innovation and New Technology, and Industrial and Corporate Change.

Franco Malerba

Franco Malerba is Professor of Industrial Economics at Bocconi University (Milan). He is Director of CESPRI (Research Centre on Innovation and Internationalization) at Bocconi University, a leading international center in the field He has been President of the International Schumpeter Society and he is currently President of EARIE (European Association of Research in Industrial Economics). He is Editor of the Journal *Industrial and Corporate Change* and Advisory Editor of *Research Policy* and the *Journal of Evolutionary Economics*. He is member of the Advisory Board of SPRU (University of Sussex), CRIC (University of Manchester) and the Max Plank Institute at Jena. He holds a PhD in Economics from Yale University, and has been visiting professor in several major universities.

He has published books and articles in the economics of innovation; industrial dynamics, industrial economics; theory of the firm; competition and industrial dynamics; European computer industry; European software industry; European microelectronics industry; European telecommunications industry; Italian national system of innovation; competition, industrial and technology policies; European public policy.

His research collaborations include the European Commission, OECD, American National Science Foundation, ENEA (Italian Energy Agency) Italian Ministry of Science and Technology, Italian Ministry of Industry, Confindustria, Assolombarda, Lombardy Region, American Enterprise Institute.

With Cambridge University Press he has published in 2004 the book *Sectoral systems of innovation*.

Ron Martin

Professor Ron Martin holds a Personal Professorship in Economic Geography in the University of Cambridge, and is a Fellow of the Cambridge-MIT Institute there. His current interests include the study of regional competitiveness; the life-cycles and evolutionary dynamics of clusters; regional dimensions of financial systems; the geographies of the new knowledge economy; and the geography of labour markets. He has published 25 books and more than 150 papers on these and related themes. He was recently editor of *Transactions of the Institute of British Geographers*, and co- editor of *Regional Studies*. He is presently an editor of the *Cambridge Journal of Economics* and the *Journal of Economic Geography*. He also edits the Regional Development and Public Policy book series (Routledge). He was awarded the British Academy's Special Thanksgiving to Britain Senior Research Fellowship in 1997–1998, and was elected an Academician of the British Academy of Social Sciences in 2001. In 2003, he was selected by the American Economic Association as one of the world's most cited economists over the 1990–2000 decade. In 2005 he was elected a Fellow of the British Academy.

Peter Maskell

Peter Maskell is Professor at Copenhagen Business School, PhD in Regional Economics and Doctor (Habilitation) in Business Economics. He is presently Director of the Danish Research Unit of Industrial Dynamics (DRUID) and Chairman of the board of DIME: The European Union Network of Excellence on "Dynamics of Institutions and Market in Europe". He is a member of Academia Europea and serves on the board of Danish and foreign incorporated enterprises. He has previously been Chairman of the Danish Social Science Research Council; member of the European Science Foundation's Standing Committee for the Social Sciences; the Danish Parliament's Standing Committee on Research; and Vice President of International Affairs of Copenhagen Business School and chairman of their Research Committee. He has published books and numerous articles in scientific journals on industrial development, innovation, competitiveness, learning, and economic geography. He is reviewer for a large number of scientific journals as well as several international publishers in these fields.

Fabio Montobbio

Fabio Montobbio is associate professor of Political Economy at the University of Insubria, Varese and senior researcher at CESPRI, Bocconi University, Milan. His PhD from the University of Manchester is on technological spillovers, competitiveness and structural change. His research interests are patent economics, the measurement of knowledge spillovers, the economics of science and sectoral patterns of innovation and structural change. He has published in *World Development, Cambridge Journal of Economics, Journal of Evolutionary Economics, Structural Change*, and *Economic Dynamics*.

Kelley Porter

Kelley Porter is an assistant professor of strategy and entrepreneurship at Queen's School of Business at Queen's University in Ontario, Canada. Kelley completed her PhD in Industrial Engineering at Stanford University. She received her MA in Sociology from Stanford University and her BA with honors from Wellesley College, where she majored in Psychology and minored in Economics. Prior to starting at Stanford, Kelley spent two years working as a Research Associate at Harvard Business School, where she wrote cases about the strategic challenges facing high technology firms. Her research lies at the intersection of entrepreneurship, strategy, and organization theory. She is interested in the role that founders' backgrounds play in science-based entrepreneurship, the commercialization of university-based research, and differences in these strategies across regions and countries.

Walter W. Powell

Walter W. Powell is Professor of Education, and Sociology, Organizational Behavior, and Communication at Stanford University. He is also an external faculty member at the Santa Fe Institute. He works in the areas of organization theory, social networks, and economic sociology. He is particularly interested in the processes through which knowledge is transferred from research universities into commercial development by startup firms, and the role of networks in facilitating and hindering innovation processes. He is currently working on various studies of the evolving institutional and network stucture of the life sciences field, and an analysis of the transfer and circulation of managerial practices in the San Francisco Bay Area nonprofits community.

AnnaLee Saxenian

AnnaLee Saxenian is Dean and Professor in the School of Information Management and Systems (SIMS) and Professor in the Department of City and Regional Planning at the University of California, Berkeley. She is an internationally recognized expert on economic development in information technology; and she has written extensively on the social and economic organization of production in technology regions like Silicon Valley. Her current research explores how immigrant engineers and scientists have transferred technology entrepreneurship to regions in China, India, and Taiwan. Her publications include *Regional Advantage: Culture and Competition in Silicon Valley and Route 128* (Harvard University Press, 1994), *Silicon Valley's New Immigrant Entrepreneurs* (1999), and *Local and Global Networks of Immigrant Professionals in Silicon Valley* (2002.) Saxenian holds a Doctorate in Political Science from MIT, a Master's in Regional Planning from the University of California at Berkeley, and a BA in Economics from Williams College in Massachusetts.

Olav Sorenson

Olav Sorenson is Professor of Strategy and International Management at London Business School. He also serves as a Senior Editor at Organization Science, and an Associate Editor at Management Science. He previously held positions at the University of Chicago's Graduate School of Business and the UCLA Anderson Graduate School of Management. Prof. Sorenson received his AB from Harvard and his MA and PhD degrees from Stanford. He primarily studies topics in organizational ecology and economic sociology. His research on social networks and industrial geography has appeared in the *American Journal of Sociology, Administrative Science Quarterly, Research Policy*, and the *Journal of Evolutionary Economics*. He also co-edited the 2003 volume of Advances in Strategy Management on the theme of "Geography and Strategy."

Michael Storper

Michael Storper is Professor of Economic Sociology at the Institute of Political Studies ("Sciences Po") and member of the Center of Sociology of Organizations (CSO) in Paris He is also Professor of Economic Geography at the London School of Economics, and Professor of Regional and International Development in the School of Public Affairs at UCLA. He received his PhD in Economic Geography at the University of California at Berkeley. His research concentrates on industrial location and regional economic development and policy. A good amount of his research is comparative, concentrating on western Europe and Brazil Currently he is working on globalization processes and the ways that they are affected by flows of knowledge, at world scale and in the European Union.

He has recently served on the US National Academies Committee considering the causes and consequences of outsourcing and offshoring to the US economy. Recent research has also considered on the role of face-to-face contact in the contemporary economy; on the social structures of growth in different regions around the world; and on the way that regions face globalization processes.

Peter Sunley

Peter Sunley is Professor in Economic Geography at the University of Southampton. He is joint author of Putting Workfare in Place: Local Labour Markets and the New Deal published in 2005 by Blackwell. He holds an MA and PhD from the University of Cambridge. He was previously a lecturer and senior lecturer in geography at the University of Edinburgh. His academic work has been published in journals including *Environment and Planning, Transactions of Institute of British Geographers*, the *Journal of Economic Geography, Economic Geography*, and *Regional Studies*.

Anthony J. Venables

Tony Venables is Professor of International Economics at the London School of Economics, director of the international trade research program at the Centre for Economic Performance and has co-directed the international trade program at the Centre for Economic Policy Research. Previous experience includes work as research manager of the trade group in the research division of the World Bank and as advisor to the UK Treasury.

He has published extensively in the areas of international trade and spatial economics, including work on trade and imperfect competition, economic integration, multinational firms, and economic geography. Publications include *The spatial economy; cities, regions and international trade*, with M. Fujita and P. Krugman (MIT press, 1999), and *Multinationals in the World Economy* with G. Barba Navaretti (Princeton 2004).

Kjersten Bunker Whittington

Kjersten Bunker Whittington is a doctoral candidate in the Department of Sociology at Stanford University. Her research focuses on the intersection of science, the scientific labor market, and social stratification. Her dissertation investigates how gender disparities in scientific productivity vary across employment sectors and other organizational contexts and settings. Kjersten's doctoral work is supported by fellowships from the National Bureau of Economic Research (NBER) and the Association for Institutional Research (AIR).

List of Figures

List of Tables

1

Clusters, Networks, and Innovation: Research Results and New Directions

STEFANO BRESCHI AND FRANCO MALERBA

1.1 Clusters and Innovation: The Main Conceptual Traditions

During the past decade or so, the geography of economic activities and the analysis of clusters have resurged as key issues in the research agendas of scholars from quite diverse economic fields. Although the idea dates back to Marshall (1920) and has been developed subsequently by other economists, such as Perroux (1950), Hirschman (1958), and Jacobs (1961) to mention a few, the resurgence of geography is not casual and reflects a deep trend in contemporary economies. Without rehashing the controversy between regional economists and new economic geographers (Martin and Sunley, 1996), the rediscovery of space and territory springs from the increasing awareness that variations across regions in economic growth and performance ultimately depends on a set of factors and resources – knowledge, capabilities, skilled human capital, institutional and organizational structures – which are specific to certain locations and relatively immobile in space.

Partly triggered by such awareness, and partly as a reaction to Krugman's (1991) authoritative dismissal of knowledge-related factors as measurable agglomeration forces, an increasing number of industrial and innovation economists have undertaken the task of carefully studying the geographic dimension of innovative activities and its implications for economic clustering, particularly those clusters of small and medium-sized enterprises in technology-based or high-technology industries. This has typically involved a blending of creative empirical work and appreciative theorizing, with important contributions coming not only from economics, but also from sociologists, geographers and organizational scholars. Moreover, as these developments were unfolding, regional economists and policy makers have also started giving technology a prominent place in their research and policy agendas. Following successful cases in the United States (e.g. Silicon Valley) as well as Europe (e.g. Baden-Württemberg), many regions have been trying to mimic these examples, setting up science parks, technopoles, venture capital and financial innovation support schemes. At the supranational level, the European Union also launched several programs with the aim of supporting regional innovation policies, particularly those directed to small and medium-sized enterprises.

As a result of these growing research efforts and policy experiments, a number of different theoretical frameworks have been developed to analyse the geographical dimension of innovation and its implications for the clustering of economic activities.

A very influential line of research has developed around the notion of *localized knowledge spillovers*, which has been proposed as one of the key explanatory factors for the clustering of innovative firms. Contrary to Krugman and others, who believe that knowledge flows are either unmeasurable or are spatially unbounded in a world increasingly linked by information highways, this literature forcefully claims that the transmission of new knowledge tends to occur more efficiently among closely located actors. In turn, the importance of spatial proximity in lowering the costs of knowledge transmission has to do with some basic properties of the knowledge base relevant for firms' innovative activities, particularly its complexity and its tacit nature. Due to these features, knowledge can only be effectively transmitted through interpersonal contacts and interfirm mobility of workers, both of which are eased by close geographical and cultural proximity. Since Jaffe's (1989) seminal paper, this emerging field of research has reached some very robust conclusions. Several empirical works have convincingly shown, with reference to the US and Europe, that the production of innovations presents a strong tendency to cluster in locations where key knowledge inputs are available (Audretsch and Feldman, 1996), that knowledge tends to spill over locally and takes time to diffuse across geographic distance (Jaffe et al., 1993) and that the extent of spatial clustering varies across industries depending on the stage of the industry life cycle and the importance of tacit knowledge (Feldman and Audretsch, 1999). Notwithstanding the important findings and the remarkable success achieved in obtaining mainstream acceptance, this stream of literature has somewhat tended to overlook other important factors and conditions that account for the clustering in some areas of innovative firms and, more generally, of firms in technology-based or high-technology industries. These sets of factors have been examined by a number of different approaches, sharing the common aim of thoroughly examining what makes firms located in clusters more innovative than isolated firms and what accounts for the uneven spatial distribution of technological capabilities.

In the first place, a wide variety of theoretical insights have come from the fields of *economic geography* and *regional economics*. A (possibly incomplete) list of such approaches include works on technological districts and new industrial spaces (Storper and Harrison, 1991; Storper, 1992), the research group formed around the notion of innovative milieux (Capello, 1999), the French school on *proximité* (Rallet and Torre, 1999), the localized learning capabilities approach (Maskell and Malmberg, 1999), and numerous case studies and historical accounts of successful high-technology districts and clusters (see for example, Saxenian, 1994). While it is not possible here to account for the nuances of the arguments put forward by these various perspectives, we can briefly mention what are some major common elements underpinning them. First, learning through networking and by interacting is seen as the crucial force pulling firms into clusters and the essential ingredient for the ongoing success of an innovative cluster. The ways firms learn in innovative clusters embrace user–producer relationships, formal and informal collaborations, interfirm mobility of skilled workers and the spin-off of new firms from existing firms, universities, and public research centers. More generally, a key feature of successful high-technology clusters is related to the high level of embeddedness of local firms in a very thick network of knowledge sharing, which is supported by close social interactions and by institutions building trust and encouraging informal relations among actors. The possibility for individual firms to tap into the body of localized knowledge and capabilities depends in a fundamental way on the ability to establish and maintain effective social links and lines of communication. At the collective level, the effectiveness with which knowledge can be shared is conditioned by the existence of common norms, conventions and codes for exchanging and interpreting knowledge. In this perspective, geographical proximity often overlaps and combines with institutional, organizational, and technical prox-imity in fostering processes of collective learning. Besides offering an indus-trial atmosphere favorable to innovation and entrepreneurship, and a social capital supporting trust and co-operative relationships, a further key feature of technology-intensive clusters is related to the availability of a common set of resources, some exogenously given, like universities and public research centers, and some others endogenous to the clusters' development, like a pool of specialized and skilled labor, whose main effect is that of reducing the costs and the uncertainties associated with firms' innovative activities.

From a different perspective, *evolutionary theory* has added to these insights a focus on technology, knowledge, learning, and capabilities. For evolutionary theory, learning and knowledge are key elements in the change of the economic system. 'Boundedly rational' agents act, learn, and search in un-certain and changing environments. Relatedly, competences correspond to specific ways of packaging knowledge about different things and have an intrinsic organizational content, so that different agents know how to do different things in different ways. Thus, learning, knowledge, and compe-tences entail agents' heterogeneity in experience, competences, and organ-ization and their persistent differential performance (Nelson, 1995; Dosi, 1997; Metcalfe, 1998). For evolutionary theory, the environment and condi-tions in which agents operate may drastically differ. Evolutionary theory stresses major differences in opportunities conditions related to science and technologies. The same holds for the knowledge base underpinning innovative activities, as well as for the institutional context. Thus the learning, behavior and capabilities of agents is constrained and 'bounded' by the technology, knowledge base and institutional context in which firms act. Heterogeneous firms facing similar technologies, searching around similar knowledge bases, undertaking similar production activities and 'embedded' in the same institutional setting, share some common behavioral and organizational traits and develop a similar range of learning patterns, behavior and organizational forms. For example, a specific technological regime defines the nature of the problems firms have to solve in their innovative activities, affects the model form of technological learning, shapes the incentives and constraints to particular behavior and organization and affects the basic processes of variety generation and selection and therefore the dynamics of evolution of firms (Nelson and Winter, 1982; Malerba and Orsenigo, 1997). Thus, in the analysis of clusters evolutionary theory and the capability approach has added a major focus on sectors and their major differences in the innovation and production processes that affect firms embedded in a specific industry. In particular, some key drivers of agglomeration are sector-specific, leading to distinct patterns of concentration (Breschi, 2000). Thus, cross-sectoral differences in agglomeration can be explained on the grounds of underlying differences in the processes of technological and organizational learning. The latter are, in fact, likely to affect the relative importance of phenomena such as localized knowledge spillovers; inter- vs. intraorganizational learning; knowledge complementarities fuelled by localized labor mobility; innovative explorations undertaken through spin-offs, and, more generally, the birth of new firms.

Finally, an important line of research on clusters of innovation has developed around the concept of *innovation system* (Freeman, 1987). This approach has considered innovation as an interactive process among a wide variety of actors. It has stressed the point that firms do not innovate in isolation, so that innovation could be conceptualized as a collective process. In this process, firms interact with other firms as well as with other organizations such as universities, research centers, government agencies and financial institutions. Moreover, the action of firms is strongly shaped by the existing set of institutions, such as the intellectual property right regime, public policies and norms of behavior (Carlsson, 1997; Edquist, 1997). Although there is nothing inherently spatial in the idea that innovation develops through the interactions among different actors, the set of firms, organizations and institutions involved in such process form in many cases a sort of 'national' community, so that it makes sense to talk about *national innovation systems* (Nelson, 1993). Quite recently, this approach has branched out into two directions. On the one hand, it has been recognized that the borders defining the set of relevant actors and interactions may have a regional dimension and therefore it is possible to identify different 'regional' innovation systems, even within the same country (Braczyk *et al.*, 1998). On the other hand, it has also been suggested that both the principal institutional actors and how the involved actors are connected to each other may significantly differ across industries so that innovation systems also have a 'sectoral' dimension (Malerba, 2004).

This brief account of the main recent conceptual traditions related to the analysis of clusters of innovation would be, however, quite incomplete without reference to what is perhaps the most recent approach that has debuted on the analytical stage, that is the *social network* approach. As the short review above should have made clear, all the theoretical perspectives share the common view that interactions, formal and informal relations and, more generally, network effects are the key mechanisms through which external economies benefit local firms and are ultimately responsible for the emergence, growth, and success of a cluster of innovative firms. Actually, the idea that the level of embeddedness and social integration of businesses in a local community is crucial for the success of a cluster is by no means new and it has been strongly emphasized by most regional economists and economic geographers. What is entirely new, however, is something quite different: the attempt to model and measure empirically all sorts of network effects that are thought to be at the heart of a well-functioning cluster, using the tools and methodologies offered by social network analysis and graph theory. Although it is not yet clear whether the social-network approach constitutes just a methodology or a new theoretical framework, the number of papers that are taking, more or less explicitly, a 'network' approach to the study of innovative clusters (and not only) is taking off. This trend is important enough in our view to justify the emphasis to the notion of network given in the title to this book. As a final caveat, it is worth stressing that we have deliberately avoided engaging in providing a further definition of what is a *cluster*. Definitions of this kind abound in the literature. In this book, we have decided not to commit to any of them, but preferred instead to focus on the variety of *processes* that drive the emergence, growth, and successful development of spatial agglomerations of industrial and innovative activities. It is from a better comprehension of such processes that we expect to derive robust insights to define and classify the different typologies of *clusters* of innovation.

The next sections provide a broad guide to the main themes addressed by the contributions in this book and offer some general lessons and new research results that can be drawn from them.

1.2   The Main Themes: A Guide to This Volume

This book contains a broad collection of chapters, that reflect most of the recent and new conceptual traditions to the analysis of clusters of innovation mentioned above. Some of the chapters have been already published in a special issue of the journal *Industrial and Corporate Change* (2001, vol. 4) entirely devoted to the geography of innovation. Some others have already been published in other issues of *Industrial and Corporate Change* and the *Journal of Economic Geography*. The remaining chapters are new contributions. Overall, the book is an attempt to relate different perspectives in order to understand the spatial clustering of firms and innovation in a deeper and more critical way. The book is organized along five lines, which correspond to different parts of the book. The different conceptual traditions discussed above and the most recent developments in them are reflected in the chapters in Part I. Then, the next three parts of the book are concerned with more specific aspects: the wide variety of existing clusters and the diversity in the process of their emergence (Part II); the role of different network types, international mobility and the social setting (Part III); and a discussion on the role of spatial proximity and on the broad notion of localized knowledge spillovers (Part IV). Two chapters providing a discussion on policies related to clusters and innovation conclude the book (Part V).

1.2.1   *Recent Developments in Theorizing Clusters, Networks, and Innovation (Part I)*

In order to have a deeper and more complete understanding of clusters, networks, and innovation, most authors recognize the need to use a set of differentiated tools – both theoretical and empirical – ranging from network theory, to evolutionary dynamics of learning and capabilities in specific sectoral contexts, and to innovation systems – local and regional ones. This is reflected by the three chapters of Part I in this book, which concern, respectively, the study of networks, the role of sectors as differentiated drivers of knowledge accumulation by firms, and the regional systems of innovation.

In particular, the chapter by Robin Cowan, *Network Models of Innovation and Knowledge Diffusion*, has the purpose to introduce the reader to the main results and challenges in network modelling. Cowan claims that the use of network analysis in economics has grown rapidly, because network models overcome several of the shortcomings of more traditional market models. This is particularly the case in the context of innovation, when the transmission of knowledge plays such an important role. In general, while codified knowledge can be diffused globally, without reference to underlying connection structures, tacit knowledge has very different properties, because its diffusion depends heavily on the network of agents through which it spreads. Thus, to understand and analyse the dynamics of innovation and diffusion network models provide a promising avenue. The chapter by Cowan discusses the reasons of the current interest in networks, related to the emergence of network technologies and the role of network externalities and the distribution of information; to the real boundaries of firms in terms of market and non-market relationships; and to the expanding knowledge base of industries that requires the access and integration of different types of knowledge.

Network models from Ising types of models to random graphs to small-world models. The chapter then focuses on the relationship between networks and innovation, by discussing the main empirical contributions and the related models of knowledge transfer: as a barter and as a broadcast. Finally, the chapter tackles theoretically one of the key issues discussed in this book – network formation – and does it by discussing both the game theoretical literature concerning the stability and efficiency of networks and the literature (more evolutionary in spirit) in which every agent learns, is connected to every other, but links are activated probabilistically.

The next chapter *On Sectoral Specificities in the Geography of Corporate Location* by Giulio Bottazzi, Giovanni Dosi, and Giorgio Fagiolo adds a different perspective and asks to what extent agglomeration forces are location specific but independent of individual sectors and technologies and to what extent sector-specific drivers of agglomeration are relevant. They claim that analysis of clusters has to take this last factor into consideration: cross-sectoral differences in agglomeration forces are – at least partly – explained on the grounds of underlying differences in the processes of technological and organizational learning. The latter are, in fact, likely to affect the relative importance of phenomena such as localized knowledge spillovers; inter- vs. intraorganizational learning; knowledge complementarities fuelled by localized labor mobility; innovative explorations undertaken through spin-offs, and, more generally, the birth of new firms. Bottazzi, Dosi, and Fagiolo propose a relatively simple and empirically testable model apt to disentangle the relative impact of location-specific and industry-specific observed locations. The model yields empirically testable predictions on the equilibrium distribution of the diverse relevance of agglomeration forces across industrial sectors. They apply it to the evidence on the geographical distribution of Italian business units across a set of industries that might be considered archetypes of distinct regimes of technological learning: leather products, transport equipment, electronics, and financial intermediation services. The results are indeed consistent with the view that intersectoral differences in economies of agglomeration might be (at least partly) explained by differences in innovation patterns and learning regimes displayed by firms belonging to diverse industrial sectors.

Finally, in the chapter *Regional Knowledge Capabilities and Open Innovation: Regional Innovation Systems and Clusters in the Asymmetric Knowledge Economy* Philip Cooke brings to the book the regional innovation system perspectives on clusters. He first provides a review of the origins of regional innovation systems thinking and gives a systematic account of the idea and content of regional innovation systems, related to advances made by regional scientists, economic geographers and innovation scholars. Then, the chapter moves into an analysis of conditions and criteria for empirical recognition and judgement as to whether actual cases of innovation activity warrant the designation of 'regional innovation system' or not. Then the analysis is applied to two contrasting European exemplars. Later, a revised analysis of regional innovation systems and their relationship to clusters under knowledge economy conditions is offered. Reflecting recent theorization of regional innovation systems and clusters, new challenges that underline the importance for global competitiveness of regional innovation systems are identified. These connect 'asymmetric knowledge' and 'open innovation' in new ways that privilege a Penrosian-inspired theorization of 'regional knowledge capabilities'. Finally, Cooke claims that much of the research field of regional innovation systems placed undue attention upon the role of the public policy in supplying the soft infrastructure of innovation support for enterprises. Regional innovation policies in Europe were often orchestrated by the European Commission, but national governments have pursued such policies more consciously in the twenty-first century some, notably Sweden, Finland, Italy, and the UK. This supports a key hypothesis of this chapter that herein lies the source of Europe's innovation gap with the US, for such reliance on public intervention signifies major market failure deriving from asymmetric knowledge, because markets for innovation services have yet to be widely recognized by European entrepreneurs (in contrast to the US). The future requires the widespread evolution of public innovation support systems with a stronger institutional and organizational support from the private sector.

1.2.2   The Wide Variety of Existing Clusters and the Diversity in the Process of Their Emergence (Part II)

Many contributions emphasize the need to concentrate more analytical and empirical efforts to understand the conditions and the process leading to the emergence of new technology-based clusters. Much of the existing literature largely overlooks this question, by focusing on the study of well-accomplished regional systems, like Silicon Valley. Similarly, most of the attempts to create new clusters have often tried to replicate locally the set of conditions found in existing successful regions. On the contrary, the key point in several chapters of this book is that the examples provided by mature and successful regional systems are likely to be of little help to address the question of how to spark entrepreneurship and let new clusters emerge and thrive.

   Among the critical conditions for sparking off the growth of a new cluster, the availability of a highly skilled labor force and of university-trained human capital has been identified as one of the most important factors. If the existence of a pool of skilled workers is a key ingredient for successful clusters, also the localized mobility of people (either among firms or from existing firms, universities, and public research centers to new firms) is equally relevant. Spin-offs are equally important. The mobility of skilled workers represents, in fact, the crucial source of new firm formation as well as the main mechanism through which technical and market knowledge flows locally. These remarks suggest therefore that the working of regional labor markets (and, more specifically, the labor markets for technical, manager-ial, and academic employees) is a very promising area, which deserves more careful study, both with reference to nascent and to established clusters.

These issues are reflected in Part II of the book, which moves from the broad conceptual and empirical analyses of Part I to the analysis of specific clusters and specific mechanisms of cluster emergence and formation.

Part II of the book opens with the chapter *'Old Economy' Inputs for 'New Economy' Outcomes: Cluster Formation in the New Silicon Valleys* by Timothy Bresnahan, Alfonso Gambardella, and AnnaLee Saxenian. The key issue addressed is to investigate the forces that account for the emergence of new clusters of technology-based firms. A key distinction in the chapter is that starting a cluster is quite different from sustaining a cluster in terms of processes and economics. In examining the emergence of clusters, the authors draw upon and summarize the findings of a large study on a number of nascent clusters, both in the US and outside the US (e.g. Ireland, Taiwan, Israel, India, and Scandinavia). The chapter claims that the existing theories about clusters of innovative activities, shaped as they are by cases of suc-cessful regions and focused on network effects and the resulting agglomer-ation economies, can explain very well the working of a well-established cluster (such as Silicon Valley), but are unable to tell how nascent clusters start and take hold. The reason is that none of the elements yielding increasing returns and positive-feedback network effects is yet in place in a cluster at its beginning. Although no recipe can be given for starting and sustaining a cluster, the chapter argues that some deep regularities arise from the cases studied. In the first place, a plentiful supply of skilled labor is a critical pre-condition in forming the basis for entrepreneurship. In this respect, univer-sities may certainly play a crucial role, but the supply of skills can come from other sources, including large incumbent firms and foreign-educated people. Moreover, the relevant skills include not only technical, but also managerial ones. In the second place, the successful start of a cluster seems also to involve the ability (and the fortune) to take advantage of technological and market opportunities not yet exploited. In most of the clusters analysed (with the exception of the Scandinavian countries), this has involved a positioning in technological and product spaces of the ICT industry that were comple-mentary to those in the leading clusters (i.e. Silicon Valley). For many of these rapidly growing clusters, the establishment of co-operative connections with the leading centers of technology and demand has represented the most important mechanism for sparking off entrepreneurial opportunities in exist-ing and new ICT niches and segments. These two elements – highly skilled labor and connections to technological and market opportunities – feature in all the nascent clusters in ICT. The transition from the early phase of cluster emergence to a well-structured cluster yielding positive network effects implies a long and risky process of firm building and market building. In other words, the mere growth in the number of firms located in a cluster is unlikely to give rise to those agglomeration economies associated with existing successful regions, unless coupled with significant and systematic efforts and investments by the early actors in the cluster to build the organizational and technological capabilities required for growth, and to create and nurture those institutions (e.g. venture capital) that fuel the development of the cluster.

The chapter that follows by Maryann Feldman goes in depth into the discussion of one case of cluster emergence: the US Capitol region. In *The Entrepreneurial Event Revisited: Firm Formation in a Regional Context*, Feldman starts from the important point that the examples provided by well-developed and fully functioning regional innovative systems, such as Silicon Valley, may provide little help to devise appropriate policies for regions lacking industrial capabilities and an entrepreneurial tradition. Rather, a more fruitful approach for these regions is to look at the conditions and factors that spark entrepreneurship and foster the initial development of a new cluster. The chapter examines the specific case of the US Capitol region, which was able to transform, during the 1980s and the 1990s, into one the most successful clusters of Internet- and biotechnology-related firms. Tracing back the origins of the cluster to the beginning of the 1970s, the author notes that the region was, at that time, almost completely lacking those supportive conditions, like the availability of venture capital, business services, social capital, and universities engaged in industry-oriented research, that are typically associated with local environments promoting the formation of new firms. On the other hand, a distinctive feature of the region was the presence of a number of government agencies and research institutions, mostly related to the health and defense departments, which constituted a reservoir of skilled and yet idle employees. The critical factor unleashing entrepreneurial forces has thus to be found, according to the author, in a series of exogenous shocks, mainly related to policy initiatives such as the downsizing in federal employment, the public procurement and outsourcing for services, changes in intellectual property regime, and policies supporting small and medium-sized enterprises. Overall, the effect of these shocks was to provide incentives as well as opportunities for employees in the public sector, but also from the private industry, to engage in the formation of new companies. Most of these newly founded firms localized in the region, because of the locational inertia of entrepreneurs and the need to locate near the originating laboratory or agency in order to secure contracts, licenses, and partnerships. Moreover, even though the earliest start-ups were mainly service firms acting as government contractors, later generations of new firms and spin-offs realized the opportunities to develop commercial products and to engage in autonomous R&D activities. Although further research is needed before generalizing, the paper stresses two broad implications that can be derived from the case examined. First, the transition from a State-anchored region to a private sector high-tech cluster was a rather spontaneous and bottom-up process of reaction and adaptation to changes that were exogenous to the regional system. Secondly, the conditions supporting entrepreneurship lagged, rather than led the development of the cluster. They developed over time, following the region's success and being actively built by pioneering entrepreneurs attempting to cope with and to adapt to changes in the local environment.

Then, in *The Firms That Feed Industrial Districts: A Return To the Italian Source*, Mark H. Lazerson and Gianni Lorenzoni explore the heterogeneous nature of the firms within the Italian industrial districts and the interfirm relationships and business groups that criss-crossed them. Until recently, these organizational aspects have received scant attention in most of the industrial district literature, which has instead largely highlighted local industrial policy and the role of private and public associations in sustaining economic growth. In most of the literature there has been a tacit assumption that the enterprises that comprise the district are mostly organizationally homogeneous and that their strategy and structure are shaped by local municipal policies and the dominant norms of the community. Lazerson and Lorenzoni criticize the prevailing view that industrial districts always developed in opposition to large firms. They claim that many industrial districts have greatly benefited from technology and skill transfers initiated by large firms and that the success of industrial districts often depends on importing intellectual, organizational, and technological inputs from outside the local area. They base their study on the Prato textile district; the Carpi knitwear district; the Bologna machine-packaging district; and Mantova's Castel Goffredo women's stocking district, as well as on several other significant Italian districts. They claim that no industrial district has ever emerged from a set of industrial policy initiatives promoted by either public or private organizations. The larger firms of the districts – albeit small by most standards – often orchestrate subcontracting relations, explore commercial avenues, and invest in research and development. These diverse activities link leading firms to both distant and local actors, putting them in a strategic position to respond quickly to external market demand, while realigning the productive resources of less-sensitively located actors. A notable strength of industrial districts is their capacity to combine organizational heterogeneity and homogeneity. Too much homogeneity may actually undermine the dynamism of districts by discouraging diversification and openness to new ideas. Leading firms with loose attachments to distant networks introduce district firms with new ideas and concepts that are continually refined and sharpened because of the ubiquity of redundancy, proximity, and transactional intensity. Redundancy derives from the large number of highly specialized firms that perform similar but slightly different functions, which forces firms to both mimic each other and distinguish themselves by developing incremental process and product improvements. Proximity produces spontaneous social and professional interaction between entrepreneurs and employees engaged in the same industry both at home and at work, facilitating the diffusion of information. Transactional intensity obligates firms to have continuous relations with each other, offering many more points of contact and information than agents working within hierarchical organizations where information is often purposely limited. This is one reason why leading firms often encourage their supplier firms to develop multiple relations with other final firms, rather than seeking to hold them hostage. Despite the very different social, political, and legal background of Italian industrial districts the variety of governance mechanisms used to manage interorganizational market relationships are not markedly different from those found by other researchers in very different settings.

Finally, the chapter by Steven Klepper, *Employee Start-Ups in High-Tech Industries*, starts from the recognition that from Fairchild Semiconductors in Silicon Valley, many spin-offs have been created and therefore asks why employees of high-tech firms leave to found firms in the same industry, as the 'fairchildren' did in Silicon Valley. Klepper first reviews three theories about spin-offs. First, 'agency theories', in which spin-offs are modelled as capitalizing on discoveries that employees make in the course of their employment in incumbent firms. Agency costs related to innovation impede employees from contracting with their firms to develop the discoveries, leading to spin-offs. Secondly, 'organizational capability theories' in which spin-offs develop innovations that incumbents are slow to pursue because of organizational limitations. These difficulties create opportunities for spin-offs. Finally, 'employee-learning theories' in which spin-offs exploit knowledge their founders learned in their prior employment to compete with their employees and other firms in their industry. Each theory is evaluated based on the empirical evidence. The evidence does not seem to support completely any of the three theories. On the basis of this evidence, a different theoretical perspective is proposed: spin-offs are like children. This theory starts with a variant of the employee-learning theory, and uses the concepts of reproduction and inheritance linked to the evolutionary models by Nelson and Winter (1982). Firms are assumed to be governed by routines, and organizations can reproduce, requiring the transplant of some routines of the existing firm to the new firm by one or more employees. But only some employees are able to reproduce. Because high-technology firms have more functions than low-tech firms, they have more routines to manage, more employees with access to routines and therefore more spin-offs than low-tech organizations. Spin-offs inherit a subset of routines of their parents and therefore they will perform a subset of the functions of their parents. They will inherit routines more suited to their activity than other kinds of start-ups and therefore they will outperform other types of start-ups and have longer survival. When spin-offs grow and expand they take on new routines. Therefore, they will tend to depart from their origins and therefore from their parents, diverging further and further from their parents. Similarly, their performance will also change. As a firm ages, it will differ more from its parent, leading to a greater diversity in the innovation it pursues. Therefore, spin-offs are a source of diversity.

1.2.3 *The Role of Different Network Types, International Mobility and the Social and Institutional Setting (Part III)*

A further point of convergence of many of the studies in this book is that, by putting a lot of emphasis upon the role of proximity, a good part of the existing approaches ends up looking at clusters as isolated and self-contained entities, not paying attention to external relations, the specificity of various types of networks and institutions, and the social structure that characterizes a network. This is what the chapters in Part III aim to do.

In particular, external linkages are vital in order to establish and maintain a dense local network of relationships, for both emerging and established clusters. These linkages, however, may differ in the two cases. For *emerging* clusters, external links allow to get access to knowledge, skills, contacts, capital, and information about new technological opportunities and new markets. The mobility of labor across large distances, particularly through the repatriation of scientists, engineers, and managers trained elsewhere, is a crucial means to establish these external links. For *established* clusters, external links with other regional systems or with sources of new knowledge and technology may allow an upgrade of the industrial base (by specializing and developing distinctive and highly complementary capabilities) and to reduce the risk of lock-in (by keeping the cluster open to radical new ideas and technologies from outside).

In general, for most authors of this book the major challenge for future analysis lies in the empirical analysis of network structures. But data requirements for this type of exercise are quite substantial. Patent databases are rich enough, but provide evidence of only one type of information flow, and so construction of large, detailed databases is a major task ahead, and may concern formal alliances, various types of formal and informal linkages, labor mobility, and so on. Moreover, research on networks is being done in a wide variety of fields: psychology, sociology, strategic management, so that a very rich research environment has to be created for communication between, and the integration of, all these disciplines.

The chapters in Part III of the book discuss the role of various factors in shaping clusters, networks, and innovation. AnnaLee Saxenian and Jinn-Yuh Hsu add a new key factor responsible for the emergence of a cluster: the international mobility of highly skilled technical and managerial labor. In *The Silicon Valley–Hsinchu Connection: Technical Communities and Industrial Upgrading,* Saxenian and Hsu provide a careful analysis of how knowledge and skills can be transferred across large distances and thus contribute to the reciprocal industrial upgrading of regions located far away in space. The chapter examines two frequently cited cases of successful high-tech clusters, namely Silicon Valley in California and the Hsinchu-Taipei region of Taiwan, suggesting that the dominant accounts for the emergence of successful new regions, such as Taiwan's Hsinchu, by focusing exclusively upon local factors, such as the role of state policies, the availability of skills and specialized inputs, and the competition and vertical co-operation among local firms, or by stressing the sourcing strategies of multinational corporations, fall short of explaining the emergence of indigenous innovative capabilities in peripheral areas. Although the role played by all these factors should not be overlooked, the authors argue that a key ingredient to their success has been the contributions given by a community of US-educated engineers who have built social and economic linkages between Silicon Valley and Hsinchu economies. This technical community formed during the 1970s and the 1980s as US-educated Taiwanese engineers started to organize collectively and form professional networks and organizations. The reversal of this 'brain drain', spurred by the accelerated growth of the economy in the 1980s, thus brought back to Taiwan an increasing number of returnees with strong professional and personal ties to Silicon Valley. Moreover, a growing population of new 'argonauts', constantly travelling between the two regions and including venture capitalists as well as engineers from companies with activities in both regions, also contributed to establish and co-ordinate a sustained flow of technical knowledge, skills, contacts, capital, and information about new opportunities and new markets. The development of this transnational technical community has also transformed the relationship between the Silicon Valley and Hsinchu economies from a one-way to more decentralized two-way flows of technology, skills, and capital, allowing producers of both regions to collaborate and to develop distinctive but highly complementary capabilities. The case studied suggests to the authors some important implications. First, multinational corporations may no longer be the privileged vehicle for transferring knowledge and skills across national borders, particularly in those contexts requiring close communications and timely response. These needs are better served by international technical communities, organizing production and innovation at the local and the global levels. Relatedly, localization and globalization have to be seen as increasingly complementary and mutually reinforcing phenomena, in which transnational communities of practice play the crucial role of recombining specialized components and knowledge produced at different localities. Finally, the Taiwanese case suggests to policy makers that investments in education and training and policies creating local conditions favorable to entrepreneurial activity by foreign-educated engineers and scientists can be at least as important, to foster a region's participation in global technology and production networks, as are attempts to attract foreign investments.

In *The Institutional Embeddedness of High-Tech Regions: Relational Foundations of the Boston Biotechnology Community*, Kelley Porter, Kjersten Bunker Whittington, and Walter W. Powell examine the biotechnology industry and focus on the Boston area, one of the largest concentrations of dedicated biotechnology firms in the world, with a rich array of public research organizations. They start from the statement that the joint and contingent effects of geography and network connections are crucial to the innovative capacity of high-tech clusters, and then enquire what types of network relations are most critical. They ask whether informal personal ties and occupational relations provide more open pathways to enhance the flow of ideas than more formal, contractual affiliations; whether the institutional form of the dominant organizations shape the organizational practices of the members of a regional community, determining the nature of spillovers; how the overlap of multiple types of networks across a diverse array of organizations creates an ecosystem with a distinctive character and accompanying norms that define membership in this community. To address these questions, they combine four unique data sets that account, in various ways, for the organization of the life-sciences community in the greater Boston metropolitan area, and aim to trace technology networks and the array of university–industry linkages in the life sciences, spanning both formal connections and informal flows. They claim that most current research on science networks focuses on just one type of relationship among contractual ties, patent or publication citation networks, or academic entrepreneurs. Thus, research does not know how networks are overlaid on one another, and which types of linkages are generative and which ones provide the relational glue that sustains relationships over time. A full understanding of the development of a regional economy or an industrial district requires insight into how multiple networks stitch together a community, generating multiple independent pathways through which ideas, people, and resources can travel. In short, Porter, Bunker, and Powell argue that the intersection of multiple networks – embeddedness in Granovetter's term – is the wellspring of successful technology clusters. They begin with formal linkages as a starting point, and then use a dataset on contractual ties as a basis on which to identify organizational founders, members of scientific advisory boards, and inventor networks. The goal is to discern how the overlap of these four different networks – alliances, founding teams, science boards, and inventors – constitutes the nexus of a community of practice in the Boston community.

Olav Sorenson in *Social Networks and the Persistence of Clusters: Evidence from the Computer Workstation Industry* argues that firms cluster not because geographic concentration necessarily benefits them, but rather because social networks constrain where entrepreneurs locate and what types of businesses they start. Entrepreneurship involves opportunity recognition, and resource mobilization. Perceiving the potential for profits from opening a new venture in a particular industry typically requires both familiarity with the way in which the industry works and access to private information regarding market conditions. Those individuals most likely to consider starting a firm in an industry either have experience working in the industry or a related business. Even after deciding to attempt entry, the nascent entrepreneur must successfully assemble a variety of resources – tacit knowledge, financial capital, and skilled labor – to begin operations. Therefore, those individuals most capable of assembling the resources to pursue their idea in a particular location are likely to have strong ties to the local community. Since social connections themselves tend to cluster in geographic and social space, these constraints on where entrepreneurs can start firms imply that the spatial pattern of new entrants reifies the geography of industry – production tends to remain clustered into 'industrial districts' even if a more dispersed configuration would be more efficient. The chapter by Sorenson examines computer workstation manufacturing. An examination of the dynamics of entry into and exit from this industry suggests that firms within an industry cluster within a small number of geographic regions not because this spatial configuration enhances the efficiency of production, but rather because social networks constrain where entrepreneurs found new firms and what types of businesses they enter. Social connections to existing industry participants increase the likelihood that a nascent entrepreneur perceives an opportunity in the industry. Moreover, upon recognizing the possibility for a new venture, ties to the industry importantly facilitate the mobilization of the resources, including tacit knowledge and skilled labor, necessary to begin operations. Given that these important social connections rarely extend far in space, those most likely to perceive opportunities within an industry and those most capable of acting on them reside in close proximity to existing firms within an industry. As a result, entrepreneurship tends to reinforce the existing geographic distribution of an industry. Sorenson also advances some explanation of why network constraints account for interindustry variation in the degree of geographic concentration. First, dispersion might simply result from a process of diffusion: some firms manage to escape the confines of the existing regions in which the industry resides. Thus these remote entries may represent a form of entrepreneurial arbitrage. Alternatively (or additionally), the proportion of *de alio* entrants might influence the speed at which an industry diffuses. Whereas these dynamics place severe constraints on where entrepreneurs in an industry might arise, the arrival of *de alio* entrants likely depends more on the existing distribution of related industries. Hence, the prevalence of *de alio* entrants early in an industry's history might play an important role in determining its level of dispersion. In addition to these industry dynamics, other characteristics, such as the technology being deployed, may also influence the importance of social networks, and concomitantly the rate at which production of a particular type diffuses across space. Once one might expect social networks to play an even stronger role in access to tacit knowledge in industries drawing on information of a relatively high degree of average complexity, thereby slowing its dispersion.

1.2.4 The Meaning and Effects of Proximity and Localized Knowledge Spillovers (Part IV)

The extent and localization of knowledge spillovers remain quite high in the agenda of analysis of clusters, networks, and innovation. At a more theoretical level, some authors point out that the dichotomies of knowledge vs. information and tacit vs. codified knowledge, seem to provide an oversimplified explanation for the high degrees of localization of knowledge creation and diffusion. In particular, more theoretical and empirical works have to be devoted to examining the sharing rules and the codes used by the technical and epistemic communities and the role they play in mediating the transmission of knowledge across different firms and institutions. This line of research would then permit one to gain a more precise and detailed understanding of the role that geographical proximity plays in the creation of language and codebooks that define the boundaries of the technical communities and would also permit evaluation of under what circumstances physical proximity does not constitute an insurmountable obstacle to the long-distance transmission of (apparently tacit) skills and knowledge. Moreover, to the extent that the codification process entails costs and can be strategically manipulated to exclude competitors, one could go beyond the often idealized model of cluster as providing an unrestricted and free pool of knowledge and address the more realistic question of assessing how much co-operation and how much competition among firms and among networks of firms takes place in clusters. This is what Part IV of the book intends to do.

In *Buzz: Face-to-Face Contact and the Urban Economy*, Michael Storper and Anthony J. Venables claim that despite the major reduction in transportation costs and the rise and variety of information that can be communicated in different ways and speed, face-to-face contact remains central to co-ordination in the economy. They argue that existing models of urban concentrations are incomplete unless grounded in the most fundamental aspect of proximity; face-to-face contact. Face-to-face is particularly important in environments where information is imperfect, rapidly changing, and not easily codified. They claim that face-to-face contact has four main features: it is an efficient communication technology; it can help to solve incentive problems; it can facilitate socialization and learning; and it provides psychological motivation. Thus face-to-face has unique behavioral and communicational properties that give it specific advantages as a technology of communication, co-ordination, and motivation. In sum, the various theories of agglomeration and the persistence of cities refer to transactional structures and circumstances that necessitate close contact between persons, and to the various outcomes of proximity between agents. Then they develop two game-theoretic models that illustrate why agents engage in face-to-face contact: in the first, face-to-face contact overcomes incentive problems in the formation of working partnerships, in the second it allows actors to assess others' qualities and to form 'in groups' for more efficient partnering and higher innovation. Finally, they place these ideas in a wider context and compare them to other mechanisms of co-ordination of activity in different contexts related to the fluidity of the environment and to the type of knowledge used in co-ordination. Compared to markets, firms or networks, face-to-face contact – buzz – is a relevant mode of co-ordination when the environment is fluid and knowledge is tacit and specialized. In these situations, the combined effects of face-to-face contacts – buzz – generates increasing returns for the people and the activities involved.

In *The Geography of Knowledge Spillovers: Conceptual Issues and Measurement Problem*, Stefano Breschi, Francesco Lissoni, and Fabio Montobbio provide a critical reassessment of the theoretical concept of localized knowledge spillovers and the econometric literature, based on the knowledge production function that in recent years has made large use of such a notion. The main claim of the authors is that, in spite of the undeniable merits of this literature in drawing attention to regions as a meaningful unit of analysis to study flows of knowledge, the insistence upon knowledge spillovers as the major analytical category to explain the localized nature of innovative activities risks diverting research from other mechanisms governing knowledge flows and to induce misleading policy implications. In particular, the authors criticize the argument by which what benefits firms located in highly innovative clusters is a pool of publicly available knowledge, whose accessibility is, however, bounded in space due to the tacit nature of the relevant knowledge and the consequent need to adopt informal means of knowledge transmission. The point raised in the chapter is that this theoretical proposition contains a number of logical contradictions and leaves many questions open. On the one hand, it is argued, recent developments in the economics of knowledge show that tacitness is not an inherent characteristic of knowledge, but refers to the way knowledge itself is transmitted within an epistemic community. When conceptualized in this way, tacitness may become a powerful exclusionary means, which can be wilfully manipulated to prevent a number of actors from understanding the content of scientific and technical messages. Depending on the sharing rules agreed upon by the epistemic community and the incentives facing individual agents, localized knowledge flows may encompass a large number of intermediate cases between the two extremes of pure private and pure public goods, such as price-excludable public goods, common property, and club goods. In addition, such a perspective allows one to decouple geographical and cognitive proximity and so provide a rationale for knowledge links taking place among agents located far away in space. On the other hand, the chapter also argues that the dominant position associating localized knowledge flows to pure knowledge externalities has also obscured the wide variety of mechanisms through which knowledge is exchanged among agents, many of which give rise to pecuniary, rather than pure knowledge externalities. In particular, the authors point to the need of investigating, with new methodologies and empirical indicators, the role played by localized and competing networks of firms, by the labor market and the interfirm mobility of skilled workers, and by the contractual arrangements linking local universities and firms.

Finally, in *Comparative Localization of Academic and Industrial Spillovers*, James D. Adams deals with the question of measuring the spatial extent of knowledge spillovers from academic and industrial research. Using a very detailed survey on slightly more than 200 R&D laboratories owned by US manufacturing firms, Adams is able to quantify the learning efforts undertaken by R&D laboratories to absorb knowledge spillovers from other firms and universities, and to identify precisely the most important channels through which spillovers flow, like conferences and meetings, joint research and patent licensing, hiring of engineering graduates, and faculty consulting. The most important result from Adams' analysis is that spillovers from university research are far more localized than one would expect on the basis of the geographic distribution of university R&D, and more localized than spillovers from industrial research. This suggests that firms tend to take advantage of local universities for research, consulting, and human capital, while they search for distant knowledge when more applied and industry-oriented research is involved, especially in the case of larger laboratories and firms. In addition to this, the evidence reported by Adams shows that while the production of laboratory patents benefits from localized knowledge spillovers, especially from local universities, spillovers are weaker for new products, thus indicating that the need for co-location with academic research tends to be greater during the early phases of research. Overall, the findings reported in Adams' chapter have very important policy implications, as they point to the paradox that the form of knowledge, i.e. academic research, that is usually regarded as more of a public good than any other is also the most spatially localized. Adams suggests that the solution of this puzzle is to see the localization of university research as an effective way to diffuse public knowledge. In addition, he also conjectures that while state and regionally funded universities serve local interests through training and dissemination, with unavoidable duplications of efforts, research with a more basic and wider scope should be financed at the national and international levels. This is a question that needs further scrutiny, but one that surely deserves much attention.

1.2.5   Policy Implications for Clusters, Networks and Innovation (Part V)

A final point concerns public policy and the role of government. In this respect, the chapters presented in this book show a remarkable convergence in pointing out the ineffectiveness of public policies attempting to direct the formation of new clusters through top-down interventions, such as techno-poles, science parks, and firm incubators. Rather, government policies can play a very important role in cluster development by accommodating the formation of new firms, the investments in education and the provision of support infrastructures. This is particularly important in the case of several European regions where the intervention of public actors has been quite heavy and directive.

In Part V some of these issues are examined in depth. Peter Maskell in *Towards a Knowledge-Based Theory of the Geographical Cluster* aims to investigate the public-policy implications for clusters when knowledge creation becomes key. Maskell claims that the reason for the existence of the cluster can be found in the enhanced knowledge creation that takes place along its horizontal and vertical dimensions. He distinguishes 'Marshallian' horizontal clusters where the learning advantages stem from the intrinsic variation between independent co-localized firms with similar capabilities from 'Smithian' vertical clusters where division of labor, interaction, information asymmetries, and co-ordination costs takes place among firms within a cluster. He also suggests that the boundaries of a cluster can be defined by the interdependence between certain kinds of economic activities on the one hand and their appropriate institutional framework on the other. An institutional endowment favorable towards one kind of economic activity can be hostile to others. The very reasons why cognitive distance might be small within the cluster makes the cognitive distance very great between clusters. When access to dissimilar bodies of knowledge is required in product innovation, too much clustering becomes perhaps a burden and further clustering ceases. Maskell considers the policy challenges and options relevant in three different stages of the cluster's life cycle, keeping in mind the discussion about the existence, growth, and boundaries of a cluster advanced previously. Each stage merits a set of specific public policies distinctively different from what will be generally beneficial at the other stages. At the infant stage, when firms with complementary or similar capabilities by experimentation or conjecture have started to reap some of the benefits of co-location, the relevant public policy options are mainly market conformist by supporting what is already in the making and by helping to provide inputs in short supply: targeted labor-mobility improving measures, specific educational efforts, vocational training programs, dedicated initiatives to enhance creativity and collaboration, physical infrastructure improvements, actions to develop competent and sensitive venture. Most of the abundant policy ambitions and initiatives to support and develop clusters in recent years have been concerned with the next, mature stage of cluster development. The arguments question the value of these initiatives and view them as being at least partly misdirected, because local learning largely takes care of itself. Only outward-looking measures may require specific policy support in order to help firms to monitor and grasp categorically new knowledge (especially if differently organized) and to widen the horizon and extend the reach of the local actors. Finally, when clusters become stagnant, or start to decline, the policy challenge shifts from being supportive to becoming creatively destructive by dismantling institutions molded to accommodate and support yesterday's economic structures, by assisting communities when faced with the need to unlearn and by providing cognitive and economic space for new waves of entrepreneurial activity that might subsequently help put the cluster on a new and promising track.

The final chapter by Ron Martin and Peter Sunley, *Deconstructing Clusters: Chaotic Concept or Policy Panacea?*, has a more general focus, by reassessing in a critical way the very notion of a cluster and its often enthusiastic and widespread adoption as a regional planning policy tool. After tracing the popularity of the cluster metaphor to its vague and generic character that makes it easily applicable to a wide variety of contexts, and to its undeniable appeal to policy makers of both developed and peripheral regions more and more pre-occupied with boosting regional competitiveness and innovation, Martin and Sunley point to the many deficiencies and limitations that surround this notion. First, they point out that a major source of ambiguity is related to the definition of what actually constitutes a cluster. Neither the well-known Porter's definition nor the many other definitions proposed in the literature have any clear implications for what the geographical as well as industrial boundaries of clusters should be. The net result of this lack of clarity is that the cluster concept has become a sort of chaotic one, being equally applied to largely different types of industrial localizations and for processes that operate at different geographical scales. Secondly Martin and Sunley also criticize the cluster approach as a theory of competition and regional development. Beside the fundamental problems in understanding what is meant by regional 'competitiveness', they point out that the cluster approach, with its emphasis on the importance of factors external to firms, has quite obscured the importance of firm-based learning and, more generally, the accumulation of capabilities within the boundaries of firms, without, however, investigating in depth the functioning of all sorts of linkages and interactions that are assumed to be so important. Moreover, a fundamental limitation of the cluster theory is that it tends to abstract clusters from the rest of the economic landscape, not situating cluster development within the overall dynamics and evolution of industry and innovation and the wider process of regional development. In the third place, Martin and Sunley show how this conceptual confusion reflects upon the attempts to empirically identify and delimit clusters. These vary from 'top-down' approaches that rely on quantitative data, mostly census-type geographical data collected at the level of administrative spatial units, to 'bottom-up' exercises that apply qualitative and highly subjective methodologies. The result of this variety in the ways to identify clusters is that even a simple count of clusters within a country may go from a mere handful to several dozens. From the perspective of public policies, Martin and Sunley stress how this conceptual and empirical elusiveness does not permit adoption of the cluster framework as a solid basis for public intervention. In particular, they strongly oppose the idea that it is possible to identify successful cluster 'blueprints' that can be implemented in different economic, social and institutional contexts. Moreover, they also point out the many risks of failure involved in policy strategies too much oriented towards supporting local and regional specialization. These are all conclusions that most, if not all the contributions in this book are likely to share.

1.3   Some Broad Lessons and New Research Directions on Clusters, Networks, and Innovation

What are the main lessons that can be learned from this book? And which are the main research indications that could be drawn from them? Undoubtedly, the authors in this book broadly share the analytical view that *economies of agglomeration and networks effects* are key explanatory variables for the emergence, growth, and success of a cluster of innovations and innovators. To these two factors, this book adds a series of other important points that can be summarized in the following:

a. *Various research traditions and tools* have to be used in order to examine clusters, networks, and innovation in depth and in a complete way. Regional economics, the new economic geography, networks analyses, the innovation system tradition, evolutionary theory, and the capability approach, all provide a different but complementary support to the analysis of clusters and innovation.

b. Similarly, for an analysis of a cluster, *different types of networks* and their relationships have to be examined. In this way it is possible to disentangle relevant and complementary information on the types of knowledge created and diffused, on the types of linkages and relationships and on their differential effects on innovation.

c. The analysis of the *emergence and dynamics of clusters* has to become one of the major items in the research agenda. Clusters should not be examined only in a static framework and at a given point in time. Rather, clusters have specific stages of development and transformation. Their identification is a very important pre-condition for any serious analytical study. In particular, while many analyses have been focused on established successful clusters, the start-up and emergence phases prove to be crucial and are characterized by different processes and mechanisms compared to the stability or maturity stages.

d. *Knowledge and learning of the variety of different players* are key elements for an understanding of the rise, growth, and transformation of a cluster. They also provide explanations for the innovativeness and the organization of a cluster, as well as for the horizontal and the vertical interactions and the division of labor among firms.

e. *The accumulation of capabilities in key (large) actors* is a fundamental process in the growth and development of a cluster. During the initial stage of a cluster, some (large) firms may emerge as global players in terms of international leadership and rate of innovation. The presence of these key actors has major implications for the creation of new firms through spin-offs, human capital formation, and the creation of new skills.

f. *Sectoral specificities* have to be taken into consideration for an explanation of differences in agglomeration economies across areas. Different industries and services have different patterns of firms' agglomeration, depending on the specificities of their technological regimes and sectoral systems of innovation.

g. *Labor-market characteristics and spin-offs are major elements in cluster development.* The availability of a highly skilled labor force and university-trained human capital, as well as of localized mobility of people, effective labor markets for technical and managerial people and spin-offs are quite relevant for the working and growth of a cluster.

h. *Disentangle as much as possible the notions of proximity and spillovers and move beyond them to deeper concepts such as face-to-face contacts, social networks, and labor mobility.* The literature on localized knowledge spillovers has had the undeniable merit of drawing the attention on the spatial dimension of innovative activities. But the very success of this approach has somewhat hindered the search for the channels and mechanisms through which knowledge spillovers flow. Perhaps it is now time to capitalize on the notion of knowledge spillovers and move beyond it. On the one hand, new analytical tools are being developed to explicitly model and empirically measure the networks of social linkages and contacts that are so crucial for the functioning of a cluster. On the other hand, it is now very clear that more analytical and empirical attention should be devoted to the study of some key local institutions, especially to the working of the local labor market and to the set of rules governing the relations among employers and employees.

i. *International specialization and demand linkages matter very much for the growth of clusters.* Clusters may position themselves differently on international markets in terms of sectoral, technological, and product specialization. Not only do these differences greatly affect the specific organization of a cluster because of differences in the underlying knowledge and learning processes, but they may also greatly affect its development and success. In particular, the link with a large and advanced demand and the complementarity with existing clusters or international leaders may positively affect the growth of a cluster. On the contrary, cluster emergence through competition with existing leaders on the same products and markets has not always proven successful, particularly if the cluster is located in countries different from the leading ones.

j. Localization and globalization coexist in a cluster. High-tech clusters have both a local dimension and an international one. These dimensions interact at various levels – knowledge, technologies, products, individuals, firm, institutions, and so on – and have to be taken into account for an explanation of the dynamics of the cluster.

k. The effect of the national context on clusters is often significant. Clusters are embedded in specific national systems of innovation and production that differ in terms of development, actors, structure, government policy, and legal and social institutions. These differences do shape the start, growth, and organization of a cluster.

l. The emergence of local institutions is very important in the initial phases of a cluster and may be crucial for its subsequent growth and success. In the initial phase, cluster-specific institutions and non-firm organizations may spring up and become key elements in the working and growth of a cluster. The processes of emergence (and eventual transformation) of these institutions and non-firm organizations are usually affected by, and in turn affect, national non-firm organizations and institutions (such as government policy and national regulations) and international ones (such as multinational corporations).

m. Co-evolution and path dependence are key elements in the explanation of the emergence and growth of clusters and of their differences. It is the dynamic interplay of all the variables examined so far – knowledge, technologies, market structure, institutions, labor market, social setting, proximity advantages – that lead to emergence of specific clusters in specific areas. Co-evolutionary processes and path dependence lead to differential growth and specific dynamics of agglomeration and clustering.

n. Thus, the replicability of successful clusters by public policy is often doomed to failure. The previous point, corroborated by the evidence in this book, points to the difficulty in replicating successful clusters. Several chapters of this book indeed point to some factors that are common to most high-technology clusters, thus representing strong regularities and therefore broad indications for public policy. However, the actual replicability of successful clusters may be something different. Because the emergence of successful clusters is, in fact, the result of coevolutionary and path-dependent processes, the identification of single factors (which indeed does represent a major step forward in the analysis and in public policy suggestions) may not imply necessarily the understanding of a 'complete recipe' for the triggering off of a phase of clusters' emergence and growth. And, moreover, this complete recipe is not what public policy should aim at in the first place. In fact, all the policy indications stemming from this book clearly point to the role of accommodating policies and to the creation of support infrastructure (in terms of education, institutions, and so on), rather than to a well-structured, articulated and complete set of policy interventions aiming to directly affect the dynamics of a cluster.

o. Finally, public policy should be *sensitive to the life cycle of a cluster*, and therefore differ according to the specific stage a cluster is actually in. Public policy has to be supportive (but not dirigist) in the early stage, outward looking in the mature stage and creatively destructive in the declining stage.

We think that these are the most important lessons that can be drawn from the contributions in this book. At the same time, these lessons also represent clear indications for future research in the realm of clusters, networks, and innovation.

References

Audretsch, D. B. and Feldman, M. P. (1996), 'R&D spillovers and the geography of innovation and production', *American Economic Review*, **86**(3): 630–640.

Braczyk, H., Cooke, P., and Heidenreich, M. (eds) (1998), *Regional Innovation Systems*, London: UCL Press.

Breschi, S. (2000), 'The geography of innovation: a cross-sector analysis', *Regional Studies*, **34**(3): 213–229.

Capello, R. (1999), 'Spatial transfer of knowledge in high technology milieux: learning versus collective learning processes', *Regional Studies*, **33**(4): 353–365.

Carlsson, B. (1997), *Technological systems and industrial dynamics*, Dordrecht: Kluwer Academic Publishers.

Dosi, G. (1997), 'Opportunities, incentives and the collective patterns of technological change', *Economic Journal*, **107**(127): 1530–1547.

Edquist, C. (1997), *Systems of innovation*, London: Frances Pinter.

Feldman, M. P. and Audretsch D. B. (1999), 'Innovation in cities: science-based diversity, specialisation and localised competition', *European Economic Review*, **43** (Special issue): 409–429.

Freeman, C. (1987), *Technology policy and economic performance: Lessons from Japan*, London: Frances Pinter.

Gordon, I. R. and McCann, P. (2000), 'Industrial clusters: Complexes, agglomeration and/or social networks', *Urban Studies*, **37**(3): 513–532.

Hirschman, A. O. (1958), *The strategy of economic development*, Clinton, MA: Yale University Press.

Jacobs, J. (1961), *The death and life of great American cities*, New York: Random House.

Jaffe, A. B. (1989), 'Real effects of academic research', *American Economic Review*, **79**(5): 957–970.

Jaffe, A. B., Trajtenberg, M., and Henderson R. (1993), 'Geographic localisation of knowledge spillovers as evidenced by patent citations', *Quarterly Journal of Economics*, **108**: 577–598.

Krugman, P. (1991), *Geography and trade*, Cambridge, MA: MIT Press.

Krugman, P. (1998), 'What's new about new economic geography?', *Oxford Review of Economic Policy*, **14**(2): 7–17.

Malerba, F. (2004), *Sectoral systems of innovation*, Cambridge: Cambridge University Press.

Malerba, F. and Orsenigo, L. (1997), 'Technological regimes and sectoral patterns of innovative activities', *Industrial and Corporate Change*, **6**: 83–117.

Martin, R. and Sunley, P. (1996), 'Paul Krugman's geographical economics and its implications for regional development theory: a critical assessment', *Economic Geography*, **72**: 259–292.

Marshall, A. (1920), *Industry and trade*, London: Macmillan.

Maskell, P. and Malmberg, A. (1999), 'Localised learning and industrial competitiveness', *Cambridge Journal of Economics*, **23**(2): 167–186.

Metcalfe, S. (1998), *Evolutionary economics and creative destruction*, London: Routledge & Kegan Paul.

Nelson, R. (1993), *National innovation systems*, Oxford: Oxford University Press.

Nelson, R. (1995), 'Recent evolutionary theorizing about economic change', *Journal of Economic Literature*, **33**: 48–90.

Nelson, R. and Winter, S. (1982), *An evolutionary theory of economic change*, Cambridge, MA: The Belknapp Press of Harvard University Press.

Perroux, F. (1950), 'Economic space: theory and applications', *Quarterly Journal of Economics*, **64**(1): 89–104.

Porter, M. (1998), *On competition*, Harvard: Harvard Business School Press.

Rallet, A. and Torre, A. (1999), 'Is geographical proximity necessary in the innovation networks in the era of global economy?', *GeoJournal*, **49**(4): 373–380.

Saxenian, A. (1994), *Regional advantage. Culture and competition in Silicon Valley and Route 128*, Harvard: Harvard University Press.

Storper, M. (1992), 'The limits to globalization: technology districts and international trade', *Economic Geography*, **68**: 60–93.

Storper, M. and Harrison, B. (1991), 'Flexibility, hierarchy and regional development: The changing structure of industrial production systems and their forms of governance in the 1980s', *Research Policy*, **20**: 407–422.

PART I

2

*Network Models of Innovation and Knowledge Diffusion**

ROBIN COWAN

Introduction

Much of modern microeconomics is built from the starting point of the perfectly competitive market. In this model, there are an infinite number of agents – buyers and sellers, none of whom has the power to influence the price by his actions. The good is well defined, indeed it is perfectly standardized. And any interactions agents have is mediated by the market. That is, all transactions are anonymous, in the sense that the identities of buyer and seller are unimportant. Effectively, the seller sells 'to the market' and the buyer buys 'from the market'. This follows from the standardization of the good, and the fact that the market imposes a very strong discipline on prices. Implicit here is one (or both) of two assumptions. Either all agents are identical in every relevant respect, apart, possibly, from the prices they ask or offer; or every agent knows every relevant detail about every other agent. If the former, then obviously my only concern as a buyer is the prices asked by the population of sellers, since in every other way they are identical. If the latter, then each seller has a unique good, and again what I am concerned with is the price of it. In either case, we see that prices capture all relevant information and are enough for every agent to make all the decisions he needs to make.

It is commonplace to observe that we seldom see a perfectly competitive market. We never see infinite numbers of agents, and obviously someone is able to influence prices, else how would they be set, and how would they change? (See the debate between Becker, 1962, 1963; and Kirzner, 1962, 1963, on this issue.) But that alone does not say that the model is a bad approximation. More important is that while it may be possible, in principle, for any agent to interact with any other, in fact this is far from the case in practice. Typically, any agent only interacts with a very small proportion of the population. The 'global market' does not really exist. Interactions tend to be quite localized in many senses. It is also the case, though, that we don't have perfect information about other agents, neither is it the case that they are identical. Moreover, this non-identicality may matter – it may be economically relevant. Agents are in different physical locations, one from another. In some ways this is easily handled by adding to the definition of a good its location, and then including the price of transportation in the information set. But more complex changes have to be made, for example, when agents are competing: address models take account of the fact that when agents are close together they may have to compete harder with each other than when they are far apart.[1] Agents may use different standards or technologies. If a good exhibits network externalities or increasing returns to adoption, two agents will create externalities for each other if they use the same standard or technologies, but not if they do not. But often this is not an anonymous effect: it is true that there is a global network externality to telephone use, but there is a much stronger local externality: the value of a telephone is much higher if my friends own them than if they do not, regardless of aggregate behavior. The identity of who is using which technology makes a difference to its economic value to any particular agent. Similarly, the history that a pair of agents shares can have a significant effect on the nature of their interactions. If we have interacted many times and the experience has been good, trust is created and we can have certain kinds of interactions (based on a hand-shake, for example). If we have no history, or even more so if we have had bad experiences in the past, hand-shakes will not be enough, and there may be some types of interactions that we simply cannot arrange. In each case, more than just the price of the good matters.

In each of these cases, with the possible exception of history, the phenomenon can be represented as an issue of space and distance. Geographical space is the most natural. Issues of transportation costs are easily understood in this context, and the degree of competition among sellers is relatively well understood as it is affected by distance (see Anderson *et al.*, 1992). However, technologies or standards exist in a space of technical attributes; preferences exist in a Lancasterian characteristic space and so on. The point then can be seen that the distance between two agents affects their interactions. If, for example, agents are close together in technology space, they may be able to share hardware, software, or information. These interactions may be impossible if the agents are far from each other in technology space – the software is not compatible across hardware problems; the technologies have different operating features, so information about how to make one of them efficient will not apply to the other, and so on.

As pointed out above, address models can be used to capture some of these phenomena. But when coupled with other issues that have been studied by economists in recent decades, there may be a more natural way to approach some of these problems.

2.1 Knowledge Distribution

Distance and transportation costs are clearly relevant when talking about physical goods. Surprisingly, they are also relevant when discussing something as intangible as knowledge or information. In many economic models, knowledge is assumed to be a public good: once discovered and publicized, it is freely available to all in the economy. The presence of the Internet and the World Wide Web should make the 'globally available' aspect of knowledge even stronger. Consider patents. Patents are highly codified data and are by definition stored in a public database, the most important of which (USPTO and EPO) are now searchable online. Thus, anyone with an internet connection can read any patent granted in the US or Europe (and many other jurisdictions as well). Diffusion of the knowledge or information contained in patents should be a truly global phenomenon. But the work of Jaffe *et al.* (1993) shows quite clearly that this is not the case. The diffusion of information is a process embedded in location. Distance is important in knowledge diffusion – the closer we are to the location of the originator of knowledge, the sooner we learn it.

This result has been revisited by Breschi and Lissoni (2003). Jaffe *et al.* looked at diffusion over geographical distance; Breschi and Lissoni add social distance. Knowledge diffusion is not only a geographically spatial phenomenon, it is also a 'socially spatial' phenomenon. That is, the more closely connected socially I am to the originator of a piece of knowledge, the more quickly I will learn about it. What these results strongly suggest is that knowledge diffusion is taking place to a very large extent by personal contact. Knowledge is passed informally through face-to-face contacts, and direct interactions. One explanation for this is that much relevant knowledge is tacit, or at least not codified, which means that it cannot be broadcast, and can only be transmitted locally, through direct interactions. So space matters for knowledge diffusion, and social space may matter as much as or more than geographic space. 'Social space' can only be sensibly understood in the context of social networks.

2.2   Behind the Current Interest in Networks

In economics, interest in networks has been fuelled by three different developments, all of which occurred in the last decades of the twentieth century.

2.2.1   Network Technologies

Since the early 1980s, economists have been interested in technologies that function as part of a network. The prototypical example is the telephone. A single telephone has no value, but when connected to a network of other telephones, it has. We see many examples of these sorts of technologies, particularly associated with information and communication: telephone; telefax; e-mail; and so on. Two of the main issues in the economics literature on this subject have been the presence of network externalities and standardization. For an artifact to join a network, it must be able to communicate with the other artifacts that make up that network. Some form of interoperation standards must be in place. In the early days of e-mail, the first large commercial network, Compuserve, was unable to connect to the BITNET, which was the main e-mail form used over the Internet. Thus, a potential e-mail user had to decide which network to join. More generally, who you are connected to, and who you want to be connected to is a question of which standard to adopt. It is worth observing, since this issue will arise again below, that many of these network technologies are concerned with the distribution of information. Information is diffused using these technologies, and physical networks form as agents decide which standard to adopt, and thus which other agents it will be possible to communicate with. Networks form as agents adopt technologies. Some of these networks reside in physical infrastructure, others are more virtual, for example the network of people sharing information about a computer operating system or programming language. Network issues are thus at the heart of many of the new technologies.

2.2.2   Boundaries of the Firm

In the last couple of decades there has been a resurgence of interest in the boundaries of the firm (see, for example, Holmstrom and Roberts, 1998). There seems to have been a trend whereby the monolithic, vertically integrated firm has slowly dissolved as more and more of its activities are outsourced. This began simply with parts, as a firm faced the 'make-or-buy' decision for the parts of its assembly. The 'raw materials' that came into the firm became less 'raw'. This is a relatively minor change, but does involve creating relationships with suppliers based not only on price but also on trust, since, a low-quality shipment of parts (whether deliberate or not, on the part of the supplier) could be disastrous. Firm boundaries have since become even more porous: firms now outsource not only parts, but also design. Parts manufacturers are likely to know more than parts users about how to design parts efficiently and for efficient production, so it is sensible that they have a strong hand in this design process. Again, though, even more than with parts supply, with design supply firms and their suppliers need a particular kind of relationship. Long-standing relationships, partial co-operation, joint ventures all are forms that emerged as the former vertically integrated firms attempted to take advantage on the human capital and competencies of their suppliers. These are market relationships only to a small degree. They demand direct interactions, and a significant amount of stability, to ensure that the transactions can take place effectively.

2.2.3   The Expanding Knowledge Base

One explanation for the deeper outsourcing is the expanding knowledge base of industries. Granstand (1998) summarizes several studies that reach the following conclusions: In recent decades, large, technology-based firms in particular have expanded their technology bases into a wider range of technologies. This technological diversification has been one of the fundamental causes of firm growth. In addition, because an expanding technology base demands an expanding knowledge base, this technological diversification has been a leading cause not only of an increase in R&D expenditure, but also of an increase in external technology sourcing (see also Granstand and Sjölander, 1990). Generally, we can see that as the range of a firm's technologies expands, the firm must learn about them, how to use the new technologies, how to develop them, how to integrate them into existing products, and how to create new products from them. Thus, not only does a firm need more knowledge, it needs more types of knowledge. Initially in any case, it can be difficult to develop this knowledge in-house. Because of its nature, knowledge, and especially new knowledge can be difficult to acquire in the market, so firms seek some form of collaboration with other firms that already have the knowledge. Firms sought arrangements to outsource not only production and design, but now also R&D. The rise of strategic R&D alliances since 1980 has been very striking (see Hagedoorn, 2002). Having a portfolio of alliances acts as insurance for a firm wishing not to be taken by surprise by new technology developments. It also gives the firm rapid access to disparate and varied information should it need it (for a discussion of the motivation behind the rise in strategic alliances see, for example, Narula and Hagedoorn, 1999). Firms act to create links with other firms with the goal of transmitting knowledge across those links. In a more extreme version, we see the rise of the networked organization. This is sometimes viewed as an intermediate organizational form, between markets on the one hand, and hierarchies on the other. The central idea is that the 'organization' takes advantage of a large amount of autonomy between nodes, but at the same time uses links between those nodes to transmit value between them. Clearly, this organizational form precludes the idea of global interaction in the sense that any firm can interact with any other. Indeed, part of the structure demands that firms interact only with a relatively circumscribed subset of the entire population.

What we observe, taking these issues together, are occasions in which an agent interacts with only a small part of the population. Further, these interactions are not (entirely) market mediated, but take place rather over more direct connections, and long-lived connections can be more effective than temporary ones. Finally, the identity of the agents can make a difference to the nature and success of the interaction. This sounds much like the description of a network: agents are nodes, they are linked to particular other nodes, and interactions take place only over these direct links.

2.3 The Economics of Networks

2.3.1 *Empirically*

There is now a sizeable empirical literature that uses this approach for industry studies: Silicon Valley, and the computer industry more generally (Saxenian, 1991; Langlois and Robertson, 1992); Japanese business groups (Imai, 1989; Lincoln and Gerlach, 1998); the biotech industry (Powell *et al.*, 1996; Orsenigo *et al.*, 2001); Italian industrial districts (Pyke *et al.* 1992; Lazerson and Lorenzoni, 1999); the automobile industry (Dyer, 1996); the fashion industry (Uzzi, 1997). All of them observe that the 'peculiar' properties of these industries can be understood by analysing the agents' behavior as part of a network structure, and that an important part of the way these industries function is determined by precisely who interacts with whom. Social capital, developed by direct interactions between agents, permits the agents to circumvent many of the problems implicit in anonymous markets such as opportunistic behavior, imperfect information and incomplete contracts, the transmission of tacit knowledge, knowledge spillovers, and so on. The social capital developed through network interaction therefore reduces transaction costs, and can serve to make the industry more efficient in many ways.

2.3.2 *Theoretically*

In addition to the relatively recent empirical work on networks, there has been a slightly longer tradition of abstract network analysis. Roughly speaking, analytical models have been of two types: Ising models and random graphs.

2.3.2.1 *Ising Models*   In an Ising model, agents are located at fixed points in a regular integer space, for example at the integers on a line or at integer co-ordinates in Euclidian two dimensions. Agents are directly connected to their n nearest neighbors in the physical space. These structures are often called nearest-neighbor networks or graphs. The networks are clearly very regular, and have high levels of local co-ordination, and typically, are locally very dense. They do, however, have relatively long average paths between pairs of agents. The general model was developed in 1925 (Ising, 1925) to study ferromagnets, and therefore its analytic properties are relatively well understood. In economics, it has been used to study a wide variety of situations: macrodynamics (Durlauf, 1993); technology diffusion (Allen, 1982; An and Kiefer, 1993); criminal behavior (Glaeser *et al.*, 1996); the effectiveness of prices (Föllmer, 1974). All this work takes advantage of the fact that in the Ising model local interactions are very neatly defined, and only distance, between locations, rather than absolute location matters.

Nonetheless, complex patterns of aggregate behavior can emerge from local interactions.

2.3.2.2 Random Graphs At the other extreme of network structures, economists have used random graph models to study, for example, coalition formation (Kirman, 1983; Ionnides, 1990); technology diffusion (Steyer and Zimmermann, 1998); learning (Ellison, 1993); strategy revision (Blume, 1995). In these graphs, any agent is connected with some probability to any other agent in the population, regardless of location. Consequently, the networks that emerge have no spatial patterns in the space in which agents are physically located. An alternative interpretation is that agents are not located in physical space, but rather only in network space, so any notion of distance is only distance in the network. In addition, there is essentially no local coherence, and generally graphs are not locally dense, even in network space. On the other hand, random graphs are known to have low average path lengths: the path in network space between two agents is, on average, low.

From the point of view of knowledge creation and diffusion, the focus on these extreme forms of network structure draws attention to the contrast in the properties of local density and path length. It is often asserted that innovation is facilitated by agglomeration of human capital. A location in which many agents are working on related issues creates a critical mass of knowledge workers so that they become an epistemic community, in which a common language emerges, problem definitions become standardized, and problem-solving heuristics emerge and are developed. In this type of situation, Marshal's idea that knowledge is "in the air" applies strongly. Agglomerations having these features foster innovation. (See the empirical studies referred to above.) Applying the network model, this situation is present if the network of agents exhibits high local density, or equivalently high 'cliquishness'. That is, if there are (relatively small) groups of agents who are closely and heavily interconnected. As we have seen, this is true in a nearest-neighbor graph, but not in a random graph.

By contrast, knowledge diffusion is most rapid when path lengths are short. Diffusion is about spreading a piece of knowledge to all agents in the economy, and this will happen fastest (and with least degradation) when it takes few steps between the originator of the knowledge and its recipients. Short path lengths, associated with the random-graph structure make this happen most quickly.

Thus there appears to be a tension between knowledge creation and knowledge diffusion. The tension is resolved by the network structure known as the small world. This is a network structure that is at the same time highly cliquish and with short paths between agents. It lies between the nearest-neighbor network and the random network.

2.3.2.3 Small Worlds Economists focused on Ising and random-graph models partly because they had been extensively explored in other disciplines, but more because there was no obvious way to characterize systematically structures that lay between these two extremes. Watts and Strogatz (1998) develop a one-parameter class of random-graph models in which the parameter could be used to scale between the regular graph of the Ising model and the random graph of random-graph theory. The algorithm for generating a graph was as follows: create a regular nearest-neighbor graph. Fix the parameter p. Examine each link in the network, and with probability p rewire one end of that link, connecting it to an agent chosen randomly from the population (in the process checking to ensure that agents are not connecting to themselves, and that any pair of agents is connected at most once). This algorithm scales between the regular, nearest-neighbor graph (if $p = 0$) and the random graph (if $p = 1$), but also has the feature that it does so without changing the density, or total number of connections in the graph. This is illustrated in Fig. 2.1.

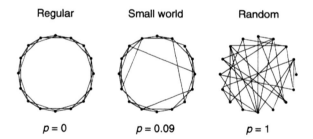

Fig. 2.1 Transition from a locally ordered structure to a random graph, dependent on p

This algorithm provides a way of finding the small world. Small worlds are characterized by two structural parameters: cliquishness and path length. Cliquishness captures the idea that 'my friends are friends of each other', that is, of local density. Formally, average cliquishness is defined as

$$C = \frac{1}{N} \sum_{i} \sum_{j,l \in \Gamma_i} \frac{X(j,l)}{\| \Gamma_i \| (\| \Gamma_i \| -1)/2},$$

where $X(j,l) = 1$ if $j \in \Gamma_i$ and $X(j,l) = 0$ otherwise; Γ_i is the set of neighbors of i (those to whom he is directly connected), and $\| \Gamma_i \|$ is the size of that neighborhood.

Average path length is formally defined as

$$L(p) = \frac{1}{N} \sum_{i} \sum_{j \neq i} \frac{d(i,j)}{N-1},$$

where $d(i,j)$ is the length of the shortest path between i and j.

Not surprisingly, as p increases, since the local coherence necessarily falls with the introduction of random links, cliquishness decreases. Similarly, since a random link is a potential short-cut, average path length also falls. Crucially, though, the latter falls much faster than the former. This is illustrated in Fig. 2.2, where we observe that for values of p between roughly 0.01 and 0.1, cliquishness is close to that of a nearest-neighbor graph, while path length is close to that of a random graph. In this region, conditions are favorable both for knowledge creation and for knowledge diffusion.

2.4   Small Worlds and Innovation

Diffusion involves passing information or knowledge from one agent to another. There are many possible microeconomic models of this process. Empirical studies have revealed two striking ones. Allen (1983) observes what he calls 'collective invention' in the steel industry in Cleveland (UK) in the nineteenth century. (There are many other significant examples of the same phenomenon, see Cowan and Jonard, 2004 for a brief discussion.) In a situation of collective invention, competitors in an industry share technical information relatively freely with each other. Technical advance by one firm is essentially broadcast to other firms in the region. The broadcast takes place

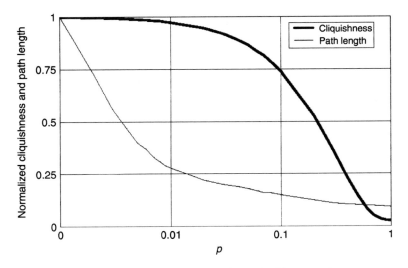

Fig. 2.2 Cliquishness and path length as determined by network structure

sometimes through local publication (Nuvolari, forthcoming), or through presentations at meetings (Allen, 1983). The most popular modern example is open-source software development. Again, technical advances made by one developer are broadcast to a group of fellow-developers, and so a common undertaking to improve the technology exists.

The second microeconomic model of knowledge transfer is identified by von Hippel (1998). He observes a form of knowledge barter in a variety of industries. Technical managers of plants meet informally and discuss the technical problems they are faced with. Information passes among them outside any sort of market context. There is a caveat, however, which is that for information passed there is a quid pro quo – it seems to be accepted that if a person receives information but does not pass any out, he is eventually excluded from the interactions. Dyer and Nobeoka (2000) find similar strictures against free riding in the Toyota network—firms that do not freely share their knowledge are sanctioned. In the Toyota network sanctions are formal, whereas in von Hippel's work they seem to be socially governed. In both cases, though, knowledge transfers can be seen as a form of barter, in which agents effectively trade knowledge and information.

Recent papers by Cowan and Jonard (2003, 2004) examine these knowledge-transfer mechanisms using an underlying network structure to govern who interacts with whom.

2.4.1   Knowledge Transfer as Barter

Consider a population of N agents. Each agent has direct connections to, on average, n other agents. An agent is characterized by the set of agents to whom he is directly connected, and a knowledge endowment. Knowledge is of several types, so agents' endowments are represented by a vector. When agents meet, they trade knowledge in a barter arrangement, exchanging knowledge of different types. The 'exchange' however, only increases knowledge levels due to the non-rivalrous property of knowledge as a good. It is also the case that knowledge transfer is not complete. Absorptive capacity is not perfect (see Cohen and Levinthal, 1989 for a discussion of this issue).

Specifically, consider two agents i and j. Their respective knowledge endowments are $v_i = (v_{i,1}, v_{i,2} \ldots v_{i,K})$ and $v_j = (v_{j,1}, v_{j,2} \ldots v_{j,K})$. If i and j meet they make all possible trades, and we can describe how their knowledge vectors evolve in the following way. The K knowledge types are partitioned into pairs (m,n) such that $v_{i,m} > v_{j,m} + c$ and $v_{j,n} > v_{i,n} + c$. Then

$$v_{i,m}(t+1) = v_{i,m}(t);$$
$$v_{i,n}(t+1) = v_{i,n}(t) + a(v_{j,n}(t) - v_{i,n}(t));$$
$$v_{j,m}(t+1) = v_{j,m}(t) + a(v_{i,m}(t) - v_{j,m}(t));$$
$$v_{j,n}(t+1) = v_{j,n}(t),$$

where a is the absorptive capacity, and c is the per trade transaction cost. Absorptive capacity is less than one, which implies that the post-trade knowledge levels do not converge completely. Agent j is able to learn only part of what i has to teach. A corollary of this is that as knowledge travels along a multiagent chain, from i to j to k and so on, the knowledge degrades. Thus, transmitting knowledge over a long chain is costly not only in terms of time, it is costly in terms of the diminution of the quantity of knowledge.

The dynamics of the model are very simple: Each period one agent is chosen randomly. At random, he selects one of his direct connections, and with that agent makes all possible trades. Over time, agents' knowledge endowments change as they trade. The question of interest is how aggregate knowledge levels grow with these underlying microeconomics, and how aggregate growth is affected by network architecture. To answer that question, the model is simulated, using the Watts–Strogatz algorithm to create the networks over which this process takes place.

At the beginning of each run of the simulation a network of agents is created using the Watts–Strogatz mechanism for a given value of p. Each agent is endowed with a knowledge vector $v_i = (v_{i,1}, v_{i,2} \ldots v_{i,K})$, where $v_{i,K}$ is drawn from a uniform $[0,1]$ distribution. Each period in simulation time a randomly drawn agent attempts trade with one of the agents to whom he is directly connected. The simulation is run until all possible trades have been exhausted, and then restarted with a new p value.

In a model like this, where no new knowledge is being created, it is clear that short path lengths should facilitate aggregate knowledge growth. Short path lengths imply that the knowledge that does exist is spread rapidly and widely through the population, and this would constitute a source of rapid growth in aggregate knowledge. This implies that a random network should be highly efficient. The results are different, however. It is the small-world network that is most effective in long-run aggregate knowledge growth.

The industrial districts literature argues that cliquishness is good for knowledge creation, as described above. But none of these effects is explicitly included in this model. The value of cliquishness arises from a different source. One of the disadvantages of a barter economy is the requirement that potential traders satisfy a double coincidence of wants. When this fails, potentially improving transfers do not take place. Cliquish network structures mitigate this problem, because within a clique there are typically several indirect but still short paths between any two agents. Thus, if i and j cannot trade due to a failed double coincidence of wants, the desired knowledge of j can still be transmitted to i if they share a common neighbor. This will be the case if the network is cliquish. Thus, the local redundancy of cliquish graphs is an effective way of circumventing problems arising from the double coincidence of wants constraint.

The time series of knowledge levels for different network structures shows interesting patterns. In a random network, there is no discernible geographic structure, but path lengths are short. Here, diffusion is very rapid early in the history, but the process is exhausted at relatively low knowledge levels as the double coincidence of wants constraint starts to be violated. In a network that is very regular, such as the nearest-neighbor network, the graph is locally dense but path lengths are long. This implies that diffusion is slow. But because of the local density, the double coincidence of wants issue does not bite, so aggregate knowledge growth can continue for a long time. In the small-world region, the network is locally dense, but has relatively short paths. The latter should imply rapid initial growth; the former should imply continued growth. Indeed, we observe these features of the small-world structure. Growth in the small world is relatively rapid early on (though not quite as rapid as the random world) and it continues for a very long time.

The small-world results are affected by absorptive capacity. The small world has value because it combines short path lengths with local redundancy. Redoing the experiment with different values for absorptive capacity shows that the optimal network structure, as measured by p in the rewiring algorithm, becomes more and more random, that is, the optimal value of p increases with absorptive capacity. This occurs because the relative importance of path length and cliquishness changes as absorptive capacity changes. This can be seen by considering the extreme case of $a = 1$. In this case, if i trades with j, the two become identical. A third agent, k, therefore, is indifferent between trading with i and trading with j. Thus, if k has a link to j, there is no value to k to have a link to i. This says that there is no value to cliquishness – k would be better to have a link to someone that j is not connected to.

2.4.2   Knowledge Transfer as Broadcast

The model just described saw knowledge transfer as taking place through a bilateral barter exchange. A contrasting situation exists where agents engage in local broadcasting of their new knowledge. This can be modelled using a similar underlying structure, but changing the knowledge dynamics (Cowan and Jonard, 2003).

Consider a population of N agents each having direct connections to, on average n other agents. An agent is characterized by the set of agents with whom he has direct connections, referred to as his neighbors, and by a scalar knowledge stock. In each period, one agent innovates and broadcasts his knowledge to his neighbors. This knowledge is received by his neighbors, and partially absorbed. The population of agents is heterogeneous in two respects: ability to innovate and ability to absorb. Thus, the characterization of an agent also includes his idiosyncratic innovation ability, b_i and his idiosyncratic absorptive capacity, a_i. The knowledge of an agent can increase for two reasons: the agent can innovate, a process that takes place exogenously; or the agent can receive new knowledge from a recent innovator. The knowledge dynamics for an innovator are simply

$$v_i(t + 1) = (1 + b_i)v_i(t).$$

If j is a neighbor of i, and i innovates, i then broadcasts to j. Agent j's knowledge increases as:

$$v_j(t + 1) = \max\left(v_j(t),\, v_j(t) + a_j(v_i(t) - v_j(t))\right),$$

and the knowledge of i is unchanged.

As in the previous section, in each run of the simulation a network is created for a particular value of p; agents are assigned random absorptive capacities, random innovation abilities, and random initial knowledge levels.

The model can be used for two purposes: to compare the performance characteristics of different network structures, and to ask how innovation and diffusion over fixed network compares with random diffusion such as an epidemic model. A slight modification of the model lets us approximate an epidemic model of diffusion. In the model as described, any time a particular agent innovates, he broadcasts his knowledge to the same set of n agents. These agents are his (unchanging) neighbors. Suppose instead that when an agent broadcasts, he broadcasts to n agents chosen at random from the entire population. Here, agents do not have a fixed set of neighbors, so the distribution of knowledge in the first stage is completely random, as it is in the standard epidemic model. Comparing this model to the one described above will give an indication of the value of a fixed network as a diffusion vehicle.

In this model, similarly to the barter model discussed above, the magnitude of absorptive capacity has an important effect on the results. When absorptive capacity is low ($a < 0.5$) small worlds dominate in terms of long-run knowledge levels. The region of $0.01 < p < 0.1$ produces the highest long-run aggregate knowledge levels. However, when absorptive capacity is high ($a > 0.5$) the random world ($p = 1$) dominates, and the extent to which it dominates increases with a.

Absorptive capacity also affects the comparison between networked and random, epidemic diffusion. If absorptive capacity is low, a fixed network performs better than random diffusion, no matter the value of p. By contrast, when absorptive capacity is high, random diffusion is better than almost all network structures. The value of the network comes from the repetition of interaction, which is most valuable when to convey knowledge effectively takes more than a single interaction.

Small worlds perform well as structures over which to diffuse knowledge and support innovation. But there are situations in which the small world is not optimal. If the knowledge and the community of agents surrounding it is such that transmitted knowledge is easy to absorb, then a random world, which has short paths between agents, is most efficient. However, a more general result is that networks *per se* are a good thing – they perform better than a world in which knowledge is diffused to random agents each time. It is important to note here that this is all in the context of networks with constant density. So random diffusion does not mean broadcasting to the entire economy, but rather to a randomly chosen subset of it.

Both of the models just described were models of diffusion. In a variation of the barter model Cowan *et al.* (2004), introduce innovation by the knowledge recipients. Here, agents are not merely passive receivers of knowledge but they actively attempt to use their new knowledge to make innovations. In this model, if i innovates and then broadcasts to j, then if $v_i(t) > v_j(t)$ the knowledge level of j changes as:

$$v_j(t) = v_j(t)\left[1 + \left(\frac{v_j(t)}{v_i(t)}\right)^\gamma \left[1 - \left(\frac{v_j(t)}{v_i(t)}\right)^\gamma\right]\right].$$

If the recipient is well below the broadcaster in knowledge level, it may be difficult for the recipient to understand the message, and so absorption is low. At the other extreme, if the recipient is close to the broadcaster, there is little new in the message. At intermediate positions, it is possible (particularly if γ is large), for the recipient to receive the information, innovate and finally achieve a knowledge level higher than the broadcaster. We understand this situation to represent an industry in which innovative potential is large.

In this model the small-world effect is not present. The value of cliquishness tends to be outweighed by the effects of short paths. However, the value of short paths depends heavily on the parameter γ. When γ is small, so the industry has little innovative potential, knowledge advance is largely through imitating those who exogenously innovate. Short paths are valuable, and the random graph is most efficient. However, if γ is large, the reverse is true. In this case, leap-frogging becomes an important phenomenon and agents who do so make big advances. They can rapidly leave the rest of the population behind. This means that their broadcasts are too esoteric for others to understand, and thus contribute little to aggregate population growth. This feature is highly attenuated, though, if the network is cliquish. Within a clique, agents tend to be similar to each other, so relatively few agents get left behind, and cliques advance rapidly together. Cliquish structures produce the highest growth rates.

The same argument explains the comparison of a network structure with random broadcasts. Again, the value of γ is important. When innovation potential is high, networks perform better than a homogeneous mixing. When γ is low, the reverse is true. Again, it has to do with agents getting too far ahead of the rest of the population, and so contributing little to aggregate growth.

This can be interpreted as relating to the industry life cycle. In a new industry, innovative potential is high, as there are many avenues unexplored, and many discoveries yet to be made. This corresponds to a high γ, and so suggests that the optimal network structure for communication will be cliquish. By contrast, in a mature industry, dominant designs exist, innovation is more exploitation than exploration, and so innovative potential is much lower. This can be represented by a low γ, and so the optimal network structure will be random. These results fit well with the discussion of absorptive capacity. In a new industry, typically knowledge is less codified, and so absorptive capacity is low. One of the features of the emergence of a dominant design is that the cost-benefit calculation for codification changes, and codification tends to be a more common activity. This will increase absorptive capacity, and so change the optimal network structure to be more random.

In spite of the wide play the notion of small worlds has had in general, in economics the efficiency properties of small worlds have been little explored. One exception is Wilhite (2001), who develops a trade model in which agents must trade only over a network structure, but in a context of imperfect information. He compares the performance of the economy, in terms of whether or not it reaches a Pareto optimal equilibrium, and importantly, how long it takes to get there, accumulating transactions costs along the path. He finds that when agents trade over a small-world network structure the economy performs better on these criteria than it does using different trading infrastructures: agents in a small world rapidly reach the Pareto optimal equilibrium (as does a complete network, which mimics perfect competition) but with very small search costs.

Recent empirical analysis of economic networks has focused to a very large extent on the network structure. In particular, economists have asked whether various networks have the small-world structure. In general, the answer is 'yes'.[2] Many examples of small-world networks in economics have been observed: patent citations among Dutch firms (BRITE/EURAM network, the 5th Framework TSER network); Dutch patent citations (Cowan and Jonard, 2003); strategic alliances (Duysters and Verspagen, forthcoming); LANL co-authorship in a variety of academic disciplines (Barabasi and Albert, 2000; Newman, 2001); patent citation in US biotech (Johnson and Mareva, 2002); interlocking corporate directorships in the US (for example, Davis *et al.*, 2003). There has been considerable work now describing economic networks, and it is clear that the small-world structure is pervasive, yet there has been little empirical work addressing the efficiency of different structures. Research along these lines could make an important contribution to our understanding of different economic structures.

2.5 Network Formation

In much of the literature that uses networks as an analytical tool the network structure is taken as given. Agents have links to other particular agents and these links do not change over time. This is clearly a very special case, as most networks evolve continuously and nodes create and destroy links to other nodes.

Roughly two strands of literature have emerged in economics to study this phenomenon. A literature based on a game-theoretic approach defines a notion of stability and asks which network structures are stable under different conditions.[3] Here, the aim is to characterize agents' incentives to form or break links, and then to look for configurations in which no agent wants to form new links or break an existing one. A central question here is whether stable networks are efficient. A second literature has a much more evolutionary approach, in which in principle every agent is connected to every other, but links are activated probabilistically. The probability of i activating a link to j depends on whether this link has been valuable in the past, so, as experience is gained with different links, the probability of choosing them changes. This model is very similar in spirit to the Hebb learning model in psychology (Hebb, 1949).

2.5.1 Pairwise Stability

In the game-theory tradition authors looks for stable network structures. Stability is determined at the agent level. If no agent wishes to destroy any of his existing links, and no pair of unconnected agents wish to form a link between them, then the structure is stable. An early example of such a model is the connection model of Jackson and Wolinsky (1996). In this model, an agent pays a cost c to participate in a link. If agents i and j are connected they receive benefits from that connection of $\delta^{d(i,j)}$, where $\delta < 1$ and $d(i,j)$ is the number of links in the shortest path between i and j. In this simple model, which network structures are stable is clearly determined by the relative sizes of c and δ. If $\delta + \delta^2(N-2)/2 < c$ costs are too big and no connections are formed – the empty network is stable. If $c < \delta - \delta^2$, connections are cheap, and the complete network is stable. For intermediate values of c, there are many possible stable networks, one of which is the star network.

Many models build on this simple connection model, and the results are relatively robust. The continued emergence of empty, complete, and star networks is striking (and in some conditions a circle or a wheel emerges as well). Very roughly speaking, the density of the stable network increases as costs of forming links decreases. But because of the nature of network structures, there tend to be critical values across which we observe dramatic changes in the emergent network architecture. Generally, stable networks are efficient, but there is a region of the parameter space (for intermediate values of the costs of forming links) in which there could be a tension between stability and efficiency: some stable networks may be efficient, but others are not.

Pairwise stability is both a strong and a weak equilibrium concept. It is strong in the sense that it characterizes a stationary state. It describes an unchanging network. But it could be weak in that it can describe fragile networks. Carayol and Roux (2003) argue that introducing a small amount of noise into the link formation algorithm is more realistic and implies that the stochastically stable state is a more reasonable solution concept. Further, they introduce the assumption that costs of link formation will be lower when partners are located near to each other (equivalently, the probability of meeting a potential partner increases as the distance between them decreases).[4] Introducing this type of preferential meeting into a simulation model of network formation implies first that many pairwise stable states (and in particular the star) are not stable, and second that the stochastically stable networks often have small-world properties.

A paper that deserves particular attention here is Goyal and Joshi (2002). This is one of the first papers to introduce solid microeconomics into a network-formation model (another early paper is Goyal and Moraga, 2001). Here, firms form bilateral relations to reduce costs, and then compete on a product market. As is observed in most industries, firms can have more than one partner, forming additional partnerships without the permission of current partners. Both the costs of forming links and the nature of product competition determine the nature of the emerging network. Using the definition of stability introduced by Jackson and Wolinsky (1996), Goyal and Joshi show that when the costs of link formation are low, the complete network is both uniquely stable and uniquely efficient under quantity competition. By contrast, if the firms are competing on prices, the empty network is uniquely stable, whereas a linked double star is uniquely efficient. If competition is described more generally by the conditions under which firms can make positive profits, then it is the strength of competition that matters. When all firms make positive profits but lower cost firms make higher profits, then under strong but not unreasonable conditions the complete network is uniquely stable. When only the lowest-cost producer(s) make positive profits, then the network takes on a dominant group architecture: there is a (small) complete subnetwork of the low-cost producers, accompanied by the remainder of firms all of which are isolated. This network structure also emerges when costs of link formation are high, and competition is Cournot. What this paper shows is that even with minimal structure relating the network structure and firms' costs (a firm's costs fall linearly with the number of its partners), the nature of competition is crucial in determining emergent network structures. Thus, we should expect very different structures to merge in different industries.

2.5.2 Network Formation by Learning

Several models of network formation have been developed in which agents make connections to other agents probabilistically, increasing the probability of connecting to a particular agent if experiences with him are positive (see, for example, Plouraboué *et al.*, 1998; Weisbuch *et al.*, 2000; Kirman and Vriend, 2001). This approach has been used to study very different phenomena, and has produced a wide array of results. And while the models within this tradition are too varied to have a 'standard, baseline model', they tend to have the feature that even though, in principle, networks evolve forever, they do tend to settle down and exhibit aggregate regularities. For example, Kirman and Vriend (2001) in a market with buyers and sellers, find that, as in real markets, the network structure stabilizes to a state in which there is significant buyer–seller loyalty, in which most buyers tend to use only one seller. At the same time, though, the network retains some fluidity, as there is a group of non-loyal buyers, who even in the long run continue to patronize a large number of sellers. This structure of a stable, relatively unchanging core of activity, accompanied by enough fluidity to prevent the network from ossifying is a typical result in these models.

There is a long line of empirical work in the strategic management literature focused on the inertia in alliance formation. It is now generally accepted that the current state of the network is an important variable for explaining future link formation. The general conclusion is that this is the result of accumulated joint experience between partners, which generates both trust and a shared cognitive space (see, for example, Powell *et al.*, 1996; Gulati, 1999; Garcia-Pont and Nohria, 2002).

2.5.3   Stable Matching and Learning

There have been attempts to strike a balance between these two extremes, in which agents are relatively rational, yet the market can, in principle, evolve forever. One example, Cowan *et al.* (2003), looks at network formation in the context of innovation and diffusion. In that model, agents have a knowledge endowment characterized by an amount and a type. Agents form pairs and as a pair innovates, adding the new knowledge to their respective stocks. Over time, pairs form and dissolves, and a network emerges. The pair formation is treated as a 'matching problem', and in each period the set of pairs is stable.[5] A stable match is one in which no two agents prefer each other to their assigned partners (if they did they would leave their assigned partners and form a pair). Put another way, a matching assignment is stable if there is no blocking coalition of size 2 (any larger blocking coalition would include a blocking coalition of size 2). The structure of the network depends heavily on the nature of innovation. If innovation is driven largely by knowledge quantities the network tends to evolve to isolated pairs of agents–partnerships never dissolve. On the other hand, if diversity of knowledge is important in innovation, agents have many different partners over time, and the resulting network is very dense. What drives this result is the assumption that if two agents work together to innovate, they learn from each other, and so become more similar to each other than they were at the beginning of the episode. This implies that if diversity in knowledge is important, if two agents repeatedly innovate together, eventually they will be too similar to be valuable to each other. This change between regimes is very abrupt, almost a phase change. There is a small region of the parameter space, though, where intermediate structures seem to emerge. In this intermediate region, where both diversity and quantity are important, small cliques of (more than 2) agents form that permit enough diversity to be preserved. This is the region in which small worlds might appear. These results fit well with the static results described above – empty networks (which in this model are approximated by isolated pairs) and complete networks (which in this model are approximated by networks in which agents are connected to roughly 60 per cent of other agents) emerge. We observe no stars here, however, and the region in which structures other than these two extremes are possible is very small.

An interesting empirical question about network formation links to the discussion of small worlds. The motivation of firms to create links that generate a cliquish structure is well known from the literature on agglomeration and industrial districts.[6] But a more interesting question is the mechanism or microeconomics motivation behind the formation of interclique links. One paper that examines this issue is Baum et al. (2003). Using data on syndicates formed in the merchant banking industry in Canada between 1952 and 1990, Baum et al. ask about the motivations of banks to form clique-spanning ties. It is possible to characterize links in a small world as one of two types – intraclique links and interclique links. Clique formation is based on the belief in the value of multilateral (as opposed to purely bilateral) arrangements. Resource pooling, risk sharing, the formation of critical masses, and so on, provide incentives to create a group of interlinked agents rather than a simple pair. To form a link with a particular agent, or to include him or her in a group, it is necessary to know about his or her competencies, needs, intentions, and resources. With this information one can judge both whether that agent would bring value to a connection and whether he or she would be interested in forming the connection. There are two sources for this information. First, past ties with that agent generate a relational embeddedness, which contributes to stability in the network structure. Secondly, common partners yield information, and this is seen as a source of structural embeddedness. Motives underlying intraclique ties seem relatively straightforward, and have been explored in other literature, for example work on agglomeration economies. More problematic are clique-spanning ties.

Baum et al. suggest three possibilities: chance, 'insurgent partnering' and 'control partnering'. 'Insurgent partnering' refers to the action of a peripheral firm that is attempting to find a more central, and thus more important place in the industry. In social network analysis terms, it observes a structural hole in the network of merchant banks, and attempts to fill it by connecting with banks on either side of it. 'Control partnering' by contrast, occurs when an already central firm attempts to strengthen its position as a leader by finding a new source of information. That is, a firm that is at the center of a subnetwork connects with another subnetwork in order to access the information there, and to control its flow throughout the larger network.

To establish which of these strategies accounts for clique-spanning ties, Baum *et al.* regress a bank's rate of clique-spanning tie formation on measures of a bank's centrality, then whether a bank occupies structural holes and several bank-specific attributes. They find that all three strategies are present, but that chance and insurgent partnering dominate. That is, a network changes from a cliquish but not globally well-connected network to a small world because peripheral firms attempt to find a more central place in the structure. They see opportunities to gain power in the industry by bringing together two more or less existing cliques.

Goyal *et al.* (2004) look at co-authorship of academic economics papers. What they observe is a striking change in the network over the last 30 years. They find that as the prevalence of co-authored papers increases, the size of the giant connected component likewise increases. It remains the case, though, that the average distance between economists in the connected component remains small. The frequency distribution of links is very skewed, and the structure of the graph is one of interlinked stars. It appears that a small world is emerging in economics itself.

2.6   Conclusions

The use of network analysis in economics is growing rapidly. Network models offer ways to overcome several of the shortcomings of more traditional market models. When those models do not apply, network modelling may provide advantages. This is particularly the case in the context of innovation, when the transmission of knowledge plays such an important role. Codified knowledge can be diffused globally, without reference to underlying connection structures, but tacit knowledge has very different properties. Its diffusion depends heavily on the network of agents through which it will spread. To understand the dynamics of innovation and diffusion, network models provide a promising avenue.

One recent development in network analysis more generally has been the introduction of the concept of a scale-free network (see, for example, Barabasi and Albert, 2000). Scale-free networks are characterized through the frequency distribution of links, which follows a power law. This is a highly skewed distribution, with very fat tails: most nodes have very few links, a few nodes have many links. This type of network, which has been observed in many natural phenomena, has the property of being very robust to the failure of random nodes. However, it is not robust to directed attacks. That is, failures of particular nodes can be catastrophic to the performance of a scale-free network. This development is only just beginning to come into economics, but it fits well with the recent work on small worlds: many networks appear to be both scale free and small world (as one example, see Riccaboni and Pammolli, 2002, who find that networks in the life sciences and ICT industries have scale-free properties). Thus, one interesting, and unaddressed question is how these two concepts fit together in the context of economics, and whether the issue of robustness has any relevance for how an industry functions. As yet, we have little idea about the efficiency properties of scale-free networks.

The next major challenge for economists lies in the empirical analysis of network structures, and particularly in understanding the efficiency properties of existing structures. Beyond case studies, the data requirements for this type of exercise are very heavy. Patent databases are rich enough, but provide evidence of only one type of information flow, and so construction of large, detailed databases is a task ahead.

Research on networks is being done in a wide variety of fields: psychology, sociology, strategic management, physics, and so on. Economics is one branch with particular interests, and so it is facile to say that economics must look outside for inspiration. Nonetheless, the interconnection between economic activity, networks, and other aspects of network-mediated behavior creates a rich research environment in which this approach will continue to yield valuable insights into the way modern economies function and perform.

Notes

* Much of the material in this chapter arises from the collaborative work done with Nicolas Jonard, and owes much to him. I also acknowledge the very helpful comments of Muge Ozman and encouraging words of Franco Malerba.

1. See Hotelling (1929) or Salop (1979) for example. But see also Anderson *et al.* (1992), especially Chapter 4, to illustrate how quickly address models become extremely difficult in terms of tractability.
2. One suspects that there may be an observation bias here though – it may be difficult to publish a paper saying that a particular network of economic agents is not a small world.
3. See for example Jackson and Wolinsky (1996); Bala and Goyal (2000); Watts (2001); Jackson and Watts (2002); Jackson and Dutta (2003); Goyal and Vega-Redondo (2004). Jackson (forthcoming) is a nice survey.
4. See also Johnson and Gilles (2000), who also discuss spatially dependent costs.
5. See Gale and Shapley (1962) on matching problems.
6. See for example, Uzzi (1997) or Baker (1990), on strategic issues of link formation.

References

Allen, B. (1982), 'Some stochastic processes of interdependent demand and technological diffusion of an innovation exhibiting externalities among adopters', *International Economic Review*, **23**: 595–608.

Allen, R. (1983), 'Collective invention', *Journal of Economic Behavior and Organization*, **4**: 1–24.

An, M. and Kiefer, N. (1993), 'Local externalities and societal adoption of technologies', *Journal of Evolutionary Economics*, **5**: 103–117.

Anderson, S. P., de Palma, A., and Thisse, J. F. (1992), *Discrete choice theory of product differentiation*, Cambridge, MA: MIT Press.

Baker, W. E. (1990), 'Market networks and corporate behaviour', *American Journal of Sociology*, **96**: 589–625.

Bala, V. and Goyal, S. (2000), 'A non-cooperative model of network formation', *Econometrica*, **68**: 1181–1229.

Barabasi, A. and Albert, R. (2000), 'Statistical mechanics of complex networks', *Review of Modern Physics*, **74**: 47–97.

Baum, J. A. C., Shipilov, A. V., and Rowley, T. J. (2003), 'Where do small worlds come from?', *Industrial and Corporate Change*, **12**(4).

Becker, G. S. (1962), 'Irrational behavior and economic theory', *Journal of Political Economy*, **70**(1): 1–13.

Becker, G. S. (1963), 'Rational action and economic theory: a reply to I. Kirzner', *Journal of Political Economy*, **71**(1): 82–83.

Blume, L. (1995), 'The statistical mechanics of best-response strategy revision', *Games and Economic Behavior*, **11**(2): 111–145.

Breschi, S. and Lissoni, F. (2003), 'Mobility and social networks: Localised knowledge spillovers revisited', CESPRI Working Paper 142, CESPRI, Centre for Research on Innovation and Internationalisation Processes, Università Bocconi, Milan, Italy.

Carayol, N. and Roux, P. (2003), 'Self-organizing innovation networks: when do small worlds emerge?', Working Papers of GRES – Cahiers du GRES 2003–8, Groupement de Recherches Economiques et Sociales.

Cohen, W. and Levinthal, D. (1989), 'Innovation and learning: the two faces of R&D', *The Economic Journal*, **99**: 569–596.

Cowan, R. and Jonard, N. (2003), 'The dynamics of collective invention', *Journal of Economic Behavior and Organization*, **52**(4): 513–532.

Cowan, R. and Jonard, N. (2004), 'Network structure and the diffusion of knowledge', *Journal of Economic Dynamics and Control*, **28**: 1557–1575.

Cowan, R., Jonard, N., and Ozman, M. (2004), 'Knowledge dynamics in a network industry', *Technological Forecasting and Social Change*.

Cowan, R., Jonard, N., and Zimmermann, J.-B. (2003), 'On the creation of networks and knowledge' in M. Gallegati, A.P. Kirman and M. Marsili (eds), *The complex dynamics of economic interaction: essays in economics and econophysics*, Berlin: Springer.

Davis, G. F., Yoo, M., and Baker, W. E. (2003), 'The small world of the American corporate elite, 1982–2001', *Strategic Organization*, **1**(3): 301–326.

Durlauf, S. (1993), 'Non-ergodic economic growth', *Review of Economic Studies*, **60**: 349–366.

Duysters, G. and Verspagenu, B. (2004), 'The small worlds of strategic technology alliances', *Technovation*, **24**: 563–571.

Dyer, J. H. (1996), 'Does governance matter? Keiretsu alliances and asset specificity as sources of Japanese competitive advantage', *Organization Science*, **7**(6): 649–666.

Dyer, J. H. and Nobeoka, K. (2000), 'Creating and managing a high performance knowledge-sharing network: the Toyota case', *Strategic Management Journal*, **21**: 345–367.

Ellison, G. (1993), 'Learning, local interaction and coordination', *Econometrica* **61**(5): 1047–1071.

Föllmer, H. (1974), 'Random economies with many interacting', *Journal of Mathematical Economics*, **1**: 51–62.

Gale, G. and Shapley, L. (1962), 'College admissions and the stability of marriage', *American Mathematical Monthly*, **69**: 9–15.

Garcia-Pont, C. and Nohria, N. (2002), 'Local versus global mimetism: the dynamics of alliance formation in the automobile industry', *Strategic Management Journal*, **23**: 307–321.

Glaeser, E., Sacerdote, B., and Scheinkman, J. (1996), 'Crime and social interaction', *Quarterly Journal of Economics*, **111**: 507–548.

Goyal, S. and Vega-Redondo, F. (2004), 'Network formation and social coordination', *Games and Economic Behavior*, forthcoming.

Goyal, S., van de Leij, M., and Moraga-González, J. L. (2004), 'Economics: an emerging small world?', mimeo, University of Essex.

Goyal, S. and Joshi, S. (2002), 'Networks of collaboration in oligopoly', *Games and Economic Behavior*, **43**: 57–85.

Goyal, S. and Moraga, J. L. (2001), 'R&D networks', *Rand Journal of Economics*, **32**(4): 686–707.

Granstand, O. (1998), 'Towards a theory of the technology-based firm', *Research Policy*, **27**(5): 465–489.

Granstand, O. and Sjölander, S. (1990), 'Managing innovation in multi-technology corporations', *Research Policy*, **19**(1): 35–60.

Gulati, R. (1999), 'Network formation and learning: the influence of network resources and firm capabilities on alliance formation', *Strategic Management Journal*, **20**: 397–420.

Hagedoorn, J. (2002), 'Inter-firm R&D partnerships: an overview of major trends and patterns since 1960', *Research Policy* **31**(4): 477–492.

Hebb, D. O. (1949), *The organization of behavior: a neuropsychological theory*, New York: John Wiley & Sons.

Holmstrom, B. and Roberts, J. (1998), 'Boundaries of the firm revisited', *Journal of Economics Perspectives*, **4**(12): 73–94.

Hotelling, H. (1929), 'Stability in competition', *Economic Journal*, **39**: 41–57.

Imai, K. (1989), 'Evolution of Japan's corporate and industrial networks', in B. Carlsson (eds), *Industrial dynamics, technological organizational and structural changes in industries and firms*, Boston: Kluwer, 123–156.

Ioannides, Y. (1990), 'Trading uncertainty and market form', *International Economic Review*, **31**: 619–633.

Ising, E. (1925), 'Beitrag zur Theorie des Ferromagnetismus', *Zeitschrift fur Physik*, **31**: 253–258.

Jackson, M. O. (forthcoming), 'A survey of models of network formation: stability and efficiency', in G. Demange and M. Wooders(eds), *Groups formation in economics; networks, clubs and coalitions*, Cambridge: Cambridge University Press.

Jackson, M. O. and Watts, A. (2002), 'The evolution of social and economic networks', *Journal of Economic Theory*, **106**:(2) 265–295.

Jackson, M. O. and Wolinsky, A. (1996), 'A strategic model of social and economic networks', *Journal of Economic Theory*, **71**: 44–74.

Jackson, M. O. and Dutta, B. (2003), 'On the formation of networks and groups' in M. Jackson and B. Dutta (eds), *Models of the strategic formation of networks and groups*, Springer.

Jaffe, A., Trajtenberg, M., and Henderson, R. (1993), 'Geographic localization of knowledge spillovers as evidenced by patent citations', *Quarterly Journal of Economics*, **63**: 577–598.

Johnson, C. and Gilles, R. P. (2000), 'Spatial social networks', *Review of Economic Design*, **5**: 273–299.

Johnson, D. K. N. and Mareva, M. (2002), 'It's a small(er) world: the role of geography and networks in biotechnology innovation', Wellesley College Working Paper 2002–01.

Kirman, A. P. (1983), 'Communication in markets: A suggested approach', *Economics Letters*, **12**: 101–108.

Kirman, A. and Vriend, N. (2001), 'Evolving market structure: an ACE model of price dispersion and loyalty', *Journal of Economic Dynamics and Control*, **25**: 459–502.

Kirzner, I. M. (1962), 'Rational action and economic theory', *Journal of Political Economy*, **70**(4): 380–385. (Reply to Becker, G. S., 'Irrational behavior and economic theory', *Journal of Political Economy*, **70**(1): (Feb.), pp. 1–13.)

Kirzner, I. M. (1963), 'Rational action and economic theory: Rejoinder', *Journal of Political Economy*, **71**(1): 84–85.

Langlois, R. and Robertson, P. L. (1992), 'Networks of innovation in a modular system: lessons from the microcomputer and stereo components industries', *Research Policy*, **21**(4): 297–313.

Lazerson, M. H. and Lorenzoni, G. (1999), 'The firms that feed industrial districts: a return to the Italian source', *Industrial and Corporate Change*, **8**(2): 235–266.

Lincoln, J. A. and Gerlach, M. (1998), 'The structural analysis of Japanese economic organization: a conceptual framework' in W. Mark Fruin (eds), *networks and markets; Pacific Rim strategies*, New York: Oxford University Press.

Narula, R. and Hagedoorn, J. (1999), 'Innovating through strategic alliances: moving towards international partnerships and contractual agreements', *Technovation*, **19**: 283–294.

Newman, M. E. J. (2001), 'The structure of scientific collaboration networks', *Proceedings of the National Academy of Sciences USA*, **98**: 404–409.

Nuvolari, A. (forthcoming), 'Collective invention during the British Industrial Revolution: the case of the cornish pumping engine', *Cambridge Journal of Economics*.

Orsenigo, L., Pammoli, F., and Riccaboni, M. (2001), 'Technological change and network dynamics: lessons from the pharmaceutical industry', *Research Policy*, **30**: 485–508.

Plouraboué, F., Steyer, A., and Zimmermann, J. B. (1998), 'Learning induced criticality in consumer's adoption pattern: a neural network approach', *Economics of Innovations and New Technology*, 6: 73–90.

Powell, W. W., Koput, K. W., and Smith-Doerr, L. (1996), 'Interorganizational collaboration and the locus of innovation: networks of learning in biotechnology', *Administrative Science Quarterly*, 41: 116–145.

Pyke, F., Becattini, G., and Sengenberger, W. (eds) (1992), *Industrial districts and interfirm co-operation in Italy*. Geneva: International Institute for Labour Studies.

Riccaboni, M. and Pammolli, F. (2002), 'On firm growth in networks', *Research Policy*, 31(8–9): 1405–1416.

Salop, S. C. (1979), 'Monopolistic competition with outside goods', *Bell Journal of Economics*, 10: 141–156.

Saxenian, A. (1991), 'The origins and dynamics of production networks in Silicon Valley', *Research Policy*, 20: 423–437.

Steyer, A. and Zimmermann, J. B. (1998), 'On the frontier: structural effects in a diffusion model based on influence matrixes', in P. Cohendet, P. Llerena, H. Stahn and G. Umbhauer (eds), *The economics of networks: Interaction and Behaviours*, 118–135, Springer.

Uzzi, B. (1997), 'Social structure and competition in interfirm networks: The paradox of embeddedness', *Academy of Management Journal*, 42(1): 35–67.

von Hippel, E. (1998), The sources of innovation, Oxford: Oxford University Press.

Watts, A. (2001), 'A dynamic model of network formation', *Games and Economic Behaviour*, 34: 331–341.

Watts, D. and Strogatz, S. (1998), 'Collective dynamics of small-world networks', *Letters to Nature*, 393.

Weisbuch, G., Kirman, A., and Herreiner, D. (2000), 'Market organisation and trading relationships', *Economic Journal*, 110: 411–436.

Wilhite, A. (2001), 'Bilateral trade and "small-world" networks', *Computational Economics*, 18: 49–64.

3

On Sectoral Specificities in the
Geography of Corporate Location

GIULIO BOTTAZZI, GIOVANNI DOSI AND GIORGIO FAGIOLO

3.1 Introduction

The very fact that 'space matters in economic activity' does not intuitively
come as any big news – irrespective of the angle from which one tries to
interpret the observed spatial distributions of firms, plants, workers, manufacturing output, etc. After all, plenty of evidence witnesses for distributions
that are very far from uniform ones, defined on whatever scale, e.g. countries,
departments, regions, states, etc.

However, on further thought, why should one expect uniform spatial
distributions of economic activities? Or, putting it somewhat more technically, what is the null hypothesis against which one should compare the
historical observations in order to corroborate the notion that space *actually*
matters in the location of economic activities, as contrasted to the opposite
one, that distributional asymmetries are simply the transient outcomes of
'spatially unbiased' random processes?

Next, even after detecting the asymmetric importance of agglomeration
forces, if any, to what extent are they *location specific* but independent of
individual sectors and technologies? Or, conversely, what is the importance
of *sector-specific* drivers of agglomeration or dispersion of economic activities
that apply across different locations within similar ensembles of production
processes and outputs?

Finally, having identified some significant intersectoral specificities in
agglomeration patterns, can one map them into some underlying distinguishing features of the knowledge bases upon which production and innovation
draw in each sector?

These are the broad motivating questions that inspire this work. Clearly, any
attempt of a thorough treatment here would be futile. Rather, what we shall try
to do in the following is, first, to propose a relatively simple and empirically
testable model apt to disentangle the relative impact of location-specific and
industry-specific observed locational patterns. Second, we shall put forward
some conjectures on the underlying determinants of the regularities displayed
by our evidence, based on Italian districts, as well as by a few other sources
concerning other countries and stemming from different methodologies.

In Section 3.2 we spell out the basics of the interpretative framework, as rooted in the recent statistical and econometric literature. Together, we briefly sketch out some theoretical questions we mean to address. The model is presented in Section 3.3 while in Section 3.4 we present some preliminary econometric results with reference to some benchmark industries (leather products, transport equipment, electronics, financial intermediation services). The model yields empirically testable predictions on the equilibrium distribution of the size of spatial clusters and on the diverse relevance of agglomeration forces across industrial sectors. Hence, we apply it to the evidence on the geographical distribution of Italian business units across a set of industries that might be considered archetypes of distinct *regimes of technological learning* (Pavitt, 1984; Dosi, 1988; Malerba and Orsenigo, 1996; Marsili, 2001). The results are indeed consistent with the view that intersectoral differences in economies of agglomeration might be (at least partly) explained by differences in innovation patterns and learning regimes displayed by firms belonging to diverse industrial sectors. Finally, in Section 3.5 we suggest a few extensions of the basic model and some directions for future work.

3.2   The Interactions Between Geographical and Industrial Characteristics as Drivers of Agglomeration and Dispersion: The General Picture

Let us start with some impressionistic evidence. *First*, note that a vast number of empirical studies about firm locational patterns in the US, Asia, and Europe, broadly show that industries are more clustered than any theory of comparative advantage might predict (cf. Krugman (1991) and Fujita *et al.* (1999) among many others).

However, *second*, a wealth of qualitative analysis suggests that seemingly agglomerative phenomena may take quite diverse forms (see, for example, the surveys and the discussions in Lee and Willis (1997), Martin (1999), and more specifically on the Italian evidence, Sforzi (1989) and Antonelli (1994)). Examples of diverse agglomeration phenomena include: (i) *horizontally diversified agglomerations*, characterized by the coexistence of many producers of similar but differentiated products; (ii) *'Smithian' forms of agglomeration*, whereby activities previously vertically integrated within individual firms undergo a process of division of labor *cum* branching out of different specialized firms; (iii) *hierarchical clusters*, which generally involve an oligopolistic core together with subcontracting networks; and (iv) what one could call *'Schumpeterian Silicon Valley'* districts, where agglomeration is driven to a good extent by complementarities in innovative efforts – partly fuelled by 'exogenous science'.[1]

A high sectoral variability in agglomeration structures and in the nature of agglomeration drivers clearly hints at the existence of large underlying sectoral and geographical specificities permeating agglomeration processes. In this perspective, a *third*, related, set of robust empirical evidence concerns the huge intersectoral differences in the revealed spatial agglomeration outcomes. As a suggestive illustration, Fig. 3.1 plots the distributions of some statistics computed on the frequency profiles of Italian business units (BUs in the following) belonging to different manufacturing sectors and located in each geographical location.[2] It is easy to see the high variability in the distribution of manufacturing sectors across geographical sites. For instance, there exists a high number of locations where business units belonging to almost all sectors are equally represented. On the contrary, for quite a large frequency of sites, agglomeration occurs only for business units belonging to a small number of sectors (in some cases 1 or 2). More generally, in more than 50 per cent of locations, quite a large fraction of sectors is not even represented. The intersectoral variability in agglomeration

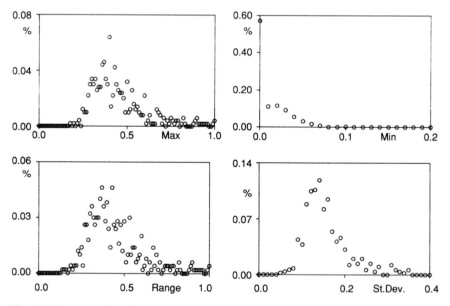

Fig. 3.1 Frequency distributions of MAX (top-left), MIN (top-right), RANGE (bottom-left) and STANDARD DEVIATION (bottom-right) statistics computed on the weighted frequency profile of Italian manufacturing business units (BUs) belonging to different industrial sectors (2-digit disaggregation) present in each geographical location in 1996. For each statistics *S*, a circle corresponding to a value *s* on the *x*-axis represents the percentage of all locations for which the statistics *S* (computed on the weighted frequency profile of BUs belonging to each industrial sector present in that location) is equal to *s*. Locations are defined in terms of Local Systems of Labor Mobility (cf. note 2, p.71). *Source:* Our elaborations on ISTAT, *Censimento Intermedio dell'Industria e dei Servizi*, 1996

profiles is robustly confirmed by the evidence on other countries such as France, the UK, and the US.[3]

Finally, *fourth*, the measures of agglomeration appear to be quite stable over time, notwithstanding a greater variability of the locations of agglomeration themselves, and notwithstanding a turbulent underlying microdynamics with persistent flows of entry, exit, and variation in the relative sizes of incumbents (Dumais *et al.*, 2002).

Taken together, the foregoing pieces of evidence suggest a picture where different drivers of agglomeration, which might be economy wide, location specific, and/or sector specific, interact over time (on possibly different time- and spacescales) leading to patterns of concentration exhibiting distinct patterns across both locations and industries.

Indeed, the main conjecture that we mean to explore is that cross-sectoral differences in agglomeration forces ought to be – at least partly – explained on the grounds of underlying differences in the processes of technological and organizational learning. The latter are, in fact, likely to affect the relative importance of phenomena such as localized knowledge spillovers; inter- vs. intraorganizational learning; knowledge complementarities fuelled by localized labor mobility; innovative explorations undertaken through spin-offs, and, more generally, the birth of new firms.

However, in order to pursue such a broad line of inquiry, a necessary preliminary task involves the identification of location-wide drivers that operate across different sectors located in any one area, as distinguished from sector-specific drivers that conversely apply across different locations.

Let us illustrate the intuition behind our analysis borrowing from the 'dartboard' metaphor from the seminal work by Ellison and Glaeser (1997), with which the following has indeed many points in common.

Suppose that the economic space is a sort of dartboard where darts of different colors are thrown (that is, economic activities belonging to different sectors are located). Here, the null hypothesis (i.e. 'agglomeration does not matter') is a distribution of darts on the board solely due to random factors. In departing from pure randomness, however, one might observe systematic patterns ultimately due to:

1. The intrinsic widespread attractiveness (or repulsiveness) of some areas on the board: hence, one will systematically find there more (or less) darts *of all* colors than what sheer randomness would predict.[4]
2. Specific patterns *distinctive of any one color* (that is, sectoral specificities) on the top of the generic locational patterns as from the point above.
3. The different *size* of different darts (that is, different degrees of lumpiness of single investments).

Ellison and Glaeser (1997, 1999) and Dumais *et al.* (2002) control for the latter, as captured by the concentration in plant size distribution, and study the importance of sector-specific agglomeration factors as compared to intersectoral, location-wide, ones (which, quite expansively, they call the 'natural advantage' of a location).[5]

Our exercise largely shares a similar spirit, albeit with some distinct features. *First*, we do *not* 'wash out' any lumpiness effect. We do it partly out of necessity and partly out of choice. The constraint is that given our small spatial units (defined in terms of local labor-mobility basins, typically smaller than most US counties) and our fine-grained sectoral partition, it is very hard to find the relevant sectoral/spatial breakdown of the data. At the same time, at a conceptual level, it is not entirely uncontroversial that one should take out the 'size effect'. In order to see this, think of, say, five entities located in one particular place that at some point merge into one. This does not mean that agglomeration has fallen, but rather that whatever forces driving agglomeration have now been internalized within a single firm.

Second, the model presented below entails an explicit dynamics whereby – in the foregoing dartboard metaphor – the possibility of throwing a dart in a particular area of the board depends upon the darts already in place (their total numbers and their colors).

Third, one tries to capture some of the turbulence observed in the empirical data by allowing a persistent process of corporate exit and entry.

Fourth, our model predicts the whole distribution over locations of, e.g. plants or employment in each sector, rather than a simple value of an 'agglomeration coefficient', as in Ellison and Glaeser (1997).

3.3 The Model

Consider an economy with one industry and a potentially infinite number of identical firms. In the economy there are $M \geq 2$ locations, labeled by $j = 1, \ldots, M$, which can be thought of as 'production sites' or 'industrial districts'. Each location j is characterized by an intrinsic 'geographical attractiveness' $a_j > 0$ and by an 'agglomeration' parameter $b > 0$, which in the first place we assume to be homogeneous across locations. The coefficient a_j captures the gain from choosing to locate in j net of any agglomeration effects. On the contrary, b measures the agglomeration strength in our economy: a larger b implies a higher incentive to a firm from locating in any location, given the number of firms that have already settled their activities in that location.

Time is discrete. Let n_j^t be the number of firms present in location j at time $t = 0, 1, 2, \ldots$. Suppose that at time $t = 0$ the size of the economy is $N \gg M$ and assume an initial distribution $\underline{n}^0 = (n_1^0, \ldots, n_M^0)$, $n_j^0 \geq 0$, $\sum_{j=1}^{M} n_j^0 = N$.

The dynamics of the economy is governed by the following simple rules. At the beginning of each time period $t \geq 1$, a firm is chosen at random among all incumbent firms to 'die' (i.e. disappear from the location where it operates). Next, a new firm enters and chooses the site where to locate its production facilities. In line with Arthur (1994, Chap. 4), we model firms' locational choices in a stochastic fashion. More precisely, we posit that a firm entering the industry at time t chooses site j with a probability proportional to:

$$a_j + b\tilde{n}_j^t, \tag{3.1}$$

where a_j is the 'intrinsic attractiveness' of site j, b is the 'agglomeration' parameter, and $\tilde{n}_j^t$ is the actual number of firms present at location j after exit has occurred (i.e. $\tilde{n}_j^t = n_j^t - 1$ if exit occurred in j and $\tilde{n}_j^t = n_j^t$ otherwise).

The state of the system is completely defined, at each $t \geq 0$, by the 'occupation' vector $\underline{n}^t = (n_1^t, \ldots, n_M^t)$. Since the state of the system at time $t+1$ only depends on $\underline{n}^t$, the dynamics of the economy is described by a finite Markov chain with state space $S = \{(n_1, \ldots, n_M) : n_j \geq 0, \sum_{j=1}^{M} n_j = N\}$.

Results on the existence of a stationary (invariant) distribution for $\underline{n}^t$ (and its characterization) are provided in the following lemma.

Lemma 1 *Define $p(\underline{n}^t; \underline{a}, b)$ as the probability that the system is in the state $\underline{n}^t$ at time $t \geq 1$ and*

$$P(\underline{n}'|\underline{n};\underline{a}, b) = \Pr\{\underline{n}^{t+1} = \underline{n}'|\underline{n}^t = \underline{n}; \underline{a}, b\}$$

as the generic element of the transition probability matrix of the associated Markov chain, where $\underline{n}, \underline{n}' \in S$. Then:

1. *Let $\Delta_h = (0, \ldots, 0, 1, 0, \ldots 0)$ the unitary M-vector with h-th component equal to 1. If $\underline{n}^{t+1} = \underline{n}' \neq \underline{n} + \Delta_k - \Delta_j$ for all $k, j = 1, \ldots, M$ then $P(\underline{n}'|\underline{n}; \underline{a}, b) = 0$. Otherwise, if there exists $k, j = 1, \ldots, M$ such that $\underline{n}^t = \underline{n}$ and $\underline{n}^{t+1} = \underline{n} + \Delta_k - \Delta_j$, then:*

$$P(\underline{n} + \Delta_k - \Delta_j|\underline{n};\underline{a}, b) = \begin{cases} \dfrac{n_j}{N} \dfrac{a_k + bn_k}{A + (N-1)b} & k = j \\[2mm] \dfrac{n_j}{N} \dfrac{a_k + b(n_k - 1)}{A + (N-1)b} & k = j \end{cases} \tag{3.2}$$

where $\underline{n} = (n_1, \ldots, n_M) \in S$ and $A = \sum_{m=1}^{M} a_m$.

2. *The Markov chain governing the evolution of $\underline{n}^t$ is irreducible and therefore admits a unique stationary distribution $\pi(\underline{n};\underline{a}, b)$ that reads:*

$$\pi(\underline{n};\underline{a}, b) = \frac{1}{\vartheta(N; A, b)} \frac{N!}{n_1! \ldots n_M!} \prod_{j=1}^{M} \vartheta(n_j; a_j, b), \tag{3.3}$$

where:

$$\vartheta(n_j; a_j, b) = \begin{cases} \prod_{b=1}^{n_j} [a_j + b(b-1)] & 1 \le n_j \le N \\ 1 & n_j = 0 \end{cases}$$

Proof. See Appendix A. ∎

Since (3.3) is invariant with respect to a rescaling of the *a*s and *b* by a common coefficient, one can set w.l.o.g. $b = 1$. Any entrant firm will then choose location *j* with probability proportional to:

$$a_j + \tilde{n}_j^t, \tag{3.4}$$

where now the 'intrinsic attractiveness' a_j might be interpreted as a relative measure of agglomeration economies. Consequently, a smaller a_j implies stronger economies of agglomeration. If $b = 1$, the invariant distribution simplifies to:

$$\pi(\underline{n};\underline{a}) = \frac{N!}{A^{[N]}} \prod_{j=1}^{M} \frac{a_j^{[n_j]}}{n_j!}, \tag{3.5}$$

where $a_j^{[n_j]} = a_j(a_j + 1) \dots (a_j + n_j - 1)$ is Pochammer's symbol.[6]

Coefficients $a_j > 0$ determine the nature of the distribution. As the values of the *a*'s get bigger, the effects of agglomeration economies wither away. In the limit, when $a_j \to +\infty$ and $a_j/a_{j'} \to 1$ for any *j* and *j'*, agglomeration economies disappear and the expression in (3.5) reduces to a multinomial distribution. On the contrary, when $a_j = 1 \forall j$, (3.5) becomes the Bose–Einstein distribution.[7]

Some remarks are in order. First, we assume that entry rates (i.e. birth rates) are positive, constant and equal to exit rates (i.e. death rates). The idea behind this assumption comes from the observation that the share of firms belonging to a given sector who enter and/or leave a given location in a relatively short period of time (e.g. a year) is typically much larger than the net growth of industry size, so that the timescale at which spatial reallocations occur is generally very short.[8] Therefore, the invariant distributions in (3.3) and (3.5) *do not* necessarily depict only the long-run state associated to some 'old' or 'mature' industry. Since each entry/exit decision made by any one firm constitutes one time step in the model, our invariant distributions describe the state of the system after a sufficiently large number of spatial reallocation events have taken place (which may well imply a relatively short real-time horizon). Invariant distributions can then be directly compared with cross-sectional empirical data because they describe a system that, for short real-time horizons, is always near its short-term stochastic equilibrium state.[9] Long-term modifications in the industrial structure might be instead captured by allowing *a* and *b* coefficients to change across subsequent phases of industry evolution, albeit on a timescale much longer than the one related to spatial reallocation decisions (i.e. indexed by t).

Second, and relatedly, we suppose that any firm remains in its location until it eventually exits from the industry. Individual locational choices might then be interpreted as being *irreversible*. However, one-step transition probabilities computed in (3.2) are also consistent with an alternative locational process involving *reversible* choices wherein: (i) there is a constant population of N firms (no entry/exit); (ii) in each time period a randomly drawn firm is allowed to switch location with probabilities proportional to (3.1), with $a_j > 0$ for all j. In both cases, the size of the industry is constant (equal to N) throughout the whole process since the net growth rate is zero. Therefore, the impact of the noise introduced in the system by any single additional decision (either due entry/exit or between-location switches), albeit quite small, does not become negligible as t becomes large. Thus, the equilibrium behavior of the system can be described, unlike models based on Polya urn schemes, by a non-degenerate stationary distribution.

In the next section, we will test the predictions of the model against data on geographical distribution of firms across Italian geographic locations (cf. note 2, p. 71). We employ (3.5) to test for the existence of persistence differences in the strength of agglomeration economies among industrial sectors.

3.4   Agglomeration Economies and Industrial Sectors: An Application to Italian Data

In this section we address the following questions. *First*: Do the theoretical distributions (derived from the model presented above) adequately replicate, for each given sector, the observed frequency distributions of firms across locations? *Second*: What is the statistical impact of intersectoral differences on the dynamics of spatial concentration?

Note that in order to start answering the latter question, one ought to disentangle two basic factors jointly contributing to the observed sector specificities in agglomeration patterns, namely: (i) agglomeration drivers that, for any given sector, are location specific and generate agglomeration benefits due to dynamic increasing returns to concentration (e.g. *ex ante* 'intrinsic' differences across geographical locations, cross-sectoral spillovers that cumulatively act upon the existing concentration patterns, etc.); (ii) agglomeration drivers that are entirely *sector specific* and promote concentration across all geographical locations (e.g. thanks to economies of agglomeration forces that are intrinsically related to the way knowledge is accumulated, innovations are generated, etc.).

In this perspective, we present here a preliminary study focusing on four sectors: (a) leather products; (b) transport equipment; (c) electronics; (d) financial intermediation.

TABLE 3.1 *The statistical classification of the considered sectors*

Sector	ISIC Class	Pavitt's group
Leather	D.19	Supplier dominated (*SD*)
Transport equipment	D.34, D.35	Scale intensive (*SI*)
Electronics	D.30, D.31, D.32, D.33	Science based (*SB*)
Financial intermediation	J.65, J.66, J.67	Information intensive (*II*)

The choice is motivated by the observation that these industries display a large intersectoral variation as to their patterns of innovation and learning regimes, as well as the average sizes of their business units (BUs in the following) and their competition patterns. More precisely, according to the descriptive taxonomy of industrial sectors firstly proposed by Pavitt (1984) and subsequently developed in Malerba and Orsenigo (1996) and Marsili (2001), these industries belong to four distinct groups (cf. also Table 3.1).

In Pavitt's terminology, the leather industry – with the partial exception of 'fashion products' – might be classified as a 'supplier dominated' (*SD*) sector, characterized by relatively small firms whose innovative opportunities largely stem from external *loci* of innovation (e.g. intermediate and capital inputs produced elsewhere). *SD* industries usually involve high product differentiation and include most of the so-called 'made-in-Italy' activities (e.g. textiles, clothing, furniture, toys, etc.).

Transport equipment is a standard 'scale-intensive' (*SI*) sector, wherein large firms generate (both internally and thanks to 'specialized suppliers') innovation in production processes and, together, master the design and production of quite complex artifacts.

Electronics typically belongs to the class of 'science-based' (*SB*) sectors. Here, innovation in both products and processes is largely generated in R&D departments of firms that often maintain strong links with universities and research centers.

Finally, financial intermediation activities are 'information intensive' (*II*) sectors, which share with science-based industry the locus of innovation (R&D departments) and, to some extent, the sources of innovative opportunities (universities and research centers). However, *II* sectors typically differ from *SB* ones as to the means of appropriating the economic rents from their innovations. While science-based industries typically appropriate innovations through patents and lead times of innovators *vis-à-vis* would-be imitators, information-intensive ones comparatively take more advantage of the tacitness of their knowledge bases (cf. Malerba and Orsenigo (1996)).

The conjecture that we begin to explore in this work is that intersectoral differences in the patterns of innovation, knowledge flows, and learning regimes, as proxied by Pavitt's categorization, map into different degrees of local agglomeration economies, once differences due to location-specific agglomeration effects have been factored out. It is indeed likely that firms' locational choices are affected in quite different ways by different appropriability means, distinct sources of innovation sources/types, as well as different channels through which technological information locally spills over. We suggest that such spatially local, sector-specific, drivers might be able to account for the observed differences of agglomeration patterns across industries.

3.4.1 Data and Methodology

The exercise employs a database provided by the Italian Statistical Office (ISTAT) from the Census of Manufacturers and Services. Data contain observations about more than half a million business units (BUs), i.e. local plants. Each observation identifies the location of the BUs at a given point of time (1996), as well as the industrial sector where it operates. Observations refer to $L = 31$ industrial sectors[10] while locations correspond to $M = 784$ 'local systems of labor mobility' (LSLM) (see endnote 2).

Let $n_{i,l}$ be the number of BUs in LSLM i operating in sector l. Denote with $n_{.,l}$ the number of BUs operating in sector l and with $n_{i,.}$ the total number of BUs belonging to i-th LSLM. Since a standard maximum likelihood procedure is not viable,[11] we shall estimate coefficients a_{il}, for any given sector l, in two benchmark cases:

1. a_{il} are homogeneous across locations, i.e. $a_{il} = \alpha_l$, where $\alpha_l > 0$ is a sector-specific parameter;
2. a_{il} are heterogeneous across locations and $a_{il} = \gamma_l \cdot \theta_{i|l}$, where γ_l is a sector-specific parameter and $\theta_{i|l}$, for any given sector, is a location-specific parameter.

Notice that in case 1 one is assuming that location-specific agglomeration drivers are homogeneous across LSLM. Under this hypothesis, BUs belonging to any given sector l would choose any given geographical site with equal probability. On the other hand, in case 2 one assumes that the geographical attractiveness of any site i can be decomposed into a factor that accounts for location- (and possibly sector-) specific (i.e. $\theta_{i|l}$) local attractiveness and a strictly sector-specific factor accounting for activity-specific increasing returns to agglomeration (i.e. γ_l).

We estimate $\theta_{i|l}$ by using data about all sectors different from l, which are assumed to be exogenous with respect to the data-generation process postulated in the single-sector model. Hence, sector distributions, in both case 1 and 2, will depend on a single parameter (α_l or γ_l) that can in turn be estimated by a standard best-fit procedure (e.g. minimization of a chi-square test between theoretical and empirical distributions).

In order to compare theoretical predictions with empirical data, let us define the marginal (site-occupancy) stationary probability distribution $\phi(h|a_{il}, A, N)$ as the probability that a site with 'intrinsic attractiveness'

$a_{il} > 0$ would host in the limit exactly $h = 0, 1, \ldots, N$ firms. From (3.5), one obtains (cf. Appendix 3B):

$$\phi(h|a_{il}, A, N) = \frac{N!}{A^{[N]}} \frac{a_{il}^{[h]}}{h!} \frac{(A - a_{il})^{[N-h]}}{(N - h)!}. \tag{3.6}$$

For each sector under analysis, we may therefore compare the theoretical distribution (3.6) with the corresponding observed frequency with which a LSLM hosting $n_{i,l} = h$ business units appears in sector l:

$$f_l(h) = \frac{1}{M} \sum_{i=1}^{M} \delta(n_{i,l}, h), \tag{3.7}$$

where $\delta(n_{i,l}, h) = 1$ if and only if $n_{i,l} = h$.

3.4.2   Results

Let us begin by unrealistically assuming that all locations are homogeneous as to their intrinsic geographical attractiveness. In this case, the process is driven only by economies of agglomeration that are themselves homogeneous across locations. More formally, for any single sector l, let $a_{il} = \alpha_l$, $i = 1, \ldots, M$ and $A_l = M\alpha_l$, $\alpha_l > 0$. Theoretical frequencies (3.6), become:

$$\varphi_l(h; \alpha_l) = \phi(h|\alpha_l, M\alpha_l, N) = \frac{N!}{(M\alpha_l)^{[N]}} \frac{\alpha_l^{[h]}}{h!} \frac{(M(\alpha_l - 1))^{[N-h]}}{(N - h)!}. \tag{3.8}$$

Notice that ϕ will now depend, for any l, on a single parameter α_l measuring the strength of the agglomeration effect (recall that a low α_l means strong agglomeration economies). For each sector under study, the agglomeration parameter will then be estimated as:

$$\alpha_l^* = \arg\min_{a_l \in \Lambda} \chi^2(f_l, \varphi_l), \tag{3.9}$$

where χ^2 is the standard goodness-of-fit test between two binned (theoretical and empirical) frequency distributions and Λ is an evenly spaced grid of values for $a_l > 0$.

As one should expect, tests of this model yield very poor agreement with data, with 'predicted' theoretical distributions $\varphi_l(h; \alpha_l^*)$ always underestimating observed distribution tails. In particular, χ^2 tests reject the hypothesis that data come from the distribution in (3.8) for any value of $\alpha_l > 0$, in all four sectors under analysis.

The reason why this is the case becomes evident if one plots, for any given sector l, the number of BUs located in the LSLM i against the total number of BUs belonging to all sectors but l (i.e. $n_{i,.} - n_{i,l}$). Under the assumption of homogeneous intrinsic geographical attractiveness, any two BUs belonging to different sectors should choose the same location with equal probability. Therefore, no statistically significant correlation should appear between $n_{i,l}$ and $n_{i,.} - n_{i,l}$ for any l. Conversely, as Fig. 3.2 shows, for any of the four chosen sectors a statistically significant positive correlation between the two variables appears: The LSLMs corresponding, say, to Milan or Turin, clearly display an *ex ante* attractiveness different from an LSLM on the Alps.

More reasonably, suppose instead that the degrees of intrinsic geographical attractiveness are heterogenous across locations and let $a_{il} = \gamma_l \cdot \theta_{i|l}$. Here, $\theta_{i|l}$ represents the strength of agglomeration economies of location i in sector l. Given the high correlation between $n_{i,l}$ and $n_{i,.} - n_{i,l}$ exhibited by

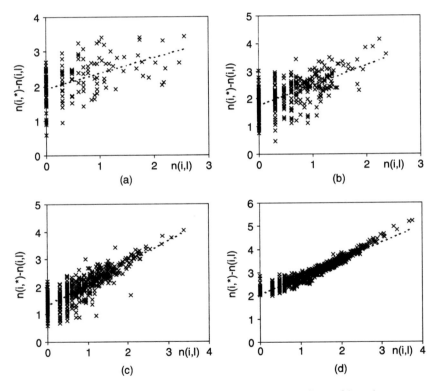

Fig. 3.2 Number of business units belonging to sector l located in a given Local System of Labor Mobility $(n_{i,l})$ vs. the total number of BUs belonging to all sectors but l $(n_{i,.} - n_{i,l})$: a) Leather products; b) Transport equipment; c) Electronics; d) Financial intermediation. All variables are in log scale. Estimated Slopes of Linear Regressions (significance of t-test $\hat{\beta} = 0$ in brackets): (a) $\hat{\beta} = 0.443$ (0.0001); (b) $\hat{\beta} = 0.798$ (0.0002); (c) $\hat{\beta} = 0.727$ (0.001); (d) $\hat{\beta} = 0.746$ (0.0000).
Source: Our elaborations on ISTAT, *Censimento Intermedio dell'Industria e dei Servizi*, 1996

the data for all sectors under study, we will assume that for any location i and sector l:

$$a_{il} = \gamma_l \frac{n_{i,.} - n_{i,l}}{\sum_{i=1}^{M} (n_{i,.} - n_{i,l})} = \gamma_l \frac{n_{i,.} - n_{i,l}}{N - n_{.,l}}, \qquad (3.10)$$

where $\gamma_l > 0$ measures industry-specific effects due to economies of agglomeration. Coefficients $\theta_{i|l}$ capture here the effect of local agglomeration drivers that, for each given sector, are location specific (as compared to agglomeration forces that, on the contrary, act at an economy-wide level). The latter include all factors that make a location intrinsically preferable compared to others, in terms of, e.g. better industrial infrastructures, sheer overall size, etc., all the way to local spillovers that generate dynamic increasing returns to agglomeration for all sectors.

Since our data-generation process refers to a single sector, we can proxy $\theta_{i|l}$ by using exogenous information about the behavior of all firms belonging to all sectors different from the one under consideration. If (3.10) holds, the theoretical frequency of finding a LSLM hosting exactly b BUs in sector l can be easily computed by averaging marginal probabilities in (3.6) over all LSLM, after having controlled for the size of each sector. The theoretical (weighted) frequency distribution for sector l then reads:

$$\psi_l(b; \gamma_l) = \frac{1}{M} \sum_{i=1}^{M} \phi(b|a_{il}, A_l, n_{.,l}), \qquad (3.11)$$

where ϕ is the probability distribution in (3.6), a_{il} are defined as in (3.10), $A_l = \sum_{i=1}^{M} a_{il}$ and $n_{.,l}$ is the number of BUs in sector l. Since ψ_l depends, for any sector l, only on γ_l, we can use the same fitting procedure we employed in the homogenous coefficients case. 'Predicted' values for γ_l are therefore computed as:

$$\gamma_l^* = \arg \min_{\gamma_l \in G} \chi^2(f_l, \psi_l), \qquad (3.12)$$

where χ^2 is defined as above and G is an evenly spaced grid of values for $\gamma_l > 0$.

Table 3.2 reports 'predicted' values for sectoral agglomeration parameters, their 5 percent confidence intervals,[12] together with χ^2 test values and tail probabilities for the difference between $\psi_l^* = \psi_l(b; \gamma_l^*)$ and f_l.

In all four sectors, 'predicted' theoretical distributions ψ_l^* fit very well with empirical frequencies. Indeed, one cannot reject the hypothesis that ψ_l^* are different from empirical distributions $f_l(b)$. As to the magnitudes of the predicted parameters, notice that 'leather', 'transport equipment', and 'electronics' sectors seem to display higher agglomeration economies (i.e. comparably small γs) as compared to 'financial intermediation'. This piece of

TABLE 3.2 *'Predicted' agglomeration parameters* $\gamma_l^* = \arg\min_{\gamma_l \in G} \chi^2(f_l, \psi_l)$.
Confidence intervals for γ_l^* *contain all* γ_l *s.t. the 5% chi-square test between* $\psi_l(h;\gamma_l)$
and f_l *is not rejected. Degrees of freedom:* $D = 50$

Sector (*l*)	γ_l^*	Confidence intervals	$\chi^2(f_l, \psi_l(\gamma_l^*))$	Prob $\{\chi_D^2 > \chi^2(f_l, \psi_l(\gamma_l^*))\}$
Leather	0.0032	(0.0026, 0.0098)	52.6760	0.3709
Transport equipment	0.0128	(0.0087, 0.0169)	58.7517	0.1855
Electronics	0.0376	(0.0301, 0.0462)	54.2862	0.3147
Financial intermediation	0.7871	(0.7101, 0.8005)	44.1767	0.7051

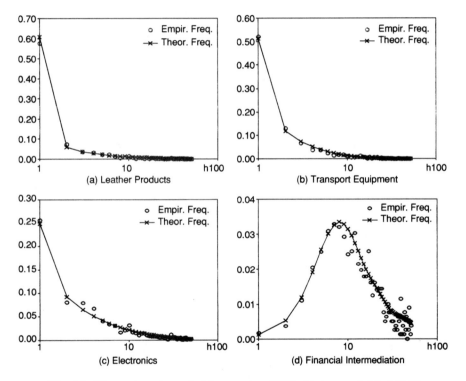

Fig. 3.3 Observed vs. theoretical frequencies of BUs (business units) in LSLM
(Local System of Labor Mobility). *Y*-axis: Frequency of LSLM hosting *h* BUs.
Source: Our elaborations on ISTAT, 1996 data

conjectural evidence seems confirmed by Fig. 3.3, where predicted (ψ_l^*) and
empirical (f_l) frequencies are plotted. While the first three sectors studied
exhibit the standard skewed shape associated to relatively high agglomeration
forces, financial intermediation is characterized by a more dispersed distribution of BUs across locations.

In order to test whether estimated coefficients statistically differ across sectors, we performed χ^2 tests for the difference between any two distributions. We first test whether any two 'predicted' distributions are different. Results reported in Table 3.3 show that theoretical distributions ψ_l^* are all statistically different from each other. Notice, however, that confidence intervals for γ_l^* partly overlap (see Table 3.2), especially as far as 'leather' and 'transport equipment' sectors are concerned. Therefore, to further explore if estimated γs really differ between sectors, we compared any two distributions $\psi_{l_1}^*$ and $\psi_{l_2}(h; \gamma_{l_1}^*)$, i.e. the distribution of sector $l_2 \neq l_1$ computed employing the 'predicted' parameter value for sector l_1. When they differ statistically, then one may reasonably conclude that $\gamma_{l_1}^* \neq \gamma_{l_2}^*$.

Results reported in Table 3.4 confirm that 'financial intermediation' exhibits agglomeration economies statistically lower than the other three sectors. Furthermore, 'electronics' appears to display intermediate values of γs, while 'leather' and 'transport equipment' are characterized by high (and not statistically different) agglomeration strength.

These results are in line with qualitative analyses on the relationships between the intersectoral patterns of innovation/learning regimes and

TABLE 3.3 *Tail probabilities for the chi-square test between $\psi_l(\gamma_l^*)$ ('predicted' distribution for sector l) and $\psi_m(\gamma_m^*)$ ('predicted' distribution for sector m). Degrees of freedom: $D = 50$*

| $\chi^2(\psi_l(\gamma_l^*),\psi_m(\gamma_m^*))$ | | *m* | | |
		Leather	Transport	Electronics	Financial
l	Leather	□	0.0523	0.0002	0.0001
	Transport	0.0523	□	0.0000	0.0000
	Electronics	0.0002	0.0000	□	0.0000
	Financial	0.0001	0.0000	0.0000	□

TABLE 3.4 *Tail probabilities for the chi-square test between $\psi_l(\gamma_l^*)$ (distribution for sector l computed at the 'predicted' value for sector l) and $\psi_m(\gamma_l^*)$ (distribution for sector m computed at the 'predicted' value for sector l). Degrees of freedom: $D = 50$*

| $\chi^2(\psi_l(\gamma_l^*),\psi_m(\gamma_l^*))$ | | *m* | | |
		Leather	Transport	Electronics	Financial
l	Leather	□	0.9942	0.0621	0.0000
	Transport	0.9598	□	0.0000	0.0000
	Electronics	0.0771	0.0000	□	0.0000
	Financial	0.0001	0.0000	0.0000	□

geographical concentration of economic activities (on Italy, cf. *inter alia* Antonelli (1994)).

The fact that agglomeration economies are relevant in the leather sector is quite in line with the evidence from other studies highlighting the high concentration of sectors that Pavitt (1984) groups under the 'supplier-dominated' heading, such as textile and leather products (cf. Ellison and Glaeser (1997), Maurel and Sedillot (1999), Overman and Duranton (2002) and Devereux *et al.* (2004)). The forces fuelling many Italian industrial districts, mostly featuring in this category, point at processes of interfirm division of labor, at knowledge complementarities, and at labor-embodied skills as factors underlying agglomeration (cf., for instance, Brusco (1982) and Piore and Sabel (1984)).

A 'scale-intensive' sector such as transport equipment shows a strong agglomeration profile although probably for different reasons, insofar as concentration is likely to display an 'oligopolistic core' often surrounded by subcontracting networks.[13]

Agglomeration economies should also appear significant in *SB* sectors, due to 'Silicon Valley' effects based on knowledge complementarities and on particular institutions fuelling 'exogenous science'. For example, on the evidence from the US, Audretsch and Feldman (1996, p. 639) note that 'a key determinant of the extent to which the location of production is geographically concentrated is the relative importance of new economic knowledge in the industry'. However, as already noted in Bottazzi *et al.* (2002), science-based sectors do not display, in Italy, striking agglomeration effects, probably due to the underlying weakness of 'fuelling' research institutions, with nothing even vaguely comparable to, e.g. Stanford, UC Berkeley, or MIT.

Finally, firms belonging to *II* industries (e.g. banks and insurance companies) do not appear to enjoy important agglomeration economies. Therefore, at least in our benchmark *II* sector, agglomeration economies implied by the existence of large fixed costs associated to the provision of specialized intermediate goods (e.g. related to extensive adoption of information and communication technology goods and services) seem to be overcome by 'monopolistically competitive' strategies of branch location near the customers (see Fujita and Hamaguchi (2001)).

3.5   Conclusions

In this chapter, we have presented a simple model of industrial clustering in which adaptive firms make locational choices in the presence of agglomeration economies. The latter stem from both standard comparative advantage arguments (making some locations inherently more attractive than others) and dynamic increasing returns to scale in agglomeration that can be both location and industry specific. We have applied the predictions of the model about the long-run distribution of the size of spatial clusters to data on Italian 'Local Systems of Labor Mobility' (i.e. a proxy for industrial districts).

In each sector under analysis, the accordance of theoretical predictions with data is quite high, with statistically significant, sector- and location-specific economies of agglomeration. In turn, we conjectured that such sectoral specificities in the strength of geographical clustering are likely to map into underlying differences in the modes of innovative exploration and knowledge accumulation.

Of course, one may think of several ways forward with respect to the foregoing analysis. First, our basic conjecture on the role of technological specificities as determinants of the intensity of agglomeration, if any, is going to be corroborated only by studying many more sectors, possibly in different countries. Second, one ought to incorporate explicit local interactions among firms and non-linear accounts of the location probabilities. Third, it would be interesting to consider intersectoral interactions in location patterns. Fourth, one should compare the results stemming from our statistical procedures with those based on different ones, such as the Ellison–Glaeser index and refinements thereof.

Existing evidence does suggest widespread phenomena of clustering of innovation activities (cf. Feldman (1994) and Cowan and Cowan (1998) among others). Moreover, technology-specific interactions between location of innovative activities and location of production have been identified in the case of multinational corporations (see, e.g. Cantwell (1989), Feldman (1994), Cantwell and Iammarino (1998) and Mariani (2002)). More generally, one observes robust links – although by no means any perfect matching – between the geographic distribution of innovative and production activities (cf. Audretsch and Feldman (1996), Lamoreaux and Sokoloff (1999), Pavitt (1999), Sutthiphisal (2002) and the literature cited therein). The foregoing study is, in many respects, complementary to such investigations and, hopefully, moves some steps ahead toward bridging the geography of location with the economics and geography of innovation.

Acknowledgements

We gratefully acknowledge the support of the research by the Italian Ministry of Education, University, and Research (MIUR, Project EFIRB03GD) and by the Sant'Anna School of Advanced Studies (Grant ERISO3GF). Comments by Thomas Brenner, Yannis Ioannides, Karl Schlag, Alan Kirman, and the participants to the conferences: 'Reinventing Regions in the Global Economy', Regional Studies Association, April 2003, Pisa, Italy; 'Computing in Economics and Finance', Society for Computational Economics, July 2003, Seattle, US; 'Clusters, Industrial Districts, and Firms: The Challenge of Globalization', Modena, Italy, September 2003, have helped along the various revisions of the work, incrementally building on Bottazzi et al. (2002).

Notes

1. Incidentally, note that most Italian districts display various combinations of forms (i) and (ii).
2. Original data refers to geographical location (Year: 1996) of a sample of more than half a million business units disaggregated with respect to the Italian ATECO 91 classification (which coincides with the 2-digit ISIC, Rev. 3, classification). Each geographical location represents a 'local system of labor mobility' (LSLM), that is a geographical area characterized by relatively high inward labor commuters' flows. LSLMs are periodically updated by multivariate cluster analyses employing census data about social, demographic and economic variables (see Sforzi (2000) for details). Frequency plots in Fig. 3.1 are computed as follows. Consider, for each LSLM, the frequency profile of manufacturing BUs present in that location and belonging to each 2-digit manufacturing sector (weighted by the relative size of each sector). For each frequency profile (location) we compute MIN, MAX, RANGE and Standard Deviation statistics and we plot their frequency distribution. Among all LSLM in the dataset (784), we consider only those hosting at least 10 BUs (about 99 per cent of the entire sample).
3. Ellison and Glaeser (1997), Cf. Maurel and Sedillot (1999), Overman and Duranton (2002) and Devereux *et al.* (2004). See Brenner (2003) for empirical evidence on industrial clustering in Germany across different manufacturing industries.
4. That is, to trivialize, one will find 'more of everything' in New York as compared to Pisa, irrespective of any finer pattern of comparative advantage.
5. Refinements and applications of this basic methodology are in Maurel and Sedillot (1999), Overman and Duranton (2002) and Devereux *et al.* (2004). See also the detailed reviews in Combes and Overman (2004) and Ottaviano and Thisse (2004).
6. This model is a variation of the Ehrenfest–Brillouin urn scheme. See Garibaldi and Penco (2000) and Garibaldi *et al.* (2002) for the case with 2 locations. A similar simplified version is in Kirman (1993).
7. Cf., e.g. Wio (1994) and Johnson *et al.* (1997). Notice also that values $a_j \leq 0$, for some j, can, in principle, be considered in order to allow for negative *ex ante* geographical benefits. However, since a negative a_j would require the empirically questionable notion of predefined upper bounds on the number of firms that can be hosted in a location, we prefer to stick to the assumption of non-negative as.
8. In the Italian case, see, e.g. Quarterly Reports by Unioncamere, 'Movimprese: Dati Trimestrali sulla Nati-Mortalità delle Imprese', *Uffici Studi e Statistica Camere di Commercio*, Italy, various years, available online at the url: http://www.starnet.unioncamere.it.
9. Cf. also Appendix B for an interpretation of this property in terms of Polya-urn schemes.
10. Data about industrial sectors are disaggregated according to the Italian ATECO 91 classification that corresponds to the 2-digit ISIC (Rev. 3) classification.

11. Unfortunately, data about sufficiently long time series of homogeneous observations are still not available at the appropriate level of disaggregation.
12. Confidence intervals contain all values of γ_l such that $\mathrm{Prob}\{\chi^2_D > \chi^2(f_i, \psi_i)\} < 0.05$, where χ^2_D is a r.v. distributed as a $\chi^2(D)$ and D are the degrees of freedom of the test.
13. We suspect that the evidence on the positive impact of production scale-economies upon spatial concentration presented in Kim (1995), is mostly confined to this group of sectors (including, of course, those that are also dependent on natural resources, such as mineral processing). In order to disentangle the different agglomeration structures, notwithstanding similar summary statistics as the degrees of agglomeration themselves, in future studies, we intend to compare our measures with the Ellison–Glaeser index, which, as mentioned, controls the concentration in terms of size of production units.

References

Antonelli, C. (1994), 'Technology districts, localized spillovers, and productivity growth: the Italian evidence on technological externalities in core regions', *International Review of Applied Economics*, **12**: 18–30.

Arthur, W. (1994), *Increasing returns and path-dependency in economics*. Ann Arbor: University of Michigan Press.

Audretsch, D. B. and Feldman, M. (1996), 'R&D spillovers and the geography of innovation and production', *American Economic Review*, **86**: 630–640.

Bottazzi, G., Fagiolo, G., and Dosi, G. (2002), 'Mapping sectoral patterns of technological accumulation into the geography of corporate locations. a simple model and some promising evidence', LEM Working Paper 2002/21, Sant'Anna School of Advanced Studies.

Brenner, T. (2003), 'An identification of local industrial clusters in Germany', Papers on Economic and Evolution No. 0304, Max Planck Institute, Jena, Germany.

Brusco, S. (1982), 'The Emilian model: productive decentralisation and social integration', *Cambridge Journal of Economics*, **6**: 167–184.

Cantwell, J. (1989), *Technological innovations and multinational corporations*. Oxford: Basic Books.

Cantwell, J. and Iammarino, S. (1998), 'MNCs, technological innovation and regional systems in the EU: some evidence in the Italian case', *International Journal of the Economics of Business*, **5**: 383–408.

Combes, P. and Overman, H. (2004), 'The spatial distribution of economic activities in the European Union', in V. Henderson and J. Thisse (eds), *Handbook of urban and regional economics*, Vol. 4. Amsterdam, North Holland, forthcoming.

Cowan, R. and Cowan, W. (1998), 'On clustering in the location of R&D: statics and dynamics', *Economics of Innovation and New Technology*, **6**: 201–229.

Devereux, M., Griffith R., and Simpson, H. (2004), 'The geographic distribution of production activity in Britain', *Regional Science and Urban Economics*, **34**: 533–564.

Dosi, G. (1988), 'Sources, procedures and microeconomic effects of innovation', *Journal of Economic Literature*, **26**: 126–171.

Dumais, G., Ellison G., and Glaeser, E. (2002), 'Geographic concentration as a dynamic process', *Review of Economics and Statistics*, **84**: 193–204.

Ellison, G. and Glaeser, E. (1997), 'Geographical concentration in U.S. manufacturing industries: a dartboard approach', *Journal of Political Economy*, **105**: 889–927.

Ellison, G. and Glaeser, E. (1999), 'The geographic concentration of industry: does natural advantage explain agglomeration?', *American Economic Review*, **89**: 311–316.

Feldman, M. (1994), *The geography of innovation*. Boston: Kluwer Academic Publishers.

Fujita, M. and Hamaguchi, N. (2001), 'Intermediate goods and the spatial structure of an economy', *Regional Science and Urban Economics*, **31**: 79–109.

Fujita, M., Krugman, P., and Venables, A. (1999), *The spatial economy: cities, regions, and international trade*. Cambridge, MA: The MIT Press.

Garibaldi, U., and Penco, M. (2000), 'Ehrenfest urn model generalized: an exact approach for market participation models', *Statistica Applicata*, **12**: 249–272.

Garibaldi, U., Penco, M., and Viarengo, P., (2002), 'An exact physical approach for market participation models', in R. Cowan, and N. Jonard (eds), *Heterogeneous agents, interactions, and economic performance*. Lecture Notes in Economics and Mathematical Systems, Berlin-Heidelberg: Springer-Verlag.

Gradshteyn, I. and Ryzhik, I. (2000), *Table of integrals, series and products*. New York: Academic Press.

Johnson, N., Kotz, S., and Balakrishnan, N. (1997), *Discrete multivariate distributions*. New York: Wiley.

Kim, S. (1995), 'Expansion of markets and the geographic distribution of economic activities: the trends in U.S. regional manufacturing structure, 1860–1987', *Quarterly Journal of Economics*, **110**: 881–908.

Kirman, A. (1993), 'Ants, rationality and recruitment', *Quarterly Journal of Economics*, **108**: 137–156.

Krugman, P. (1991), 'Increasing returns and economic geography', *Journal of Political Economy*, **99**: 483–499.

Lamoreaux, N. and K. Sokoloff (1999), 'Inventors, firms and the market for technology: U.S. manufacturing in the late nineteenth and early twentieth centuries', in D. Raff, N. Lamoreaux, and P. Temin (eds), *Learning by doing in firms, markets, and nations*. Chicago: University of Chicago Press.

Lee, R. and Willis, J. (1997), *Geographies of economies*. London: Arnold.

Malerba, F. and L. Orsenigo (1996), 'Technological regimes and firm behaviour', *Industrial and corporate change*, **5**: 51–88.

Mariani, M. (2002), 'Next to production or to technological clusters? The economics and management of R&D location', *Journal of Management and Governance*, **6**: 131–152.

Marsili, O. (2001), *The anatomy and evolution of industries: technological change and industrial dynamics*. cheltenham: Edward Elgar.

Martin, R. (1999), 'The new "geographical turn" in economics: some critical reflections', *Cambridge Journal of Economics*, **23**: 65–91.

Maurel, F. and Sedillot, B. (1999), 'A measure of the geographic concentration in French manufacturing industries', 7*Regional Science and Urban Economics*, **29**: 575–604.

Ottaviano, G. and Thisse, G. (2004), 'Agglomoration and economic geography', in Henderson, V. and J. Thisse (eds), *Handbook of urban and regional economics*, Vol. 4. Amsterdam, North Holland, forthcoming.

Overman, H. and Duranton, G. (2002), 'Localisation in U.K. manufacturing industries: assessing non-randomness using micro-geographic data', CEPR Discussion Paper 3379, Centre for Economic Policy Research.

Pavitt, K. (1984), 'Sectoral patterns of technical change: towards a taxonomy and a theory', *Research Policy*, **13**: 343–373.

Pavitt, K. (1999), *Technology, management and systems of innovation*. Cheltenham: Edward Elgar.

Piore, M. and Sabel, C. (1984), *The second industrial divide: possibilities for prosperity*. New York: Basic Books.

Sforzi, F. (1989), 'The geography of industrial districts in Italy', in E. Goodman, and J. Bamford (eds.), *Small firms and industrial districts in Italy*. London: Routledge.

Sforzi, F. (2000), 'Local development in the experience of Italian industrial districts', in I. C. Research (eds), *Geographies of diverse ties. An Italian perspective*. Rome: CNR-IGU.

Sutthiphisal, D. (2002), 'The geography of invention in high- and low-technology industries: evidence from the second Industrial Revolution', Mimeo, Department of Economics, Los Angeles: UCLA.

Wio, H. (1994), *An introduction to stochastic processes and nonequilibrium statistical physics*. Singapore: World Scientific Publishing.

Appendices

A   Proof of Lemma 1

Point 1. Let $P(\underline{n}'|\underline{n};\underline{a}, b)$ be the generic element of the transition matrix of the Markov chain that describes the dynamics of the system. Moreover, let $p(\underline{n}^t = \underline{n};\underline{a}, b)$ be the probability that the chain is in the state n at time t (in the following we will omit, for the sake of simplicity, the parameters $\underline{a}, b$).

We have assumed that in any time period only one firm will exit its current location and only one firm will enter one of the M locations (possibly including the one in which exit has occurred). Therefore, given $\underline{n}^t = \underline{n}$, the state at time $t + 1$ must necessarily be such that either (i) there exist two locations, say k' and k'', $k' \neq k''$ such that $n_{k'}^{t+1} = n_{k'}^t - 1$ and $n_{k''}^{t+1} = n_{k''}^t + 1$; or (ii) $\underline{n}^{t+1} = \underline{n}^t$, if the entrant has chosen the same location of the exiting firm. Hence if $\underline{n}^{t+1} \neq \underline{n}^t + \Delta_k - \Delta_j$ for all $k, j = 1, \ldots, M$ then $P(\underline{n}'|\underline{n}) = 0$. Otherwise, if there exist $k, j = 1, \ldots, M$ such that $\underline{n}^t = \underline{n}$ and $\underline{n}^{t+1} = \underline{n} + \Delta_k - \Delta_j$, then for any $j, k = 1, \ldots, M$:

$$\Pr\{\underline{n} + \Delta_k - \Delta_j | \underline{n}\} = \Pr\{\text{A Firm Exits from location } j\}.$$

$$\cdot \Pr\{\text{Entrant Chooses location } k | \text{A Firm Exits from location } j\}.$$

As the exiting firm is chosen at random from all incumbent firms then:

$$\Pr\{\text{A Firm Exits from location } j\} = \frac{n^t_j}{N}.$$

From (3.1), we also have that the entrant firm will find n^t_k firms in any location $k \neq j$, while (if a firm has left location j) it will find $n^t_j - 1$ firms in location j. Thus:

$$\Pr\{\text{Entrant Chooses location } k|\text{A Firm Exits from location } j\} =$$

$$= H^{-1}\begin{cases} a_k + bn^t_k & k = j \\ a_k + b(n^t_k - 1) & k = j \end{cases},$$

where H is a normalizing constant. By imposing the normalizing condition:

$$H^{-1} \cdot [\sum_{j=1}^{M} \sum_{\substack{k=1 \\ k \neq j}}^{M} \frac{n^t_j}{N}(a_k + bn^t_k) + \sum_{j=1}^{M} \frac{n^t_j}{N}(a_j + b(n^t_j - 1))] = 1,$$

we get that:

$$H = \sum_{b=1}^{M} a_b + (1 - \frac{1}{N}) \sum_{b=1}^{M} bn_b = A + (N-1)b. \qquad (3.13)$$

This proves Point 1. ∎

Point 2. For strictly positive $a_j, j = 1,\ldots,M$, each location has a strictly positive probability of receiving the entering firm, see (3.2). Therefore any state $\underline{n} \in S = \{(n_1,\ldots,n_M): n_j \geq 0, \sum_{j=1}^{M} n_j = N\}$ is reachable with a positive probability in a suitable number of steps starting from any other state. Hence, the Markov chain is irreducible and its evolution reads:

$$p(\underline{n}^{t+1} = \underline{n}) = \sum_{\underline{n}' \in S} P(\underline{n}|\underline{n}')p(\underline{n}^t = \underline{n}').$$

The invariant distribution $\pi(\underline{n};a,b)$ must therefore obey the detailed balance condition:

$$\pi(\underline{n};a,\ b)P(\underline{n}'|\underline{n}) = \pi(\underline{n}';a,\ b)P(\underline{n}|\underline{n}'), \qquad (3.14)$$

where $\underline{n},\underline{n}' \in S$ and P is the transition matrix. By using (3.14) and transition probabilities given in (3.2), one gets:

$$\pi(\underline{n} + \Delta_k - \Delta_j;a,b) = \pi(\underline{n};a,b)\frac{n_j}{n_k + 1}\frac{a_k + bn_k}{a_j + b(n_j - 1)}. \qquad (3.15)$$

The invariant distribution can thus be obtained by recursively applying (3.15) for a given initial occupancy vector in S. Let $\underline{n}^{*1} = (N,0,\ldots,0)$ be the state of the system with all firms in the first location and let $\pi^{*1} = \pi(\underline{n}^{*1};\underline{a},b)$. Now suppose to move $n_2 \geq 1$ firms from the first to the second location. By applying (3.15) recursively one obtains:

$$\pi((N - n_2, n_2, 0, \ldots, 0); \underline{a}, b) = \pi^{*1} \frac{N!}{(N - n_2)! n_2!} \cdot$$

$$\frac{\prod_{j_1=1}^{N-n_2} [a_1 + b(j_1 - 1)] \cdot \prod_{j_2=1}^{n_2} [a_2 + b(j_2 - 1)]}{\prod_{j_1=1}^{N} [a_1 + b(j_1 - 1)]}. \tag{3.16}$$

Suppose now to further move $n_3 \geq 1$ firms from the first to the third location, while keeping n_2 firms in location 2. Using again (3.15) and (3.16), one gets:

$$\pi((N - n_2 - n_3, n_2, n_3, \ldots, 0); \underline{a}, b) = \pi^{*1} \frac{N!}{(N - n_2 - n_3)! n_2! n_3!} \cdot$$

$$\frac{\prod_{j_1=1}^{N-n_2-n_3} [a_1 + b(j_1 - 1)] \cdot \prod_{j_2=1}^{n_2} [a_2 + b(j_2 - 1)] \cdot \prod_{j_3=1}^{n_3} [a_3 + b(j_3 - 1)]}{\prod_{j_1=1}^{N} [a_1 + b(j_1 - 1)]}.$$

$$\tag{3.17}$$

Notice that the result in (3.17) does not depend on the order in which firms have been moved from location 1 to locations 2 and 3. A clear pattern emerges irrespective of the sequencing of locations. Consider a generic occupancy vector $\underline{n} = (n_1, n_2, \ldots, n_M) \in S$ obtained by moving exactly $n_k \geq 1$ firms from the first to the k-th location and defining $n_1 = N - \sum_{k=2}^{M} n_k$. By recursively applying (3.15), one has:

$$\pi(\underline{n}; \underline{a}, b) = \frac{\pi^{*1}}{\prod_{i=1}^{N} [a_1 + b(i - 1)]} \frac{N!}{n_1! \ldots n_M!} \prod_{j=1}^{M} \vartheta(n_j; a_j, b), \tag{3.18}$$

where:

$$\vartheta(n_j; a_j, b) = \begin{cases} \prod_{b=1}^{n_j} [a_j + b(b - 1)] & 1 \leq n_j \leq N \\ 1 & n_j = 0 \end{cases}. \tag{3.19}$$

Notice that, if $n_j = 0$ for some j, then $\vartheta(n_j; a_j, b) = 1$ because no factors are generated.

Since π has to be invariant under symmetric permutations of n and a one can rewrite (3.18) as:

$$\pi(\underline{n}; \underline{a}, b) = Z(\underline{a}, b, N) \frac{N!}{n_1! \cdots n_M!} \prod_{j=1}^{M} \vartheta(n_j; a_j, b),$$

where Z is a normalizing constant depending, in general, on $\underline{a}$, b and N.

One can see that the function in (3.19) admits the following representation:

$$\vartheta(k; x, y) = \frac{d^k}{ds^k} (1 - sy)^{-x/y}\big|_{s=0}. \tag{3.20}$$

Indeed, consider

$$\tilde{\vartheta} = \sum_{k=0}^{\infty} \frac{s^k}{k!} \vartheta(k; x, y) \tag{3.22}$$

and let us rewrite it as a degenerate hypergeometric series

$$\tilde{\vartheta}(s; x, y) = 1 + \sum_{k=1}^{\infty} \frac{s^k y^k}{k!} \prod_{b=0}^{k-1} \left(\frac{x}{y} + b\right) = {}_2F_1(b/a, w; w; b) \tag{3.22}$$

for a generic (positive) w. Following Gradshteyn and Ryzhik (2000, p. 966), one obtains

$$\tilde{\vartheta}(s; x, y) = (1 - sy)^{-x/y} \tag{3.23}$$

and (3.20) follows.

Returning to the expression of the equilibrium distribution, using (3.20), one gets:

$$\pi(\underline{n}, \underline{a}, b) = \frac{1}{Z} \frac{N!}{\prod_j n_j!} \left(\frac{d}{ds_j}\right)^{n_j} \prod_j (1 - s_j b)^{-a_j/b}\big|_{\underline{s}=0}, \tag{3.24}$$

where $\underline{s} = (s_1, \ldots, s_M)$. Summing up over all the occupancies, one has:

$$\sum_{\underline{n}} \pi(\underline{n}, \underline{a}, b) = \frac{1}{Z} \left(\sum_j \frac{d}{ds_j}\right)^N \prod_{j=0}^{M} (1 - s_j b)^{-a_j/b}. \tag{3.25}$$

Notice also that if f_j are M differentiable functions, then the following expression holds:

$$\left(\sum_j \frac{d}{dw_j}\right)^N \prod_j f_j(w_j)\big|_{\underline{w}=0} = \left(\frac{d}{dw}\right)^N \prod_j f_j(w)\big|_{x=0}, \tag{3.26}$$

so that one obtains:

$$Z = \left(\frac{d}{ds}\right)^N \prod_{j=0}^{M} (1 - sb)^{-a_j/b}\big|_{s=0} = \frac{d^N}{ds^N} (1 - sb)^{-A/b}, \tag{3.27}$$

which, using (3.20), gives

$$Z = \vartheta(N; A, b).$$

B   Recovering the Polya Approach

Consider the stationary distribution given in (3.5). Following Johnson *et al.* (1997, Chap. 40), one can show that (3.5) can also be interpreted as the time-*t* probability distribution of a Polya entry process in which firms make *irreversible* locational choices.[14]

More precisely, suppose an industry (i.e. an urn) with a potentially infinite number of firms (i.e. balls) and M locations (i.e. ball colors or types). At time $t = 0$ the state of the system is given by the occupancy vector $\underline{n}^0 = (n_1^0, \ldots, n_M^0)$, $\sum_{i=1}^{M} n_i^0 = N^0$, where n_i^0 is the number of balls of color i in the urn. At any time period, a ball is extracted at random from the urn and put back in it together with $c \geq 1$ other balls of the same color. A standard result is that the probability that at time $\tau > 1$ the occupancy vector is $\underline{n}^\tau = (n_1^\tau, \ldots, n_M^\tau) \gg 0$, with $\sum_{i=1}^{M} n_i^\tau = N = N^0 + c\tau$, reads:

$$p(\underline{n}^\tau | \underline{n}^0, c) = \frac{\Gamma(N+1)\Gamma(N^0)}{\Gamma(N^0 + c(N-1) + 1)} \prod_{i=1}^{M} \frac{\Gamma(n_i^0 + c(n_j^\tau - 1) + 1)}{\Gamma(n_i^0)\Gamma(n_j^\tau + 1)}. \qquad (3.28)$$

If one is allowed to add only one ball at any time (i.e. $c = 1$), then $N^t = N^{t-1} + 1$ and (3.28) becomes:

$$p(\underline{n}^\tau | \underline{n}^0) = \frac{N!}{(N^0)^{[N]}} \prod_{i=1}^{M} \frac{(n_j^0)^{[n_j^\tau]}}{n_j^\tau!}, \qquad (3.29)$$

where $a^{[x]} = a(a+1)\ldots(a+x-1)$ is again the Pochammer symbol. Therefore, if $a_j = n_j^0$, the probability distribution (3.29) becomes the invariant distribution for the Ehrenfest–Brillouin model (3.5). This result allows us to directly compute (using standard results for the Polya process theory, cf. Johnson *et al.* (1997, Chap. 40)), the marginal probability that a site with intrinsic benefit a will contain – after a sufficiently long period of time – exactly k firms. Indeed, the latter marginal distribution is equal to the marginal probability that in an urn with 2 colors there will be k balls with the first color, when in the urn there are N balls and the initial number of balls of the first color was a, cf. (3.6).

Notice finally that, in contrast to the process of firms locational choice presented in Section 3.3, initial conditions (i.e. the number of firms initially present in each location) matter in the finite-time probability distribution of the Polya process. As net industry growth rate is positive (entry rate is equal to c, while exit rate is zero) locational decisions are irreversible. Therefore, dynamic increasing returns strongly affect long-run agglomeration patterns as early microevents may cumulatively reinforce the agglomeration benefit of any given location, possibly overcoming *ex ante* intrinsic comparative advantages. The impact of additional perturbations caused by entry becomes progressively negligible in the long run, thus leading to lock-in of the system.

In contrast, the Ehrenfest–Brillouin interpretation is consistent with always-reversible decisions: initial conditions never matter for the invariant distribution. As the size of any individual perturbation does not die out with time, the strength of dynamic increasing returns in much weaker than in the Polya interpretation.

Regional Knowledge Capabilities and Open Innovation: Regional Innovation Systems and Clusters in the Asymmetric Knowledge Economy

PHILIP COOKE

4.1 Introduction

In this chapter, a systematic account of the idea and content of regional innovation systems is reprised.[1] This rests intellectually on discoveries made by regional scientists, economic geographers, and innovation analysts working at the national level, who observed several features of actual innovation processes by firms and among firms and researchers that put in question received wisdom. The received wisdom was often rather influenced by philosophy and sociology of science that uncritically internalized autobiographical accounts by famous scientists. They stressed the logical progression of discovery from theory to experiment, confirmation to validation, and science to technology, but left many puzzles, not least how change occurred.[2] This is noted in the first main section of this chapter as a prelude to a brief illustrative account of the precise mechanisms operating in a specific biotechnology innovation system centered in Massachusetts. Although single cases should merely be heuristic rather than scientifically definitive, one alone is sufficient to refute conventional wisdom, rather as Karl Popper noted when a *black* swan was discovered in Australia.

Then, the chapter moves into an analysis of conditions and criteria for empirical recognition and judgement as to whether scientifically analysed, actual cases of innovation activity warrant the designation of 'regional innovation system' or not, something not always done theoretically or empirically in the national systems of innovation literature, although Malerba (1993) is a notable exception. The dichotomies attendant on the formation of a new field of study are moderated in light of more recent findings. Although, conceptually a system is either a system or it is not, in realist terms a system can be more or less systemic. Critics of dyadic conjecture confuse conceptual with real analysis. For pedagogical purposes it is important to delimit polarities conceptually then deploy the resulting framework to characterize particular empirical cases in terms of combinations of systems indicators. Though space does not allow that here, it is done in Braczyk *et al.* (1998)

and the interested reader is referred there for details. Reflecting recent theorization of regional innovation systems and clusters, however, attention is devoted in Section 4.4 to new challenges that underline the importance for global competitiveness of regional innovation systems. These connect 'asymmetric knowledge' (after Akerlof, 1970) and 'open innovation' (Chesbrough, 2003) in new ways that privilege a Penrosian-inspired (1959/1995) theorization of 'regional knowledge capabilities' as drivers of globalization impulses, rather than the reverse.

The fifth section of this chapter notes that much of the research field of regional innovation systems placed undue attention upon the role of the public policy in supplying the soft infrastructure of innovation support for enterprises. Reasons for this are given, including the fact that regional innovation policy in Europe was often orchestrated by the European Commission.[3] National governments have pursued such policies more consciously in the twenty-first century, some, notably Sweden, Finland, Italy, and the UK, with attention to regional-level imperatives.[4] This supports a key hypothesis of this chapter that herein lies the source of Europe's innovation gap with the US, for such reliance on public intervention signifies major market failure deriving from asymmetric knowledge. Simply put, markets for innovation services have yet to be widely recognized by European entrepreneurs, in stark contrast to their US counterparts. The future is seen as requiring the widespread evolution of public innovation support systems but as for their complementation by stronger institutional and organizational support from the private sector, this is far away especially in the era after the dot.com-led global economic downturn. In furtherance of this analysis, the first main section (4.2) reviews the origins of regional innovation systems thinking. This is followed by a section (4.3) that concretizes the analysis by reference to two contrasting European exemplars. In Section 4.4 a revised analysis of regional innovation systems and their relationship to clusters under knowledge economy conditions is offered. Section 4.5 draws some conclusions for policy from the foregoing analysis, before brief conclusions are drawn in Section 4.6.

4.2 Lineaments of Regional Systems – Thinking about Innovation

Although this section focuses closely upon the origins of regional innovation systems thinking, it does so with the help of a worked case analysis of what is also written of as a classic modern cluster, biotechnology in Boston (Owen-Smith and Powell, 2004). To prevent confusion, a regional innovation system usually exists administratively at the meso-level between central or federal, and local government. This is true to the meaning of 'region' that lies in the Latin word *regere* 'to govern'. Thus, saying Lombardy is a region of Italy leads us to examine the relationship between two regional subsystems, which are social and thus open systems. However, they also involve multilevel governance, knowledge, and productive interactions with external actors nationally and internationally. The two subsystems are the knowledge *generation* (or exploration and examination) and knowledge *exploitation* subsystems. These interact regionally as well as externally by means of exchange of resources, personnel and administrative authority. Such interactions facilitate knowledge transfer between the subsystems, and enhancing global knowledge flows for economic development is a primary task of innovation policy, particularly at the regional level (OECD, 2004).

But what about clusters? A well-blessed regional innovation system will not be dependent on a mono-industrial base. As well as multiple industry sectors, a region may have some clusters; naturally not all industry is organized in clusters. There are monopolistic structures, isolated branch plants, diffused public welfare services, company towns, and a whole panoply of plant-level forms. However, clusters may be among these forms. Clusters are various, as Bottazzi *et al.* (2002) present from an Italian perspective. They take at least five forms: Horizontally Diversified (e.g. 'Made in Italy' luxury goods); Vertically Disintegrated ('Smithian' with a local value chain); Hierarchical (oligopolistic); Research Driven (science-based); and Path Dependent (a Detroit-type agglomeration). They are, of course, *markets* whose main peculiarity is geographical concentration usually of a quasi-monopolistic kind. Proximity provides advantages not otherwise available, notably localized knowledge spillovers. These may take pecuniary form, as for example with the purchase of specialized local labor, or they may be non-pecuniary as when a firm does another firm a favor or can exploit reputational or trust-based rather than transaction-cost agreements. Such 'communities' may create localized collaborative 'governance' associations for common purchasing, marketing, or knowledge exchange. Hence, competition may be underpinned by certain collaborative norms. Armed with these insights we can take a microscopic, firm-based perspective on the functioning of a 'research-driven' cluster embedded within a wider regional innovation system that is globally connected. The example shows how globalization works ground-up rather than top-down in leading knowledge economy regional innovation systems. It shares regional geographic space with other clusters in biomedical devices, software, financial investment, higher education, and the remnants of 'path-dependent' clusters in textiles and precision engineering.

Consider the following. The US biotechnology firm Genzyme developed a drug to help combat the most debilitating effects of Gaucher's disease. This disease wholly undermines the physical capability of the sufferer by rendering bones brittle, but unlike osteoporosis affects also the blood, spleen, and liver so that the patient requires full hospitalization on a permanent basis. The mental faculties are not affected by the disease, hence the discovery of a drug that could manage or ideally, of course, cure the disease would return a fully functioning human being to a normal productive life. *Ceredase,* the company's recombinant DNA technology, halts progression of the disease thus enabling patients to return to a normal life provided they receive annual top-up treatment by injection of the drug. There are only some 5000 persons genetically predisposed to developing this disease in the Americas, and perhaps 10 000 world-wide. Each annual treatment cost some $300 000–$400 000 in 1999, but for each US patient, hospitalization for one year cost more than double that amount. Healthcare insurance companies could therefore be said to be the drivers of specific innovations because of the clear cost advantages successful ones bring. Absence of equivalent drivers in Europe, for example the UK, can easily be seen to have the opposite effect. Indeed, recently in that country, drug cost to the publicly funded health service was initially the excuse for not providing innovative treatment for influenza, let alone cancer.

To continue for a moment with the benign effects only of such a 'selection mechanism', the company based in Cambridge and other Massachusetts locations works closely with Senator Edward Kennedy, a local representative influential on federal government health committees. Its origins lie in Boston's Tufts University and New England Enzyme Center. It is a founding member of the Partners Healthcare System with Brigham and Women's hospital, and the Massachusetts General hospital, supported with $400 million in National Institutes of Health research funding and giving access to a large patient base for research and clinical trials (examination knowledge). Ten senior Harvard faculty are on the Partners Advisory Committee. Local interaction with the Food & Drug Administration (FDA) office in Boston is fruitful, but without biotechnology industry lobbying through the regional industry association, the Massachusetts Biotechnology Council, the local FDA office would not exist.

If necessary, specialist legal and financial services are available in the metropolitan area, as are specialist biotechnology incubation and technology park facilities. There are some 280 other biotechnology firms in the region and the business environment is both research led and entrepreneurial. Of course, it could be considered malign that a firm like Genzyme and others are incentivized to search out minority diseases with a relatively accessible genetic code that carry a very high premium, rather than more common ones with more complex genetic disorders. But given the massive research costs of biotechnology, it is hard to see a market model of innovation selecting a different course. The alternative would involve unlimited and long-term public funding that might not produce desired results, something that could be said historically to denote the 'crusade against cancer'.

What is striking about the Boston biotechnology case is how important are localized, metropolitan, and 'regional' in the sense of State of Massachusetts-wide institutional and organizational interactions across a wide range of partnership settings. But non-regional, 'national', or federal interactions are crucial too. Public research funding for the Boston biotechnology cluster was at least $1.5 billion per year in 2002, and most of that was federal in origin, ranging from federal National Institutes of Health to Small Business Innovation Research (SBIR) grants. Moreover, the regulatory powers of the federal FDA is crucial, even if they can be more easily accessed locally through the opening of a regional office. Finally, the vast power of the US healthcare market and the healthcare insurance industry cannot be underestimated.

Then, there are the global linkages between the regional cluster and innovation partners elsewhere, from California to Europe, not least in the case of Genzyme with a Dutch CEO, and two enzyme-production plants in the UK plus other European branch operations. It constitutes, for firms like Biogen, Genetics Institute, Quintiles, LeukoSite, Millennium,[5] and the many others, a multilevel innovation, governance and regulatory system. This is the advantage of taking a *regional* innovation systems (RIS) approach. The rich picture of interactions in the cluster can be set on the canvas of wider, global innovation interactions. For example, such are the regional knowledge capabilities of this bioscience innovation system that it attracted R&D presence from Abbott, Amgen, AstraZeneca, Pfizer, Sanofi-Aventis, and Novartis as well as Wyeth's two operations 2000–2004. Novartis from Switzerland has committed $4.25 billion over ten years to its Novartis Institutes of Biomedical Research. These aim to access leading-edge knowledge from cluster firms, research institutes, and medical schools in post-genomic drug discovery, concentrating on the key therapeutic areas of cardiovascular disease, diabetes, infectious diseases, functional genomics, and oncology.

Hence, it is evident that the bioscientific innovation system in Massachusetts, and particularly its core knowledge cluster in Cambridge is exerting a global influence upon industry organization. This is a reversal of the 'scale' perspective that sees multinationals orchestrating the world's economic geography. It reminds us of Penrose's (1959/1995) point about the *metamorphosis* wrought upon industry organization by the rise of knowledge networks in specific geographical centers that are outside the control of the firm. As we shall see, 'open innovation' of this kind has spread from biotechnology and post-genomics to electronics, energy, and even homecare products as testified by Procter & Gamble's replacement of its R&D division by C&D (Connect & Develop).[6] Capturing this tendency early, the concept of a regional innovation system is still relatively new, its first usage dating from a paper published by the present author (Cooke, 1992) and reviewed similarly in the first collection of papers on the subject (Braczyk et al. 1998; Cooke, 1998). The development path of the concept was almost entirely from regional science and economic geography. Indeed, authors like Lundvall (1992) were strangely hostile to the concept, again being strongly wedded to a Listian 'national' economy notion that seems increasingly questionable nowadays. There had been a lengthy tradition of published research on technical change and regional development in the UK by, for example, Oakey (1979) and in the US by Rees (1979) although one of the earliest papers on the subject was that of Thomas (1975). The late Morgan D. Thomas made a major contribution to innovation research in relation to growth poles, after Perroux (1955). The linkage to innovation research is underlined for this school since, as Andersen (1994) showed, Perroux developed the growth pole concept after reading Schumpeter's (1942/1975) work on disruptive economic change and the swarming effects of radical innovation upon growth processes. Perroux's contribution was to highlight the economic geography of what Dahmén (1950) called 'development blocks' from where (Porter, 1990, 1998) admits he got the idea of clusters.

In the case of Rees (1979) and Cooke (1992), the moves towards studying regional innovation evolved differently. Undoubtedly, Thomas's (1975) work influenced the former, but of greater direct significance was that of Vernon (1966) on the product life cycle, something Porter (1980) also worked with when analysing corporate strategy. Rees extended the notion of the product life cycle to that of the regional life cycle, stressing the importance of intensive technology regions to innovation and the negative effects of low technological intensities upon regions that become branded as mature technology 'branch plant' regions. This was also the aspect of innovation and the problems caused by industry restructuring in contexts of low innovativeness that stimulated the present author's interest (see, for example, Cooke, 1980, 1985). The fact that Wales was precisely one of those regions at the end of the product life cycle, although it had once been a globally significant innovator in metallurgical and mining industries, is undoubtedly connected to the intellectual interests of the three authors originating there. In the Cooke (1985) paper there is a detailed analysis of the then fairly novel idea and practice of regional innovation policy, set in the context of government policies seeking to 'clone' Silicon Valley and the early IT industry, but drawing on the 'technopole' policy in France and exposing it to critique. The problem observed was the lack of systemic network development around decentralized government research laboratories. Rather, these stood like 'cathedrals in the desert', often in agglomeration but not clustering and not creating synergies through spin-off and subcontracting activities. This, it was concluded, was not the model to imitate in regions such as Wales and the learning value was principally of the developmental weaknesses of linear, centralized and hierarchical growth pole and technopole thinking.

The alternative had to be non-linear, decentralized and heterarchical, something that this author had found in what was coming to be called 'Third Italy' (Bagnasco, 1977). Working with a Portuguese colleague on the industrial districts of Portugal and Emilia-Romagna, and analysing their contrasts in entrepreneurship and innovativeness with Wales, Cooke and da Rosa Pires (1985) discovered for themselves the value of interfirm networking and regional policies responsive to small firm needs, particularly in Italy. This occurred at approximately the time that the ground-breaking book by Piore and Sabel (1984) on the same subject had been published. Other regional scientists also began writing about network relations of this kind in new technology regions, particularly in Silicon Valley and most notably Saxenian (1981, 1994) and subsequently Scott (1986). But, of course, both the Third Italy and Silicon Valley were easily seen to be unique and untranslateable, despite the multitude of efforts to clone them by consultants and technology policy makers nearly everywhere. Most regions then had relatively weak administrations, little experience or competence in innovation support, little or no high-technology industry, and few, if any, industrial districts. But the question that now had to be answered was whether, underlying these diverse cases of regional economic success there was a generic and generalizable model. To test this out Cooke and Morgan (1990, 1993, 1994a) secured funding to investigate regional innovation networking in Wales and Baden-Württemberg. The latter region was chosen because it had a comparable, though larger-scale, industry structure to that of Wales, dominated by automotive and electronics engineering as well as a mix of large and smaller firms in supply chains. Yet there the resemblance ended, since the German region remains the more prosperous and innovative one. So the research question could be summarized as what's the special ingredient? Both regions could be shown to have industry clusters as defined by Porter (1998):

Geographic concentrations of interconnected companies, specialised suppliers, service providers, firms in related industries, and associated institutions. . . . in particular fields that compete but also co-operate (ibid. p. 197)

These were stronger in the automotive industry, linked also to machine-tools in the German case, while in Wales it was electronics that had the stronger cluster-like character, even though this had evolved around FDI, something Porter (1990) erroneously considered impossible until he reconsidered in Porter (1998). But while the electronics cluster in Wales could be considered 'competitive', the German automotive one was considerably more endogenously 'generative' and this innovative capability was an important clue to understanding differences in performance.[7]

In the late 1980s, the first fruits of the research and theorization of national innovation systems (Freeman, 1987) became widely available and the present author had invited this key figure to Cardiff to address his Masters class in Regional Development. Shortly after, a chapter by Lundvall on 'Innovation as an Interactive Process' was published in the collection of Dosi et al. (1988). While the ideas of neither, notably Freeman's on networks nor Lundvall's on interactive learning, were cited in Cooke (1992) they were understood and found useful in designing comparative research. Problems lay in the relative generality of their concepts of national innovation systems, their blind spot about regions, and a kind of stylized empiricism rather than detailed empirical research in what was nevertheless path-breaking work. Thus, it was crystal clear that there was a distinct need for new and detailed empirical research inside firms and innovation support organizations to get a better understanding of the nature of and extent to which co-operation and partnership operated in a market context and to determine the extent to which they contributed to greater innovativeness and competitiveness. What the national innovation systems research had never done was to schematize systems typologically but rather, presented everywhere studied as rather unique. This was something we also considered a weakness and a long-term aim was to overcome it, fulfilled in the publication of Braczyk *et al.* (1998) but prefigured in Cooke (1992) and Cooke and Morgan (1994*b*).

So what is the relationship between a National System of Innovation (NSI) and a Regional Innovation System (RIS)? This is, of course, a large question, needing a further chapter. However, some thought was given to this in Cooke *et al.* (2000). There, it was suggested, lies a powerful, persisting role for NSIs to set scientific priorities, fund basic research, and university-level training. RISs may influence or even disburse certain allocations, but without major tax-raising and tax-retaining powers, which few if any real systems have, there is an NSI monopoly. But this is a functional division based on historic path dependence. In evolutionary terms, things can change. Thus, what is presently, following Arrovian theorems, justified in terms of market failure (of investment in basic research) may evolve into something else, such as market non-failure consequent on radical privatization and incentivization of basic research investment, probably through private foundations as happens noticeably in bioscience and medicine. Or regions may wrest more taxation control from central government and amass budgets sufficient to set and fund their own, democratically achieved, basic research priorities.[8] In relational terms, regional lobbies make a difference, as in the US pork-barrel system of defense-science allocations that disproportionately favored certain regions. In Germany and the UK expensive decisions to build new synchrotrons have similarly been lobbied to Berlin and Oxford as biotechnology rises up the political agenda at the expense of nuclear research. Finally, as advanced industry inclines more to the cluster than the corporate model of industrial research organization, specialized RISs will necessarily develop intimate relationships with centers of major scientific policy and funding within the NSI, of the kind currently enjoyed by corporate heads. RIS governance thus becomes a litmus test of industry capability, and in many cases, new actors, such as university rectors may take their place, as in Austin, Texas with Sematech and MRC or Sheffield (UK) where advanced titanium research has caused Boeing to make a first R&D move off-shore (Cooke, 2002).

4.3   The Conceptual System and the Real System

There is confusion among many economists, and others tutored in neo-classical economics, about the distinction between a conceptual and a real system. The former may include such obvious idealizations as 'perfect competition', 'equilibrium', 'the real world is just a special case', and so on.

The latter will describe an actually existing system, with all its flaws and complexities. Iteration between conceptual and real systems is normally conducted by drawing on dichotomous thinking, aimed at covering polarities, in relation to which real cases are then measured. In the research process described thus far, earlier empirical research was, as usual, also necessary to assist delineation of conceptual systems. Thus, at this point, the research approach contained five key, linked concepts. The first was 'region' which we have seen was meant as a meso-level political unit that might have some cultural or historical homogeneity but which at least had some statutory powers to intervene in and support economic development, particularly innovation. The second was 'innovation', where the broad notion promulgated by the neo-Schumpeterian school, of which Freeman and Lundvall were leading exponents, as commercialization of new knowledge in respect of products, processes, and organization was a good starting point, but one that needed to be tested by detailed empirical research in firms. Third was the concept of 'network', which was conceived of as a set of reciprocal, reputational, or customary trust, and co-operation-based linkages among actors that coalesces to enable its members to pursue common interests, in this case in respect of innovation, after which it may continue with new projects, evolve with changed members or disappear. Fourth, the concept of 'learning' was prominent, particularly that related to 'institutional learning' where new levels and kinds of knowledge, skills, and capabilities could be embedded in the routines and conventions of firms and innovation support organizations and old ones discarded or forgotten as Johnson (1992) usefully put it.[9] Finally, 'interaction' was key, in the sense of regular means of formal and informal meeting or communicating focused on innovation such that firms and relevant network organizations and members could *associate* to learn, critique, or pursue specific project ideas or practices of collective and individual economic, commercial, or communal relevance.

In conducting the comparative European research, initially in two very differently performing regions from the innovation viewpoint, and analysing the results of interviews with senior managers of firms, government, and intermediary 'governance' organizations, it became possible to speak of regional innovation systems, the strengths and weaknesses of which could be measured along the five axes. Indeed 'systemness', which is a conceptual as well as a real construct where the ideal and real are much closer together in something like a central heating system than they are in respect of regional innovation, can be shown to be present or not in part or the whole of these dimensions. Hence, whether or not a region has an innovation system can be determined, as can the nature of whatever systemic innovation interaction, networking and learning capacity it does, in fact, possess. Analysing these dimensions against, on the one hand, interactive governance, meaning good knowledge flows among intermediaries and with firms, and on the other hand, interfirm interaction, networking, learning, and so on, enabled a judgement about the nature and extent of systemness to be made.

Thus, Baden-Württemberg could be shown to be a clear instance of a *heterarchical* regional innovation system because research results showed that firms had many vertical and horizontal, market and non-market, trustful and skeptical relations with each other. More than this, they had comparable relationships with intermediaries and government departments, who themselves worked through networks. Of course, in both dimensions, there were power relations; thus Daimler-Benz was able to animate and influence networks at the highest possible level inside and beyond the region. Equally, as the authoritative institution, the *land* government was more influential than any other public body in the region. But that did not mean that actions important for innovation were only initiated by them, nor that those that were always succeeded. A fine instance of the latter was the *land* initiated policy for Baden-Württemberg to become the first region in Germany or elsewhere in interactive television. A large budget was earmarked and leading large firms in telecoms, computing, and TV were organized into a policy network. Small and medium-sized firms were not highlighted in this process despite critics' arguments that 'content is king', the technology is not, and the innovative new media firms were in the *mittelstand*. Predictably, telecoms firms (Deutsche Telekom) found it impossible to agree standards or much else with computing firms (IBM, Hewlett-Packard) and the TV company could not work with either. Hence the attempt to 'create' a new media network among global players in the region was a failure.

However, an alternative narrative can be provided where the networks already exist and a member highlights an innovation issue. The case concerns the early 1990s impact on the possible future industrial fabric by the advent of Toyota's new luxury car, the Lexus. Keep in mind the *land* is home to Mercedes and Porsche and had Audi in the region also. Mercedes expressed its fears that it would be uncompetitive both to its industry association and the government. The reason was that Mercedes still designed and even produced far more parts and components in-house than the industry average in Germany. One way of reducing costs was to subcontract responsibility for innovation to the supply chain. This idea was discussed with the automotive trade association and the regional industry minister's office. The ministry, on the advice of the association, commissioned US consultants (A. D. Little) to explore the capability of regional *mittelstand* firms to take on an extra R&D burden. It transpired that most were used to receiving designs from the customer and producing to order, also few had R&D offices or staff. So to stimulate greater integration of innovation in the external system of production the ministry agreed to subsidize model projects in which suppliers would learn to innovate by interaction. Suppliers expressed fears that they would lose precious know-how to competitors, so agreement was reached that sensitive knowledge needed to innovate would be held by the Fraunhofer

Institute acting as a trusted third party member of the project networks. The outcome was a more systemic regional innovation process involving more open innovation and one that has contributed to the strengthening of Mercedes' global competitive strength.

The key point here is that such interaction could take place rapidly because a variety of key players were present in proximity and accordingly were familiar with each other's reputations and capabilities. Thus, as well as large customer firms and extended supply chains, there were numerous research institutes such as the Fraunhofer Society, well equipped in applied automotive research, the Max Planck Institutes if more fundamental research knowledge was needed, the regional branch of the German automotive industry association, the technology centers of the Steinbeis Foundation scattered throughout the higher education system of the *land,* and numerous engineering and other technical consultancies. The systemic nature of these nodes in the network could relatively easily be exploited given a challenge such as the one described.[10]

In a different setting such as that of Wales, where industry restructuring more comparable to that occurring in Germany's older industries in the Ruhr, the role of the State is much stronger because of market failure in the declining sectors. Unlike Baden-Württemberg, Wales had pressed for a powerful economic development agency to manage the transition to new industries. Modelling itself on the Irish Development Authority, the Welsh Development Agency went full speed for a Foreign Direct Investment strategy. The ingenuity of this rather basic approach was to target Japan rather than the US as the Irish and, later, Scottish development agencies had done. Relatively few European regional development agencies either existed or pursued such strategies so the competitive field was not as strong as it subsequently became. Around 60 Japanese and other south-east Asian companies were attracted from 1975 onwards. The challenge that evolved as this rebuilding process developed also concerned supply chains and innovation, neither of which were strong in automotive and electronic engineering. Gradually, through discussion, a 'sourcing' policy was adapted to become a supplier-development program and innovative forums of candidate and approved suppliers aimed at establishing standards, quality criteria, and innovation with customers was formed by the development agency. Where gaps in the supply chain were found, the agency persuaded FDI supply firms to locate in what were becoming automotive and electronics clusters. Later, small R&D divisions were established by some of the FDI firms and contract research was placed in universities. Skills problems were tackled by involving training colleges and intermediaries in the forums. A regional innovation strategy, part-funded as a pilot by the European Commission, was produced with full industry involvement.

But State agencies were co-ordinating all these policies and the systemic promotion of innovation was somewhat *hierarchical* as a consequence. Market failure had meant that, despite attempts to build up the innovation capability of the regional economy, most FDI firms were at the mature end of the product and hence regional life cycle. By the beginning of the millennium, the problems of devoting a great deal of attention to FDI in mature sectors like automotive components, televisions, and telecom equipment, and failing to create a good environment for entrepreneurship in innovative 'new economy' sectors were revealed. Wales scores low on new economy businesses and its FDI firms like Sony and Panasonic began to downsize and shift mature production to China, Poland, Slovakia, and the Czech Republic. Unlike Ireland and Scotland, where the pursuit of high technology eventually led to secondary and indigenous business growth in, for example, business and leisure software, not least because skills development in high technology creates knowledge that is also suitable for entrepreneurship in new economy fields where barriers to entry are low, in Wales the government was late in trying to lead an entrepreneurship crusade. The key problem remains a dearth of growing mid-size businesses either producing or investing in future-oriented business sectors, and while consciousness of the importance of innovation may have risen, for example as inputs to the production of plans and strategies, for the moment the outputs remain rather disappointing.[11]

There are many more regions in Europe and elsewhere with a story more similar to that of Wales than Baden-Württemberg. In a further research study (Cooke et al., 2000) funded by the TSER program of the European Commission, eleven regions in the EU and in Eastern and Central Europe were examined with a common research methodology to establish the extent to which regional innovation systems existed. Of these, only four were good candidates. Two are those already discussed above and the others are the Basque Country in Spain, with a State-led structure very much like that of Wales and a still rather weak innovation performance (see also Cooke and Morgan, 1998), and Styria in Austria where there is also a strong public innovation support infrastructure but much of it devoted to university spin-out and cluster formation. Elsewhere, in regions like Friuli in Italy or Wallonia in Belgium, where there were signs of growth these seemed almost to be occurring despite rather than because of government actions. In Brabant in Holland, SME innovation was evident but there was no regional administration and the same applies to the Tampere region in Finland where, like Styria university spin-offs supplying Nokia performed well with stimulus from the national innovation system promotion of incubation and science parks. Industries in regions restructuring towards raising research links with universities as a means of augmenting 'regional knowledge capabilities' have performed better than those in regions like Wales, Wallonia, or North Rhine Westphalia that evolved outsourcing down the value chain (Cooke et al., 2004). The Centro region in Portugal also has market-based low-technology industrial districts that are now seen to be extremely vulnerable to export trading conditions and 'offshoring', but cannot be said to have the character of a regional innovation system. There are networks but they are somewhat clientelistic and opportunities for upgrading through commercializing university research are scarce. Lower Silesia in Poland has potential, based on its universities, but has little regional systemic innovation capability, unlike the Féjer region in Hungary that has a burgeoning regional supply-chain culture developing around US FDI in automotive and electronics engineering but no regional government or strong research base. It is notable that automotive and electronics FDI had a limited propulsive effect in restructuring older industrial regions in Western Europe and is now increasingly performing that mature product life cycle function in the East, while gradually attenuating its presence in its previous host regions. The best lesson the East can learn from the West is to seek to develop regional innovation systems that promote endogenous development in immature sectors that may nevertheless benefit from certain kinds of skills development and knowledge transfer from advanced users and producers of, say computers, pharmaceuticals, and telecommunications. For the moment, it is these learner regions that adapt rather than imitate or simply act as production platforms that develop the most, as happened to some degree in Ireland and the Asian 'tigers'.

4.4   Regional Knowledge Capabilities, Asymmetric Knowledege and Open Innovation: New Challenges for Regional Innovation Systems and Clusters

As knowledge economy imperatives of the kind highlighted in Dunning (2000) and Cooke (2002) become magnified, such that the corporate valuation of intangible goods is much higher than previously, the employment of highly qualified labor more pronounced, and the measures of knowledge inputs and outputs (R&D and patents) have risen exponentially, a Penrosian *metamorphosis* in the sourcing of productive knowledge has evolved. This has spatial expression in regional innovation systems and clusters. This thesis is logically and empirically supported in the following five interlinked propositions:

- First, Chandlerian internal economies of R&D scale become diseconomies confronted with demands for new, interdisciplinary research. Informal knowledge networks spawned a research industry as hypothesized by Stankiewicz (2001). This consolidated around *networks* of research institutes, university centers of excellence, public laboratories, engineering and management consultants, clinical research organizations, and so on.
- Second, project-based research was increasingly conducted in regional settings and clusters characterized by both knowledge *specialization* and *diversification*. Debate on knowledge spillovers (e.g. Breschi and Lissoni, 2001; Henderson, 2003; Rosenthal and Strange, 2003; and Audretsch and

Dohse, 2004) strongly suggests geographical knowledge concentrations display cyclical difference in the prominence of one over the other over time in the evolution of the cluster. This is caused by the interplay between initial, say, laboratory discoveries that may lead to 'pipeline' transactions when legally binding, confidential, contractual business is being transacted with firms, which is later subject to 'open science' conventions.

- Third, Akerlof's (1970) perspective, actually on 'asymmetric information' but 'asymmetric knowledge' is more theoretically consistent here, adds to the analysis in its recognition of the non-uniformity, non-universality, non-ubiquity, and sheer 'stickiness' of the kind of knowledge routinely valuable in research (as exploration and examination knowledge) and innovation (as exploitation knowledge; see March, 1991). In Akerlof's terms, the learning agent finds itself in a world of potential 'lemons'. The argument of relevance here is that a producer, retailer, or professional investor in a specialist field will generally have significantly greater knowledge of that field than a consumer of the product or service in question. In Akerlof's famous case of the used-car industry, the consumer, with only partial, amateur knowledge always faces the *risk* of purchasing a 'lemon'. The importance of the insight is that it provides a fundamental reason why markets are imperfect, particularly regionally so, and indeed points to a basic cause of market failure. In our context, a 'learning organization' or even a 'learning region' faces a significant risk in accessing superior knowledge sources. Uncertainty, time, and expertise are the main constraints upon overcoming asymmetric knowledge.

- Fourth, this insight helps explain the rise of 'regional knowledge capabilities' as an effect of both potentially disruptive innovation supply, and of demand for scarce knowledge capabilities that may increasingly be found in or near universities, but not only there. The process is represented in Table. 4.1. To explain what the table shows, it suggests the following.

In the early stage (1) of a technology, there will be few firms or academics with the requisite combination of scientific and commercialization expertise for technology exploitation. However, when the two come together and the market potential of what has been discovered is realized, there will be a 'pipeline'-type transaction to patent, arrange investment, and create a firm (Zucker *et al.*, 1998). This was how Genentech, Biogen, Hybritech, etc., began in specific academic settings that have since

TABLE **4.1** *Characterization of successful and potentially successful knowledge clusters*

	Specialization	Diversification
Pipeline	1. Embryonic	4. High Success
Open Science	2. Innovative	3. High Potential

become clusters.[12] Once this process has begun, the sector remains specialized but new firms, often retaining close affiliation with their home university, open 'channels'. Knowledge spillovers are thus accessed to create highly innovative environments around 'open science' conventions. Stage-three knowledge production occurs when diversification begins and specialist suppliers, on the one hand, but more importantly, new technology research lines and firms form – for example, after a research breakthrough – on the other. Large research budgets are by now attracted to leading centers and this stimulates further 'open science' communication, cross-fertilization through knowledge spillovers and further new-firm formation. Fourth, after this, many serious entrepreneurial transactions occurring through 'pipeline' relations take place, trialling proves successful and licensing deals for marketing a product are regularly struck between big pharma and entrepreneurial firms. Thereafter, further R&D outsourcing to leading research institutes or specialist firms is further engaged and a potentially successful bioregion can be said to have become a highly successful one. It is a classic example of the power of 'increasing returns'.

- Fifth, this model works well for the iterative process of taking exploration knowledge through its examination phases to ultimate exploitation as a commercial product through academic entrepreneurship. But is it generic, in other words does it also apply to knowledge-to-product processing in the completely different context of a project originating inside the large firm? If so, we have an explanation of the modern innovation process that satisfies both the exigencies of markets and conventions of 'open innovation'. To test this, let us briefly elaborate a case from homecare products firm Procter & Gamble (P&G) briefly noted by Chesbrough (2003). In 1999, P&G established a Director of External Innovation under a program called 'Connect & Develop'. Internal research by the firm's nearly 9000 scientists continued, but if after three years research results were not utilized they were made available to other firms, including direct competitors. 'P&G's R&D department used to be like the Kremlin. Now we're more like the Acropolis – all ideas are welcome and get a fair hearing.' Thus, Nabil Sakkab, Senior Vice President of Research and Development in Procter & Gamble's Fabric and Home Care division, describing the way P&G's R&D department has transformed itself into an externally focused 'Connect & Develop' – C&D (rather than R&D) organization. Although retaining significant R&D capability, with approximately $2 billion invested annually, the company created some 20 different global 'communities of practice' bringing distinctive scientific capabilities together, encouraging and rewarding knowledge transfer from one business area to another. P&G leads in the reapplication of technologies, products, and business models from suppliers, universities, entrepreneurs, and institutes. 'C&D is about shared risk and interdependence', explains Sakkab, 'we'll license, we'll collaborate where it makes sense.'[13]

Thus, finally, a *regional knowledge capabilities* model of regional growth has been advanced based upon a Penrosian (1959/1995) 'knowledge capabilities' platform and Chesbrough's (2003) 'open innovation' perspective. These are *explained* by 'asymmetric knowledge' endowments after Akerlof (1970) and, in turn, *explain* the rise of regional innovation systems, on the one hand, and clusters, on the other, as spatial forms of 'constructed advantage' (Foray and Freeman, 1993) in the knowledge economy. Constructed advantage arises from the formation of quasi-monopolistic network linkages among distinctive 'communities of practice' or 'epistemic communities' (Haas, 1992) of consequence to innovation such as universities, industry, and government in a given territory.[14]

Now, when it comes to instances of regional innovation systems, and within them, clusters, should they exist, we begin to see that asymmetric knowledge must also extend to kinds of 'regional knowledge' based on institutions and organizations. Those with good 'regional knowledge capabilities' for the knowledge economy are likely to be more like the idealization on the left side of Table. 4.2. Actually, cluster characteristics may more often display certain 'entrepreneurial' characteristics from the right side, in combination with certain 'collaborative' norms from the left. The discussion is constructed in relation to 'infrastructural issues' that are contextual to innovation, and 'superstructural issues' including both 'institutional' norms, values and the like, and 'organizational' characteristics more microgovernance focused and microindustrial for consistency with the original version of this contribution (see also, Cooke *et al.*, 1997).

Before discussing this, two key innovation policy issues for regions arise, the first concerns whether possessing cultural elements belonging more to the right side of Table. 4.2, policy might be more focused on removing obstacles to entrepreneurship than designing innovation-system interactions. For an entrepreneurial culture is also a form of constructed advantage.[15] Secondly, for regional policy agencies recognizing that they are unquestionably 'institutional' rather than 'entrepreneurial' can regional knowledge economy weaknesses be overcome by adopting a 'learning region' posture? This, in effect, is what happened in much of the world that tried to 'clone' Silicon Valley in the 1980s. Akerlof (1970) would lead us to infer this to be difficult because of asymmetric knowledge for even a 'learning organization' let alone a 'learning region', and indeed most such efforts failed. But not all, especially when aligned with regional knowledge capabilities; thus Kista in the Stockholm region grew to 29 000 high-tech jobs by adapting 'open innovation' to Ericsson's telephony capabilities and 'open innovation' requirements. The same could be said around Helsinki and elsewhere in Finland in regard to Nokia's comparable capabilities. South East Asian high-tech clusters based

TABLE **4.2** *Conditions for higher and lower regional innovation systems potential*

Regional Innovation Systems Potential	
HIGHER	LOWER
Infrastructural Level	
Autonomous Taxing and Spending	Decentralized Spending
Regional Private Finance	National Financial Organization
Policy Influence on Infrastructure	Limited Influence on Infrastructure
Regional University–Industry Strategy	Piecemeal Innovation Projects
Superstructural Level	
Institutional Dimension	
Co-operative Culture	Competitive Culture
Interactive Learning	Individualistic
Associative-Consensus	Institutional Dissension
Organizational Dimension (Firms)	
Harmonious Labor Relations	Antagonistic Labor Relations
Worker Mentoring	Self-Acquired Skills
Externalization	Internalization
Interactive Innovation	Stand-alone R&D
Organizational Dimension (Policy)	
Inclusive	Exclusive
Monitoring	Reacting
Consultative	Authoritative
Networking	Hierarchical

in research parks were also successful. The common element is that they are cases of playing to strengths. 'Learning-by-cloning' seems unsuccessful but 'learning-by-adapting' possibly less so if applied intelligently and appropriately. Let us now look at key conditions more or less favorable to regional innovation-system formation.

4.4.1 Infrastructural Issues

The first infrastructural issue concerns the degree to which regional financial competence is present. This includes private and public finance. Where there is a regional stock exchange, smaller firms may find opportunity in a local capital market. Where regional governments have jurisdiction and competence, a regional credit-based system in which the regional administration can be involved in co-financing or provision of loan guarantees, will be of considerable value, something extremely important about the German system where the private sector avoids high risk. Hence, secured 'proximity capital' can clearly be of great importance especially as lender–borrower interaction and open communication are seen to be increasingly important features in modern theories of finance. Hence, regional governance for innovation entails the facilitation of interaction between parties, including, where appropriate and available, the competences of member-state and EU resources. This can help build up capability, reputation, trust, and reliability among regional partners.

However, regional *public* budgets are also important for mobilizing regional innovation potential. We may consider three kinds of budgetary competence for those situations where at least some kind of regional administration exists. First, regions may have competence to administer *decentralized spending*. This is where the region is the channel through which central government expenditure flows for certain items. Much Italian, Spanish, and French regional expenditure is of this kind, although there are exceptions, such as the Italian Special Statute regions and for some Spanish regions. A second category applies to cases where regions have *autonomous spending* competence. This occurs where regional assemblies determine how to spend a centrally allocated block grant (as in Scotland and Wales in the UK) or where, as in federal systems, they are able to negotiate their expenditure priorities with their central state and, where appropriate, the EU. The third category is where regions have *taxation authority* as well as autonomous spending competence since this allows them extra capacity to design special policies to support, for example, regional innovation. The Basque Country in Spain has this competence as does Scotland. Clearly, the strongest base for the promotion of regional innovation is found where regions have regionalized credit facilities and administrations with autonomous spending and/or taxation authority.

A further infrastructural issue concerns the competence regional authorities have for controlling or influencing investments in hard infrastructures such as transport and telecommunications and softer, knowledge infrastructures such as universities, research institutes, science parks, and technology-transfer centers. Most regions lack the budgetary capacity for the most strategic of these, but many have competences to design and construct many of them or, if not, to influence decisions ultimately made elsewhere in respect of them. The range of possibilities is enormous in this respect, so we classify broadly into types of infrastructure over which regions may have more or less managerial or influence capacity. If we think of our three cases, then the federal systems in Germany and the US have most influence over infrastructural decisions, including roads and even airport policies; in Germany basic research funding frequently has a regional (*land*) component, and in the US also, management and funding of public universities is devolved. In the UK case, regions in England (but not Northern Ireland, Scotland, and Wales) have only had regional development agencies since April 1999. So the infrastructural autonomy enjoyed in the federal system is absent except for the construction, mainly privately, of science and technology parks, whose location is regulated by local government.

4.4.2   Superstructural Issues

Three broad categories of conditions and criteria can be advanced in respect of superstructural issues. These refer, in general, to mentalities among regional actors or the 'culture' of the region and can be divided into the *institutional level*, the *organizational level for firms*, and the *organizational level for governance*. Together, these help to define the degree of *embeddedness* of the region, its institutions, and organizations. Embeddedness is here defined in terms of the extent to which a social community operates in terms of shared norms of co-operation, trustful interaction, and 'untraded interdependencies' (Dosi, 1988) as distinct from competitive, individualistic, 'arm's length exchange', and hierarchical norms. The contention here is that the former set of characteristics is more appropriate to systemic innovation through network or partnership relationships. It is widely thought that American entrepreneurship involves this cultural characteristic, but in biotechnology, as in other cases of high technology, there is co-operation as well as competition, as we have seen. The resurgence of the Boston's Route 128 is caused by Massachusetts' life sciences clustering and innovation support policy from which biotechnology and biomedical instruments industries, in particular, have benefited (Porter, 1998; Best, 2001).

Therefore, if we look, first, at the institutional level, the 'atmosphere' of a co-operative culture, associative disposition, learning orientation, and quest for consensus would be expected to be stronger in a region displaying characteristics of systemic innovation, whereas a competitive culture, individualism, a 'not invented here' mentality and dissension would be typical of non-systemic, weakly interactive innovation at regional level. Moving to the organizational level of the firm, those with stronger systemic innovation potential will display trustful labor relations, shopfloor co-operation and a worker-welfare orientation with emphasis upon helping workers improve through a mentoring system, and an openness to externalizing transactions and knowledge exchange with other firms and organizations with respect to innovation. The weakly systemic firm characteristics would include antagonistic labor relations, workplace division, 'sweating', and a 'teach yourself' attitude to worker improvement. Internalization of business functions would be strongly pronounced and innovativeness might be limited to adaptation. Regarding the organization of governance, the embedded region will display inclusivity, monitoring, consultation, delegation, and networking propensities among its policy makers while the disembedded region will have organizations that tend to be exclusive, reactive, authoritarian, and hierarchical.

But equally, aspects of the right side institutions and organizational features like competitive and individualistic culture, self-acquired skills and even 'stand-alone R&D' might, despite evidence advanced by Chesbrough (2003) that it is becoming rarer by the day, fit certain American stereotypes of the entrepreneurial (as compared to a more European 'institutional') regional innovation system that is more dependent on public-sector facilitation. Silicon Valley, with its enormous innovation capability but also the wreckage of 400 000 lost jobs, 2001–2003, comes to mind (Bazdarich and Hurd, 2003). In outline, these characteristics are summarized in Table. 4.2. To repeat, both sets of conditions are ideal types in the sense that it is unlikely that any region fits either side. Rather, it is a useful heuristic enabling the tracking of tendencies by regions towards one or other pole, perhaps signifying an element of convergence influenced either by globalization processes, the policy effects of state governments or, in the EU, European Union programs.

4.5   Problems with Public Regional Innovation Systems

We can say that regional innovation systems are both rare and newly discovered. In Europe, where research has been concentrated, they are dependent on public institutions to a significant degree. This is true even in accomplished regional economies such as Baden-Württemberg, but normal in many cases where industrial restructuring is pronounced, and there are many cases where it is hard to discern systemic regional innovation. Nevertheless, Vence (2001), using EU data showed that innovative regions performed best in the EU 1980–1995 in relation to productivity and employment growth by firms. This is consistent with findings discussed already from Rosenthal and Strange (2003) and Audretsch and Dohse (2004). The 'new economy' sectors of ICT, biotechnology, and media have in common proximity to as well as some presence inside large cities. This intracity presence is particularly true for new media and leisure software (computer games) firms, as occurs in New York and Los Angeles, as described in Braczyk et al. (1999). For ICT and biotechnology, especially the latter, location in clusters closer to leading-edge university research is most important. Hence, Cambridge and Oxford, at about one-hour's drive from London, have ICT or biotechnology clusters, as does Uppsala in relation to Stockholm, and Lund in cross-border relation to Copenhagen.

These places are dependent on public research funds for basic scientific investigation but exploitation and commercialization of research findings is looked after by venture capitalists, corporate venturing arms of larger firms, contracts and milestone payments by big pharmaceutical, media or ICT firms, business angels, patent lawyers, specialist corporate lawyers, merchant banks, consultants, and accountants. In and near to great cities are found a rich private infrastructure of innovation support whose presence has become particularly visible during the period of emergence and consolidation of what have been identified as the 'new economy' sectors. Although leading corporations involved in the marketing of computing, telecommunications, varieties of software, pharmaceuticals, and media products and services exist outside clusters, they also have a presence in many of them, either through establishing localized plants or offices, or even more commonly through acquisition, a contractual relationship or other form of partnership. But, having also outsourced much leading-edge research to smaller technology firms, it is these suppliers that display high levels of clustering to access knowledge spillovers, opportunities for tacit knowledge exchange and other 'untraded interdependencies', more generally. Such settings create highly innovative milieux and in Europe the support infrastructure is beginning to learn to be as aggressive in pursuit of innovation opportunities capable of being realized as substantially profitable investments as the model that emerged earliest in California. But they are, as yet, few in number and far behind the originators of what we may refer to as the new economy or, more in tune with Winter's (1984) usage, Entrepreneurial Regional Innovation System (ERIS) actors.

In the earlier version of this chapter (Cooke, 2001) there was a lengthy discussion concerning the new institutional and organizational norms associated with these industries compared to so-called 'old economy' industries. By now, that has become more or less conventional wisdom but also the new norms contained 'knowledge economy' traits like overvaluation of intangible assets that saw the downfall, with massive losses, of firms like Enron, WorldCom, and Global Crossing to name a few. The knowledge economy raises new ethical as well as economic issues. The key distinctions are now filed under the rubric of 'open innovation', something the lineaments of which could be observed in reference to a firm, Xerox, discussed at length by Chesbrough (2003) as a kind of inadvertent pioneer of it. To repeat, the transformation was away from a model of preferred industry organization in which centralized corporate structures pursued constant returns from scale economies, accompanied by inflation, where core technologies were mature and disruptive change unwelcome, and headquarters decisions could be locked-in to a specific piece of machinery, often the original source of the corporation's existence. Probably the classic example is Xerox, based in Rochester, NY, exploiting an original copier technology incrementally, maximizing share value but also firm value. Thus:

Virtually Xerox's entire workforce of 125 000 was focused on selling one type of product; the office copier. They represented decades of corporate investment – hundreds of millions of dollars – in embedded training, technology, and customer service. (Hiltzik, 2000, p. 392)

This is by way of comparison with Apple, itself spawned (we would say now through 'open innovation') by Xerox through its investment in the Palo Alto Research Center or Xerox PARC where the Alto, predecessor of the Macintosh, originated. Open innovation meant first-mover advantage by a small start-up like Apple gave increasing returns, based on Moore's Law of the falling price of microprocessors, in disruptive technologies where knowledge was enacted upon itself to create productivity and enhanced value (Castells, 1996; Cooke, 2002), a definition of the knowledge economy production paradigm. Although Xerox PARC was set up by the parent firm as an innovative R&D laboratory, few products other than laser printers were successfully marketed by Xerox, but most of PARC's other innovations became mainstays of Silicon Valley and the ICT part of the 'new economy'.

Echoed here is our earlier discussion of the centrality of venture capital to the firms that help move knowledge from its exploration, through the examination process to its final exploitation under open innovation. Pioneered in biotechnology, the 'open innovation' business model subsequently spread to ICT, electronics, energy, and now even household care products. It is a model in which investors became willing to invest in *ideas* on the promise, or in the hope, of profits. Thus, ideas, knowledge, and research had themselves become speculative targets. In accounts of the rise of firms like Cisco Systems, Netscape, Yahoo, Google, and Oracle, all founded in Silicon Valley, great importance is given to firms like Kleiner, Perkins, Caulfield & Byers, and other, lesser venture capital houses such as Sequoia Capital, Sierra Ventures, Technology Venture Investments, New Enterprise Associates, and the Mayfield Fund, all clustered in Sand Hill Road, Palo Alto. Kleiner Perkins (KP) investments in some 230 firms had in 1997 market capitalizations worth $125 billion, 1997 revenues of $61 billion and employed 162 000 people, mostly but not exclusively in Silicon Valley.

However, by July 2004, although the portfolio had risen to over 400 companies the total market value of investments was down to $80 billion. In brief, a key role in entrepreneurial innovation had been taken, for good or ill, by an aggressive scouring of research laboratories by venture capitalists (VCs) some of whom, like KP, had in effect, built their own clusters of start-up firms that are advised to trade with each other in Japanese *keiretsu* style. An empirical indication of the *keiretsu* approach to proximity in venture capital investment used to be shown by analysis of the location of the investments of KP, the leading *keiretsu* investor (www.kpcb.com).[16] Of the 230 firms in which the company retained equity in the early 2000s, 59 per cent or 134 were located in Silicon Valley, 25 were located elsewhere in California, and 71 outside that State. Of those in Silicon Valley, 20 were in Mountain View, 18 in Sunnyvale, 16 in San Jose, 14 each in Palo Alto and San Mateo, and 7 each in Santa Clara and Redwood City. These locations are easily within an hour's drive of Sand Hill Road where KP has its head office, many are within an hour's walk. Not only is geographical proximity at the heart of this model of industry organization, clustering activity between firms in the *keiretsu* family is the rationale for the performance enhancement of the equity holdings. These firms were key buyers and sellers of 'open innovation' through R&D outsourcing. This underline's Zook's (2000) observation about the high positive correlation between Internet firms and venture capitalists in the US, which is that they do not like to be more than an hour's drive away from their investments because they are then able to engage in hands-on management of the investment.

These shifts, first towards dynamic 'new economy' business growth occurring in few knowledge-capable regions, then the disappointment as billions of dollars were wiped from these very technology stocks from 2001, followed by accounting scandals and ethical crises have led to new search procedures on the part of regional innovation policy makers. In the more sophisticated cases these increasingly adopt three new search modes:

- There is evidence of disaffection with 'success recipes', that is, with either direct study visits to global innovation hotspots to bring the alchemy home. It especially applies to 'learning region' contexts that may be unsuited to the application of unique species of 'constructed advantage', especially in institutional contexts that are less entrepreneurial than the originator. This is also pronounced with respect to indirect learning of single recipes claimed to work well anywhere, an exemplar being the selling of a 'clusters' recipe. Cluster policies have been poor performers in most contexts where policy has been invoked to build up the most attractive of them, notably ICT, but also biotechnology. The ICT-led stock market decline was the proximate cause of problems here, but also the appeal of academic entrepreneurship and university spinout businesses was clearly oversold. This has been replaced by a more analytical knowledge-appreciation and rigorous questioning about regional and local applicability of exogenous models.

- Furthermore, the appropriateness of exogenous models in general is a claim that has been put under the spotlight. Examples of more generative approaches based on assessment of regional needs and capabilities has become more evident. Mention was made of models listed in Cooke (2004a) which include diverse asset-exploitation such as 'filial networks' and 'advanced institutes' to integrate useful research into regional economies. Further examples involve 'knowledge laboratories' utilizing endogenous cultural assets for economic development purposes, and 'lighthouse projects' engaging professional and lay communities to express demand for e.g. innovative digital mobile telephony services.

- Finally, this suggests a more rigorous attempt to connect regional innovation strategies with regional knowledge capabilities. This has come to the fore with the formation of regional science councils developing regional science policies as infrastructure for regionalized innovation. The constructing of advantage using regional knowledge assets is also moving ahead with such ideas as 'Art Cities', 'cultural clusters', and related cultural innovation system building (Lazzeretti, 2004). The quest for regional knowledge capabilities in a context typified by asymmetric knowledge has led to a greater focus in constructing advantage not so much on regional learning from exemplars but regional innovation based on identifying knowledge with generative potential.

Hence, a reassessment of the impact of the 'new economy' and the discontents it provoked have been presented. The initial conclusion is that a distinctive mode of induced innovation was established in the 1990s that temporarily proved to be effective at raising the rate of new firm formation around new economy sectors, but really, thus far, only those sectors and, with exceptions, not for very long. This gave the US, where the model was set in place in Silicon Valley in the 1970s but developed significantly and bravely, some would say recklessly, in the 1990s, a lead that may yet expand further in the first decade of the twenty-first century, except in mobile, convergent (multimedia) telephony where Europe leads although South East Asia threatens. Such growth is strongly clustered as are the effects of the economic downturn that followed the boom. However, a new model, based on 'open innovation' has also consolidated. Thus, firms continue to agglomerate around universities or centers of creative knowledge like film studios. Learning was the central attraction where knowledge capital could have rapidly escalating value. Now it is clear that knowledge itself is the direct magnet. The more knowledge-based clusters thrive, the more imbalanced the economy is likely to become spatially and in distributional terms and the more important it becomes to seek ways of moderating this without killing the golden goose. This is an important challenge confronting economic policy makers everywhere for the foreseeable future.

4.6   Conclusions

Even though the gloss has gone from some new economy stocks as the inevitable cyclicality of all markets reasserted itself for dot.coms and mobile-telephony firms in the year 2000, something has happened to make systemic innovation a key resource for the venture capital community in the US and a little of Europe. The prominence of the US in this respect helps understanding of the innovation gap regularly experienced by the EU in that regard. It was shown in the introduction how markets incentivize the quest for exploitation of research and its transformation into commercialized innovations. It was then shown how relatively regionalized such processes are even in the US but that there, systemic innovation is endemic and mostly marketized. Of course, big federal budgets fuel the whole process through the funding of basic research. For the moment, that will remain the case although large corporations have begun to reveal an appetite to take such early-stage investment risks, notably in pharmaceuticals, where venture capitalists show reluctance.

Recognition of the importance of systemic innovation at the regional level was shown to be a relatively recent phenomenon in Europe. However, research shows that much of the responsibility for supporting it in European regions rests on the not always adequate shoulders of government functionaries at a variety of levels, including to a growing extent, that of the region. It is not difficult to draw the conclusion that these institutional regional innovation systems (IRIS), where they exist, are uncompetitive with the entrepreneurial systems (ERIS) operating in the US, on their own ground. However, lessons about 'asymmetric knowledge' are slowly being learned and a search for latent knowledge capabilities set in process. The experimentation with institutional borrowing was not the fault of personnel but policy that in Europe sought to provide what in Italy are called 'real services'. This was because, as elsewhere to varying degrees, there remains market failure in the provision of private innovation support infrastructures of the 'soft' variety. The obvious policy conclusion to be drawn from this analysis was that policy should stimulate the growth of strong private investing organizations that would have the profit motive as the incentive to be more proactive than public systems have shown themselves to be capable.

The processes operating with such speed and relative success to induce commercial innovation from research laboratories in places like Silicon Valley and Boston can be reasonably clearly detected. Elite universities have, in leading cases, highly professional technical liaison offices, backed by experienced exploitation and commercialization personnel. There is abundant investment capital and places to invest it. There are regulatory mechanisms covering things like stock-options that give greater incentives than is the case normally in Europe. It is evident from work conducted by the science ministry in the US and UK (Sainsbury, 1999) that smaller, innovative firms in the US find a support initiative such as SBIR, with its research council-like peer-review system, valuable at the early, research or 'proof of principle' stage of innovation. Firms in the EU who know about SBIR have pressed the Commission to introduce something similar. Even though SBIR is (early-stage) public investment, it is consistent with the time-economies of new economy firms. This should be contrasted with the European example noted in Cooke (2001), recently rediscovered elsewhere by the present author, where banks require innovative SMEs to have won a grant as a condition for even considering a *loan* application let alone equity. Thus, grant dependence is reinforced by institutional inertia in the face of risk. Without seeking simply to imitate the new economy model of systemic innovation, it is clearly desirable that some account is taken of its key elements in redesigning innovation policy in Europe to begin to close the gaps that opened up even after the downturn between the innovation performances of the two competitor economies of the US and the EU.

Notes

1. In the earlier version of this chapter (Cooke, 2001), knowledge about regional innovation system performance was cross-sectional, but with the publication of Cooke *et al.* (2004) some longitudinal analyses of these phenomena are now

available. These are set within an evolutionary economics perspective that invites broader theoretical reasoning. A Penrosian regional 'knowledge capabilities' perspective helps capture important insights for future understanding of economic development, in which 'asymmetric knowledge' is reinforced by 'open innovation'.

2. This has been partly resolved by insights such as that of Latour (1998) distinguishing the relative certainty, stability, and detachment of 'science' and the uncertainty, instability, and disruptiveness of 'research'. In a 'knowledge economy' the economic value of 'research' for innovation is markedly enhanced.

3. The European Commission's 'Third Report on Economic and Social Cohesion' (2004) advocates regional innovation systems as delivery mechanisms for regional policy under knowledge economy conditions.

4. Thus, Sweden's national technology agency NUTEK was downgraded in favor of VINNOVA (The Swedish Agency for Innovation Systems) because of failure to promote regional innovation, something VINNOVA is charged with doing. Finland's and Italy's national governments are promoting non-university-centered regional innovation resulting from ground-up experiments. In Finland a *filial model* based on research networks of innovation professors has been disseminated from Seinajöki, where it originated, to five other regions. While in Italy, the so-called 'Pisa model' (OECD, 2001) based on Institutes of Advanced Study has also been disseminated in five regional experiments (Cooke, 2004*a*). In the UK, regional development agencies were set up in the English part in 1999, and supplied by the UK Department of Trade & Industry with cluster, innovation, and venture capital seed-funding.

5. Consolidation of ownership in the Cambridge cluster means that Biogen is now Biogen-IDEC, Genetics Institute is now an R&D arm of Wyeth, and LeukoSite was absorbed by acquisition into Millennium, all between 2001 and 2004.

6. For further detail, see below p. 94.

7. 'Generative growth' is cognate to the neo-classical notion of 'endogenous growth' but does not share its individualistic perspective. Rather, in a more evolutionary manner it presumes firms and institutions interact around resources and organization, sometimes embarking on collaborative practices the better to compete utilizing knowledge networks rather than 'stand-alone' idealizations of competition (see Penrose, 1959/1995).

8. See reference to regional science policy in the UK and even regional science foundations in German *länder* in Cooke (2004*d*).

9. In Section 4.5 an argument is developed that is more skeptical of the value of a commitment to 'learning' without an equivalent commitment to organizational or governance change to accommodate it. This is a key policy lesson that innovation systems approaches are far less prone to than 'learning economy' or 'learning region' ones. At the heart of the learning dilemma lies the 'asymmetric knowledge' problem. Resolution of this for *firms* entails 'open innovation' in centers with regional knowledge capabilities, conceivably organized as regional innovation systems with clusters. In this sense, Johnson's discovery of the innovative value of 'unlearning' was prescient.

10. Latterly, Germany's Japan-like economic stagnation has been echoed in continuing, relatively modestly successful attempts to build new technology platforms in biotechnology, multimedia, and photonics in Baden-Württemberg.

Politically, the rise to membership of the *land* government of radical liberals (neoconservative) has seen the closure of some 90 intermediary institutions that knitted the *land*'s network economy together. Among these is the respected Centre for Technology Assessment, a research center that pioneered dissemination of knowledge on regional innovation systems.

11. If anything, the fate of Wales's innovation system has been worse than that of many. From 1998 to 2004 the Welsh economy lost some 50 000 manufacturing jobs, many in the FDI sector. The Welsh Assembly, with much of Wales newly qualified for ERDF Objective 1 status, put into effect ambitious 'endogenous growth' programs, involving an Entrepreneurship Action Plan, a Knowledge Exploitation Fund, a public-private venture capital fund *Finance Wales*, and a *Technium* incubator program. Policy 'powerhouses' such as a significantly enlarged Welsh Development Agency, Training Agency (*ELWa*) and the Tourist Board were charged with implementing these policies. So poor have been the results of these efforts to build a new SME-based innovation system that on July 14, 2004 it was announced that all three agencies would close in April 2006 and their functions be absorbed into the Welsh Assembly's Ministry of Economic Development.

12. Thus, DNA synthesis was pursued from the outset in biotechnology in three-way tie-ups between academics, pharmaceuticals firms, and venture capitalists (Herbert Boyer and Stanley Cohen in San Francisco; Walter Gilbert in Cambridge, MA; and Ivor Royston in San Diego) each contracted to 'big pharma', respectively Eli Lilly, Novo Nordisk, and Eli Lilly, and venture capital, respectively Kleiner Perkins Caufield & Byers (KPCB; account manager Robert Swanson), Sofinnova, and KPCB (account manager Brook Byers)

13. Most of this account relies upon a description of P&G's replacement of R&D by C&D taken from the company website: http://www.eu.pg.com/news/2002/europeanresearch2002.html

14. It is thus cognate with, but recognizes the probability of temporary disharmonies rather than the stable consensus found in Etzkowitz and Leydesdorff's (1997) idea of the 'Triple Helix'.

15. Sidney Winter (1984) wrote about this in an article that differentiated entrepreneurial and institutional technology regimes. For elaboration in relation to innovation systems see Cooke (2004*b*, *c*)

16. Since the dot.com downturn and Japan's prolonged period of economic stagnation, KP have rebadged their '*Keiretsu Companies*' mission as '*Portfolio Companies*'.

References

Akerlof, G. (1970), 'The market for 'lemons': qualitative uncertainty and the market mechanism', *Quarterly Journal of Economics*, **84**: 488–500.

Andersen, E. (1994), *Evolutionary economics*, London: Pinter etc.

Audretsch, D. and Dohse, D. (2004), 'The impact of location on firm growth', CEPR Discussion Paper no. 4332. London: Centre for Economic Policy Research.

Bagnasco, A. (1977), *Tre Italie: la problematica territoriale dello sviluppo Italiano*, Bologna: Il Mulino.

Bazdarich, M. and Hurd, J. (2003), *Anderson forecast: inland empire and bay area*, Los Angeles: Anderson Business School.

Best, M. (2001), *The new competitive advantage*, Oxford: Oxford University Press.

Bottazzo, G., Dosi, G., and Fagiolo, G., (2002), 'On the ubiquitous nature of agglomeration economies and their diverse determinants: some notes', in A. Curzio and M. Fortis (eds), *Complexity and industrial clusters*, Heidelberg: Physica-Verlag.

Braczyk, H., Cooke, P., and Heidenreich, M. (eds) (1998), *Regional innovation systems*, London: UCL Press.

Braczyk, H., Fuchs, G. and Wolf, H. (eds) (1999), *Multimedia and regional economic restructuring*, London: Routledge.

Breschi, S. and Lissoni F. (2001), 'Localised knowledge spillovers versus innovative milieux: knowledge "tacitness" reconsidered', *Papers in Regional Science*, **80**: 255–273.

Castells, M. (1996), *The rise of the network society*, Oxford: Blackwell.

Chesbrough, H. (2003), *Open innovation*, Boston: Harvard Business School Press.

Cooke, P. (1980), 'Dependent development in UK regions with particular reference to Wales', *Progress in Planning*, **15**: 1–62.

Cooke, P. (1985), 'Regional innovation policy: problems and strategies in Britain and France', *Environment and Planning C: Government and Policy*, **3**: 253–267.

Cooke, P. (1992), 'Regional innovation systems: competitive regulation in the new Europe', *Geoforum*, **23**: 365–382.

Cooke, P. (1998), 'Introduction: origins of the concept', in H. Braczyk, P. Cooke, and M. Heidenreich (eds) *Regional innovation systems*, London: UCL Press.

Cooke, P. (2001), 'Regional innovation systems, clusters and the knowledge economy', *Industrial and Corporate Change*, **10**: 945–974.

Cooke, P. (2002), *Knowledge economies: clusters, learning and cooperative advantage*, London: Routledge.

Cooke, P. (2004*a*), 'The role of research in regional innovation systems: new models meeting knowledge economy demands', *International Journal of Technology Management*, **27**: 1–26.

Cooke, P. (2004*b*), 'The regional innovation system in Wales: evolution or eclipse?', in P. Cooke, M. Heidenreich, and H. Braczyk (eds), *Regional innovation systems* (2nd edn), London: Routledge.

Cooke, P. (2004*c*), 'Integrating global knowledge flows for generative growth: life sciences as a knowledge economy exemplar', in OECD (eds), *Global knowledge flows and economic development*, Paris: Organisation for Economic Co-operation & Development.

Cooke, P. (2004*d*), 'Biosciences and the rise of regional science policy', *Science and Public Policy*, **31**: 1–13.

Cooke, P. and da Rosa Pires, A. (1985), 'Productive decentralisation in three European regions', *Environment and Planning A*, **17**: 527–554.

Cooke, P. and Morgan, K. (1990), 'Learning through networking: Regional innovation and the lessons of Baden-Württemberg', *Regional Industrial Research Report No. 5*, Cardiff: University of Wales.

Cooke, P. and Morgan, K. (1993), 'The network paradigm: new departures in corporate and regional development', *Environment and Planning, D: Society and Space*, **11**: 543–564.

Cooke, P. and Morgan, K. (1994*a*), 'The regional innovation system in Baden-Württemberg', *International Journal of Technology Management*, **9**: 394–429.

Cooke, P. and Morgan, K. (1994*b*), 'The creative milieu: a regional perspective on innovation', in M. Dodgson and R. Rothwell (eds), *The handbook of industrial innovation*, Cheltenham: Edward Elgar.

Cooke, P. and Morgan, K. (1998), *The associational economy: firms, regions and innovation*, Oxford: Oxford University Press.

Cooke, P., Uranga, M., and Etxebarria, G. (1997), 'Regional innovation systems: institutional and organizational dimensions', *Research Policy*, **26**: 475–491.

Cooke, P., Boekholt, P., and Tödtling, F. (2000), *The governance of innovation in Europe*, London: Pinter.

Cooke, P., Heidenreich, M., and Braczyk, H. (eds) (2004), *Regional innovation systems* 2nd edn, London: Routledge.

Dahmén, E. (1950), *Entrepreneurial activity and the development of Swedish industry, 1919–39*, Homewood: American Economic Assoc. (English Translation, 1970).

Dosi, G. (1988), 'The nature of the innovation process', in, G. Dosi, C. Freeman, R. Nelson, G. Silverberg, L. Soete, (eds) *Technical change and economic theory*, London: Pinter.

Dosi, G., Freeman, C., Nelson, R., Silverberg, G. and Soete, L. (eds) (1988), *Technical change and economic theory*, London: Pinter.

Dunning, J. (eds) (2000), *Regions, globalization and the knowlege-based economy*, Oxford: Oxford University Press.

Etzkowitz, H. and Leydesdorff, L. (eds) (1997), *Universities and the global knowledge economy*, London: Pinter.

European Commission (2004), *Third report on economic and social cohesion*, Brussels: CEC

Foray, D. and Freeman, C. (1993), *Technology and the wealth of nations: the dynamics of constructed advantage*, London: Pinter.

Freeman, C. (1987), *Technology policy and economic performance – lessons from Japan*, London: Pinter.

Haas, P. (1992), 'Introduction: epistemic communities and international policy coordination', *International Organisation*, **46**: 1–37.

Henderson, V. (2003), 'Marshall's scale economies', *Journal of Urban Economics*, **53**: 1–28.

Hiltzik, M. (2000), *Dealers of lightning: Xerox PARC and the dawn of the computer age*, New York: Harper.

Johnson, B. (1992), 'Institutional learning', in B. Lundvall (eds) *National systems of innovation: towards a theory of innovation and interactive learning*, London: Pinter.

Latour, B. (1998), From the world of science to the world of research, *Science*, **280**: 208–209.

Lazzeretti, L. (eds) (2004), *Art cities, cultural districts and museums*, Florence: Firenze University Press.

Lundvall, B. (eds) (1992), *National systems of innovation: towards a theory of innovation and interactive learning*, London: Pinter.

Malerba, F. (1993), 'The national system of innovation: Italy', in R. Nelson (ed.), *National innovation systems: a comparative analysis*, Oxford: Oxford University Press.

March, J. (1991), 'Exploration and exploitation in organisational learning', *Organisation Sciences*, **2**: 71–87.

Oakey, R. P. (1979), 'Technological change and regional development: a note on policy implications', *Area* **11**: 340–344.

OECD (2001), *The Pisa model*, Paris: Organisation for Economic Co-operation & Development.

OECD (2004), *Global knowledge flows and economic development*, Paris: Organisation for Economic Co-operation & Development.

Owen-Smith, J. and Powell, W. (2004), 'Knowledge networks as channels and conduits: the effects spillovers in the Boston biotechnology community', *Organisation Sciences*, **15**: 5–21.

Penrose, E. (1959/1995), *The theory of the growth of the firm*, Oxford: Oxford University Press.

Perroux, F. (1955), 'Note sur la notion de pôle de croissance'. *Economie Appliquée* **8**: 307–320; (English translation in I Livingstone (eds.) (1971), *Economic policy for development*, Harmondsworth: Penguin: 278–289).

Piore, M. and Sabel, C. (1984), *The second industrial divide*, New York: Basic Books.

Porter, M. (1980), *Competitive strategy*, New York: Free Press.

Porter, M. (1990), *The competitive advantage of nations*, New York: Free Press.

Porter, M. (1998), *On competition*, Cambridge: Harvard Business School Press.

Rees, J. (1979), 'Technological change and regional shifts in American manufacturing', *Professional Geographer*, **31**: 45–54.

Rosenthal, S. and Strange, W. (2003), 'Geography, industrial organisation, and agglomeration', *The Review of Economics & Statistics*, **85**: 377–393.

Sainsbury, D. (1999), *Biotechnology clusters*, London: Department of Trade and Industry.

Saxenian, A. (1981), 'Silicon chips and spatial structure: the industrial basis of urbanization in Santa Clara County, California', (paper to conference at American University, Washington D.C. on *'New Perspectives on the Urban Political Economy'*, May).

Saxenian, A. (1994), *Regional advantage: culture and competition in Silicon Valley and route 128*, Cambridge: Harvard University Press.

Schumpeter, J. (1942/1975), *Capitalism, socialism and democracy*, New York: Harper Torchbooks.

Scott, A. J. (1986), 'High technology industry and territorial development: the rise of the Orange County complex'. *Urban Geography*, **7**: 3–45.

Stankiewicz, R. (2001), 'The cognitive dynamics of technology and the evolution of its technological system', in B. Carlsson (eds.), *New technological systems in the bio-industry: an international comparison*, Dordrecht: Kluwer.

Thomas, M. D. (1975), 'Growth pole theory, technological change, and regional economic growth', *Papers of the Regional Science Association*, **34**: 3–25.

Vence, X. (2001), 'Innovative capacity and employment creation in European regions: the relevance of Regional Innovation Systems', paper to Second International Conference, *'Employment and Innovation'*, Institute of Regional Development, Seville, April 23–24.

Vernon, R. (1966), 'International investment and international trade in the product cycle', *Quarterly Journal of Economics*, **80**: 190–207.

Winter, S. (1984), 'Schumpeterian competition in alternative technological regimes', *Journal of Economic Behaviour and Organisation*, **5**: 287–320.

Zook, M. (2000), 'Grounded capital: venture capital's role in the clustering of Internet firms in the US', paper to *Association of Collegiate Schools of Planning* Conference, Atlanta, November 1–5.

Zucker, L., Darby, M., and Armstrong, J. (1998), 'Geographically localised knowledge: spillovers or markets?' *Economic Inquiry*, **36**: 65–86.

Part II

5

'Old Economy' Inputs for 'New Economy' Outcomes: Cluster Formation in the New Silicon Valleys

TIMOTHY BRESNAHAN, ALFONSO
GAMBARDELLA AND ANNALEE SAXENIAN

5.1 Introduction

This chapter discusses the sources of success in regional clusters of entrepreneurship and innovation like Silicon Valley. It draws from the results of a two-year research project carried out by a large international and interdisciplinary team. The project has looked at how different forces, including public policy, business strategy, and institutions at regional and national level have combined to encourage the emergence, growth, and maintenance of clusters, and how they might achieve the level of positive feedback and ongoing success of Silicon Valley itself. Our viewpoint has been comparative. We have used both in-depth case studies and statistical methods to analyse examples of early, preliminary, and partially successful development of regional clusters in information and communications technology (ICT), inside and outside the United States.

The topic of this chapter has been difficult to attack until now, both for practical and conceptual reasons. On the practical side, international comparison of Silicon Valley imitators has suffered the difficulties of comparing a roaring success to some bitter failures. Where Silicon Valley is entrepreneurial, decentralized, and only loosely and flexibly connected to broader national institutions, many efforts at imitation have been government sponsored, top-down or tightly linked to established firms, perhaps 'national champions'. This wide divergence makes an analytical approach difficult, for one cannot easily investigate success drivers for getting over the positive feedback hump by looking at places that have been a roaring success or at places where so little of the logic is right.[1] As a result, opinion in the policy arena has fractured, with some believing that there is a magic formula for creating a new cluster of innovation and others thinking that the Silicon Valley model is unique and inimitable outside the United States. Much of the same 'all good/all bad' thinking characterizes analyses of Silicon Valley as well. At one stage, the region and its companies could do no wrong, at another, no right.

Against this background, the mission of our project has been to analyse a number of different attempts to gain national economic advantage from regional clusters of development in ICT. We have sought to avoid both the hagiographic 'SV is great' mode and the hypercritical 'there is no new economy' mode. Our main goal has been to assess and possibly identify the sources of long-term economic growth in clusters of industrial activity.

We define a regional cluster simply as a spatial and sectoral concentration of firms; and we measure success by the ability of the cluster as a whole to grow, typically through the expansion of entrepreneurial start-ups. In our project, we have then identified a number of nascent clusters of technology-based innovative activity around the world. They are all distinguished by entrepreneurship and growth, and they all have substantial focus on ICT. In short, they are all 'success stories', and in this sense they are all 'young Silicon Valleys'. Indeed, as we shall see below, one nascent cluster in our study is the Silicon Valley of four decades ago, and we asked one of its 'father founders', Gordon Moore, to recount this story. With that one exception, however, we do not yet know if the other centers that we have looked at will achieve the level of commercial and technological success of the mature Silicon Valley. It is not even clear whether these nascent clusters will build sophisticated support and service industries (like venture capital) and experienced entrepreneur-mentors that would make founding a new firm as easy in them as it is in Silicon Valley today.

Our sampling scheme allows us to take up two kinds of questions, but it rules out others. It lets us examine the similarities and differences among emerging clusters, but does not let us contrast these nascent clusters with failed efforts to get clusters going. The reason for this is simple. Unsuccessful cluster attempts, such as Malaysia's Multimedia Super Corridor, have typically failed to provide useful contrasts for the same reason as earlier literature failed. The similarities and differences among the nascent clusters we have selected, however, provide a rich field for investigating other analytically important questions. For instance, what factors are systematic and what are unique features of the western United States in these emerging regional clusters? Answering this question is critical for breaking out of the 'recipe' mode of analysis that has served policy formation so badly in recent decades.

Specifically, our study examines the forces that create new clusters of entrepreneurship-led growth. More broadly it is an empirical investigation into the microeconomics of growth and trade. Our international and interdisciplinary team has compared nascent regional clusters both inside and outside the United States. We pose two interrelated questions. First, how did these 'imitators' of Silicon Valley initially become centers of ICT-related growth; and second, what accounts for the subsequent success (or lack thereof) of these clusters to ensure that success builds on success in a self-reinforcing fashion. The goal is to understand how factors including national and regional policy, business strategy, and national and regional institutions combine to encourage the growth of regional clusters.

Our team has included the Stanford SIEPR-affiliated economists Tim Bresnahan, Kevin Davis, Michael Horvath, and Scott Wallsten; business people/entrepreneurs, notably Ralph Landau and Gordon Moore; and management specialists and economists from other universities or institutions who work on the development of technology clusters, including AnnaLee Saxenian from Berkeley, Suma Athreye from the Open University in the UK, Ashish Arora from Carnegie Mellon University, Erran Carmel from American University, Catherine de Fontenay from the University of New South Wales, Alfonso Gambardella from the Sant'Anna School of Advanced Studies, Tamah Morant from the University of North Carolina, John Richards from McKinsey & Co., and Salvatore Torrisi from the University of Camerino.

We have looked at a number of different clusters: outside the US in Ireland, Cambridge, UK, Israel, Scandinavia, India, and Taiwan, and, within the US, Northern Virginia in the present and Santa Clara County (Silicon Valley) in the 1960s. In spite of their significant differences, India, Ireland, and Israel are the prototypical cases of nascent ICT clusters that we have in mind.[2] They have all exhibited a significant acceleration in the production of ICT (especially software and services) during the 1990s. Their ICT growth has been exceptional according to practically all major indicators: annual double-digit growth in the number of new firms, in ICT revenues and employment, in exports; increasing share of ICT of total exports of the country (up to one-third of total exports in the case of Israel). Taiwan has shown a similar pattern in the manufacturing of PCs and related businesses. In the advanced world, Northern Virginia has shown similar features, including double-digit growth figures. Our two special cases are the two European regions. While Cambridge, UK has all the features of a cluster in the sense we are defining it here, it does not match the patterns, and particularly the growth figures, of the other regions that we have looked at. This is not to say that Cambridge, UK has not been successful. But compared to the other regions (including Silicon Valley), the growth figures have simply not been the same. The Scandinavian story, as we shall see, is interesting because it is the only case in which growth was triggered by a whole different vertical ICT market, wireless hardware.

Our team of researchers has worked with the data on these clusters and we have also visited each of the regions to interview key actors. We have met a number of times over the course of a two-year period in order to review and compare preliminary results and analysis as well as to jointly develop conclusions. In what follows, we discuss the key findings of the entire research.

5.2   Agglomeration Economies and External Effects

Many of the existing theories of clusters of innovative activity focus on external effects and the resulting agglomeration economies.[3] One central feature of clusters of innovative activity is external effects among the technology firms located there. A local external effect is anything that raises the return to particular firms located in a region as a result of the location of other firms in the same region. External effects can be *direct*, as when managers or technologists learn about market or technical developments from colleagues in neighboring firms, when firms in closely related industries serve as one another's customers or suppliers, and so on. External effects can also be *indirect*, as when key inputs are in abundant supply or when the overall level of commercial technology activity is high. These indirect external effects arise from increasing returns to scale in the supply of key inputs such as venture capital, which may locate where entrepreneurship is dense but support the development of new entrepreneurial firms; a thick labor market in technical personnel; or commercially oriented activities in universities or national laboratories, to name just a few. Both direct and indirect external effects generate positive feedback loops that ensure that technology-related firms locate in regions where other technology firms are already located.[4]

These external effects have (at least) two distinct implications. One implication is for economic growth, both within a region and in the broader economy. External effects among innovative firms inventing general-purpose technologies are highly levered mechanisms for increasing the rate of growth of an overall economy. By raising the rate of return to invention, either direct or indirect external effects can, if the field of the invention is important enough, push the commercialization of valuable technologies faster and closer to markets. Similarly, in the case of indirect external effects the economic return to key inputs such as highly skilled labor, the knowledge to be found in universities or the market judgement of venture capitalists can be raised by clustering among firms. A second implication of external effects is that nothing succeeds like success under external effects, and the private return to participation in these clusters of innovation by entrepreneurs, venture capitalists, technologists, and those in the key supplier industries can be enormous.[5] These two points—external economies of scale, and the resulting capture of the rents by producers and the regions in which they are located and headquartered—explain the great interest in agglomeration economies.[6]

But network analysis alone cannot explain how regional clusters emerge. The existence of external effects explains why a region would like to have entrepreneurial-led growth and why the world's consumers would like to have more clusters founded. But examining the positive feedback in an existing successful cluster does not tell you *how* a cluster begins. Moreover, while clusters of entrepreneurial-led growth are valuable social institutions, we know little about why clusters begin where they do or how many clusters will emerge within a given industry. There is a strong element of social increasing returns to scale in the argument, which one would normally expect to lead to a limited number of clusters in any particular industry or technology. Understanding how nascent clusters overcome these limits has been an important part of our study.

The positive feedback logic of the theory and of established and successful clusters makes it difficult for analysts to identify a starting point. Positive feedback, when it is working, appears as a virtuous cycle, and, when it is not working, as a difficult chicken-and-egg problem. For a region that is not yet succeeding, 'nothing succeeds like success' is an empty remark. The related more analytical observation that all of the elements of success (entrepreneurship, venture capital, etc.) feedback to one another positively does not communicate what it is important to get started. Our analysis, by looking at the nascent clusters that exhibit significant signs of growth, lets us address the question of how to start. We return to this question of the factors leading to the start of a cluster in Section 5.3.

The second aspect of external effects, namely the possibility of social increasing returns and the resulting producer rents, also contains the analytical temptation to draw a false dichotomy that positions 'old economy' explanations of growth as alternatives to 'new economy' ones. Here we do not need to linger on a sophisticated distinction between what is old and what is new economy. For the purposes of our discussion the common sense with which these expressions are currently used is sufficient. 'Old economy' is a shorthand for a number of concepts: organizational and firm-building activities, investment in general and industry-specific human capital, larger companies and related economies of scale at the level of the firms, lengthy periods of investment in capability before their exploitation. 'New economy' means instead entrepreneurship, economies of scale at the level of regions or industries rather than firms, external effects, etc.[7] Our point is that a strong opposition between old and new economy explanations of growth can lead to some analytical errors. Should we seek to explain the success of clusters *only* by external effects? Is this newly discovered feature of supply so important that it trumps all others? Much 'new economy' thinking goes down this false dichotomy path, drawing a distinction between the positive-feedback forces that are at work in a cluster–guarantors of instant success in the most fervid 'new economy' thinking–and the supposedly 'ordinary' or 'old economy' work of firm building, market building, invention, and commercialization.

The studies carried out in our project show that it is an error *either* to focus only on the external effects and conclude that new economy logic supersedes old, *or* to conclude that there is nothing to the positive-feedback external effects story at all. Instead, in the construction and maintenance of successful clusters, the new economy and old economy elements act as complements to one another; neither one can succeed without the other. Many governments have made the analytical error of focusing far too much on the second aspect of external effects, and have viewed clusters of innovative activity as no more than a ticket to producer rents. This has provided the intellectual foundation for largely failed policies that attempt to jump-start growth in clusters by directive policy. In our study, we have taken another look at that kind of policy, but do not dwell on it. Instead, we focus on places–and governments– that have got the mix of policies close to right.

5.3 Starting a Cluster

The first step in understanding the complementary relationship between external effects and ordinary investments is to step back from the already-built, successful Silicon Valley cluster of the present. We need to look, instead, at clusters in the making, whether in Silicon Valley in the 1950s and 1960s, or regions like those that we have looked at in our SIEPR project, e.g. Ireland, Israel, India, Northern Virginia, and Taiwan in the present. In each of these cases we found that there are some external effects at the nascent stage. Yet very important forces for success arise in the ordinary business challenges of building firms and building markets.

Put simply, our argument is that the processes of starting and sustaining a cluster have different economics. Starting a cluster involves, first, building the economic fundamentals for an industry or technology, and, second, finding the spark of entrepreneurship to get it going. Both of these are supported by a number of common elements in the regions that we examined—and it is striking how similar all the nascent clusters are to one another in this regard, and how much more similar to one another they are than to the current established and thriving Silicon Valley cluster. It is particularly significant that the Silicon Valley of 40 years ago is also closer to today's nascent clusters than either is to the Silicon Valley of today.

Many similarities between today's successful clusters and the Silicon Valley of the 1960s arise because founding a new cluster, or the early firms in a new cluster, is a very different entrepreneurial and economic activity from founding a firm in an established cluster. New clusters, including Silicon Valley in the 1960s, offer substantially less support to entrepreneurship in the start-up or pioneering phase than does a mature cluster like Silicon Valley today. External effects—namely benefits to particular technology firms that arise from the presence of other firms or of support structures like venture capital—play only a small role in the early phases. Such benefits typically come later in the development of a cluster.

Among others, one similarity across the new clusters that we have examined is that they have taken advantage of a new technological and market opportunity that had not already been exploited: the integrated circuit industry in the Silicon Valley of the 1960s; the Internet- and network-security markets exploited in Ireland and Israel today; specific opportunities like software demand following the YK2 or the Euro problem in India; the hardware and equipment opportunities in new kinds of devices like cellphones and PDAs embraced in Scandinavia and Taiwan. The rationale for this is not hard to guess. Markets with substantial producer rents, like ICT today, are characterized by powerful forces that make a direct assault on an existing market position unpromising. In the first place, the advanced technological capabilities and market connections of incumbents may offer a commanding lead. These markets often have barriers to entry created by the deployment of commercialization assets in established markets. At the same time, there can be market forces associated, for example, with *de facto* standard setting, as in much of computing, or political forces that protect existing national champions, as in parts of telephony, which make entry difficult. Broadly speaking, the lesson from our case studies is that to blossom, the new-cluster entrepreneurs have to turn away from established sources of rents to define new ones, and (at least initially) make their relationship with existing technologies and clusters complementary rather than competitive.

In this respect, practically all the technologies developed in the new clusters that we have looked at in our study are complementary to existing ICT technologies, mostly sold by US-based firms or US-linked multinationals. Since ICT is used in large complex systems, it is important for the new entrants to have their inventions and advances linked with other inventions and advances. At the same time, this means that the new clusters can take advantage of the sizable and growing demand for the leading technologies. Our clusters in Ireland, India, Israel, and Taiwan come from regions that, for one reason or another, have easier potential interactions with the US market (language, cultural connections, diaspora, etc.). They have then been able to take great advantage of the significant US demand for ICT products, services, and components, during the 1990s. Combined with other factors that we shall highlight below (particularly underemployed skilled labor), this has given rise to a powerful mechanism for sparking off growth opportunities in some ICT niches and segments.

At one level, this is no more than the obvious remark that 'demand is important for growth'. In a debate overemphasizing supply-side factors like agglomeration economies and external effects, however, this remark is often overlooked. That market and demand factors lead to linkages to the US does not reflect a 'US-centric' view. The linkages with the US are merely a powerful example for pointing out how important it can be to be connected to a sizable and growing source of demand. Finding the source of demand that may spark off the growth of the cluster can be critical for its rise, and in many respects it should be one of the policy focuses in this arena.

In brief, to obtain growth one cannot point only to the 'surfing' of agglomeration economies, but also to the underlying 'wave' of technological and market opportunity. For many of the regions that we have examined in our project, the wave was the great expansion of ICT following the commercialization of the Internet.

Another similarity across our new clusters is the degree of investment, effort, and building needed to set up the background for an innovation cluster's take off. To take up our earlier remarks again, development of the ICT businesses is not the magic exploitation of some 'new economy' rules. Instead, it takes years of firm-building and market-building efforts. The long-term investment in education of a skilled labor force has been critical in a number of regions, notably in Taiwan, Ireland, India, and Israel. The supply of highly skilled workers can come from any of a number of sources, but needs to be plentiful: Stanford-trained scientists and engineers to Silicon Valley, military training and Russian émigrés to Israel, alumni of 'beltway bandit' federal contractors in Virginia, and an educated population earning far less than world-standard wages in Ireland and India. While it is critical to invest in the assets that will permit the emergence of a cluster, there is no magic recipe (take one great university, 47 venture capitalists, and . . .) that works. Instead, a number of different routes exist to building the backdrop—technology opportunity, educated labor, flow of entrepreneurial talent, etc.[8]

Sometimes these long-term investments in national or regional capabilities can grow for a long time in what seems like a low-return mode before the take off into cluster growth.

The story of early entrepreneurship and the early integrated circuit industry seen from the perspective of Fairchild and Intel illustrates this point very well. This is the story of the developments that put the Silicon in Silicon Valley, though there was the beginning of a high-tech cluster in Santa Clara County before these times.[9] What was important in determining the success of the early Silicon Valley back in the 1960s? Moore and Davis (2001) bring forward several elements. First, there was a rich technological opportunity in the semiconductor business. Second, there were immediately available markets such as consumer electronics and defense. The creation of general-purpose semiconductors led quickly to sales in those markets, where the value of a miniaturized component was clear. There was also the prospect of whole new uses of semiconductors in information technology industries, a real prospect for long-term growth. Both the technological and the market opportunity were separate from the existing high-tech (tube-based) electronic industry, and provided an advantage to producers located far from existing sellers.

How was this technological and market opportunity exploited? The Moore–Davis story is as far as can be imagined from one in which young entrepreneurs instantly succeed in a supportive environment of external effects. None of the modern institutions of Silicon Valley existed, so none of the incoming benefits of external effects were there. No mentoring from experienced entrepreneurs now working as venture capitalists, no easy access to the required skills or to wise and experienced thoughts about business models, no networks of connections to supply partners and marketing partners–none are part of the early period story. Instead, the story is one of investment in human capital, firm-building and market-building processes that took a long time and quite serious effort and risk. Allowing for changed circumstances, this same element is present in many of our regions. Building a new capability at the firm level that will lead to local increasing returns and positive feedback does not involve anticipating or exploiting those high-payoff features, it involves investing in the key assets that will permit later collective payoffs.

To summarize, the forces underlying the emergence of a cluster differ from those needed to ensure its continued growth. While increasing returns and external effects can keep a cluster going, the initial spark is more difficult to obtain and more risky to pursue. Our research suggests that these include the importance of being linked to a sizable and growing demand as well as the availability of a proper supply of key factors like, in the case of ICT, skilled labor. Other critical factors are firm- and market-building capabilities. These require significant and systematic efforts by the 'pioneers' of the cluster to promote organizational and technological capabilities of various sorts, create new firms and institutions, etc. Finally, another factor is plain 'luck'. Founders such as Moore recognize that there was considerable uncertainty at the beginning about the potential size of rents and the appropriate firm and industry structure to pursue them. Similarly, the opportunities for many of the newer clusters involved a particular matching of regional supply capability to world demand.

In fact, there is a logical argument for suggesting that luck plays a role in this context. We noted that nascent clusters, and the entrepreneurs operating there, have to bet on new trajectories before they manifest their potential. But this also means that they have to bet on an opportunity before it is clear to everybody else that it is indeed an opportunity. Some degree of risk is therefore unavoidable. At the same time, this means that only some of these opportunities (and most likely few of them) will materialize. Many attempts at creating new clusters and successful new firms in certain industrial or technological trajectories will fail, and they will fail in spite of the fact that the key actors have done all the right things that are to be done in these contexts. In this area it appears that luck and skill are complements; those initiatives that embody a superior business model or technology are more likely to find the 'luck' they need.

This string of similarities across our cases corroborates our earlier remark that the 'new economy'/'old economy' distinction is a false dichotomy. There are two errors. It is just as incorrect to say that clusters of innovative activity can take off as if by magic as it is to deny the huge national and regional advantages that accrue from the existence of an established Silicon Valley cluster. The truth is that old economy hard work, both in company building and in regional investments such as education, and new economy external effects are complements—each is more valuable with the other than without it. There is a great deal of truth to the 'external effects' theory that entrepreneurship is easier in a cluster than outside of it. This is the realization of the theoretical idea of 'social increasing returns to scale'. Yet that certainly does not mean that the world can support only one cluster, and the growing pressure on the limited stocks of skilled labor and land in the US and Silicon Valley are powerful forces favoring the emergence of new clusters.

5.4   No 'Recipes' but Some Deep Regularities

5.4.1   Highly Skilled Technical Labor

All our regional stories point to the importance of highly skilled labor as a pre-condition for the growth of an ICT-based entrepreneurial cluster— Taiwan, Ireland, India, and certainly Israel. In some cases, underemployed skilled labor is close to being the 'only' factor (India, but also Ireland or

Israel), or at least the one that spurred the rest. Further, some of our other stories reveal that there is a role for universities both as a source of skilled labor and of technologies that are exploited for export and growth–e.g. Cambridge, UK and Silicon Valley in the 1960s.[10]

Taken as a group, however, these stories are not at all encouraging of the simple 'recipe' view of universities and higher education in starting a cluster. Our cases demonstrate that there are a number of different ways to achieve a supply of skilled labor and that it is the ultimate outcome (a highly skilled labor supply), not the particular mechanism (a university) that matters. Large firms can also play a critical role in growing the skill base. While the role of universities like Stanford or Berkeley has been widely emphasized in the Silicon Valley story, one should not neglect the potential training provided by established firms like Hewlett-Packard or Intel. Large firms often nurture technical competencies. For example, individual researchers can use equipment or they can be part of research teams that would hardly be available outside the leading companies. Similarly, many offer managerial training, and possibly even managerial connections. Moreover, this technical and managerial training can encourage spin-offs. This raises a classical problem of 'private' vs. 'social' interest. As pointed out by Moore in his study with Davis, established companies warn against spin-offs. Even though Moore himself notes that one can benefit from spin-off supplier industries (e.g. chip-manufacturing equipment), established companies clearly look unfavorably to the spillovers that they create by training people who would then use these competencies outside the firm.

Our stories pointed out other sources of training, apart from universities and large firms. In Northern Virginia the development of sophisticated technical capabilities in ICT, and particularly in communication technologies, has stemmed from the existing bases of competencies provided by years of contract research for the government and the defense department in the area. Government contracts have for many years nurtured contractor firms, and the related technical skills in such firms. Once defense procurement slowed down, and new Internet-related and other communication technology opportunities rose, skilled labor in these fields were available in the area, and this implied the supply of skills that were fruitfully used for launching the cluster. In Israel, the military proved to be the key supply of technical skills, along with some leading technical universities (and particularly the Israel Institute of Technology, or Technion). Finally, the supply of skills can come from outside the region. The clusters in Taiwan and India have drawn heavily on US-educated Chinese and Indian engineers. In Israel as well, immigration (largely from Russia) has been an important source of skill. Similarly, the nascent Silicon Valley attracted engineers from all over the United States (Bresnahan et al., 2001; de Fontenay and Carmel, 2001; Moore and Davis, 2001; Saxenian, 2001).

In sum, the conventional wisdom lumps education, skilled labor, and universities in a single idea and often overlooks alternative mechanisms for achieving a skilled labor pool. It is therefore important to stress that a university *per se* is not essential to the emergence of a successful cluster. This qualification is useful for at least two reasons. The first one is that it brings further support to the rejection of a formulaic recipe for the rise of the clusters. Putting a university at the center of the cluster can help, but it is neither a necessary nor a sufficient condition. Second, there can be different sources of skills in different regions, and–given that it is the availability of the skills that matters–regions can look for the most appropriate way (or mix thereof) for acquiring skilled labor, from universities to larger firms and other local as well as distant institutions. The policy implication is also straightforward–forming or attracting skilled labor, rather than a particular means for doing it, is the crucial aim.

5.4.2   Managerial Labor

The contributions of returning expatriates also suggest that the key human-capital investments are managerial as well as technical. Most of the nascent clusters we have analysed are focused on ICT–as is much of the activity in Silicon Valley. They therefore offer difficult management and marketing challenges because these sectors present non-trivial problems of commercialization of scientific and technical opportunity.

Firms in new clusters and sectors develop sources of non-technical (or not narrowly technical) human capital in a variety of ways. Silicon Valley itself, being perhaps more 'first' than the other clusters, has produced an indigenous supply of scientist-managers and engineer-managers by having scientists and engineers learn a second skill set (management), often by experience, in the early stages. Of course, as Silicon Valley matured, it used a number of other models to create dual-knowledge-base managers, including more experiential training (think of Steve Jobs or Larry Ellison) mentoring by experienced entrepreneurs or venture capitalists of younger managers-to-be, and career moves from established firms in the industry (in and out of Silicon Valley) into new entrepreneurial firms.[11]

Later-growing clusters have not needed such heroic means of creating managerial capabilities as did the early Silicon Valley. ICT markets are more established, and technical people native to a region can achieve training in a number of ways that introduce them both to the management problems of ICT enterprise and to world markets. Multinational enterprises (MNEs) have played an important initial role in this regard–e.g. Taiwan, and possibly Ireland, certainly Israel.[12] Potential engineer-managers can work in MNEs in their home region and gain experience in a second skill set, while also learning about world markets. This mechanism for building managerial human capital can later be deployed in indigenous firms. This is an advantage of late development.

A second source of the same human capital building arises through the return of expatriate engineers and managers working in established clusters elsewhere, especially in Silicon Valley itself. When repatriated, these individuals bring with them experience and knowledge of management in ICT firms, in this case even in ICT start-ups. And, since their work was overseas (often in the largest market, the US) they return with connections to and knowledge of ICT markets. This mechanism is the long-distance analog of the one that has been going on within Silicon Valley for some time, namely development of human capital within established companies followed by a spinout or a movement of experienced workers to a new firm. The difference is that these spinouts and this labor mobility go to a place where the engineer or manager would like to live—India, Israel, or Taiwan—rather than to a site just a few miles away.

5.4.3   New Firm Formation and Firm Building

We have already noted that firm-formation and firm-building capabilities are important elements of successful clusters. In this respect, the studies in our project show that there is a difference between the growth of firms and the growth in the number of firms in a cluster. Growth in the number of firms may not lead to the sustained creation of substantial economic rents. Similarly, growth in the size of the high-tech sector, as in the early phases in Taiwan and partly the current phase in India, does not necessarily ensure continued growth. The question is whether some firms in the clusters emerge out of the class of small entrepreneurial start-ups and stake out independent positions in world markets.

To be sure, growth of firms could be a signal rather than a cause of success. A firm that pioneers an important innovation or one that generates a new market will most likely grow. In turn, the growth of local firms can be critical for the success of a cluster. Growing firms create demand for other types of employment and not just technology (e.g. manufacturing, marketing). Moreover, as many technology markets have shown today, most of the rents are downstream. Companies with market power have the resources to make additional investments, with further implications for growth. More generally, larger companies, like Intel or Hewlett-Packard in Silicon Valley, Ericsson and Nokia in Scandinavia, produce backward and forward linkages that systems of smaller firms may not be able to produce, at least to the same extent. These are all important factors for sustaining the growth opportunities.

Our regional studies show that the growth of firms is not a natural outcome of the rise of a cluster. For instance, the new companies could be consulting or service firms established by individuals whose primary job is elsewhere (e.g. university professors). In these cases the effort on firm building would be more limited than those by individuals who would make primary bets on their companies. Also, some entrepreneurs prefer not to have their firms grow. Growth implies new management challenges, possible decentralization of powers and greater tension, risk, or responsibilities. It is not uncommon in some locales, as in our case of Cambridge, UK, to find individuals who are not interested in these challenges. If commitments to firm building are important this could limit the growth of a cluster, particularly compared with the risks and investments in firm building made by the early founders of Silicon Valley and by some of the entrepreneurs that populate the Indian, Israeli, or Taiwanese scene today. In sum, we suggest that the growth of companies, and not just the growth in the number of firms, is a signal of the success of the cluster. These are the firms that will become one of the sources of increasing returns for the continuous growth of the cluster, in the form of training for potential spinouts, development of managerial and technical competencies, along with various forms of backward and forward linkages.

The growth (or lack thereof) of local firms may also stem from comparative advantage. Indian engineers and Cambridge boffins may be reacting to the incentives they face, and supplying only what is economically efficient to the world economy (in these cases, the services of highly skilled individuals). Over time, this would lead to a classical gain from trade, i.e. wages for highly skilled labor far closer to the global level for labor of that type. Israeli high-tech companies, for example, are often bought by American firms and moved to the US as soon as they reach a certain size and stage in their evolution. This may not be bad for the Israeli economy if the companies are paid the right price, notably the present value of the company given its expected opportunities. If the market for companies showed few imperfections in this respect, the gains from trade could produce notable benefits. If they remained in Israel, these companies might be limited by the size of the domestic market. Since development and commercialization (unlike initial research) benefit from exploitation of larger markets, there may be an advantage from selling the companies once they reach the stage when a large market becomes an important asset. This then shifts the problem from a general pre-occupation with the acquisition of the best domestic firms, toward the potential imperfections in the international market for companies.

Another regional path is specialization in the creation of new innovative companies, with acquisition and commercial development of those companies or the technologies they create by established firms outside the region. Success on this path requires a fertile field of technological opportunity. If the field matures or is exhausted there may be limits to creating rents from selling new technologies. This too can be seen as a problem of setting the right price for the technology, or for the acquired company. Research suggests that asymmetric information leads to payments for technology licenses that are below the actual present value of the firm and to the acquisition of technology firms at prices below their long-term contribution (Arora *et al.*, 2001). Yet even under these conditions comparative advantage may still be critical. It may be that focusing on the early part of the innovation cycle is the right specialization for Israeli companies. In turn, the advantages of specialization would increase if the imperfection of the global technology markets were reduced, and the companies sold for a price closer to the 'right' price.

5.4.4   Connection to Markets

We have already noted that our emerging ICT clusters in Israel, India, Ireland, and Taiwan all had significant ties with the Unites States, which helped them to exploit the ICT-intensive US growth of the second half of the 1990s. In this respect, it was critical for these regions to position themselves in product spaces that were complementary to the main sources of demand (notably Silicon Valley and the US) rather than directly competing with them (Arora et al., 2001; de Fontenay and Carmel, 2001; Saxenian, 2001).

Our case studies suggest that there can be two patterns of connecting to markets and sources of demand. The first one is that of the emerging countries mentioned above. Here the linkage is given by the relationships with the main market (the US), and the complementarity of the products of the clusters with the existing leading technologies, particularly those produced in the US themselves. The second model is the one epitomized by our case of the Scandinavian countries. The key here is to position the companies in areas not covered by the existing leaders, once again the US firms. The problem is even more complex because, as the Scandinavian stories in our project point out, the issue is not simply to cover products not produced by the leaders. In ICT, the leaders–and particularly the US firms–have been able to occupy entire vertical markets, and in most cases they have occupied them on a global scale. This has left little room for other global players to occupy even parts of these vertical markets. The only opportunity left was to occupy other vertical markets, with potentially global, or at least continental demand, which had not been occupied by the leaders (see Richards, 2001).

Some leading European firms, and particularly the Scandinavian companies Ericsson and Nokia, successfully pursued this strategy. In this respect, the study by John Richards (2001) in our project shows that the success of the Scandinavian model depended in good part on the same factors that we have highlighted in other cases–highly educated workforce, supply of technically and managerially skilled people, and connection to demand (particularly continental demand). The peculiarity of the model, however, is that it focused on a vertical market that was not occupied by the leading US firms, notably the wireless hardware segment of the ICT business. Moreover, as we shall also see later, the opportunities in this area were further raised by one of the most successful institutional European accomplishments in the ICT business during the last decade, i.e. the establishment of the GSM standard for communication throughout the continent. This was a key event for creating a continental demand, which enhanced the growth of this segment and benefited the producers that had occupied this area.

The connections to market and to the leading areas world-wide also open up the question of the potential advantage of being 'out of town' that may accrue to newcomers or to latecomers. The point is that being 'out of town' may imply lower stakes in existing technologies and activities, and this may help new clusters to seek new sources of rents or to tap new product spaces and technologies. Of course, with the advantages of being 'out of town' for novelty come disadvantages for connectedness to world markets. One particular disadvantage of not being connected to the leading clusters, or to the leading centers of technological growth, is that of not being able to take advantage of some of the results of external effects, such as the availability of the 'right' labor. But this also explains the rise of some of the new regions that we have discussed in this chapter. As noted, some of them were indeed 'out of town', but they all had local sources, or characteristics—such as excess supply of skilled labor—that made up for the disadvantage they faced.

Thus, on the one hand, countries like Israel, India, Ireland, and Taiwan compensated for the disadvantages of being out of town by virtue of focusing on activities that were complementary to those of the United States. They then combined the advantages of being out of town, which enabled them to focus on new areas, with the ability to link with the sources of growth (whether demand or technical linkages and the like). On the other hand, the Scandinavian model implied that the companies had the opportunity (and possibly the fortune) of exploiting a new vertical market, and in this process they also built up the new linkages (technical, with demand, etc.) that were critical for the rise of the new cluster.

In these last several sections, we have emphasized the deep regularities cutting across all our study regions in the domains of human capital of two kinds: market connection and new-firm formation. In emphasizing the deep similarities, we do not want to gloss over the considerable differences across these countries in institutions and in market mechanisms. These matter considerably for the ways in which the various deep capability-building goals were accomplished in different places.

5.5   Co-operation vs. Competition among Clusters in the World Economy

The new clusters that emerged in the late 1990s have had to deal with the dominance of the most important existing technology areas by US firms, largely firms located in the western US. From the perspective of rich places like Northern Virginia or Israel, or poorer places like Taiwan or Ireland, or vastly poorer places like India, linkages to established centers of technology are very important in the growth phase. Maintaining these linkages can be a difficult management problem for companies that have to do something new, but at the same time have to find ways to stay linked to the old. The best solutions appear to be participation in a world-wide production network that is an extension of the Silicon Valley network itself.

We have already noted the importance of finding a new area of technology or product area in which to succeed. This involves co-operation with existing firms and sales of complementary rather than competing products–at least in the short term. This pattern is not, however, a policy recommendation so much as it is an observation of why and how certain more narrowly imitative policies are likely to be ineffective. The real policy implications arise from thinking carefully about the particular sources of advantage for a nascent cluster and why that source might yield short-term complements with the potential to become long-term substitutes.

All the nascent regions we have examined have escaped from the belief that co-operation with existing richer economies is 'colonialist'. Linkages with the US have been critical to all, in one way or another. India and Taiwan are linked to the US via outsourcing of software services and manufacturing, respectively. Israel and Taiwan are also linked to the US by a returning group of expatriates who have worked there, and who see the benefits of long-distance collaboration. There is, in these cases, a flow of people and ideas back and forth between the existing cluster and the nascent ones.[13] The diaspora has been particularly valuable to the nascent clusters that we have looked at in emerging markets. Technology transfer (in the narrow sense) is not very important in these cases. Rather, what is transferred is primarily organizational models, a valuable piece of understanding for a nascent cluster, and the opportunity to apply that knowledge in a new domain.

This pattern of connection-led growth varies across the areas we study. India began simply by arbitraging the differences in engineering labor costs between that country and the US in outsourcing. There are no guarantees that such an activity will lead to entrepreneurship-led growth, though many valuable assets (such as knowledge of and connections to the US market and up-to-date technical skills) were gained in the process. Taiwan similarly began as a source of low-cost labor for manufacturing PCs, which had become too expensive to make in Silicon Valley. This was strongly complementary to Silicon Valley, and, combined with economic and institutional arrangements inside Taiwan that permitted and encouraged entrepreneurship, led to considerable growth of technical and market capabilities and ultimately an indigenous industry. Entrepreneurs in Ireland, Israel, and Northern Virginia have been content to position themselves as niche players, producing in areas where they have an advantage (either individually or regionally) and thinking of themselves as linked to and complementary to Silicon Valley.

This pattern has also meant a significant departure from earlier relationships between the US and other countries' high-tech industries. For example, the pattern looks different from the more competitive, and even confrontational, relationship between the US and Japan in semiconductors in the 1980s. The increasing competitiveness of Japanese semiconductor memory producers directly threatened the market position of the US producers. The case of Cambridge, UK provides another contrast. The Cambridge cluster looks more similar to Silicon Valley in terms of product space than the other emerging countries that we have examined. At the same time, while Cambridge has certainly grown, its growth rates have been steady and 'normal' compared to those of some of the emerging countries, and of Silicon Valley itself. This is why we think of Cambridge as a 'partial' success story when compared to such high-growth clusters.[14] The products of firms in Cambridge were similar to those of Silicon Valley, with its first-mover advantage, and so could only cover spaces in the world-wide market that were not already exploited by the leader. By contrast, companies in the emerging countries engaged in complementary activities. This allowed them to avoid competing directly with Silicon Valley, while taking advantage of the growth rates of the latter through their complementary relationships.[15]

The world-wide economic forces that have enabled these complementary patterns between the US and the emerging countries in ICT are important. First, the ICT industries grew more rapidly and in a more varied way than could have been anticipated. A number of technologies turned out to have significantly larger markets than originally anticipated—the PC and associated complementary hardware and software, and the Internet and associated close complements come immediately to mind. Further, many of these new technologies raised rather than lowered the demand in existing markets—the Internet has dramatically increased the demand for PCs and for mainframe computers along with the demand for telecommunications transport and switching services, for example. All this has provided tremendous market and technical opportunities, and put pressure on the existing innovation-supporting resources, notably engineering labor and conveniently located land, in the existing successful clusters in the US.

Immigration and the physical expansion of Silicon Valley have provided partial offsets to these powerful forces, but both face real limits. Not everyone wants to live in the United States, and what had once seemed a vast expanse of cheap land used in fruticulture was discovered to be a valley—with walls. Out of people and out of conveniently located land, Silicon Valley was in a position to co-operate with nascent clusters.

The countries and regions that responded come from the 'also rans' of economic development in the twentieth century. Apart from the Scandinavian countries and Northern Virginia, all were relatively poor and peripheral. Why have the less-advanced economies responded so well to these opportunities? Even more interestingly, why have many richer countries (e.g. the continental European countries and Japan) been less responsive than these 'also rans'? The first part of the answer was largely given in the previous pages. In particular, our regions offered underemployed skilled labor and connections with the US that helped match their excess supply of skills with the excess demand for (ICT) skills in the US. While our analysis does not extend to countries like Germany, France, and Japan, it is clear that they also offered ample, if not greater, supplies of both technical and managerial skills. A strong possibility for explanation is that the human capital in these other countries had substantially higher opportunity costs. A German engineer has lucrative opportunities in existing industries such as automobile, chemicals, and electronics. The incentives to set up a risky new venture in a new industry could not easily match the gains from working in such established industries.

To summarize, as new firms or regions emerge in a context where leading firms, regions, and countries exist, the former have advantages and disadvantages. The 'also rans' can exploit the opportunities created by the markets and institutions in the ICT sector, if they are well connected to them, without bearing the costs of creating them. However, because the major product spaces have been filled, they can only serve niche markets or focus on complementary activities. But what about the longer- (or medium-) term future? The initial successes imply that competencies are gradually accumulated. The longer- (medium-) term implications are not straightforward. Will there eventually be competition with the leaders? In the specific context we are analysing here (India, Taiwan, etc.) the situation is still fluid, and it is difficult to give definitive answers.

One cannot rule out *a priori* that some leading companies in the emerging countries will eventually compete with companies in the leading countries. The leaders, however, will probably keep moving up the frontier. The situation may turn out to be like the classical one in product markets wherein mature products are taken up by the followers, and the leaders develop more advanced technologies. However, other trajectories are possible. For example, firms in the new countries may specialize according to comparative advantage. The Indian firms, for instance, may further their initial comparative advantage of being able to organize large-scale projects for developing relatively lower end software at low costs. Comparative advantage has certainly played a role in Taiwan, which has developed sophisticated chip-manufacturing capabilities complementary to chip design in the US. The improved functioning of global markets may affect these processes as well. For example, it may be easier today to operate an international market in firms. This would favor the acquisition of companies overseas, and reinforce the existing division of labor, as noted earlier in the case of Israel.

5.6   Policy Issues and Conclusions

The core of good advice to policy is concrete understanding of the forces driving the economy. Two very different bodies of understanding have been brought to bear on high-tech, entrepreneurial-led growth. Should we understand the foundation of new regional clusters of entrepreneurial activity using new economy theories of increasing returns, or should we focus on comparative advantage? Our answer is an element of each. Much of the opportunity for new regions arises because old regions find themselves running up a steeply rising supply curve of land and of highly skilled labor. Even the very substantial migration of highly skilled labor to the existing Silicon Valley cluster has crashed into this classical diminishing-returns phenomenon. As a result, many of the policy implications are simple and classical: invest in education, have open market institutions, tolerate and even encourage multinationals, tolerate and even encourage a brain drain. For similar reasons, we find no support for the wisdom of protectionist, infant industry, national champion or directive industrial policy programs. Yet that is not the end of the story. The mechanism by which entrepreneurial-led growth takes off and becomes a contributor to regional and even national development is one with a strongly increasing-returns flavor. Once clusters are founded, they do indeed deliver the kinds of opportunities emphasized in the increasing-returns framework. But the big issue is how to start a cluster, and what can policy do (and not do) in this respect.

For one, our case studies clearly show the foolishness of directive public-policy efforts to jump-start clusters or to make top-down or directive efforts to organize them. Clusters of innovative activity do not respond well to being directed, organized, or jump-started, entrepreneurship being a quirky thing. For example, the study by Scott Wallsten in our project (Wallsten, 2001) could not empirically find any effect of a public-sponsored program as important as the Small Business Innovation Research (SBIR) program in the US on high-tech employment in US counties (see also Wallsten, 2000). In contrast, accommodative government policies can be an important part of cluster development. Apart from public investments in areas like education, governments played an important supporting (though not leading) role in making entrepreneurship easier in many of our regions, notably in Ireland, Taiwan, Virginia, and Israel.

A powerful policy lesson from all of our cases is that none of our clusters engaged in protectionism or 'strategic trade policy'—even while attempting to capture greater shares of rent-producing activities or sectors. In fact, it was the openness of many of these regions to the world economy that has allowed success in the market-connected model. Rather than seek to offer firms a protected domestic market, which in the cases we study would have led to suboptimal scale, these regions have sought to define new niches and maintained a strong export orientation.

One of the most effective policies for regional development that we have encountered in our analyses has been that which encouraged the creation of the GSM standard. The GSM standard was critical for the growth of a continental wireless hardware market in Europe that benefited the Scandinavian firms first, and firms from other European countries later on. Yet the purposes of the policy were not set to encourage regional growth in Scandinavia. The rise of the Scandinavian model, built around the two leading firms Ericsson and Nokia, relied on several of the factors that we have already discussed for the other countries or regions—a substantial supply of skills and a strong policy for education; the role of the larger firms in encouraging the supply of skills; the ability to cover a niche (wireless hardware, and possibly wireless Internet software and services) that has eventually become quite important. The formation of a European standard was, however, key for creating a sizable demand. Public policy was not the only factor that gave rise to the standard. It was, however, an important one, as with many standard-setting processes (whether technical, legal, or else) that require the co-ordination of different actors. In sum, rather than interventionist policies, often directed toward the formation of the clusters themselves, and of their firms, the creation of the conditions for the clusters to arise, like a continental demand, can be a much more effective mechanism for promoting the opportunities of growth.

A natural end to our journey into the potentially new microdeterminants of economic growth suggested by the cases of regions like Ireland, India, Israel, or Taiwan is to summarize the key findings of our research. Notably, novel factors at the turn of the century are adding relevant new dimensions and relevant new determinants of growth. These include greater opportunities to exploit external effects, as well as economies of scale at the level of regions or industries, rather than mainly at the level of the firms. Yet, the importance of old economic factors, and related determinants of growth, has not vanished. Even within the context of the new models, old economy ingredients, like firm-building capabilities, connection to markets and demand, along with the supply of skills (both technical and managerial), are critical for the new economy forces (external effects, agglomeration economies, etc.) to reach their full potential. In particular, these factors are critical forces for the initial push that is required to start any new entrepreneurial-led growth process. Old economy factors are crucial for new economy outcomes.

This also speaks to public policy. Direct, top-down policies are most likely to fail. Particularly worrisome are policies that would direct at a level of detail such as picking the specific industries or technologies to be sponsored. The right policies have elements of a 'benign neglect', and they allow for a significant decentralization in the choice of the initiatives. They would focus instead on the enabling conditions like the creation of suitable demand and markets (including formation of standards), openness, competition for encouraging the success of skilled people and people with entrepreneurial ambitions, along with policies focused on key supply-side factors and institutions, and on education in the first place.

The stories of the emerging regions that we have studied in our project have also shown that one driver of entrepreneurship in these areas has been the low opportunity costs of local human capital. When human capital has high opportunity costs because of alternative productive uses (employment in large established firms in leading industries like ICT itself, automobile, chemicals, etc.), this is hardly an issue for public policy. The question is far more serious when the opportunity costs for local human capital comes from artificially high wages in relatively unproductive jobs—e.g. excessive levels of employment in public administration, or in intermediaries of various sort, which is typical, for instance, of countries like Italy or Japan. The right policies for new-cluster formation will fight such 'unproductive' opportunity costs, to allow for the full blossoming of true opportunities for their human capital.

Acknowledgements

This chapter draws on the results of a two-year research project, 'Silicon Valley and its Imitators', organized by the Stanford Institute for Economic and Policy Research (SIEPR), and carried out by an international and inter-disciplinary team. In drafting this chapter we benefited from specific, and most helpful comments by Scott Wallsten, along with several fruitful discussions with other team-mates of the project, and particularly Ashish Arora, Suma Athreye, Kevin Davis, Michael Horvath, Gordon Moore, John Richards, and Salvatore Torrisi. A special acknowledgement goes to Ralph Landau for his intellectual suggestions and for his encouragement in pursuing this research. All errors remain ours.

Notes

1. The study that overcomes this difficulty most successfully (Saxenian, 1994) looks only at one country and still finds itself comparing a region (Silicon Valley) wherein many structures support entrepreneurship to one (Route 128) where few structures do.
2. Of course, when we mention India we do not mean the entire country but the few regions that have shown a significant growth of ICT during the 1990s.
3. Some of the classical references are Krugman (1991), and more recently Porter (1998). Saxenian (1994), which we quoted earlier, is another classical citation. Arthur (1990) discusses specifically increasing returns in the context of 'Silicon Valley locational clusters'. There are also, of course, the classical, early references to agglomeration economies that date back to Marshall (1920), Perroux (1950), Myrdal (1957), and Hirschman (1958). Finally, Jaffe *et al.* (1993) and Audretsch and Feldman (1996) provide evidence of the extent of geographically localized knowledge spillovers.
4. The direct/indirect language follows the standard usage in external effects theories. This mirrors the classical Marshallian distinction, which pointed out three sources of external economies: a thick labor market; specialized input producers (and related increasing returns), which arise because close-by producers entail larger local markets; knowledge spillovers and 'untraded interdependencies'.
5. This is how thoughtful analysis of agglomeration economies and external effects states what those concepts can explain. See, for example, Fujita *et al.* (1999), who argue against use of '*ad hoc* dynamics' to take models too far past the question 'When is a spatial concentration of economic activity sustainable?'
6. For example, in our project, Horvath (2001) deals with the distribution of venture capital in the US, and finds that the venture capital industry is highly

concentrated geographically, and that the funds tend to be invested close to where they are collected. This is suggestive of the fact that a venture capital industry tends to arise where there is a large market of potential users. In this respect, it looks very much like a specialized supplier industry in the Marshallian sense that arises locally because of larger local markets (an indirect external effect, using our earlier terminology).

7. This form of organization distinction, rather than the sectoral one, underlies our use of the old/new economy language.

8. In our project, the story of Taiwan is told in Saxenian (2001); Arora *et al.* (2001) discuss India and Ireland; de Fontenay and Carmel (2001) studied Israel.

9. Hewlett-Packard, for example, was established years earlier and it was growing at the time of the founding of the integrated circuit industry in Silicon Valley.

10. Athreye (2001) discussed the story of Cambridge, UK in our project.

11. If anything, this problem was quite clear in the view of the early Silicon Valley, when Gordon Moore and the others, as emphasized in his story, had to hire a fully fledged manager, Ed Baldwin, outside of their technical group, who took up the management for the company and taught them stuff that is nowadays commonly taught in MBA courses (Moore and Davis, 2001).

12. The more traditional role of MNEs in providing technology transfer and a mechanism for connecting to world markets is not crucial in our cases (e.g. Arora *et al.*, 2001; de Fontenay and Carmel, 2001).

13. The role of social structures and community ties may also be strong. This is particularly true within bodies of entrepreneur-managers who participate in a brain drain and then a reverse brain drain (Arora *et al.*, 2001; Saxenian, 2001, 2002) or who have common experiences, e.g. in the military (de Fontenay and Carmel, 2001).

14. Another possible explanation of Cambridge's only 'partial' success is the lack of market access. No mechanism like returning expatriates created strong links to major markets and the domestic market was small (Saxenian, 1988).

15. See Athreye (2001) for details on the Cambridge, UK case.

References

Arora, A., Fosfuri, A., and Gambardella, A. (2001), *Markets for technology: the economics of innovation and corporate strategy.* Cambridge, MA: MIT Press, forthcoming.

Arora, A., Gambardella, A., and Torrisi, S. (2001), 'In the footsteps of the Silicon Valley? Indian and Irish software in the international division of labour,' Working Paper, Stanford Institute for Economic Policy Research (SIEPR), Stanford, CA: Stanford University.

Arthur, B. (1990), 'Silicon Valley locational clusters: when do increasing returns imply monopoly?,' *Mathematical Social Sciences*, **19**: 235–251.

Athreye, S. (2001), 'Agglomeration and growth: a study of the Cambridge hi-tech cluster,' Working Paper, Stanford Institute for Economic Policy Research (SIEPR), Stanford, CA: Stanford University.

Audretsch, D. B. and Feldman, M. P. (1996), 'Knowledge spillovers and the geography of innovation and production,' *American Economic Review*, **86**: 630–640.

Bresnahan, T., Morant, T., and Wallsten, S. (2001), 'Northern Virginia's high-tech corridor and the economics of regional development,' Working Paper, Stanford Institute for Economic Policy Research (SIEPR), Stanford, CA: Stanford University.

De Fontenay, C. and Carmel, E. (2001), 'Israeli's Silicon Wadi: the forces behind cluster formation.' Working Paper, Stanford Institute for Economic Policy Research (SIEPR), Stanford, CA: Stanford University.

Fujita, M., Krugman, P., and Venables, A. J. (1999), *The spatial economy: cities, regions and international trade.* Cambridge, MA: MIT Press.

Hirschman, A. O. (1958), 'The strategy of economic development,' *Yale Studies in Economics*, no. 10.

Horvath, M. (2001), 'Imitating Silicon Valley: regional comparisons of innovative activity based on venture capital flows,' Working Paper, Stanford Institute for Economic Policy Research (SIEPR), Stanford, CA: Stanford University.

Jaffe, A., Trajtenberg, M., and Henderson, R. (1993), 'Geographic localization of knowledge spillovers as evidenced by patent citations,' *Quarterly Journal of Economics*, 63: 577–598.

Krugman, P. (1991), *Geography and trade.* Cambridge, MA: MIT Press.

Marshall, A. (1920), *Principles of economics*, 8th edn. London: Macmillan.

Moore, G. and Davis K. (2001), 'Learning the Silicon Valley way,' Working Paper, Stanford Institute for Economic Policy Research (SIEPR), Stanford, CA: Stanford University.

Myrdal, G. (1957), *Rich lands and poor*, World Perspectives Series, vol. 16. Harper Brothers: New York.

Perroux, F. (1950), 'Economic space: theory and applications,' *Quarterly Journal of Economics*, 64: 89–104.

Porter, M. E. (1998), 'Clusters and the new economics of competition,' *Harvard Business Review*, Nov.–Dec., 77–90.

Richards, J. (2001), 'Clusters, competition, and "global players" in ICT Markets: the case of Scandinavia,' Working Paper, Stanford Institute for Economic Policy Research (SIEPR), Stanford, CA: Stanford University.

Saxenian, A. (1988), 'The Cheshire Cat's grin: innovation and regional development in England,' *Technology Review*, Feb./Mar. 1988.

Saxenian, A. (1994), *Regional advantage, culture and competition in Silicon Valley and route 128.* Cambridge, MA: Harvard University Press.

Saxenian, A. (2001), 'Taiwan's Hsinchu region: imitator and partner for Silicon Valley,' Working Paper, Stanford Institute for Economic Policy Research (SIEPR), Stanford, CA: Stanford University.

Saxenian, A. (2002), *The new argonauts: how entrepreneurs are linking technology markets in a global economy.* Cambridge, MA: Harvard University Press, forthcoming.

Wallsten, S. (2000), 'The effects of government–industry R&D programs on private R&D: the case of the small business innovation research program,' *Rand Journal of Economics*, 31: 82–100.

Wallsten, S. (2001), 'The role of government in regional technology development: the effects of public venture capital and science parks,' Working Paper, Stanford Institute for Economic Policy Research (SIEPR), Stanford, CA: Stanford University.

6

The Entrepreneurial Event Revisited:
Firm Formation in a Regional Context

MARYANN P. FELDMAN

6.1 Introduction

Entrepreneurship and new-firm formation are central to current thinking about economic growth, especially at the regional level and specifically in the formation of regional clusters of industrial innovation. Start-up firms are the embodiment of innovation, especially for radical new technologies that are not easily absorbed into existing firms (Audretsch, 1995). New industries such as semiconductors, microcomputers, biotechnology, and information and communications technologies (ICT) have largely developed in geographically defined clusters, and although this phenomenon is certainly not new, places with such colorful names as Silicon Valley, Medical Alley, or Research Triangle have captured the public imagination as the vehicle for industrial change and economic development. A focal point for development policy is creating attributes that mimic the characteristics of successful locations. Typically, government policy aims to leverage the presence of local research universities, increase the availability of venture capital, encourage a culture of risk taking, and create strong local informational and business development networks.

Once established, industrial clusters benefit from virtuous, self-reinforcing processes. A critical question is how these entrepreneurial processes begin, take hold and transform a regional economy. Conditions that we observe in defined clusters tell us how these systems function and the policy prescriptions that follow from studying these environments may not be appropriate for regions that are trying to develop an entrepreneurial environment.[1] Dubini (1989) characterized the environment for entrepreneurship as either munificent or sparse. An important concern is how environments lacking an entrepreneurial tradition change and became munificent. Conventional wisdom about the factors that promote entrepreneurship is drawn from analysis of munificent environments. Rather than viewed as causal factors, strong local networks, active research universities, and abundant venture capital may be attributes of successful entrepreneurship in established clusters.

The genesis or initial formation of firms, the building of institutions and social relationships appears to be a distinct phenomenon. Teubal and

Andersen (2000) argue for an appreciation of stages of regional development and propose evolutionary models that incorporate the rich context, diversity of experience, and uniqueness of regional systems. Increasingly, the actions of individuals as agents of change are not included in our examination of regional economies (see Appold, 2000, for a review). This is at odds with our understanding of the importance of economic agents (Kay, 2000), the coevolution of technology and institutions (Nelson, 1998), and the way in which entrepreneurs actively interact with their local environments (Saxenian, 1994).

This chapter examines what Shapero (1984) described as the entrepreneurship event – the decision to engage in the formation of a company–and considers the ways in which this decision may be influenced by the regional context. This chapter also focuses on the transformation of one local environment that was able to develop an entrepreneurial culture and subsequent industrial clusters where no recognizable climate of entrepreneurship existed before. The specific case considered here is the development of the US Capitol region,[2] recognized as a birthplace of the Internet and as a prominent center for biotechnology and telecommunications. By any number of measures, this region previously lacked the attributes that conventional wisdom associated with an entrepreneurial environment. We focus on the evolution of the region and specifically on the phase transition from an environment characterized as sparse to one that would now be characterized as munificent. By considering the early entrepreneurial efforts through which biotechnology and ITC took root in the region, the approach taken is 'appreciative history-friendly theorizing' (Malerba et al., 1999; Teubal and Andersen, 2000). The emphasis incorporates a role for individual entrepreneurs as agents of change who make decisions to start companies, shape local environments and institutions, and develop the resources and relationships that further their interests. It is argued in this chapter that viewing entrepreneurs as agents of change is critical to understanding not only the entrepreneurship event but also the creation of a positive local environment. The findings suggest that many of the conditions the literature indicates should be in place to promote entrepreneurship appear to lag rather than lead its development and thus question our understanding of the dynamics of regional change and the implied policy prescriptions.

The next section of the chapter considers the characteristics of entrepreneurial 'hot-beds' highlighted in the literature, and then examines whether these factors existed in the Capitol region before early entrepreneurial activity in biotechnology or ICT. Section 6.3 provides an interpretive history of the genesis of entrepreneurship in the Capitol region. Section 6.4 reconsiders the supportive factors the literature suggests promote entrepreneurship and argues that these factors not only followed the initial success but that they were also built by the efforts of entrepreneurs. Section 6.5 concludes with an examination of the conditions that may be associated with the acceleration of entrepreneurship. The intention is to provide prescriptive information for those regions that are trying to spark entrepreneurship and an economic transition.

6.2   Entrepreneurial Environments

Entrepreneurship has emerged as an important topic in economic development. Defined as the act of organizing resources to initiate commercial activity, entrepreneurship has been studied extensively from a variety of perspectives (see Bhide, 1999). One of the most notable features of entrepreneurship is its propensity to cluster spatially. Alfred Marshall (1890) noted this tendency and described the contextual factors associated with it (see Feldman, 2000). More recently, Michael Porter's (1990) diamond of interrelated localized competition, demanding customers, linked supporting industries and supportive government policy provides a set of factors that improve the functioning of firms. Porter (1990, pp. 655–656) perceives a strong role for government in providing a context for cluster development; however, he does not address the topic of how policy might influence entrepreneurship or the practical question of how to promote entrepreneurship. Others in the literature have addressed this question and a conventional wisdom has developed. For example, Florida and Kenny (1988) describe a social structure of innovation that promotes the formation of new firms. Others, like Bahrami and Evans (1995), describe the rich entrepreneurial environment of Silicon Valley as an ecosystem of institutions, venture capital, social capital, and entrepreneurial spirit that reduces the difficulty of starting a new firm. These factors form a conventional wisdom in the popular press and public discourse.[3]

Table 6.1 provides a summary of environmental characteristics that conventional wisdom typically associates with locations strong in entrepreneurial initiative and some of the work highlighting these conditions.[4] Each of these characteristics will be examined in turn and, in particular, will be related to the Capitol region in the formative years around 1970. Studies of the development of technology clusters typically find that there is a long time

TABLE 6.1 *Characteristics of entrepreneurial places*

Environmental characteristic	Representative authors
Availability of venture capital	Bruno and Tyebjee (1982); Florida and Kenney (1988); Sapienza (1992)
Supportive social capital	Bearse (1981); Roberts (1991); Abetti (1992); Flora and Flora (1993)
Entrepreneurial expertise/support services	Bruno and Tyebjee (1982); Malecki (1990)
Research universities as growth engines	OTA (1984); Raymond (1996)

lag between early business initiatives and the realization of commercial success (Link, 1995; Trajtenberg, 2000). The choice of the year 1970 as a baseline is admittedly somewhat arbitrary. It is selected due to data availability as well as to give a sufficiently long timeline in order to observe how the region has changed. However, it is not completely arbitrary, as we will see below in the discussion of what particular events contributed to the explosion of biotechnology and IT in the region. The objective of the next section is to provide a broad overview of the initial conditions characterizing the region in the early 1970s and then to move through the successful changes and developments as the biotechnology and IT sectors began to emerge.

6.2.1   Venture Capital

'Venture capital appears in virtually every inventory of necessary conditions for entrepreneurship' (Malecki, 1997a, p. 174). In addition to providing funding, venture capital also provides management expertise for companies that have the potential to develop into significant economic entities but whose creators may have little initial commercial experience. Venture capital is also considered an important indicator of the innovative potential of a regional economy. Considerable state and local public policy initiatives have been directed towards developing public venture capital programs or towards attracting private venture capital to regions.

The measurement of venture capital typically considers the number of equity deals completed in a region in a given year and the amounts of equity involved. By this measure, in 1971 there were three investments in the Capitol region for a total of $1.5 million. Of course, in 1971, the venture capital industry in the US was in its infancy with 68 equity deals for approximately $50 million nationally. The Capitol region accounted for 4 per cent of the deals and 3 per cent of the capital invested.

Another indicator of the venture capital industry is the number of venture capital firms located or headquartered in a location. In 1976, Bill Gust was recruited from Silicon Valley to the Capitol region to run a venture fund for the Bonaventure family. This appears to be the first venture capital firm in the region. Gust notes that there was little activity to invest in locally and the initial investments that he made were in Silicon Valley or along Massachusetts' Route 128 where there was more promising activity. Thus, we can see, anecdotally and by venture capital comparisons, that the Capitol region had little activity in the early 1970s and thus it cannot have been part of the initial environment.

6.2.2   Supportive Social Capital

When Marshall (1890) wrote that the 'secrets of the industry are in the air' he was most likely referring to the intangible non-pecuniary factors that facilitate information sharing and the flow of ideas. Accommodating social capital, the aligned characteristics of thick local networks and a supportive local culture is central to our conceptualization of conditions that promote local cluster development (see Ashiem, 2000, for a review). These factors are part of the success story of the Italian industrial districts and clusters of technology-intensive regions in the United States (Lazerson and Lorenzoni, 1999). For example, Roberts (1991), in writing about Route 128, emphasizes social and institutional support for entrepreneurship and the existence of a culture that promotes risk taking and creativity. Saxenian (1994) highlights the adaptive nature of supportive social capital in Silicon Valley that facilitated entrepreneurial activity and firm formation.

Social capital as a qualitative indicator of local networks and connectedness is difficult to quantify. We may, however, rely on quotes from individuals who were in a position to assess the depth of social capital in the region or to analyse proxy measures such as the composition of the local employment base, or evidence of collective or government action aimed at supporting or promoting entrepreneurship. These proxy measures combined with individual actor's assessments reveal that in $c.$ 1970 the Capitol region did not have social capital that was supportive of entrepreneurship.

In large part, the economy of the Washington region owes its existence to the US federal government and, correspondingly, the region has largely been dominated by government employment. In 1970, two-thirds of the local economy was dependent either directly or indirectly on federal expenditures, and half the workforce was employed in the government sector (Stough, 1999). The region benefited from a strong presence of federal laboratories and agencies such as the National Institutes of Health (NIH), the United States Food and Drug Administration (FDA), the Agricultural Research Service, the National Institute of Standards and Technology (NIST), the National Science Foundation (NSF), and the Department of Defense, including the Pentagon and the Defense Advanced Research Projects Agency (DARPA).[5]

Federal employment is typically stable and offers job security and benefits that would not be expected to promote a social culture supportive of entrepreneurship. Star scientists in the region were interested primarily in doing basic research that would bring academic rather than commercial rewards (Desrochers and Feldman, 2000). Attempts to start a business were seen as selling out and betraying scientific integrity (Eaton et al., 1998). There was not much interest in the commercial application of the region's resources and the business community was noted to have little 'understanding or appreciation of the power of technology for creating small companies on little capital'.[6]

There were many individuals with high levels of individual intellectual capital in the region and they most likely were part of social networks. The relevant question for an environment that promotes entrepreneurship would be the presence of local linkages between individuals that would advance industrial activity or promote commercial interests. One frequently cited example of the type of social capital that promotes entrepreneurship is the Home Brew Computer Club in the San Francisco Bay area, which began as an informal forum for individuals from different educational, social, and professional backgrounds to get together and discuss their common interest in personal computer technology in the early 1970s. The Home Brew Computer Club is cited as an important institution in the development of the personal computer industry (Segaller, 1998). Although such organizations have formed more recently in the Capitol region, interviews have not revealed that any social or special interest groups of this type existed during the formative phase of the industry.[7]

One proxy for social capital may be governmental activity or other types of collective action to promote or encourage entrepreneurship such as interest or advocacy groups or technology councils. One structural limitation in the Capitol region is a jurisdictional problem as the region covers three states – Virginia, West Virginia and Maryland–as well as the federal District of Columbia. The fact that the region spans three states and the federal district gives it a special nature particularly because each state is constitutionally responsible for the welfare and education of its constituents (Stough, 2000, p. 10) and by extension economic development. This makes it difficult to co-ordinate government action across the jurisdictions even though they compose one region in terms of a unified labor market with strong interrelationships. Indeed, the two states of Maryland and Virginia are well known as competitors rather than collaborators and have been known to engage in bidding companies away from one another rather than promoting a regional agenda (Anderson, 1996). Following a national trend, both states actively began promoting entrepreneurship in the mid-1980s, the midpoint of the period examined in this chapter. Nevertheless, before this time, the support for entrepreneurship was small and reinforcing social capital largely did not exist. The combination of secure federal jobs, star scientists' disdain for commercial activity, and weak government and social support for new business ventures created an environment that, if not outright hostile, did little to promote entrepreneurship or foster an entrepreneurial spirit until the mid-1980s when we began to see a change.

6.2.3   Entrepreneurial Support Services

Entrepreneurial expertise or support services provide resources to navigate a fledgling company with information about issues such as intellectual property, business formation, and legal requirements, as well as routine accounting and business compliance issues. Indeed, small firms are typically not able to engage these resources in-house. Access from their local external environment may augment a small firm's internal capabilities.

In the 1970s and 1980s, Washington, DC certainly had a large concentration of lawyers but their expertise was not in corporate law or focused areas such as patent law that would facilitate new, high-technology business. Business support services may be represented by the presence of large corporations who are their major clients (Malecki, 1990). Yet in 1970, there were only three Fortune 500 companies headquartered in the Capitol region: Fairchild Hiller, a producer of defense aircraft (no. 299); Black and Decker, a manufacturer of household tools (no. 395); and EASCO, an aluminum producer (no. 448). The lack of a group of executives and managers and the earlier absence of well-known business schools in the region has been documented previously (Feldman, 1994).

6.2.4 Research Universities

Research universities figure prominently in descriptions of Route 128 and Silicon Valley, yet others have noted that not every research university has spawned technology-intensive economic development (Feller, 1990; Feldman, 1994). We observe that universities have different academic cultures and offer various incentives and rewards for entrepreneurial activity. While the Capitol region is home to several prominent research universities, such as Johns Hopkins University, the University of Maryland, Georgetown, and George Washington, among others, none of them had taken a role in technology transfer in the 1970s. Most notably, Johns Hopkins University was the single largest recipient of federal R&D expenditures, even larger than MIT, which is credited with the genesis of Route 128 (Roberts, 1991) or Stanford University credited with the development of Silicon Valley (Leslie and Kargon, 1997). In contrast to these two well-known examples, Johns Hopkins did not have policies to encourage commercial activity and the academic culture was relatively hostile to academic entrepreneurship (Desrochers and Feldman, 2000). In addition, the intellectual property that was developed at federal labs was not available for commercial use.

6.3 Entrepreneurship Comes to Washington: An Interpretive History

In the 30 intervening years the region has undergone what might be best conceptualized as a transition or phase change from an economy characterized by little entrepreneurial activity to a fully functioning entrepreneurial environment. The Capitol region has established technological leadership based on entrepreneurial activity in biotechnology and the Internet[8] – two new industries that have seeded and established themselves in the past 20 years. In this section, each of these cases is considered in turn. First, we describe our study methodology and consider some methodological issues related to our approach.

6.3.1   Methodology and Methodological Issues

Our analysis is an interpretive summary based on interviews with entrepreneurs in biotechnology and ICT. An important component of the interviews has been gathering information on where entrepreneurs were employed prior to starting their own companies, what the motivation was for starting their own companies, what resources they used in developing their companies and technologies, and the subsequent spin-off activity these entrepreneurs have generated.[9]

There are some methodological issues to mention. First, it is important to note that this is a retrospective study. We are limited by being able to identify firms that are in existence now or that were at one time prominent enough to leave a trace. While we are able to trace these firms back in time to their founding, we have no knowledge of similar firms that were started but may have failed or been acquired or merged into other firms prior to our study.[10] This approach does allow us to consider the roots of successful entrepreneurship and the ways in which entrepreneurial activity took hold, but it cannot address the failure of enterprises that died without leaving a record. While each of these companies has its own unique and compelling founding story, the objective is to discern trends and patterns.

6.3.2   The Employment Histories of Capitol Region Entrepreneurs

The Capitol region is generally recognized as the third largest concentration of biotech companies in the United States (PricewaterhouseCoopers, 1998). Leading companies in the region include Human Genome Sciences (HGS) and Celera Genomics Corporation, two key actors in the international effort to map the human genome. In addition, another local company, MedImmune, is currently the world's eighth largest dedicated biotech company with six FDA approved products on the market. In total, there are approximately 300 small and medium-sized biotech firms currently in the region as of 2001.

Table 6.2 provides an overview of the genesis of new firm start-ups in biotech in the Capitol region, with the name of the founding entrepreneurs and their prior place of employment. We chose the mid-1970s to be the date for the establishment of the industry as Stanley Cohen and Herbert Boyer invented their genetic engineering techniques in 1973. These techniques have given rise to the modern commercial biotech industry. The earliest entrepreneurs in the Capitol region started firms during this recognized time of high economic opportunity stemming from Cohen and Boyer's techniques when many of the prominent national firms such as Amgen and Genentech were formed. The entrepreneurs documented in Table 6.2 were previously employed at large firms. Unlike other regions, the pharmaceutical industry did not have any significant presence in the region, thus individuals

TABLE 6.2 *Origins of bioscience companies in the region*

	Entrepreneur(s)	Prior organization(s)	Type	Company founded
1973–1980	Thomas M. Li	NIH	G	Biotech Research Labs
	Stephen Turner	Becton Dickinson	L	Bethesda Research Labs, Inc. (Life Technol.)
	Larry Cunnick	Hazelton Labs		BIOCON, Inc.
	Les Kirkegaard	Litton Bionetics	L	Kirkegaard & Perry Labs, Inc.
	Albert Perry	Litton Bionetics	L	Kirkegaard & Perry Labs, Inc.
1981–1985	James Whitman	HEM Research, Inc.	P	Advanced Biotechnologies, Inc.
	Augustine Cheung	University of Maryland Baltimore	U	Cheung Labs, Inc. (now Celsion, Inc.)
	Sam Wohlstadter	Amgen, Inc. (Founder)	S	IGEN International, Inc.
	Richard Massey	Amgen, Inc.	S	IGEN International, Inc.
	Michael Hanna	NIH	G	Perimmune, Inc. (now part of Intracel, Inc.)
	Richard G. Smith	HEM Research, Inc.	P	Lofstrand Labs Limited
	Solomon Graham	HEM Research, Inc.	P	Quality Biological, Inc.
	P. Thomas Iype	NIH	G	Biological Research Faculty & Facility, Inc.
	Floyd Taub	NIH	G	Digene, Corp.
	Stephen Turner	Bethesda Research Labs	P	Oncor, Inc.
	Martha Knight	NIH	G	Peptide Technologies, Inc.
	Richard Radmer, 5 other scientists	Martin Marietta	L	Martek Biosciences Corp.
1986–1990	M. James Barrett	Life Technologies, Inc.	S	Genetic Therapy, Inc.
	French Anderson	NIH	G	Genetic Therapy, Inc.

	Gregory Merril	Western Maryland College (Undergrad. student)	U	High Techsplanations, Inc. (now HT Medical, Inc.)
	Larry Tamarkin	NIH	G	CytImmune Sciences, Inc.
	Wayne Hockmeyer	WRAIR, Praxis Biologics	G	MedImmune, Inc.
	Franklin H. Top	WRAIR, Praxis Biologics	G	MedImmune, Inc.
	Craig Wright	WRAIR	G	Univax
	Ripley Ballou	WRAIR	G	Univax
	Sean O'Neil	Pharmacia Diagnostics	L	Washington Biotechnology
	William Tew	Johns Hopkins Uni. School of Medicine	U	Chesapeake Biological Laboratories, Inc.
	Paul Silber	Mary Kay Cosmetics, Toxicology Division	L	In Vitro Technologies, Inc.
	Alex Titomirov	Russian Academy of Sciences (Ph.D. candidate)	U	Informax, Inc.
1991–1995	John Holaday	WRAIR, Medicis Pharmaceutical Corp.	G	EntreMed
	John Magnani	BioCarb	S	GlycoTech
	Christopher Kemp	NIH	G	Kemp Biotechnologies
	Ronald Crystal	NIH	G	Gen Vec
	Craig R. Smith	Johns Hopkins Uni. School of Medicine, Centocor, Inc.	U	Guilford Pharmaceuticals, Inc.
	Se-Jin Lee	Johns Hopkins University	U	MetaMorphix
	Akira Komoriya	FDA	G	OncoImmunin, Inc.
	Beverly Packard	FDA	G	OncoImmunin, Inc.
	Randall Kincaid	Human Genome Sciences		Veritas, Inc.
	Floyd Taub	Digene Corp.		Dovetail Technologies, Inc.
	Craig Wright	Univax		Novavax

(Continued)

TABLE 6.2 (*Continues*)

	Entrepreneur(s)	Prior organization(s)	Type	Company founded
1996–1998	Paul O.P. Ts'o	Johns Hopkins Uni.	U	Cell Works Inc.
	Mark Zimmer	IGEN International, Inc.	S	Claragen, Inc.
	Aprile Pilon	NIH	G	Claragen, Inc.
	Karl Johe	NIH	G	NeuralStem Biopharmaceuticals, Ltd
	John Commissiong	NIH	G	NeuroTrophic Research Corp.
	Wei Wu He	Human Genome Sciences, Inc.	S	Origene Technologies, Inc.
	Gilbert Jay	American Red Cross Holland Lab.	NP	Origene Technologies, Inc.
	Robert Garrity	NIH	G	Biological Mimetics, Inc.
	Peter Nara	NIH	G	Biological Mimetics, Inc.
	George Lin	NIH	G	Biological Mimetics, Inc.
	Richard Feldman	NIH	G	Genome Dynamics, Inc.
	Irving Weinberg	Johns Hopkins Uni.	U	PEM Technologies, Inc.
	M. James Barrett	Genetic Therapy, Inc.	S	Sensors for Medicine and Science, Inc.
	Arthur Colvin	Life Technologies, Inc.	S	Sensors for Medicine and Science. Inc.
	Scott Meissner	Human Genome Sciences, Inc.	S	Teleclone, Inc.

Key: S = start-up firm; L = large firm; U = university; G = government agency; NP = non-profit; P = private firm, not able to classify.

previously employed at prominent suppliers to the National Institutes of Health (NIH) formed the earliest firms related to biotech. The presence of the NIH in the Capitol region is a defining characteristic as the US agency with the mission to oversee health and medical research. It employs a large number of researchers at the agency's home campus in Bethesda, MD. The NIH has proven to be a spawning ground for new company start-ups, especially in the last 10–15 years. Other government institutes and agencies, such as the Walter Reed Army Institute for Research (WRAIR) and the US Food and Drug Administration have also been a significant source of biotechnology entrepreneurs. Although recently the region's universities have spawned new companies, this did not occur at the earliest stages. From this table we begin to see that while the initial entrepreneurs came from government institutions and large corporations, the new start-up firms became particularly fruitful in generating second-, third-, and fourth-generation start-ups.

The ICT industry also has a strong presence in the Capitol region with a concentration in Northern Virginia. According to some sources, the region may be regarded as the birthplace of the Internet.[11] Prominent companies in the region include MCI, AOL, NexTel, Teligent, and Wintel. Over 400 small and medium-sized enterprises (SMEs) located in the area are ICT firms.[12] Companies in the region supply half of the total world-wide Internet backbone (PricewaterhouseCoopers, 1998).

Table 6.3 provides a sampling of ICT start-ups in the region with the name of the founding entrepreneurs and their prior place of employment. The modern computer-networking technologies that are the backbone of the Internet and ICT emerged in the early 1970s from the US Department of Defense Advanced Research Projects Agency (variously called ARPA and DARPA) (see Kahn and Cerf, 1999, for more detail). Individuals leaving the Department of Defense (DOD) and the military services formed the earliest start-ups. In addition, individuals from private industry both within the region and outside figure prominently. Local universities are notably absent from this list.

While biotech and ITC are very different industries, the objective here is to discern patterns in the origins of the companies and to explore the temporal development of entrepreneurial activity. Several notable patterns emerge. First, entrepreneurs hail from a variety of different organizations. Government agencies served an important incubator function in both industries; however, they were not the sole source of entrepreneurial talent. There is evidence of great diversity in the backgrounds of the entrepreneurs. Secondly, the earliest start-ups were service firms that were not originally involved in the types of R&D activities that generate new industries. Firms such as Bethesda Research Labs and AMS were not launched as product development firms although they have evolved in that direction over time. Thus, the industry had rather humble beginnings – not the type of start-up that would attract much attention from investors, the media or local

TABLE 6.3 *Origins of ICT companies in the region*

	Entrepreneur(s)	Prior organization(s)	Type	Company founded
1968–1980	Harry Kaplowitz	Xerox Corporation	L	Infodata Systems, Inc.
	William McGowan	Private Business Consultant	P	MCI Communications Corporation
	J. R. Beyster	Westinghouse	L	SAIC
	Patrick Gross	DOD, GE	G	AMS
	Frank Nicolai	DOD	G	AMS
	Charles Rosetti	DOD, Boston Consulting Group	G	AMS
	Ivan Selin	DOD	G	AMS
	Mario Morino	Navy	G	Morino Associates
	Fritz Volgenau	US Regulatory Commission, DOD	G	SRA, International
1981–1985	Sterling Williams	Manufacturing Data Systems, Inc.	P	Sterling Software
	William Melton	College (Master's degree in Asian Studies and Chinese Philosophy)	U	Verifone
	Ed Bersoff	Army	G	BTG
	Steve Walker	DOD	G	Trusted Information Systems
	Katherine K. Clark	Blue Cross and Blue Shield of the National Capital Area	L	Landmark Systems Corporation
	Patrick McGettigan	Blue Cross and Blue Shield of the National Capital Area	L	Landmark Systems Corporation
	John R. Lennon	Advanced Technology, Inc.	L	Techmatics
	Thomas Hewitt	Kntron-PRC, CSC, Boeing computer	L	Federal Sources
	Stephen M. Case	Pepsi, Procter & Gamble	L	AOL
	James Kimsey	Army	G	AOL

1986–1990	Terence Mathews	Mitel. Northern Telecom	S	Newbridge Networks
	Morgan O'Brien	Lawyer	P	Nextel
	Mark R. Warner	MCI and Venture Capitalist	S	Nextel
	Richard L. Adams	Federal employee	G	UUNet
	Earl W. Stafford	Air Force	G	Unitech
	Harry Hagerty	Founder of DSC Communications	S	Globalink
	Michael Saylor	DuPont	L	MicroStrategys
	Martin Schoffstall	NYSERNet (Founder – Syracuse)	S	PSINet
	William L. Schrader	NYSERNet (Founder – Syracuse)	S	PSINet
	Ram Mukunda	Intelesat	P	Startec Global Communications
	Robert E. LaRose	Advanced Technology, Inc. (founder), Syscon Corporation	P	Universal Systems, Inc.
	Michael Doughney	Tandem Computers, Computer Time Share Corp.	L	Digex
	Doug Humphrey	IBM	L	Digex
1991–1995	Brian Thompson	MCI	S	LCI
	Jack McDonnel	Verifone	S	Transactions Network Systems
	Jeong Kim	Naval Research Laboratory (contract with Allied Signal)	G	Yurie Systems
	Scott E. Stouffer	Telecommunications Techniques Corp. (subsidiary of Dynatech Corp.)	P	Visual Networks
	Steve Chaddick	Founder of AT&T Tridom	P	Ciena
	David Huber	General Instrument Corp.	L	Ciena
	Patrick Nettles	Blyth Holding, Inc.	P	Ciena
	Jack Slevins	COMSAT Radiations Systems	L	Comdisco

(Continued)

TABLE 6.3 (*Continues*)

	Entrepreneur(s)	Prior organization(s)	Type	Company founded
	Daniel Lynch	Founder of Interop	S	CyberCash
	William Melton	Founder of Verifone/Transactions Network Solutions	S	CyberCash
	Neil Hazard	MCI	S	Primus Telecommunications Group
	Sunil Paul	AOL	S	FreeLoader
1996–1997	Brandy Thomas	Mercer Management Consulting	P	Cyveillance
	Christopher Young	Mercer Management Consulting	P	Cyveillance
	John Puente	Digital Communication Corporation	L	Orion Network Systems
	Alex J. Mandl	AT&T	L	Teligent
	Jane A. Dietze	Goldman Sachs & Co.	L	Torso
	Jamie Hamilton	FreeLoader	S	Torso
	Jeffrey S. Hosley	AOL	S	Torso
	David Huber	Founder of Ciena	S	Corvis
	Doug Humphrey	DIGEX (founder)	S	Skycache
	Elias Shams	Yuri Systems	S	Telezoo

Key: S = start-up firm; L = large firm; U = university; G = government agency; NP = non-profit; P = private firm, not able to classify.

economic development officials. Thirdly, entrepreneurship picks up momentum. Over time, generations of new firms spun-off from the earliest start-ups and entrepreneurs who cashed in from one new venture created other new companies.

Between 1970 and 1990, the Capitol region was affected by a series of exogenous shocks to its employment structure. Some of these shocks were government policy initiatives, such as the downsizing of the federal government, the initiation of federal outsourcing, especially services that could be adapted to the commercial sector, and changes that allowed access to intellectual property in high-opportunity sectors. In addition, the favorable treatment of small firms with regard to securing government contracts or financing provided a further impetus for firm formation.

6.3.3 Federal Downsizing and Outsourcing

From 1970 to 2000, the employment structure in the Capitol region changed precipitously. Beginning during the Carter administration, there was a pronounced downsizing in federal employment that continued during the Reagan presidency. The reasons were a perceived general dissatisfaction with the large size of federal government and the efficiency of the private sector relative to the public sector. As a result, federal employment became less secure and employment conditions and future prospects deteriorated. Most importantly, compensation levels for members of the senior service declined. During the 1980s, public sector pay scales lagged badly behind those of comparable executives in the private sector (National Commission on the Public Service, 1990). Many of the affected individuals were victims of location inertia – they had strong personal ties to the region. In addition, other regions that offered alternative technology-intensive private sector employment had significantly higher housing costs, which also limited mobility. Individuals in the prime of their careers found entrepreneurship a viable employment option. The threshold for such risk taking was lowered by the exogenous shocks mentioned earlier – when the federal 'cushion' was not so comfortable, the incentive to leave government employment was higher.

Opportunities for entrepreneurship were provided simultaneously as federal jobs were downsized. The Civil Service Reform Act of 1978, which defined limits on the size of the federal workforce, contained an initiative to outsource the production of goods and services to the private sector. Thus, there was an incentive as well as a relatively low risk level for highly skilled individuals to leave federal employment and start firms to provide goods and services to their former employers. For example, the procurement of design services for personnel systems reconfiguration, redesign of government payment, and distribution systems were awarded to contractors in the Capitol region (Stough, 2000). These contractual arrangements created a need for proximity to the federal government that favored local firms.

Federal procurement spending in the metropolitan Washington area grew by 114.3 per cent from 1983 to 1997, creating enormous opportunities for private sector firms (see Table 6.4). Nationally, federal procurement spending increased by 3.1 per cent during this time (Haynes *et al.*, 1997, p. 149). Most importantly, the Reagan administration was responsible for a pronounced defense build-up that was coupled with this outsourcing to the private sector. The so-called Star Wars or Strategic Defense Initiative (SDI) was materially different from other defense build-ups as it focused on the technical and software attributes of armaments systems such as electronics, design, and systems management. Thus, SDI funded broad-based technical expertise rather than armaments production.[13] While this initiative stimulated economic growth throughout the United States, the Capitol region was one of the major beneficiaries (Stough *et al.*, 1998).

For example, the earliest ITC entrepreneurs were systems integrators who provided a customized set of arrangements of procured items such as computer components and software to create a functioning deliverable product. These firms began working as contractors on complex government computing services and telephone systems, and moved to the forefront of Internet development, electronic commerce, and satellite communications and wireless telephony. The ARPANET was built and developed by DOD contractors who invented the technology as they built the system. When the federal government removed commercial restriction on the use of the

TABLE 6.4 *Federal procurement increased in the Capitol region, 1983–1997 (real dollars in billions; 1982–1984 = 100)*

Year	Value of procurement contracts
1983	2.771
1984	3.244
1985	3.801
1986	4.060
1987	4.410
1988	3.719
1989	3.556
1990	4.109
1991	4.758
1992	4.733
1993	5.093
1994	5.655
1995	6.214
1996	6.947
1997	7.626

Source: adapted from Stough *et al.* (1998, p. 8).

Internet in 1989, two for-profit companies were spun-off from then non-profit Internet service providers (ISPs). UUNET was re-formed as a for-profit firm and PSINET was spun-off from NYSERNET.[14]

The Capitol region was affected by other exogenous changes that affected entrepreneurship. The changes in employment structure and incentives were coupled with new opportunities for the commercial exploitation of intellectual property rights that accrued from publicly funded research. These legislative changes created new commercial opportunities that have lured many scientists into starting their own companies. Most companies appear to have started with personal funds rather than venture capital, a finding that is consistent with the literature (Bhide, 1999; D. G. Blanchflower, A. Oswald, and A. Stutzer, unpublished manuscript).

6.3.4   Federal Legislation that Favored Small Business Formation

Table 6.5 provides an overview of a series of US policy initiatives that favored small business in general but especially technology-intensive start-ups. Considered together with the downsizing of the federal workforce, these initiatives provided a mechanism for new-firm formation.

In 1980, in response to declining American competitiveness, a new era in the transfer of publicly funded intellectual property to industrial firms began with the passage of the Stevenson–Wydler Technology Innovation Act, and the Bayh–Dole University and Small Business Patent Act. These policies were based on a belief that private access to and ownership of public research would ensure that research results would be widely disseminated and have the largest effect on commercial development, and subsequent economic growth. The Stevenson–Wydler Act in 1980 facilitated the transfer of technologies that originated in federal labs. The many federal labs in the Capitol region were thus allowed to license their innovations to private firms. This allowed employees of those labs, faced with potential downsizing, to license technology that could form the basis for a new firm. Similarly, the Bayh–Dole Act in 1980 allowed universities to retain ownership rights to intellectual property arising from federally funded research and license the right to use this property to private firms. This provided an incentive to promote commercial development of university research discoveries.

The Small Business Innovation Development Act of 1982 established the Small Business Innovation Research (SBIR) Program. Under this Act, all federal agencies with an annual R&D budget greater than $100 million are required to set aside a percentage of R&D funds for small businesses. Small businesses, according to the Act, was defined as a firm with less than 500 employees and less than $2.5 million in annual sales. Thus, the Act greatly increased the funding available to technologically oriented small businesses. Lerner (1996) estimates that the SBIR program has provided over $6 billion to small, high-technology firms between 1983 and 1995.

TABLE 6.5 *Major US policy initiatives favoring science-based entrepreneurship*

Name and date	Description	Implication for entrepreneurship
Stevenson–Wydler Technology Innovation Act (1980)	Facilitate the transfer of technologies that originated and are owned by Federal Laboratories to the private sector.	Employees could become entrepreneurs by licensing technology developed at Federal Labs. Other firms could view Federal Labs as a source of technology for transfer.
Bayh–Dole University and Small Business Patent Act (1980)	Permitted small businesses, universities and not-for-profit institutions to retain title to inventions resulting from federally funded grants and contracts.	Encouraged universities to actively engage in technology transfer to license inventions to industry. Allowed federal contracts to engage in commercialization.
Small Business Innovation Development Act (1982)	Established the Small Business Innovation Research Program within major federal agencies.[a]	Increased funding available for technologically oriented small businesses.
National Co-operative Research Act (1984)	Eased anti-trust penalties on co-operative research.	Facilitated joint projects and made it easier for small firms to find niche markets with emerging technologies.
Federal Technology Transfer Act (1986)	Amended the Stevenson–Wydler Act to authorize Co-operative Research and Development Agreements (CRADAS) between federal agencies and private firms.	Allowed small firms to extend R&D capabilities by collaborating with federal labs and agencies on commercialization.
National Competitiveness Technology Transfer Act (1989)	Part of a Department of Defense authorization bill, amended the Stevenson–Wydler Act to allow government-owned contractor-operator labs to participate.	Increased the pool of potential partners and research projects.

Defense Conversion, Reinvestment and Transition Assistance Act (1992)	Initiated the Technology Reinvestment Project (TRP) to provide technology development, deployment, and training needs of companies adversely affected by defense conversion.	Allowed firms that previously engaged in defense-related business to initiate new product lines.

Source: Venture Economics special tabulations.

[a] All federal agencies with an R&D budget greater than $100 million are required to set aside a certain percentage of R&D funds for small businesses, defined as those with less than 500 employees and less than $2.5 million in annual sales.

The 1986 Technology Transfer Act amended the Stevenson–Wydler Act to authorize Co-operative Research and Development Agreements (CRADAs) between federal agencies and private firms and specifically gave a major boost to the Capitol region's technology community (Stough, 1999). The Federal Technology Transfer Act allowed companies to form partnerships with government agencies for the first time. This new ability to form CRADAs resulted in the creation of an array of new firms, especially in the biotechnology sector. Enterprising scientists licensed technology out of their own university or government research labs to start new companies and chose to locate the new companies near their existing homes. In other cases, venture capitalists and executives in large companies recognized the commercial potential in research and either licensed the technology directly or formed a partnership with the scientist to jointly develop new products or services based on the technology. Although each federal agency maintains its own records, it appears that the first CRADAs went to companies in the Capitol region. It would also seem that in order to maintain such a partnership, at least in the initial stages, firms would need to locate near their federal lab or government-agency partners.

In conclusion, entrepreneurship in the region was a response to exogenous factors: underemployed skilled labor brought about by changes in federal employment policy coupled with new opportunities for the private sector to contract with the federal government and commercialize new technologies. The two cases considered here responded to different pressures. The advent of entrepreneurship was reactive and adaptive. While both sectors benefited from great opportunity for commercial products, biotechnology was more influenced by CRADAs and opportunities for licensing and joint product development, while ITC benefited more from outsourcing opportunities. In both cases, locational inertia kept the entrepreneurs in the area. Over time, the region developed supporting conditions that the literature associates with entrepreneurial environments. The next section considers the ways in which these factors developed.

6.4   Supportive Conditions Follow

An evaluation of the Capitol region now finds that the conditions the literature associates with a rich and thriving entrepreneurial environment are in place. There are professional associations that support entrepreneurial activity, a strong local venture capital industry with a net inflow of investments, and supportive universities. This section considers the development of these factors.

6.4.1   Available Venture Capital

By all indications, venture capital lagged rather than led entrepreneurship in the Capitol region. Figure 6.1 demonstrates the growth of venture capital in Virginia, Maryland, and the District of Columbia. We observe that there was little venture capital investment in the Capitol region in the early 1970s, but that it has increased substantially over time. At the initial start-up phase, entrepreneurs started by pursuing commercial projects that did not require

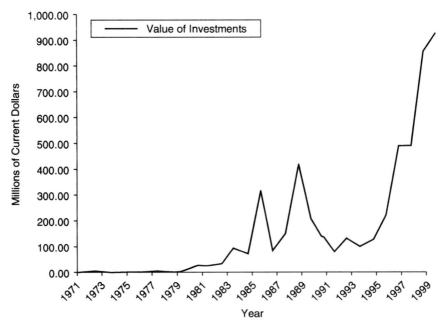

Fig. 6.1 Value of venture capital investments in the region.
Source: Venture Economics special tabulations.

high levels of investment and were unlikely to generate the types of large profits that would interest venture capitalists. They started with government contracting, producing rather mundane bread-and-butter products, such as medical test kits and reagents for biotechnology, or services such as computer system integrations and maintenance work in ICT. In addition, the growing number of related firms in the region provided opportunities for subcontracting work and asset sharing, thus making it easier for the start-up firms to bootstrap and steadily grow without large doses of new capital.

Of course, over this period, the amount of funding for venture capital grew significantly at the national level. Figure 6.2 presents the percentage of national venture capital (VC) that was invested in Capitol-region firms. For perspective, consider that the region was home to an average of 3.3 per cent of the US population during this time. There are periods of high intensity in the 1980s that represent deals in specific companies in biotech and ITC. It is noteworthy that since the early 1990s there has been an upward trend of VC investment in the region. Venture capital seeks opportunity and when there are potentially profitable investment opportunities, VC in a region may then

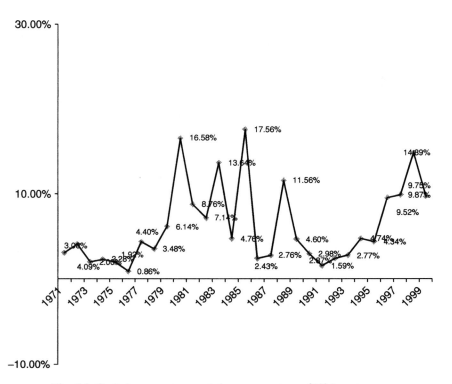

Fig. 6.2 Capitol-area venture capital as a percentage of US investments.
Source: Venture Economics special tabulations.

be attracted. The need of venture capitalists to monitor the new firms in which they invest makes close geographic proximity valuable (Gompers and Lerner, 1999).

There are now approximately a dozen VC firms headquartered in the region and firms located elsewhere have opened branches. In March 1999, Silicon Valley Bank, which primarily provides debt financing, opened a branch office in Northern Virginia with the comment, 'We are trying to be ahead of the curve. As far as new startups, this is a real hotbed' (Montgomery and Bacon, 1999). Successful entrepreneurs have also reinvested in companies in the region. In 1986, a group of business leaders formed the Mid-Atlantic Venture Association (MAVA) to facilitate the flow of capital to entrepreneurs. Other venture capital funds and venture angel groups have also been formed by successful entrepreneurs and companies in the region have formed corporate venture funds.

6.4.2 Supportive Social Capital

Over time, individual start-up companies grew, went public, or were bought out and the dynamics of the region changed as well. Most notably, local entrepreneurs who made large fortunes engaged in institution building to support their activities and to encourage further entrepreneurship. Also important was the emergence of networks of supportive social capital that began as membership or sponsorship organizations. These activities were primarily private sector initiatives, financed with private funds. These initiatives working with state and local government programs resulted in cross-fertilization and a common mission to promote the development of industry in the Capitol region.

Ceruzzi (2000) documents the development of a community of consulting firms in proximity to the US Pentagon, around the newly opened Route I-495, the Washington Beltway. The earliest government contractors were labeled with the unflattering name of 'Beltway Bandits'. The name was coined in the 1970s to reflect the location of the community of consulting firms around the Washington Beltway whose work proved lucrative. The firms formed a trade association, the Professional Services Council, to address and defuse this type of criticism and promote their interests. Once established, the organization served as a focal point for common benefit. Ceruzzi reports that the term 'Beltway Bandits' eventually became the name of a Fairfax county softball team, implying a sense of perverse pride in the term. The use of similar terms such as 'Nerds and Geeks' provide definition to a social group or network. The term 'Beltway Bandits' implies a unique local group.

A group of Virginia businesspeople organized a broad campaign to advocate state tax increases in order to address a noted shortage of technology workers and provide greater infrastructure funds (Baker, 1995). This initiative attempted to build infrastructure to support the development of local industry. Rather than seeking specific requests for their own business, the business leaders were promoting a broader, collectively responsible social agenda (Feldmann, 1997). The group, called 'Virginia First', argued that the drop in per capita state spending in Virginia from 22nd in the nation in the mid-1980s to 43rd in the mid-1990s was troublesome and would not provide sufficient resources for future economic growth.

Other private-sector-driven initiatives have provided venues for inter-action and information sharing. For example, the Indian CEO High Tech Council of Washington was formed as a social and networking organization. This organization, despite its name, links a membership of 950 high-level executives, the vast majority of whom are not Indian. This was a private sector effort to provide a venue where entrepreneurs could interact with their peers.[15] Another initiative is the Potomac Knowledge Way Project with a mission to increase the region's awareness and understanding of the Internet. Specifically,

the Potomac Knowledge Way was a not-for-profit leadership organization that acted as a catalyst, thought leader and idea incubator to help the Greater Washington region to be a global leader in advanced telecommunications, content, and Internet-related industries, and the new opportunities their convergence is creating in the region.[16]

Initiatives undertaken include the weekly *Netpreneur News*, which has a subscription of 7000 individuals.[17] In addition, state and local government formed technology councils such as Northern Virginia Technology Council (NVTC) and the Maryland High-Tech Council to promote networking and local industry interaction.

Older-style quasi-public organizations such as the Washington Board of Trade and the Greater Baltimore Committee have broadened their agendas and spun-off new organizations directed at technology-intensive industry. Other government-financed programs found greater success by collaborating with the privately organized networks (Guidera, 1996).

Legislative programs also followed and addressed the needs of industry. For example, in 2001, the state of Maryland passed 12 legislative acts focusing on providing a supportive environment for technology-based eco-nomic development. These cover the full gamut of infrastructure develop-ment, training programs, and tax incentives.

6.4.3   Entrepreneurial Expertise and Support Systems

The literature has emphasized the importance of support services. While it is true that agglomeration economies broadly conceived often play a crucial role for the start-up firms, the emergence of the Capitol region as a dynamic private-sector economy demonstrates that entrepreneurs adapt and assemble what they need as they build their ventures. Rather than talk about specific support services, the emergence of systems to support entrepreneurship was spontaneous and followed the region's success.

Entrepreneurs have also mentored the development of industry. Several entrepreneurs sold their companies and then started private incubators to nurture other companies. These founders were motivated to share their expertise and to build the region – 'to give something back', as one said. In addition, at least three angel networks have formed in the last five years by cashed-out entrepreneurs. The Private Investors Network (PIN), the Capital Investors Club, and the Washington Dinner Club are organizations of experienced entrepreneurs who actively invest in new companies and offer management advice. An industry devoted to outsourcing services to start-ups has also come into prominence, holding seminars and breakfast meetings to recruit clients.

6.4.4   Universities as Growth Engines

Universities in the region have responded to the increased entrepreneurial activity by offering new programs and building branch operations closer to commercial activity. For example, Johns Hopkins University offers a Masters degree in biotechnology in Silver Spring, MD, about 50 miles away from the main Baltimore campus. Virginia Tech University opened a branch campus in Northern Virginia about 250 miles from their main campus. The draw has been the number of workers seeking additional training, the opportunities for industry-funded research and interaction with industry. In particular, local universities have benefited from the philanthropy of local entrepreneurs. For example, George Mason University began in Fairfax, VA in 1950 as a commuter school. It has grown into Virginia's second-largest university with 18 doctorate programs and a focus on technology. Donors have given the university millions of dollars to endow 43 professorial chairs, allowing the university to recruit high-profile professors (O'Harrow and Lipton, 1996). All of the universities in the area have responded with incubators and other programs to encourage entrepreneurship.

6.5   Reflective Conclusions and Appreciative Theorizing

The economic success of Silicon Valley in terms of individual wealth creation, corporate profits, and job creation has been so impressive it has pushed government officials in locations across the United States to try to imitate or replicate its success. Many US government policies are aimed at replicating the conditions that exist in the region today in the belief that their local areas may also capture the benefits of new high-technology firm formation and the attendant economic growth. As a result, many regions attempt to identify themselves as the next Silicon Valley. However, much of this prevailing conventional wisdom is based on a snapshot of the advanced

stage of Silicon Valley's development, i.e. on the workings of a fully functioning innovative system. Looking at a successful region in its full maturity,
however, may not provide prescriptive information about the process of how
such regions do develop. That is to say, the conditions that we associate with
an entrepreneurial environment are the result of a functioning entrepreneurship and do not illuminate the early efforts by which such entrepreneurship
first took hold and the cluster initially developed.

A critical question is how regions change and develop into areas with
higher growth potential. Is replication of a mature entrepreneurial environment sufficient to foster entrepreneurship? Saxenian (1994) analyses Silicon
Valley from the perspective of how this regional industrial system adapted to
restructuring in the semiconductor and computer industry, and establishes
the importance of social relationships in defining the capacity of the region to
evolve and accommodate new demands. The example presented here represents an examination of how one region, initially lacking an entrepreneurial
tradition, accomplished the transformation to a functioning rich regional
system. Such a transformation entails a fundamental shift or phase change
from an inert innovative system to a more active system. Certainly, the
Capitol region was the site of large government research infrastructure,
classified as a state-anchored region using Markusen's (1996) typology. In
this regard, the concentrations of resources and highly skilled labor plus
access to sophisticated, demanding technology users were pre-existing conditions in the region. The transformation to private sector entrepreneurial
growth did not appear to represent movement along a technological trajectory (Kenney and von Burg, 1999), but instead was a sustained effort at
capacity building that involved human agency, adaptation, and evolution.
Not only this, a critical point was reached in the development of the region
where it jumped from virtually no high-technology start-up activity to intense
activity with start-ups per year numbering in the hundreds.

Certainly, in the development of an industrial system of innovation, there
are many individual complex stories and personal motivations. The prevailing wisdom was that government employees and contractors could never
become successful private businesses–the incentives were very different.
Government workers were, the logic went, too removed from the pressures
of the market and were not profit oriented. Government contracts followed a
practice of placing a low bid in order to get the job and then making a profit
by demonstrating a need for change orders in the absence of competition.
This is a very different philosophy from trying to do a job right the first time
and completing a job at lowest cost. However, the earliest entrepreneurs in
biotechnology and ITC were government contractors and employees who
proved this logic wrong. What is critical is that the region did provide
opportunity for individuals. They began working for the government but
then realized that they could adapt their products for dual-use commercial
markets. Therefore, they developed commercial products and with this

development came innovations and they eventually succeeded. In essence, this was a phase change from latent to active entrepreneurship.

The entrepreneurial event in the Capitol region was a response to and adaptation to change, that were exogenous to the regional system. In this regard, federal policies such as downsizing created slack and surplus resources that could find new and more productive uses. Thus, the gales of Schumpeter's creative destruction were unleashed. Policies that created a supply of potential entrepreneurs would not have been sufficient. A complementary set of government policies aimed at creating demand for ICT and biotechnology services, through government procurement policies that facilitated the transition. Other exogenous conditions were the policies that provided mechanisms or tools to enable companies to access resources. These affected the supply of new ideas by creating access to intellectual property from government investment.

Both biotechnology and ITC are high-opportunity technologies that face growing product demand and are attractive to investors. This indicates that firms working in these technologies faced favorable market conditions. The degree to which this is exogenous may be debated. Good entrepreneurs may create their own opportunity and thus define the industry. The idea that technology development is endogenous to cluster development and that the actions of key individual change agents define both the cluster and the industry seems to warrant more investigation. Abbate (2000) finds that the attributes of the Internet reflect the characteristics and values of the individuals involved in its development. This suggests that companies, regions and industries may benefit from the same factors and decisions – their evolution may be intricately interwoven. Currently, a myriad of economic development policies attempt to encourage entrepreneurship. Nevertheless, we have shown that rather than being actively promoted and encouraged by economic development policies, the early stages of these activities had much more humble and pedestrian beginnings. The conditions that we associate with entrepreneurship developed over time. In the early stage of these new technologies, the way in which they would develop was unclear and it would have been difficult to anticipate the types of specific assistance that entrepreneurs needed. Individual entrepreneurs were in the best position to move the technology, the industry, and the region forward. This is not to say that there is no role for local government policy in promoting entrepreneurship. No early examples presented themselves in this region; however, we have not directly examined that question.

Are there general lessons to be learned from the development of the Capitol region or is this, and every other, case unique? Certainly, this region benefited from high average individual and household incomes and higher than average education levels, giving it very different resource endowments from other underdeveloped regions that face the lack of an entrepreneurial culture. The general lesson is that entrepreneurs adapt, and when they are successful, they build the types of resources that support their activities. A distinction should be drawn between the conditions that support innovation and the conditions that support entrepreneurship. The two concepts are certainly related: entrepreneurship is one way in which innovation is realized as firms are formed to commercialize and advance new ideas. External environments and resources may make it easier for innovation to be realized but may not be sufficient to induce new firm formation, which is where the concepts diverge.

Once established, industrial clusters become virtuous, self-reinforcing circles. Yet, we know less about the conditions and factors – the initial spark or the entrepreneurial events–that influence the establishment of these clusters. Context, institutions, and social relationships are certainly areas for public policy intervention in terms of creating a supportive and positive environment for entrepreneurship. Specifically relevant are the conditions that affect the decisions of individuals to become entrepreneurs, and the ways in which an entrepreneurial culture develops and takes hold. Much of the economic development discourse appears informed by attempts to replicate the characteristics associated with a fully functioning regional system in what may be considered a mechanistic economic development machine – line up the inputs and economic development will follow. Such a view ignores the rich context, diversity of experience, uniqueness, and adaptativity of regional systems.

Our understanding of regional economic systems may be enhanced by a consideration of entrepreneurs as economic agents who actively interact with their local environments, adapt to new situations, crises, or opportunities using place-specific assets, and, finally, build and augment local institutions. Certainly, this is not the last word on this topic. It is my hope that this historically informed appreciative theorizing will inspire others to take a more detailed look. It is only through an appreciation of the nuances of cluster development that we may begin to inform policy.

Acknowledgements

Prepared for the international conference on Regional Economic Development: New Interpretative Paradigms and New Policy Instruments, sponsored by LIUC University. The author wishes to acknowledge comments and suggestions from the anonymous referees and the editors as well as Johanna Francis, Diana Hicks, Ed Malecki, Franco Malerbo, Joshua Schaff, Roger Stough, Kingsley Haynes, Gunner Elliason, Pierre Desrochers, and participants at a research seminar at George Mason University. This chapter is indebted to the individuals who agreed to interviews and generously shared their time and expertise in identifying salient issues as well as providing and validating information. Special thanks to Bob Starzynski, former editor of *TECHCapital*, and Thomas Kusner, formerly of Venture Economics, for sharing data and information.

Notes

1. Much of our understanding of the development of environments for entrepreneurship is based on the analysis of successful regions after they have achieved success. Historians document the development of these areas, yet this line of inquiry has not been well integrated into how we conceptualize regional change and economic development.

2. The US Capitol region is considered here as the Consolidated Metropolitan Statistical Area (CMSA) that includes Washington, DC, Northern Virginia, and the Maryland suburbs including Baltimore City and its environs. Two counties in West Virginia were added in 1990.

3. See for example, Lohr (1999) or a recent speech in the state of Maryland that stresses the examples from successful regions (www.inform.umd.edu/pres/speech_techshow.html).

4. The environments that support entrepreneurship, especially in technology-intensive firms, have been subject to extensive study (see Malecki, 1997*b*, for a review).

5. Other authors have found that high levels of federal expenditures are associated with technology-based economic development (Glasmeier, 1988; O'hUallachain, 1989*a,b*; Markusen *et al.*, 1991).

6. Quote from William M. Gust, currently Managing General Partner of Anthem Capital LP, who came to the region in 1978 from Silicon Valley to manage the Boventure Company, Inc., a family-owned venture capital business.

7. It is difficult retrospectively to investigate the existence of social networks. Our interviews did not uncover any evidence of formal or informal organizations that attempted to unite individuals along some common interest.

8. Within the region, there is evidence of geographic differentiation. Biotechnology is primarily concentrated in the Maryland suburbs in Gaithersburg and along the I-270 corridor. The Internet companies are concentrated in the Northern Virginia suburbs.

9. Beginning in 1996, we began investigating the origins of biosciences in the region (Eaton *et al.*, 1998; Feldman and Ronzio, 1999). We maintain a database of bioscience companies that tracks their growth and development. When it became clear that the concentration of ICT companies in Northern Virginia followed a similar pattern of development, we began similar interviews of ICT companies. Roger Stough at George Mason University monitors these companies and has provided information and suggestions.

10. Such a study would involve access to a source of historical data on firms such as tax or employment records to discern when the firms came into existence and when they ceased to exist. This approach would be limited because the smallest and most typical form of start-up, the sole proprietorship, might not be captured.

11. For example, the Virginia Economic Development Partnership (http://yesvirginia.org/wva-be.html) uses this slogan.

12. There is no accepted definition of the ICT industry and estimates of the numbers of entities in the region vary widely and appear to be influenced by media hype. This is the author's conservative estimate.

13. This affected ITC as well as biotechnology. Consider the firm Martek that is a spin-off from the defense contractor Martin Marietta and was funded by DOD.
14. UUNET was formed as a non-profit organization by a grant from the UNIX Users Group (USENIX) acquired by Metropolitan Fiber Networks in 1995, which was acquired by WorldCom in 1996. WorldCom merged with MCI to form MCI WorldCom in 1998.
15. See www.c2mm.com/indianceo/indianceo.htm for more details.
16. This quote is taken from the organization's web page: http://knowledgeway. org/.
17. The Potomac Knowledge Ways project officially ceased operations in March 2000, as was the organization's original intention. The Netpreneur Project is now operated out of and supported by the Morino Institute.

References

Abbate, J. (2000), *Inventing the Internet*. Boston, MA: MIT Press.
Abetti, P. A. (1992), 'Planning and building the infrastructure for technological entrepreneurship,' *International Journal of Technology Management*, 7: 129–139.
Anderson, T. (1996), 'Maryland develops plan to beat Virginia: a new economic development strategy will focus on making Maryland business-friendly,' *Washington Technology* (www.wtonline.com/archive/1996_APRIL_25/front_news/front_-news3.html).
Appold, S. A. (2000), 'The control of high-skill labor and entrepreneurship in the early US semiconductor industry,' *Environment-and-Planning*, **A32**: 2133–2160.
Ashiem, B. (2000), 'Industrial districts: the contributions of Marshall and beyond,' in G. Clark, M. Feldman, and M. Gertler (eds), *Oxford handbook of economic geography*. Oxford: Oxford University Press, pp. 413–431.
Audretsch, D. B. (1995), *Innovation and industrial evolution*. Boston, MA: MIT Press.
Bahrami, H. and Evans, S. (1995), 'Flexible re-cycling and high-technology entre-preneurship,' *California Management Review*, 37: 62–89.
Baker, P. (1995), 'Giving Allen the business on colleges: executives say extra $200 million a year is needed for education,' *Washington Post*, July 25, A1.
Bearse, P. J. (1981), *A study of entrepreneurship by region and SMSA size*, Philadelphia: Public/Private Ventures.
Bhide, A. V. (1999), *The origin and evolution of new business*. Oxford: Oxford University Press.
Bruno, A. V. and Tyebjee, T. T. (1982), 'The environment for entrepreneurship,' in C. A. Kent, D. L. Sexton, and K. H. Vesper (eds), *Encyclopedia of entrepreneurship*. Prentice Hall: Englewood Cliffs, NJ, pp. 288–307.
Ceruzzi, P. (2000), 'Tysons Corner, Virginia,' *Knowledge, Technology and Policy*, **13**: 86–102.
Desrochers, P. and Feldman, M. (2000), 'The practical application of "truth for its own sake": a short history of university–industry technology transfer at the Johns Hopkins University', Working Paper.
Dubini, P. (1989), 'The influence of motivations and environment on business start-ups: some hints for public policies,' *Journal of Business Venturing*, 4: 11–26.

Eaton, B., Feldman, M., Gerstley, L., Connolly, M., and Mangels, G. (1998), 'Biosciences in Maryland: A closer look,' MDBio.

Feldman, M. P. (1994), 'The university and high-technology start-ups: the case of Johns Hopkins University and Baltimore,' *Economic Development Quarterly*, **8**: 67–77.

Feldman, M. P. (2000), 'Location and innovation: the new economic geography of innovation, spillovers, and agglomeration,' in G. Clark, M. Feldman, and M. Gertler (eds), *Oxford handbook of economic geography*. Oxford: Oxford University Press.

Feldman, M. P. and Ronzio, C. R. (1999), 'Closing the innovative loop: moving from the lab to the shop floor in biotech,' Johns Hopkins University Institute for Policy Studies, Occasional Paper no. 22.

Feldmann, L. (1997), 'In Virginia, businesses argue for taxes,' *Christian Science Monitor*, September 9, 4.

Feller, I. (1990), 'Universities as engines of R&D-based economic growth: they think they can,' *Research Policy*, **19**: 335–348.

Flora, C. B. and Flora, J. L. (1993), 'Entrepreneurial social infrastructure: a necessary ingredient,' *Annals of the American Academy of Political and Social Science*, **529**: 48–58.

Florida, R. and Kenney, M. (1988), 'Venture capital-financed innovation and technological change in the USA,' *Research Policy*, **17**: 119–137.

Glasmeier, A. K. (1988), 'Factors governing the development of high tech industry agglomerations: a tale of three cities,' *Regional Studies*, **22**: 287–301.

Gompers, P. A. and Lerner, J. (1999), *The venture capital cycle*. Cambridge, MA: MIT Press.

Guidera, M. (1996), 'Start-ups finding it easier to get paired with "Angels"; University of Maryland's Dingman Center joins investor network in matchmaking effort,' *Baltimore Sun*, August 21, 1C.

Haynes, K., Fuller, S. S., and Qiangsheng, L. (1997), 'The Northern Virginia economy: the changing role of federal spending,' *Research in Urban Economics*, **11**: 145–161.

Kahn, R. E. and Cerf, V. G., (1999), 'What is the internet (and what makes it work)?,' paper prepared for the Internet Policy Institute, December.

Kay, N. (2000), 'Searching for the firm: the role of decisions in the economics of organization,' *Industrial and Corporate Change*, **9**: 683–707.

Kenney, M. and von Burg, U. (1999), 'Technology, entrepreneurship and path dependence: industrial clustering in Silicon Valley and Route 128,' *Industrial and Corporate Change*, **8**: 67–103.

Lazerson, M. H. and Lorenzoni, G. (1999), 'The firms that feed industrial districts: a return to the Italian source,' *Corporate and Industrial Change*, **8**: 235–266.

Lerner, J. (1996), 'The government as venture capitalist: the long-run effects of the SBIR program,' NBER Working Paper no. W5753.

Leslie, S. and Kargon, R. (1997), 'Recreating Silicon Valley,' *Business History Review*.

Link, A. N. (1995), *A generosity of spirit: the early history of the Research Triangle Park*. Research Triangle Park, NC: Research Triangle Foundation of North Carolina.

Lohr, S. (1999), 'Paradox of the internet era; behemoths in a Jack-be-nimble economy,' *New York Times*, September 12.

Malecki, E. J. (1990), 'New firm formation in the USA: corporate structure, venture capital, and local environment,' *Entrepreneurship and regional development*, **2**: 247–265.

Malecki, E. J. (1997*a*), *Technology & economic development*. Essex: Addison Wesley Longman.

Malecki, E. J. (1997*b*), 'Entrepreneurs, networks, and economic development: a review of recent research,' in J. A. Katz (eds), *Advances in entrepreneurship, firm emergence and growth*, Vol. 3. Greenwich, CT: JAI Press, pp. 57–118.

Malerba, F., Nelson, R., Orsenigo, L., and Winter, S. (1999), 'History-friendly models of industry evolution: the computer industry,' *Industrial and corporate change*, **8**: 3–40.

Markusen, A. (1996), 'Sticky places in slippery space: a typology of industrial districts,' *Economic geography*, **72**: 293–313.

Markusen, A., Hall, P., Campbell, S., and Dietrich, S. (1991), *The rise of the gunbelt*. New York: Oxford University Press.

Marshall, A. (1890), *Principles of economics*. London: Macmillan.

Montgomery, D. and Bacon, J.A. (1999), 'How green is our valley?,' *Virginia Business*, March (www.virginiabusiness.com/vbmag/yr1999/march99/howgreen.html).

National Commission on the Public Service (1990), *Leadership for America: rebuilding the public service. The Report of the National Commission on the Public Service and the Task Force Reports to the National Commission on the Public Service, Paul A. Volcker, Chairman*. Lexington, MA: Lexington Books.

Nelson, R. (1998), 'The agenda for growth theory. a different point of view,' *Cambridge Journal of Economics*, **22**: 497–520.

O'Harrow, R., Jr and Lipton, E. (1996), 'George Mason U. embroiled in debate about its mission,' *Washington Post*, February 14, A1.

O'hUallachain, B. (1989*a*), 'The identification of industrial complexes,' *Annals of the Association of American Geographers*, **74**: 420–436.

O'hUallachain, B. (1989*b*), 'Agglomeration of services in American metropolitan areas,' *Growth and change*, **20**(3): 34–39.

OTA (Office of Technology and Assessment) (1984), *Technology, innovation, and regional economic development*. Washington, DC: US Government Printing Office.

Porter, M. (1990), *The competitive advantage of nations*. New York: Free Press.

PricewaterhouseCoopers (1998), *Toward a new economy: merging heritage with vision in the Greater Washington region*. Potomac Knowledge Ways Project: Washington, DC (http://knowledgeway.org/voice/newecon/homepage.html).

Raymond, S. (eds) (1996), 'The technology link to economic development,' *Annals of the New York Academy of Sciences*, 787.

Roberts, E. B. (1991), *Entrepreneurs in high technology*. New York: Oxford University Press.

Sapienza, H. J. (1992), 'When do venture capitalists add value?,' *Journal of Business Venturing*, **7**: 9–27.

Saxenian, A. (1994), *Regional advantage*. Cambridge, MA: Harvard University Press.

Segaller, S. (1998), *Nerds 2.0.1: a brief history of the Internet*. New York: TV Books.

Shapero, A. (1984), 'The entrepreneurial event,' in C. A. Kent (ed.), *The environment for entrepreneurship*. Lexington, MA: Lexington Books, pp. 21–40.

Stough, R. R. (1999), 'Building and embedding an innovative culture in the regional economy,' paper presented at the Seventh Annual Conference on the Future of the Northern Virginia Economy, George Mason University, May 26.

Stough, R. R. (2000), 'The new generation technology economy: comparative regional analysis and the case of the US National Capital Region,' paper presented at the American Association for the Advancement of Science meeting in Washington, DC, February 2000.

Stough, R. R., Campbell, H., and Haynes, K.E. (1998), 'Small business entrepreneurship in the high technology services sector: an assessment of edge cities of the US National Capital Region,' *Small Business Economics*, **10**: 61–74.

Teubal, M. and Andersen, E. (2000), 'Enterprise restructuring and embeddedness: a policy and systems perspective,' *Industrial and corporate change*, **9**: 87–111.

Trajtenberg, M. (2000), 'R&D policy in Israel: an overview and reassessment,' paper presented at the NBER Summer Institute.

7

The Firms that Feed Industrial Districts: a Return to the Italian Source

MARK H. LAZERSON AND GIANNI LORENZONI

7.1 Introduction

A century ago, Alfred Marshall's (1923) encounter with the spatially clustered agglomerations of small firms in Lancashire's cotton and Sheffield's cutlery industries inspired him to coin the term industrial district. Today, the industrial district has once again become a central framework for conceptualizing economic and social action. Economists and geographers have shown how local-firm agglomerations generate external economic efficiencies by supporting both large and stable markets in labor skills and equipment and cheaper subsidiary trades and related services, and promote greater use and development of specialized machinery and organizational methods (Romer 1987; Storper and Scott 1989; Krugman 1991). Applied economists have argued that regional industrial clusters make firms more internationally competitive (Porter 1990; Saxenian 1994). Political economists have heralded the industrial district as the foundation stone for a meso-level industrial policy in which community institutions both reconcile the interests of business and labor and promote continuous product and process improvements in manufacturing (Piore and Sabel, 1984; Best, 1990; Locke, 1995).

Today, industrial districts outline the landscapes of both advanced capitalist democracies – Japan (Friedman, 1988), the United States (Saxenian, 1994), Germany (Herrigel, 1996), and Denmark (Kristensen, 1992) – and developing countries: Brazil (Schmitz, 1995), Mexico (Rabellotti, 1993), and India (Cawthorne, 1995). But it has been primarily in Italy where an international debate has raged among both scholars and policy makers on industrial districts as an alternative development model to the large, vertically integrated hierarchical firm (Piore and Sabel, 1984; Pyke *et al.*, 1990; Pyke and Sengenberger, 1992).

Italy's northeast and north-central regions are covered by geographically specific, small-firm industrial conglomerations where tens of thousands of well-paid artisans have produced fashion goods, furniture, machine tools, and ceramics that have conquered world markets. In the 1990s, Castel Goffredo made 39 per cent of the pantyhose sold in Europe and 17 per cent of that sold in the world (Ugolini, 1995). Bologna accounted for a disproportionate percentage of Italy's production of packaging machinery, a sector in which it ranked number four in the world (United Nations, 1995, pp. 172–173). Industrial districts furnished about 30 per cent of Italy's exports and employed 16 per cent of its manufacturing workers (Montedison and Cranec Catholic University of Milan, 1998) and disproportionately numbered among the country's wealthiest provinces.

The organizational structure of Italian industrial districts in large measure has rested on outsourcing production to mostly independent subcontractors. While vertically integrated firms have existed in many industrial districts, they too usually relied to varying degrees on subcontracting. Firms transacted extensively with other firms, a reflection of the extreme division of labor across firms used to achieve economies of scale, with each firm specialized in just a few of the production phases necessary to make a completed product. Economies of scale are often captured by small production batches, reflecting customized demand for a wide variety of models, sizes, and colors that often cannot be profitably satisfied by mass-manufacturing methods. Another crucial factor has been the industrial district's ability to achieve dominance in economies of time, which can be defined as the ability to design, manufacture, and deliver customized products rapidly. Capacity subcontracting in which firms undertake overflow work for other firms has also been common in industrial districts, but is secondary in importance to task specialization.

In light of these unique capacities, Piore and Sabel's (1984, p.32) description of district firms as organizationally amorphous and gelatinous appears quite puzzling, since the production of highly complicated goods requires firms to engage in long-term planning and investment in capital and skilled labor.

Firms that had underestimated a year's demand would subcontract the overflow to less well situated competitors. But the next year the situation might be reversed, with winners in the previous round forced to sell off equipment to last year's losers. Under these circumstances, every employee could become a subcontractor, every subcontractor a manufacturer, every manufacturer an employee.

Sabel's (1991, 1993, 1994) more recent writings have recognized the complex and structured nature of subcontracting relationships, yet his anarchistic vision of industrial districts in which 'the lead firm and supplier on one project can trade places on the next' appears unchanged (1995, p. 155). But even if the situation they described may have once reflected the reality of industrial district firms, it certainly no longer does. The small mechanical engineering firms of Modena that had shaped Sabel's (1982) early impressions of industrial districts had changed considerably by the end of the 1980s. Franchi and Rieser (1991, pp. 464–465; SNAMM, 1993) who studied over 200 small mechanical engineering firms in Modena during a seven-year period concluded:

Decentralized production still is a dominant feature of industrial districts, but it is usually organized by a lead firm.... Rather than having a pyramidal structure where each type of firm is subordinate to a higher level, the district is a composite weave of firms having different choices and varying degrees of independence. (1991, pp. 464–465)

Lead firms and suppliers were increasingly specialized, and although some subcontractors market a finished project, it was a relatively rare occurrence when a subcontractor overnight became the lead manufacturer. Lead firms tended to orchestrate a disproportionate amount of the economic activity, both in terms of quantity and quality. They provided the district with much of its propulsive and dynamic character, exploiting their external sources of information about changes in markets and technologies and transmitting them to local subcontractors through relatively well-defined networks.

In this chapter we explore the heterogeneous nature of the firms within industrial districts and the interfirm relationships and business groups that criss-crossed them. These organizational aspects have received scant attention in most of the industrial district literature, which has instead largely highlighted local industrial policy and the role of private and public associations in sustaining economic growth (Goodman and Bamford, 1989; Pyke et al., 1990; Pyke and Sengenberger, 1992). Most of this literature has tacitly assumed that the enterprises that comprise the district are mostly organizationally homogeneous and that their strategy and structure are shaped by local municipal policies and the supposedly dominant norms of the community. While local institutions and broader social-structural features undoubtedly shape and constrain economic behavior within industrial districts, we wanted to emphasize the central role of entrepreneurial agency.

Our focus on both the firm and district in which it is embedded offers a rather different panorama from that which has emerged in other studies of Italian industrial districts. First, we criticize the prevailing view that industrial districts have always developed in opposition to large firms. Actually, many industrial districts have greatly benefited from technology and skill transfers initiated by large firms. Secondly, we point out that the success of industrial districts often depends on importing intellectual, organizational, and technological inputs from outside the local area. Thirdly, we express doubts about whether the district's alleged social and cultural homogeneity accounts for the absence of the costly co-ordinating and transaction problems that institutional economists have attributed to outsourcing (Williamson, 1975, 1985; Chesbrough and Teece, 1996). Finally, such homogeneity may actually undermine the dynamism of districts by discouraging diversification and openness to new ideas.

In our study we have selected firms located in Italian industrial districts that have figured prominently in the literature: the Prato textile district near Florence in Tuscany; the Carpi knitwear district in the province of Modena;

and the Bologna machine-packaging district – the last two located in Emilia-Romagna. We have also included Mantova's Castel Goffredo women's stocking district in the Lombardy region, and have referred to several other significant Italian districts that outside of Italy are little known. Our data is drawn from our own empirical investigations in these districts over the last ten years, primary statistical information gathered by the Italian government, and research conducted by others.

7.2   What is an Industrial District?

Giacomo Becattini (1979, 1989, 1990, 1991), an economist whose original readings of Marshall's writings framed the early industrial district research agenda, defined industrial districts as a spatially and culturally identifiable area in which both employers and employees live and work. His ideal-type industrial district is comprised of numerous small firms engaged in primary and auxiliary activities related to a single industrial category and situated in a community clearly demarcated by its geography, history, and culture. Such a community engenders cultural, social, and political homogeneity and co-operative and trusting behavior in which economic action is regulated by a series of implicit and explicit rules governed by both tacit social conventions and explicit rules and regulations enforced by public and private organizations.

Geographers Storper and Scott (1989) have instead focused on identifying spatially dense agglomerations of industry-related firms. For them, Hollywood and Wall Street are as much industrial districts as are Prato and Carpi. Storper and Scott's less teleological definition of industrial districts has, in large measure, been embraced by a recent Italian legal reform that defined an industrial district as any provincial area in which the number of employees within a specific industrial sector is 30 per cent above the national average and where small firms having fewer than 100 employees predominate (Legge 5, number 317 of October 5, 1991[1]).

While we are agnostic about industrial district definitions and their boundaries, we agree with Becattini that Italian industrial districts share historical and political specificities. Italy's retarded national unification has marked its industrial districts with strong regional social, political, and cultural attachments. Because of the relative geographic immobility of Italians living in the country's central and northern regions, many entrepreneurs and employees have lived their entire lives in the same communities where their grandparents, their parents, and they themselves were born. The result is a form of social homogeneity that is relatively uncommon to other dynamic economic agglomerations such as Silicon Valley, where most of the entrepreneurs come not only from different regions but from different countries (Saxenian, 1994). How this factor affects Italian industrial districts shall be considered later in the chapter.

7.3 Origins of Industrial Districts

Definitional disputes about industrial districts obscure the more significant question of how they first developed. Because the early work on industrial districts developed from an economic tradition that stressed the presence of two distinct sectors – modern manufacturing and traditional, artisanal production, it has long been assumed that an adversarial relationship exists between small firms and large firms (Berger, 1980a,b, 1981; Piore and Sabel, 1984; Perrow, 1994). In addition, much of the earlier research on the entrepreneurial roots of Italian industrial districts has highlighted its rural origins, especially the influence of share-cropping (Paci, 1980). Later research, however, has cast doubt on this excessively narrow explanation, pointing out how industrial district entrepreneurs have had a diversity of agricultural and urban backgrounds (Forni, 1987; Guenzi, 1997). Our own reading points to the many occasions when relatively large manufacturing companies provided the pre-conditions for industrial districts through transferring technology and skills to an area, which helped cement the foundation for small-firm growth.

Until a combination of war, sharp recessions, and loss of old markets resulted in widespread factory closures and industrial restructuring at the end of the 1940s, the Prato cloth industry remained dominated by large, vertically integrated wool mills. Skilled workers who lost their jobs then opened specialized microfirms, a process that continued until the early 1970s when the few remaining vertical firms decentralized their activities (Lorenzoni, 1980; Dei Ottati, 1994a). Castel Goffredo's rise to prominence as Europe's hosiery center was fueled by Noemi, a large vertically integrated company that had been the area's only producer of women's hosiery from 1924 until the 1950s (Testa, 1993). Although Castel Goffredo once enjoyed a rich artisanal tradition in silk production, it had long disappeared by the time Noemi opened its doors (Testa, 1993). When Noemi went bankrupt its former employees opened small workshops where they applied their industrial skills, often backed by capital amassed by relatives and friends working in the region's rich agriculture[2] (Belfanti, 1995).

In Carpi, too, several large firms helped spawn an industrial culture in a semi-rural area and played an indirect role of making it a thriving center for the production of knitwear, machine-tools, and medical supplies. At the turn of the twentieth century Truciolo, a state-owned company, was established in Carpi, employing hundreds of workers and bringing modern manufacturing organization to the area's traditional straw-hat industry (Cigognetti and Pezzini, 1994). When it closed in 1931, its former employees opened small, straw-hat firms. These in turn were converted at the end of World War II to making ready-made knitwear, applying the same organizational principles used in the straw-hat industry (Cappello and Prandi, 1973).

World War II also marked the occasion when the former Truciolo factory was reopened to house the munitions operations of Magneti-Marelli – today Italy's largest manufacturer of car electrical components – that had been transferred there from Milan to escape Allied aerial bombardments. At the end of the war it returned to Milan, leaving behind many highly skilled machinists who opened various machine-tool firms that would soon form a sizeable industrial district specialized in wood-working tools (Solinas, 1994). One of these former machinists who learned to make molds at Magneti-Marelli eventually established several large firms that would spawn the disposable medical-supply industry district in Mirandola – a town ten miles from Carpi (Solinas, 1994).

Similar stories of large firms spawning industrial districts of small firms apply to Belluno, which has become a major district for eyewear; Lumezzane, a metallurgy district; and Manerbio, a textile district (Belfanti, 1996, 1997). These districts overlapped with communities in which Putnam (1993) uncovered a secular history of strong civic culture comprised of dense networks of voluntary co-operative organizations. While we cannot speculate here about how these endogenous factors influenced economic development, it should be recognized that a series of exogenous factors have all played a critical role in encouraging industrialization in north-east and north-central Italy (Fontana, 1997).

7.4   Small Firms

The prevalence of small firms in most Italian industrial districts in large measure reflected their predominance throughout Italian manufacturing. In 1991, 63 per cent of Italy's manufacturing work force was employed in firms with fewer than 99 employees and 39 per cent in firms with fewer than 19 employees (ISTAT, 1995, p. 79). In 1991 the average manufacturing company had only 9.53 persons in its work force (ISTAT, 1995, p. 79).

In both Prato, with its 9000 textile firms and 42 000 employers and employees,[3] and in Carpi, with its 2600 knitwear firms and 16 000 employers and employees,[4] more than 50 per cent of the workforce was employed in firms with ten or fewer persons (Bigarelli and Crestanello, 1994). On the other hand, in the highly automated and capital intensive women's stocking industry of Castel Goffredo – one-third of the 6000 persons employed in 340 firms worked in establishments with more than 100 employees (Furlotti et al., 1997) and in the Bologna machine-packaging industry, comprising approximately some 300 firms, one-third of the 7100 strong labor force worked in firms with more than 500 employees (Franchi et al., 1996). Thus, in some districts large firms held a dominant position.

In all of the industrial districts the very largest firms in terms of employment were also those that required substantial capital investments, which can mean in some cases that they were subcontractors. In the highly parcellized

Prato fabric district the largest firms were concentrated in finishing and dyeing operations that normally run 24 hours a day to amortize the expensive equipment. These firms were mostly subcontractors working for fabric manufacturers, but they were widely viewed as being the most profitable within the sector. Similarly in the small-sized motorcycle industry, the largest firms by employment were subcontractors producing the key components – brakes, clutches, engines, and frames – for assembly by smaller manufacturers, whose competitive strength rested primarily on their market reputation and distribution channels.

Product specialization was one reason for the predominance of small manufacturing firms in Italy, but another was the high costs of using hired labor imposed by labor law and social-security legislation. As a consequence, employers outsourced many of their labor-intensive activities to smaller firms that paid marginally lower taxes, enjoyed greater freedom to hire and fire labor and substituted family members for paid labor (Lazerson, 1995). The dearth of large capital markets in Italy had for a long time restricted opportunities for large firms, while small state-subsidized loans and simplified legal and tax procedures facilitated the creation of small businesses. A large market of suppliers and distributors serving small manufacturers' specialized needs also minimized overhead and entry costs.

An abundance of small firms tells little about the level of industrial concentration within the districts, for even the very largest firms outsourced extensively to small firms. Industrial economists assume that market concentration in an industrial sector arises when eight firms control more than 45 per cent of the market (Bain, 1968). In some sectors, evidence supported Harrison's (1994) claim that market share within industrial districts had become increasingly concentrated. By the early 1990s, seven of Castel Goffredo's largest firms sold 50 to 60 per cent of Italy's pantyhose production, a sharp rise in concentration compared to the 1980s (Testa, 1993, p. 137; Furlotti et al., 1997, p. 18). By 1998, a single company produced nearly 40 per cent of all the district's output because of consolidation in the industry.[5] Substantial market concentration also existed in Bologna's machine-packaging industry, where approximately 35 per cent of Italian producers were located. The four largest firms captured 43 per cent of the industry's turnover and the eight largest 50 per cent (ERVET, 1993, p. 2–13). On the other hand, in the knitwear district of Carpi the 15 largest firms accounted for 30 per cent of sales in the area, only marginally higher than in the early 1980s (Bigarelli and Crestanello, 1994). In Prato, the five largest mills represented only 8 per cent of total sales within the district, little changed from 6 per cent ten years ago.[6]

Whether increased market concentration also creates larger companies in terms of employee size depends on a number of factors. In Castel Goffredo average firm size increased from nine persons in 1981 to 22 in 1991 principally because new forms of capital-intensive technology and automation allowed several different manufacturing tasks to be undertaken by a single employee, thereby eliminating many of the advantages of subcontracting labor-intensive activities (Polettini and Salan, 1991). As a result, the very largest firms became increasingly vertically and horizontally integrated, and used fewer subcontractors. Several of the largest manufacturers also moved into retail operations through franchise operations. In contrast, the average firm size in the machine-packaging industry between 1984 and 1993 decreased from about 70 persons per firm to 54, reflecting both a decline in firm size among the largest firms and an increase in the number of smaller firms (ERVET, 1993, pp. 2–9). What appeared to be occurring here was that pressures to achieve economies of time in engineering highly complex and customized components for packaging manufacturing encouraged highly skilled technicians to start small spin-off firms with subcontracts from their former employers (Lipparini, 1995, p. 83).

7.5   The Boundaries of the District

Increasingly, industrial district production comprised goods partially or even completely manufactured outside of the district. In Prato, 33 of the district's 50 largest wool manufacturers reported that they regularly purchased fabric or yarn outside of Prato (Balestri and Toccafondi, 1994, pp. 10, 34). The same survey also found that 80 per cent of these firms imported fabric and yarn from foreign sources and that another 25 per cent invested or planned to invest abroad (Balestri and Toccafondi, 1994, p. 50). A more ambitious 1993 survey based on 319 Prato firms concluded that 50 per cent of final firms subcontracted to firms in northern Italy, while 60 per cent purchased yarn from outside the district (IRIS, 1994). Growing dependence on firms located outside of Prato was caused by shrinking demand for carded-wool yarn, the district's most important product.

Carpi's knitwear firms search for cheaper and more abundant labor meant that 38 per cent of their output was outsourced to non-district subcontractors, located primarily in the neighboring regions of Veneto and Lombardy, but also in the more distant Marches and Apulia regions (Bigarelli and Crestanello, 1994). Overall, 40 per cent of those working for Carpi firms were employed by subcontractors in other regions of Italy (Bigarelli and Crestanello, 1994). In the early 1990s, foreign outsourcing still remained relatively marginal to the industry, comprising just 3 per cent of Carpi's total production (Bigarelli and Crestanello, 1994).

Another study that canvassed 6000 firms in Italy's major apparel districts confirmed that developments in Carpi and Prato formed pieces of an emerging pattern:

Outsourcing to other Italian regions is fairly widespread ... in all regions and among all final enterprises. Micro-enterprises send 25 percent of their processing (work) outside the region (almost always to neighboring regions), small enterprises send 40 per cent, and all the others send approximately 50 per cent. (Brusco and Bigarelli, 1995, p. 20)

In Castel Goffredo, the women's stockings district, the elasticized thread for all of the stockings made by the very largest producer was prepared in two large plants located in the distant region of Abruzzo, some 300 miles away from Castel Goffredo. These two plants were also expected to start producing large quantities of finished stockings. This same company also owned a modern manufacturing plant in Faenza – about 140 miles from Castel Goffredo – which made finished stockings.

Nor were districts self-sufficient in generating investment capital. In the province of Modena 10 per cent of the labor force worked for international firms (Fiorani, 1995, pp. 104–107). In Mirandola's medical-supply district all of the leading manufacturers were foreign pharmaceutical companies that had acquired locally owned firms (Baroncelli, 1998). Bologna's machine-packaging industry also had a long history of attracting foreign producers, the most important one being Tetra-Leval, the world's largest packaging firm with Swedish origins. ACMA, once one of Bologna's largest packaging companies, was throughout the 1960s and 1970s a subsidiary of the American conglomerate American Machine & Foundry (Lipparini, 1995, p. 97). In 1992, Castel Gofreddo's second-largest stocking producer Filadoro was sold to the American conglomerate Sara Lee.

We have highlighted both the extent of manufacturing outside of the district and the presence of foreign capital in some industrial districts to underscore both the district's permeable boundaries and its attractiveness to external firms. Nevertheless, we demur at Amin and Robins' (1991) and Harrison's (1994) claims that multinational firms are writing the final chapter on industrial districts. Yes, the transfer of production elsewhere proceeds apace in the districts, but it is Janus-faced. In Prato, the low value added and intermediate phases of production were increasingly subcontracted to non-district firms, but the higher-value activities of design, final inspection, marketing, and distribution remained concentrated within the district (Dei Ottati, 1996, p. 7). In Carpi, capital-intensive activities such as weaving and embroidery were normally undertaken locally, as were the final critical phases of ironing, inspection, and packaging (Brusco and Bigarelli, 1995; Lazerson, 1995). Samples or prototypes were still produced in both Carpi and Prato because the need to make last-minute design modifications and the importance of highly skilled and trustworthy subcontractors favored local manufacturing. Knitwear products characterized by short production runs and frequent style changes were more likely to be produced locally than standardized year-round clothing items, such as tee shirts, jeans, and underwear, manufactured in large batches for inventory (Brusco and Bigarelli, 1995).

The consequences of foreign investment on the district's organizational structure were equally disparate, undercutting claims of a one-dimensional logic driving local acquisitions by multinationals (Harrison, 1994). Sara Lee, which once snapped up local firms at high prices, was now trying to resell Filadoro – its Castel Goffredo stocking plant – back to Italian investors because its new corporate strategy opposed apparel manufacturing (Tait, 1998, p. 28).

Harrison (1994) focused on acquisitions of local packaging-machinery firms in Bologna and Modena by foreign multinationals and claimed that such changes presaged qualitative changes in interfirm relations within the district. In particular, he pointed out that Bologna-based SASIB – an Olivetti-controlled multinational and Italy's second-largest manufacturer of cigarette-packaging machinery – in an attempt to favor its own subsidiaries treated local firms shabbily by using arm's-length bargaining, squeezing them over prices, depriving them of vital information, and eventually abandoning them altogether. Policies reminiscent of those used in the American motor industry (Helper, 1991). But Lipparini (1995, p. 154) argued that SASIB was never a typical Bologna packaging firm because it had relatively few network ties to other machine-packaging firms. On the other hand, there were several other foreign-owned Bologna-based packaging-machine firms – Corazza, Wrapmatic, Cassoli – that retained local management and solidified their ties to local suppliers.[7]

From a historical perspective the role of foreign multinationals in the machine-packaging district appears benign. During the 1960s and 1970s when the machine-packaging company ACMA was still under American control, it helped germinate many of the local, owner-controlled companies that have formed the district's backbone (Lipparini, 1995, p. 97). In 1988 ACMA was purchased by GD, an Italian-owned company that has been the country's largest manufacturer of cigarette-packaging machines.

Certainly, foreign companies have been attracted to industrial districts by the promise of cheap assets, proximity to important markets, and access to new technologies. But multinational firms in the machine-packaging industry also invested in the Bologna–Modena area to tap into the local production network, according to a Tetra-Laval executive – the large food-packaging company – in 1993, after the company transferred two-thirds of its packaging-machinery production and a division of its world research and development headquarters to Modena.

In Emilia-Romagna there is a web of small- and medium-sized firms and artisanal workshops in the mechanical-engineering sector capable of supplying all of the necessary components to optimize the performance of our equipment. This combination of technical knowledge, craft skills, and innovation represents a winning card that is difficult to find anywhere else. (Bonicelli, 1993, p. 18)

7.6   The Cultural Homogeneity of the District

Harrison (1994) objected to foreign companies in industrial districts because of their supposedly pernicious effects on interfirm networks. But others have worried more about their threat to the district's cultural homogeneity. Becattini (1979, 1987, 1990, 1991), Piore and Sabel (1984), and others (Best, 1990; Dei Ottati, 1991, 1994b) have repeatedly stressed how cultural homogeneity lubricates social relations among economic actors, reinforces consensus and group loyalty among both entrepreneurs and employees, assures the social ostracism of rule violators, provides a common language to speed information exchange, and establishes the basis for a co-operative ideology that is not solely based on material enrichment. For instance, Sabel and Piore (1984, pp. 267–268) wrote: '[F]ear of punishment by exclusion from the community is probably critical to the success of the explicit constraints on competition', and community rules 'balance competition among firms, so as to encourage permanent innovation' (Sabel and Piore, 1984, p. 29). Best (1990, p. 208) believed that private associations, municipalities, and regional subcultures were surrogates for organizing interfirm governance, a kind of 'collective entrepreneur' promoting co-operation, enforcing social norms of fair play, and stimulating economic growth. Dei Ottati (1991, p. 57) in turn analogized the district to a community market governed by public and private associations, suffused by 'an implicit code of behavior acquired by socialization'.

The strongly functionalist imagery of much of the industrial district literature that presents the district as a gemeinschaft may stem from both a research selection bias that has favored the most successful industrial districts and a failure to consider longitudinal data (Amin, 1989; Blim, 1990). Even more important is that while the functional aspects of socially homogenous communities have been heralded their dysfunctional aspects have been completely ignored (Merton, 1936). The isolated mountain community portrayed in Banfield's (1956) classic study of southern Italy was extremely homogenous, yet co-operation, trust, and economic development were stifled. Studies of life in Mafia villages have revealed how cultural homogeneity insulates organized crime in Italy from competing value systems and punishes those with different ideas (Gambetta, 1993). In small communities social solidarity based on kinship and social ties has often retarded economic progress, especially when introduced by outsiders who are easily ostracized.

Cultural homogeneity can be equally insidious when entrepreneurs belong to the same social clubs, come from the same schools, and pray in the same churches. Granovetter (1973) signaled how such strong social ties may restrict economic exchange and opportunity far more than weak ones. Several empirical studies of industrial districts have provided support for Granovetter's thesis. In Poni's (1998) historical research on Bologna's silk industry, which prospered between the sixteenth and seventeenth centuries only to virtually disappear by the end of the eighteenth century, businessmen, workers, farmers, and peasants, and even the Catholic Church joined together to defend the city's silk-making monopoly. But it was precisely this unwavering loyalty to community rules that foreclosed alternative possibilities that would have allowed Bologna to compete with silk producers from other cities and pursue alternative industrial paths. Following the local silk industry's collapse Bologna remained impoverished and without industry for nearly 100 years.

Grabher (1993) blamed the precipitous decline of the German Ruhr on the excessively consensual approach of its business, labor, and political elites. Glasmeier (1994), too, partially attributed the decline of the Swiss watch industry to the closed mind-set existing in the small towns of the Jura Mountain, which treated advances in technology and marketing charily. When everyone is performing the same routines and exposure to new ideas is limited, new skills are not learned, new investments are not made, and new technologies are not invented (Nelson and Winter, 1982).

7.7 Community and Co-operation

The decline of Bologna's important silk industry in the eighteenth century demonstrates that overwhelmingly adherence to local economic norms and institutions may actually be counterproductive for the local economy. On the other hand, there are also many cases where community membership proved inadequate in generating economic co-operation. Wilkinson's (1993, p. 10) reconsideration of Marshall's paradigmatic industrial district of Leicester uncovered rampant individualism, cutthroat competition, and deteriorating wages and working conditions: The 'effect of this on the relationship amongst firms made the hosiery industry incapable of effective cooperation at almost any level and for any purpose.' Passaro's (1994) study of Solofra, a rare analysis of a southern Italian industrial district, also confirms that personal distrust is not incompatible with high firm densities and deep-rooted cultural homogeneity.

Solofra is an important leather-tanning community near Naples, where the vast majority of the owners of the district's 150 small firms – 70 per cent of which have a workforce of fewer than ten individuals – were born and raised in the local area (Passaro, 1994). Nevertheless, distrust among Solofra's employers was so intense that many hesitated to dismiss their employees for fear that they would reveal production secrets to their new employers. It is not surprising then that only 18 per cent of its entrepreneurs believed that location in the leather-tanning district was a positive factor (Passaro, 1994). Distrust of one's competitors may also explain Solofra's organizational preference for horizontal and vertical integration, in contrast to that of Santa Croce sull'Arno, a much larger leather-tanning and finishing area between Pisa and Florence, where decentralized production reigned (Bartolini, 1994). Clearly, Solofra's entrepreneurs had little sympathy with Marshall's (1922, p. 271) musings about the benefits of untrammeled flows of information within industrial districts; they did not want the secrets of production to be in the air.

Solofra undoubtedly suffers from the many maladies of southern Italian underdevelopment. But even within the best-functioning Italian industrial districts co-operation among entrepreneurs is difficult to police. In Prato, excess production capacity in carded wool intensified price competition among weaving subcontractors and eventually undermined the trade association's suggested prices. Industrial district theorists like Dei Ottati (1995, 1996) have always pointed to the price list as a significant example of the informal rules that regulate market exchange within the district. Coleman's (1990, pp. 107–108) assertion that forms of social closure such as community-based membership can enforce adherence to rules of economic exchange, must be tempered by the recognition of their fragility in the face of cyclical pressures.

In Castel Goffredo, we learned of a verbal agreement among many of the major pantyhose manufacturers in which it was agreed that no wage increase would be offered to any competitor's employee seeking to change jobs, a measure intended to halt an inflationary wage spiral among skilled workers. But Filadoro, one of the very largest manufacturers regularly violated this code, luring highly skilled workers away from its competitors with impunity. The owners of this firm were ostracized, but nonetheless achieved substantial financial success.

7.8   Local and Distant Networks

Castel Goffredo appeared to satisfy many of the conditions under which a community moral code can be enforced by social control. Admittedly, its population of 8500 inhabitants was larger than the Maltese villages studied by Boissevain (1974, p. 123), who concluded that once a town exceeded 4000 people everyone could no longer know one another. But the entire community of women's hosiery entrepreneurs comprises no more than 1000 persons, nearly all of whom live within a 15-mile radius in a semi-rural area. Many of the owners who supported the hiring code had frequented the same schools and parish of the owners and executives of the offending company. Discussion with company owners also indicated that knowledge of the violation was quite widespread (Gambetta, 1988). These facts make one doubt the effectiveness of a community enterprise code in places many times larger than Castel Goffredo.

Our research in Castel Goffredo also revealed how in some situations local networks are overshadowed by the influence of distant networks. One of Filadoro's strengths was its special relationship with Dupont Corporation, because it was one of the first stocking producers to use Lycra. Dupont supposedly granted Filadoro more favorable prices and marketing treatment than its competitors, many of whom were unable to procure sufficient quantities of Lycra. At least in this case, Filadoro's external networks seemed more valuable than its local ones, which it was in the process of minimizing by cutting back on local subcontractors and expanding its internal production capacity. While Filadoro was certainly an exception to the rule, the example underscores the importance of external firm networks to the operations of many industrial districts. In our interviews, both manufacturers and suppliers in Castel Goffredo reported that they gained some of their most valuable information about both local firms and market conditions from purchasing agents for foreign buyers and representatives of equipment manufacturers. These external agents who enjoyed continuous contacts with many of the producers often helped link Castel Goffredo's neighboring suppliers and manufacturers.

The power of external networks in Castel Goffredo also undermined another agreement promoted by the largest pantyhose manufacturer to halt the widespread Italian practice of evading taxes by selling goods to whole-salers and retailers free of value-added tax. Unreported sales actually posed a major accounting burden for large manufacturers, who already benefited from numerous tax deductions. Such accounting practices also made the companies appear less valuable than they actually were, which affected their sale value. But for stocking distributors, especially the many small ones, untaxed sales were highly lucrative, often accounting for 50 per cent of turnover. They, therefore, resisted the reform, and within two weeks the largest manufacturer caved in. This episode raised a whole series of intriguing questions about the relationship between local producers and distributors and marketing agents, which have been ignored in most accounts of indus-trial districts that focus excessively on manufacturing.

In Castel Goffredo, evidence of indiscriminate interfirm co-operation was not very strong. But there were frequent examples of process-based trust in which firms regularly tested each other's reliability and probity, moving from small, discrete exchanges exposing them to minimal risks to more open-ended deals that potentially subjected them to greater harm because of undertaking uncollateralized obligations. Similar phenomena were observed by Uzzi (1997) during his study of embedded ties in New York City's garment district, Lorenz (1988) among subcontractors in southern France, and Larson (1992) in her investigation of interfirm alliances used by some American high-technology firms. Ring (1996) called such patterns of deepen-ing transactional reciprocity 'resilient trust'. On the other hand, Williamson (1993) said such relationships represented 'calculativeness' rather than trust because they involved a self-interested appraisal that weighed risks and benefits. It is doubtful whether calling these highly uncertain economic exchanges a form of economic calculation accurately respects that term's accepted lexical (Merriam-Webster, Inc., 1961) or historical meaning (Weber,

1981). Such a narrow analysis also restricts our knowledge of crucial facets of economic action that extend beyond discrete transactions of goods and services to touch the deeper and broader social relationships that shape economic institutions.

Co-operation and trust among firms in the district appear to arise from a process of reciprocal relations that individual firms have constructed over time with each other, rather than a universal resource buried in the district's substratum that can be accessed by all of its denizens. Admittedly, the dead weight of past personal and family histories embedded within a clearly demarcated social field make such forms of reciprocity less costly and haphazard than in places lacking these layers of social density. But whether these factors generate economic action depend upon the actions of real flesh and blood entrepreneurs. In the next section, we consider the role of such entrepreneurs in Prato in escaping the economic straitjacket that was partly of the district's own making.

7.9 Confronting Crisis in an Industrial District: The Case of Prato

By the mid-1980s demand for carded wool, Prato's bread and butter, had declined precipitously. Fashion changes, better-heated offices and homes, and new competition from developing countries required ever lighter and sophisticated textiles that penalized carded wool, a rather bulky material. But Prato's subcontractors lacked both the necessary skills and machinery to satisfy the new demands of their manufacturer-customers. So Prato's textile manufacturers were forced to turn to external suppliers for imitation leather and fur, non-woven fabrics, and plant fibers like linen, cotton, and silk (Dei Ottati, 1996).

Eventually, a significant number of Prato's subcontracting firms were able to switch their production to worsted wool and non-wool fabrics, partially offsetting the decline in carded-wool production (Dei Ottati, 1996). Indeed, carded-wool production declined so drastically that a number of manufacturers who still depended upon it were forced to become partners in spinning mills to gain access to adequate supplies. This rapid transformation was promoted neither by subcontractors nor by private associations but by Prato's well-established manufacturing firms. A review of these developments challenges three powerful myths about industrial districts: that change is endogenously produced; that relationships among firms are symmetrical; and that public and private associations can substitute for private entrepreneurs in governing the district.

In reaction to incipient signs of shrinking demand for carded-wool, many of the largest manufacturing firms started in the late 1970s to reorganize their key subcontractors into business groups, either by purchasing an equity interest or by pressuring them to align their activities more closely with their principal customers (Balestri, 1994; Balestri and Toccafondi, 1994;

IRIS, 1994 ; Dei Ottati, 1995, 1996). In the latter case, the wool mills would use various strategies such as promising them long-term work, guaranteeing their bank loans, and in some situations loaning them machinery.

More than 20 per cent of carded-wool spinning mill subcontractors were partially owned by the wool mills whom they serve (SPRINT, 1995, p. 13). Such joint-ownership agreements were most common in the strategically important capital-intensive production phases such as finishing and spinning. A survey of Prato's 50 leading fabric manufacturers reported that 24 of them had acquired a financial interest in related firms and another 14 had agreed long-term accords with subcontractors in Prato (Balestri and Toccafondi, 1994, pp. 48–49).

European Wool and the Best Group[8] were two firms we studied that had reorganized their subcontractors in order to introduce new fabrics and technology to Prato. The former emphasized external suppliers that were better integrated with its own production needs; the latter had tightened its supplier relationships to enhance interfirm co-ordination. Both firms had purchased controlling interests in some key suppliers. European Wool imported new technology in the form of elasticized cotton jeans from Biella, a textile district in northern Italy (Locke, 1995). European Wool had actually begun manufacturing elasticized fabrics prior to the carded-wool crisis in the hope of ending its dependence on a single product. But it discovered that straying from carded-wool products proved very difficult. First, prospective buyers doubted European Wool's ability to make cotton fabrics because Prato's reputation and comparative advantage was limited to carded-wool. Prato was not seen as a market for cotton fabrics. Second, the technical skills and machinery required to produce both elasticized cotton fabric and garments were unavailable in Prato, compelling European Wool to work with subcontractors outside the district. For several years European Wool tottered, only stabilizing after it had obtained a large contract from a prestigious fashion house.

Once its success was confirmed European Wool used its market power to pressure several Prato subcontractors to switch to cotton. European Wool introduced a fabric that was bulk-dyed in various colors, which allowed it to use skills common to Prato's carded-wool dyeing. Close proximity to fabric dyers was crucial because the many nuances in fabric shades required continuous visits to the dye works. Prato's tradition of rapid, informal contracting also permitted fast responses to changing market requirements. European Wool even expected that one day the denim textile maker in northeast Italy in which it owned an equity interest could be transferred to Prato.

The Best Group, one of Prato's 50 largest and fastest growing wool mills, compelled its subcontractors to switch to new fabrics by tightening its relationships with 15 key subcontractors, three of which were linked by minority equity ownership agreements. In consideration of Best's oral promise to provide them with long-term work, these subcontractors invested in costly new machinery chosen in co-ordination with Best to assure that it would accurately reproduce the customers' fabric prototypes. Many of Best's decisions were heavily influenced by its largest customers such as the British emporium Marks & Spencer, which had imposed stringent quality terms and delivery times. Eight Best employees visited the subcontractors daily to supervise and monitor output, while others measured, inspected, and analysed each bolt of fabric. In addition, Best, like most other major wool mills, placed most of its quality-control inspectors in the refinishing plants of its subcontractors.

Some could interpret Best's control mechanisms as a *de facto* hierarchy formed to combat shirking and dishonesty (Stinchcombe, 1985). Others may interpret them as a hybrid system of price, authority, and trust (Bradach and Eccles, 1989). But Best understood them as mechanisms to maximize interorganizational learning and rapidly alert subcontractors to problems. As the eponymous owner of the company explained: 'For me, my supplier is my future, and I must do everything to rescue him when he makes a mistake. If an error is made, the decision of how to divide the cost of damages is determined by our relationship based on common sense. If it is a very small supplier then I can't in all fairness make him pay, but if it is a large one it is a different story.' Similar variations of incomplete relational contracting have been reported by Dore (1983) in his studies of Japanese industrial networks.

Best was totally dependent upon his suppliers: fabric uniformity required a single subcontractor for each production task, making it impractical to play one against the other by dividing orders among them. Best also apprised its subcontractors early on about its plans to prepare them for the 200 semi-annual sample changes. If Best's unwillingness to pit one subcontractor against another raised prices, it was seen as an acceptable cost for creating a better integrated manufacturing network. Elsewhere, too, Brusco and Bigarelli (1995, p. 16) have noted how the salience of price in interfirm relationships has diminished: 'Price variations between customers and subcontractors linked by long-term relationships are much lower than market-price variations: prices rise less sharply when the market booms and tend not to drop as sharply when the market is sluggish.' In the end, the decisive element was not price competition, as Schumpeter (1962, p. 84) wrote, 'but the competition from a new commodity, a new technology, a new source of supply, a new type of organization.'

Prato's recent experience permits one to compare it to some other industrial districts that proved unable to change their stripes. According to Lazonick (1990), the English cotton industry in Lancashire collapsed because there were both too many small, specialized firms and a dearth of vertically integrated and solvent large firms capable of industrial modernization. His strongly Chandlerian interpretation of Lancashire's woes with its stress on the importance of large, vertically integrated firms needs to be reinterpreted in light of Prato's experience. Leading firms with good information and strong finances can shake smaller and less secure firms out of their routine torpor, though there is no evidence that they must be vertically integrated. One of the strengths of the leading Prato wool manufacturers was to invest primarily in design and marketing and relatively little in fixed production capital. Their frequent contact with buyers from all over the world made them highly sensitive to changing market signals. On the other hand, the subcontractors' substantial investments in equipment, their relatively small size, highly specialized nature, and dependence on manufacturers for both information and market access minimized their institutional capability to promote change.

7.10   Governance Mechanisms

The relationships that European Wool and the Best Group forged with their suppliers moves our discussion forward to how firms within industrial districts organize or govern economic transactions with other firms. Probably the most prominent interorganizational feature of industrial districts is the frequency of interfirm transactions stemming from manufacturers' extensive dependence on other firms for the production of components and semi-finished goods. Even in Castel Goffredo's women's stocking industry where the technology increasingly favored horizontal integration, there were still 275 production firms engaged as subcontractors for 28 manufacturers (Polettini and Salan, 1991, p. 82).

Oliver Williamson (1975, 1985) has argued that when a company locates near a supplier upon whom it relies for specific assets, meaning purchases of specialized labor skills, products, and services, it risks greater vulnerability: suppliers can suddenly withdraw their services, raise prices, or modify the quality of their goods. Individually drafted legal contracts and close monitoring may avoid some of these problems, but only at great expense. Much better, according to Williamson, would be for this company to expand its own organization to provide these services and products, and apply hierarchical rather than market power.

But in the face of Williamson's admonitions over the last 30 years, most entrepreneurs in Prato's textile industry, Carpi's knitwear industry, and Bologna's machine-packaging industry disintegrated their production organization by relying ever more on subcontracting to lower labor costs, expand economies of scale, to raise quality and promote innovation. Interviews with manufacturers and subcontractors indicated no evidence of high transaction costs stemming from frequent use of lawyers, non-transparent pricing, excessive transportation expenses, or opportunism arising out of bilateral monopolies (Lazerson, 1988, 1995). On the contrary,

Carpi knitwear companies that hesitated to adopt subcontracting were punished by lower profits (Bursi, 1987).

Subcontracting remained the preferred mode of transacting in the district. But can one then conclude that pure market mechanisms governed these relationships? Dei Ottati (1991, p. 68), the only district theorist who has confronted the problems of organizational governance in depth, wrote that the industrial district's social characteristics combined with its competitive markets has avoided the transaction costs problems posed by Williamson: '[C]oordination...is achieved mainly by the two "invisible hands" – the market and the community – by a combination of the price system and the practice of mutual adaptation.' Dei Ottati says the small numbers bargaining problem thrown up by Williamson that undermines competitive markets is not a factor in the district because of large numbers bargaining: when trust is abused incompliant partners can be easily substituted and specialized skills and machinery redirected. She also says that the district shines because of its neo-classical economic strengths: investment risks are relatively modest in small firms, barriers to entry low, and rapid demand change leads to brief and short-lived transactions (Dei Ottati, 1994c).

The weakness of Dei Ottati's neo-classical defense of industrial districts with its highly unorthodox community market concept is that industrial districts boast a range of highly sophisticated and specific goods that can only be produced when there is continuous co-ordination between manufacturers and their suppliers: goods that Williamson (1975, pp. 27–28) calls asset specific because they depend on firms possessing intimate knowledge of each other's idiosyncrasies. But even more crucially, substantial empirical evidence indicates that subcontracting in industrial districts has been governed by long-term relationships rather than by arms-length bargaining between anonymous buyers and sellers.

Long-term relationships certainly prevailed where technologically sophisticated, customized production required joint problem solving and continuing mutual readjustments. Lipparini's study (1995, p. 112) of a group of 25 major final manufacturers of packaging machinery and their suppliers in Bologna calculated that the average relationship lasted 10 years. It also found that dependence upon suppliers for unsubstitutable components or co-produced and co-designed parts had risen since the 1980s as manufacturers tried to gain economies of scale by relying more on specialized component makers (Lipparini, 1995, pp. 158–184). Similar developments have been observed in the Japanese automobile industry, where manufacturers were highly dependent upon the technical skills of component makers (Saki, 1995).

But even in so-called traditional industries such as women's stocking and textile production the large variety of fabrics, sizes, thicknesses, colors, and models, combined with the importance of timely deliveries and satisfactory performance make the substitutability of subcontractors impractical. In

Castel Goffredo, our survey of 70 women's hosiery producers reported stable relationships averaging 10 years or more. In Prato, 86 per cent of the district's carded, woolen-yarn subcontractors characterized their relationship with their woolen-mill customers as 'stable over time and limited in number' (SPRINT, 1995, p. 13). Over 40 per cent of these 380 suppliers of carded woolen-yarn regularly depended upon their largest customer to buy at least one-half of their output (SPRINT, 1995, p. 13).

Admittedly, the transactions of district manufacturers and subcontractors can still be framed in terms of a classical market where the goods are fungible, buyers and sellers easily substituted, and price considerations foremost. But these firms usually offer lower-quality and less-innovative products and are also relatively smaller. Increasingly, key elements of classical markets have diminished in salience. Arms-length dealings are uncommon when firms have enjoyed long-term relationships. Extensive search mechanisms in which parties attempt to maximize profit by choosing the least expensive or highest-paying contract are also rare. Because decentralized production often involves incomplete contracting where the terms of the contract need to be constantly renegotiated, cost represents only one dimension of the equation. For example, in the clothing and textile industry manufacturers expect additional orders for a particular line if demand is strong. When this is the case, the manufacturer nearly always must return to the same subcontractors who produced the original item to insure that the new orders will be homogeneous with the earlier batch. Although this permits the subcontractor to exploit the manufacturer, such behavior is rare because of the expectation of reciprocity built into long-term relationships.

The foregoing examples demonstrate that trust or good faith represents an element governing subcontracting relationships in the district. But it must be underlined that trust is carefully interspersed with control mechanisms. For example, Prato manufacturers usually trust only small, family-operated weaving firms that have no hired help and with whom they have had long-term relationships to weave costly cashmere wool into cloth. Even then, manufacturers weigh the cashmere yarn before sending it out, and reweigh and scientifically analyse it again after it has been woven into cloth. As was already mentioned, it is common for technicians from the manufacturer to roam freely throughout the subcontractors' workshops to check on procedures and quality. Manufacturers permanently station quality-control inspectors, who check every yard of cloth, on the premises of finishing subcontractors. Other mechanisms by which manufacturers exercise control over even trusted subcontractors is by lending them machinery, co-signing bank loans on their behalf, orally promising them long-term orders, and purchasing shares in their firms. These various governance mechanisms permit flexible market arrangements, while avoiding fixed hierarchical structures.

7.11   Discussion

In our chapter we have sought to place firms at the forefront of our research, which we believe remain the central organizational actors in industrial districts. Important as institutional arrangements are in industrial districts – business associations, regional and local policies – it should be recalled that no industrial district has ever emerged from a set of industrial policy initiatives promoted by either public or private organizations. Even Brusco (1982), an early observer of the originality of Italian industrial districts who has emphasized public economic development policies, acknowledged that there is no solid evidence that they have stimulated economic growth, and that many of them have been deeply flawed (Brusco and Righi, 1989; Brusco, 1997). Other Italian economists have also questioned the overall effectiveness of many of these local industrial policies (Prometeia, 1991; Provincia di Modena, 1993).

By bringing firms out of the shadow of the district, we have underscored the organizational complexity of the industrial district. Our evidence indicates that the larger firms of the districts – albeit small by most standards – often orchestrate subcontracting relations, explore commercial avenues, and invest in research and development. These diverse activities link leading firms to both distant and local actors, putting them in a strategic position to respond quickly to external market demand, while realigning the productive resources of less-sensitively located actors. Although we have no evidence, it is very likely that an individual firm's survival is very much connected to the relationships it has forged with other firms. Further research into the combined effects on firms of geography and relationships could enrich the organizational ecology perspective, in particular its understanding of firm establishments (Hannan and Freeman, 1989).

A notable strength of industrial districts is their capacity to combine organizational heterogeneity and homogeneity. Leading firms with loose attachments to distant networks help pollinate district firms with new ideas and concepts that are continually refined and sharpened because of the ubiquity of redundancy, proximity, and transactional intensity. Redundancy derives from the large number of highly specialized firms that perform similar but slightly different functions, which forces firms to both mimic each other and distinguish themselves by developing incremental process and product improvements. Proximity produces spontaneous social and professional interaction between entrepreneurs and employees engaged in the same industry both at home and at work, facilitating the diffusion of information. Transactional intensity obligates firm actors to have continuous relations with each other, offering many more points of contact and information than agents working within hierarchical organizations where information is often purposely limited (Simon, 1945). This is one reason why leading firms often encourage their supplier firms to develop multiple relations with other final firms, rather than seeking to hold them hostage.

Despite Italian industrial districts' very particular social, political, and legal heritage, the governance mechanisms used to manage interorganizational market relationships are not markedly different from those found by other researchers in very different settings. Uzzi's (1996, 1997) study of the New York City garment industry noted that while some firms used arms-length bargaining focused on price, others used a mix of embedded relationships that varied in the length and intensity of the ties. In the world of investment banking, Baker (1990) uncovered a pattern of hybrid interfaces in which corporations used a mix of hierarchical and market choices to select invest-ment banks to underwrite deals. This allowed firms to leverage both rela-tionship power and market efficiency. Similarly, leading firms in industrial districts engaged in a series of long-term relationships with local suppliers to maintain sufficient autonomy to exploit external contacts when dictated by market conditions. Explanations of interfirm co-operation based on the cultural homogeneity of the district have failed to make this distinction and have fallen into the trap of the oversocialized economic actor, which Gran-ovetter (1985) criticized for mistakenly assuming that the identification of a set of dominant social values can predict how economic agents will behave.

In addition to presenting a more realistic view of Italian industrial districts than the prevailing one of consensual islands of market felicity, we have also suggested that the rise of industrial districts is due to factors other than Italian particularism. Skill and technology transfers initiated by large corporations, as well as subcontracting policies, have done much to spark small-firm develop-ment. Our insistence on the often decisive and at times casual role of large firms behind industrial district development may prove bothersome to those who have heralded industrial districts as prefiguring a democratic society based on a free association of small independent producers (Piore, 1990; Perrow, 1994). But if successful industrial districts are as much a product of large firms diffusing technology and knowledge at the local level as they are of historical path dependencies and imagined cultural communities, then the promise of reproducing them tomorrow in economically underdeveloped areas is that much greater. Some evidence has already emerged of how the location of large furniture companies in southern Italy has sparked the creation of numerous small firms, where there once were none (Belussi, 1998). Undoubtedly, the industrial districts of north and central Italy have been enriched by the residual patrimony formed from collaborative economic endeavors such as share-cropping and co-operatives (Silverman, 1968; Put-nam, 1993). But this does not mean that other areas do not possess their own social resources that can be exploited to achieve small-firm development.

Schmitz (1995, p. 23) indicated that it has been the large Brazilian shoe factories, most using traditional assembly lines, that have taken the greatest strides towards industrial districts: '[F]ordist expansion contributed significantly to the growth of the local supply industry, and the proximity of the suppliers enhances the prospects for flexible specialization, particularly in its small-firm variant.' He also noted that unlike larger firms, small firms neither contributed to nor participated in local self-help institutions. In the Agra shoe district of India, Knorringa (1996) reached similar conclusions and pointed out how larger firms, often multinationals, imported new technology into the district and opened distribution channels for some of the local producers.

It is often said that network arrangements exist because they are efficient. But this explanation cannot explain why they only arise under certain conditions nor why they sometimes fail. They are certainly conditioned by economic rationality, but they also benefit from various moral economies or conventions that are too often excluded from economists' equations (Favereau, 1989). Long-term relationships, personal reputation, sweat equity, and family-based firms claim a special status within the economic calculus of many industrial districts. On the other hand, the standard economic conventions of written contracts, extensive search activities, arms-length bargaining, and price-based bargaining are less frequently encountered. Similar arrangements are common among marginal minority groups operating at the interstices of the larger economy (Portes and Sensenbrenner, 1993). But the Italian examples indicate that network organizations or business groups occupy a critical place at the very nerve centers of advanced capitalism. They are not cases that can be dismissed as intermediate or unstable forms slowly evolving toward Anglo-Saxon models. In response to new global and technological challenges and a trend toward the internationalization of markets, Italian industrial districts have emerged strengthened, and the commitment to community and place renegotiated rather than abandoned.

Notes

1. See also *Gazzetta Ufficiale*, Serie generale n. 118 of May 22, 1993, Decreto of April 21, 1993: 'Determinazione degli indirizzi e dei parametri di riferimento per l'individuazione, da parte delle regioni, dei distretti industriali.'
2. This information is based on interviews with owners conducted by one of the authors during autumn, 1991.
3. Information provided by Unione Industriale Pratese (the industrialists manufacturing association) in February, 1997.
4. Italian industrial employment statistics aggregate all those occupied in industry to include owners and related family members, as well as employees.
5. Data obtained from the director of production of Golden Lady, the leading manufacturer.
6. Data obtained by authors from the Prato Industrial Association, April 18, 1996.
7. Based on discussions with Andrea Lipparini, who has conducted extensive research on the packaging industry in Bologna.
8. The names of the firms are fictitious.

References

Amin, A. (1989), 'Specialization without growth: small footwear firms in Naples,' in E. Goodman and J. Bamford (eds), *Small firms and industrial districts in Italy.* London: Routledge, pp. 239–258.

Amin, A. and Robins, K. (1991), 'These are not Marshallian times,' in R. Camagni (ed.), *Innovation networks: spatial perspectives.* London: Bellhaven Press, pp. 105–118.

Bain, J. (1968), *Industrial organization.* New York: John Wiley.

Baker, W. (1990), 'Market networks and corporate behavior,' *American Journal of Sociology* **96**: 589–625.

Balestri, A. (ed.) (1994), *Terzo rapporto sul sistema economico pratese, 1993.* Prato: SPRINT (Sistema Prato Innovazione Tecnologica).

Balestri, A. and Toccafondi, D. (1994), *Imprenditori e distretti industriali: I nuovi volti dell'industria tessile pratese secondo i suoi protagonisti.* Prato: Pratofutura.

Banfield, E. (1956), *The moral basis of an amoral society.* New York: The Free Press.

Baroncelli, A. (1998), 'La dualite organisationnelle des enterprises d'un district industriel: Le cas du biomedical de Mirandola P. Bardelli, T. Froehlicher, and S. Vendemini (eds), in *La metamorphose des organisations: Connivences d'acteurs, contrats et cooperations interentreprises.*

Bartolini, S. (1994), 'Dinamiche di concentrazione della proprietà a Santa Croce sull'Arno,' in M. Bellandi and M. Russo (eds), *Distretti industriali e cambiamento economico locale.* Turin: Rosenberg & Sellier, pp. 201–212.

Becattini, G. (1979), *Scienza economica e trasformazioni sociali.* Florence: La Nuova Italia.

Becattini, G. (1987), *Mercato e forze locali: il distretto industriale.* Bologna: Il Mulino.

Becattini, G. (1989), 'Sector and/or districts: Some remarks on the Conceptual Foundations of Industrial Economics,' in E. Goodman and J. Bamford (eds), *Small firms and industrial districts In Italy.* New York: Routledge.

Becattini, G. (1990), 'The Marshallian industrial district as a socio-economic notion,' in F. Pyke *et al., Industrial districts and inter-firm cooperation in Italy.* Geneva: International Institute for Labor Studies, pp. 37–51.

Becattini, G. (1991), 'The industrial district as a creative milieu,' in G. Benko and M. Dunford (eds), *Industrial change and regional development.* London: Belhaven Press, pp. 102–116.

Belfanti, C. M. (1995), *Cento anni di storie della Casa Rurale e Artigiana di Castelgoffredo.* Mantova: Casa Rurale di Castelgoffredo.

Belfanti, C. M. (1996), 'Due secoli di storie del distretto industriale di Lumezzane', in A. Cova and G. Rumi (eds), *Brescia e il suo territorio.* Milan: Cariplo Bank, pp. 503–528.

Belfanti, C. M. (1997), 'Mezzadri, artigiani, operai: personaggi in cerca d'autore alle origini del distretto industriale', in C. M. Belfanti and T. Maccabelli (eds), *Un paradigma per i distretti industriali: radici storiche, attualità e sfide future.* Brescia: Grafo, pp. 31–38.

Belussi, F. (1998), 'Salotti, sulle ali del distretto' *Osservatorio dell'economia materana* 1, February, pp. 12–26.

Berger, S. (1980*a*), 'Discontinuity in the politics of industrial society,' in S. Berger and M. Piore (eds), *Dualism and discontinuity in industrial societies.* Cambridge: Cambridge University Press, pp. 132–149.

Berger, S. (1980*b*), 'The traditional sector in France and Italy,' in *Dualism and discontinuity in industrial societies*. Cambridge: Cambridge University Press, pp. 88–131.

Berger, S. (1981), 'The uses of the traditional sector in Italy: why declining classes survive,' in F. Bechhofer and B. Elliot, *The petite bourgeoisie: comparative studies of the uneasy stratum*. London: Macmillan, pp. 71–89.

Best, M. (1990), *The new competition: institutions of industrial restructuring*. Cambridge: Harvard University Press.

Bigarelli, D. and Crestanello, P. (1994), 'Strategie di diversificazione e di riorganizzazione produttiva a Carpi negli anni Ottanta,' in M. Bellandi and M. Russo (eds), *Distretti industriali e cambiamento economico locale*. Turin: Rosenberg & Sellier, pp. 183–200.

Blim, M. (1990), *Made in Italy: small-scale industrialization and its consequences*. New York: Praeger.

Boissevain, J. (1974), *Friends of friends: networks manipulation and coalitions*. Oxford: Basil Blackwell.

Bonicelli, E. (1993), 'La svedese Tetra Pak crede nell'Italia e sposta a Modena il centro di ricerca.' *Il Sole – 24 Ore*, June 1, p. 18.

Bradach, J. and Eccles, R. (1989), 'Price authority and trust: from ideal types to plural forms.' *Annual Review of Sociology*, **15**: 97–118.

Brusco, S. (1982), 'the Emilian model: productive decentralization and social integration.' *Cambridge Journal of Economics*, **6**: 167–184.

Brusco, S. (1997), 'Tavola Rotanda,' in C .M. Belfanti and T. Maccabelli (eds), *Un paradigma per i distretti industriali: radici storiche, attualita e sfide future*. Brescia: Grafo, pp. 225–247.

Brusco, S. and Bigarelli, D. (1995), 'Industrial structure and training needs in the knitwear and clothing sectors in Italy – a regional analysis, (1993).' Unpublished paper available from authors, Economics Department, University of Modena.

Brusco, S. and Righi, E. (1989), 'Local government, industrial policy and social consensus: The case of Modena (Italy).' *Economy & Society*, **18**: 405–424.

Bursi, T. (1987), *Indagine sulle condizioni economico-finanziarie delle imprese emiliano-romagnole del tessile/abbigliamento (1982–1986)*. Carpi: CITER.

Cappello, S. and Prandi, A. (1973), *Carpi: tradizione e sviluppo*. Bologna: Il Mulino.

Cawthorne, P. (1995), 'Of networks and markets: the rise and rise of a South Indian town, the example of Tiruppur's cotton knitwear industry.' *World Development*, **23**(1): 43–56.

Chesbrough, H. and Teece, D. (1996), 'When is virtual virtuous: organizing for innovation,' *Harvard Business Review*, Jan–Feb, pp. 65–74.

Cigognetti, L. and Pezzini, M. (1994), 'Dalla lavorazione delle paglie all'industria delle maglie: la nascita del distretto industriale di Carpi,' in M. Bellandi and M. Russo (eds), *Distretti industriali e cambiamento economico locale*. Turin: Rosenberg & Sellier, pp. 107–126.

Coleman, J. (1990), *Foundations of social theory*. Cambridge, MA: Harvard University Press.

Dei Ottati, G. (1991), 'The economic bases of diffuse industrialization.' *International studies of management & organization*, **21**(1): 53–74.

Dei Ottati, G. (1994*a*) 'Prato and its evolution in a European context,' in R. Leonardi and R. Nanetti (eds), *Regional development in a modern european economy: the case of Tuscany*. London: Pinter, pp. 116–139.

Dei Ottati, G. (1994*b*), 'Trust, interlinking transactions and credit in the industrial district.' *Cambridge Journal of Economics*, **18**: 529–546.

Dei Ottati, G. (1994*c*), 'Cooperation and competition in the Industrial district as an organization model.' *European Planning Studies*, **2**(4): 463–483.

Dei Ottati, G. (1995), *Tra Mercato e comunita: aspetti concettuali e ricerche empiriche sul distretto industriale*. Milan: Franco Angeli.

Dei Ottati, G. (1996), 'Economic changes in the district of Prato in the 1980s: towards a more conscious and organized industrial district.' *European Planning Studies*, **4**(1): 35–52.

Dore, R. (1983), 'Goodwill and the spirit of market capitalism: *British Journal of Sociology*, **34**: 459–482.

ERVET (1993), *Macchine automatiche per l'imballaggio e il confezionamento*. Bologna: Ente Emilia-Romagna per la valorizzazione del territorio.

Favereau, O. (1989), 'Marches internes, marches externes.' *Revue Economique*, **2**: 273–328.

Fiorani, G. (1995), *Modena e le medie citta d'Europa: uno studio sui vantaggi localizzativi*. Modena: Comune di Modena.

Fontana, G. L. (1997), 'Radici storiche dei sistemi produttivi del Veneto,' in C. M. Belfanti and T. Maccabelli (eds), *Un paradigma per i distretti industriali: radici storiche, attualita e sfide future*. Brescia: Grafo, pp. 45–70.

Forni, M. (1987), *Storie familiari e storie di proprieta: itinerari sociali nell'agricoltura italiana del dopoguerra*. Turin: Rosenberg & Sellier.

Franchi, M., Brusco, S., Cainelli, G., Forni, F., Malusardi, A., and Rigetti, R. (1996), 'Developments in the Districts of Emilia-Romagna,' in F. Cossentino, F. Pyke, and W. Sengenberger (eds), *Local and regional response to global pressure: the case of Italy and its industrial district*. Geneva: International Institute for Labour Studies, pp. 17–36.

Franchi, M. and Rieser, V. (1991), 'Le categorie sociologiche nell'analisi del disreto industriale: tra comunita e razionalizzazione.' *Stato e Mercato*, **33**: 451–476.

Friedman, D. (1988), *The misunderstood miracle*. Ithaca: Cornell University Press.

Furlotti, R., Polettini, P., and Salan, A. (1997), *Il distretto industriale della calzetteria femminile: 2nd censimento generale delle imprese*. Castel Foffredo (Mantova): Centro Servizi Calza di Castel Goffredo.

Gambetta, D. (1988), 'Can we trust trust?', in D. Gambetta (ed.), *Trust: making and breaking cooperative relations*. Oxford: Basil Blackwell, pp. 213–237.

Gambetta, D. (1993), *The Sicilian Mafia: the business of private protection*. Cambridge: Harvard University Press.

Glasmeier, A. (1994), 'Flexible districts, flexible regions? The institutional and cultural limits to districts in an era of globalization and technological paradigm shifts', in A. Amin and N. Thrift (eds), *Globalization, institutions, and regional development in Europe*. Oxford: Oxford University Press, pp. 118–146.

Goodman, E. and Bamford, J. (eds) (1989), *Small firms and industrial districts in Italy*. New York: Routledge.

Grabher, G. (1993), 'On the weakness of strong ties: the ambivalent role of inter-firm cooperation in the decline and Reorganization of the Ruhr,' in G. Grabher (ed.), *The embedded firm: on the socioeconomics of industrial networks*. London: Routledge, pp. 255–277.

Granovetter, M. (1973), 'The strength of weak ties.' *American Journal of Sociology*: 1360–1380.

Granovetter, M. (1985), 'Economic action and social structures: the problem of embeddedness.' *American Journal of Sociology*, **91**: 481–510.

Guenzi, A. (1997), 'La storia economica e i distretti industriali marshalliani: qualche considerazione su approcci e risultati,' in C. M. Belfanti and T. Maccabelli (eds), *Un paradigma per i distretti industriali: radici storiche, attualita e sfide future*. Brescia: Grafo, pp. 19–29.

Hannan, M. and Freeman, J. (1989), *Organizational ecology*. Cambridge: Harvard University.

Harrison, B. (1994), *Lean and mean: the changing landscape of corporate power in the age of flexibility*. New York: Basic Books.

Helper, S. (1991), 'How much has really changed between United States' automakers and their suppliers?' *Sloan Management Review*, **32**(4): 15–28.

Herrigel, G. (1996), *Industrial constructions: the sources of German industrial power*. Cambridge: Cambridge University Press.

IRIS (Istituto di Ricerche e Interventi Sociali) (1994), *Societa economia e territorio a Prato: Indagine per il nuovo piano regolatore*. Prato: Comune di Prato.

ISTAT (1995), Annuario di statistico italiano: 7th censimento generale dell'industria, del commercio, dei servizi e dell'artigiano 21 ottobre, (1991), vol. 1, book 1: Rome: ISTAT.

Kristensen, P. H. (1992), 'Industrial districts in West Jutland,' in F. Pyke and W. Sengenberger (eds), *Industrial districts and local economic regeneration*. Geneva: International Institute for Labor Studies.

Knorringa, P. (1996), *Economics of collaboration: Indian shoemakers between market and hierarchy*. Thousand Oaks, CA: Sage Publications.

Krugman, P. (1991), *Geography and trade*. Cambridge: MIT Press.

Larson, A. (1992), 'Network dyads in entrepreneurial settings: a study of the governance of exchange relationships.' *Administrative Science Quarterly*, **37**: 76–104.

Lazerson, M. (1988), 'Organizational growth of small firms: an outcome of markets and hierarchies?' *American Sociological Review*, **53**: 330–342.

Lazerson, M. (1995), 'A new phoenix?: Modern putting-out in the Modena knitwear industry.'*Administrative Science Quarterly*, **40**: 34–59.

Lazonick, W. (1990), *Competitive advantage on the shop floor*. Cambridge, MA: Harvard University Press.

Lipparini, A. (1995), *Imprese, relazioni tra imprese e posizionamento competitivo*. Milan: Etas Libri.

Locke, R. (1995), *Remaking the Italian economy: policy failures and local successes*. Ithaca: Cornell University Press.

Lorenz, E. (1988), 'Neither friends nor strangers,' in D. Gambetta (eds), *Trust: making and breaking cooperative relations*. Oxford: Blackwell, pp.194–210.

Lorenzoni, G. (1980), *Lo sviluppo industriale di Prato*. In *Storia di Prato* III Prato: Edizioni Cassa di Risparmi e Depositi.

Marshall, A. (1922), *Principles of economics* (8th edn). London: Macmillan.

Marshall, A. [1923] (1970), *Industry and trade*. New York: Kelley.

Merriam-Webster, Inc. (1961), *Webster's new collegiate dictionary*. Springfield, MA: G. & C. Merriam Co.

Merton, R. (1936), 'The unintended consequences of purposive social action.' *American Sociological Review*, 1: 894–904.

Montedison and Cranec Catholic University of Milan (1998), *Il ruolo dei distretti industriali nel 'made in Italy.'* Available from the Ufficio Studi of Montedison, Milan.

Nelson, R. and Winter, S. (1982), *An evolutionary theory of economic change.* Cambridge: Harvard University Press.

Paci, M. (1980), 'Struttura e funzioni della famiglia nello sviluppo industriale periferico,' in M. Paci (ed.), *Famiglia e mercato del lavoro in un'economia periferica.* Milan: Franco Angeli, pp. 9–70.

Passaro, R. (1994), 'Le strategie competitive delle piccole imprese di una area interna del Mezzogiorno: Il caso del settore conciario a Solofra.' *Piccola Impresa/Small Business*, 3: 85–112.

Perrow, C. (1994), 'Small-firm networks,' in N. Nohria and R. Eccles (eds), *Networks and organizations: structure, form & action.* Cambridge: Harvard Business School Press, pp. 445–470.

Piore, M. (1990), 'Work, labor and action: work experience in a system of flexible production', in F. Pyke, G. Becattini, and W. Sengenberger (eds), *Industrial districts and inter-firm cooperation in Italy.* Geneva: International Institute for Labor Studies, pp. 52–74.

Piore, M. and Sabel, C. (1984), *The second industrial divide.* New York: Basic Books.

Polettini, P. and Salan, A. (eds) (1991), *Il sistema produttivo di Castel Goffredo: rilevazione generale delle imprese nel settore della calzetteria femminile.* Mantova: Amministrazione Provinciale di Mantova.

Poni, C. (1998), 'Confrontare due distretti industriali urbani: Bologna e Lyon nell'eta moderna,' in V. Giura (ed.), *Gli insediamenti economic e le loro logiche.* Naples: Edizioni Scientifiche Italiane, pp. 125–155.

Porter, M. (1990), *The competitive advantage of nations.* New York: The Free Press.

Portes, A. and Sensenbrenner, J. (1993), 'Embeddedness and immigration: notes on the social determinants of economic action.' *American Journal of Sociology*, 98: 1320–1350.

Prometeia (1991), *Le politiche per l'artigianato in Emilia Romagna: Secondo rapporto dell'Osservatorio Regionale sull'Artigianato.* Milan: Franco Angeli.

Provincia di Modena (1993), *Tavola di concertazione sull'economia modenese: primo rapporto sulla situazione economica della provincia di Modena, giugno, 1993.* Modena: Assessorato Programmazione e Pianifazione Territoriale.

Putnam, R. (1993), *Making democracy work: civic traditions in modern Italy.* Princeton: Princeton University Press.

Pyke, F., Becattini, G., and Sengenberger, W. (eds) (1990), *Industrial districts and inter-firm cooperation in Italy.* Geneva: International Institute for Labor Studies.

Pyke, F. and Sengenberger, W. (eds) (1992), *Industrial districts and local economic regeneration.* Geneva: international Institute for Labor Studies.

Rabellotti, R. (1993), 'Is there an "industrial district model"?: Footwear districts in Italy and Mexico compared.' *World Development*, 23(1): 29–41.

Ring, P. S. (1996), 'Fragile and resilient trust and their roles in economic changes.' *Business and Society*, 35: 148–175.

Romer, P. (1987), 'Growth based on increasing returns due to specialization.' *American Economic Review*, 77: 56–62.

Sabel, C. (1982), *Work and politics: the division of labor in industry*. New York: Cambridge University Press.

Sabel, C. (1991), 'Moebus-strip organizations and open labor markets: some consequences of the reintegration of conception and execution in a volatile economy,' in J. Coleman and P. Bourdieu (eds), *Social theory for a changing society*. Boulder, CO: Westview Press, pp. 23–54.

Sabel, C. (1993), 'Studied trust: building new forms of cooperation in a volatile economy,' in R. Swedberg (ed.), *Explorations in economic sociology*. New York: Russell Sage Foundation, pp. 104–144.

Sabel, C. (1994), 'Learning by monitoring,' in N. Smelzer and R. Swedberg (eds), *The handbook of economic sociology*. Princeton: Princeton University Press, pp. 137–165.

Sabel, C. (1995), 'Turning the page in industrial districts,' in A. Bagnasco and C. Sabel (eds), *Small and medium-size enterprises*. New York: St. Martin Press, pp. pp. 134–161.

Saki, M. (1995), *Suppliers' Associations in the Japanese Automobile Industry: Collective Action for Technology Diffusion*. Discussion paper 1147. London: Center for Economic Policy Research.

Saxenian, A. L. (1994), *Regional advantage: culture and competition in Silicon Valley and route 128*. Cambridge: Harvard University Press.

Schmitz, H. (1995), 'Small shoemakers and Fordist giants: tales of supercluster.' *World Development*, **23**(1): 9–28.

Schumpeter, J. A. (1962), *Capitalism, socialism, and democracy*. New York: Harper & Row.

Silverman, S. (1968), 'Agricultural organization, social structure and values in Italy: amoral familism reconsidered.' *American Anthropologist*, **70**: 1–20.

Simon, H. (1945), *Administrative behavior: a study of decision-making processes in administrative organization*. New York: The Free Press.

SNAMM (1993), *Piccole imprese crescono, 1985–1992: una ricerca sulle piccole imprese metalmeccaniche nella provincia di Modena*. G. Fiorani, M. Franchi, and V. Rieser (eds). Modena: Sindacato Nazionale Artigiani Metalmeccanici Manifatturieri.

Solinas, G. (1994), 'Grande imprese e formazione di competenze: l'industria meccanica di Carpi,' in M. Bellandi and M. Russo (eds), *Distretti industriali e cambiamento economico locale*. Turin: Rosenberg & Sellier, pp. 127–148.

SPRINT (1995), *Nicchie di mercato per un distretto industriale: guida al settore della filatura cardata di Prato*. Prato: Sistema Prato Innovazione Tecnologica.

Stinchcombe, A. (1985), 'Contracts as hierarchical documents,' in A. Stinchcombe and C. Heimer (eds), *Organization theory and project management*. Oslo: Norwegian University Press, pp. 121–171.

Storper, M. and Scott, A. (1989), 'The geographical foundations and social regulation of flexible production complexes,' in J. Wolch and M. Dear (eds), *The power of geography: how territory shapes social life and social reproduction*. Boston: Unwin and Hyman, pp. 21–40.

Tait, N. (1998), 'Sara Lee poised to sell textile arm,' *Financial Times*,' January 5, p. 28.

Testa, F. (1993), *Le dinamiche competitive nel settore della calzetteria femminile*. Padova: CEDAM.

Ugolini, M. (1995), *La natura dei rapporti tra imprese nel settore delle calze per donna*. Padova: CEDAM.

United Nations (1995), *1994 international trade statistics yearbook*, Vol. II. New York: United Nations.

Uzzi, B. (1996), 'The sources and consequences of embeddedness for the economic performance of organizations: the network effect.' *American Sociological Review*, **61**: 674–698.

Uzzi, B. (1997), 'Social structure and competition in inter-firm networks: the paradox of embeddedness.' *Administrative Science Quarterly*, **42**: 35–67.

Weber, M. (1981), *General economic history*. New Brunswick, NJ: Transaction.

Wilkinson, F. (1993), 'A history of destructive competition and aborted cooperation: the Midlands hosiery industry.' Unpublished paper on file with the author at the Department of Applied Economics, Cambridge University.

Williamson, O. (1975), *Markets and hierarchies*. New York: Free Press.

Williamson, O. (1985), *The economic institutions of capitalism*. New York: Free Press.

Williamson, O. (1993), 'Calculativeness, trust, and economic organizations.' *Journal of Law & Economics*, **36**: 453–486.

8

Employee Start-ups in High-Tech Industries

Steven Klepper

8.1 Introduction

Where do entrants come from? One place is incumbent firms in the same industry. Employees commonly leave their employers to start firms in the same industry, which will be called spin-offs. In some industries, spin-offs are legion. Indeed, in the semiconductor industry so many spin-offs can be traced back to one firm alone, Fairchild Semiconductor, that they have been dubbed Fairchildren. Some observers characterize spin-offs as parasites feeding off the innovative efforts of their parents, aided by 'vulture' capitalists that help them get started. Ironically, Fairchild's most famous offspring, Intel, has maintained this position, going to great extremes to harrass employees that leave to start their own firms (Jackson, 1998, pp. 211–338). Scholars who share this view of spin-offs fear the effects spin-offs may have on the ability and incentives of incumbent firms to innovate and thus to be able to compete with the likes of Japanese firms blessed with lifetime employment (Florida and Kenney, 1990, pp. 79–97). Other scholars, however, see spin-offs as the font of innovation. To them, the Fairchildren jumped a sinking ship and led the semiconductor industry to new glory fuelling the juggernaut known as Silicon Valley.

Wherein lies the truth about spin-offs? Are they the rapacious plunderers their critics would have or the paragons of innovation their supports claim? The answer presumably lies in a better understanding of the motives of spin-offs in innovative, high-tech industries and the process governing their formation. Why, in fact, do employees of high-tech firms leave to found firms in the same industry? Is it mainly to exploit innovations they worked on for their employers? Is it mainly because of the inability of their employers to perceive and/or act upon promising technological developments in their industry? Is it mainly to exploit human capital they acquired as a byproduct of their employment? Each of these perspectives has been featured in recent theoretical work. They raise fundamental questions concerning organizational behavior, entry, competition, and innovation. But which of them accords most closely with what is known about spin-offs?

In the last 20 years, empirical studies of entrepreneurship, especially of high-growth and high-tech start-ups, have mushroomed. Few studies, though, have focused narrowly on spin-offs. Perhaps fuelled by this void, new theories have been crafted and others adapted to explain spin-offs. In the last year or so, a flurry of new empirical studies, still in working paper form, of high-tech spin-offs (Chesbrough, 2000; Chesbrough and Rosenbloom, 2000; Franco and Filson, 2000; Klepper and Sleeper, 2000) and a new book on high-growth start-ups (Bhide, 2000) have added considerably to our understanding of spin-offs. Coupled with prior work, a picture is beginning to emerge about the forces governing spin-offs and their social implications. The purpose of this chapter is to bring this picture into focus.

The various theoretical perspectives bearing on spin-offs are first discussed. Distinctive implications of each concerning the initial strategies of spin-offs, the firms most likely to spawn them, their timing, and their performance are assembled. The empirical evidence from the spin-off studies and those of high-tech and high-growth start-ups of all kinds is then used to assess these implications. The evidence suggests the importance of spin-offs exploiting skills their founders acquired in their prior employment. A theory marrying the concepts of reproduction and inheritance with the evolutionary modelling of organizations pioneered by Nelson and Winter (1982) is fashioned to provide a novel interpretation of the empirical findings. The theory is used to address the social implications of spin-offs regarding technological change, highlighting themes about diversity and duplication of effort raised by Dick Nelson in his various writings about capitalism as an engine of progress (Nelson, 1981, 1990, 1991). Further explorations that could fill in important gaps in our knowledge about spin-offs are discussed in the conclusion.

8.2   Theoretical Perspectives

A number of theories have been developed to account for spin-offs. They are not, however, the only theories that can explain spin-offs. Small and large firms have often been observed to specialize in different types of innovations. Relatedly, certain types of innovations seem to pose problems for larger incumbent firms and cause the leaders of industries to be displaced. While theories designed to address these phenomena have not been designed to explain spin-offs, it seems reasonable to imagine that the same types of innovations that small firms specialize in or that are difficult for incumbent firms to master could provide distinctive opportunities for spin-offs. As such, these theories are reviewed along with those that directly address spin-offs.

Four theoretical perspectives are distinguished. In the first one, spin-offs are modelled as capitalizing on discoveries that employees make in the course of their employment in incumbent firms. Various types of agency costs associated with innovations impede employees from contracting with their firms to develop the discoveries, leading to spin-offs. In the second perspective, spin-offs are portrayed as developing innovations that incumbents are slow to pursue because of organizational limitations. Different theories stress different kinds of innovations that challenge incumbent capabilities, but the common perspective of these theories is that these difficulties create opportunities for spin-offs. The third perspective stresses the connection between spin-offs and employee learning. Spin-offs are viewed as exploiting knowledge their founders learned in their prior employment to compete with their employers and other firms in their industry. In the last theoretical perspective, predictions about spin-offs are developed based on analogizing spin-offs to children. Each perspective is reviewed in turn.

8.2.1   Agency Theories

Three agency theories are reviewed. The first, by Wiggins (1995), develops a model to explain why certain types of innovations would be developed by smaller, owner-managed firms rather than larger firms in which ownership and control are separated. Many spin-offs are initially managed by their owners, and thus Wiggins' model provides a natural way to explain spin-offs. The second theory that is reviewed, by Anton and Yao (1995), develops a model that is designed to explain spin-offs. Although beginning from a somewhat different vantage point, it yields very similar implications to Wiggins (1995). The third theory, by Bankman and Gilson (1999), addresses why start-ups of any kind are ever financed by venture capitalists.

The theories share a common premise. They imagine that an employee makes a valuable discovery while working for an incumbent firm. The classic case is an R&D employee that comes across a valuable idea or invention. The discovery is known initially only by the employee, although in Anton and Yao (1995) the firm may later learn it. Neither party can establish property rights to the discovery. The discovery can be more profitably developed by the employer than a firm started by the employee, reflecting scale, scope, tax, or other informational advantages that would also make it optimal socially for the employer to develop the discovery. Asymmetric information pertaining to the discovery impedes the ability of the employee to contract with the employer to develop it. In each model, the analysis focuses on when it is more profitable for the employee to develop the discovery in his or her own firm rather than contracting with the employer to develop it.

In Wiggins (1995), effort by the employee must be expended in order for the discovery to be developed. The employer can only observe if the development is successful, which requires both effort by the employee and luck. To motivate the employee to expend effort, the employer offers the employee a payment per unit of development time based on the profits from the development. The share of the profits offered to the employee is greater the lower the probability of successful development of the discovery to compensate for the greater risk of failure. Wiggins assumes that if the discovery is successful, the employer can exploit its legal control over the firm and its accounts to cause the profits associated with the discovery to appear to be zero. The only deterrent against doing this is that in the extreme no one will work for the firm, causing it to lose any future profits from its invested capital. The analysis focuses on the kinds of discoveries for which the benefits of misrepresenting profits as zero exceed the costs. These discoveries will be developed by employee-owned firms and hence could provide the impetus for spin-offs.

Key factors include the length of time it takes to develop the discovery, the probability of successful development and the capital intensity of the employer's business. No payment is made until the development of the discovery is completed and the employer can tell if it has been successful. Therefore, the length of the development period conditions the payment owed to the employee. So does the probability of successful development, with the payment greater the lower the probability of success. The amount of future profit the employer will forfeit if no one works for it is proportional to the amount of capital invested. Therefore, the employer will be more likely to renege on its payment to the employee on discoveries that take longer to develop, are riskier, and that involve less capital-intensive businesses. Wiggins identifies the first two conditions with path-breaking innovations and innovations that open up new lines of business, which can take a long time to judge if successful. Hence, these are the kinds of innovations that employees can do better by developing them in their own firms, suggesting that spin-offs will specialize in path-breaking innovations and ones opening new submarkets within an industry.

In Anton and Yao (1995), even if the employee does not reveal his or her discovery to the employer, the employer may subsequently learn it on its own. The source of the firm's discovery cannot be determined objectively, so the firm can only contract to pay the employee based on whether it learns the discovery. In contrast to Wiggins (1995), there is no uncertainty regarding the value of a discovery nor any difficulty in enforcing a contract concerning payment for learning the discovery, but the employer cannot determine if any particular employee has made a (valuable) discovery before it is revealed. The employee has three options: contract with the firm to reveal his/her discovery and not develop it in his/her own firm, reveal the discovery and contract with the firm not to develop it in his/her own firm, or develop it in his/her own firm.

If an employee has not made a discovery (but another has) and he/she contracts with an employer to reveal this discovery, the employer will still have to pay the employee if it learns the discovery on its own. To discourage contracting by employees who have not made discoveries, contracts will have to stipulate a payment by the employee to the employer if the latter does not learn a discovery. This requires the employee to have sufficient wealth to fund such a payment, on the order of the R&D budget needed to learn the discovery. If path-breaking innovations require greater R&D budgets, contracts for path-breaking innovations will not occur, and, similar to Wiggins, such innovations will lead to spin-offs.

Even without sufficient wealth, an employee could choose to reveal voluntarily a valuable discovery and then contract with the employer not to start his/her own firm in competition with the employer. If the employer's advantage in developing the innovation were sufficiently great, the reduced profits experienced by the employer from competition would exceed the profits the employee could make by developing the discovery in his/her own firm. Otherwise, it would always pay the employee to develop the discovery in his/her own firm. Employers will have larger advantages in developing innovations that exploit distinctive complementary assets they possess, making such innovations more amenable to contracting. Consequently, innovations that do not require distinctive complementary assets would be more likely to lead to spin-offs. Anton and Yao note that innovations opening up new submarkets not serviced by incumbents are likely to make less use of employer complementary assets. Hence, by a different route, they end up at the same place as Wiggins – path-breaking innovations and innovations opening up new submarkets will lead to spin-offs.

Anton and Yao discuss why contracting with a venture capital firm is not likely to solve contracting problems with employers. Thus, if the contracting problems are not sufficiently serious to undermine contracting with the employer, why would spin-offs financed by venture capitalists ever occur? Stated alternatively, if employers have advantages over venture capitalists in developing discoveries, why would venture capitalists ever outbid employers to develop employee discoveries? This is the question addressed by Bankman and Gilson (1999).

Their answer derives from the activities employees engage in to maintain rights to a discovery. They need to devote effort to preventing other employees from learning of their discovery, which directly reduces the effort they devote to their employer's goals. It may also reduce the productivity of other employees that could benefit from knowing the discovery. If employers always outbid venture capitalists for discoveries, employees would never have to bear the risk of starting their own, venture-capital-backed firms. If employers bid less than venture capitalists to develop ideas, however, Bankman and Gilson assume more risk-averse employees would still contract with the employer. They further assume that with less compensation for discoveries, such employees would expend less effort to keep their discoveries secret, yielding savings to employers. Not knowing which employees are more risk averse, Bankman and Gilson argue that the optimal firm policy would be to bid less than venture capitalists to develop ideas, balancing the loss of projects with the savings from less employee effort devoted to keeping discoveries secret. Less risk-averse employees would then opt for venture-capital-backed spin-offs. Similar to Wiggins and Anton and Yao, innovative discoveries lead to spin-offs, but it is the nature of the discoverer and not the innovation that conditions whether a spin-off occurs.

The main implication of the agency theories is that the impetus for spin-offs is the development of particular innovations. In Anton and Yao (1995) and Bankman and Gilson (1999) the innovations grow out of research undertaken by the parents of the spin-offs. Presumably, these will be innovations that relate to their parents' activities, although the models of Wiggins and Anton and Yao suggest the innovations are more likely to be path-breaking or ones that open new submarkets. The parents may also develop the innovations depending on whether they make the requisite discovery themselves, in which case the spin-offs will compete directly with their parents. At a minimum, the spin-offs will develop innovations their parents would also be interested in pursuing.

8.2.2 Organizational Capability Theories

Another way to explain spin-offs is by focusing on difficulties encountered by incumbent firms, which provide opportunities for new firms to enter an industry. If the incumbent's difficulties are organizational in nature, individual employees would not be plagued by the same difficulties and would be natural candidates to start new firms to take advantage of the opportunities missed by incumbents. Various theories of this ilk are reviewed in order to generate predictions concerning spin-offs.

Organizational difficulties can be caused by many factors. Rather than delve into the causes, one way to conceptualize organizational difficulties is simply to accept that periodically organizations undergo crises. Cooper (1985, p. 79) conjectures that organizations undergoing crises would be likely sources of spin-offs and thus will have higher rates of spin-offs. Brittain and Freeman (1986) associate crises with a firm being taken over by a firm from another industry, by a new CEO being hired from outside the firm, or by a slowdown in the firm's rate of growth. They conjecture that each of these factors will increase a firm's spin-off rate.

Most of the theories that attempt to explain the decline of industry leaders implicate certain types of innovations as especially difficult for incumbent firms to evaluate and implement. Henderson and Clark (1990) feature the challenges posed by 'architectural' innovations that alter the way the components of a product are configured. Tushman and Anderson (1986) feature 'competence-destroying' innovations whose development requires competencies not possessed by established firms. Christensen (1993) features innovations that appeal to new users of a product, which pose problems for established firms because of their undue reliance on their own customers for feedback on innovations.[1] Bhide (2001) argues that established firms have a comparative advantage in pursuing less-ambiguous projects and screen out ideas that are more difficult to lay out in a business plan. As long as such projects require modest initial capital that can be financed by employees and their family and friends (who are especially well positioned to evaluate the skills and judgement of the employees), they will provide distinctive opportunities for spin-offs.

These theories thus have implications regarding the types of activities spin-offs will initially pursue, the kinds of organizations that will spawn them, and the relationship of spin-offs with their parents prior to their formation. They imply spin-offs will pursue particular types of innovations – architectural, competence-destroying, opening new submarkets, or ones involving modest capital and vague business plans. Most imply that organizations spawning spin-offs have or will experience difficulty. They all suggest that founders of spin-offs will have been frustrated with their prior employers' unwillingness to pursue ideas they perceived to be promising. All the theories imply spin-offs will develop innovations their parents do not want to pursue, suggesting that parents will not initially perceive spin-offs as a competitive threat.

8.2.3   Employee-Learning Theories

A number of theories discuss the role that employee learning plays in spin-offs. Two proposed models of spin-offs that feature employee learning, while others offer conjectures about employee learning and spin-offs.

Franco and Filson (2000) develop a model of industry evolution in which the only entry is by spin-offs. Firms produce a homogeneous product but differ in the quality of their technical knowledge, with more knowledgeable firms having higher profits and longer expected survival. Firms hire R&D workers to try to improve their knowledge. Each R&D worker has an exogenous probability of learning his or her firm's knowledge. The only way an R&D worker can capitalize on this knowledge is by starting his/her own firm, which is profitable as long as the firm's knowledge is sufficiently good. The better a firm's knowledge, then the lower the wage R&D workers will accept to work for the firm because of the greater prospects of starting their own firm, which enables firms to appropriate the full expected value of their R&D. The model implies that more knowledgeable firms will spawn more spin-offs. It also implies that initially spin-offs will use the same technology as their parents and thus will produce identical products to their parents. Spin-offs will initially have the same expected profits and survival prospects as their parents, thus more innovative and long-lived parents will have more innovative and long-lived spin-offs.

Klepper and Sleeper (2000) also feature learning in a model of a differentiated product industry. To develop a variant of an industry's product, firms must make an investment in R&D and marketing know-how. Assuming all firms charge the same price, buyers purchase the variant that comes closest to their ideal type. Depending on their backgrounds, some firms invest in multiple variants that do not directly compete with each other. A firm and its employees that work on a particular product variant learn from the firm's R&D and marketing efforts, enabling them to develop a related variant at a cost less than the initial one. Firms initially choose product variants that leave no room for profitable entry by non-spin-offs, but spin-offs can enter because they have lower costs and thus need less market share than non-spin-offs to be profitable. Similar to Bankman and Gilson (1999), it is assumed that many employees do not have the inclination or organizational skills to start their own firm, but those that do will exploit the available opportunities for spin-offs by entering with a product similar to one they worked on for their firm. They will differentiate their product from their firm's to render retaliation by their firm unprofitable. Incumbent firms have the same capabilities as spin-offs and could pre-empt them. As long as the probability of firms having employees with the requisite organizational skills and inclination to start their own firms is sufficiently low, however, the costs of pre-emption will exceed the expected benefits, and firms will be better off gambling that they will not lose market share to spin-offs.

Klepper and Sleeper's model has a number of implications for spin-offs. Spin-offs produce a product similar to, but differentiated from, that of their parents. They have a smaller market than their parents – they produce one of possibly multiple product variants produced by their parents, and they have a lower initial market share than the related product of their parents. Their product is sufficiently differentiated not to jeopardize the viability of their parents' related market. Their parents could have but will not produce the spin-off's product variant because it would cannibalize its own market, suggesting a tension between the founders of spin-offs and their parents prior to the formation of the spin-offs. Each product variant produced by a firm is an independent source of spin-offs, so the broader the product line of a firm, then the greater the number of spin-offs it would be expected to spawn. The richer a firm's know-how associated with a product variant, the lower the organizational skills required for employees to start profitably a spin-off and thus the greater the expected number of spin-offs from the firm producing a related product variant. Finally, after the initial entry of firms, unexpected demand growth would be needed to induce entry of non-spin-offs but not spin-offs, whereas an unexpected decline in demand would not affect non-spin-off entry (because it was already expected to be zero) but could compromise the profitability of spin-off entry, suggesting that spin-offs will be more responsive to unfavorable than favorable entry conditions.[2]

Other theories do not involve full models of spin-offs but offer conjectures that relate to employee learning. Garvin (1983, p. 12) notes that a firm's knowledge must be embodied in human versus physical capital for it to be accessible to employees. Based on the logic of the product life cycle (cf. Klepper, 1996), he conjectures that as industries mature, firms devote more effort to improving the production process and know-how becomes more embodied in physical capital, lowering the rate of spin-offs. Cooper (1985, p. 78) conjectures that since spin-offs typically start off small, smaller firms will provide more useful lessons for employees to start their own firms, implying that smaller firms will have higher spin-off rates per employee. Some have speculated that in regions with more firms in an industry, the spin-off rate will be higher because of the greater supply of knowledgeable employees needed to form organizational and initial management teams (Garvin, 1983, p. 8; Cooper, 1985, p. 79). Cooper (1985, p. 78) also sees the breadth of knowledge of the founders of a spin-off as a key factor conditioning its performance.

Thus, employee-learning theories have implications regarding the initial strategies of spin-offs, the types of firms that spawn them, the market conditions conducive to their formation, and the factors that condition their performance. They envision spin-offs either pursuing the same overall strategy as their parents or focusing on one of their parents' activities. Consequently, they will either compete directly with their parents or more narrowly in one of their parents' activities. In the latter case, however, they will pursue ideas their parents do not want to pursue and as such might have been a source of tension, and they will distance themselves from their parents in a way that will not directly threaten them. More innovative and successful firms, and possibly firms with a broader product line, will be richer learning environments and thus will spawn more spin-offs. While such firms might be expected to be larger, smaller firms might serve as a more useful role model and could spawn more spin-offs per employee. Employees may learn more in industries with less-mature technologies and it may be easier for them to act on what they learn in regions with a greater density of firms, so both conditions might be more conducive to spin-offs. Favorable conditions for entry might not be a prerequisite for spin-offs but unfavorable entry conditions could compromise spin-offs. Finally, more innovative and successful firms will breed more progressive and better-performing spin-offs.

8.2.4   *Theories of the Heritage of Spin-offs*

The last category of theories is not very well developed. It does, however, suggest a couple of interesting predictions.

It is predicated on the idea of spin-offs having a heritage, with spin-offs conceptualized as children and the employers of their founders as parents. Using this perspective, Dyck (1997) makes a distinction that is not prominent in the other spin-off theories, namely that some spin-offs are planned in the sense that their parents are supportive and helpful. Parental involvement and support is generally helpful to children, suggesting by analogy that planned spin-offs will outperform unplanned ones.[3] Cooper and Gimeno-Gascon (1992) also conjecture that a spin-off's heritage will affect its performance. Spin-offs with more founders that worked together in

the same parent organization are expected to have more valuable experience
to draw upon, leading to better performance.

8.2.5   Summary

The main implications of the various theories are brought together in Table
8.1. They are summarized along four dimensions – the nature of the spin-
offs, the kinds of firms that are parents of spin-offs, the timing of the spin-
offs and the performance of the spin-offs – with each dimension further
broken down into subsidiary categories.

The first dimension concerns the nature of spin-offs, including their initial
strategy, market focus, and relationship with their parents. The agency and

TABLE 8.1 *Predictions of the theories*

Nature of spin-offs

Initial strategy

Develop distinctive innovations	Tushman and Anderson (1986), Henderson and Clark (1990), Christensen (1993), Anton and Yao (1995), Wiggins (1995)
Develop innovations with vague business plan, modest capital	Bhide (2001)
Develop innovations of any kind financed by venture capital	Bankman and Gilson (1999)
Copy parent's technology	Franco and Filson (2000)
Develop variant of parent's product with small initial market	Klepper and Sleeper (2000)

Initial market focus

New submarket	Christensen (1993), Anton and Yao (1995), Wiggins (1995)
Same as parent	Franco and Filson (2000)
Variant of parent's product	Klepper and Sleeper (2000)

Relationship with parent

Frustration before formation of spin-off	Tushman and Anderson (1986), Henderson and Clark (1990), Christensen (1993), Cooper (1985), Klepper and Sleeper (2000)
Pose no initial threat to parent	Tushman and Anderson (1986), Henderson and Clark (1990), Christensen (1993), Klepper and Sleeper (2000)
Direct challenge to parent	Franco and Filson (2000)
Possible aid from parent	Dyck (1997)

Parents

Innovativeness/ success
Above average   Franco and Filson (2000), Klepper and
                                           Sleeper (2000)

Slow to pursue new submarkets   Christensen (1993)
Soon to lose market share   Tushman and Anderson (1986),
                                           Henderson and Clark (1990)
Recent crisis, change in leadership,   Cooper (1985), Brittain and Freeman
  slowed growth   (1986)

Breadth of product offerings
Above average   Klepper and Sleeper (2000)

Size
Smaller firms have more spin-offs per   Cooper (1985)
  employee

Location
Higher spin-off rate of firms in densely Garvin (1983), Cooper (1985)
  populated regions

Timing of spin-offs

Characteristics of market
Spin-offs greater in younger, less-mature Garvin (1983)
  markets

Entry conditions
High rate of creation of new submarkets Garvin (1983), Christensen (1993),
  raises spin-off rate   Anton and Yao (1995), Wiggins (1995)
Conditions favoring non-spin-off entry   Klepper and Sleeper (2000)
  have less effect on spin-offs than
  conditions adverse to non-spin-off
  entry

Spin-off performance

Parent and spin-off performance
Positively related   Franco and Filson (2000), Klepper and
                                           Sleeper (2000)

Parental involvement
Helpful to spin-off   Dyck (1997)

Founding team
Multiple founders that worked together   Cooper (1985)
  in same organization improves spin-off
  performance

organizational capability theories imply that spin-offs will initially develop some kind of innovation. In most of these theories the innovation is distinctive, although Bankman and Gilson (1999) stress the distinctiveness of the innovators rather than the innovations and in Bhide's (2001) theory the ideas pursued by spin-offs are neither well spelled out nor involve much capital. The learning theories, in contrast, predict spin-offs will produce the same or a subset of the products of their parents. Regarding their initial market focus, the theories of Anton and Yao (1995), Wiggins (1995), and especially Christensen (1993) predict that spin-offs will enter new submarkets, while the learning theories predict spin-offs will initially occupy the same or a subset of their parents' markets. The organizational capability theories and the learning theory of Klepper and Sleeper (2000) predict that prior to their formation, the founders of spin-offs will be frustrated with their parents. These theories also imply that parents will not initially be threatened by their spin-offs because they either could not or would not have chosen to do the same things as their spin-offs. In contrast, the learning theory of Franco and Filson (2000) implies spin-offs will directly challenge their parents, whereas Dyck's (1997) theory suggests that some spin-offs will actually be aided by their parents.

The second dimension in Table 8.1 concerns the nature of the firms that spawn spin-offs. The learning theories predict that more innovative and successful firms will spawn more spin-offs, whereas the theories featuring limits on organizational decision making imply that firms spawning more spin-offs will recently have experienced crises or will subsequently decline. The learning theory of Klepper and Sleeper (2000) predicts that firms with a broader product line within an industry will spawn more spin-offs, Cooper (1985) predicts that smaller firms will spawn more spin-offs per employee, and a few theories emphasize the importance of regional conditions for spin-off rates.

The third dimension concerns the timing of spin-offs. Garvin (1983) predicts a higher spin-off rate in younger, less-mature markets. The various theories that associate spin-offs with new submarkets, including Garvin (1983), Christensen (1993), Anton and Yao (1995), and Wiggins (1995), imply that a high rate of creation of new submarkets will lead to a greater rate of spin-offs. The learning theory of Klepper and Sleeper (2000) implies that conditions favorable to non-spin-off entry will have less impact than unfavorable conditions on the rate of spin-offs.

The last dimension concerns the performance of spin-offs. The learning theories of Franco and Filson (2000) and Klepper and Sleeper (2000) predict a positive relationship between a parent and spin-off's performance. Dyck (1997) suggests that parental involvement in spin-offs will improve their performance. Cooper (1985) predicts that spin-offs with teams of founders that worked together in the same organization will perform better than spin-offs with either single founders or founders that did not work together.

8.3   The Evidence

Two sets of studies concerning high-tech spin-offs are reviewed. The first set includes Brittain and Freeman (1986), Franco and Filson (2000), and Klepper and Sleeper (2000). These studies analyse, respectively, spin-offs of Silicon Valley semiconductor producers in 1955–1981, US commercial rigid-disk drive producers in 1977–1997, and US commercial laser producers in 1961–1994. All the producers and their spin-offs are identified using business directories, trade sources, and genealogical trees, which are also the sources for more detailed information about spin-offs and their parents. All three studies examine the factors that influenced the rate at which firms spawned spin-offs. Franco and Filson also analyse the performance of disk-drive spin-offs and their parents, and Klepper and Sleeper examine the initial strategies of the laser spin-offs and the relationship of the spin-offs to their parents.

The second set of studies also focus on high-tech spin-offs. They do not develop databases that are as comprehensive about spin-offs as the first set, but use both interviews and archival sources to collect detailed information about both spin-offs and sometimes other types of start-ups. Christensen (1993) chronicles in considerable detail the evolution of the hard disk-drive industry from its inception through 1989, which serves as a useful supplement to Franco and Filson's study. Boeker (1988) analyses 51 semiconductor firms in Silicon Valley, 45 of which were spin-offs. He considers how their initial strategies were influenced by the strategies of their parents and the functional specialties of their founders. Chesbrough (2000) analyses how the performance of 35 planned spin-offs from Xerox was influenced by Xerox's involvement in managing them, and Chesbrough and Rosenbloom (2000) consider the performance of six of the spin-offs in greater detail. Walsh *et al.* (1996) analyse the factors that influenced the performance of 35 start-ups, most of which were spin-offs, in the semiconductor silicon industry over its 45-year history. Last, a genealogical tree of San Diego biotechnology firms compiled by Mitton (1990) is used to make some computations about biotech spin-offs.

The information from these studies is supplemented by numerous studies of high-tech and high-growth start-ups. Three studies that collected detailed information from interviews and archival sources are particularly informative. Cooper (1971) studies the origins of approximately 250 high-tech start-ups in Silicon Valley in the 1960s, which covered all the high-tech start-ups he could find there. Roberts (1991) examines the origins, decisions, evolution, and performance of high-tech spin-offs from MIT, including the MIT labs, and from firms located in Boston and elsewhere. Finally, Bhide (2000) examines the origins, strategy, evolution, and performance of a large sample of high-growth start-ups from predominantly the fastest growing firms in *Inc.* magazine.

The evidence from the various studies is reviewed following the organization of Table 8.1.

8.3.1   Nature of Spin-offs

The laser study addresses each of the three issues concerning the nature of spin-offs in Table 8.1 and is thus considered first. A total of 465 firms were studied, of which 79 were spin-offs. Data were compiled for each producer on which of nine major types of lasers it produced each year. Most of the spin-offs initially produced only one of the nine types of lasers. Only 13 of the 79 spin-offs initially produced a laser type that its parent had not already produced, and in seven of these cases the parent produced or researched the laser for itself or the military before its spin-off (but did not produce it commercially before its spin-off). Only nine parents provided any help to their spin-offs, so the overlap between the lasers of the spin-offs and their parents was not due to the involvement of the parents. The average firm produced only two lasers over its lifetime, so the overlap was also unlikely to be due to chance. It appears that spin-offs entered independently of their parents producing a product similar to one produced by their parents. Although some of the nine laser types were developed after the start of the industry and created new uses for lasers, few spin-offs produced these (or any other) of the lasers before their parents, suggesting that spin-offs did not generally focus on new submarkets.

Detailed data were collected on the initial products and strategies of about 30 of the spin-offs. Most tended either to do contract research or produce a custom variant of one of their parent's lasers or to produce a higher or lower power version of their parent's laser. Few began with anything that could be called a significant innovation. Consistent with such modest strategies, few parents discontinued production of their spin-off's initial laser after the formation of the spin-off, and only two instances were found of parents suing their spin-offs.

The pattern in disk drives is somewhat different. Franco and Filson report a number of examples of spin-offs incorporating distinctive technological features of their parents' drives in their own. They also acknowledge, however, that a number of spin-offs entered new submarkets before their parents. Christensen (1993) provides detailed information about thisphenomenon. Three new submarkets for disk drives emerged corresponding to the shrinking of disk drives initially from 14 to 8 in., then from 8 to 5.25 in., and then from 5.25 to 3.5 in. Each smaller drive was purchased by manufacturers of smaller computers – first minis, then personal computers, and then notebooks and laptops. Of the 39 start-ups that entered between 1973 and 1989, most of which were spin-offs, 21 initially entered a new submarket, and, according to Christensen, generally before their parents. He claims that the smaller drives did not pose the kind of technical challenges to incumbents envisioned in architectural and competence-destroying innovations. They were not costly to develop, the incumbents were the first to develop prototypes of the new drives, and the incumbents introduced state-of-the art versions of the drives when they finally introduced them. Rather, he attributes the slow response of incumbents to relying too centrally on their customers for feedback about the new drives. Whatever the reason, it appears that approximately half the disk-drive spin-offs pursued a distinctive innovation that opened up a new submarket. This contrasts sharply with lasers.

The initial strategies of Silicon Valley semiconductor producers were analysed in Boeker (1988).[4] Firms were classified according to whether they pursued a strategy of being a product innovator, fast follower, low-cost producer, or niche producer. The prior positions of founders were determined, with those in technical positions predicted to be more likely to pursue a product-innovation strategy, those in production positions predicted to pursue a low-cost producer strategy, and those in marketing and sales predicted to pursue either a fast follower or niche strategy. The initial strategy of spin-offs was influenced by their parent's strategy, but the strongest influence on their initial strategy was exerted by their founder's prior position in the industry. This suggests that in devising their initial strategies spin-offs drew primarily on the prior functional experiences of their founders rather than the technologies of their parents.

The broader literature on high-tech and high-growth start-ups provides a useful backdrop to the findings from the laser, disk-drive, and semiconductor industries. Similar to lasers, most studies find a close correspondence between the markets served and technologies used by start-ups and their parents (Cooper, 1984, pp. 160–161). Cooper (1971, p. 19), for example, reports that 85.5 per cent of the high-tech start-ups in Silicon Valley in the 1960s produced for a similar market or used a similar technology to their parents. Also similar to lasers, many high-tech and high-growth start-ups began by doing either contract research or custom production or by producing only a modestly different product from their parents (Braden, 1977, pp. 27–29; Roberts, 1991, pp. 166–168; Bhide, 2000, p. 32). Another common finding, which was not analysed in any of the spin-off studies, is that a majority of founders report being frustrated with their prior employers due to their ideas being rejected or to what they perceived to be bad management (Cooper, 1971, p. 23; Amit and Muller, 1994; Bhide, 2000, p. 57).[5] Finally, consistent with Boeker's findings for the semiconductor industry, Roberts (1991, pp. 104–106) finds that founders of spin-offs that had worked at the MIT labs did not often directly transfer technology they worked on at the labs but generally indicated that an important aspect of their spin-off's work was based on technologies they learned at the lab.

These findings suggest that, with the exception of about half of the disk-drive producers, spin-offs did not generally introduce significant innovations in their products, nor did they pursue very ambitious strategies. They produced products closely related to ones their parents produced, or in the case of disk drives ones their parents apparently developed but chose not to produce. They relied less on distinctive technologies of their parents and more on the experiences of their founders to craft their initial strategies. Finally, although they did not appear to be terribly innovative or challenging to the competitive positions of their parents, founders of spin-offs commonly reported frustration with their parents as a major reason for leaving to start their own firms.

8.3.2   Parents

One of the strengths of the three spin-off studies is that they have a natural comparison group for the firms that spawned spin-offs, namely the firms that did not spawn spin-offs. All three studies exploit this by estimating logit, probit, and hazard models of the determinants of firm spin-off rates.

In disk drives, the firms with superior technology, measured by the density of information that could be stored per square inch, and the firms that were first to produce the smaller disk drives spawned more spin-offs (Franco and Filson, 2000). In semiconductors, early producers in major product groups also spawned more spin-offs (Brittain and Freeman, 1986). In lasers, longer-lived firms spawned more spin-offs. The primary reason is that the rate of spin-offs increased sharply with the years a firm produced a laser through year 14, after which it declined, and only the more successful firms had production runs of 14 or more (Klepper and Sleeper, 2000).[6] Calculations for San Diego biotech firms indicate a similar rise in the rate of spin-offs through their first 10 years (this was the maximum age of firms in the sample).

While these findings suggest that more innovative and successful firms spawned more spin-offs, they do not preclude the possibility that parents may have been declining or about to decline when they spawned their spin-offs. Brittain and Freeman (1986) provide some support for this in semiconductors. They find that the lower a firm's recent growth rate relative to its historical rate, the greater its rate of spin-offs. In contrast, Franco and Filson (2000) find that a firm's growth rate did not negatively affect its spin-off rate in the disk-drive industry. Klepper and Sleeper (2000) analyse the extent to which the period right after a firm ceased producing a type of laser was a fertile period for spin-offs. They find this to be a particularly infertile period, with spin-off rates as low as when firms first began producing the laser. According to Brittain and Freeman (1986), other possible indicators of crises include a firm being taken over by another from outside its industry, a new CEO coming from outside the firm, or a slowed rate of growth, all of which they find increased the spin-off rate of semiconductor firms. Klepper and Sleeper (2000), however, find that acquisitions by either laser or non-laser firms increased a firm's spin-off rate comparably, and many of the firms acquired by laser companies were successful. Moreover, the laser firms that spawned the most spin-offs were the most successful firms in the industry, and they spawned spin-offs throughout their lifetimes.

Both Brittain and Freeman (1986) and Klepper and Sleeper (2000) analyse whether semiconductor and laser firms with broader product lines spawned more spin-offs.[7] Both find that they did. Klepper and Sleeper analyse this further by looking separately at how the rate at which firms spawned spin-offs producing particular lasers was affected by the firm's experience producing that same laser versus all other lasers. They find only the former mattered. This suggests that spin-offs drew on targeted knowledge of their parents, and each distinct laser a firm produced was an independent source of spin-offs.

Franco and Filson (2000) examine whether the size of disk-drive producers affected their spin-off rate, which it did not. This corresponds to the mixed findings that have been reported concerning the effect of firm size on the spin-off rate of firms per employee (Feeser and Willard, 1989, p. 432). Klepper and Sleeper analysed how the location of firms affected their spin-off rate. The most densely populated area of laser producers is Silicon Valley, which contained about 15 per cent of the producers and accounted for almost 30 per cent of the spin-offs. Even after controlling for all other factors, firms in Silicon Valley still had a higher rate of spin-offs than firms located elsewhere, although firms in other densely populated areas did not have above average spin-off rates. Among the 23 spin-offs with parents in Silicon Valley, 20 also located in Silicon Valley,[8] suggesting that spin-offs may have played an important role in the concentration of the industry around Silicon Valley.

The evidence strongly indicates that firms with richer and broader knowledge spawned more spin-offs. Even in the disk-drive industry, where a substantial fraction of firms entered new submarkets before their parents, the better disk-drive firms spawned more spin-offs, suggesting that even spin-offs entering new submarkets exploited knowledge from their parents. The higher rate of spin-offs in acquired firms is an intriguing finding, and it is not clear how this fits with the rest of the evidence. The sharp rise in the spin-off rate in both laser and biotechnology firms through middle age is also an intriguing finding, as is the finding in lasers of a pronounced decline in the spin-off rate after firms passed through middle age. The initial rise may reflect that learning increases over time, which is consistent with Robert's (1991, pp. 110–111) findings that spin-off founders with longer tenure at the MIT labs exploited their lab experience in their spin-offs to a greater degree. The decline in the spin-off rate after a certain age is more challenging to explain, but it may reflect that if workers have not left after a certain point, they are unlikely ever to leave. This merits further investigation.

8.3.3   Timing of Spin-offs

Garvin (1983) argues from anecdotal evidence that spin-offs are more likely in young industries that do not use capital-intensive production methods. Klepper and Sleeper analyse this in lasers. Consistent with Garvin's findings, they find a sharp fall off over time in the spin-off rate in the two (of the nine) laser types that were eventually produced in the largest volumes and had the most attention devoted to improving their production processes.

Both Brittain and Freeman (1986) and Klepper and Sleeper (2000) analyse how entry conditions affected the spin-off rate. Brittain and Freeman found no clear effect of the overall entry or exit rate on the spin-off rate in semiconductors. Klepper and Sleeper probe this further in the laser industry by dividing the non-spin-off entry rate into two variables, one for above-average values and the other for below-average values. They find that the former had little effect but the latter a strong positive effect on the spin-off rate, consistent with unfavorable entry conditions having more effect than favorable conditions on the spin-off rate.

8.3.4.   Performance of Spin-offs

The only one of the three spin-off studies that analyses the performance of the spin-offs is Franco and Filson (2000). Two models are estimated. One is a probit model of the probability of spin-offs surviving the next year, with all firm-years pooled. The other is a hazard model of the length of survival of spin-offs. In the probit model, the richness of the spin-off's technology, but not whether it was a first mover, increased its survival probability. Although its parent's technology and whether it was a first mover were not expected to influence the spin-off's survival after controlling for the spin-off's technology and first-mover status, the parent's technology was negatively related to and its first-mover status was positively related to its spin-off's survival probability. In the hazard model, the spin-off's survival was modelled as a function of the parent's technology, first-mover status and sales growth rate at the time of its spin-off, and also whether the founder of the spin-off had founded a prior disk-drive firm. Similar to the probit estimates, the early-mover variable was positively related to the spin-off's survival probability, as was the growth variable, whereas the technology variable was negatively related to the spin-off's survival probability. Prior founding experience did not affect the spin-off's length of survival, which is consistent with prior findings (Schollhammer, 1991; Starr and Bygrave, 1991; Walsh et al., 1996, p. 150).

These findings are mixed concerning the connection between the performance of spin-offs and their parents. This may partly reflect the unexpected way the industry developed. The new, smaller drives that were pioneered by some of the spin-offs were improved at a sufficiently rapid rate that producers of the drives ended up dominating the industry. Consequently, anything that influenced whether a spin-off was an early producer of a new drive enhanced its survival. Franco and Filson (2000) show that early-mover parents were more likely to spawn early-mover spin-offs, which could explain the greater longevity of spin-offs from early mover parents. The results concerning the technology variable are harder to explain, but the failure of this variable to play its predicted role is consistent with the findings reviewed earlier that suggest that spin-offs rely primarily on the specific experiences of their founders rather than the technology of their parents. There were too few disk-drive start-ups that were not spin-offs for Franco and Filson to test whether spin-offs survived longer than other types of start-ups. Sleeper (1998) analyses this for lasers, and finds that spin-offs survived much longer than other kinds of start-ups and survived comparably to the most qualified experienced entrants. Walsh *et al.* (1996) similarly find that start-ups in the semiconductor silicon industry whose founders had industry experience and training and/or experience in materials survived longer. Thus, having founders with industry experience appears to enhance the performance of spin-offs.

Chesbrough's (2000) findings concerning Xerox's planned spin-offs provide a further idea about why a parent's technical knowledge might not positively affect the performance of its spin-offs. Xerox's spin-offs were constituted as separate firms to develop technologies that did not fit into Xerox's main businesses. They varied in terms of the share of their equity held by Xerox, the number of non-Xerox members on the board of directors, whether their initial CEO was from Xerox, and whether they sold their products through Xerox's salesforce. Spin-offs with a smaller number of outside directors, a Xerox CEO and that sold through Xerox's saleforce had lower initial growth rates, suggesting that Xerox's involvement in its spin-offs was harmful. This may reflect the need for many new businesses to change their strategy in response to initial feedback, which could be inhibited by too much reliance on a parent's mindset and technology (cf. Chesbrough and Rosenbloom, 2000). Indeed, this is one of Bhide's (2000, pp. 53–68) main findings. Even the most successful firms in his sample often began with little in the way of substantive business plans or capital. In many instances, they discovered something unexpected after starting their businesses that prompted a substantial reorientation of their activities. Bhide finds that an important trait that distinguished successful entrepreneurs was their ability to adapt opportunistically to unexpected developments. It is not much of a leap to imagine that being encumbered by a mindset inherited from a parent could inhibit this ability.

Many studies of high-tech and high-growth start-ups have searched for factors that could explain differences in their performance. The methods of these studies are diverse and sometimes questionable, but one result comes through repeatedly. Spin-offs with multiple founders perform better than those with a single founder (Cooper and Bruno, 1977; Cooper, 1985; Roberts, 1991, p. 258). Roberts (1991, pp. 269–271) explores the pathways by which this operated among his spin-offs. He finds that larger founding teams did not have appreciably more technical experience but had greater marketing and administrative experience than single founders. Their firms devoted more attention and effort to marketing and administration than the firms of single founders, which in turn improved their performance. This implies that founders' contributions to their spin-offs work primarily through their functional specialties and not through the specific technologies of their parents.

These findings suggest that spin-offs benefit from the experience of their founders and the more diverse those experiences, then the better the performance of spin-offs. Although more successful firms spawn more spin-offs, it is less clear how attributes of parents, including their technologies, affect the performance of their spin-offs. In the extreme, too much allegiance to a parent's mindset could even be harmful.

8.3.5   Summary of Major Themes

The evidence on spin-offs is limited, and studies do not always cover the same issues or reach the same conclusions. But a few broad themes come through from the studies that seem worth summarizing as a prelude to further discussion about the spin-off theories.

First, spin-offs appear to draw on particular experiences of their parents and founders in devising an initial business strategy. Even in disk drives, where a number of spin-offs ventured into new submarkets before their parents, they appear to have drawn on prior innovative efforts of their parents. Secondly, more innovative, successful firms with broader product lines spawn more spin-offs. These firms appear to have richer environments from which employees can draw. Thirdly, being able to draw upon the experiences of their founders gives spin-offs a competitive advantage over other kinds of start-ups, and the broader the experiences of a spin-off's founders, then the better its performance. Fourthly, and related to the third theme, in guiding their spin-offs founders appear to draw primarily on their prior experiences related to their functional positions rather than the specific technologies of their parents.

8.4   Interpretations and Implications

Now that the findings of the empirical studies have been drawn out and summarized, each of the theoretical perspectives can be evaluated. As discussed below, perhaps not surprisingly the evaluation suggests that all of the perspectives are lacking in some ways. A considerable amount of the evidence, though, supports the importance of employee learning in spin-offs. To redress shortcomings of the employee-learning models concerning what employees learn, an evolutionary model is sketched out that makes explicit the knowledge founders bring to their spin-offs. It is shown that the model can accommodate the main empirical findings of the studies. The model is also used to discuss the social implications of spin-offs regarding techno-logical change.

8.4.1   *The Theoretical Perspectives*

While four theoretical perspectives were laid out, the fourth has not been very well developed nor tested. Consequently, only the first three perspec-tives are considered.

Consider first the agency theories. The essential idea of these theories is that spin-offs develop innovations that originate in efforts by their parents. They do not end up being pursued by their parents because of various contracting problems that lead employees to develop the innovations in their own firms. This basic story does not resonate well with the findings. Most high-tech start-ups seem to begin humbly, without very ambitious plans. An exception is the disk-drive firms that pioneered the smaller disk drives, but even their experiences do not appear to conform very well with the premise of the agency models. The innovations they developed were actually pioneered by the incumbent firms, who showed prototypes of the new, smaller drives to their customers. It does not appear that at this point any employees had defected to produce these drives on their own. They left only after the incumbent firms declined to develop the new drives beyond the prototype stage, and this does not seem to have had anything to do with contracting or incentive problems concerning their employees or with ven-ture capitalists outbidding the firms to develop the new drives.

A number of other findings suggest that founders of spin-offs do not generally capitalize on discoveries financed by their employers. Many em-ployees seem to leave firms out of frustration with not being able to get their firms to develop their ideas. While this could reflect some kind of contracting difficulty, it indicates that the employees commonly reveal their 'discoveries' before starting their own firms. Anton and Yao (1995) predict employees will reveal their discoveries only if they can work out a contract with their employers to develop the innovations, and Bankman and Gilson (1999) presume that employees go to considerable lengths to keep their discoveries secret, particularly if they are willing to consider developing them in their own firms (with venture capital financing). The fact that employees are often frustrated with their employers suggests something more fundamental than a contracting breakdown. Indeed, one does not have to look beyond the disk-drive industry for breakdowns that seemingly had little to do with contracting difficulties.

The findings about the performance of spin-offs and start-ups also suggests that their initial ideas are often not very important in determining their long-term fates. It is not technologies they appropriate from their parents but the broad experiences of their founders that seem to determine their performance. Anton and Yao's theory also features the possibility that parents may develop the same innovations as their spin-offs, and all the agency theories feature the difficulties of establishing property rights to the kinds of innovations developed by spin-offs. This suggests that it might be common for parents to challenge their spin-offs both competitively and legally. While no doubt many examples of such challenges can be cited, the laser study was the only one that examined this in some depth, and little evidence was found about parents challenging their spin-offs in any way. No doubt some spin-offs capitalize on discoveries financed by employers, but this does not seem like the modal pattern.

Consider next the organizational capabilities theories. This group of theories is a mixed bag. At one end of the spectrum are the theories of Henderson and Clark (1990) and Tushman and Anderson (1986). These theories feature innovations that either fundamentally alter the way a product's components are configured or require different competencies than incumbent firms possess. They were not designed to account for spin-offs but to explain why industry leaders sometimes have difficulty maintaining their leadership. At the other extreme of the spectrum is Bhide's (2001) theory, which does address more directly the kinds of employee ideas that employers would be reluctant to pursue. In his theory, established firms use decision-making procedures that favor projects that can be well spelled out in a business plan, suggesting that spin-offs will develop ideas that are not easily amenable to description and that can be financed by employees. In the middle between these two extremes are the theories of Garvin (1983) and Christensen (1993), which feature how the emergence of new submarkets can provide distinct opportunities for spin-offs.

If one had to choose between the extreme views, Bhide's theory would clearly be favored. None of the studies generated evidence suggesting that spin-offs commonly start out in the vanguard of architectural and competence-destroying innovations. Their beginnings are generally much too humble for such ambitious innovations. Moreover, if spin-offs pioneered innovations that were difficult for incumbent firms to master, it might be expected that spin-offs would be spawned by firms experiencing difficulty. However, the opposite appears to be the case. In all three of the industries studied carefully – semiconductors, disk drives, and lasers – the most innovative and successful firms with the broader product lines spawned the most spin-offs. They do not seem to have been either slowing down or declining around the time of their spin-offs.

The disk-drive industry is an outlier that provides some support for the submarket theories of Garvin and Christensen. Approximately half of the disk-drive spin-offs did pursue notable innovations, albeit ones that incumbents apparently had developed first through the prototype stage. Furthermore, they pursued innovations their parents were reluctant to develop, which apparently frustrated the developers of the innovations enough to start their own firms (Christensen, 1993, p. 563). All of this fits the theory.

One difficulty with this theory, however, is that it appears to explain primarily just the spin-offs in the disk-drive industry. The laser spin-offs entered very similar markets to their parents, and the broader evidence on high-tech and high-growth start-ups suggests a similar pattern. Moreover, the best firms spawned the most spin-offs, including in disk drives. While this is not necessarily inconsistent with the submarket theory, it is not exactly supportive of it either. It suggests that the best firms provide the best training ground for employees inclined to start their own firms. A training ground conjures up the image of employees learning, which is the domain of the employee-learning theories. Thus, at a minimum there appears to be more to spin-offs, even in the disk-drive industry, than incumbent firms blinded to new opportunities because of relying too much on their customers to evaluate new disk drives.

The variant of the employee-learning theory developed by Klepper and Sleeper (2000) also provides an alternative explanation for the disk-drive industry, and an explanation that reconciles disk drives with lasers and much of the other evidence. If incumbent firms anticipated the potential cannibalization of their main markets that did ultimately result from the smaller disk drives, they would have had less incentive than their spin-offs to pursue these markets, which could explain why their spin-offs ended up pioneering them. Christensen (1993, p. 563) claims the markets for the smaller drives were so uncertain initially that the potential for cannibalization could not have been anticipated, but then it is not clear what information the spin-offs had about these markets that justified their boldness. Moreover, it is not hard to envision how incumbents might have been less inclined than their spin-offs to risk further development of drives with very uncertain prospects if one possibility, which at least one incumbent seems to have recognized from the outset (cf. Christensen, 1993, p. 563), was that their customers might turn out to be buyers of the new drives.

Much of the evidence resonates with the employee-learning theories, particularly the variant in which spin-offs exploit narrow aspects of their parents' experiences. This variant readily explains the common finding that high-tech start-ups do not stray far from their parents, and that they generally have humble beginnings. It can also explain the common frustration of spin-off founders with their parents and the fact that more innovative and successful firms with broader product lines spawn more spin-offs. It can also explain some of the idiosyncratic findings, such as the asymmetric effect of entry conditions on the rate of spin-offs in the laser industry, and possibly also the effect of acquisitions and location on firm spin-off rates (Klepper and Sleeper, 2000).

The learning theories, though, have a major weakness. They cannot explain the main findings concerning the performance of spin-offs and start-ups. The only prediction that comes out of the learning theories concerning the performance of spin-offs is that their performance should be related to the performance of their parents. In the one study on disk drives that tested this prediction, the results were mixed. No support was provided for the idea that spin-offs learn about their parent's technologies–the quality of a parent's technology *negatively* affected its spin-off's survival prospects. Indeed, many of the findings suggest that founders of spin-offs do not exploit knowledge about their parents' specific technologies. Rather, founders appear to draw more narrowly on their experiences, which are bounded by their functional positions and training. The learning theories are actually quite silent on exactly what founders of spin-offs learn from their employers and how they use this in their own firms. The fact that better firms spawn more spin-offs certainly suggests that the quality of a parent's experience conditions what employees learn, but exactly how this occurs is a black box in the learning theories.

This same feature of the learning theories limits their usefulness for assessing the implications of spin-offs for technological change. The learning theories are principally theories about how firms start, not about how they perform over time. This is equally true about the other theories that were reviewed. If one wants to evaluate how spin-offs affect technological change, which surely is one of the major reasons for analysing spin-offs, then something more is needed.

Rather than stop at this point, a crude attempt is made to describe a theory of spin-offs that can begin to address the implications of spin-offs for technological change. The main point of this exercise is not theory building. Indeed, the model focuses almost entirely on the supply side, with the demand side modelled only implicitly. Moreover, it incorporates many simplifying assumptions that abstract from important aspects of the competitive landscape. The model's usefulness lies in providing a kind of structure and vocabulary to address how employees passing down what they know through their spin-offs can have profound implications for technological change.

8.4.2 *An Evolutionary Account of Spin-offs*

A natural way to generalize the employee-learning theories is by exploiting the metaphor of spin-offs as children and employers as parents. Parents give birth to their spin-offs, which inherit various characteristics from their parents. Dyck (1997) basically conceives of spin-offs in this way. But rather than exploit theories of parenting and child behavior, as he does, the proposed model combines the ideas of reproduction and inheritance with the notion of organizational routines developed in Nelson and Winter (1982). This makes for a novel approach, as little use has been made of the ideas of reproduction and inheritance in evolutionary modelling in the social sciences (Nelson, 1995, p. 54).

The firm is assumed to be governed by routines. Separate routines are used for each distinct product the firm produces. Each product, in turn, requires separate routines for R&D, marketing, management, and the other main functions involved in operating a business. These routines are originally installed by the firm's founders and the original management team they hire. They prescribe procedures that all members of the firm must adhere to when making decisions.[9] Founders will adopt the rules they are familiar with from their past experiences. The better the quality of these past routines and the closer the environment in which they were used to the firm's activities, then the better the firm's performance. The firm's overall perform-ance is based not just on the quality of its individual routines, but on its entire set of routines. Routines will perform better when they are combined with other routines governing complementary functions – e.g. R&D routines will perform better when combined with marketing routines.

Organizations can reproduce. They can reproduce on their own or in combination with other organizations. Reproduction requires one or more employees to transplant the routines he or she knows to a new firm, namely the spin-off. For now, let the number of employees that join the new firm as founders and the number of firms that contribute founders to the new firm be a random variable. Only some employees will ever reproduce. The rest either lack the organizational skills or risk preferences needed to start their own firms. They are sterile. Reproduction has a cost. It will not occur unless the offspring is expected to perform well enough to recoup the cost. This depends on two factors. One is the quality of the routines an employee knows that will be inherited by the offspring. This quality depends not only on the quality of the firm's routines in the employee's domain but also the length of time the employee has had to learn the routines. The higher the quality of the routines an employee knows, then the greater the expected performance of his/her spin-off and hence the higher the employee's prob-ability of reproduction at any given moment, *ceteris paribus*. Reproduction also requires a supportive environment (industry). If conditions fall below a cutoff, all reproduction ceases. Otherwise, reproduction is as specified above. For simplicity, it is assumed that if an employee reproduces, then the firm replaces the employee but maintains the same routines. This could be relaxed to allow replacements to influence the firm's routines according to the routines they used in their prior employment.

Firms compete for market share. The worst performers do not capture enough market share to cover their costs and they shrink and die, whereas the best performers are profitable and grow. Among other things, growth involves taking on new products. Internal growth requires hiring new employees and installing new routines based on the experiences of the new employees and the leaders of the firm. Growth can also occur through merger. If two firms merge, they select the best routines in areas where they overlap and let go the employees whose routines are no longer employed. In areas where they do not overlap, they use the routines employed by the contributing organization. Employees that have been let go have higher reproduction rates because they have lower opportunity costs of reproduction.

The model has a number of implications that seem to accord with the evidence on spin-offs. First, high-tech organizations have more routines than low-tech ones because they have more functions, such as R&D, to manage. Therefore, they will have more employees with access to routines, hence will spawn more spin-offs than low-tech organizations. This could explain why scholars of spin-offs and start-ups have been preoccupied with high-tech industries (Garvin, 1983). Second, since spin-offs inherit a subset of the routines of their parents, they will perform a subset of the functions performed by their parents. This could explain the finding in lasers that spin-offs initially produce one of their parent's lasers. A transplanted routine will not perform the same way it did in its original firm because it will be surrounded by different other routines that also condition its behavior. This could explain why spin-offs are differentiated from their parents even in areas where they initially overlap. The combination of spin-offs initially pursuing only a subset of their parent's activities and doing even those differently from their parents can help explain the finding in lasers that spin-offs did not appear to threaten or otherwise affect their parents very much.

Spin-offs will inherit routines more suited to their activity than other kinds of start-ups and thus will outperform other types of start-ups. This could explain the longer survival of spin-offs than other kinds of start-ups. Spin-offs with more founders will have more complementary routines to draw upon and thus will perform better than spin-offs with less founders, which could explain the better performance of spin-offs with larger founding teams. Spin-offs that inherit better-quality routines will perform better, and since these same routines govern the performance of parents, the performance of spin-offs will be positively correlated with the performance of their parents in the spin-off's domain. This could explain certain aspects of Franco and Filson's (2000) findings concerning disk-drive spin-offs.

Better-performing firms will have better routines, and employees with access to better routines will be more likely to reproduce. Therefore, better-performing firms will spawn more spin-offs, which was found in all three spin-off studies. Firms with broader product lines have more employees and routines and thus will have a higher reproduction rate, which could explain the findings about product breadth in semiconductors and lasers. As firms age initially, employees will come to know their routines better, causing their reproduction rate to rise. This could explain the initial rise in the spin-off rate of laser and biotech firms with age. Firms replace employees that leave with new employees, some of whom will be sterile. Since only fertile employees reproduce, over time the percentage of a firm's employees that are sterile must rise and approach one. This could explain the decline in firm spin-off rates that occurred in lasers after age 14. If industry conditions worsen sufficiently, no reproduction will take place, but otherwise industry conditions do not affect reproduction rates. This could explain the asymmetric effect of demand conditions on the spin-off rate in lasers. Finally, if firms are acquired, some employees are let go and this increases their reproduction rate, which could explain why firms that are acquired have higher spin-off rates.

So it would seem that the model can accommodate a wide range of the evidence on spin-offs. It is not worth making too much of this. Explanations of the model for certain patterns, such as acquired firms having higher spin-off rates and demand conditions having an asymmetric effect on spin-offs, follow rather transparently from assumptions. The point of the model, however, was not to construct a sophisticated theory but to provide a way to address the implications of spin-offs regarding technological change. To do that requires one more observation about the model.

When a firm grows and expands its scope, it takes on new routines. These new routines will have an effect on how the rest of the firm's routines operate to condition its performance. Thus, as firms grow, their performance will change. The further they grow, the more they will tend to depart from their origins and thus their parents. Thus, it can be expected that as spin-offs grow they will diverge further and further from their parents, and for that matter other firms as well. This would be expected to cause them to make decisions about all matters, including innovation, that differ from their parents and the other firms in their industry. They will see things differently from other firms and as a result develop innovations that differ from other firms in the industry. To the extent that firms are all descended from the same parents, their managers will all have been exposed to the same routines, and there will be considerable overlap in their decisions and thus innovations. Nonetheless, as they age, firms would be expected to become less similar, leading to a greater diversity in the innovations they pursue.

The importance of perceptions and the routines underlying them is nicely illustrated in Shane (2000). He considers how eight different groups made use of the same licensable invention. The members of each group differed in terms of their training and expertise. As a result, they had very different perceptions of how the licensable invention could be exploited and pursued radically different innovations based on the invention. Not surprisingly, they differed greatly in their economic success. These were simple groups, and their routines could be associated with individuals. They had different routines because the members of the groups had different training and experience, and this led them to develop different innovations from the same technology.

Another example of how differences in perceptions and routines affect a firm's choices comes from Boeker's (1997) study of how the hiring of top managers affected the products produced by semiconductor firms. The direction of causality is unclear, but firms that hired new executives tended to adopt some of the products of the executive's prior employer. If the firms wanted to grow by increasing their scope, hiring a new top manager to install new routines from his old employer would logically lead the firm to mimic some of the practices of the top manager's prior employer. The influence of the new top manager was greater for more experienced managers that reported to their prior firm's CEO and for hiring firms with smaller and less-experienced management teams, suggesting that experience conditions the quality of the routines a manager is able to transplant to a new firm and the receptivity of the firm to the transplant. This is consistent with the assumption in the model that more experienced employees have more knowledge about routines to transfer to a spin-off.

These examples illustrate the fundamental point that organizations have different routines and these routines change over time, which will cause innovations to vary across organizations and within organizations over time. Applied to spin-offs, it implies that spin-offs will develop different innovations from their parents as well as other firms in their industry. Furthermore, spin-offs appear to have distinctive fitness that enables them to survive longer than other kinds of start-ups and perhaps even longer than experienced entrants. As they prosper and gain experience, they will become even more differentiated from other firms in the industry, leading them to develop more distinctive innovations. Expressed alternatively, spin-offs will be a source of diversity. Assuming firms cannot fully appropriate the returns to their innovations due to imitation and other forces, the more diverse the innovations developed in an industry then the greater the benefits that will accrue to society. Interpreted in this light, spin-offs will stimulate an industry's rate of technological change.[10]

This is a novel conclusion to come out of a learning type of model. Learning models typically imply that firms undertake too little R&D because the prospects of employees leaving and imitating their technology undermines their incentives to undertake R&D. Franco and Filson (2000) sidestep this implication by assuming that R&D workers accept lower wages at firms with richer technologies, which allows firms to appropriate the full value of their innovative efforts. But at best this makes spin-offs neutral in terms of their implications for technological change. Spin-offs fare no better in the agency theories. The only theories that see spin-offs playing a productive social role are those that see them overcoming some kind of organizational deficiency in decision making. Such deficiencies are controversial, though, and the evidence suggests this has limited applicability to spin-offs.

This interpretation of spin-offs resonates with themes Dick Nelson has championed for many years. Economists have long pointed to the twin welfare theorems to defend capitalism. Dick has argued, though, that in everyday conversation they reveal a more basic faith in the diversity of approaches to innovation that capitalism fosters (Nelson, 1981). He has also stressed the potential wasteful duplication of effort inherent in technological competition in capitalistic systems (Nelson, 1990, 1991). The evolutionary account of spin-offs maps into both points. Spin-offs are an inherent source of innovative diversity in capitalistic systems. They also provide an inexpensive way for good routines to be duplicated. To the extent that spin-offs exploit the experiences of their founders, as embedded in their parents' routines, and not the specific technological achievements of their parents, they will have minimal effects on the incentives of their parents to innovate. All told, they can be a powerful force promoting technological change.

No doubt this view of spin-offs is both too simplistic and too optimistic, but it begins to provide a vocabulary and way of thinking that casts spin-offs in a new light. Moreover, it resonates with popular views of Silicon Valley as an extraordinary engine of progress. Spin-offs are an essential feature of the landscape there, and if they were on balance harmful it is hard to see how Silicon Valley could have been so successful. Hyde (2000) seems to recognize this in his treatise on the legal treatment of mobile high-tech workers. He advocates a legal position of weak property rights to information, narrow definitions of trade secret, and non-enforcement of convenants not to compete that would allow workers broad latitude to exploit their experience. He recognizes the many technological benefits that can come from workers changing jobs, with spin-offs being a prime example.

Spin-offs are a distinctive form of entry, and they may help explain a number of the patterns documented by Geroksi (1995) regarding entry (cf. Klepper and Sleeper, 2000). The empirical findings implicate spin-offs in many other important processes as well. But having spun a highly stylized tale of spin-offs involving reproduction and inheritance, ample illustrations have been provided about the potential importance of spin-offs to move on.

8.5   Conclusion

The growing theoretical and empirical literature on spin-offs provides many insights into the forces underlying their formation. Employee learning appears to play a key role in the formation of spin-offs and the kinds of firms that spawn them. But many questions remain about employee learning.

The most basic concerns what exactly employees learn that they use when they start spin-offs. Do employees learn only from the activities they are involved in or can they learn from the general experiences of their employers? Is the amount they learn affected by the nature of the technologies their employer uses and the kinds of innovations it develops? Is it influenced by the employee's tenure at the firm? These questions could be probed by collecting information about the tenure and positions of the founders of spin-offs and the technologies of their parents.

A related set of questions that could be explored with data on founders and the performance of their spin-offs pertain to what founders exploit that they have learned from their parents. Do they directly transfer technology from their parents? Is the amount of knowledge they transfer to their spin-offs affected by other founders? Is it affected by whether the founders previously worked together? Is it affected by how long they worked for their parents?

Very little is known about how spin-offs evolve over time. Do they take on similar activities to their parents as they grow? Does it depend on the positions the founders held in their parent firm(s)? Do they change their strategy as they grow, and if so, what conditions the extent of the change?[11] Are many parents involved in their spin-offs after the spin-offs are formed? How often do they help finance their spin-offs? Do many parents challenge their spin-offs legally? What characteristics of spin-offs and parents affect whether they are involved in legal challenges? Nearly all of these questions have counterparts in terms of the performance of spin-offs, so if more data were assembled about founders and parents then the determinants of the performance of spin-offs could also be explored further.

The few spin-off studies that have been conducted cover a very narrow range of industries, but even they exhibit sufficient differences to suggest that employee learning may be operative to a greater degree in some industries and settings than others. Exploring this idea further will require data from more industries, just as expanding the range of issues considered will require more data. Some insight can be gained from the spin-off studies about where such data might be found. Two of the studies relied on firm compilations done by others. Researchers will need to be alert to shortcuts such as these to assemble the necessary information for a broader range of industries. Hopefully, the significance of the issues raised by spin-offs and the great many outstanding questions about them will galvanize the search for more data and also the development of more sophisticated theories about how employee learning affects spin-offs and the rate of technological change.

Acknowledgements

I thank John Miller for many helpful discussions and Amar Bhide and two anonymous referees for comments. Support is gratefully acknowledged from the Economics Program of the National Science Foundation, grant no. SBR-9600041.

Notes

1. Garvin (1983) has proposed a theory of spin-offs that also features the role of new submarkets in providing the impetus for spin-offs. He does not directly address difficulties incumbents may have in pursuing new submarkets, but he

envisions that new submarkets will provide distinctive opportunities for spin-offs because employees of incumbent firms are especially well positioned to learn about them on a timely basis.

2. The theory can also address the effects on a firm's spin-off rate of acquisitions (if they affect the market positioning of the firm), location (if the geographic density of firms affects the ability of employees to form founding and initial management teams), and its background prior to entry (if it affect the richness of the firm's knowledge).

3. Dyck develops other intriguing predictions about planned versus unplanned spin-offs and also about spin-off siblings. These are not listed, however, because they have been tested only on religious organizations (Dyck, 1997), which have limited relevance to high-tech spin-offs.

4. This issue was not analysed by Brittain and Freeman (1986).

5. While this may be a *post hoc* rationalization, Cooper (1971, p. 23) reported that a sizable percentage of the founders in his sample were sufficiently frustrated to quit their jobs before contemplating starting their own firms.

6. In addition, the total years a firm produced a laser increased its spin-off rate at every point in its lifetime, although this effect was not statistically significant.

7. In conformance with their theoretical model, Franco and Filson (2000) treat the disk-drive industry as a homogeneous product industry and thus do not analyse this issue.

8. Nearly all studies find a similar pattern of spin-offs locating close to their parents (cf. Cooper, 1971, p. 18; Roberts, 1991, p. 64).

9. Heath *et al.* (1998) provide concrete illustrations of various organizational routines and the roles they play in overcoming individual cognitive limitations.

10. Relatedly, practices such as lifetime employment could actually retard an industry's rate of technological change, particularly regarding innovations that require considerable novelty.

11. Boeker (1989) has analysed some of these questions for semiconductor start-ups.

References

Amit, R. and Muller, E. (1994), ' "Push" and "pull" entrepreneurship,' in W. D. Bygrave, S. Birley, N. C. Churchill, E. Gatewood, F. Hoy, R. H. Keeley, and W. E. Wetzel, Jr (eds), *Frontiers of entrepreneurship research, 1994*, Wellesley, MA: Babson College, pp. 27–42.

Anton, J. J. and Yao, D. A. (1995), 'Start-ups, spin-offs, and internal projects,' *Journal of Law, Economics, and Organization*, **11**: 362–378.

Bankman, J. and Gilson, R. J. (1999), 'Why start-ups?,' *Stanford Law Review*, **51**: 289–308.

Bhide, A. V. (2000), *The origin and evolution of new business*. Oxford: Oxford University Press.

Bhide, A. V. (2001), 'Taking care: ambiguity, resource pooling and error control,' Mimeo, Columbia Business School.

Boeker, W. (1988), 'Organizational origins: entrepreneurial and environmental imprinting at the time of founding,' in G. Carroll (ed.), *Ecological models of organizations*. Cambridge MA: Ballinger, pp. 33–51.

Boeker, W. (1989), 'Strategic change: the effects of founding and history,' *Academy of Management Journal*, **32**: 489–515.

Boeker, W. (1997), 'Executive migration and strategic change: the effect of top manager movement on product-market entry,' *Administrative Sciences Quarterly*, **42**: 213–236.

Braden, P. L. (1977), *Technological entrepreneurship*. Ann Arbor, MI: University of Michigan.

Brittain, J. W. and Freeman, J. (1986), 'Entrepreneurship in the semiconductor industry', unpublished manuscript.

Chesbrough, H. (2000), 'Creating and capturing value from technology: the case of Xerox's spin-off companies,' Mimeo, Harvard Business School.

Chesbrough, H. and Rosenbloom, R. S. (2000), 'The role of the business model in capturing value from innovation: evidence from Xerox Corporation's technology spinoff companies,' Mimeo, Harvard Business School.

Christensen, C. M. (1993), 'The rigid disk drive industry: a history of commercial and technological turbulence,' *Business History Review*, Winter, 531–588.

Cooper, A. C. (1971), *The founding of technologically-based firms*. Milwaukee: The Center for Venture Management.

Cooper, A. C. (1984), 'Contrasts in the role of incubator organizations in the founding of growth-oriented companies,' in J. A. Hornaday, F. A. Tardley, Jr, J. A. Timmons, and K. H. Vesper (eds), *Frontiers of entrepreneurship research, 1984*. Wellesley, MA: Babson College, pp. 159–174.

Cooper, A. C. (1985), 'The role of incubator organizations in the founding of growth-oriented firms,' *Journal of Business Venturing*, **1**: 75–86.

Cooper, A. C. and Bruno, A. V. (1977), 'Success among high-technology firms,' *Business Horizons*, April, 16–22.

Cooper, A. C. and Gimeno-Gascon, F. J. (1992), 'Enterpreneurs, processes of founding, and new-firm performance,' in D. L. Sexton and J. D. Kasarda (eds), *The state of the art of entrepreneurship*. Boston, MA: Pws-Kent, pp. 301–340.

Dyck, B. (1997), 'Exploring organizational family trees,' *Journal of Management Inquiry*, **6**: 222–233.

Feeser, H. R. and Willard, G. E. (1989), 'Incubators and performance: a comparison of high- and low-growth high-tech firms,' *Journal of Business Venturing*, **4**: 429–442.

Florida, R. and Kenney, M. (1990), *The breakthrough illusion*. New York: Basic Books.

Franco, A. M. and Filson, D. (2000), 'Knowledge diffusion through employee mobility,' Federal Reserve Bank of Minneapolis, Staff Report 272.

Garvin, D. A. (1983), 'Spin-offs and the new firm formation process,' *California Management Review*, January, 3–20.

Geroski, P. A. (1995), 'What do we know about entry?,' *International Journal of Industrial Organization*, **13**: 421–440.

Henderson, R. A. and Clark, K. B. (1990), 'Architectural innovation: the reconfiguration of existing systems and the failure of established firms,' *Administrative Science Quarterly*, **35**: 9–30.

Heath, C., Larrick, R. P., and Klayman, J. (1998), 'Cognitive repairs: how organizational practices can compensate for individual shortcomings,' *Research in Organizational Behavior*, **20**: 1–37.

Hyde, A. (2000), 'Working in Silicon Valley: economic and legal analysis of a high-velocity labor market,' Mimeo, Chapters 2 and 3.

Jackson, T. (1998), *Inside Intel*. New York: Penguin Putnam.

Klepper, S. (1996), 'Entry, exit, growth, and innovation over the product life cycle,' *American Economic Review*, **86**: 562–583.

Klepper, S. and Sleeper, S. (2000), 'Entry by spinoffs,' Mimeo.

Mitton, D. G. (1990), 'Bring on the clones: a longitudinal study of the proliferation, development, and growth of the biotech industry in San Diego,' in N. C. Churchill, W. D. Bygrave, J. A. Hornaday, D. F. Muzyka, K. H. Vesper, and W. E. Wetzel, Jr (eds), *Frontiers of entrepreneurship research, 1990*. Wellesley, MA: Babson College, pp. 344–358.

Nelson, R. R. (1981), 'Assessing private enterprise: an exegesis of tangled doctrine,' *Bell Journal of Economics*, **9**: 524–548.

Nelson, R. R. (1990), 'Capitalism as an engine of progress,' *Research Policy*, **19**: 193–214.

Nelson, R. R. (1991), 'Why do firms differ, and how does it matter?,' *Strategic Management Journal*, **12**: 61–74.

Nelson, R. R. (1995), 'Recent evolutionary theorizing about economic change,' *Journal of Economic Literature*, **33**: 48–90.

Nelson, R. R. and Winter, S. G. (1982), *An evolutionary theory of economic change*, Cambridge, MA: Harvard University Press.

Roberts, E. B. (1991), *Entrepreneurs in high technology*. New York: Oxford University Press.

Schollhammer, H. (1991), 'Incidence and determinants of multiple entrepreneurship,' in R. Ronstadt, J. A. Hornaday, R. Peterson, and K. H. Vesper (eds), *Frontiers of entrepreneurship research, 1991*. Wellesley, MA: Babson College, pp. 11–24.

Shane, S. (2000), 'Prior knowledge and the discovery of entrepreneurial opportunities,' *Organization Science*, **11**: 448–469.

Sleeper, S. D. (1998), 'The role of firm capabilities in the evolution of the laser industry: the making of a high-tech market,' Ph.D. dissertation, Carnegie Mellon University.

Starr, J. A. and Bygrave, W. D. (1991), 'The assets and liabilities of prior start-up experience: an exploratory study of multiple venture entrepreneurs,' in R. Ronstadt, J. A. Hornaday, R. Peterson, and K. H. Vesper (eds), *Frontiers of entrepreneurship research, 1991*. Wellesley, MA: Babson College, pp. 213–227.

Tsai, L. B. (1997), 'The spatial aggregation of automobile manufacturing activities in the Midwest,' Mimeo.

Tushman, M. L. and Anderson, P. (1986), 'Technological discontinuities and organizational environments,' *Administrative Science Quarterly*, **31**: 439–465.

Walsh, S. T., Kirchhoff, B. A., and Boylan, R. L. (1996), 'Founder backgrounds and entrepreneurial success: implications for core competence strategy application to new ventures,' in P. D. Reynolds, S. Birley, J. E. Butler, W. D. Bygrave, P. Davidson, W. B. Gartner, and P. P. McDougall (eds), *Frontiers of entrepreneurship research, 1996*. Wellesley, MA: Babson College, pp. 146–154.

Wiggins, S. N. (1995), 'Entrepreneurial enterprises, endogenous ownership, and the limits to firm size,' *Economic Inquiry*, **33**: 54–69.

Part III

9

The Silicon Valley–Hsinchu Connection: Technical Communities and Industrial Upgrading

AnnaLee Saxenian and Jinn-Yuh Hsu

9.1 Introduction

Silicon Valley in California and the Hsinchu-Taipei region of Taiwan are among the most frequently cited 'miracles' of industrialization in the information technology (IT) era. Since the region's transformation from an agricultural valley into the birthplace of the semiconductor industry in the 1950s, Silicon Valley firms have pioneered a wide range of new, technology-related industries. The regional economy has adapted flexibly to fast changing markets, and local producers continue to define the state-of-the-art in successive generations of technology – from semiconductor equipment, personal computers (PCs), and networking hardware and software, to biotechnology, multimedia software, and Internet-related infrastructure and services.

Taiwan's technology achievements are more recent, but no less impressive. The Taipei area, which served as a source of cheap labor for foreign consumer electronics multinationals as late as the 1970s, is known today as a global center of IT systems design and manufacturing. Local companies dominate the markets for a large and growing range of computer-related products, from notebook computers, motherboards and monitors to optical scanners, keyboards and power supplies (Fig. 9.1). In addition, Taiwan's state-of-the-art semiconductor foundries account for two-thirds of global output. Not surprisingly, the industry has grown dramatically in the past two decades (Fig. 9.2). Taiwan's IT sector now ranks third in the world, with a total output of US$34 billion in 1998, ahead of larger nations like South Korea, and behind only the United States and Japan.

The IT industries in the United States and Taiwan are differently specialized and remain at different levels of technological development. As a result, the dominant accounts of their success treat them in isolation. For some scholars, national economic success in information-technology industries is evidence of the dynamism of free markets (Gilder, 1989; Lau, 1994; Callon, 1995). These accounts identify high levels of human capital formation, domestic entrepreneurship and market competition in either Taiwan or the US to explain the successes of their respective technology industries. Others argue that activist states are responsible for the successes. In this view, the

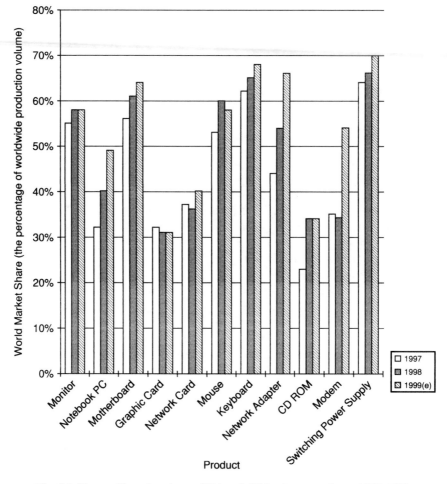

Fig. 9.1 The world market share of Taiwan's IT hardware products, 1997–1999.
Source: MIC

intervention of agencies like the US military and aerospace agencies and Taiwan's Industrial Technology Research Institute (ITRI) explain the dynamism of the new industries (Borrus, 1988; Wade, 1990; Kraemer *et al.*, 1996; Mathews, 1997).

Recently, analysts have moved beyond the simple state–market debate to examine other determinants of economic performance such as the geography of production. These explanations of success look at subnational units. For example, Taiwan's technology sector is concentrated in the 50-mile industrial area linking Taipei to the Hsinchu Science-based Industrial Park. The Hsinchu region, like Silicon Valley, appears as an exemplar of Marshallian

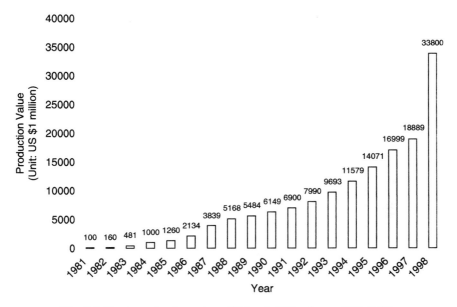

Fig. 9.2 Yearly production value of Taiwan's IT hardware, 1981–1998.
Sources: Huang (1995); http://mic.iii.org.tw/english/asiait/issues/special/1998/98sp-1.htm

external economies, in which the localization of skill, specialized materials and inputs, and technological know-how generate cost reductions for individual firms and increasing returns to the region as a whole (Krugman, 1991).

Yet the concept of external economies cannot account for qualitative, as opposed to quantitative, sources of growth. In particular, it overlooks the contributions of technological innovation to regional growth. So, for example, the 'new' economic geography cannot explain why Taiwan outperformed Singapore in the IT industry in the 1990s. Both were poor economies and destinations for electronics foreign direct investment (FDI) in the 1960s and 1970s. While Singapore is now a leading supplier of hard-disk drives, PCs, and multimedia cards, it has fallen far behind Taiwan's proliferation of indigenous PC and integrated circuit (IC) producers that continually innovate and upgrade their manufacturing capabilities. Many observers claim that Taiwan's expertise in designing and manufacturing PCs is now unparalleled, even in the US.

Taiwan's technological achievements are reflected in international comparisons of patenting.[1] While all the Asian newly industrializing economies ranked low in the 1980s, Taiwan received US patents at an accelerating rate in the 1990s and surpassed not only Singapore but also Korea and Hong Kong in the number of patents granted per capita (Fig. 9.3). In fact, Taiwan, along with Israel, now ranks ahead of all of the G7 countries except the US and Japan in patents per capita (Trajtenberg, 1999).

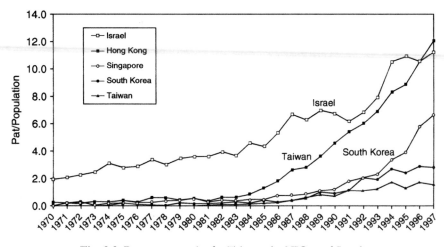

Fig. 9.3 Patents per capita for Taiwan, the NICs, and Israel.
Source: http://www.nber.org/papers/w7022

Silicon Valley and Hsinchu might also be viewed as industrial clusters, in which competition and vertical co-operation among local firms account for rising productivity, innovation, and new-firm formation (Porter, 1998). Both regions boast high rates of entrepreneurship and hundreds of small and medium-sized enterprises (SMEs) alongside larger technology companies with multiple backward and forward linkages. And independent accounts of the performance of producers in these regions stress their flexibility, speed, and innovative capacity relative to their leading competitors (Callon, 1995; Ernst, 1998).

The most convincing accounts document how the decentralization of the industrial systems of Hsinchu and Silicon Valley ensures the flexibility and innovative capacity needed to compete in a volatile market environment (Saxenian, 1994; Hsu, 1997; Lin, 2000). Levy and Kuo (1991), for example, compare the 'bootstrap' strategy of Taiwan's small, specialized PC firms with the high-volume PC assembly strategy of the vertically integrated Korean conglomerates. They suggested that the propensity for risk-taking and ex-perimentation in Taiwan's SMEs produced an ongoing stream of innovation and the opportunity for some firms to achieve technological mastery and grow large. The competitive advantages of this 'bootstrap' strategy were confirmed in the 1990s as Korea's *chaebol* fell increasingly behind the accel-erating PC product life cycle and were forced to source key components from Taiwan (Chung, 2000).

Yet this approach suffers from its focus on regions in isolation. It over-looks the growing role of international trade and investment in economic growth – and cannot explain the emergence of successful new regions such as Taiwan's Hsinchu that are located far from established centers of technology and skill. Mounting evidence suggests the need to examine the organization of production at the *global*, as well as the local level. Scholars have documented, for example, the way that global corporations organize their supply chains, or international production networks, and the opportunities this provides for industrial upgrading in less-advanced economies.

The success of Taiwan's PC producers, from this view, derives from their role as original equipment manufacturers (OEMs) for the leading US and Japanese PC companies – a relationship that stimulates knowledge creation, technology transfer, and improved domestic capabilities (Borrus, 1997; Dedrick and Kraemer, 1998; Ernst, 1998).[2] Analyses of global production networks represent an important conceptual advance because they demonstrate a powerful mechanism for industrial upgrading in remote locations like Taiwan. However, the focus on the sourcing strategies of multinational corporations overlooks the emergence of indigenous entrepreneurship and innovation in the periphery during the 1990s, particularly in places like Taiwan.

The connection between technology producers in the United States and Taiwan is both more extensive and more decentralized than these top-down accounts suggest. The central and largely unrecognized actors in this process are a community of US-educated engineers who have built a social and economic bridge linking the Silicon Valley and Hsinchu economies. These highly skilled Taiwanese immigrants are distinguished from the broader Chinese diaspora (or 'overseas Chinese business networks') by shared professional as well as ethnic identities and by their deep integration into the technical communities of both technology regions.

The development of a transnational community – a community that spans borders and boasts as its key assets shared information, trust, and contacts (Portes, 1996) – has been largely overlooked in accounts of Taiwan's accelerated development. This chapter argues that the contributions of this international technical community have been key to the successes of more commonly recognized actors: government policy makers and global corporations. Both rely heavily on the dense professional and social networks that keep them close to state-of-the-art technical knowledge and leading-edge markets in the United States. The connection to Silicon Valley, in particular, helps to explain how Taiwan's producers innovated technologically in the 1980s and 1990s independently of their OEM customers.

The development of an international technical community has also transformed the relationship between the Silicon Valley and Hsinchu economies. In the 1960s and 1970s, capital and technology resided mainly in the US and Japan and were transferred to Taiwan by multinational corporations seeking cheap labor. This one-way flow has given way in the 1990s to more decentralized two-way flows of skill, technology, and capital. The Silicon Valley–Hsinchu relationship today consists of formal and informal collaborations between individual investors and entrepreneurs, SMEs, as well as the division of larger companies located on both sides of the Pacific. A new generation of venture capital providers and professional associations serve as intermediaries linking the decentralized infrastructures of the two regions. As a result, by the 1990s Hsinchu was no longer a low-cost location yet local producers continued to gain a growing share of global technology markets.[3]

9.2   Technical Communities and Industrial Decentralization

The emergence of new centers of technology, like Taiwan, in locations outside of the advanced economies has been possible because of radical transformations in the structure of the IT sector. The dominant competitors in the computer industry in the 1960s and 1970s were vertically integrated corporations that controlled all aspects of hardware and software production. Countries sought to build a domestic IBM or 'national champion' from the bottom up. The rise of the Silicon Valley industrial model spurred the introduction of the PC and initiated a radical shift to a more fragmented industrial structure organized around networks of increasingly specialized producers (Bresnahan, 1998).

Today, independent enterprises produce all of the components that were once internalized within a single large corporation – from application software, operating systems, and computers to microprocessors and other components. The final systems are in turn marketed and distributed by still other enterprises. Within each of these horizontal segments there is, in turn, increasing specialization of production and a deepening social division of labor. In the semiconductor industry, for example, independent producers specialize in chip design, fabrication, packaging, and testing, as well as different segments of the manufacturing materials and equipment sector. A new generation of firms emerged in the late 1990s that specializes in providing intellectual property in the form of design modules rather than the entire chip design. There are, for example, over 200 independent specialist companies in Taiwan's IC industry alone (Fig. 9.4).

This change in industry structure appears as a shift to market relations. The number of actors in the industry has increased dramatically and competition within many (but not all) horizontal layers has increased as well. Yet this is far from the classic auction market mediated by price signals alone; the decentralized system depends heavily on the co-ordination provided by cross-cutting social structures and institutions (Aoki, 2000). While Silicon Valley's entrepreneurs innovate in increasingly specialized niche markets, intense communications in turn ensure the speedy, often unanticipated, recombination of these specialized components into changing end-products. This decentralized system provides significant advantages over a more integrated model in a volatile environment because of the speed and flexibility as

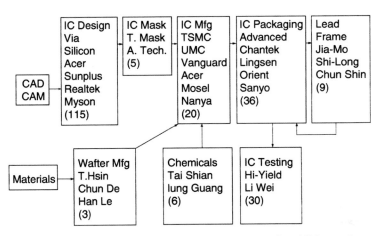

Fig. 9.4 The structure of Taiwan's IC industry (no. of establishments).
Source: ERSO/ITRI (1999)

well as the conceptual advances associated with the process of specialization and recombination.[4]

The deepening social division of labor in the industry creates opportunities for innovation in formerly peripheral regions – opportunities that did not exist in an era of highly integrated producers. The vertical specialization associated with the new system continually generates entrepreneurial opportunities. By exploiting these opportunities in their home countries, transnational entrepreneurs can build independent centers of specialization and innovation, while simultaneously maintaining ties to Silicon Valley to monitor and respond to fast-changing and uncertain markets and technologies. They are also well positioned to establish cross-regional partnerships that facilitate the integration of their specialized components into end-products.

The social structure of a technical community thus appears essential to the organization of production at the global as well as the local level. In the old industrial model, the technical community was primarily inside the corporation. The firm was seen as the privileged organizational form for the creation and internal transfer of knowledge, particularly technological know-how that is difficult to codify (Kogut and Zander, 1993). In regions like Silicon Valley, where the technical community transcends firm boundaries, however, such tacit knowledge is often transferred through informal communications or the interfirm movement of individuals (Saxenian, 1994). This suggests that the multinational corporation may no longer be the advantaged or preferred organizational vehicle for transferring knowledge or personnel across national borders. An international technological community provides an alternative and potentially more flexible and responsive mechanism for long-distance transfers of skill and know-how – particularly between very different business cultures or environments.

The remainder of this chapter documents the evolution of the transnational community linking Hsinchu and Silicon Valley and the concomitant process of industrial upgrading. It traces the origins of a technical community among Taiwanese engineers in the US in the 1970s and 1980s, the subsequent institutionalization of the linkages between Silicon Valley and Hsinchu, and the emergence in the 1990s of mutually beneficial collaborations between specialist producers located in the two regions. It provides recent survey data to document the nature and scale of the interactions within this cross-regional community. A concluding section re-examines the relationship between technical communities and regional development and briefly suggests policy lessons.

9.3   The Construction of a Taiwanese Technical Community in Silicon Valley

The modern 'brain-drain' from Asia to the United States dates to the Immigration Act of 1965, often referred to as the Hart–Celler Act. Prior to 1965, the US immigration system limited foreign entry by mandating extremely small quotas according to nation of origin. Hart–Celler, by contrast, allowed immigration based on both the possession of scarce skills and on family ties to citizens or permanent residents. It also significantly increased the total number of immigrants allowed into the country. Taiwan, like most other Asian countries, was historically limited to a maximum of 100 immigrant visas per year. As a result, only 47 scientist and engineers immigrated to the US from Taiwan in 1965. Two years later, in 1967, the number had increased to 1321 (Chang, 1992).

Taiwanese students came to the US by the thousands during the 1970s and 1980s. In fact, Taiwan sent more doctoral candidates in engineering to the US during the 1980s than any other country, including entire graduating classes from Taiwan's most élite engineering universities: National Taiwan University, National Chiaotung University, and Tsinghua University. These students were lured by the ample fellowship money available for graduate studies at US universities and pushed by the limited professional opportunities in Taiwan at the time. Most stayed in the US after graduation, recognizing that there would be little demand for their skills back home. Taiwanese policy makers complained bitterly at the time about losing the 'best and brightest' to the United States.

The influx of highly skilled immigrants coincided with the growth of a new generation of technology industries in Silicon Valley. As the demand for technical skill in the electronics industry exploded, it attracted recent graduates to the region. By 1990, one-third of all scientists and engineers in Silicon Valley's technology industries were foreign-born, primarily from Asia (Saxenian, 1999). By 2000, there were approximately 9000 US-educated

Taiwanese engineers and scientists working in Silicon Valley, the majority of whom arrived prior to 1990.

Early Chinese immigrants to Silicon Valley saw themselves as outsiders to the region's mainstream technology community. While most held graduate degrees in engineering from US universities and worked for established technology companies, they often felt personally and professionally isolated. Some responded to this sense of exclusion by organizing collectively.[5] They typically found one another socially first, coming together to celebrate holidays and family events. Over time, they turned the social networks to professional purposes, creating associations to provide resources and role models to assist the advancement of individuals within the technology community.

The Chinese Institute of Engineers (CIE) is commonly regarded as the 'grandfather' of the Chinese professional organizations in Silicon Valley. A small group of Taiwanese immigrants started a local branch of CIE (an older, New York-based organization) in 1979 to promote communication and co-operation among the region's Chinese engineers. Its early growth built on pre-existing social ties, as most of its members were graduates of Taiwan's top engineering universities. These alumni relations, which seemed more important to many Taiwanese immigrants when living abroad than they had at home, provided an important basis for solidarity among the region's immigrant engineers. The San Francisco Bay Area chapter of CIE quickly surpassed the original New York chapter to become the largest in the country, reflecting the shifting center of technology production in the United States.

The CIE is a scientific and educational organization whose goal is the exchange of engineering information. However, the initial meetings of the Bay Area chapter focused heavily on teaching members the mechanics of finding a job or starting a business, getting legal and financial help, and providing basic management training to engineers who had only technical education. Over time, CIE also became an important source of role models and mentors for newly arrived immigrants. Gerry Liu, who co-founded Knights Technology with four Taiwanese friends reports:

When I was thinking of starting my own business, I went around to call on a few senior, established Chinese businessmen to seek their advice. I called David Lee ... I contacted David Lam and Winston Chen. I called up Ta-lin Hsu. They did not know me, but they took my calls. I went to their offices or their homes, they spent time with me telling me what I should or shouldn't be doing.[6]

Liu was one of the first generation of Taiwanese to start a company in Silicon Valley, and he has in turn become a role model for later generations of Chinese immigrants.

CIE was just a start. In subsequent years, Silicon Valley's Taiwanese immigrants organized a variety of other technical and business associations, including the Chinese American Semiconductor Professionals Association, the Chinese American Computer Corporation, the Chinese Software Professionals Association, and the North American Taiwanese Engineers Association. These organizations are among the most vibrant and active in the region. Like the CIE, they combine elements of traditional immigrant culture with distinct high-technology practices: they simultaneously create ethnic identities and facilitate the professional networking and information exchange that aid success in Silicon Valley's decentralized industrial system (Saxenian, 1999).

Taiwanese engineers like Gerry Liu turned increasingly to entrepreneurship in the 1980s and 1990s, in response both to the perception of a 'glass ceiling' in the established companies and to the emergence of supportive ethnic networks and role models. It is difficult to accurately measure the rate of immigrant entrepreneurship, but data on the number of Chinese CEOs in the region serves as a useful proxy. While Chinese engineers were the chief executives of 9 per cent of all Silicon Valley companies started between 1980 and 1984, they were running 20 per cent of those started between 1995 and 1999. By 1999, Chinese were at the helm of 2001 Silicon Valley-based technology companies, or 17 per cent of the companies started in the region since 1980. The next largest group of foreign-born CEOs was Indians, who were running 774 firms, or 7 per cent of the total (Saxenian, 1999).

First-generation immigrants from Taiwan thus constructed a technical community in Silicon Valley, one that met both social and professional needs. This is not to suggest that they became a self-contained ethnic enclave. While many Taiwanese engineers socialize primarily with other Taiwanese immigrants and support one another when they start businesses, they also work closely with immigrants from other countries as well as with native-born engineers. There is growing recognition as well that while a start-up might be spawned with the support of ethnic networks, it must become part of the mainstream in order to grow. The most successful Chinese businesses in Silicon Valley today are those that draw on ethnic resources, at least initially, while integrating over time into the mainstream technology and business networks.[7]

It is worth noting as well that immigrant engineers from mainland China, a fast-growing presence in Silicon Valley in the 1990s, are creating their own social and professional associations rather than joining those established by their Taiwanese predecessors. This divide underscores the dangers of overstating the power of race or nationality in creating cohesive ethnic identities, which is often done in discussions of the business networks of the overseas Chinese. Collective identities are constructed over time, often through the kinds of face-to-face social interactions that are facilitated by geographic, occupational, or industrial concentration. The initial social connections often have a basis in shared educational experiences, technical backgrounds, language, culture, and history. Once established, these concentrations promote the frequent, intensive interactions that breed a sense of commonality and identification with members of the same group – and at the same time, exclude others, even of similar racial characteristics.[8]

9.4   Institutionalizing the Silicon Valley–Hsinchu Connection

Policy makers in Taiwan began to recognize that the 'brain-drain' could become a potential asset as they sought to upgrade the island's position in the international economy in the 1970s. They sponsored frequent technical meetings and conferences that brought together engineers based in both the United States and Taiwan.[9] They actively recruited Taiwanese engineers in the US to return home, either temporarily or permanently. And drawing heavily on policy advice from overseas Chinese, they developed strategies to upgrade the technological capabilities of the private sector and to promote new-firm formation and competition in the emerging information technology industries. In the 1970s and 1980s, government agencies in Taiwan aggressively transferred state-of-the-art technology from the US, created a venture capital industry long before it became fashionable elsewhere in the world, and developed other measures to diffuse technology, including the formation of the Hsinchu Science-based Industrial Park.

By exploiting this overseas resource, Taiwan's policy makers unwittingly supported the extension of Silicon Valley's Chinese network to include their counterparts in Taiwan. Frequent advisory meetings and technical interactions supported the creation of personal and professional relationships between engineers, entrepreneurs, executives, and bureaucrats on both sides of the Pacific. One indicator of this process is the list of recipients of the Chinese Institute of Engineers (USA) Annual Awards for Distinguished Service and for Achievement in Science and Engineering, which reads like a who's who of Chinese technologists based in the US and Taiwan over the past three decades.[10] In short, an unintended consequence of Taiwan's outward-looking technology strategy was creation of an international technical community, one that is now self-sustaining.

The accelerated growth of the Taiwanese economy in the 1980s, combined with active government recruitment, ultimately spurred a reversal of the 'brain-drain'. Lured primarily by the promise of economic opportunities as well as the desire to return to families and contribute to their home country, growing numbers of US-educated engineers returned to Taiwan in the 1990s. Approximately 200 engineers and scientists returned to Taiwan annually in the early 1980s. A decade later, more than 1000 were returning annually. According to the National Youth Commission, by 1998 more than 30 percent of the engineers who studied in the US returned to Taiwan, compared to only 10 percent in the 1970s (see Fig. 9.5).

The Silicon Valley–Hsinchu business connection was institutionalized in 1989 with the formation of the Monte Jade Science and Technology

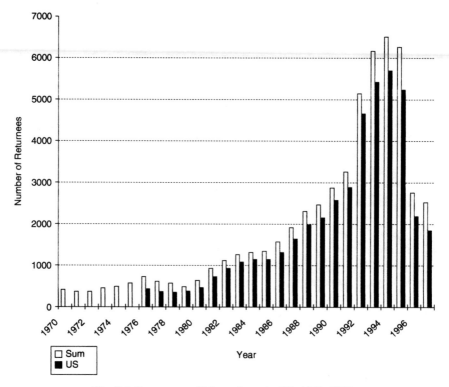

Fig. 9.5 Returnees to Taiwan from the US, 1970–1997.
Source: National Youth Commission, Taiwan

Association. Monte Jade was started in 1989 by a group of senior Taiwanese executives with the intention of promoting business co-operation, investment, and technology transfer between Chinese engineers in the Bay Area and Taiwan. The name Monte Jade, after the highest mountain peak in Taiwan, was chosen to signify 'cross cultural and technological foresight and excellence at the highest level'. Today, the organization has 150 corporate members in the Silicon Valley branch, including the leading Taiwanese technology companies, and 300 individual members, almost all of Taiwanese origin.

The primary objective of Monte Jade is to 'open up opportunities for professionals and corporations at both ends of the Pacific to network and share their valuable experiences'. While officials claim that there is no financial connection between Monte Jade and the Taiwanese government, the informal connections are clear. Monte Jade's main offices are in the same office suite as the Science Division and the local representatives of the Hsinchu Science-based Industrial Park. Proximity supports close and on-going interactions, and these interactions are by no means unintentional. A founding member described his vision for Monte Jade:

I felt that at the time we were right in the throes of a huge change in the Valley in terms of what Chinese-Americans role could be. Many of us had worked hard and long as engineers, had managed to get to the point where we were either head of the company or a key member of the management team of a company. It was very clear that the Chinese American contribution can [sic] go far beyond engineering and scientific contribution into the business domain ... what you need is a forum so that people can help each other, mentoring the younger generation, in terms of how to manage, how to run a business, how to get capital, and so on. ... At that time Taiwan was doing quite well ... the economic miracle had created a lot of wealth so a two-way bridge was needed between here and Taiwan.

He went on to note that these ties could not have developed earlier because Taiwan had not developed to the point that people like him could contribute. If they had gone back during the 1970s, he said, 'they would have been sweeping floors'.[11]

Monte Jade sponsors a large annual meeting that typically draws an audience of more than 1000 Chinese engineers from both the US and Taiwan for a day of technical meetings as well as an evening banquet. There are also smaller monthly dinner meetings as well as a variety of social events, both planned and unscheduled. These social gatherings, which typically include family members, are often as important as the professional activities in building shared identities. One indication of the association's success is that its monthly newsletter, which is in Chinese, can be easily found in both Silicon Valley and Hsinchu.

Monte Jade actively promotes entrepreneurship as well – a reflection of the extent to which the Taiwanese immigrants have adopted the Silicon Valley business model. The Annual Monte Jade Investment Conference draws hundreds of aspiring entrepreneurs, venture capitalists, and other service providers from the United States, Taiwan, and the rest of Asia. A special committee of the board of directors offers assistance to individual members who are considering starting companies regarding corporate for-mation, growth, and development. It also helps member firms with the flow of investment funds, technology transfer, and mergers and acquisitions. One executive reports building connections with individuals from the Taiwan Stock Exchange in order to help a new Silicon Valley company go public in Taiwan. Another claims that Monte Jade has been critical to giving confidence to a new generation of entrepreneurs, both in the US and Taiwan, because 'most of us know each other socially and we tend to refer problems and situations back and forth. This definitely helps our businesses.'[12]

While the Hsinchu Science Park was not the cause of Taiwan's success in IT, its success reflects the fast expanding ties between the two regions. After its first eight years (1980–1988) the Park was home to only 94 companies with under $2 billion in annual sales collectively, and it attracted only a handful of US-educated engineers per year. By the early 1990s, as the 'brain-drain' reversed, the Park became a destination for hundreds of returnees annually and they started new companies at an accelerating rate. The Park was attractive to engineers from the US in part because of its location close to the headquarters of ITRI and ERSO as well as two of Taiwan's leading engineering universities, and because it offered a range of fiscal incentives for qualified technology investments.[13] Equally important, the Park provided returnees with preferential access to scarce, high-quality housing and to the only Chinese-American school in Taiwan – both of which are located on the park grounds.

While only 184 Taiwanese had returned from the US to work in the Hsinchu Science Park in 1989, a decade later the total had increased more than 15-fold to 2840. And these returnees were disproportionately likely to start their own companies. Some 40 percent of the companies located in the Science Park (110 companies out of a total of 284) in 1999 were started by US-educated engineers, many of whom had considerable managerial or entrepreneurial experience in Silicon Valley. These returnees in turn actively recruited former colleagues and friends from Silicon Valley to return to Taiwan.

Take Miin Wu, who immigrated to the US in the early 1970s to pursue graduate training in electrical engineering. Like virtually all of his classmates from National Taiwan University, he took advantage of the ample fellowship aid available in the US at the time for poor but talented foreign students. After earning a doctorate from Stanford University in 1976, Wu recognized that there were no opportunities to use his newly acquired skills in economically backward Taiwan and he chose to remain in the US. He worked for more than a decade in senior positions at Silicon Valley-based semiconductor companies including Siliconix and Intel. He also gained entrepreneurial experience as one of the founding members of VLSI Technology.

By the late 1980s, economic conditions in Taiwan had improved dramatically and Wu decided to return home. In 1989, Wu started one of Taiwan's first semiconductor companies, Macronix Co, in the Hsinchu Science-based Industrial Park, with funding from H&Q Asia Pacific. He initially recruited 30 senior engineers, mainly former classmates and friends from Silicon Valley, to return to Taiwan. This team provided Macronix with the specialized technical skills and experience to develop new products and move into new markets quickly. Wu also transferred elements of the Silicon Valley management model to Macronix, including openness, informality, and the minimization of hierarchy – all significant departures from traditional Taiwanese corporate models. Macronix went public on the Taiwan stock exchange in 1995 and the following year became the first Taiwanese company to list on NASDAQ. The firm is now the sixth largest semiconductor maker in Taiwan, with over $500 million sales and some 3300 employees.

Although most Macronix employees and its manufacturing facilities are based in Taiwan, the firm has an advanced design and engineering center in Silicon Valley, and Wu regularly recruits senior managers from the Valley.

Macronix has also established a corporate venture capital fund that invests in promising start-ups based both in Silicon Valley and Taiwan. The goal of these investments is not to raise money but to develop technologies related to their core business. In short, Miin Wu's activities bridge and benefit both the Hsinchu (Taiwan) and Silicon Valley economies.

In addition to permanent returnees like Wu, a growing population of 'astronauts' work in *both* places and spend much of their lives on airplanes. While their families may be based on either side of the Pacific (most often they stay in California because of the lifestyle advantages), these engineers travel between Silicon Valley and Hsinchu once or even twice a month, taking advantage of the opportunities to play middlemen, bridging the two regional economies. This includes many Taiwanese angel investors and venture capitalists as well as executives and engineers from companies like Macronix with activities in the two regions. This lifestyle is, of course, only possible because of the improvements in transportation and communications technologies. However, it does not mean these 'astronauts' are rootless. Their dense personal networks and intimate local knowledge of both Silicon Valley and Hsinchu play a central role in co-ordinating economic linkages between the two regions.

Even engineers who remain in Silicon Valley are typically integrated into the transnational community. Many work for start-ups or large firms with activities in both regions. Some moonlight as consultants on product development for Taiwanese firms. Others return to Taiwan regularly for technical seminars sponsored by government agencies or professional associations like CIE.

As engineers travel between the two regions they carry technical knowledge as well as contacts, capital, and information about new opportunities and new markets. Moreover, this information moves almost as quickly between these distant regions as it does within Hsinchu and Silicon Valley because of the density of the social networks and the shared identities and trust within the community. These transnational ties have dramatically accelerated the flows of skill, know-how, and market information between the two regions. In the words of a Silicon-Valley-based Taiwanese engineer:

If you live in the United States it's hard to learn what is happening in Taiwan, and if you live in Taiwan it's hard to learn what is going on in the US. Now that people are going back and forth between Silicon Valley and Hsinchu so much more frequently, you can learn about new companies and new opportunities in both places almost instantaneously.[14]

In the words of another engineer who worked for IBM in Silicon Valley for 18 years before returning to Taiwan: 'There's a very small world between Taiwan and Silicon Valley' (Barnathan, 1992). Others say Taiwan is like an extension of Silicon Valley. The former CEO of Acer America claims that the continuous interaction between the Hsinchu and Silicon Valley has generated 'multiple positive feedbacks' that enhance business opportunities in both regions.[15]

Taiwanese returnees like Miin Wu have accelerated the transfer of organizational models from Silicon Valley as well. An engineer who returned from the US in 1993 and now works for Taiwan Semiconductor Manufacturing Company (TSMC) reports that the corporate culture of TSMC is more American than Taiwanese (Gargan, 1994). This is true of most Hsinchu-based technology companies, which have adopted variants of the Silicon Valley management model with its relative informality, minimization of hierarchy, and orientation toward entrepreneurial achievement.

While Taiwan's traditions of entrepreneurship, collaboration, relationship-based business, and resource sharing among SMEs have provided fertile ground for many aspects of Silicon Valley management models (Hamilton, 1997), others, such as the heavy reliance on family ties, have largely been abandoned. As a result, Taiwanese businessmen are often far more comfortable than their Asian counterparts setting up branches in Silicon Valley. Virtually all of the leading Taiwanese companies have research labs or design operations in the region.

9.5   Cross-Regional Collaborations and Industrial Upgrading

A community of Taiwanese returnees, 'astronauts', and US-based engineers has become the bridge between Silicon Valley and Hsinchu. What was once a one-way flow of technology and skill from the United States to Taiwan has become a two-way thoroughfare allowing producers in both regions to collaborate to enhance distinctive but complementary strengths of these comparably decentralized industrial systems. Fred Cheng, who runs Win-bond North America, claims that: 'The best way to start a technology company today is to take the best from each region, combining Taiwanese financial and manufacturing strength with Silicon Valley's engineering and technical skill.'[16] This appears to be a classic case of the benefits of comparative advantage. However, the economic gains from specialization and trade depend on the social structures and institutions that ensure flows of information and facilitate joint problem-solving between distant producers.

These cross-Pacific collaborations extend the localized processes of innovative upgrading through experimentation and recombination that occur *within* each region. The producers in both Silicon Valley and Hsinchu are organized to respond to uncertainty rather than to try to predict or plan for it. Taiwan's PC makers, for example, typically source components and parts from over 100 different local suppliers and subcontractors (Lin, 2000). The extensive social division of labor provides systems firms with the flexibility to shift rapidly, as they did in the early 1990s from low-margin desktop PCs into more profitable notebooks, and the specialization of producers allows each to remain at the leading edge of design and/or manufacturing capabilities.

Today, Taiwan manufactures PCs for the dominant computer firms from Dell and Compaq to Sony and Toshiba. More recently, Taiwanese producers have shifted into manufacturing mobile phones and information appliances.

This adaptation requires shifting patterns of collaboration, with new combinations emerging as markets shift and as local producers develop new technical capabilities. Taiwanese firms began producing CD-ROMs, modems, and TFT-LCDs in the 1990s, for example, and while they remain technological imitators in these products, they are now leading producers in each market. In short, Taiwan excels at both incremental product innovation and rapid development and commercialization.

The integration of the technical communities in Silicon Valley and Hsinchu has facilitated a new division of labor between the two regions. In some cases this is reflected in the location of divisions within a firm. Manufacturing-oriented firms like Macronix are based in Hsinchu and maintain design centers in Silicon Valley. Alternatively, Integrated Silicon Structures Inc. (ISSI), which designs ICs, is headquartered in Silicon Valley but works very closely with its manufacturing division in Hsinchu. Today, more than 67 Taiwanese technology firms have operations in Silicon Valley, including not only large established companies like Acer but also more recent start-ups like Via Technology. Division managers in these firms are typically well connected in the local labor market and technical community, while also maintaining close working relationships with their colleagues in the main office. Winbond's Fred Cheng, for example, has worked in Silicon Valley for 20 years, but knows Taiwan's technology community very well because he travels to headquarters at least 10 times a year.

The transnational community thus allows companies like Winbond to avoid the problems that many corporations face when they establish operations in Silicon Valley. Foreign firms need to be able to integrate into the region's social networks to gain access to up-to-date technology and market information, while simultaneously maintaining the ability to communicate quickly and effectively with decision-makers in the headquarters (Weil, 2001). More hierarchical European and Asian corporations often face difficulties developing such a two-way bridge to Silicon Valley.

The cross-regional collaborations between Hsinchu and Silicon Valley frequently involve vertical partnerships between producers at different stages in the supply chain. Take the relationship between Taiwan's foundries and their Silicon Valley equipment manufacturers. Steve Tso, a senior vice president in charge of manufacturing technology and services at TSMC, worked at semiconductor equipment vendor Applied Materials in Silicon Valley for many years before returning to Taiwan. He claims that his close personal ties with senior executives at Applied Materials provide TSMC with an invaluable competitive advantage by improving the quality of communication between the technical teams at the two firms – in spite of the distance separating them.

The interactions between TSMC and Applied Materials engineers are continual, according to Tso, and, for the most part, must be face-to-face because the most advanced processes are not yet standardized and many of the manufacturing problems they face are not clearly defined. Tso travels to Silicon Valley several times a year, and reports that teams of TSMC engineers can always be found in the Applied Materials' Silicon Valley facilities for training on the latest generations of manufacturing equipment. Engineers from Applied Materials, likewise, regularly visit TSMC. He argues that this close and ongoing exchange helps TSMC develop new process technologies quickly, while minimizing the technical problems that invariably arise when introducing new manufacturing processes. It also keeps his firm abreast of the latest trends and functions in equipment design.[17]

A comparable level of collaboration is required between the semiconductor foundries and their customers, the firms that design the integrated circuits. According to Tso, the engineers from Silicon Valley-based customers like AMD, National Semiconductor, S3, and Trident can always be found in the TSMC offices in Hsinchu, which are flexibly divided in order to allow their customers' technical teams to work closely with TSMC teams. Likewise, TSMC engineers spend significant amounts of time in their customers' facilities in Silicon Valley.

Taiwan's other leading semiconductor foundry, United Microelectronics Corporation (UMC), has gone a step further and institutionalized collaboration with Silicon Valley's 'fabless' chip designers. United Integrated Circuits Corporation (UICC) joins UMC with more than eight Silicon Valley design firms including Oak Technology, Trident Semiconductor, Opti, ISSI, and ESS – all of which were started by Chinese entrepreneurs. Each of the US partners holds 5–10 percent share in the $600 million fab, with UMC holding the 40 percent balance. UICC guarantees the design firms with secure foundry space even in the case of industry-wide capacity shortages, and it ensures UMC the capital it needs to build the fab as well as guaranteeing full capacity utilization.

A new breed of venture capitalists mediates these cross-regional collaborations (Saxenian and Li, 2001). Like their Silicon Valley-based predecessors, these transnational financiers often have technical training and work experience in either Taiwan or the United States. However, unlike older generations of venture capitalists, whose networks and investments tend to be very close to home, these investors see their role as bridging geographically distant centers of skill and excellence. In the words of Peter Liu (co-founder of WIIG who went on to start another venture firm, WI Harper):

WI Harper distinguishes itself from its Sand Hill counterparts through its personal and professional ties with key management in Asia. . . . In Asia it is very difficult to get good information, and through our established network of contacts we are in an excellent position to help the companies in which we invest. . . . We see ourselves as the bridge between Silicon Valley and Asia. (Hellman, 1998)

Ken Tai is a good example. Tai was a co-founder of Multitech, the forerunner of Acer, along with several classmates from Taiwan's Chaio-tung University. After working for 17 years at Acer, he worked for two start-ups before starting his own venture capital firm, InveStar. In 1996, its first year of operations, InveStar invested $50 million in Silicon Valley companies. Like Peter Lui, Tai sees his firm as a bridge linking Silicon Valley's new product designs and technology and Taiwan's semiconductor manufacturing and system integration capabilities.

The new technology is all in Silicon Valley, but when you want to integrate that technology into a final product, Taiwan is the best place. Taiwan is the best place to integrate technology components together in a very efficient way because it excels at production logistics and information handling.

Tai goes on to describe InveStar's role as an intermediary in this process:

When we invest in Silicon Valley startups we are also helping bring them to Taiwan. It is relationship-building...we help them get high-level introductions to the semi-conductor foundry and we help establish strategic opportunities and relationships in the PC sector as well. This is more than simply vendor–customer relationships. We smooth the relationships.[18]

The case of Platform Technology, a Silicon Valley start-up founded by US-educated Chinese entrepreneur Paul Tien, illustrates the benefits of the cross-Pacific relationships.[19] InveStar provided Platform with $3 million in 1996 when the firm was already several years old and was struggling to find customers, in spite of its state-of-the-art audio chip design. The InveStar partners also introduced Tien to senior executives at the leading PC companies in Taipei. Platform became known within Taiwan's technology circles, and got so many design wins that it quickly became one of the world's largest producers of audio chips. Platform was also having problems with the manufacturing process at its foundry, TSMC. As a small US-based start-up they could not get the attention of the giant chip manufacturer. Once again, the InveStar partners intervened by calling their friends at TSMC to ensure that Platform's calls were returned and that its problems were addressed immediately.

Or take the start-up Allayer, which was formed in Silicon Valley in 1997 to focus on the design of high bandwidth networking ICs. One of Allayer's investors and largest shareholders is Acer Capital America, the venture arm of Taiwan's Acer Group. The President of Acer Capital America, Ronald Chwang, sits on the Allayer Board of Directors and has actively helped them establish a partnership with D-Link, Taiwan's leading manufacturer of networking hardware, as well as with their OEM suppliers (foundries) TSMC and UMC. As a result, Allayer is now in the process of establishing an R&D subsidiary in Taiwan to design IC products to meet the special requirements of the local network industry, while also enhancing technical support and co-operation with other customers like D-Link.

These examples suggest that Taiwan's transnational entrepreneurs are well positioned to quickly identify promising new market opportunities, raise capital, build management teams and establish partnerships with other specialist producers – even those located at great geographical distances. The speed of personal communications and decision-making within this community as well as their close ties to Silicon Valley accelerates learning about new sources of skill, technology, capital, and about potential collaborators. It also facilitates timely responses. This responsiveness is difficult for even the most flexible and decentralized multinational corporations.

While Silicon Valley and Hsinchu remain at different levels of development and differently specialized, the interactions between the two regions are increasingly complementary and mutually beneficial. As long as the United States remains the largest and most sophisticated market for technology products, which seems likely for the foreseeable future, new product definition and leading-edge innovation will remain in Silicon Valley. However, Taiwanese companies continue to enhance their ability to design, modify, and adapt as well as rapidly commercialize technologies developed elsewhere. As local design and product development capabilities improve, Taiwanese companies are increasingly well positioned to take new product ideas and technologies from Silicon Valley and quickly integrate and produce them in high volume at relatively low cost.

9.6   Concluding Comments

The Taiwanese experience demonstrates that the social structure of a technical community is as important to organizing production at the global level as it is at the local level. Moreover, it suggests that the multinational corporation is no longer the privileged vehicle for transfers of knowledge and skill. A transnational technical community allows distant producers to specialize and collaborate to upgrade their capabilities, particularly when the collaborations require close communications and joint problem-solving. The trust and local knowledge that exist within technical communities, even those that span continents, provide a competitive advantage in an environment where success depends on being very fast to market. And rather than competing for a relatively fixed market, these specialists are jointly growing the market by continually introducing new products, services, and applications. As a result, while the relationships between producers in the two regions have deepened over time, they remain complementary and mutually beneficial rather than zero-sum.

The case also suggests that localization is not at odds with the globalization of economic activity. Rather they are mutually reinforcing. Globalization is increasingly a process of integration of specialized components through collaboration at an international level. This is best viewed as a process of recombination in which firms specialize in order to become global, and their specialization in turn allows them to be better collaborators. The best environments for breeding such specialist firms are the decentralized industrial systems of places like Silicon Valley and Hsinchu. Just as the social structures and institutions *within* these regions encourage entrepreneurship and learning at the regional level, so the creation of a transnational technical community facilitates collaborations between individuals and producers in the two regions and supports a process of reciprocal industrial upgrading.

The enduring importance of the technical community linking Silicon Valley and Hsinchu is reflected in current survey data (see Appendix). Silicon Valley's Taiwanese engineers and scientists continue to travel to Taiwan regularly (7.3 per cent travel to Taiwan more than five times a year for business purposes, 22 per cent travel between two and four times a year). The great majority (85.3 per cent) have friends and colleagues who have returned to Taiwan to work or start a company, with 15.8 per cent reporting more than 10. They regularly exchange information with friends and colleagues in Taiwan about technology and about job opportunities in both locations. More than one-third (38.9 per cent) have helped to arrange business contracts in Taiwan, one-quarter of them (24 per cent) have served as advisors and consultants for Taiwanese companies, and one-fifth (19.2 per cent) have invested their own money in start-ups or venture funds in Taiwan. Many have caught the Silicon Valley bug as well, with 58.8 per cent reporting that they plan to start their own business sometime in the future, and 50 per cent that say they would consider locating their business in Taiwan.

Transnational communities are not unique to Taiwan. Transnational entrepreneurs have been important actors in the development of new technology industries in Israel, India, and China. In each of these cases, engineers and entrepreneurs with ties to Silicon Valley's technical community have built the long-distance bridges that allow them to take advantage of specialized skill and resources in their home regions, while simultaneously maintaining a presence in Silicon Valley. And in each of these cases, venture capitalists and ethnic social networks and professional associations have played a central mediating role in the process (Autler, 2000; Saxenian, 1999; Teubal, 2000).

As governments around the world clamor to establish venture capital industries and technology parks in efforts to replicate the Silicon Valley experience, the Taiwanese case suggests that new centers of technology and entrepreneurship cannot be created in isolation. Rather they require ongoing connections to the US market – often through integration into Silicon Valley's technical community. The Taiwanese case also suggests that regions seeking to participate in global technology networks should devote as much attention to expanding education and training, creating institutions to support new firm formation, and building ties to Silicon Valley as to attempting to lure foreign investment.

Acknowledgement

We gratefully acknowledge the financial support of the Chiang Ching-Kuo Foundation and the Public Policy Institute of California.

Notes

1. The limits of patent data as a measure of innovation are well known. They are used here as a rough indicator of the differential technological performance of these economies.
2. An OEM arrangement is one in which the brand name company (the customer) provides detailed technical blueprints and most components that allow the contractor (the supplier) to produce according to specifications. Observers site the shift to ODM (original design manufacturing) in Taiwan as evidence of industrial upgrading because the contractor takes on the responsibility for design and most component procurement as well.
3. Taiwan's IT manufacturing capacity began shifting to regions of coastal China in the late 1990s to take advantage of significantly lower-cost labor, but the continued superiority of Taiwanese management and technology means that the business is still controlled by Taiwan-based firms.
4. It is possible to specialize without innovating, and it is possible to innovate without changing the division of labor. However, it seems that the deepening social division of labor enhances the innovative capacity of a community: expanding opportunities for experimentation generate ideas, these ideas are in turn combined to make new ideas, and so forth in a dynamic and self-generating process. This suggests that specialization increases innovation and ultimately economic growth.
5. Ironically, many of the distinctive features of the Silicon Valley business model were created during the 1960s and 1970s by engineers who saw themselves as outsiders to the mainstream business establishment in the East coast. The region's original industry associations like the American Electronics Association were an attempt to create a presence in a corporate world that Silicon Valley's emerging producers felt excluded from. These organizations provided role models and support for entrepreneurship similar to that now being provided within immigrant communities.
6. Interview, Gerry Liu, January 22, 1997.
7. This parallels Granovetter's (1995) notion of balancing coupling and decoupling in the case of overseas Chinese entrepreneurs.
8. This emphasis on the construction of professional identities differs from the often-cited role of *guanxi* in Chinese business relationships. See Hsu and Saxenian (2000).
9. This section draws heavily from account provided in Meany (1994). For more detailed accounts of the development strategies for Taiwan's technology industry, see Liu (1993) and Chang *et al.* (1994, 1999).
10. For the list of recipients, see www.cie-gnyc.org/Rwinner.htm.
11. Leonard Liu interview, April 3, 1998.
12. Lester Lee interview, July 1, 1997.

13. The incentives include low interest loans, a five-year income tax break for the first nine years of operation, the right to retain earnings of up to 200 per cent of paid-in capital, accelerated depreciation of R&D equipment, and low-cost land. This information and the data on the Park in the following paragraph comes from the Science Park Administration, Hsinchu Science-based Industrial Park.
14. C. B Liaw interview, August 28, 1996.
15. Ron Chwang interview, March 25, 1997.
16. Fred Cheng interview, March 25, 1997.
17. Steve Tso interview, March 15, 1999.
18. Ken Tai interview, May 16, 1997.
19. Herbert Chang interview, July 22, 1997.

References

Aoki, M. (2000), 'Innovation in the governance of product–system innovation: the Silicon Valley model,' Stanford Institute for Economic Policy Research, Policy Paper no. 00–003, October.

Autler, G. (2000), 'Global networks in high technology: the Silicon Valley–Israel connection,' Master's thesis, Berkeley: University of California.

Barnathan, T. (1992), 'Bringing it all back home,' *Business Week*, December 7, 13.

Borrus, M. (1988), *Competing for control: America's stake in microelectronics*. New York: Ballinger.

Borrus, M. (1997), 'Left for dead: Asian production networks and the revival of US electronics,' in B. Naughton (ed.), *The China circle: economics and technology in the PRC, Taiwan and Hong Kong*. Washington, DC : Brookings Institution Press, pp. 139–209.

Bresnahan, T. (1998), 'New modes of competition: implications for the future structure of the computer industry,' Conference paper, March.

Callon, S. (1995), Different paths: The rise of Taiwan and Singapore in the global personal computer industry,' Asia/Pacific Research Center, Stanford University, January.

Chang, P.-L., Hsu, C.-W., and Tsai C.-T. (1999), 'A stage approach for industrial technology development and implementation – the case of Taiwan's computer industry,' *Technovation*, **19**, 233–241.

Chang, P.-L., Shih, C., and Hsu, C.-W. (1994), 'The formation process of Taiwan's Ic industry – method of technology transfer,' *Technovation*, **14**, 161–171.

Chang, S. L. (1992), 'Causes of brain drain and solutions: the Taiwan experience,' *Studies in Comparative International Development*, **27**, 27–43.

Chung, M. K. (2000), 'One best way? Niche market player or global Market player: the case of the Korean and Taiwanese electronics industries,' Paper presented at the International Conference on Business Transformation and Social Change in East Asia, Taiwan, Tunghai University, June 2–3.

Dedrick, J. and Kraemer, K. (1998), *Asia's computer challenge: threat or opportunity for the United States and the World?* New York: Oxford University Press.

ERSO/ITRI (1999), *Taiwan semiconductor industry – 1999 Edition*. Electronic Research and Service Organization, Hsinchu, Taiwan: Industrial Technology Research Institute.

Ernst, D. (1998), 'What permits David to defeat Goliath? The Taiwanese model in the computer industry,' unpublished paper, BRIE, Berkeley: University of California.

Gargan, E. (1994), 'High tech Taiwanese come home,' *New York Times*, July 19, C1–2.

Gilder, G. (1989), *Microcosm: the quantum revolution in economics and technology*. New York: Simon & Schuster.

Granovetter, M. (1995), 'The economic sociology of firms and entrepreneurs,' in A. Portes (ed.), *The economic sociology of immigration*. New York: Russell Sage.

Hamilton, G. (1997), 'Organization and market processes in Taiwan's capitalist economy,' in M. Orru *et al.* (eds), *The economic organization of East Asian capitalism*. Thousand Oaks, CA: Sage, pp. 237–293.

Hellman, T. (1998), 'WI Harper International: Bridge between Silicon Valley and Asia,' Graduate School of Business, Stanford University, SM-39.

Hsu, J.-y. (1997), 'A late industrial district? Learning networks in the Hsinchu Science-based industrial park,' doctoral dissertation, Department of Geography, Berkeley: University of California.

Hsu, J.-y. and Saxenian, A. (2000), 'The limits of guanxi capitalism: transnational collaboration between Taiwan and the US,' *Environment and Planning A*, **32**: 1991–2005.

Huang, C. (1995), 'R.O.C.: republic of computers,' *Common Wealth Magazine*, June 1, 221–224 (in Chinese).

Kogut, B. and Zander, U. (1993), 'Knowledge of the firm and the evolutionary theory of the multinational corporation,' *Journal of International Business Studies*, **24**(4): 625–646.

Kraemer, K., Dedrick, J., Hwang, C.-Y., Tu, T.-C., and Yap, C.-s. (1996), 'Entrepreneurship, flexibility, and policy coordination: Taiwan's computer industry,' *Information Society*, **12**: 215–249.

Krugman, P. (1991), *The geography of trade*. Cambridge, MA: MIT Press.

Lau, L. J. (1994), 'The competitive advantage of Taiwan,' *Journal of Far Eastern Business*, Autumn, 90–112.

Levy, B. and Kuo, W.-J. (1991), 'The strategic orientation of firms and the performance of Korea and Taiwan in frontier industries: lessons from comparative case studies of the keyboard and personal computer assembly,' *World Development*. **19**(4): 363–374.

Lin, T. (2000), 'The social and economic origins of technological capacity: A case study of the taiwanese computer industry,' Doctoral dissertation, Temple University, Sociology Department, January.

Liu, C.-Y. (1993) 'Government's role in developing a high-tech industry: the case of taiwan's semiconductor industry,' *Technovation*, **13**: 299–309.

Mathews, j. A. (1997), 'A Silicon Valley of the East: Creating Taiwan's semiconductor industry,' *California Management Review*, **39**(4): 26–54.

Meany, C. S. (1994), 'State policy and the development of Taiwan's semiconductor industry,' in J. Aberbach *et al.* (eds), *The role of the state in Taiwan's development*. London: sharpe , pp. 170–192.

Porter, M. (1998), 'Clusters and the new economics of competition,' *Harvard Business Review*, November–December, 77–90.

Portes, A. (1996), 'Global villagers: the rise of transnational communities,' *American Prospect*, March–April, 74–77.

Saxenian, A. (1994), *Regional advantage: culture and competition in Silicon Valley and route 128*. Cambridge, MA: Harvard University Press.

Saxenian, A. (1999), *Silicon Valley's new immigrant entrepreneurs*. Public Policy Institute of California: San Francisco, CA (www.ppic.org/publications/PPIC120/index.html).

Saxenian, A. and Li, C.-Y. (2001), 'Bay-to-bay strategic alliances: the network linkages between Taiwan and the US venture capital industries,' *International Journal of Technology Management*, forthcoming.

Trajtenberg, M. (1999), 'Innovation in Israel, 1968–97: A comparative analysis using patent data,' Working Paper no. 7022, Cambridge, MA: National Bureau of Economic Research.

Teubal, M. (2000), 'Globalization and firm dynamics in the Israeli software industry: a case study of data security,' The Hebrew University.

Wade, R. (1990), *Governing the market: economic theory and the role of government in East Asian industrialization*. Princeton, NJ: Princeton University Press.

Weil, T.(2000), 'Why and how European companies reach out to Silicon Valley,' in F. Sachwald (eds), *The new American challenge*, notes de l' Insitut Français des Relations Internationales, le Documentation française, October 2000.

Appendix. The Silicon Valley–Hsinchu Technical Community

The following data are from a web survey of foreign-born professionals in Silicon Valley conducted during May 2001.

Taiwanese sample, n = 180. Of this group, 85 percent have postgraduate degrees (Masters or Ph.D.), 92 percent of which were obtained in the US, and 78 per cent are in technical, scientific, or engineering fields.

How many of your friends and/or colleagues have returned to Taiwan to work or start a company?

None	14.7 percent
1–9	69.5
10–20	10.5
21	5.3

How often have you travelled to Taiwan for business purposes on average during the past three years?

5 or more times a year	7.3 percent
2–4 times a year	22.0
Once a year	31.2

How often do you exchange information about the following with family, friends, classmates, or business associations outside of the US?

	Jobs in the US	Jobs in Taiwan	Technology
Regularly	12.0 percent	7.6 percent	15.2 percent
Sometimes	69.6	62.0	66.3
Never	18.5	30.4	18.5

Have you ever served as an advisor or a consultant for a company from Taiwan?

Yes	24 percent
No	76

Have you helped others arrange business contracts in Taiwan?

Yes	38.9 percent
No	61.1

Have you invested your own money in start-ups or venture funds in Taiwan?

Yes, more than once	12.2 percent
Yes, only once	5.0
Never	80.8

Do you have plans to start your own business on a full-time basis?

Yes, this year	3.2 percent
Sometime in the future	55.6
Never	12.7
Don't know	28.5

Would you consider locating your business in Taiwan?

Yes	50 percent
No	50

10

The Institutional Embeddedness of High-Tech Regions: Relational Foundations of the Boston Biotechnology Community

KELLEY PORTER, KJERSTEN BUNKER WHITTINGTON,
AND WALTER W. POWELL

10.1 Introduction

The biotechnology industry exemplifies many of the key features of science-based clusters. Biotechnology firms in both the US and Europe are located in a small number of geographic regions. Within these clusters, there are extensive relations between firms and public research organizations, including universities, government laboratories, and research hospitals. In the United States, the strength and robustness of the three leading biotechnology clusters – the San Francisco Bay Area, the Boston Metropolitan area, and San Diego County – stem from the joint contributions of both public and private organizations to scientific and technical advance (Owen-Smith *et al.*, 2002). The combination of dense social networks and geographic co-location has been critical to the genesis of these high-tech regions (Bunker Whittington *et al.*, 2005).

Research in both economics and sociology has made notable strides in accounting for the factors that generate regional advantage. A rich literature has chronicled the tendency for the research and development efforts of organizations to leak out and aid the innovation efforts of other organizations (Jaffe, 1986, 1989). Such spillover effects occur broadly across industries (Jaffe *et al.*, 2000), but are accelerated within regions (Jaffe *et al.*, 1993). These effects are further amplified when key participants in a region are public research organizations, committed to norms of open science and information disclosure (Dasgupta and David, 1994; Owen-Smith and Powell, 2004). Studies of regional advantage have also emphasized the myriad dense connections that knit together high-tech clusters (Saxenian, 1994; Kenney, 2000). The effects of propinquity are further increased when strategic alliances connect local participants (Almeida and Kogut, 1999). Consequently, both Brown and Duguid (2000) and Kogut (2000) argue that in a technology cluster, the network of relationships among participants is the primary source of knowledge.

Thus, we know that the joint and contingent effects of geography and network connections are crucial to the innovative capacity of high-tech clusters. But what types of network relations are most critical? Do informal personal ties and occupational relations provide more open pathways to enhance the flow of ideas than more formal, contractual affiliations? Does the institutional form of the dominant organization shape the organizational practices of the members of a regional community, determining the nature of spillovers? How does the overlap of multiple types of networks across a diverse array of organizations create an ecosystem, with a distinctive character and accompanying norms that define membership in this community? To address these questions, we combine four unique data sets that account, in various ways, for the organization of the life-sciences community in the greater Boston, Massachusetts metropolitan area.

Boston is home to one of the largest concentrations of dedicated biotechnology firms in the world.[1] In addition, Boston has a rich array of public research organizations, including research universities (Harvard, MIT, Tufts), research hospitals (Brigham and Women's, Massachusetts General), and medical research institutes (Dana Farber Cancer Center). During the 1990s, the Boston area also developed a very active venture capital sector that funded biotech start-up firms (Powell *et al.*, 2002). By the beginning of the twenty-first century, the Kendall Square neighborhood in Cambridge, Massachusetts was home to the world's largest single, geographically concentrated cluster of biotech firms. Kendall Square is also home to MIT and the Whitehead Institute for Biomedical Research, an international leader in the Human Genome Project. More recently, multinational pharmaceutical firms such as Pfizer and Novartis have moved R&D facilities to Kendall Square, as has the Los Angeles-based company Amgen, the largest biotech firm in terms of annual sales. In sum, by one accounting (Owen-Smith and Powell, 2004), the Boston region had a total of 57 independent, dedicated biotech firms, 19 public research organizations, including universities and hospitals, and 37 venture capital firms between 1988 and 1999. This diverse set of organizations is linked by a wide array of formal and informal relationships.

The Origins of Biotech in Boston.   The initial burst of organizational foundings in Boston occurred in the late 1970s and early 1980s. The year 1980 is often cited as a watershed year, as a trio of events generated widespread attention to biotechnology. Savvy analysts, however, argue that the acceptance that occurred in 1980 was the icing on the cake because considerable university and company activity was already underway (Mowery *et al.*, 2004). In 1980, the Supreme Court approved the patenting of genetically engineered biological material in the Diamond v. Chakrabatty case, while the US Congress passed the Bayh–Dole Act, allowing US universities to retain intellectual property rights to the commercial applications based on basic research funded by federal grants. In the fall of 1980, the Bay Area company Genentech had a hugely successful initial public offering. These events are regarded as a catalyst to the legitimation of biotechnology (Teitelman, 1989; Robbins-Roth, 2000).

The emergence of biotechnology in the Boston area was not a smooth process, however. Unlike in California, where biotechnology was regarded as the new alchemy, in Boston there was much more contention (Watson, 2003: Chap. 4). In the summer of 1976, the city of Cambridge, MA passed a ban on research involving DNA, based on fears that researchers would contaminate the local water supply. In early 1977, the city council overturned this ban. In the interim, however, Harvard researcher, entrepreneur, and Nobel laureate Walter Gilbert moved his work to the United Kingdom. One of Boston's most notable firms, Biogen, co-founded by Gilbert, established its legal charter in Luxembourg to avoid local restrictions and controversies.

The relative absence of a venture capital community and the strong presence of public research organizations also stamped Boston in other ways. Three of the major early firms – Biogen, Genzyme, and Genetics Institute – had unusual developmental trajectories. Biogen soon settled in Cambridge, MA after its European legal origins. The company chose a strategy of licensing its lead development projects to large pharmaceutical companies rather than pursuing the more independent and risky path chosen by firms founded in California. Genzyme was very much influenced by 'refugees' from the health care corporation, Baxter, most notably Henri Termeer, from Baxter's blood plasma division (Robbins-Roth, 2000; Higgins, 2005). Genetics Institute (GI) followed the more upstart approach of California biotechs, attempting to develop a genetically engineered medicine that was a biotech alternative to an existing pharmaceutical product for heart attacks. GI lost out in this race to the Bay Area firm Genentech, and was subsequently acquired by the large corporation, American Home Products (Powell and Brantley, 1996). Many GI scientists, however, refused to accept their loss of autonomy, and continued to both publish and patent under the GI name. Eventually, American Home Products and Wyeth merged, and GI re-emerged as the biotech branch of Wyeth. We have documented that Boston-based biotech companies have focused more on orphan drugs and medicines for well-defined patient groups than have Bay Area biotechs, which have aimed their R&D efforts at larger markets with first-to-the-world medicines (Owen-Smith and Powell, 2005). We contend this distinction between delivering therapeutic treatments for known populations and 'swinging for the fences' reflects the strong public research organization imprint in Boston and the significant venture capital influence in the Bay Area.

10.2   Tracing Technology Networks

Relations between US universities and industry have a deep and long-standing history (Geiger, 1986; Rosenberg and Nelson, 1994). This 'knowledge plus' orientation of American research universities has contributed to the rapid development of a number of key science- and technology-based industries, particularly in information and communications technologies and in the biomedical field. University–industry interfaces may well be more extensive in the field of biotechnology than any other science or technology sector. Unlike in other technology fields, universities have continued to play a fundamental, driving role in biotech, long after initial discoveries emerged from university laboratories and were commercialized by science-based companies (Powell, 1996; Mowery *et al.*, 2004). The array of university–industry linkages in the life sciences spans both formal connections and informal flows. A partial list includes:

- the movement of university graduates into commercial firms;
- consulting relations between faculty and companies;
- licensing of university technologies;
- industry gifts supporting university research and student training;
- faculty entrepreneurship leading to the founding of new companies;
- faculty involvement on scientific advisory boards;
- co-patenting between university and industry scientists;
- formal contractual partnerships to pursue joint R&D, product or prototype development,and clinical trials.

In detailed work on the specific area of tissue engineering, Murray (2002, 2004) has chronicled a wide range of relationships that promote knowledge transfers between university labs and biotech firms. Joint authorship, the sharing of research tools and equipment, mentoring relations, and personnel movement all contribute to the creation and maintenance of a closely linked technological community.

Most current research on science networks focuses on just one type of relationship – contractual ties, patent or publication citation networks, or academic entrepreneurs (Powell *et al.*, 1996; Fleming *et al.*, 2004; Shane, 2004). Thus, we do not know how networks are overlaid on one another, and which types of linkages are generative and which ones provide the relational glue that sustains relationships over time. In previous work, we have argued that formal contractual relationships are but 'the tip of an iceberg', and are built on prior informal relations that may stem from common graduate school training, post-doctoral experience, or professional careers (Powell *et al.*, 1996). Murray (2004) suggests that, in addition to intellectual capital, academics who start biotech firms bring social capital through their local laboratory networks and their wider, cosmopolitan affiliations with co-authors and colleagues. In his research on the high-tech sector in Boston in the early 1990s, Gulati (1995) also found that business relations commonly grew from prior friendship ties. There are, however, other forms of affiliation than friendship or business; moreover, relations that begin as formal partnerships can become cemented through friendship, just as friends may become business partners. A full understanding of the development of a regional economy or an industrial district requires insight into how multiple networks stitch together a community, generating multiple independent pathways through which ideas, people, and resources can travel. In short, we argue that the intersection of multiple networks – precisely what Granovetter (1985) termed embeddedness – is the wellspring of successful technology clusters.

Collecting data on multiple networks, however, is a daunting task. And discerning the extent to which one type of association is either related to, or amplifies, another type of affiliation is even more challenging. We attempt this task here in order to explore the relational foundations of the Boston biotechnology cluster. We begin with formal linkages as a starting point, using a dataset on contractual ties as a basis on which to identify organizational founders, members of scientific advisory boards, and inventor networks. Our goal is to discern how the overlap of these four different networks – alliances, founding teams, science boards, and inventors – constitutes the nexus of a community of practice in the Boston region.

Alliances.   We begin with a database that covers the formal contractual ties involving 482 dedicated biotechnology firms (DBFs) over the period 1988–1999 (Powell *et al.*, 1996; Powell *et al.*, 2005).[2] The data on biotech firms, their partners, and the associated interorganizational relations among them were drawn from *Bioscan*, an industry source published six times a year. The organizational data include firm age, size, public status, reasons for exit (when applicable), and contractual ties. Tie data allow us to calculate measures of network experience, diversity, and centrality, as well as to classify individual linkages by the type of business activity they entail. These linkages represent annual snapshots of the formal network that constitutes the 'locus of innovation' in biotechnology. We extract from this global network the 114 organizations located in Boston, and the alliances among them (Owen-Smith and Powell, 2004).

Founding Teams.   This group of 114 Boston-based organizations, along with their collaborators, serves as the foundation for three complementary, more relational datasets that capture different kinds of collaborations. The first is a detailed database on organizational foundings. We were able to obtain complete information on the founders for 52 of the 57 dedicated human biotech firms established in the Boston area. Founders were identified on a company's web site, designated as such in press releases, or reported in a firm's filing with the Securities and Exchange Commission (SEC). There are 131 individuals involved in creating biotech companies over the period 1980 to 1997. Fifty-four per cent of the founders are from local Boston organizations.[3] The average number of founders per DBF is 2.5, although 13 companies have only one founder. More than half (52 per cent) are faculty from universities, and the large majority (48 out of 67) are from Boston-area universities. Interestingly, nearly all university-based founders retain some form of affiliation with their universities. For example, none of the six scientists who came together to start Biogen left their primary jobs. Other founders come from a business background, typically as pharmaceutical executives (15 per cent) or venture capitalists (12 per cent). Others come from a scientific background, either as post-doctoral fellows or scientists at an established company (17 per cent). A small number (4 per cent) are serial entrepreneurs who have started more than one company and have both prior science and business experience. Only 34 per cent of the founders work full time for the biotech start-up, the others hold a part-time affiliation and retain their affiliation with their 'home' organization. Unlike the contractual linkages, which we restrict to Boston because of their large number, we include both founders and scientific advisory board members whose former and/ or primary affiliations are from within as well as outside the Boston area.

Scientific Advisory Boards. We supplement the founders' database with information on the scientific advisory boards (SABs) established by these companies. Firms create science advisory boards in order to access cutting-edge research, evaluate the clinical development prospects for research that is underway, create linkages to practitioner and patient communities, as well as consolidate ongoing relations with prestigious research scientists (Audretsch and Stephan, 1996). We have information on the advisory boards of 45 of the 57 Boston biotech firms.[4] The average size of a scientific advisory board is 8.8, with variation ranging from a low of two to a high of 26. In total, there are 366 scientists on the advisory boards, with approximately one-third from Boston-area institutions. Of the 366 individuals on SABs, 319 sit on only one Boston DBF, 37 on two boards, nine serve on three, and one scientist is a member of four Boston-based SABs. Among these board members, 47 are also founders of Boston-area DBFs.[5]

Inventor Networks. To capture less formal linkages, we turn to data on research collaborations. We collect data on co-assigned patents by inventors at both dedicated biotech firms and research universities in the greater Boston area.[6] Our focus is only on those patents that are assigned to more than one inventor. These represent, we think, interesting examples of scientific collaborations that allow us to understand the impact of research on the development of a biotech cluster. The co-inventor science network also highlights the critical role played by founders, scientific advisory board members, and scientists that move between universities and companies.

The patent data consist of inventor-level information from United States patents filed between 1976 and 1998 from universities and DBFs in the Boston region. The academic sample includes all 'Research One' universities in the Boston region (Harvard, Tufts, Boston University, and MIT).[7] To gain information on the individuals involved with each patent, the patent numbers were obtained by matching Boston-area DBF and university names with patent assignees from the United States Patent and Trademark Office database. Patent numbers for these organizations were then matched with the NBER inventor data obtained from the United States Patent and Trademark Office (Hall *et al.*, 2001).[8]

Multiple inventions by the same person require the confirmation of similar names. Inventions are considered to be from the same person when two inventors match in first, middle, and last name (or part thereof, in the case of missing middle or first names). Importantly, however, two names are only considered a match if they have similar first, middle and last names and a similar city and state, assignee name, or the same primary and secondary technology class. We also locate Boston biotechnology founders and their scientific advisory board members in the inventor network. Of the 131 founders and the 366 scientific advisory board members, 67 (51 per cent) and 67 (18 per cent) have been granted patents that were assigned to Boston universities and DBFs.

The data for this analysis represent actor-by-actor networks, derived from two-mode affiliation data, where the inventors are the actors and each patent is the event. In this way, a connection between inventors is assumed on the basis of their collaborative research activity. Most patents represent a costly and time-consuming process of collaboration between two or more inventors. The lengthy two-plus year timeline between a filed and issued patent, and the considerable cost in filing, render patents a less common form of dissemination, compared to publishing or conference presentations. As such, co-patenting represents a strong partnership linking scientific research with commercial application.

bWe focus our analysis of the patent collaboration network on the largest, weakly connected component in a network (White and Harary, 2001; Moody and White, 2003). This structure, the 'main component', represents the greatest concentration of co-inventors, and the largest hub of patenting collaboration in the Boston region.[9] Of the 57 firms in our Boston sample, just 14 appear in the main component at least once between 1976 and 1998. Three universities – Harvard, MIT, and Boston University – also appear in the main component. Between 1976 and 1998, there are 907 inventors who have been assigned 896 patents in the Boston main component: 67 per cent ($N = 610$) of the inventors are listed on patents assigned to universities, 29 per cent ($N = 266$) are on patents granted to biotechnology firms, and 4 per cent are to scientists who patent with both firms and universities. Of the 67 founders and 67 advisors who have patents, 15 and 13, respectively, are located in the main component.

10.3   Visualizations of the Networks

We turn now to graphical representations of the four network databases we have assembled.[10] Our aim is to provide 'maps', or visual images of the networks at key points in their emergence and evolution.[11] We draw inferences from the representations of each data set, and then culminate by locating the firms and universities, company founders, and scientific advisory board members in the co-patent network. Recall that our goal is to understand how multiple networks overlap, as well as to explicate the intersection of university and commercial science. We believe this embeddedness is crucial to the development and growth of successful high-tech clusters. For readers who are unfamiliar with network visualizations, allow us to suggest how the pictures should be viewed. The software we employ, Pajek, utilizes algorithms that represent centrality in a network of affiliations. The nodes are the actors – be they individuals or organizations – and the lines are forms of affiliation – contractual linkages, founding teams, advisory boards, and co-patenting. With this program, nodes repel one another and lines pull nodes together. Thus, our representations are stable configurations that reflect a local equilibrium – the overall pattern and density of affiliations as the field is captured at rest. Hence, the visualizations are referred to as minimum-energy drawings. These representations create real clusters of tightly connected participants, which are central to the formation and durability of the overall network. As an illustration, Harvard scientists sit on numerous scientific advisory boards. Because of these connections, Harvard is centrally located in the advisory board network. A line, or edge, links the Harvard node with each of the DBF nodes. The more Harvard faculty that sit on the board of a particular DBF, the shorter the line connecting Harvard and that DBF. We use the visualizations to discern which individuals and organizations provide the foundation of the network, and which function as its backbone over time.

The Boston Contractual Network. We begin with formal linkages among organizations in the Boston area, conceiving of these connections as one indicator of membership in a regional community. We have shown in previous work that both membership and position in the local network have a significant effect on the volume of patenting by biotech firms (Owen-Smith and Powell, 2004; Bunker Whittington *et al.*, 2005). Figure 10.1 presents a series of images of the Boston network in 1988. The shape of nodes in the network represents organizational type – triangles represent public research organizations (PROs), circles indicate DBFs, and squares reflect the position of venture capital (VC) firms. No pharmaceutical companies are located in Boston during this time period.

Note several interesting features of Fig. 10.1. First, consider the Boston network at the upper left. In 1988, this network is relatively sparse with the bulk of organizations isolated from the network of formal relationships. The ties that do exist, though, form a dominant main component.[12] More interestingly, note the critical role that PROs (triangles) play in connecting the main component of the network and the relative absence of VC firms (there are few squares and only one is connected even peripherally to the main component). Six public research organizations (MIT, BostonUniversity,Tufts,Harvard, the Dana Farber Cancer Center, Massachusetts General Hospital, and the New England Medical Center) are

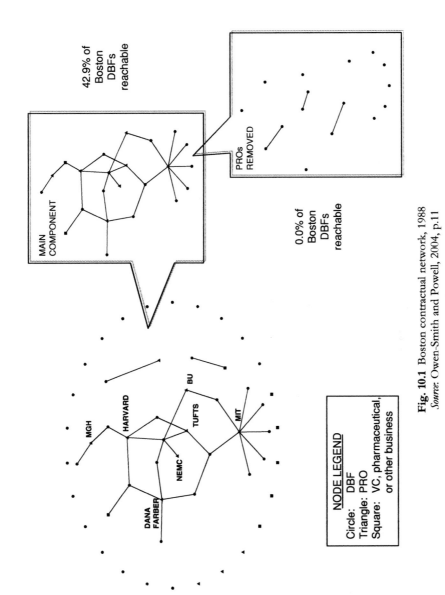

Fig. 10.1 Boston contractual network, 1988

Source: Owen-Smith and Powell, 2004, p.11

centrally positioned; they are among the most connected organizations. Four biotech firms (circles) are also well connected. These are the companies Biogen, Genetics Institute, Genzyme, and Seragen. But overall, in 1988, the Boston biotechnology community is rather sparsely connected internally by formal collaborations. While the main component contains nearly 43 per cent of active Boston-area DBFs, the network is heavily dependent for its cohesiveness upon key public research organizations. Removing these organizations from the network results in the complete collapse of the main component. Put differently, the formal, contractual network dissembles without universities and research hospitals. Figure 10.1 suggests that, early in its development, the Boston biotechnology community was weakly linked with less than half of all local DBFs reachable through formal network channels. The early coherence of this regional network is dependent upon the very active engagement of local public research organizations.

As a point of comparison, Fig. 10.2 reprises Fig. 10.1 to present the Boston network in 1998. By then, more than 71 per cent of Boston DBFs were connected to the main component. More importantly, the network itself has undergone a marked change as local biotech firms began working directly with one another, rather than forming indirect 'chains' through shared ties to PROs. Local VC firms are also much more engaged; their presence is apparent in the portion of the corridor to the right of MIT. PROs (particularly MIT, BU, Harvard, and Brigham and Women's Hospital) still play an important role in 1998, but their dominance is declining, as evidenced by the image of the component with PROs removed.

Specifically, consider the final frame of Fig. 10.2, which illustrates that nearly 36 per cent of Boston DBFs remain connected in a component that does not rely on public organizations. Indeed, the growth of biotech-to-biotech ties and the increasing support of local VCs suggest that Boston has undergone a transition from its early dependence upon PROs to a more market-oriented regime where small science-based firms and venture capital play key connective roles.

In related work (Owen-Smith and Powell, 2004), we have shown that the Boston biotech community changed in another key respect as well. The network of contractual affiliations also spread out over the 1990s, with alliances to organizations outside Boston growing rapidly in number and density. This growing reach is accompanied by a similar shift from PRO dominance to commercial leadership. This expansion notwithstanding, the Boston biotech community was clearly anchored by universities and research institutes. These early institutional underpinnings came from organizations with a strong commitment to the norms of open science, where practices of publishing and wide dissemination of research results are paramount (Dasgupta and David, 1987, 1994; Powell, 1996). Interestingly, then, the rapid emergence of commercial biotechnology in Boston owes a considerable debt to public science. We turn now to three other sets of relations in order to examine more fully the Boston community.

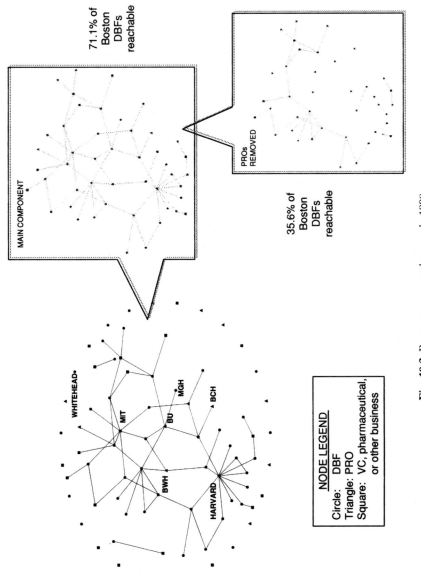

Fig. 10.2 Boston contractual network, 1998

Source: Owen-Smith and Powell, 2004, p.14

The Structure of Founding Teams.   We have collected data on the founders of biotechnology firms in Boston, tracing their biographies back to their undergraduate training (Porter, 2004). These career history data allow us to construct a founder affiliation network,[13] in which we link the newly founded firm with the organization that a founder belongs to either concurrently with or immediately prior to the creation of the biotech company.[14] A new biotech company typically requires some combination of scientific competence in the life sciences, some business experience in either the pharmaceutical industry or high-tech fields, and venture capital involvement (Porter, 2004).

Figure 10.3 presents an early picture of the founder affiliation network in 1983. Circles represent DBFs, triangles are PROs, and squares are venture capital, pharmaceutical, or biomedical companies. This visualization shows six hubs, representing the founding teams of Biogen, Advanced Magnetics, Integrated Genetics, Creative Biomolecules, Genzyme, and T Cell Science. These groups would be unconnected were it not for MIT that connects to Integrated Genetics, Genzyme, and Biogen, where Nobel Laureate and MIT faculty member Phillip Sharp was a co-founder. These three firms, along with Repligen and Applied Biotechnology, have one or more MIT faculty members on their founding teams.

Figure 10.4 portrays the Boston sector a decade and a half later, in 1997. We see Millennium, the genomics company, Cubist, Argule, Mitotix, and CpG ImmunoPharma as key new entrants to the network. Again, MIT is an important bridge, linking Cubist, Millennium, and Genetix. Harvard appears as another major bridge, also connecting Millennium, Genetix, Boston Life Sciences Inc., and Leukosite.

Figure 10.5 depicts the founder network for all years – 1976 to 2003. Because this visualization is incredibly dense and crowded when we include all relationships, we display the network with only those organizations that have two or more founder linkages. In this summary figure, the centrality of both MIT and Harvard is readily apparent, as these are the two most extensively linked organizations. Slightly more than one-quarter (26 per cent) of biotech firms in Boston were founded exclusively by faculty from Harvard or MIT.

These figures highlight how the backgrounds of founders of Boston companies have shifted over time. This transition is reflected in the changes in both the shape and position of the nodes in Figs. 10.3 and 10.4. Note in Fig. 10.3 the important role played by VCs in establishing firms. In the early 1980s, about 30 per cent of the start-ups had a venture capitalist on the founding team. By 1997, the role of VCs decreased and the importance of founders with prior experience in biotechnology rose. VCs returned to the more standard job of investor and biotech veterans provided the business expertise. Thus, throughout the 1980s and 1990s, Harvard and MIT remained the key source of scientific ideas, while those providing business acumen shifted from venture capital to biotech executives.

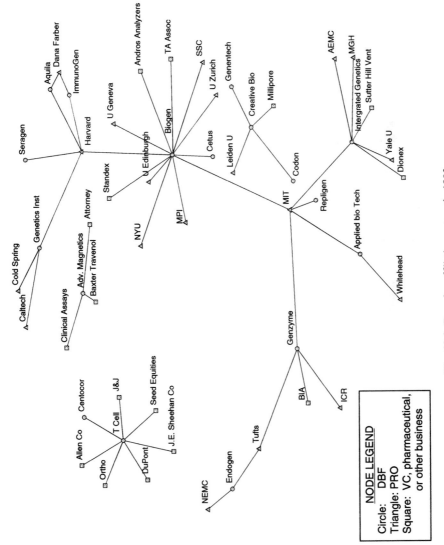

Fig. 10.3 Founder affiliation network, 1983

NODE LEGEND

Circle: DBF
Triangle: PRO
Square: VC, pharmaceutical, or other business

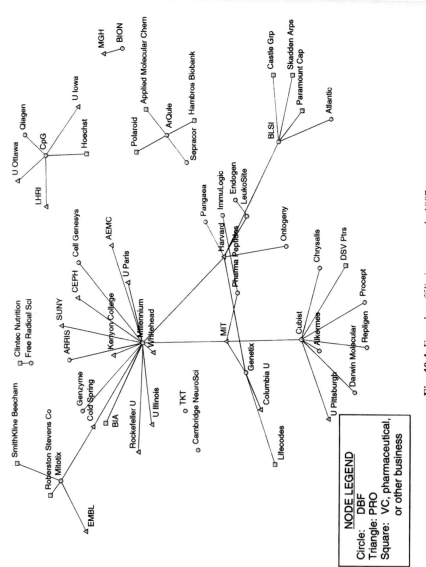

Fig. 10.4 Founder affiliation network, 1997

NODE LEGEND

Circle: DBF
Triangle: PRO
Square: VC, pharmaceutical, or other business

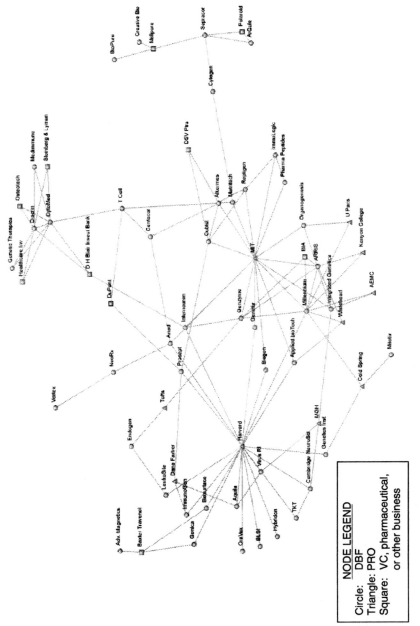

NODE LEGEND

Circle: DBF
Triangle: PRO
Square: VC, pharmaceutical,
or other business

Fig. 10.5 Founder affiliation network, only nodes with two or more links – 1978–2003

The scope of scientific advisory boards.   We have collected data on the scientific advisory boards for as many Boston-area firms as are available through public sources. Membership on these boards changes over time, as the composition shifts to reflect new areas of research by a growing firm, as well as the movement of research into clinical development and eventual product launch. In contrast to the group of founders, there is a much more pronounced presence of physicians on SABs.[15] Given turnover on SABs, and variation in the pace of foundings of new companies across time, we had to make choices about how to represent the network linkages that are created through scientific board membership. Obviously, different representations are possible. We selected three 'snapshots' for this set of affiliations. We chose 1984 to represent an early period in the development of Boston biotech, 1997 as a portrait of a more developed stage, and a representation across all years (1978–2003) that includes only those organizations with three or more advisory board member connections.[16] These graphics serve as compliments to the pictures of the founding team networks.

We conceptualize the SAB affiliation network as an organization-to-organization tie; thus, a professor at Harvard who sits on the board of Millennium creates a Harvard–Millennium affiliation. On average, a DBF's scientific advisory board reaches 11 different organizations. Because the focus is on a company's board, the representations will have some of the appearance of a hub and spoke figure, with DBFs at the center. In the early years of biotech in Boston, Fig. 10.6 portrays several pioneering firms – Biogen, Creative Biomolecules, Sepracor, and Endogen – as well-connected hubs. Note, however, that the most centrally linked organizations in 1984 are Harvard, Tufts, and MIT. Again, we see the central, generative role of public research organizations.

Biogen reached out widely for its scientific advisors, drawing on scientists from Scotland, Belgium, Sweden, Germany, and Switzerland, as well as Wisconsin and MIT. Endogen has advisors from Harvard, Tufts, and several Boston hospitals and institutes, as well as Stanford. In contrast, Creative Biomolecules drew from areas throughout the United States, including Tulane, Miami, Connecticut, but added advisors from Boston-based Tufts and Harvard. Sepracor, Integrated Genetics, and Advanced Magnetics all have advisors from both Harvard and MIT. Only one firm, Cambridge Medical, is isolated from the main component; it draws its advisors from a set of organizations markedly different from other Boston DBFs.

Fast forward to 1997, depicted in Fig. 10.7. This dense network displays a new generation of Boston companies, including Millennium, with quite a large board, Ariad, Interneuron, and Hybridon. Note the number of triangles (PROs) at the center of the network; these firms provide the most scientists and physicians to serve on SABs. Once again, Harvard and MIT are at the very middle, joined by Massachusetts General Hospital (MGH), and the Dana Farber Cancer Center nearby. A handful of other public research

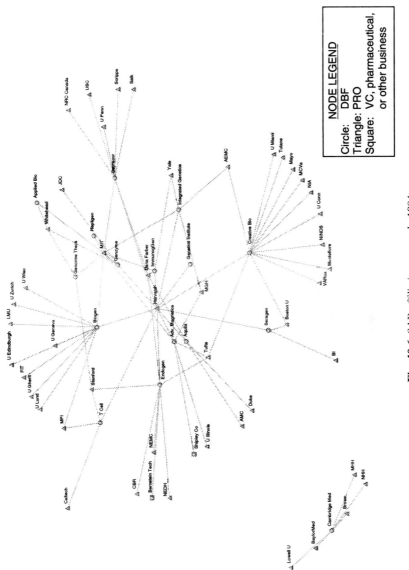

NODE LEGEND
Circle: DBF
Triangle: PRO
Square: VC, pharmaceutical, or other business

Fig. 10.6 SAB affiliation network, 1984

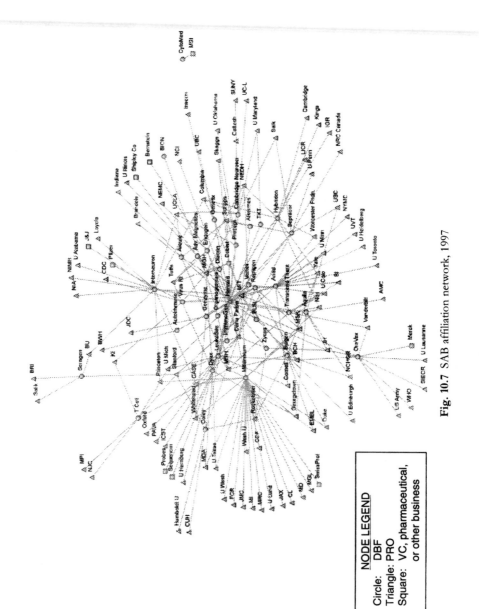

Fig. 10.7 SAB affiliation network, 1997

NODE LEGEND

Circle: DBF
Triangle: PRO
Square: VC, pharmaceutical,
                or other business

organizations from Boston, including Tufts University, the Whitehead Institute, and Boston's Children's Hospital, and New York City, specifically Memorial Sloan Kettering Hospital (MSK), Mt. Sinai Hospital (MSH), and Rockefeller University, are also densely connected. Thus, while Boston PROs remain central, by 1997 an elite group of New York City PROs are contributing advisory board members to Boston DBFs.

Figure 10.8 is the summary representation of advisory boards from 1976–2003, for organizations with three or more linkages. There is a notable absence of any square-shaped nodes in the figure, which points to the lack of involvement of scientists or executives from pharmaceutical companies on DBF boards. Repeated contacts on scientific advisory boards occur only between PROs and DBFs. Not surprisingly, Harvard is the most central organization in this network, providing the most SAB members. MIT, Massachusetts General Hospital (MGH), and Dana Farber are also very active. Boston DBFs avail themselves of the deep knowledge in local PROs, and venture outside the region rather infrequently.

The Inventor Network. The founders of biotech firms, the scientific advisory board members of these companies, and research scientists in Boston-area universities and firms are all actively engaged in a variety of ongoing collaborations and forms of interaction.[17] To drill deeper into the underlying scientific structure of the Boston region, we examine the patent co-inventor network to discern linkages among Boston scientists in both universities and firms.

Once again, we focus our analysis of this collaborative network on the main component, where patenting collaboration is most concentrated. Figure 10.9 is a visualization of the co-patenting network, with 907 inventors. A white circle is a university inventor and a gray circle an inventor at a DBF. There are 599 inventors from universities, 257 from DBFs, and a select group of 23 who have patents assigned to both Boston universities and DBFs. To help locate these few individuals, they are represented by squares. Not surprisingly, these scientists play important bridging roles, connecting the academic and commercial communities, and facilitating the flow of ideas and resources from the university lab to commercial development. These scientists are translators in a dual sense – they are familiar with the mores of both university science and science-based companies, and their research translates from the laboratory bench to clinical treatment.

We also highlight two smaller groups in this co-inventor network. There are 15 founders of Boston DBFs who have been granted US patents and are located in this main component. Thirteen scientific advisory board members also appear in the main component. In percentage terms, these individuals are quite rare, comprising 1.7 per cent and 1.4 per cent of the main component population, respectively. We label founders with triangles, and SAB members with diamonds. While these individuals are few in number, their critical role

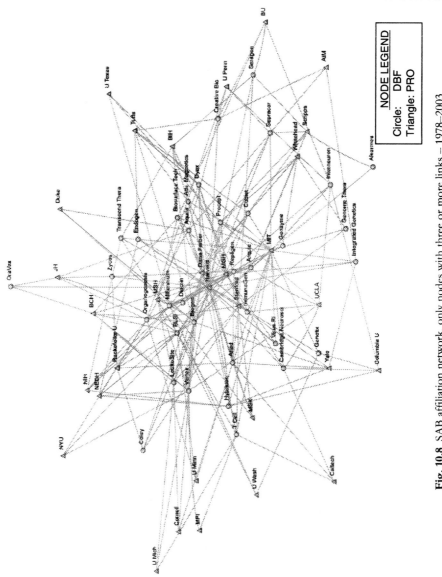

Fig. 10.8 SAB affiliation network, only nodes with three or more links – 1978–2003

NODE LEGEND
Circle: DBF
Triangle: PRO

as connectors that stitch together the overall scientific network is readily apparent in Fig. 10.9.

Figure 10.9 has an expansive center, or pump, that appears to 'supply' the overall network. At the very center of the map is a square, Prof. Robert Langer of MIT, who is the most active co-patentor in our network with 86 co-invented patents, as well as a co-founder of a company and a member of four DBF advisory boards. The group around him is tightly bunched, like a grape cluster. His close collaborators are both university and DBF scientists, a select few scientists who have moved from MIT to companies, and a handful of advisory board members. The traffic out of this central core connects with the rest of the network.[18]

Connected to the central group are five distinctive clusters, which we have labelled. To the north of the 'Langer core cluster', is group 1, where all inventors have an affiliation with Genetics Institute, a leading Boston DBF in the 1980s that became a division of a succession of large pharmaceutical corporations in the 1990s. Clearly, one reason the large firms had strong interest in GI was its stock of patents. Group 2, the cluster to the far right of the figure, includes inventors from Genzyme, Biogen, and Harvard. This cluster reflects another early founding group, as these two firms are the most notable first-generation Boston DBFs. The small cluster 3 consists of teams of Harvard and MIT scientists. Cluster 4 is an interesting mix of biotech companies that are all tied to MIT through founders. This group of scientists comes from CytoMed, Genzyme, Integrated Genetics, T Cell Science (now Avant), Virus Research Institute, and Transkaryotic Therapies. The very large cluster 5 to the left of the figure is a university group made up of MIT scientists, save for five Boston University inventors. In contrast to the advisory board networks where Harvard faculty played such a central role, the inventor network is dominated by MIT scientists.

Figure 10.9 also portrays the critical role of a small number of people located in multivocal positions as founders, advisory board members, and patentors with both universities and DBFs. Removing the 15 DBF founders and 13 scientific advisory board members from the main component drops connections between clusters 3, 4, and 5 completely. Likewise, removing the 23 individuals who patent across university and industry lines disconnects clusters 1 and 2 from the rest and considerably breaks done the rest of the network. Without these 51 individuals (5.6 per cent of the full network), the main component of the inventor network unravels, falling into separate strands. Unlike the previous network visualizations (done at the organizational level), which show a burgeoning field with multiple, independent pathways, Fig. 10.9 is much less robust. The inventor network is highly dependent upon the activities of a select few scientists.[19]

We provide an alternative representation of Fig. 10.9, rotating the flat horizontal network and presenting it vertically, with the most connected individuals at the top in Fig. 10.10. To scale the figure, we use the conventional

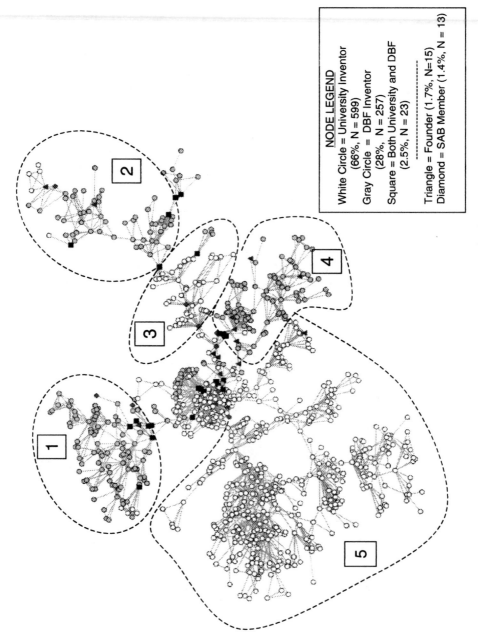

NODE LEGEND

White Circle = University Inventor
(66%, N = 599)
Gray Circle = DBF Inventor
(28%, N = 257)
Square = Both University and DBF
(2.5%, N = 23)

Triangle = Founder (1.7%, N=15)
Diamond = SAB Member (1.4%, N = 13)

Fig. 10.9 Boston patent co-inventor network, 1976–1998

network measure of betweenness centrality (Freeman, 1979) and array the nodes by standard deviation.[20] Those at the bottom level represent scientists who have a betweenness centrality score that is at the mean of the group or below. Each subsequent level brings the threshold up one standard deviation of betweenness centrality. At the peak, we find Prof. Langer, whose betweenness centrality is 19 standard deviations above the mean. Note how over-represented founders, advisors, and inventors who patent with universities and DBFs are in the top echelons. Between 31 per cent and 59 per cent of these individuals are two standard deviations above the mean in betweenness centrality, while only 9 per cent and 10 per cent of the DBF and university scientists are. Figure 10.10 emphasizes the important role these individuals play in bringing together science and commerce.

10.4   Comparisons Across Networks

The diverse, cross-cutting linkages that characterize the Boston biotechnology community share common topological features, while showing important differences in institutional detail. Structurally, all the network maps display similar typologies, with a relatively small number of highly connected organizations or individuals at the center, linking a diverse set of less-connected organizations. All four networks – contracts, founders, advisors, and inventors – are anchored by public research organizations. Given that these four networks are primarily oriented for commercial purposes, the centrality of universities and hospitals is remarkable. One might argue that this involvement reflects the growing commercialization of research universities and hospitals; indeed, an active line of research and commentary makes exactly this claim (Slaughter and Leslie, 1997; Krimsky, 2003). In contrast, we stress that PROs stimulate economic growth precisely because they have largely pursued public science, generating valuable spillovers. Universities contribute most effectively to economic growth when they act like universities and enhance the stock of basic science. Too much attention to commercial prospects, policies of exclusive licensing, or unequal rewards for faculty pursuing proprietary interests make universities vulnerable to corporate capture, and in the long run, render them less consequential (Nelson, 2001; Owen-Smith and Powell, 2003).

The imprint of the different public research organizations varies in interesting ways. In the contractual network, particularly in the 1980s, research hospitals, MIT, Harvard, Tufts, and Boston University were particularly crucial. In the founder affiliation network, MIT and Harvard were the primary source of entrepreneurs. Relatively absent from this network were Tufts and Boston University, which had faculty involved in only a few foundings. On science advisory boards, Harvard was the key contributor of faculty. Research hospitals were active in this capacity as well, highlighting the role SABs play in evaluating clinical efficacy. MIT faculty were also

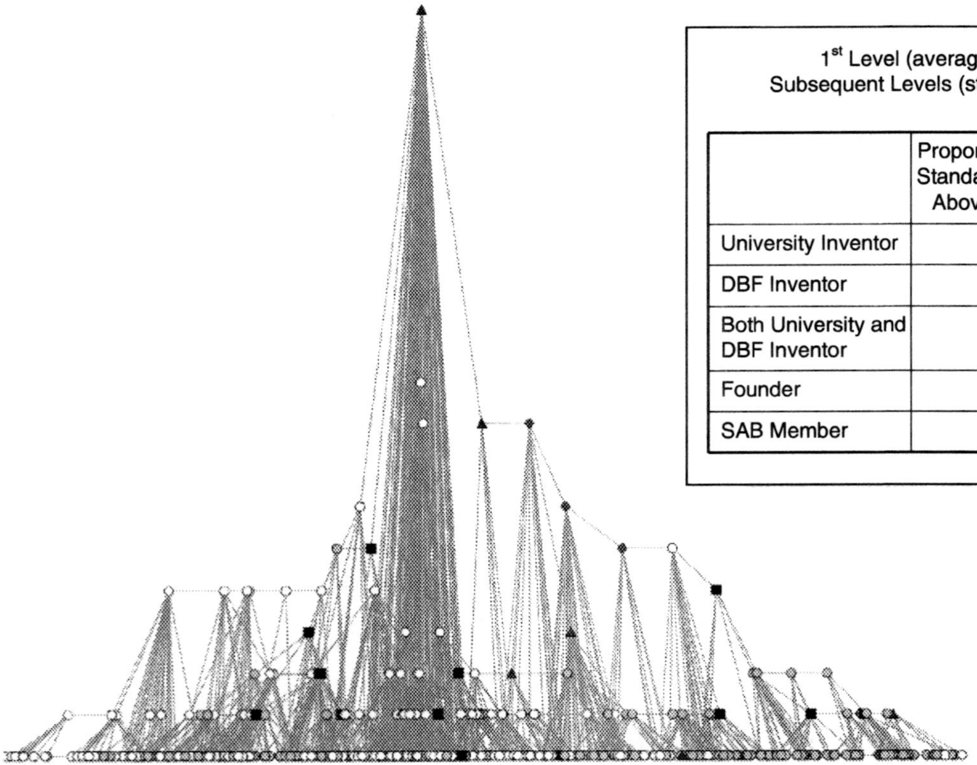

	Proportion at least 2 Standard Deviations Above the Mean
University Inventor	10%
DBF Inventor	9%
Both University and DBF Inventor	59%
Founder	33%
SAB Member	31%

1st Level (average): 0.01
Subsequent Levels (std dev): 0.04

Fig. 10.10 Betweenness centrality distribution of the patent co-inventor network, 1976–1998

involved, but clearly their energies are more focused on invention. The co-patenting network was dominated by MIT in two key respects, a MIT lab formed the core of the network, and MIT faculty represent more than 66 per cent of all the inventors in the main component network.

We have presented snapshots of three of the networks at two points in time, so we can discern how the relationships evolved as the field of biotechnology matured. The contractual network underwent a dual shift. One transition was from PRO dominance to a more commercial focus, with strong influence by venture capital firms and first-generation biotechs. The second change was from a regional focus to a global focus, with many more alliances with organizations outside of Boston (Owen-Smith and Powell, 2004). The network of founders continued to be dominated by Bostonians, although Fig. 10.4 does show that over time more founders came from outside Boston. When they do, however, they inevitably pair with local founders. Thus, the success of biotechnology in Boston has not been a lure for 'outsiders' to come and start new companies there. Rather, established organizations, such as Pfizer, Novartis, and Amgen, have relocated R&D facilities there, hoping to share in, to use Marshall's (1920) felicitous phrase, 'the secrets of industry that are in the air'. In addition, the established firms want to draw on the rich talent pool in the Boston area, and the fluid labor markets where movement between public and private science is active.

The scientific advisory board affiliation network is, perhaps obviously, more cosmopolitan from the outset. Scientists from Europe and leading US universities and medical centers are well represented, and their presence increases over time. As biotech firms develop medicines for specific thera-peutic indications, it is critical for them to recruit thought leaders in that area of medicine, regardless of their physical location. Still, the advisory boards have a very strong Harvard stamp, and a lighter but notable imprint from Massachusetts General Hospital, Dana Farber, and MIT.

Our initial intuition was that the more formal ties, such as the contractual alliances and memberships on scientific advisory boards, would represent more closed relationships and thus less-expansive networks. In contrast, we considered the more personal relationships, such as co-patenting among inventors, likely to be more open, given the lack of contractual obligations. Thus, we anticipated that the inventor network would have more open path-ways. Interestingly, we find just the opposite results. The inventor network has a very tightly clustered topology, and the removal of a few key participants unravels the network. This type of structure reflects the fact that most individ-ual scientists have limits on the number of colleagues, post-doctoral fellows, and students they can collaborate with, and that such collaborations have a repeated games character to them, which deepens existing relations rather than extends collaborations out to new participants. The contractual and SAB networks become, over time, so expansive that their typologies are distinguished by multiple independent pathways, rendering them robust against collapse if several key participants choose to exit. The embeddings of multiple networks create a very dynamic regional economy in biotechnology, with these multiple connections providing ample opportunities for the circulation of ideas and resources.

10.5   Implications for High-Tech Regions

Thoughtful analysts of industrial clusters have stressed the extent to which every successful cluster has relatively unique features, thus generalizations across regions are difficult and usually at a very high level of abstraction. We have shown how dependent the Boston biotech community is on personal relations among research scientists, strong ongoing affiliations among universities, hospitals, and firms, and reciprocal flows of ideas and personnel. Replicating this level of connectivity in other areas would be extremely difficult, to mandate it or attempt it with policy levers would be foolish. Not surprisingly, then, biotechnology is a very agglomerated industry, with the lion's share of activity concentrated in a handful of locales.

Nevertheless, it is useful to extend beyond the Boston case and consider which institutional features are essential to the region's success and what elements are idiosyncratic to biotechnology and Boston. We take up that challenge in this section.

How Generalizable is Biotechnology?   The life sciences are an unusual science-driven industry, in that basic research done at universities and DBFs continues to be critical to the field's development. Many other technology-based fields have their origins in university or corporate labs, but subsequent development is far removed from the initial discovery process. For example, Gordon Moore, a founder of Intel, argues that the early origins of the semiconductor business in Silicon Valley were not greatly influenced by scientists at Stanford, and that the development of the field owed more to a supply of skilled labor produced by other firms (Moore and Davis, 2004). Whether university science played an important role in the creation of the semiconductor industry is a debatable point, but clearly downstream development was driven by forces of demand and competition. In contrast, biotech firms compete in an environment in which product competition is less intense, product development is extremely protracted (5–10 years to 'produce' a new medicine), and the name or brand of a company has no effect whatsoever on a patient's decision to take a medicine or therapy.

Another way of capturing the institutional idiosyncrasies of biotech is to consider how strongly a field like information and communication technology (ICT) is demand-driven, shaped by technological and market opportunities (Bresnahan *et al.*, 2001). Developing new products that have strong complementarities with existing leading technologies is essential in ICT. In contrast, the focus of biotech has been to use novel science to develop first-to-the-world medicines and therapies. These new medicines seldom have any complementarities with existing drugs, and often there is no competing therapeutic regimen for the illness that biotech firms tackled. This absence of 'typical' demand features was particularly notable in the early decades of the industry; today as the number of firms has grown and large multinational pharmaceutical companies have entered biotech in a significant way, there is growing competition in specific therapeutic areas. Still, a key force shaping industry evolution is the supply of scientific excellence, which is a primary reason public research organizations continue to exert such a strong influence.

Finally, biotech is unusual in that it is a field where all the relevant skills – scientific, clinical, manufacturing, legal, financial, regulatory, sales, and distribution – are not readily assembled in a single organization (Powell and Brantley, 1992). As a consequence, organizations turn to collaborations with others in order to combine skills. Complementarities are important in biotech, but at the organizational level, rather than the product market.

Unique Features of Boston.   Analysts of regional advantage stress that there are relatively few common institutional conditions that typify successful clusters (Bresnahan *et al.*, 2001). Clearly, Boston has several valuable and unique assets. The metropolitan area is home to numerous universities and colleges, and is one of the most educated areas of the United States. The Boston metropolitan area ranks fifth in the US in share of the population over the age of 25 with college degrees and third in percentage with college degrees between ages of 25 and 34 (Glaeser, 2003, p. 5). Thus, there is an abundant supply of well-educated human capital for organizations to draw on, and a rich stock of scientific knowledge generated by several of the world's leading universities.

Yet despite these knowledge assets, Boston has not always been a successful region. Indeed, the city has had to survive shifts from a maritime and fishing center in the early nineteenth century to a factory town in the late nineteenth century to a new economy center in the late twentieth century.[21] Between 1920 and 1980, Boston's population declined by 25 per cent. In 1980, Boston was a declining city in a middle-income metropolitan area located in a cold climate, with a reputation for high taxes and heavy regulation. By 2000, Boston was a center for information technology, financial services, and biotechnology, and ranked as the eighth richest metropolitan area in the US (and the richest one not located in the New York City region or the Bay Area).

The series of crises and restructurings do not tell a story of constant success, however, but one of obsolescence and recovery. Common to the different eras of reinvention is the supply of skills (Glaeser, 2003). Boston is in many respects a rather insular town, with a distinctive history and accent. The cold weather, stiff taxes, and difficult driving conditions do not attract large numbers of businesses to move there. Unlike regions that have used tax incentives or public initiatives to attract high-tech companies, the Boston area 'grows its own'. The attractive inputs for Boston are college students, PhD candidates, and post-doctoral fellows, drawn from all over the world. The availability of an educated work force and the supply of ideas and ingenuity have been Boston's signature.

Organizational Diversity.   A notable feature of the Boston region is the diverse set of organizations involved in the life sciences. Universities, research institutes, hospitals, and small firms combined to get the cluster started in the 1970s and 1980s, local venture capital was attracted to this activity in the 1990s, and major pharmaceutical concerns established footholds in the first years of the twenty-first century. This heterogeneity is important in that it promotes experimentation and flexibility. Without a single dominant actor, there is no fixed recipe, instead multiple bets are placed in a milieu that becomes competitive and forward looking. We have stressed that the dense networks that connect these diverse organizations afford multiple, independent pathways through which ideas and resources can flow, facilitating research progress.

Open Science.   Intense competition can lead to rivalrous, cutthroat behavior. In Boston, however, scientific competition created a virtuous cycle, rather than a vicious one, enabling researchers and clinicians to build on the accomplishments of others. The key feature of Boston is the predominance of research organizations committed to norms of open science. Research is published, debated in seminars, and applications are patented. Papers and patents are simultaneously publicly available sources of information and valuable commodities. The strong public science emphasis, even if rooted in private science commercialization efforts, allows ideas to be debated, honed, and utilized by others. Add to this mix the research and clinical focus of top-tier research hospitals, and an orientation toward public health is enhanced. The Boston area has been an expansive cluster in large part due to its open science orientation.

We emphasize that the public science research community that generates knowledge and the private science commercial regime that produces new medicines are now inextricably linked. The intellectual capital of academic and clinical researchers made possible the commercial world of biotechnology in Boston. The vitality of both the commercial and academic communities, however, rests on the public science world remaining committed to the widest possible dissemination of research results.

The growth of biotechnology in Boston has been fuelled by the multiple overlapping networks that connect universities, hospitals, and science-driven companies. This community is simultaneously collaborative and competitive. World-class science is intensely rivalrous. The great German sociologist, Max Weber (1946), observed that science is not democratic, but rather an aristocracy of merit. The contemporary life sciences represent a new hybrid of science and commerce, in which research spillovers have fuelled the emergence of a new industry. The most important lesson we take from our analysis of the Boston biotechnology community is that this productive nexus is deeply dependent upon both organizational heterogeneity and open science.

Notes

1. The other significant large biotech cluster is the San Francisco Bay Area. This region has more firms in number, and some of the oldest and most established companies, such as Genentech and Chiron. The Bay Area is also more geographically dispersed, with several smaller, local clusters in Palo Alto, South San Francisco, and Emeryville in the East Bay. While larger in scale, the Bay Area is not as tightly agglomerated as Boston. Some analyses even treat the Bay Area as three separate regions, according to the major metropolitan areas of Oakland, San Francisco, and San Jose (DeVol et al., 2004), although we think this division is misleading. The most distinctive difference between Boston and the Bay Area is the notable presence of medical research institutes in Boston, and the major concentration of venture capital in the Bay Area (Owen-Smith and Powell, 2005).

2. We define a dedicated biotech firm as an independently held, profit-seeking entity involved in human therapeutic or diagnostic applications of biotechnology.

3. By contrast, the Bay Area is much more a magnet for outsiders to start companies, as well as open to less-veteran entrepreneurs (Porter, 2004).

4. The remaining 12 firms either do not have SABs or information about them is unavailable. Murray (2004) reports that 83 per cent of the firms in her sample of 12 biotech companies have scientific advisory boards.

5. Note that we count only Boston SABs and Boston founders. Some of these individuals also serve on SABs of firms in other regions, and several have been founders of DBFs outside of Boston.

6. At present, we lack the complete data to include patent activity by research hospitals.

7. 'Research One' is a designation of research intensity that was previously applied to US universities by the Carnegie Foundation. In order to qualify as a research one institution, a campus had to receive at least $40 million per year in federal R&D funding, while granting at least 50 Ph.D. degrees.

8. The NBER inventor data contains lists of inventors sorted by patent number, making it useful to quickly gather inventor names from patent numbers obtained elsewhere.

9. To non-network analysis readers, consider that you are trying to connect a series of dots representing individuals or organizations. The main component represents the dots that can be linked without ever lifting a pen.

10. We use Pajek, a freeware program developed by Vladimir Batagelj and Andrej Mrvar, to develop meaningful and replicable visual representations of these two networks. Pajek implements two minimun-energy, or spring-embedded, network drawing algorithms based on graph-theoretic conceptions of distance and the physical theory of random fields. We draw on one or both of these two algorithms (Kamada and Kawai (KK), 1989; Fruchterman and Reingold (FR), 1991) to create images that position nodes by reference to the overall pattern of

connections in the network. These images locate isolates on the periphery of the image while situating more connected nodes centrally. Figures 10.1–10.8 are optimized with FR alone, while the density of Figs. 10.9 and 10.10 is aided by an optimization using FR followed by KK. For more information on the algorithms or their use for visualization, see Owen-Smith *et al.*, 2002; Powell *et al.*, 2005, and http://vlado.fmf.uni-lj.si/pub/networks/pajek.

11. To ease the viewing of our network graphics, we shorten or abbreviate names of key institutions whenever possible. The Appendix provides a code to convert abbreviations into full names.

12. In every year for which we have data, the Boston network is characterized by a main component, which should be regarded as the largest, coherent, minimally connected network structure. In graph-theoretic terms, the main component is the largest group of organizations reachable through indirect paths of finite length. Thus, a tie to the main component represents the minimum level of connectivity necessary to enable an organization to access information through the largest portion of the network.

13. In using the terminology 'affiliation network', we do not refer to the traditional network methodology term, which implies a two-mode actor-by-affiliation network. Rather, we refer literally to linkages that exist between organizations based on their founders' prior and current affiliations. For example, a link exists between Biogen and Harvard because of founder Walter Gilbert's involvement with both organizations. Thus, the founder networks (and those of the scientific advisory board, presented next) can be conceptualized as affiliation-by-affiliation networks.

14. The network includes the formal affiliations of founders to other organizations in the five-year period leading up to and including the founding year. These affiliations remain in the dataset for a period of five years from the firm's date of founding.

15. Some founders and advisory board members have multiple degrees and have founded or served with more than one company. Hence, counting degrees is somewhat tricky. Nevertheless, among the founders there are 82 PhDs and 31 MDs, while advisors have been awarded 245 PhDs and 174 MDs.

16. Because the scientific advisory board affiliation network is considerably denser than the founder affiliation network (due to the large number of board members), we display the SAB all-years graph with *three* or more linkages as compared with the all-years founder network that draws from *two* or more.

17. For example, in addition to the relationships we have analysed here, company board of director linkages, shared experiences as postdoctoral fellows in specific labs, or common mentor–mentee relations also provide avenues for the flow of ideas and resources.

18. In a presentation at MIT back in 2001, Powell argued that a critical skill in biotechnology was the ability to be 'multivocal', that is to be regarded as excellent at both science and commerce, and have one's actions interpreted accordingly by those with more specialized skills. For many companies, this is a challenging task, although those that acquire such capability reap considerable rewards (Powell *et al.*, 2005). Fiona Murray asked if any scientists are 'born multivocal', referring to the experience of PhDs and postdocs in a high-profile, well-connected lab such as

Langer's who go from his lab to leading positions in firms. We are pleased to present research results that confirm Prof. Murray's intuition.

19. In separate analyses, we have removed the most connected organizations from the overall founder and SAB networks, and the networks remain linked. Only the inventor network is sensitive to the removal of the most connected members.

20. Freeman's measure of betweenness considers nodes central to the extent that they sit on indirect connections between other organizations and thus can facilitate, appropriate, or impede information and resource flows in a network.

21. Here, we draw extensively on Glaeser's (2003) fascinating analysis of Boston's economic history.

References

Almeida, P. and Kogut, B. (1999), 'Localization of knowledge and the mobility of engineers in regional networks.' *Management Science*, 45: 905–917.

Audretsch, D. B. and Stephan, P. (1996), 'Company-scientist locational links: the case of biotechnology.' *American Economic Review*, 86: 641–52.

Bresnahan, T., Gambardella, A., and Saxenian, A. (2001), 'Old economy inputs for new economy outcomes.' *Industrial and Corporate Change*, 10(4): 835–860.

Brown, J. S. and Duguid, P. (2000), 'Mysteries of the region: knowledge dynamics in Silicon Valley,' in Chong-Moon Lee *et al.* (eds), *The Silicon Valley edge*, Stanford, CA: Stanford University Press, pp. 16–45.

Bunker Whittington, K., Owen-Smith, L., and Powell, W. W. (2005) 'Spillovers and embeddedness: the contingent effects of propinquity and social structure.' Working Paper, Stanford University.

Dasgupta, P. and David, P. (1987), 'Information disclosure and the economics of science and technology,' in G. R. Feiwel (ed.), *Kenneth Arrow and the ascent of economic theory*, New York: New York University Press, pp. 519–542.

Dasgupta, P. and David, P. (1994), 'Toward a new economics of science.' *Research Policy*, 23(5): 487–521.

Devol, R., Wong, P., Ki, J., Bedroussian, A., and Koeyn, R. (2004) 'America's biotech and life science clusters: San Diego's position and economic contributions.' *Milken Institute Research Report*. Santa Maria, CA: Milken Institute.

Fleming, L., Cofer, L., Marin, A., and McPhie, J. (2004), 'Why the Valley went first: agglomeration and emergence in regional innovation networks,' in J. Padgett and W. W. Powell (eds), *Market emergence and transformation*, forthcomming.

Freeman, L. C. (1979), 'Centrality in social networks: conceptual clarification.' *Social Networks*, 1: 215–239.

Fruchterman, T. and Reingold, E. (1991), 'Graph drawing by force-directed replacement.' *Software–Practice and Experience*, 21: 1129–1164.

Geiger, R. (1986), *To advance knowledge: the growth of American research universities, 1900–1940*. New York: Oxford University Press.

Glaeser, E. L. (2003) 'Reinventing Boston: 1640–2003.' NBER Working Paper 10166.

Granovetter, M. (1985), 'Economic action and social structure: the problem of embeddedness.' *American Journal of Sociology*, 91: 481–510.

Gulati, R. (1995) 'Does familiarity breed trust? The implications of repeated ties for contractual choice in alliances.' *Academy of Management Journal*, **38**(1): 85–112.

Hall, B. H., Jaffe, A. B., and Tratjenberg, M. (2001), 'The NBER patent citation data file: Lessons, insights and methodological tools.' NBER Working Paper 8498.

Higgins, M. (2005), *Career imprints: Creating leaders across an industry*. San Francisco, CA; Jossey-Bass.

Jaffe, A. B. (1986), 'Technological opportunity and spillovers of research-and-development – evidence from firm patents, profits, and market value.' *American Economic Review*, **76**: 984–1001.

Jaffe, A. B. (1989), 'Real effects of academic research.' *American Economic Review*, **79**: 957–970.

Jaffe, A. B., Trajtenberg, M., and Henderson, R. (1993), 'Geographic localization of knowledge spillovers as evidenced by patent citations.' *Quarterly Journal of Economics*, **63**: 577–598.

Jaffe, A. B., Trajtenberg, M., and Fogarty, M. S. (2000), 'Knowledge spillovers and patent citations: evidence from a survey of inventors.' *American Economic Review*, **90**: 215–218.

Kamada, T. and Kawai, S. (1989), 'An algorithm for drawing general undirected graphs.' *Information Processing Letters*, **31**: 7–15.

Kenney, M. (ed.) (2000), *Understanding Silicon Valley: the anatomy of an entrepreneurial region*. Stanford, CA: Stanford University Press.

Kogut, B. (2000), 'The network as knowledge: generative rules and the emergence of structure.' *Strategic Management Journal*, **21**: 405–25.

Krimsky, S. (2003), *Science in the private interest*. Lanham, MD: Rowan and Littlefield.

Marshall, A. (1920), *Principles of economics* (8th edn) London: Macmillan.

Moody, J. and White, D. R. (2003), 'Social cohesion and embeddedness: a hierarchical conception of social groups.' *American Sociological Review*, **68**: 103–127.

Moore, G. and Davis, K. (2004), 'Learning the Silicon Valley way,' in T. Bresnahan and A. Gambardella (eds), *Building high-tech clusters: Silicon Valley and beyond*. Cambridge. UK: Cambridge University Press, pp. 7–39.

Mowery, D. C., Nelson, R. R., Sampat, B., and Ziedonis, A. (2004), *Ivory tower and industrial innovation*. Stanford, CA: Stanford University Press.

Murray, F. (2002), 'Innovation as co-evolution of scientific and technological networks: Exploring tissue engineering.' *Research Policy*, **31**(8–9): 1389–1403.

Murray, F. (2004), 'The role of academic inventors in entrepreneurial firms: Sharing the laboratory life.' *Research Policy*, **33**(4): 643–659.

Nelson, R. R. (2001), 'Observations on the Post-Bayh dole rise of patenting at American universities.' *Journal of Technology Transfer*, **26**(1/2): 13–19.

Owen-Smith, J., Riccaboni, M., Pammolli, F., and Powell, W. W. (2002), 'A Comparison of U.S. and European university-industry relations in the life sciences.' *Management Science*, **48**: 24–43.

Owen-Smith, J. and Powell, W. W. (2003), 'The expanding role of university patenting in the life sciences.' *Research Policy*, **32**(9): 1695–1711.

Owen-Smith, J. and Powell, W. W. (2004), 'Knowledge networks as channels and conduits: the effects of spillovers in the Boston biotechnology community.' *Organization Science*, **15**(1): 5–21.

Owen-Smith, J. and Powell, W. W. (2005), 'Accounting for emergence and novelty in Boston and Bay Area biotechnology,' in P. Braumerhjelm and M. Feldman (eds), *Cluster genesis: the emergence of technology clusters and the implication for government policies*, forthcoming.

Porter, K. (2004), *You can't leave your past behind: the influence of founders' career histories on their firms*. Ph.D. dissertation, Department of Industrial Engineering, Stanford University.

Powell, W. W. (1996), 'Inter-organizational collaboration in the biotechnology industry.' *Journal of Institutional and Theoretical Economics*, **152**: 197–215.

Powell, W. W. and Brantley, P. (1992), 'Competitive cooperation in biotechnology: learning through networks?' in N. Nohria and R. Eccles (eds), *Networks and organizations*, Boston, MA: Harvard Business School Press, pp. 336–394.

Powell, W. W. and Brantley, P. (1996), 'Magic bullets and patent wars: new product development and the evolution of the biotechnology industry,' in T. Nishiguchi (ed.), *Competitive product development*. New York: Oxford University Press, pp. 233–260

Powell, W. W., Koput, K. W., and Smith-Doerr, L. (1996), 'Interorganizational collaboration and the locus of innovation: networks of learning in biotechnology.' *Administrative Science Quarterly*, **41**: 116–145.

Powell, W. W., Koput, K. W., Bowie, J. I., and Smith-Doerr, L. (2002), 'The spatial clustering of science and capital: accounting for biotech firm – venture capital relationships.' *Regional Studies*, **36**(3) (May 2002): 299–313.

Powell, W. W., White, D. R., Koput, K. W., and Owen-Smith, J. (2005) 'Network dynamics and field evolution: the growth of inter-organizational collaboration on the Life Sciences'. *American Journal of Sociology*, **110**(4): 1132–1205.

Robbins-Roth, C. (2000), *From alchemy to IPO*. Cambridge, MA: Perseus Publishing.

Rosenberg, N. and Nelson, R. R. (1994), 'American universities and technical advance in industry.' *Research Policy*, **23**: 323–348.

Saxenian, A. (1994), *Regional advantage: culture and competition in Silicon Valley and Route 128*. Cambridge, MA.: Harvard University Press.

Shane, S. (2004), *Academic entrepreneurship: university spinoffs and wealth creation*. Cheltenham, UK: Edward Elgar.

Slaughter, S. and Leslie, L. (1997), *Academic capitalism*. Baltimore: Johns Hopkins University Press.

Teitelman, R. (1989), *Gene dreams: Wall Street, academia, and the rise of biotechnology*. New York: Basic Books.

Watson, J. D. (2003) *DNA: The secret of life*. New York: Knopf.

Weber, M. (1946), 'Science as a vocation,' in H. Gerth and C. W. Mills (trans and eds), *From Max Weber: essays in sociology*. New York: Oxford University Press.

White, D. R. and Harary, F. (2001), 'The cohesiveness of blocks in social networks: node connectivity and conditional density.' *Social Methodology*, **31**(1): 305–359.

Appendix I: Abbreviations of names in network images*

Abbreviation	Formal Name, Location
AEMC	Albert Einstein Medical College, NYC
AMC	Animal Medical Center, NYC
Aquila	Cambridge Biosciences, Aquila Biopharm, Boston
Baylor Med	Baylor College of Medicine, Houston TX
BCH	Boston Children's Hospital
BI	Beth Israel Hospital, Boston
BLSI	Boston Life Sciences Inc.
BMS	Bristol-Myers Squibb, NYC
BRI	Biometric Research Institute, Arlington VA
BU	Boston University
BWH	Brigham and Women's Hospital, Boston
CASE	Case Western Reserve University, Cleveland OH
CBR	Center for Blood Research, Boston
CCF	Cleveland Clinic Foundation
CDC	Centers for Disease Control, Atlanta GA
CEPH	Centre d'Etude du Polymorphisme Humain, France
CL	Channing Laboratory, Boston
Cogito	Cogito Learning Media, Boston
CSHL	Cold Spring Harbor Laboratories, NYC
CUH	Charité University Hospital, Berlin
DRCR	Damon Runyon Cancer Research Fund, NYC
EMBL	European Molecular Biology Laboratories, Heidelberg
FCR	Frederick Cancer Research and Development Center, National Cancer Institute
FIT	Federal Institute of Technology, Zurich
Genome Thera	Collaborative Research, Genome Therapeutics, Boston
HCA	Columbia/Health Corporation America, Nashville TN
ICR	Imperial Cancer Research, London
ICST	Imperial College of Science and Technology, London
IGR	Institut Gustave-Roussy, Desmoulins, France
J&J	Johnson and Johnson, New Brunswick NJ
JAX	Jackson Laboratories, Bar Harbor ME
JDC	Joslin Diabetes Center, Boston
JH	Johns Hopkins University, Baltimore MD
JMC	Jefferson Medical College, Philadelphia PA
KI	Karolinska Institute, Stockholm
Kings	Kings College, London
LHRI	Loehs Health Research Institute, Ottawa
LICR	Ludwig Institute for Cancer Research, New York

LMU	Ludwig Maxilians-Universität-München
Mayo	Mayo Clinic, Rochester MN
MCVa	Medical College of Virginia
MD	Max Delbruck Center, Berlin
MDA	M.D. Anderson Hospital, Houston TX
MGH	Massachusetts General Hospital, Boston
MGL	Mammalian Genetics Lab, Great Falls MT
MHH	Methodist Hospital of Houston
MI	McLaughlin Institute
Montefiore	Montefiore Hospital of Houston
MPI	Max Planck Institute
MRC	Medical Research Council, UK
MSH	Mt. Sinai Hospital, NYC
MSI	Molecular Simulations Institute
MSK	Memorial Sloan Kettering, NYC
NCHGR	National Center for Human Genome Research
NE Nuclear	New England Nuclear, Boston
NEDH	New England Deaconess Hospital, Boston
NEMC	New England Medical Center, Boston
NHH	National Heart Hospital, London
NIA	National Institute on Aging
NINDS	National Institute of Neurological Disorders and Stroke
NJC	National Jewish Center
NRC-Canada	National Research Council of Canada
NYMC	New York Medical Center
Ortho	Ortho Biologics, a division of J&J
PAVA	Palo Alto Veterans Association Hospital
SALK	Salk Institute, La Jolla CA
Scripps	Scripps Research Institute, La Jolla CA
SIECR	Swiss Institute for Experimental Cancer Research
Skaggs	Skaggs Institute, La Jolla CA
SSC	Swiss Science Council
SUNY	State University of New York
T Cell	T Cell Sciences, Avant, Boston
TKT	Transkaryotic Therapeutics, Boston
U Colo	University of Colorado
U Conn	University of Connecticut
U Mich	University of Michigan
U Minn	University of Minnesota
U Penn	University of Pennsylvania
U Vt	University of Vermont
U Wisc	University of Wisconsin
UBC	University of British Columbia
UCL	University College – London

USC	University of South Carolina
VA Rox	Veterans' Admin. Hospital, W. Roxbury MA
Virus RI	Virus Research Institute, Boston
Wash U	Washington University, St. Louis MO
Worcester Fndn.	Worcester Foundation for Biosciences, Worcester MA
WHO	World Health Organization

* For biotechnology companies, we have dropped second names such as Pharmaceuticals, Biologics, and Technology, and shortened companies whenever possible. In the case of merged companies, or those with name changes, we include a shortened version of their most familiar name.

11

Social Networks and the Persistence of Clusters: Evidence from the Computer Workstation Industry

OLAV SORENSON

Organizations of like kind often cluster geographically into a few, relatively concentrated regions, frequently referred to as industrial districts or agglomerations. Hence, for example, the automobile industry in the United States resides in and around Detroit, film production and distribution companies generally call Los Angeles home, and the shoe industry concentrates heavily around the cities of Boston, Milwaukee, and St. Louis (for a lengthy list of additional examples, see Porter, 1990). Though people have long been aware of this spatial clustering of production – consider for example the centuries-long reputations of particular regions for artisan products, such as Geneva for watches or Porto and Madeira for sweet wines – scholars first became interested in understanding these patterns in the mid-1800s.

The preponderance of the theories offered to explain the geographic concentration of production essentially argues that these clustered spatial distributions represent an efficient means of organizing production. Early accounts of industrial districts thus pointed to the importance of minimizing transportation costs. German economic geographers explaining the dense cluster of heavy manufacturers in Bavaria, for example, noted that their location allowed these firms easy and relatively cheap access to coal and iron ore, critical inputs in these industries (Weber, 1909/1928). More recently, in response to the obvious failure of transportation costs to explain the clustering of high-tech and service industries, scholars have resurrected Marshall's (1890) insight that the clustering of similar firms may itself provide benefits to the organizations that reside in these districts – through the sharing of critical resources, such as skilled labor, specialized suppliers, or efficiency-enhancing innovations.

Though compelling on the surface, these theories depend on a model of human behavior at odds with empirical accounts of how firms arrive at their locations in physical space. Whether minimizing transportation costs or drawing on the benefits of locating near similar firms, these theories portray the decision of where to locate the firm as one of rational evaluation of and selection from the myriad of possible locations. Empirical research on how existing firms and entrepreneurs decide where to locate their firms, however, raises questions as to the plausibility of such an assumption. Rather than searching for the best possible location, founders of new firms simply exhibit geographic inertia – they nearly always start their firms in the same communities in which they have been living and working (Cooper, 1970; Figueiredo *et al.*, 2002; see Mitton, 1990 and Haug, 1995, on biotechnology start-ups, and Klepper, 2002, on the automobile industry). Even existing firms often fail to behave in a manner consistent with optimizing economic performance. In a survey of managers in Michigan, for example, more than half indicated that they had chosen their plant locations for personal reasons, rather than to exploit some favorable local economic condition (Katona and Morgan, 1952).

So, if those deciding where to locate plants and firms do not make these decisions with an eye to economic forces, why do firms in so many industries cluster into a few, dense regions? This chapter argues that firms cluster not because geographic concentration necessarily benefits them (though it may in some cases), but rather because social networks constrain where entrepreneurs locate and what types of businesses they start. Entrepreneurship involves two stages: (1) opportunity recognition, and (2) resource mobilization. Perceiving the potential for profit from opening a new venture in a particular industry typically requires both familiarity with the way in which the industry works and access to private information regarding market conditions. Hence, those individuals most likely to consider starting a firm in an industry either have experience working in the industry or a related business (Sorenson and Audia, 2000). Even after deciding to attempt entry, the nascent entrepreneur must successfully assemble a variety of resources – tacit knowledge, financial capital, and skilled labor – to begin operations. Given the uncertainty of the fledgling venture, social networks play a critical role in mitigating the market failure that would otherwise occur. Therefore, those individuals most capable of assembling the resources to pursue their idea in a particular location likely have strong ties to the local community (Sorenson and Audia, 2000; Stuart and Sorenson, 2003). Since social connections themselves tend to cluster in geographic and social space, these constraints on where entrepreneurs can start firms imply that the spatial pattern of new entrants reifies the geography of industry – production tends to remain clustered into 'industrial districts' even if a more dispersed configuration would be more efficient (Sorenson and Audia, 2000; Sorenson and Stuart, 2001).

Though earlier research has provided empirical support for these dynamics in footwear manufacturing (Sorenson and Audia, 2000) and biotechnology (Stuart and Sorenson, 2003), this study extends the prior work in two respects. First, it documents these processes in yet another industry: computer workstation manufacturing. Given that many, recalling Saxenian's (1994) rich description of the industry, have pointed to it as an example of a case in which clustered firms benefited from access to information spillovers, this industry seems like a particularly interesting setting in which to test the alternative hypothesis of network constraints on entrepreneurship. Secondly, the heterogeneity of entrant types allows us to examine whether these processes influence entrepreneurs more strongly than existing firms. Both the biotechnology and footwear manufacturing industries lacked sufficient numbers of *de alio* entrants to determine whether these existing firms behave differently from *de novo* entrants. As one would expect, network constraints operate most strongly among entrepreneurs (*de novo* entrants). This finding may also provide some traction on why some industries disperse to a greater degree than others. In particular, industries with a large number of *de alio* entrants may disperse more rapidly because these existing firms can solve the resource mobilization problem without drawing on social connections to industry incumbents.

11.1   Social Networks and Industrial Geography

Descriptions and theories of the entrepreneurial process typically divide it into two stages. First, the nascent entrepreneur perceives an opportunity for a new business. Upon identifying an opportunity, the next challenge involves assembling the resources necessary to create an organization capable of exploiting that opportunity. Social networks importantly enable each of these stages.

11.1.1   *Social Networks and Opportunity Identification*

Social networks aide in the opportunity identification process both by providing individuals access to private information and by directing their attention. In fledgling industries, even the existence of the enterprise itself may escape the media's attention. Only individuals with some connection to the business – whether through prior employment, experience at a firm that interacts with the new industry, or through an acquaintance involved with it – will likely consider these ventures (Sorenson, 2003). Those lacking these connections thus do not even recognize it as a potential opportunity; they simply do not conceive of it. Indeed, such an effect may partially account for the consistent 'legitimation' effect posited and documented by organizational ecologists (cf. Hannan and Carroll, 1992; Carroll and Hannan, 2000). When only a few firms exist in an industry, entry rates typically remain low. Though the paucity of firms may also exacerbate the difficulty of the resource mobilization process (because critical resource holders question the legitimacy of this type of business), small numbers of firms in an industry (particularly if these firms also have few employees) implies that a correspondingly meager number of nascent entrepreneurs have awareness of the business as a potential venture.

Even in more mature lines of business, potential entrepreneurs frequently require access to private information to determine the potential value of their ideas. Firms operating within an industry will seek to conceal their success, as well as the practices that have made them successful. Private companies simply avoid making such information widely available, but public firms can also limit the accessibility of this information by designing their public accounting statements to camouflage sensitive data. Despite these efforts, incumbent firms likely find it difficult to stem the flow of information completely. Many individuals, such as the managers of these incumbent firms, require access to the relevant information to perform their jobs properly. And little prevents these individuals from either using the information themselves or from passing it along to their friends (Sorenson, 2003). Hence, individuals with these direct ties to incumbent firms have better information on the likely profitability of a new venture.

Social networks can also play a role in opportunity identification beyond simply providing access to private information by directing the potential entrepreneur's attention. At any given time, an individual might consider starting a new venture in literally thousands of different lines of business. Why, when an opportunity does exist, do only certain individuals see it? Most nascent entrepreneurs probably scan the environment passively – open to opportunities that they come across, but not actively and systematically considering the entire range of businesses they might enter. Under these conditions, information about potential opportunities likely arises through conversations with friends and daily activities. Those connected in some way to an industry direct the most attention to it, and hence most likely recognize the potential to address an underserved market or to exploit a new strategy.

11.1.2   Social Networks and Resource Mobilization

Once the incipient entrepreneur believes he or she has identified a potentially profitable opportunity, he or she must bring together a variety of resources to form an organization to exploit it. At the very least, establishing a firm typically requires financial capital – to purchase equipment and cover operating expenditures until the venture begins generating revenue – and labor. Moreover, the level of resources necessary to enter an industry generally rises as the industry matures. Over time, the efficiency of production increases due to a combination of capital investments, improvements in human capital specific to the business and the accumulation of tacit knowledge through learning by doing. If entrants hope to compete with incumbent firms, they must obtain access to each of these elements. Existing social relations assist in the mobilization of each of these three types of resources: (1) tacit knowledge, (2) financial capital, and (3) human capital.

Social networks probably operate most strongly in channelling the flow of tacit knowledge. By its definition, tacit knowledge defies codification, making it difficult to transfer except through face-to-face contact. Despite its stickiness (and perhaps even because of it), tacit knowledge underlies the profitability of firms in many industries. Over time, incumbents evolve better procedures for operating, both in terms of the production process and in terms of how they organize and what strategies they pursue. Start-ups with access to the existing knowledge in the industry thus enjoy a large advantage relative to those that must rediscover it (Liles, 1974; Sorenson and Audia, 2000; Klepper, 2001, 2002). Despite this obvious value, tacit knowledge resists market-based exchange. Potential buyers would question the quality of the information, and sellers could not easily assuage their fears without disclosing the valuable information itself. Moreover, even if one could devise a solution to this market failure, the effective transfer of complex, tacit information requires the high bandwidth offered by sustained direct communication (Nelson, 1959). Individuals thus gain access to the knowledge either through direct experience or via strong social connections to those with the relevant experience.

In both budding industries and in concentrated, mature ones, the restricted geographic availability of this critical resource limits the ease across regions of founding a new venture within an industry. Business-specific tacit knowledge resides predominantly within the existing firms in an industry. Nascent entrepreneurs thus require strong social connections to organizations currently operating in the industry, a condition that virtually requires that entrepreneurs emerge from the ranks of current employees (Sorenson and Audia, 2000). Developing these strong ties and maintaining them depends on frequent and intimate interaction, circumstances unlikely to exist except among co-workers and close, personal friends.

Though more efficient markets act to distribute financial and human capital, two factors make these resources difficult to access without the assistance of social networks. First, new ventures in any industry represent an inherently uncertain investment. Not only do these fledgling enterprises face considerable risk, but also the exact nature of this risk generally eludes quantification (a situation referred to as 'ambiguity' in the decision-making literature). When faced with such ambiguous prospects, investors exhibit a strong preference for better-understood investment alternatives (i.e. they exhibit 'ambiguity aversion'; cf. Ellsberg, 1961; Fox and Tversky, 1995). Secondly, potential investors and employees face an information asymmetry problem when dealing with a potential entrepreneur. The budding founder knows more about the quality of his or her idea (and its odds for success) than they do. Given the entrepreneur's obvious incentives to exaggerate the attractiveness of the venture, these resource providers, moreover, cannot simply depend on the entrepreneur's judgement (Akerlöf, 1970). Together, uncertainty and information asymmetry beget a friction in the flow of financial and human capital that social networks can help to lubricate.

Social connections between nascent entrepreneurs and capital holders increase the likelihood that a fledgling venture receives financial backing by mitigating the perceived risk associated with investing in it. At least two factors contribute to this effect. On the one hand, individuals generally have greater confidence in the reliability of information received from trusted parties; hence, a social connection can reduce the salience of information asymmetry between the entrepreneur and the investor. Venture capitalists thus demonstrate a strong preference for backing the start-ups of those with whom they have prior experience or that come to them through referrals by close contacts (Fried and Hisrich, 1994). On the other hand, lacking a strong connection, consistent information across multiple independent sources might offer the investor some assurance as to the veracity of the information available on a potential investment (Sorenson and Stuart, 2001). Though the availability of financial capital in general may vary little from region to region, the importance of social relations to obtaining financing tends to bind entrepreneurs to those regions in which they have contacts.

In addition to financial capital, entrepreneurs must also recruit human-capital holders to join their proposed ventures. Given the uncertainties faced by new firms, it probably takes considerable persuasion on the part of the entrepreneur to convince skilled employees to tether their fates to that of a new company. Unlike investors who can diversify away much of the firm-specific risk, employees remain vulnerable to the vagaries assailing the firm to which they attach themselves. Absent trust in the company founder and confidence in his or her ability and judgement, employees will unlikely leave relatively secure positions to join a start-up. Strong social connections thus facilitate the recruitment of skilled personnel by engendering this trust.

As with tacit knowledge, the ability to recruit skilled labor depends on the strength of an individual's connections to industry incumbents. Workers primarily acquire industry-specific skills by working in the industry. Through the course of their jobs they both learn new skills themselves through trial-and-error and absorb the cumulative knowledge of past workers via com-munication with their co-workers and exposure to the firms' operating routines. Once employees have acquired these valuable skills, they tend to remain employed within the industry because their value to a firm – and hence the wage they would likely earn – would decline rapidly if they moved to a new industry to which their skills no longer applied. Hence, the pool of human capital that entrepreneurs would typically wish to access resides in the incumbent firms in an industry; those wishing to recruit these individuals require strong connections to those firms and individuals to lure them away from their secure employment.

11.1.3   The Geography of Social Networks

If social networks connected individuals at random without regard for physical distance, then these processes would not necessarily influence the geographic distribution of industries. People do not, however, interact at random – they interact most commonly and most frequently with those who live in close geographic proximity and with whom they share backgrounds, interests, and affiliations (also referred to as social proximity). The similar patterns – relating social and physical distance to the likelihood of a social connection – reflect the fact that both emerge from influencing the probability of a random initial meeting. To initiate a relationship, two individuals must meet in time and space. Both geographic and social locations strongly shape a person's activities; hence, proximity on these dimensions elevates the probability of a chance encounter (Blau, 1977). Moreover, these factors continue to influence the likelihood of forming and maintaining a relationship even after an initial contact. People appear to prefer to interact with those from similar social backgrounds and with related interests (Lazarsfeld and Merton, 1954). And geographic proximity strongly influences the durability of social connections by reducing the costs associated with maintaining them (Stouffer, 1940; Zipf, 1949).

Numerous empirical studies confirm the relationship between the distance separating two individuals and the likelihood of a tie. Some of the earliest work in this genre investigated the role of propinquity in determining marital partners (Bossard, 1932) and friends (Festinger et al., 1950). A great deal of subsequent research has confirmed that proximity, particularly social proximity, structures interpersonal interaction (for a review, see McPherson et al., 2001). Social similarity, for instance, explains most of the variation in social networks in the 1985 General Social Survey (Marsden, 1988). More recently, researchers have begun to study economic relationships, revealing that they too follow this pattern. For example, floor traders on an options exchange interact most frequently with those situated near them on the floor (Baker, 1984). Corporate board interlocks most commonly appear among firms with geographically proximate headquarters (Kono et al., 1998). And venture capital firms exhibit a strong tendency to invest in new ventures located close to their offices (Sorenson and Stuart, 2001). Local interactions appear as common in economic contexts as in social ones.

Together, these factors suggest that social networks severely constrain where new firms in an industry will appear. Connections to existing industry incumbents increase the likelihood that a nascent entrepreneur perceives an opportunity in that line of business because these ties direct their attention to the business and provide them with private information that increases their likelihood of recognizing an opportunity. Upon seeing the possibility for a new venture, ties to the industry importantly facilitate the acquisition of valuable tacit knowledge and the recruitment of skilled labor, thereby improving the odds that the entrepreneur successfully builds a firm and begins operations. Given that these important social connections rarely extend far in space, both those most likely of perceiving opportunities within an industry and those most capable of acting on them reside in close proximity to existing firms within an industry. Moreover, the importance of these relationships binds these individuals to these regions. As a result, the geographic distribution of entrepreneurship tends to reinforce the existing industry topography.

11.2   Computer Workstation Manufacturers

It all happened in a narrow window in 1980–81. The technologies became available that allowed us to bring [the workstation] to market effectively. –William Poduska, CEO, Apollo Computer (Thames, 1984)

Apollo Computer, a new start-up located near Boston, announced the first workstation, the Apollo Domain in October 1980, and delivered its first shipment to Harvard University in March 1981. This new type of machine comprised multiple recently developed technologies – including a 32-bit microprocessor, a high-speed local area network, large shared virtual memory resources, and Winchester hard drives – into a single, integrated system. Though each of the components only improved incrementally on prior technology, the combination proved novel.

Workstations today have relatively homogenous product characteristics, but these features evolved over time. Early machines varied greatly in the specifics of their configurations: Manufacturers used a variety of micropro-cessors, most originally developed for other purposes. Some companies used existing operating systems, such as UNIX, while others developed their own proprietary system software. Firms even differed in the manner in which they rendered graphics with some choosing raster-based imaging, creating pic-tures with series of lines, while others defined graphics one pixel at a time in bit-mapped images.

Given this variety in product characteristics, this study defines the industry instead according to product functionality. Identifying members of an indus-try at the early stages always involves a substantial degree of judgement because firms and products have yet to converge on an archetypical form. Early automobile producers, for example, experimented not just with engine types (using electric and steam in addition to gas combustion; cf. Kirsh, 2000), but also in terms of body design (Carroll and Hannan, 1995). To address this difficulty, organizational ecologists have often relied on the classifications of some outside experts – at least implicitly in the sense that directories, presumably compiled by experts, often define firm membership in an industry. An alternative involves returning to the definition typically used in economics: an industry comprises firms with highly substitutable products. At any point in time, then, producers within an industry should offer products of relatively similar functionality; the approach used here follows this line of reasoning.

For the purpose of classifying firms as workstation producers, I define workstations as distributed computing machines primarily intended for a single user. This definition importantly distinguishes workstations from three other classes of machines: terminals, servers, and personal computers. Though terminals have evolved to include substantial local processing power for rendering graphics, they still rely on a mainframe for general processing power. Servers, on the other hand, though also operating in a distributed environment, clearly have been designed with the intention of attending to more than one user. Meanwhile, personal computers sit at the opposite end of the spectrum – though intended for a single user, they do not draw on distributed resources.

Using this definition, *Data Sources*, a catalog of computers and computer-related products, provided information on which firms could be considered computer workstation manufacturers (Sorenson, 2000, details how this definition guided classification at the level of the product characteristics). Advertisements and product announcements in *IEEE Graphical Computing and Applications*, annual corporate reports, the *IDC Processor Survey*, and Lexis-Nexis searches supplemented this primary source by identifying workstations omitted from *Data Sources* (particularly in the first few years) and by providing additional firm-level information. All firms that produced a computer workstation for at least one year between 1980 and 1996 enter the dataset. In total, the data include 175 distinct firms that operated in the industry for 677 firm-years.

11.2.1   The Geography of Founding

Early computer workstation manufacturers arose in three regions – in the suburbs surrounding Boston, on the peninsula of the San Francisco Bay, and in southern California between Orange County and San Diego. Figure 11.1 depicts the geographic distribution of workstation manufacturers as of 1984 (the size of the circle markers correspond to the square root of the number of firms in the MSA). Despite the entry and exit of numerous participants, the geography of production in computer workstation manufacturing does not shift greatly over time. A glance at Fig. 11.2, which illustrates the dispersion of firms in 1996, reveals a similar geographic distribution of workstation manufacturers (with the same square root scaling of circles to density). Though production disperses somewhat across the United States, economic activity within the industry remains clustered around Boston, San Jose, and San Diego, particularly if one weights larger firms more heavily.

Though this graphical evidence appears to support the general supposition that founding tends to replicate the existing geographic distribution of the industry, it does not allow us to account for other factors that might influence the rate of new-venture initiation. Statistical analysis of founding typically uses count models to assess the effects of various factors on entry rates (Hannan and Carroll, 1992). Researchers turn to count models for two reasons: First, in most cases one does not know the risk set of potential entrants – that is, who might found a firm (for an example of research on

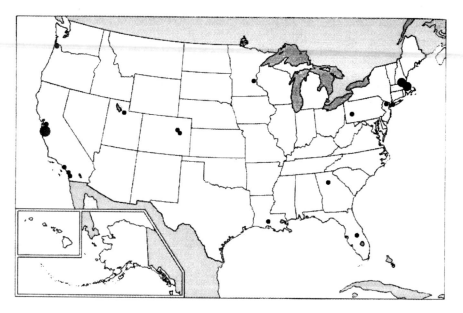

Fig. 11.1 Distribution of workstation manufacturers in 1984

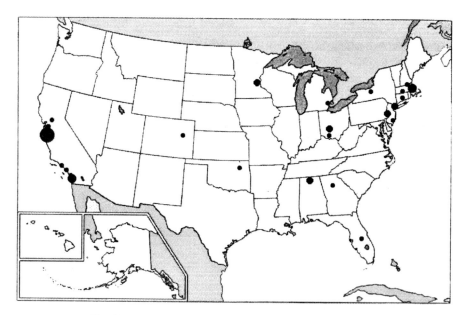

Fig. 11.2 Distribution of workstation manufacturers in 1996

spin-offs with a known risk set, see Brittain and Freeman, 1986). We, therefore, cannot investigate the transition to entrepreneurship directly but must rather make inferences jointly about the potential to become an entrepreneur and the probability of transition from the realized attempts (actually entries). Secondly, when examining entries, one would like to use an estimation procedure with an error distribution that matches that found in the data. Count models typically exhibit much longer right-hand tails than one would find in a normal (or even log normal) distribution. Analysis here proceeds using a type of count model, negative binomial regression (see Cameron and Trivedi, 1998, for a detailed review), estimating the rate at which entrants to the computer workstation industry arrive in a particular region.

Metropolitan Statistical Areas (MSAs) define the geographic units of analysis. These regions aggregate communities with a high degree of cross-employment (i.e. that belong to a common labor market). Though these regions seem appropriate for capturing the localized processes described above, when defining semi-arbitrary boundaries one must always worry about the choice of region definition. Has one erroneously excluded important influences from the unit of analysis? One can, nonetheless, reduce the importance of regional boundaries by treating space continuously when calculating independent variables (i.e. giving greater weight to factors just outside the boundary than those located at some distance from the focal unit). Hence, the models use distance-weighted density measures when estimating the importance of the proximity of existing firms to the entry rate in a region. Regions do not enter the analysis until they experience at least one entry event; thus, the models exclude from estimation communities that never host a workstation manufacturer.

The primary variable of interest is the local density of computer workstation manufacturers. Firms located in an MSA receive equal weight in this measure; as in traditional organizational ecology density terms, it amounts to a count of the local number of firms operating in the industry in the region. In addition, each computer workstation manufacturer outside the MSA also contributes to the density term proportional to its inverse distance from the geographic center of the MSA. Equation (11.1) provides the formula used for its calculation:

$$LD_{it} = \sum_j \frac{x_j}{\left(1 + d_{ij}\right)},\tag{11.1}$$

where x denotes a vector of firm-level attributes (in this case, simply a vector of ones) and d refers to the spherical distance between a firm, j, and the center of the MSA, i, in hundreds of miles (Sorenson and Audia, 2000).

The models also include several variables to control for other factors. *MSA Population*, a simple count of the number of individuals living in an MSA in a particular year, controls for the distribution of people across the United States. Both in terms of the size of the local market and in terms of the availability of labor, one would expect more firms in regions with more people. *National density*, the national count of workstation manufacturers, and its square, account for the broader industry dynamics. Organizational ecologists have argued and offered a great deal of evidence that the founding rate of organizations within an industry should first increase with the number of firms in an industry – as legitimacy spurs entry – and then decline with increasing numbers of rivals – as competition for resources inhibits resource mobilization (Hannan and Carroll, 1992). Table 11.1 describes the variables used in the entry analysis.

Table 11.2 reports the results of the analysis. The first column presents a baseline model; though population clearly influences where firms appear, the usual effects of national density do not appear. Model 2 includes the weighted local density term. The inclusion of this term improves the model significantly; computer workstation manufacturers more likely enter communities where larger populations of incumbents currently reside. Specifically, each local incumbent (or its equivalent in distance-weighted firms in neighboring regions) increases the entry rate by nearly 5 per cent; a one standard deviation rise in local density corresponds to a nearly 60 per cent increase in entry rates.

Models 3 and 4 split the analysis according to the type of entrant. Although many companies enter the computer workstation industry as new (*de novo*) firms dedicated to the production of workstations (e.g. Apollo or Sun), many others – referred to as *de alio* firms – had already been operating in related markets and decided to diversify into the manufacturing of computer workstations (e.g. HP and IBM). The account described above for how social networks might constrain the geography of entrepreneurship and hence engender the persistence of industrial clusters holds force primarily with respect to the founding of new (*de novo*) firms. Hence, the third column estimates the effect of local density on the founding rate of *de novo* firms, while the fourth column repeats the analysis for firms entering from other industries. As expected, the arrival rate of new firms exhibits far greater sensitivity (more than double) than the transition rate of existing firms diversifying into the industry to the local density of firms within the industry.

TABLE 11.1 *Descriptive statistics for entry rate models*

Variable	Mean	Standard deviation	Minimum	Maximum
MSA ENTRIES	0.25	0.63	0.00	5.00
MSA POPULATION	14.07	0.97	11.85	16.00
FIRM DENSITY / 10	4.76	1.60	0.20	7.60
FIRM DENSITY^2 / 1000	2.52	1.45	0.00	5.78
LOCAL FIRM DENSITY	13.83	10.30	1.13	51.27

TABLE 11.2 *Negative binomial regression estimates of MSA entry rates*

Variable	Model 1 All firms	Model 2 All firms	Model 3 *De novo*	Model 4 *De alio*
MSA POPULATION	0.342 ••	0.397 ••	0.448 •	0.383 ••
	(0.128)	(0.126)	(0.195)	(0.147)
FIRM DENSITY/10	0.187	0.057	−0.071	0.170
	(0.032)	(0.316)	(0.466)	(0.390)
FIRM DENSITY^2/1000	−0.200	−0.221	−0.366	−0.244
	(0.358)	(0.351)	(0.549)	(0.425)
LOCAL FIRM DENSITY		0.045 ••	0.064 ••	0.030 •
		(0.012)	(0.019)	(0.014)
CONSTANT	−6.631 ••	−7.436 ••	−8.871 ••	−7.961 ••
	(1.974)	(1.940)	(3.007)	(2.293)
ALPHA	2.155	1.746	0.729	2.412
	(0.629)	(0.552)	(1.089)	(0.841)
LOG-LIKELIHOOD	−287.3	−280.6	−113.9	−226.5

118 entries across 53 MSAs; • $p \le 0.05$, •• $p \le 0.01$

11.2.2 Location and Performance

Though these founding patterns support the thesis that existing social relations restrict where new firms in an industry typically arise, thereby reifying the geographic distribution of the industry, founding rates alone do not allow us to rule out the alternative hypothesis – that firms locate to optimize their performance (Sorenson and Audia, 2000). Indeed, much of the so-called new economic geography seeks to explain why competing firms might benefit from locating near one another. Three forces may operate here. First, firms in industrial districts might benefit from an extended division of labor (Romer, 1987). Geographic concentration allows for the development of highly specialized suppliers. These suppliers may achieve economies of scale in the production of various components, and pass these savings on to the manufacturers that purchase their wares. Secondly, agglomerations of firms within a single industry may profit from labor pooling (Diamond and Simon, 1990). Employees within these regions, perceiving less risk to developing highly specialized skills (since they could presumably take them to another local firm within the industry), might invest more in upgrading their human capital, allowing their employees to realize productivity gains. Thirdly, firms in industrial districts could enjoy returns from the sharing of information. Only one firm must bear the cost of acquiring new knowledge, but all firms can then potentially benefit from this resource (Arrow, 1962). Given Saxenian's (1994) vivid accounts of information sharing among engineers in

Silicon Valley, many have pointed to the computer workstation industry as an example of one case in which firms profit from these knowledge spillovers.

Regardless of the particular source of these benefits to collocation, all suggest that firms located near similar others should outperform those in more sparsely populated regions. Hence, if one found that locating the firm in a dense cluster of rivals appeared to detract from firm performance, it would suggest that these agglomeration externalities fail to account for the persistence of industrial clusters (Sorenson and Audia, 2000). It also notably suggests that entrepreneurs and managers may not act rationally (in the sense of maximizing the expected performance of the firm) when making their decisions of where to locate their firms. Hence, let us turn to an analysis of performance.

The analysis of firm performance here focuses on persistence within the market as an indicator of organizational success. Though perhaps less nuanced than profitability, survival offers a relatively unambiguous measure of performance. Industry participants profiting in a market are unlikely to leave, and equity and debt markets typically constrain the length of time that a firm can afford to remain in any market in which it loses money. To account properly for left censoring (the fact that many firms have not yet failed at the end of the observation window), the analysis uses event-history methods to estimate the instantaneous probability of exit (Tuma and Hannan, 1984). In particular, the analysis uses the Weibull model, in which time (age) dependence varies as an exponential function of duration.

Once again, the analysis focuses on the effects of *local density*, this time calculated with respect to a particular firm (see eqn (11.1), and includes several control variables to account for other factors influencing firm performance. *Size* measures the scale of organizational operations in the natural log of 1996 dollars; larger firms may benefit from economies of scale in R&D, manufacturing and/or marketing. *Entry age*, the natural log of the number of years (plus one) the firm operated before entering the computer workstation industry, captures the potential benefits or disadvantages accruing to *de alio* entrants. *Vertical integration*, a tally of the number of subcomponents the firm manufacturers in-house, accounts for any effects associated with the choice of vertical scope, while *diversification*, a count of the number of non-workstation products the firm markets in the computer industry captures potential economies of scope (as well as outside opportunities). *Density* and its square capture the effects of legitimation and competition on firm performance (Hannan and Carroll, 1992). Table 11.3 provides the descriptive statistics for the variables appearing in the exit rate analysis.

Table 11.4 reports the results of the analysis. The baseline results, model 5, reveal that, consistent with prior studies, firm exit rates decline with size and – having adjusted for scale – rise with age. The negative coefficient for entry age also indicates that firms entering from other markets enjoy an advantage relative to *de novo* entrants (Carroll *et al.*, 1996, found similar results in the

TABLE 11.3 *Descriptive statistics for exit rate models*

VARIABLE	MEAN	STANDARD DEVIATION	MINIMUM	MAXIMUM
AGE	2.84	2.96	0.00	14.00
SIZE	16.48	2.36	9.39	22.77
ENTRY AGE	15.01	20.11	0.00	115.00
VERTICAL INTEGRATION	2.40	1.90	0.00	8.00
DIVERSICATION	2.90	5.40	0.00	32.00
FIRM DENSITY / 10	5.02	1.63	0.20	7.60
FIRM DENSITY^2 / 1000	2.78	1.54	0.00	5.78
LOCAL FIRM DENSITY	3.75	3.24	0.01	12.24

TABLE 11.4 *Weibull estimates of firm exit rates*

VARIABLE	MODEL 5	MODEL 6	MODEL 7
AGE	0.246••	0.281••	0.290••
	(0.080)	(0.082)	(0.083)
SIZE	−0.176••	−0.193••	−0.192••
	(0.056)	(0.058)	(0.059)
ENTRY AGE	−0.233•	−0.224•	−0.222•
	(0.115)	(0.118)	(0.121)
VERTICAL INTEGRATION	−0.064	−0.087	−0.068
	(0.091)	(0.098)	(0.099)
DIVERSICATION	−0.109	−0.097	−0.139
	(0.324)	(0.333)	(0.326)
FIRM DENSITY / 10	−0.279	−0.324	−0.246
	(0.357)	(0.368)	(0.362)
FIRM DENSITY^2 / 1000	0.463	0.341	0.270
	(0.339)	(0.361)	(0.364)
LOCAL FIRM DENSITY		0.274•	0.281•
		(0.150)	(0.151)
LOCAL FIRM DENSITY × ENTRY AGE			0.051
			(0.038)
CONSTANT	1.368	2.130	−8.871••
	(1.281)	(1.304)	(3.007)
LOG-LIKELIHOOD	−139.0	−131.7	−113.9

175 firms with 122 exits; • $p \leq 0.10$, •• $p \leq 0.05$

automobile industry). Firm scope appears to have little effect on exit rates, and national population density fails to have its expected effect. Model 6 adds the weighted density measure to capture the effects of collocation. Rather than improving firm performance, locating near rivals degrades firm performance – presumably because firms compete over a variety of local resources, such as skilled labor and access to high-quality suppliers. Since *de novo* firms appeared most sensitive to the local firm proximity, model 7 tests whether these firms might benefit more from clustering by interacting entry age with local firm density. Though the positive coefficient would be consistent with greater susceptibility by *de alio* firms to local competition, the estimate fails to meet the critical level for statistical significance at even a 0.1 level.

The negative of consequences on locating near rivals should not surprise us. Each of the factors cited as an advantage to collocation also has a flip side. Drawing on common labor markets engenders competition over the highest-quality employees, thereby inflating wages. Common suppliers offer price advantages to firms using them, but also make it difficult for one firm to differentiate its products from another's. And information spills out of the firm as often as it spills in. Regardless of the specific source of this disadvantage, the lack of evidence for performance benefits to clustering implies that agglomeration externalities cannot explain geographic concentration in the computer workstation industry, and lends further credence to an explanation based on the constraints that social networks place on entrepreneurs.

11.3   Discussion

An examination of the dynamics of entry into and exit from the computer workstation manufacturing industry suggests that firms within an industry cluster within a small number of geographic regions not because this spatial configuration enhances the efficiency of production, but rather because social networks constrain where entrepreneurs found new firms and what types of businesses they enter. Social connections to existing industry participants increase the likelihood that a nascent entrepreneur perceives an opportunity in the industry. Moreover, upon recognizing the possibility for a new venture, ties to the industry importantly facilitate the mobilization of the resources, including tacit knowledge and skilled labor, necessary to begin operations. Given that these important social connections rarely extend far in space, both those most likely to perceive opportunities within an industry and those most capable of acting on them reside in close proximity to existing firms within an industry. As a result, entrepreneurship tends to reinforce the existing geographic distribution of an industry.

Though the theory posited here explains why industries should cluster, it cannot easily explain variation in the degree to which they concentrate geographically. Some industries, such as footwear production, have remained clustered in a few regions over centuries, while others, such as hand-tool fabrication and medical instruments, have dispersed relatively rapidly (for information on the relative dispersion of various industries in the US, see the appendix of Krugman, 1991). Can network constraints account for this heterogeneity? At least three avenues of theory development might allow network-based accounts to explain interindustry variation in the degree of geographic concentration.

First, dispersion might simply result from a process of diffusion. Some firms manage to escape the confines of the existing regions in which the industry resides. These remote entries may represent a form of entrepreneurial arbitrage. For example, an individual with employment experience in an industry as well as deep social connections in a region currently lacking businesses of that type may leverage his connections to disparate groups (a type of 'structural hole' in Burt's, 1992, terminology) to profit from locating in a region with lower factor market competition. Or, as existing firms expand, they might naturally reach into new regions when opening new plants. Over time, the firms and divisions these entrepreneurs and incumbents open disperse the availability of knowledge about the industry and skilled labor. Hence, a slow diffusion process might explain a positive relationship between the age of an industry and its degree of geographic dispersion.

Alternatively (or additionally), as the results here hint, the proportion of de alio entrants might influence the speed at which an industry diffuses. Whereas these dynamics place severe constraints on where entrepreneurs in an industry might arise, the arrival of de alio entrants likely depends more on the existing distribution of related industries. For example, many early automobile manufacturers hailed from the ranks of bicycle producers, carriage builders, and engine manufacturers (Carroll et al., 1996). To the extent that these industries each had their own somewhat independent geographic distributions, one might expect the automobile industry to arise initially in a greater number of locations than an emerging industry drawing on a narrower range of existing firms, and hence disperse more rapidly.

The data here on the workstation industry suggest that de alio firms serve as the geographic pioneers, first bringing production to a region, potentially seeding later entry into the region by entrepreneurs. Notably, only 11 of the 53 firms first producing computer workstations in a particular MSA enter de novo, and five of those enter in the first two years of the industry when industry incumbents still have little to offer in the way of know-how or experienced personnel. Hence, the prevalence of de alio entrants early in an industry's history might play an important role in determining its level of dispersion.

In addition to these industry dynamics, other characteristics, such as the technology being deployed, may also influence the importance of social networks, and concomitantly the rate at which production of a particular type diffuses across space. Several researchers (e.g. Hansen, 1999) have noted that certain types of knowledge might prove particularly difficult to transfer in the absence of strong, social connections. For example, complex tacit knowledge – comprising many elements interacting in a sensitive manner – defies transmittal in the absence of direct ties because errors in transfer frequently destroy the value of the knowledge (Sorenson *et al.*, 2003). Hence, one might expect social networks to play an even stronger role in access to tacit knowledge in industries drawing on information of a relatively high degree of average complexity, thereby slowing its dispersion. In support of such an idea, Sorenson (2004) found a positive cross-sectional relationship between the level of informational complexity in an industry's patents and its degree of geographic concentration.

Though framed as an alternate explanation for the persistence of industrial clusters, the larger lesson of this research and other studies like it concerns the desirability of geographic concentration in production. A variety of careful case studies have described the way in which industrial districts operate, and a growing number of analytic models show how these dynamics might prove beneficial to society. Two (somewhat related) items, however, seem lacking: (1) a healthy skepticism regarding whether clustering benefits firms and/or society in general, and (2) systematic empirical comparisons of the performance of collocated versus isolated firms. The results here, as well as in footwear manufacturing and biotechnology, suggest that firms do not benefit from locating near rivals. Though the returns to agglomeration may appear elsewhere – for example, in the form of higher wages or lower unemployment rates – we need more research to inform policy makers who, with an eye toward Silicon Valley and other successful regions, often view clusters as a panacea for economic development.

References

Akerlöf, G. A. (1970), 'The market for "lemons": quality, uncertainty and the market mechanism'. *Quarterly Journal of Economics*, **84**: 488–500.

Arrow, K. J. (1962), 'The economic implications of learning by doing'. *Review of Economic Studies*, **29**: 155–173.

Baker, W. (1984), 'The social structure of a national securities market'. *American Journal of Sociology*, **89**: 775–811.

Blau, P. M. (1977), *Inequality and heterogeneity: a primitive theory of social structure*. New York: Free Press.

Bossard, J. S. (1932), 'Residential propinquity as a factor in marriage selection'. *American Journal of Sociology*, **38**: 219–224.

Brittain, J. W. and Freeman, J. (1986), 'Entrepreneurship in the semiconductor industry'. Mimeo.

Burt, R. S. (1992), *Structural holes: the social structure of competition*. Cambridge, MA: Harvard University Press.

Cameron, A. C. and Trivedi, P. K. (1998), *The regression analysis of count data*. Cambridge: Cambridge University Press.

Carroll, G. R., Bigelow, L., Seidel, M. D., and Tsai, L. (1996), 'The fates of de novo and de alio producers in the American automobile industry, 1885–1982'. *Strategic Management Journal*, **17**: 117–137.

Carroll, G. R. and Hannan, M. T. (1995), 'Automobile manufacturers', in G. R. Carroll and M. T. Hannan (eds), *Organizations in industry*. New York: Oxford University Press, pp. 195–214.

Carroll, G. R. and Hannan, M. T. (2000), *The demography of organizations and industries*. Princeton, NJ: Princeton University Press.

Cooper, A. C. (1970), *The founding of technologically-based firms*. Milwaukee, WI: The Center for Venture Management.

Diamond, C. A. and Simon, C. J. (1990), 'Industrial specialization and increasing returns to labor'. *Journal of Labor Economics*, **8**: 175–201.

Ellsberg, D. (1961), 'Risk, ambiguity and the Savage axioms'. *Quarterly Journal of Economics*, **75**: 643–669.

Festinger, L., Schacter, S., and Back, K. W. (1950), *Social pressure in informal groups*. New York: Harper.

Figueiredo, O., Guimarães, P., and Woodward, D. (2002), 'Home-field advantage: location decisions of Portuguese entrepreneurs'. *Journal of Urban Economics*, **52**: 341–361.

Fox, C. R. and Tversby, A. (1995), 'Ambiguity aversion and comparative ignorance'. *Quarterly Journal of Economics*, **110**: 585–603.

Fried, V. H. and Hisrich, R. D. (1994), 'Toward a model of venture capital investment decision making'. *Financial Management*, **23**: 28–37.

Hannan, M. T. and Carroll, G. R. (1992), *Dynamics of organizational populations*. New York: Oxford University Press.

Hansen, M. T. (1999), 'The search-transfer problem: the role of weak ties in sharing knowledge across organization subunits'. *Administrative Science Quarterly*, **44**: 82–111.

Haug, P. (1995), 'Formation of biotechnology firms in the Greater Seattle region: an empirical investigation of entrepreneurial, financial, and educational perspectives'. *Environment and Planning A*, **27**: 249–267.

Katona, G. and Morgan, J. N. (1952), 'The quantitative study of factors determining business decisions'. *Quarterly Journal of Economics*, **66**: 67–90.

Kirsch, D. (2000), *The electric vehicle and the burden of history*. New Brunswick, NJ: Rutgers University Press.

Klepper, S. (2001), 'Employee startups in high-tech industries'. *Industrial and Corporate Change*, **10**: 639–674.

Klepper, S. (2002), 'The evolution of the automobile industry and Detroit as its capital'. Working paper, Carnegie Mellon University.

Kono, C., Palmer, D., Friedland, R., and Zafronte, M. (1998), 'Lost in space: The geography of corporate interlocking directorates'. *American Journal of Sociology*, **103**: 863–911.

Krugman, P. (1991), *Geography and trade*. Cambridge, MA: MIT Press.

Lazarsfeld, P. F. and Merton, R. K. (1954), 'Friendship as a social process: a substantive and methodological analysis,' in M. Berger, T. Abel, and C. H. Page (eds), *Freedom and control in modern society*. New York: Van Nostrand, pp. 18–66.

Liles, P. R. (1974), *New business ventures and the entrepreneur*. Homewood, IL: Richard D. Irwin.

Marsden, P. V. (1988), 'Homogeneity in confiding relations'. *Social Networks*, **10**: 57–76.

Marshall, A. (1890), *Principles of economics*. London: MacMillan.

McPherson, J. M., Lovin, L. S., and Cook, J. M. (2001), 'Birds of a feather: homophily in social networks'. *Annual Review of Sociology*, **27**: 415–444.

Mitton, D. G. (1990), 'Bring on the clones: a longitudinal study of the proliferation, development, and growth of the biotech industry in San Diego', in N. C. Churchill, W. D. Bygrave, J. A. Hornaday, D. F. Muzyka, K. H. Vesper, and W. E. Wetzel, Jr. (eds), *Frontiers of entrepreneurship research 1990*. Wellesley, MA: Babson College, pp. 344–358.

Nelson, R. R. (1959), 'The simple economics of basic scientific research'. *Journal of Political Economy*, **67**: 297–306.

Porter, M. E. (1990), *The competitive advantage of nations*. New York: Free Press.

Romer P. (1987), 'Growth based on increasing returns to specialization'. *American Economic Review*, **77**: 56–62.

Saxenian, A. (1994), *Regional advantage*. Cambridge, MA: Harvard University Press

Sorenson, O. (2000), 'Letting the market work for you: an evolutionary perspective on product strategy'. *Strategic Management Journal*, **21**: 577–592.

Sorenson, O. (2003), 'Social networks and industrial geography'. *Journal of Evolutionary Economics*, **13**: 513–527.

Sorenson, O. (2004), 'Social networks, informational complexity and industrial geography', in D. Fornahl and C. Zellner (eds), *The role of labor mobility and informal networks for knowledge transfer*, Amsterdam: Kluwer Academic, pp. 79–96.

Sorenson, O. and Audia, P. G. (2000), 'The social structure of entrepreneurial activity: geographic production of footwear in the United States, 1940–1989'. *American Journal of Sociology*, **106**: 424–462.

Sorenson, O., Rivkin, J. W., and Fleming, L. (2003), 'Complexity, networks and knowledge flow'. Mimeo.

Sorenson, O. and Stuart, T. E. (2001), 'Syndication networks and the spatial distribution of venture capital investments'. *American Journal of Sociology*, **106**: 1546–1588.

Stouffer, S. A. (1940), 'Intervening opportunities: a theory relative mobility and distance'. *American Sociological Review*, **5**: 845–867.

Stuart, T. E. and Sorenson, O. (2003), 'The geography of opportunity: spatial heterogeneity in founding rates and the performance of biotechnology firms'. *Research Policy*, **32**: 229–253.

Thames, C. (1984), 'Apollo streaks through the workstation market'. *Electronic Business*, **10**: 76–86.

Tuma, N. and Hannan, M. T. (1984), *Social dynamics: models and methods*. Orlando, FL: Academic Press.

Weber, A. (1909/1928), *Theory of the location of industries*, translated by C. J. Friedrich. Chicago: University of Chicago Press.

Zipf, G. K. (1949), *Human behavior and the principle of least effort*. Reading, MA: Addison-Wesley.

Part IV

12

Buzz: Face-to-Face Contact and the Urban Economy

MICHAEL STORPER AND ANTHONY J. VENABLES

12.1 Face-to-Face Contact Remains Important

Face-to-face contact remains central to co-ordination of the economy, despite the remarkable reductions in transport costs and the astonishing rise in the complexity and variety of information – verbal, visual, and symbolic – which can be communicated near instantly. Over the past quarter century, long-distance business travel has grown faster than output and trade (Hall, 1998). There must be powerful reasons for economic agents to congregate and see each other, given the relatively high pecuniary and opportunity cost of business travel. Forces of urbanization and localization remain strong. For example, the geographical density of employment in many sectors in the US has actually increased in recent years (Kim, 2002). It has also been estimated that, in the US, 380 localized clusters of firms employ 57 per cent of the total workforce and generate 61 per cent of the nation's output and fully 78 per cent of its exports (Rosenfeld, 1996). Other researchers, using more conservative measures, still find that 30 per cent of the US workforce is accounted for by localized employment clusters (Porter, 2001). Urbanization is continuing apace in developing countries, and many cities in high-income countries are experiencing a resurgence (Scott, 2001).

Three main forces are thought to lie behind the persistence of urbanization and localization: backward and forward linkages of firms, including access to markets; the clustering of workers; and localized interactions that promote technological innovation. We argue in this chapter that analysis of these mechanisms is likely to be incomplete unless grounded in the most fundamental aspect of proximity: face-to-face (F2F) contact.

To begin with, there is widespread agreement that localized backward and forward linkages, while important in specific cases, can account for only a small part of contemporary urbanization (Gordon and McCann, 2000). More importantly, when such linkages are strongly localized, it is rarely because of high physical transport costs, and frequently because the information associated with the physical transaction is costly or difficult to transmit at great distance. Deal-making, evaluation, and relationship adjustment are heavily dependent on face-to-face contact.

The clustering of workers is considered to be a strong contributor to localization and urbanization, largely because of the increasing demand for specialized skills and more flexible, higher-turnover labor markets. Taken together, they place a premium on clustering because employers thereby gain access to a large pool of specialized labor and can avoid hoarding during downturns. Workers gain access to a greater number of potential employers, allowing them to minimize periods of unemployment and make more rapid progression up a career ladder, with greater lifetime learning and wage growth (Jayet, 1983; Rotemberg and Saloner, 2000). Underpinning these dynamics, however, are detailed processes of signalling and screening that occur largely through face-to-face contact, as well as network structures that are constructed through such contact (Granovetter, 1995).

The third group of explanations concern technological innovation. There is fragmentary but fairly convincing evidence that cities are centers of innovation in the production of ideas and knowledge and in their commercialization (Jaffe *et al.*, 1993; Feldman and Audretsch, 1999). The notion frequently adduced to explain these facts is that spatial proximity must somehow improve flows of information upon which innovators depend, creating technological 'spill-overs'. However, the mechanisms underlying these spillovers remain unclear. One avenue of inquiry has to do with the circulation of knowledgeable workers between firms, enhancing the ability of these firms to recombine knowledge, imitate best practices, and otherwise improve their products. For example, in Glaeser's (1999) model of learning, people can absorb knowledge from contact with more skilled individuals in their own industry, and the number of probable contacts an individual makes is an increasing function of city size. Large cities therefore facilitate learning, and are particularly attractive for highly talented young people who have large potential returns from learning. The hypothesis is therefore, that knowledge 'rubs off' on people in places such as Silicon Valley or the City of London. But if this is the case, it is through F2F contact that rubbing off occurs, and we require a theory of the motivations people have for engaging in F2F contact.

Jacobs (1969) advanced the idea that cities enjoy an advantage because of their economic and social diversity. This diversity, because it is highly packed into limited space, facilitates haphazard, serendipitous contact among people. Florida (2002), drawing on the classical notions of Simmel and Tönnies (Simmel, 1950), argues that the diversity found in cosmopolitan cities facilitates 'creativity' because of the openness of their networks, the liberating force of anonymity and hence resistance to hide-bound tradition. But in none of these formulations can be found a direct explanation of the F2F interaction by which cosmopolitanism and diversity have their positive effects. Nor do these approaches consider the disadvantages of anonymity and large numbers, in the form of the costs to co-ordination they may generate, or the way in which the economy overcomes these difficulties.[1]

In another vein, Alfred Marshall, one of the main inspirations for contemporary students of the 'industrial district', also suggested the importance of direct and unplanned contact between economic agents (Marshall, 1919;

Becattini, 2000). Marshall centers on belonging to a specialized producer community that diffuses the 'secrets' of industry, not the kind of cosmopolitan and haphazard city life described by Jacobs. Numerous attempts have been made to transform his notion into a theory of the milieux underlying contemporary industrial districts. All beg the question: if agents belong to a milieu, what do their interactions consist of and what are the incentives for undertaking such interactions?

In sum, the various theories of agglomeration and the persistence of cities refer to transactional structures and circumstances that necessitate close contact between persons, and to the various outcomes of proximity between agents – more effective input–output linkages, more effective labor market matching, technological spillovers. However, they do not explain precisely what individuals do in this form of encounter, nor why they do it. These encounters are, of course, face-to-face contacts between economic agents. F2F contact is thus a missing aspect of mechanisms that are considered to generate agglomeration.

This chapter contributes to the understanding of F2F contact. First, we show that F2F contact has unique behavioral and communicational properties that give it specific advantages as a technology of communication, coordination, and motivation (Section 12.2). We develop two game-theoretic models that illustrate why agents engage in F2F contact and contribute some building blocks of a microeconomic theory of F2F contact (Section 12.3). We then place these ideas in the wider context of the role of F2F contact, among other mechanisms, in co-ordinating activity in different areas of the economy (Section 12.4). Finally, we offer concluding remarks on the future importance of F2F contact.

12.2   The Specific Properties of Face-to-Face Contact

In order to consider the possible role of F2F contact in the economy, its properties as a type of behavior and interaction need to be identified. Table 12.1 lists four major properties of F2F contact: it is an efficient communication technology; it allows actors to align commitments and thereby reduces incentive problems; it allows screening of agents; and it motivates effort.

12.2.1   F2F Contact as a Communication Technology

The first row of Table 12.1 refers to the advantages of F2F contact as a *communication technology*, particularly when much of the information to be transmitted cannot be codified.

Codifiable information has a stable meaning that is associated in a determinate way with the symbol system in which it is expressed, whether it be linguistic, mathematical, or visual. Such information is cheap to transfer because its underlying symbol systems can be widely disseminated through information infrastructure, sharply reducing the marginal cost of individual

TABLE 12.1 *Face-to-face contact*

Function	Advantage of F2F	Context
Communication technology	High frequency	Non-codifiable information
	Rapid feedback	
	Visual and body language cues	R&D
		Teaching
Trust and incentives in relationships	Detection of lying	Meetings
	Co-presence a commitment of time	
Screening and socializing	Loss of anonymity	Professional groups
	Judging and being judged	Being 'in the loop'
	Acquisition of shared values	
Rush and motivation	Performance as display	Presentations

messages. Acquiring the symbol system may be expensive or slow (language, mathematical skills, etc.), as may be building the transmission system, but using it to communicate information is cheap. Thus, the transmission of codifiable information has strong network externalities, since once the infrastructure is acquired a new user can plug in and access the whole network.

By contrast, uncodifiable information is only loosely related to the symbol system in which it is expressed. This includes much linguistic, words-based expression (the famous distinction between 'speech' and 'language'), particularly what might be called 'complex discourse' (Searle, 1969). For example, one can master the grammar and the syntax of a language without understanding its metaphors. This is also true for some mathematically expressed information, and much visual information. If the information is not codifiable, merely acquiring the symbol system or having the physical infrastructure is not enough for the successful transmission of a message. Transmission of uncodifiable information may have very limited network externalities, since the successful transmission of the message depends on infrastructure that is largely committed to one specific sender–receiver pair. Bateson (1973) refers to the 'analog' quality of tacit knowledge: communication between individuals that requires a kind of parallel processing of the complexities of an issue, as different dimensions of a problem are perceived and understood only in relation to one another.

F2F encounters provide an efficient technology of transaction under these circumstances, by permitting a depth and speed of feedback that is impossible in other forms of communication. As organizational theorists Nitin Nohria and Robert Eccles (1992, p. 292) point out:

... relative to electronically-mediated exchange, the structure of face-to-face interaction offers an unusual capacity for interruption, repair, feedback, and learning. In contrast to interactions that are largely sequential, face-to-face interaction makes it possible for two people to be sending and delivering messages simultaneously. The cycle of interruption, feedback and repair possible in face-to-face interaction is so quick that it is virtually instantaneous.

This echoes the findings of sociologist Goffman (1982) that 'a speaker can see how others are responding to her message even before it is done and alter it midstream to elicit a different response'.

But it is not just the uncodifiability of much information that makes F2F a superior technology. Communication in an F2F context occurs on many levels at the same time – verbal, physical, contextual, intentional, and non-intentional. Such multidimensional communication is held by many to be essential to the transmission of complex, tacit knowledge. For example, social psychologists argue that creativity results from several different ways of processing information at one time, including not only the standard deductive way but analogical, metaphorical, and parallel methods as well (Bateson, 1973; Csikszentmihalyi, 1996). These different means of communication are mutually enriching, and lead to connections being made that cannot be had through strictly linear perception and reasoning. An extension of this is that the full benefits of diversity and serendipity are only realized through these multiple levels of communication. Linguists such as Austin (1962) and Searle (1969) develop another aspect of communicational analysis, arguing that 'language is behavior' and F2F dialog is a complex socially creative activity. In a similar vein, sociologists such as Goffman (1959) and Garfinkel (1987) show that the interaction that comes from co-presence can be likened to being on stage, playing a role, where the visual and corporeal cues are at least as important to knowing what is being 'said' as are the words themselves.

12.2.2   *Trust and Incentives in Relationships*

The second row of Table 12.1 refers to the notion that co-presence may reduce incentive and co-ordination problems that arise in economic relationships. With tacit knowledge there is always residual uncertainty and hence the need to minimize the incentives for one agent to free ride or manipulate the other. These moral hazards exist when the inherent degree of reliability of a message is low. They can sometimes be reduced through improvements in the transparency or clarity of the information itself or in how well it can be verified. But in other cases they require shaping a relationship between the interested parties. Being close enough literally to touch each other allows visual 'contact' and 'emotional closeness', the basis for building human relationships.

For example, the contemporary knowledge-based economy involves many projects in which individuals come together to acquire and exchange information. Typically, the later stages of such a project – writing the report, executing the transaction, or constructing the investment – involve codifiable information. It is the earlier stages where information is more fluid. Is the project a good idea? Should one approach be followed or another? Answering these questions requires that partners in the project undertake research and share their results. Often, neither the inputs nor the outputs of this research are observable. Thus, a partner can conscientiously research the project or simply free-ride, hoping that other members of the team will do the work.

F2F can play important roles in mitigating these incentive and free-rider problems. One reason for this is simply that it is easier to observe and interpret a partner's behavior in an F2F situation. Any message may be understood but not believed. There are strong questions of intentionality at work in communication. Knowing the intentions of another actor enables us to decode the practical consequences of what they are expressing to us (Husserl, 1968). Speech and action are tightly interrelated, but speech does not automatically reveal to us what another person intends to do (Searle, 1969). Humans are very effective at sensing non-verbal messages from one another, particularly about emotions, co-operation, and trustworthiness. Putnam (2000, p. 175) notes that 'it seems that the ability to spot non-verbal signs of mendacity offered a significant survival advantage during the course of human evolution'. Psychologist Albert Mehrabian (1981, p. iii) notes that 'our facial and vocal expressions, postures, movements and gestures', are crucial; when our words 'contradict the messages contained within them, others mistrust what we say – they rely almost completely on what we do'.

A second reason is that F2F contact may promote the development of trust. Trust depends on reputation effects or on multilayered relations between the parties to a transaction that can create low-cost enforcement opportunities (Gambetta, 1988; Lorenz, 1992). Trust also comes from the fact that partners expend time, money, and effort in building a relationship. The time and money costs of co-presence (schmoozing) can be substantial, far outweighing the cost of the message. These costs are sunk, so indicate a willingness to embark on a repeated relationship; absent a second date, the value of the first date disappears. However, to create a relationship bond, the costs must be substantial and transparent. E-mail, paradoxically, can be so efficient that it destroys the value of the message. The e-mail medium greatly reduces the cost of sending a message, somewhat reduces the cost of receiving the message, and it makes the costs mostly non-transparent. The low costs and the non-transparency greatly limit the value of the relationship bond. A return receipt only means that the recipient has opened the message, but the sender cannot be sure that enough attention has been devoted to it to absorb the content. In this sense, for complex context-dependent information, the medium *is* the message. And the most powerful such medium for verifying the intentions of another is direct F2F contact.

12.2.3   Screening and Socialization

Even if we admit, on the basis of the above argument, that F2F contact is an efficient technology of transacting, it is nonetheless very costly, not least because it is time consuming. We do not have the luxury of F2F encounters with the entire world, so need to screen out the people with whom we want to interact. How do we identify such people? One way is formal screening procedures – examination and certification. Another is the development of informal networks, in which members of the network develop and share a pool of knowledge about members' competence.

Social and professional networks of this type often – although not always – require F2F contact. One reason is that they are necessarily based on individuals losing their anonymity; a member of the group is continually judging other members of the group, being judged, and sharing judgements with members of the group. In some internationalized professions – such as academia – this does not always require co-location, although is certainly reinforced by F2F contact in the conference circuit. In other activities these information networks can only be maintained within a restricted geographical area. In such fields as fashion, public relations, and many of the arts (including cinema, television, and radio) there are international networks 'at the top', but in the middle of these professions networks are highly localized, change rapidly, and information used by members to stay in the loop is highly context dependent. In parts of the financial services and high-technology industries, local networks intersect with long-distance contact systems. In almost anything relating to business-government relations, networks have a strongly national and regional cast.

The screening of network members and potential partners is complex because much of what is most valuable about partners is their tacit know-ledge. Much of such knowledge can only be successfully communicated as metaphor (Nisbet, 1969), whose meanings are highly culture and context dependent (Lakoff and Johnson, 1980). Polanyi (1966, p. 4) argued that tacit and metaphorical knowledge is deeply embedded in specific contexts. Thus, potential partners need to 'know' each other, or have a broad common background, acquired through socialization. Sociological theory refers to socialization as the production of the individual as a social being who develops specific capacities to signal to others that he or she belongs to a certain world, and hence elicits from others the recognition of belonging.[2] Individuals learn to share the 'codes' that show that they have certain criteria of judgement, which in turn signal to others that they belong to the same social world (Coleman, 1990). This gives them the means to become members of structured milieux, to get 'in the loop'. Socialization is inevitably achieved in large measure through face-to-face contact, from family, schooling, and the social environment in one's community and workplaces.

Notice, then, that F2F performs its screening role on two timescales in the economic process: in the long run, by socializing people; in the short run, by permitting potential collaborators to evaluate others' performance in professional groups and networks.

12.2.4   'Rush' and the Motivation that Comes from F2F Contact

The final row of Table 12.1 shows another dimension of the incentive effects of F2F contact, which goes beyond verbal or visual communication. F2F communication does not derive its richness and power merely from allowing us to see each other's faces and to detect the intended and unintended messages that can be sent by such visual contact. As noted, according to Goffman (1959), F2F communication is a *performance*, a means to information production and not merely to more efficient exchange. In this performance, speech, intentions, role playing, and a specific context all come together to raise the quantity and quality of information that can be transmitted. Moreover, performance raises effort by stimulating imitation and competition. Psychologists have shown that the search for pleasure is a powerful motivating force in behavior, and certain kinds of pleasure are linked to pride of status and position: we imitate others, try to do better than them, and derive pleasure from succeeding at so doing. When we make an effort, and are on the route to success, there is a biophysical 'rush' that pushes us forward. However, all pleasure quickly recedes as it blends into the preceding 'normal' state, and it is only by once again changing this state that pleasure is found again. The search for such pride of status and position is thus a strong motivation that must be continuously renewed (Scitovsky, 1976). F2F contact provides the strongest, most embodied signals of such desire and can generate the rush that pushes us to make greater and better efforts. It is thus no surprise that even with the sophisticated computer monitoring that can be carried out on employee performance today, very few workplaces – which are essentially centers of F2F contact – have disappeared. It is not just that it is easier to monitor employees when they are present, it is also that such presence is motivating, because it contributes to desire, imitation, and competition, and the fear of shame from failure (Scitovsky, 1976; Kahneman *et al.*, 1998).

12.3   Why People Engage in F2F Contact: Two Models

With these basic properties of F2F contact in mind, we now propose two analytical models of how F2F contact improves the co-ordination of economic agents. In the first, F2F contact overcomes incentive problems in the formation of working partnerships; in the second, it allows actors to evaluate others' qualities and leads to the formation of 'in groups' that support more efficient partnering and increased motivation. These models begin the task of developing a microeconomic theory of F2F contact. They both yield the result that productivity is raised by F2F contact.

12.3.1   Incentives in Joint Projects

Game-theoretic analysis provides a way of drawing out some of the incentive issues that arise when information is fluid and actions are not observable. To illustrate, suppose that two people are considering undertaking a joint project, but they are uncertain about its ultimate value or quality. All they know, initially, is that the project is either good, yielding final payoff A, or bad, yielding zero; they both attach the same prior probability, ρ, to the project being good. The game has two stages. The first involves acquisition of information about the quality of the project, and the second involves information sharing, deciding whether or not to undertake the project, and project implementation. What are the incentives to acquire information or to free-ride, and how might they be improved by F2F contact?

At the first stage, the two individuals undertake research independently and obtain a signal of whether the project is good or bad. The signal obtained by player i may be favorable, g_i, or unfavorable, b_i. However, the signals are not accurate – a good project can send out a signal that it is bad, and vice versa. By expending effort, e_i, each player ($i = 1, 2$) can improve the quality of the signal received (details are given in Appendix 12.1).

At the second stage of the game players truthfully reveal their signals to each other.[3] Using standard Bayesian techniques they use their combined information to compute the probability that the project is good; this probability is higher the more good signals have been received and the more effort has been expended, improving the quality of the signals. They then decide whether or not to proceed. Proceeding costs C and yields payoff A if the project turns out to be good, and zero otherwise; we assume $A_\rho = C$, so (prior to research) the project yields zero expected surplus.

The incentives faced by individuals and the equilibrium outcomes are illustrated in Fig. 12.1. The axes are the effort levels of the two players, and the lines OA and OB divide the space up into three regions. Between OA and OB effort levels are such that players will, at the second stage, choose to go ahead with the project only if they have both received good signals, $\{g_1, g_2\}$. However, below OB player 1 is putting in so little effort relative to player 2 (and hence 1's signal is so unreliable) that they proceed if 2 has a good signal and 1 a bad one $\{g_2, b_1\}$. Similarly, above OA they proceed with signals $\{g_1, b_2\}$. The curves labeled EU_1 are expected utility indifference curves for player 1, increasing to the right, and kinked where they cross lines OA and OB. The best response function for player 1 to each effort level e_2 is given by the bold solid lines, $e_1 = R_1(e_2)$. We see that if e_2 is very low, then player 1 will ignore 2's signal and put in a constant amount of effort (in the region to the left of

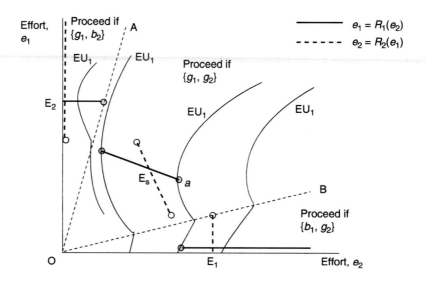

Fig. 12.1 Equilibria in a game of information acquisition and sharing

OA). Conversely, if e_2 is high enough, player 1 will free-ride, putting in zero effort (in the region below OB). At intermediate levels of e_2 player 1 puts in a positive level of effort, decreasing in e_2. Just as the solid bold lines are the best responses of player 1 to 2's effort levels, so the dashed bold lines (their reflection around the 45° line) give the best responses of player 2 to 1's effort levels.

As illustrated in Fig. 12.1, this game has three Nash equilibria, labeled E_s, E_1, and E_2, occurring where the best response functions of the two players intersect. E_s is symmetric, and involves both players putting in equal amounts of effort. E_1 and E_2 are equilibria where player 1 (respectively 2) exerts no effort; but given this, it is privately optimal for the other player to put in effort to the level illustrated. This free-riding means that little information is gathered, and at these equilibria more projects are undertaken than at E_s, the proportion of failing projects is larger, and aggregate returns lower.[4]

The multiplicity of equilibria reflects the incentives for individuals to free-ride in projects of this type. What can F2F contact do to select the symmetric equilibrium, where free-riding is reduced? F2F contact – a meeting between the players – can play two distinct roles. First, an F2F meeting prior to the start of the game may allow players to co-ordinate on this equilibrium. It is quite difficult to go into a meeting maintaining a commitment to put in no effort. This is partly because of the inherent simultaneity of the meeting: the two players are placed in a situation where neither has a mechanism to commit to making no effort. And it is partly because of the psychological effects of F2F contact; participants want to be highly esteemed by others and this is likely to be fostered by co-operation rather than conflict. With F2F it is thus difficult for one player to maintain the position that he will put in no effort and free ride on the other.

A second role that an F2F meeting can play derives from the fact that meetings are a relatively costly form of information exchange. Suppose that players can only exchange their information in a meeting. Attending the meeting has a real cost and, crucially, each player makes the decision of whether or not to attend on the basis of her *own* information: it is in the meeting that information is shared and the decision on whether or not to go ahead with the project is taken. How does this change the situation, as compared to costless information sharing? If the meeting cost is high enough then players who have done no research (as well as those who have received an unfavorable signal) will not find it worthwhile to attend the meeting. As a consequence, doing nothing is no longer privately profitable; each player has to pay a cost (that of attending the meeting) before obtaining the partner's information, and the cost is not worth paying given the original information.

In terms of Fig. 12.1, there is a change in the shape of each player's indifference curves. Critically, below OB it is no longer worthwhile for player 1 to turn up to the meeting if his signal is bad. In this event there is no prospect of sharing surplus from the project, reducing EU_1 in the region below OB, compared to above. This change in the shape of the EU_1 indifference curves means that the best response function $R(e_2)$ is extended to the right from point a. Extending it sufficiently far, point E_1 (and similarly E_2) cease to be equilibria. The best response functions now have a single intersection at E_s where both players have positive effort levels. The meeting therefore reduces the set of equilibria to the unique one at which both players make an effort.

This analysis, while highly stylized, formalizes two different possible roles that F2F meetings may have. One is as a form of pre-play communication to co-ordinate on one of the possible equilibria. The other is as a way of increasing the cost of free-riding; a player who makes no effort will not find it worthwhile to attend the meeting, and so cannot make a positive return from the project.[5]

12.3.2   *The Formation of In-Groups: Getting Into the Loop*

We argued in Section 12.2.3 that prior screening or socialization of potential partners is important. In many contexts this can be provided by formal certification and institutionalized screening mechanisms such as professional examinations. However, in other contexts – particularly in creative activities where ability is hard to formally assess and where performance criteria cannot be codified and institutionalized – such formal techniques may not be very useful. Instead, informal networks – being 'in the loop' or in the 'in-group' – may take their place as screening mechanisms.

What is the informational basis of such a group? Where *ex ante* screening and certification of individuals' ability or effort is not possible there has to be open, although not necessarily costless, membership to all. However, once in, members cease to be anonymous, knowing who is in the group, observing the performance of members, and in turn being observed by other members. This information is used to maintain the quality of the group. At its simplest, a record of failure is used as the basis for expulsion from the group. Group members are therefore continually judging and being judged, and know exactly who is 'in' and who is 'out'.

If an in-group of this type forms it will have a number of characteristics. First, it will contain a higher than average proportion of able people; high-ability people have a higher probability of undertaking successful projects, so are more likely to survive as members of the group. Secondly, members of the group will (conditional on their ability) have higher earnings than outsiders, because they are matching with (on average) higher-quality people. Thirdly, members of the group will work harder than outsiders; the earnings differential creates an incentive to stay in the group, and the probability of staying in is increased by hard work. Finally, although initial access to the group is open to all, there may be an entry cost, perhaps in the form of time and effort to become known as deserving to belong to the group. Even if this is the same for people of all abilities it will have a greater deterrent effect for the less able because their income gain from being in the group is less. This is a further self-selection mechanism that reinforces the ability composition of the in-group relative to outsiders.[6]

To model this, suppose that there is a population of size one, with exogenous death and birth rate of δ per period. The population contains two types of individual, high ability and low ability, subscripted by H and L, and the proportion of high ability in the population is $\bar{\mu}$. The size of the in-group is endogenously determined and denoted φ. The proportion of this group that is of high ability (also endogenous) is denoted μ^I, while the proportion of outsiders that are high ability is μ^O, so $\bar{\mu} = \mu^I \phi + \mu^O(1 - \phi)$ where we use superscripts I and O to denote variables for insiders and outsiders, respectively.

In each time period all individuals match into pairs to undertake a project. Matching takes place *within* each group, but is otherwise random. The success or failure of a project depends on the ability of the two partners and the effort they put in, so the probabilities of success for projects with two high-ability partners, a high-ability partner and a low-ability partner, or two low-ability partners take the following forms, for $i = O, I$:

$$\pi^i_{HH} = \rho_{HH} + f(e^i_H) + f(e^i_H)$$
$$\pi^i_{HL} = \rho_{HL} + f(e^i_H) + f(e^i_L) \qquad (12.1)$$
$$\pi^i_{LL} = \rho_{LL} + f(e^i_L) + f(e^i_L).$$

These probabilities depend on an exogenous component, $\rho_{HH} > \rho_{HL} > \rho_{LL}$, and on the effort of the individuals. We shall assume $\rho_{HH} - \rho_{HL} = \rho_{HL} - \rho_{LL}$, so that pairing with a high-ability individual is as valuable for a low-ability individual as it is for someone of high ability.[7] An individual's effort is denoted e_H^j for a high-ability person inside the group, etc., and affects probability through an increasing concave function, $f()$. Thus, a project is more likely to be successful if undertaken by high-ability and harder-working individuals.

If a project undertaken by members of the in-group fails, then both the participants in the project are ejected from the group with probability γ.[8] Since the probability of failing depends on one's partner, and partners are selected randomly from members of the group, the ejection probabilities for high-ability and low-ability people, η_H and η_L are given by:

$$\eta_H = \gamma[(1 - \pi_{HH}^j)\mu^I + (1 - \pi_{HL}^j)(1 - \mu^I)]$$
$$\eta_L = \gamma[(1 - \pi_{HL}^j)\mu^I + (1 - \pi_{LL}^j)(1 - \mu^I)]. \tag{12.2}$$

Thus, the probability of an individual in the group matching with a high-ability person is μ^I; a partnership with two high-ability individuals fails with probability $(1 - \pi_{HH}^j)$; and a partnership with one high-and one low-ability individual fails with probability $(1 - \pi_{HL}^j)$, etc.

The size and skill composition of the in-group can now be determined. The number of able people in the in-group, $\phi\mu^I$, evolves according to the differential equation

$$d(\phi\mu^I)/dt = \delta\bar{\mu}\lambda_H - (\eta_H + \delta)\phi\mu^I. \tag{12.3}$$

The first term is the flow of able people going into the group. This consists of births, δ, proportion $\bar{\mu}$ of whom are able, and proportion λ_H of whom choose to enter the group (this proportion may be unity, and is discussed below). The second term is the number of high-ability people who are ejected plus the number who die. Similarly, for low-ability people,

$$d(\phi(1 - \mu^I))/dt = \delta(1 - \bar{\mu})\lambda_L - (\eta_L + \delta)\phi(1 - \mu^I). \tag{12.4}$$

In steady state, these expressions are zero, giving the numbers of high-ability and low-ability people in the in-group, $\phi\mu^I$ and $\phi(1 - \mu^I)$, as:

$$\phi\mu^I = \frac{\delta\bar{\mu}\lambda_H}{\eta_H + \delta}, \quad \phi(1 - \mu^I) = \frac{\delta(1 - \bar{\mu})\lambda_L}{\eta_L + \delta}. \tag{12.5}$$

Equations (12.1)–(12.5) give the base case model. If we suppose that all individuals have the same effort levels ($e_H^I = e_L^I = e_H^O = e_L^O$) and all members of the population start off in the group, $\lambda_H = \lambda_L = 1$, then it is easy to show that the in-group is of higher average ability than outsiders, $\mu^I > \mu^o$, simply because high-ability people are less likely to be involved in failing projects and face ejection. The benefits from being in the group can be evaluated once we specify returns to project success or failure. Suppose then, that a successful project yields payoff 2α, an unsuccessful one yields 2β, and the payoff is split equally between the two partners. The expected payoffs to a high- and low-ability individual inside or outside ($i = I, O$) are given by,

$$u_H^i = \alpha[\pi_{HH}^i \mu^i + \pi_{HL}^i(1 - \mu^i)] + \beta[(1 - \pi_{HH}^i)\mu^i + (1 - \pi_{HL}^i)(1 - \mu^i)] - e_H^i$$
$$u_L^i = \alpha[\pi_{HL}^i \mu^i + \pi_{LL}^i(1 - \mu^i)] + \beta[(1 - \pi_{HL}^i)\mu^i + (1 - \pi_{LL}^i)(1 - \mu^i)] - e_L^i,$$

(12.6)

where we subtract the cost of effort. The present values of payoffs are,

$$V_H^O = u_H^O/\delta, \quad V_L^O = u_L^O/\delta,$$
$$V_H^I = u_H^O/\delta + (u_H^I - u_H^O)/(\delta + \eta_H), \quad V_L^I = u_L^O/\delta + (u_L^I - u_L^O)/(\delta + \eta_L).$$

(12.7)

Outsiders, in the first row of eqn (12.7), simply get instantaneous utility discounted at rate δ. Insiders (second row) get additional utility for as long as they stay in the group. Under our assumptions (and with effort levels and group-entry probabilities the same for all individuals) the instantaneous gains to being in the group are the same for high- and low-ability individuals, so $u_H^I - u_H^O = u_L^I - u_L^O$. However, the present value of being in the in-group is greater for high-ability than low-ability individuals, $V_H^I - V_H^O > V_L^I - V_L^O$. The reason is simply that they expect the benefits of group membership to last longer, as they are less likely to be involved in a failing project and to be ejected ($\eta_L > \eta_H$).

This result drives several amplification effects. Suppose that individuals choose the level of effort they put in to maximize present value payoffs (eqn (12.7)). An increase in effort increases the probability of success, and this is particularly valuable for insiders as it reduces the probability of ejection (eqns (12.2)). First-order conditions give, for outsiders and insiders, respectively,

$$(\alpha - \beta)f'(e_j^O) = 1, \quad j = H, L$$
$$[\alpha + \beta + \gamma(V_j^I - V_j^O)]f'(e_j^I) = 1, \quad j = H, L.$$

(12.8)

We see that insiders work harder than outsiders because they fear ejection from the group. This effort effect is greater for more able people because $V_H^I - V_H^O > V_L^I - V_L^O$, so has the effect of further refining the group — high-ability people work harder, are more likely to succeed, and hence have a still higher probability of staying in the group.

Finally, what proportion of new entrants to the labor force initially enter the in-group or not – how are λ_H and λ_L determined? We assume that all individuals can enter the group, but now add a cost to entry – perhaps the cost of working in a more expensive city, or of time invested in building initial contacts with the group. We model this as a fixed cost c that varies across individuals. Indexing members of the population by z, the cost takes the form, $c = \bar{c} + \tilde{c}z, z \in [0, 1]$. The proportions of high- and low-ability individuals who initially enter the in-group are obtained by finding the marginal entrant for whom the fixed cost equals the expected premium to being in the group, so:

$$\lambda_H = [V_H^I - V_H^O - \bar{c}]/\tilde{c} \quad \lambda_L = [V_L^I - V_L^O - \bar{c}]/\tilde{c}. \quad (12.9)$$

Once again, we see that the inequality $V_H^I - V_H^O > V_L^I - V_L^O$ causes a higher proportion of high ability than of low ability to enter the group initially. Entry costs therefore act as a self-selection mechanism, further increasing the ability gap between insiders and outsiders.

The results that we have outlined can be usefully summarized by a numerical example, given in Table 12.2. The first column is the base case. Using parameters given in Appendix 12.2 and an ejection probability of 0.8 per cent, the 'in-group' accounts for 18.4 per cent of the population. It contains a substantially higher proportion of able people than the population at large, and yields its members higher present value utility than is received by outsiders. This effect is greater for high- than for low-ability individuals, $V_H^I - V_H^O > V_L^I - V_L^O$. The remaining columns allow for endogenous choice of effort and costs of entry to the group. If effort is endogenous, people in the group work harder than outsiders and, since $V_H^I - V_H^O > V_L^I - V_L^O$, high-ability group members put in more effort than low-ability ones. The effect is to increase group size as failure probabilities are reduced, and to increase the proportion of the in-group that is high ability, μ^I. Column 3 gives the effect of a cost of entering the group. Although this cost is the same for high- and low-ability people the return to being in the group is greater for high-ability people. Thus, in this example, 81 per cent of high-ability people enter, compared to just 25 per cent of low ability. The

TABLE 12.2 *Group formation:* $\gamma = 0.8$

	Base	Effort	Costs of entry	Effort and entry costs
φ	0.184	0.203	0.132	0.224
μ^I	0.496	0.514	0.797	0.799
μ^O	0.293	0.283	0.258	0.194
V_H^I	6.07	6.41	6.62	7.19
V_L^I	1.44	1.73	1.56	1.7
V_H^O	5.82	6.07	5.66	5.67
V_L^O	1.32	1.57	1.16	1.17
λ_H	1	1	0.81	1
λ_L	1	1	0.25	0.37

final column gives outcomes with endogenous effort and entry costs. This case compounds the previous effects, giving the highest value of μ^I, the proportion of the in-group that is high ability.

Who are the gainers and who are the losers from this process? Rows 4–7 give the present value of individuals' utilities.[9] If no group existed, all high-ability individuals would have the same utility, as would all low-ability individuals. Existence of the group creates a gap between insiders and outsiders, and this gap is larger for high-ability individuals than low ability, and is greater when effort is endogenous and entry costs cause selection of individuals initially entering the group. Outsiders are the big losers as refinement of group membership forces them to make worse matches. The gainers from the in-group are the high-ability insiders. However, it is interesting to note that even these individuals do not want failure of a project to lead to ejection with probability 1. Varying γ, it turns out that their utility is typically maximized at some value between zero and unity. Too low, and the group is not of high enough average quality; too high, and even high-ability insiders face a significant probability of ejection.

This brings us back to our central points. F2F contact removes anonymity and allows people to judge and be judged. If you have been observed to fail then – with probability γ – you are branded an outsider, and group members will no longer seek to match with you. The magnitude of γ is, in many activities, inherently spatial. In a faceless and anonymous world $\gamma = 0$, and in-groups cannot form. F2F contact raises γ, creating the possibility of group formation. By removing anonymity F2F raises the probability of good, step-by-step iterative judgements about the abilities of others. An in-group that forms to generate and share this information improves the quality of matches made by workers, and also sharpens the incentives for individuals to succeed and increases the work effort of group members.

12.4   F2F, Buzz, and the Co-ordination of Economic Activities

12.4.1   Buzz Cities

Previous sections have highlighted the key features of F2F contact. It is a highly efficient technology of communication; a means of overcoming co-ordination and incentive problems in uncertain environments; a key element of the socialization that in turn allows people to be candidates for membership of 'in-groups' and to stay in such groups; and a direct source of psychological motivation. The combined effects of these features we term 'buzz'. We speculate that there is a superadditivity in these effects, generating increasing returns for the people and the activities involved. Individuals in a buzz environment interact and co-operate with other high-ability people, are well placed to communicate complex ideas with them, and are highly motivated. To be able to reap these benefits in full almost invariably requires co-location, rather than occasional interludes of F2F contact. It is unsurprising that people in a buzz environment should be highly productive.

Among examples of this sort of interaction are joint projects in science, engineering, and research. A large literature demonstrates the existence of localized, industry-specific knowledge spillovers within the science-and technology-based industries (Acz, 2002). Networks of firms and industries clustered within regions interact more heavily with co-located university-based scientists than with those in other regions (Darby and Zucker, 2002). This is associated with higher rates of commercialization than at long distances. Moreover, the various benefits of F2F contact that are established through long periods of co-location are durable: they have been shown to manifest themselves among people who then move away but continue to work together, and are much stronger than the contacts between long-distance partners (Breschi and Lissoni, 2003).

In many buzz cities there is also cross-fertilization between sectorally specialized networks. High technology and government have close interactions, for example, and this is why Washington DC has become a major high-technology region. Design and entertainment/communications have strong crossover effects in their development of content, and this is why places such as NY, LA, London, and Paris concentrate them together (Pratt, 2002; Scott, 2004). Higher education, finance, and government are a powerful nexus of ideas and contact networks for the socialization of elites and the co-ordination of their joint projects. These various inter-network, highly dynamic, and unplanned contact systems were alluded to by Jacobs (1969), in her intuition that urban diversity is central to certain kinds of economic creativity because of the specific advantages of unplanned and haphazard, inter-network contact. Co-location is especially important to these processes because it provides a low-cost way for new ideas and talent to make their way into existing activities, by facilitating access for newcomers and by lowering the costs of evaluation on the part of those already in the relevant loops. New relationships are hence made easier, cheaper, and much more effective than they would be without co-location.

In diversified city economies, functional agglomerations consist of pieces of different sectors sharing common input structures and common clients (Puga and Duranton, 2001). Buzz cities, we suggest, derive their agglomerative force both from the classical network agglomeration efficiencies and from the inter-network, interactive knowledge, and information-based activities including: (a) creative and cultural functions (including industries linked to this, such as fashion, design, and the arts); (b) finance and business services; (c) science, technology and high technology, and research;[10] and (d) power and influence (government, headquarters, trade associations, and international agencies) (Hall, 1998; Scott, 2001). These cities' attraction for talent and their efficiency in socializing individuals confer important advantages on their participants. Buzz cities continue to have such force today because they are the places where, more than ever; critical problems of co-ordination in the modern economy are resolved through F2F contact.

Paradoxically, buzz cities are often those we most closely associate with globalization, because they are important nodes of highly developed international business and culture networks, with high levels of international travel-and-meeting activity, and high concentrations of both high-skilled and low-skilled immigrants. They often host many multinational enterprises. The most globalized cities also seem to have the most localized buzz. This is not surprising in view of the analysis provided here. The highest levels of international business require insertion into locally grounded government and political networks in order to function efficiently.

12.4.2   Buzz and Alternative Modes of Co-ordination

Buzz is an important, or even essential, part of the way in which some activities operate, while for other activities it is unimportant. Table 12.3 offers a tentative taxonomy of alternative ways in which activities can be co-ordinated, in order to illustrate environments in which buzz is most important. The two dimensions by which activities are characterized are the kind of knowledge on which they are dependent, and the fluidity of the environment in which they operate.

In the right-hand column are activities for which information is readily available/observable, such as production and trade in basic manufactures

TABLE 12.3 *Modes of co-ordination (proximity requirement in italics)*

Environment of coordination	Knowledge used in co-ordination		
	SPECIALIZED/PRIVATE		UBIQUITOUS/ TRANSPARENT
	TACIT	CODIFIED	
STABLE	Bureaucracy/firms. Specialized networks for search/matching. (*HIGH*) Financial services	Bureaucracy/firms (*LOW*) Car industry (mass production).	Markets. (*LOW*) Basic manufactured inputs or services
FLUID	Buzz (*HIGH*) Culture, politics, arts, academia, new technologies, advanced finance	Organized networks for search/ matching (*MEDIUM*) Aerospace, pharmaceuticals	Markets. (*LOW*) Commodities (e.g. oil)

and commodities. Markets are the main mode through which such activities are co-ordinated. The knowledge requirement of such activities is not a force for clustering – the proximity requirement is low.

Other activities are more dependent on specialist or private information, sometimes codified, and sometimes tacit. The middle column gives cases where the information can be codified, e.g. in well-defined engineering or chemical blueprints. Such activities are frequently internalized within firms or bureaucracies. The reasons for this have been extensively analysed in the literature on the boundaries of the firm (Holmstrom and Roberts, 1998). For example, intangible assets such as proprietary knowledge, reputation, or goodwill can be dissipated if traded through arms-length transactions between firms. Internalization within an organization does not necessarily imply a high spatial proximity requirement.

Where information is largely codified but the environment is subject to significant fluctuation there may also be organized networks to facilitate search and matching of partners. This may create pressures for agglomeration due to the transactions costs associated with managing the input–output relations designed to cope with fluctuations in the environment. F2F contact is likely to be an important element of co-ordination, of both the market and contractual relations in the organized project system at hand. But the nature of F2F contact in this case is fundamentally different from the F2F contact that is used in finding partners. Instead, such F2F is about monitoring the project organization, where the partners and the purposes of the collaboration (its intended outputs) are already defined. Such monitoring may require the rapid-fire interaction and parallel processing of F2F contact, but it rarely involves the incentive problems of joint project formation or the complex processes of getting into loops that are associated with co-location. Under some circumstances it can therefore be carried out through occasional long-distance travel. Large-scale technology development projects, as in the aerospace or pharmaceuticals industries, are an example of this use of F2F without co-location.

The left-hand column gives cases where knowledge is tacit and is typically embodied in highly skilled workers. The need to communicate this knowledge creates a high proximity requirement. All this is amplified if the knowledge is fluid or the environment uncertain, as in the bottom left-hand corner. This is the environment where buzz comes to the fore, because the uncertainty concerns not only the content of relevant information, but the purposes to which it will be put and the people who will be involved in using it.

12.5   The Future of F2F Contact and Co-location

The emphasis on F2F contact might seem paradoxical to some, since the advent of broadband Internet communications would appear, finally, to provide us the means to avoid F2F contact. The Internet has enabled certain kinds of complex communication to occur at a distance that were previously constrained by proximity, and some have gone so far as to claim that this is leading to the 'death of distance' (Cairncross, 2001).

The reality is certainly more complicated than this, however (Leamer and Storper, 2001). The history of economic geography suggests a continuing tension between two opposing forces. On the one hand, there is ongoing transformation of complex and unfamiliar co-ordination tasks into routine activities that can be successfully accomplished at remote but cheaper locations. This is reflected in the codification of information, stabilization of meanings, and the reduction of incentive problems (opening up the possibility of more complete contracting), so that less F2F contact is needed. Its principal geographical consequence is the tendency towards deagglomeration or dispersion of production. On the other hand, bursts of innovations create new activities that can only initially be carried out via complex and unfamiliar co-ordination tasks. At any given moment, these two opposing forces combine in different ways, according to the activity at hand. The borderline between those activities that are amenable to relocation at a distance due to reduction in the cost and complexity of their associated transactions, and the new complex activities that require F2F contact and other forms of geographical proximity, is in constant evolution. New technologies may facilitate dispersion of production, but they also destabilize activities, creating uncertainty, research questions, and unknown opportunities. This is an environment in which information is rapidly changing and knowledge is tacit, conducive to buzz. It leads to a prediction that though the precise mix of activities involving F2F contact and co-location will change, they will constitute an important set of such activities well into the future, and will continue to generate agglomeration of highly skilled individuals, firms, and bureaucracies in high-cost urban centers.

Acknowledgements

This chapter was orginally published in *Journal of Economic Geography*, 4: 351–370. Earlier versions of this chapter were presented at the International Seminar on Economy and Space, Faculty of Economics, Federal University of Minas Gerais (FACE/UFMG), Centre for Regional Development and Planning (CEDEPLAR), Ouro Preto, Minas Gerais, Brazil, December 6–7, 2001; as keynote address to the Third International Congress on the Dynamics of Proximity, Paris, December 2001; to the Center for Globalization and Policy Studies, UCLA, March 2002; and to the DRUID Summer Conference, June 2003. Thanks to anonymous referees and to editors of this journal for valuable comments.

Notes

1. Although the classical arguments in sociology were concerned precisely with the negative effects of the modern urban social order in the form of their notion of anomie. While sociology does have a notion of the compensating forms of 'social integration' that might aid modern anonymous actors to become part of a society, it does not ask how actors might 'co-ordinate' in the face of anonymity and large numbers.
2. The concept of socialization belongs upstream of economists' notions of human capital, screening, and selection, because it is concerned with generation of initial capacities for action and discrimination, not merely their rational deployment. See Akerlof and Kranton (2000) for models of the economics of group identity.
3. At this stage of the game there is no incentive for players to not reveal their true signal or the effort expended in obtaining the signal. A richer model might link the share of the project's surplus to effort, in which case there are incentives to misrepresent.
4. The game has a similar structure to 'chicken' in which two Californian kids drive towards each other. The last to swerve is the winner.
5. Notice that this meeting is about information sharing, not about collective decision taking. In the latter context, Osborne *et al.* (2000) argue that meeting costs can reduce the quality of decision taking by reducing attendance.
6. The model lies, in broad terms, in the class of models of neighborhood formation – interactions occur between individuals in endogenously formed groups. Such models are surveyed by Durlauf (2003). The spatial aspect of the present model derives from knowledge flows within a spatially concentrated group, the membership of which is determined primarily by ejection due to failing projects.
7. A good match has the same effect on probability for high- and low-ability people. Adding supermodularity would reinforce results that follow, while sufficient submodularity could reverse them.
8. This ejection probability is exogenous. In a more complex model it might depend on the full history of success and failure, rather than just success on the previous project.
9. Where entry costs are incurred values are reported for the median individual in the group.
10. Though, as Florida (2002) points out, there is a detailed geography of creative workers within metropolitan areas. People in the fashion, design, government, and finance sectors tend to inhabit different parts of the metropolitan space from those in science and engineering.

References

Acz, Z. (2002), *Innovation and the economy of cities*. Cheltenham: Edward Elgar.

Akerlof, G. A. and Kranton, R. E. (2000), Economics and identity. *Quarterly Journal of Economics*, CXV, 715–753.

Austin, J. L. (1962), *How to do things with words*. Oxford: Clarendon Press.

Bateson, G. (1973), *Steps toward an ecology of mind*. London: Paladin Press.

Becattini, G. (2000), *Il distretto industriale: Un nuovo modo di interpretare il cambiamento economico*. Turin: Rosenberg & Sellier.

Breschi, S. and Lissoni, M. (2003), 'Mobility and social networks: localised knowledge spillovers revisited'. CESPRI Working Paper no. 142, University Bocconi, Milan.

Cairncross, F. (2001), *The death of distance 2.0; how the communications revolution will change our lives*. Cambridge, MA: Harvard Business School Press.

Coleman, J. S. (1990), *Foundations of social theory*. Cambridge, MA: Harvard/Belknap.

Csikszentmihalyi, M. (1996), *Creativity: Flow and the psychology of discovery and invention*. New York: HarperCollins.

Darby, M. and Zucker, L. G. (2002), 'Growing by leaps and inches: creative destruction, real cost reduction, and inching up'. NBER Working Paper no. 8947, Cambridge, MA.

Durlauf, S. N. (2003), 'Neighborhood effects', in J. V. Henderson and J.-F. Thisse (eds), *Handbook of regional and urban economics*. Amsterdam: North-Holland.

Feldman, M. and Audretsch, D. (1999), 'Innovation in cities: science-based diversity, specialization, and localized competition'. *European Economic Review*, **43**: 409–429.

Florida, R. (2002), *The rise of the creative class*. New York: Basic Books.

Gambetta, D. (ed.) (1988), *Trust*. Oxford: Oxford University Press.

Garfinkel, H. (1987), *Studies in ethnomethodology*. Oxford: Blackwell.

Glaeser, E. L. (1999), 'Learning in cities'. *Journal of Urban Economics*, **46**: 254–277.

Goffman, E. (1959), *The presentation of self in everyday life*. New York: Doubleday.

Goffman, E. (1982), *Interaction rituals: Essays on face-to-face behavior*. New York: Pantheon Books.

Gordon, I. R. and McCann, P. (2000), 'Industrial clusters: complexes, agglomeration, and/or social networks?' *Urban Studies*, **37**: 513–532.

Granovetter, M. (1995), *Getting a job: A study in contacts and careers*. Chicago: University of Chicago Press.

Hall, P. (1998), *Cities in civilization*. Oxford: Blackwell.

Holmstrom, B. and Roberts, J. (1998), 'The boundaries of the firm revisited'. *Journal of Economic Perspectives*, **12**: 73–94.

Husserl, E. (1968), *The ideas of phenomenology*. The Hague: Nijhoff.

Jacobs, J. (1969), *The economy of cities*. New York: Random House.

Jaffe, A., Trachtenberg, M., Henderson, R. (1993), 'Geographic localization of knowledge spillovers as evidenced by patent citations'. *Quarterly Journal of Economics*, **63**: 577–598.

Jayet, H. (1983), 'Chômer plus souvent en région urbaine, plus longtemps en région rurale'. *Economie et Statistique*, **153**: 47–57.

Kahneman, D., Diener, E., and Schwartz, N. (1998), *Understanding well-being: Scientific perspectives on enjoyment and suffering*. New York: Russell Sage Foundation.

Kim, S. (2002), 'The reconstruction of the American urban landscape in the twentieth century'. NBER Working Paper no. 8857, Cambridge, MA.

Lakoff, G. and Johnson, M. (1980), *Metaphors we live by*. Chicago: University of Chicago Press.

Leamer, E. and Storper, M. (2001), 'The economic geography of the internet age'. *Journal of International Business Studies* (December), and NBER Working Paper no. W8450, Cambridge, MA.

Lorenz, E. (1992), 'Trust and the theory of industrial districts', in M. Storper and A. J. Scott (eds), *Pathways to industrialization and regional development*, London: Routledge.

Marshall, A. (1919), *Principles of economics*, London: Macmillan (8th edn).

Mehrabian, A. (1981), *Silent messages: Implicit communications of emotions and attitudes*. Belmont, CA: Wadsworth.

Nisbet, R. (1969), *Social change and history: Aspects of the western theory of development*. Oxford: Oxford University Press.

Nohria, N., and Eccles, R. (1992), *Networks and organizations: Structure, form and action*. Boston: Harvard Business School Press.

Osborne, M. J., and Rosenthal, J. S., Turner, M. A. (2000), 'Meetings with costly participation'. *American Economic Review*, **90**: 927–943.

Polanyi, M. (1966), *The tacit dimension*. London: Routledge.

Porter, M. E. (2001), *Clusters of innovation: Regional foundations of competitiveness*. Washington, DC: US Council on Competitiveness.

Pratt, A. C. (2002), 'Firm boundaries? The organization of new media production in SF 1996–98'. Manuscript, Department of Geography, London School of Economics.

Puga, D. and Duranton, G. (2001), 'From sectoral to functional specialisation'. Discussion Paper no 2971, CEPR, London.

Putnam, R. (2000), *Bowling alone; the collapse and revival of American community*. New York: Touchstone.

Rosenfeld, S. (1996), 'United States: business clusters', in OECD, *Networks of enterprises and local development*. Paris: Organisation for Economic Cooperation and Development, Territorial Development Service.

Rotemberg J. J. and Saloner, G. (2000), 'Competition and human capital accumulation; a theory of inter-regional specialisation and trade'. *Regional Science and Urban Economics*, **30**: 373–404.

Scitovsky, T. (1976), *The joyless economy: An inquiry into human satisfaction and consumer dissatisfaction*. New York: Oxford University Press.

Scott, A. J. (ed.) (2001), *Global city regions: Theory and policy*. Oxford: Oxford University Press.

Scott, A. J. (2004), *On Hollywood*. Princeton: Princeton University Press.

Searle, J. (1969), *Speech Acts: an essay in the philosophy of language*. New York: Cambridge University Press.

Simmel, G. (1950), *The sociology of Georg Simmel*. Glencoe, IL: The Free Press.

Appendix 12.1

Payoffs are expected monetary gains minus e_i. A good project sends out a signal that it is good with probability γ, and a false signal with probability $1 - \gamma$. A bad project sends out a false signal (that it is good) with probability β_i, and the true signal with probability $1 - \beta_i$, where $\beta_i = \left(\gamma^{-2} + e_i\right)^{-0.5}$. Thus, if no effort is expended, $\beta_i = \gamma$.

Parameter values: $A = 150$, $C = 50$, $\rho = 1/3$, $\gamma = 0.8$.

Probabilities are all computed by Bayes theorem and Fig. 12.1 is computed in Gauss.

Appendix 12.2

Parameter values: $\bar{\mu} = 0.33, \delta = 0.1, \alpha = 1, \beta = 0, \gamma = 0.8, \rho_{HH} = 0.9, \rho_{HL} = 0.45, \rho_{LL} = 0, \bar{c} = 0.15, \tilde{c} = 1$. Effort function: $f(e) = se^{0.5}, s = 0.2$.

13

The Geography of Knowledge Spillovers: Conceptual Issues and Measurement Problems

STEFANO BRESCHI, FRANCESCO LISSONI, AND FABIO MONTOBBIO

We would like to thank the participants to the 45th Scientific Meeting of the Italian Economic Association (SIE: 22–23 October, 2004 University of Bologna), Davide Castellani and Alessandra Tucci for useful comments and suggestions. Stefano Breschi gratefully acknowledges financial support from Università Bocconi and from the Italian Ministry of Education, Research and University (MIUR). Francesco Lissoni's contribution benefited from support by the Italian Fulbright Commission and the hospitality of the Sloan School of Management at MIT. The usual disclaimers apply.

13.1 Introduction

This chapter surveys the recent empirical literature that uses mainly plant-level data and panel econometric techniques to explore the existence and spatial extent of knowledge spillovers. Following Griliches (1992) the existence of two types of knowledge spillovers is considered: pure knowledge spillovers and rent (or pecuniary) spillovers. The former are pure technological externalities, whereas the latter occur when new or improved inputs are sold, but the producers cannot fully appropriate the increased quality of their products.

Despite the analytical and policy importance of this distinction, the empirical literature has not yet been able to clearly separate these two types of knowledge spillovers. Two quite distinct traditions of econometric analysis have been trying to explore the existence of knowledge spillovers. A first group of studies has focused on the concept of localized knowledge spillovers and measured the spatial boundaries of spillovers from both private and public R&D laboratories, with a special emphasis on spillovers from universities. A second group of econometric studies has focused on international knowledge spillovers through international trade and technological transfer from the foreign branches of multinational enterprises.

We survey this econometric literature and argue that the term spillover has by now become a synonym for any kind of knowledge flow or transfer (Section 13.2). In particular, we point out that it is hard from these econometric studies to understand what types of knowledge spillovers affect firms' productivity and through what mechanisms knowledge spillovers are actually transmitted. This calls for a careful reconsideration of the concept of knowledge spillovers, by drawing a clear distinction between instances of pure technological externalities and market-based channels of knowledge transfer.

The fact that knowledge, as opposed to information, is inherently tacit has been used as a key argument to support the existence and the spatially bounded nature of pure technological externalities. In Section 13.3, we provide a discussion of that assumption by arguing that, far from being an inherent property of knowledge, tacitness may actually be the result of explicit strategic choices of firms, driven by the objective to *exclude* competitors from access to strategic knowledge. Moreover, we also argue that knowledge tacitness is neither a necessary nor a sufficient condition to explain the spatial localization of knowledge spillovers. This discussion also shows that, rather than insisting on the dichotomy tacit-codified knowledge, further progress in the direction of discriminating between pure technological externalities and pecuniary spillovers should focus on the direct measurement of knowledge flows.

The last section of the chapter addresses the empirical literature that is moving towards the measurement of the most important market-based or formal mechanisms that allow knowledge transfer and diffusion. This evidence taken together suggests that knowledge does not spill over indiscriminately and also when it leaks out it follows specific firm-level, geographical, and technological trajectories that might leave a paper trail. In particular, we focus on the recent works that have pioneered the use of patent citations as 'paper trails' left by knowledge flowing between different companies and inventors.

13.2   Knowledge Spillovers: Logical Shortcomings and Empirical Traps

The distinction between pure knowledge spillovers and pecuniary externalities is, at least in principle, rather clear (Griliches, 1992). The former occur when firms profit from the R&D activities undertaken by others without compensating them for the benefits received. They represent *disembodied* knowledge spillovers, as they are not embodied in particular services or products but refer to the impact of ideas or compounds generated by some agent on the productivity of research efforts undertaken by others. Once a piece of knowledge is created it becomes part of the publicly available stock of knowledge, sustaining a process of endogenous knowledge creation and growth (Romer, 1990). A pecuniary or rent spillover occurs instead when a new or improved input is sold, but the producer cannot fully appropriate the increased quality of the product. In this case, some of the surplus is appropriated by the downstream producers, but this mechanism *per se* does not create further innovations and endogenous growth.[1]

Although the two spillover effects can be kept distinct on a theoretical ground and despite the relevance of keeping them separate for policy purposes, when it comes to empirical studies the distinction between knowledge and pecuniary externalities becomes fuzzier. In particular, studies on R&D productivity based upon Griliches' knowledge production function may overestimate the former, and underestimate the latter, because of measurement errors (Griliches, 1992). This section is devoted to review the two main traditions of empirical literature that have adopted a *knowledge production function* approach to estimate the existence and spatial extent of knowledge spillovers. Our reading of this literature is that the distinction between the two kinds of spillovers has become gradually blurred and that in the balance between the two effects most (if not all) authors have given a special (if not exclusive) emphasis on the role of pure knowledge spillovers. The point, however, is that most of the econometric tests produced so far within the knowledge production function approach are *observationally equivalent* with respect to the role of the two kinds of externalities, i.e. they are unable to separate their respective effects.

13.2.1   Econometric Studies on the Geographical Localization of Knowledge Spillovers

Apart from Thompson's (1962) early effort, Jaffe (1989) is generally acknowledged as the pioneering paper in the knowledge production function approach to the geography of innovation. Aiming to assess the *real effects of academic research*, Jaffe proposes to estimate the following, modified knowledge production function:

$$\log(P_{ik}) = \beta_{1k}\log(I_{ik}) + \beta_{2k}\log(U_{ik}) + \beta_{3k}[\log(U_{ik}) \times \log(C_{ik})] + e_{ik}$$

where P is the number of corporate patented inventions, I represents the private corporate expenditures on R&D, U represents the research expenditures of universities, C is a measure of the within-region geographic coincidence of corporate R&D labs and university research and e represents a random disturbance. The unit of observation is at the level of US states, i, and at the level of broad technological areas, k. Estimates of this model show that the number of corporate patents is positively affected by the R&D performed by local universities, after controlling for both private R&D inputs and the state size, as measured by population. Although these results seem to support the existence of localized knowledge externalities from academic research to corporate innovative activities, Jaffe cautiously notes that 'it is important to emphasize that the spillover *mechanisms* have not been modelled', by also remarking that it would be important '(...) to look more in detail at the activities of universities, moving toward an understanding of their relationship with the private sector that would really be structural' (Jaffe 1989, p. 968).

Notwithstanding these caveats, many authors have since then started replicating Jaffe's basic methodology by readily interpreting any evidence of a positive association between knowledge inputs and innovation outputs at the level of states, regions, and cities as the unequivocal manifestation of *localized knowledge spillovers*, i.e. pure technological externalities bounded in space. Audretsch and Feldman (1996) and Feldman and Audretsch (1999) are two of the most representative and influential studies in this vein. Using innovation counts, from the Small Business Innovation Data Base (SBDIB), they replicate Jaffe's original methodology by showing that, even after controlling for the geographic concentration of production, innovative activities present a greater propensity to cluster spatially in those industries in which industry R&D, university research, and skilled labor are important inputs. Acs *et al.* (1994) also find that the elasticity of innovation output with respect to university R&D is greater for small firms than for large firms, which is interpreted as evidence that small firms, while lacking internal knowledge inputs, have a comparative advantage at exploiting spillovers from university laboratories. Along similar lines, Anselin *et al.* (1997) refine Jaffe's original methodology to take into account cross-border effects, and show that university research has a positive impact on regional rates of innovation and that these effects extend over a range of 75 miles from the innovative region.

Although one might add further references to similar studies,[2] the point we want to emphasize in this chapter is related to the proper interpretation one should give to these findings. Do these results provide unequivocal evidence supporting the importance and spatial boundedness of pure technological externalities? How much of the positive effect of local R&D inputs on innovation outputs ought to be attributed to undifferentiated and disembodied knowledge spillovers, and how much of it should instead be attributed to pecuniary externalities accruing to local firms through market-based knowledge transfer? The prevailing answer that has been given to these fundamental questions, in our reading of this literature, has almost exclusively stressed the role of disembodied, uncompensated knowledge spillovers. The theoretical foundation underlying this interpretation is, in turn, based upon the following syllogism:

a. knowledge generated within innovative firms and/or universities *spills over* to other firms, i.e. it has the characteristics of a public good, freely available to all those wishing to invest in searching for it (non-excludable) and exploitable by different users at the same time (non-rivalrous);
b. knowledge that *spills over* is mainly *tacit*, i.e. highly contextual and difficult to codify, and therefore more easily transmitted through face-to-face contacts and personal relationships, which require spatial proximity;
c. knowledge spillovers are geographically localized, i.e. they represent a public good, but a *local* one, i.e. most readily available to firms located nearby the sources of knowledge.

The following quotation epitomizes the premises and the conclusion of such syllogism:

That knowledge spills over is barely disputed. (. . .) Geographic proximity matters in transmitting knowledge, because as Kenneth Arrow (1962) pointed out over three decades ago, such *tacit* knowledge is *inherently* non-rival in nature, and knowledge developed for any particular application can easily spillover and have economic value in very different applications (. . .) The *theory* of knowledge spillovers, derived from the knowledge production function, suggests that the propensity for innovative activity to cluster spatially will be the greatest in industries where tacit knowledge plays an important role. (. . .) it is tacit knowledge, as opposed to information, which can only be transmitted *informally*, and typically demands direct and repeated contacts. (Audretsch, 1998, pp. 21–23, italics added)

Far from downplaying the importance of knowledge externalities for regional development, our claim is that this theoretical framework hides a potential contradiction, and a few traps for the empirical researchers. The contradiction is unveiled by the most recent literature on the economics of knowledge, which suggests that tacitness can be a powerful key *exclusionary* means, used to prevent other actors from fully understanding the contents of scientific and technical messages (Foray, 2004). The empirical traps derive instead from the fact that standard methodologies based on the knowledge production function at the level of states, regions, and cities are hardly able to separate the effects due to disembodied spillovers from those that derive from the market exchange of rivalrous and excludable goods. Therefore, what appear to be pure externalities may turn out to be, under a more careful scrutiny, knowledge flows that are mediated by market mechanisms (Geroski, 1995).

The problem of mixing up different types of externalities emerges rather clearly in this literature when it comes to discussing the *mechanisms* through which knowledge spillovers are likely to be transmitted. Two broad mechanisms are generally identified: *social networks* and *labor mobility* (Breschi and Lissoni, 2004). Concerning the network-based mechanisms, the argument is that agents who are co-located in the same region or city are more likely to be embedded in a very thick web of social ties through which (tacit) knowledge may easily flow. The rather obvious fact that the cost of meeting personally and exchanging ideas increases with the geographical distance, coupled with the perhaps less obvious observation that the probability of establishing a social link increases with spatial (and cultural) proximity, are also often offered as key explanations for expecting thicker knowledge exchange networks among co-located agents rather than among agents who are geographically separated. Apart from observing that no evidence has been produced so far about the actual size and the density of regional networks, later on in this chapter (Section 13.3) we argue that there is nothing on theoretical grounds to let us presume that the network of knowledge exchanges ought to include *all* agents located in a region and involved in the development of a given technology. In particular, we argue that spatial proximity is not a sufficient condition for an individual to have access through interpersonal relationships to other agents' knowledge, as long as the latter are not willing to share it and keep it proprietary. In addition, this opens up the possibility of observing the coexistence of several competing networks within the same region, rather than the existence of a single, fully connected network comprising all agents.

Regarding the role of labor mobility, and more generally spin-offs and entrepreneurship, as key mechanisms for the transmission of knowledge spillovers, the following quotation reveals once again the existence of some logical inconsistencies:

> Why should knowledge spill over from the source of origin? (...) At least two major channels or mechanisms for knowledge spillovers have been identified in the literature. Both of these spillover mechanisms revolve around the issue of appropriability of new knowledge (...) *How can economic agents with a given endowment of new knowledge best appropriate the returns from that knowledge?* If the scientist or engineer can pursue the new idea within the organizational structure of the firm developing the knowledge and appropriate roughly the expected value of that knowledge, he or she has no reason to leave the firm. On the other hand, if he places a greater value on his ideas than does the decision-making bureaucracy of the incumbent firm, he may choose to start a new firm to appropriate the value of his knowledge. (Audretsch, 1998, pp. 20–21, italics added)

To the extent that knowledge is *embodied* in specific individuals and these are able to fully appropriate the value of that knowledge by founding a new firm, no spillovers take place as the knowledge is merely shifted, along with the worker, from the parent organization to the spin-off. A cluster of innovative firms may therefore emerge as a process of creation of spin-offs and new firms, without the need of invoking the existence of network-mediated knowledge spillovers as a plausible explanation for it. In this respect, social networks do play a fundamental role, but for reasons other than those usually reported. The social capital of relationships with customers and providers of complementary services is essential to mobilize the necessary inputs to establish a new venture, rather than as a vehicle of knowledge spillovers (Stuart and Sorenson, 2003).

A pure knowledge spillover may still arise from the mobility of employees, but that requires two conditions: (a) that the worker who transfers knowledge to another company or creates a spin-off does not compensate his/her former employee for the full inventory of ideas that travels with him/her (Geroski, 1995); (b) that knowledge is not embodied in the worker that leaves the firm or that his/her separation does not imply a loss of knowledge for his/her former employer. Of these two conditions, the former is especially stringent. As suggested by some authors, it is in fact possible for employers to design labor contracts that, at least to some extent, internalize the potential externalities associated with labor mobility (Pakes and Nitzan, 1983; Moen, 2001). Therefore labor mobility may well be an important source of knowledge *diffusion*, without being a source of knowledge *spillovers*.

More generally, once we reject the idea that the evidence provided by the econometric approach based on the knowledge production function can be *exclusively* interpreted as the result of pure knowledge spillovers, the relevant questions become those of assessing the impact of knowledge transfers mediated by market exchanges and of identifying the most important market-based channels through which knowledge is diffused. As a matter of fact, a few recent papers in this tradition seem to go in the direction of suggesting that market mechanisms may explain much of the influence running from academic science to local innovation activities. Building upon his own previous work on spatial econometrics, Varga (2000) estimates the innovation elasticity with respect to academic R&D for a number of US metropolitan areas characterized by markets for business services of different size, and a different degree of specialization in high-tech industries. He finds that academic R&D expenditures impact significantly on innovation only within areas where business services and the high-tech industries have achieved a substantial critical mass. These findings may be interpreted as one more hint of the importance of markets for technologies, which need sophisticated legal and consultancy services for handling licensing, research contracts, and the financial assistance both to start-ups and large R&D projects; and of the need of thick enough labor markets for scientists and engineers for the local firms to retain new talents.[3]

While Varga (2000) does not find any meaningful impact of large firms on the innovation elasticity for academic R&D, Agrawal and Cockburn (2002) do. They propose a set of cross-sectional regressions of the number of patents over the number of university publications in over 200 US metropolitan areas, for three science-based technological fields. After controlling for the size and specialization of the areas, they find that the patents–papers association is the strongest for those areas hosting at least one 'anchor tenant', namely a large, patent-intensive firm, with some absorptive capacity in the relevant technology.[4] The authors 'hesitate to draw any conclusion about a causal relationship between academic research and industrial R&D', but go on to suggest that *vertical spillovers* may exist (from universities to the local companies), which require a mediation of a large, R&D-intensive firm. One can hardly avoid making a further speculation, and guess that the anchor tenant may indeed finance the relevant academic research, and do its best to appropriate the ensuing results: while this hypothesis leaves room for the externality hypothesis (from large firms to the rest of the local economies) it implies a market transaction between the local university and the anchor tenant.

13.2.2   *The Econometrics of International Knowledge Spillovers: FDIs and Trade*

A major contribution to the study of knowledge spillovers, and of their impact on total factor productivity, has come from research on *international* knowledge spillovers.[5] This was spurred, at the beginning of the 1990s, by a wave of macroeconomic models linking technology, trade, and endogenous growth. There are models with knowledge externalities and models in which knowledge is produced as any other good, and flows incorporated in new designs without producing any external effect (lab equipment models).

The models with knowledge externalities suggest that the equilibrium path of productivity growth may differ according to the extent of the diffusion of knowledge (Grossman and Helpman, 1991; Rivera-Batiz and Romer, 1991).[6] For example, in the model of Rivera-Batiz and Romer (1991) knowledge externalities come from the availability of a stock of knowledge that can be (re)used in research. The possibility of international flows of ideas expands the stock of knowledge that can be used in research and this has a positive impact on productivity growth. Grossman and Helpman (1991) show that if spillovers are only local in scope, each country accumulates a stock of knowledge proportional to national R&D activities. As a consequence, the international allocation of R&D resources is guided by previous experience and the initial stock of technology more than human-capital costs. The model equilibria display geographical agglomeration of innovative activities, as countries with even small historical advantage in technological sectors become, through higher rates of innovation, world leaders in these markets. If technological spillovers are global in scope (i.e. there is a world-wide common knowledge base, which is a function of the amount of differentiated products in the world economy), relative abundance of human capital generates a comparative advantage in high-tech sectors because of a higher R&D performance (Grossman and Helpman, 1991, Chap. 7). However, less R&D intensive countries engaging in international trade can access a greater variety of inputs and grow faster than they would do otherwise.

Alternatively, in the 'lab equipment' models there is excludable knowledge that is transmitted through the acquisition of (a variety of) inputs (Rivera-Batiz and Romer, 1991). Importantly, Rivera-Batiz and Romer point out that from the so-called knowledge-driven models (the ones with knowledge externalities) 'one might conclude that flows of ideas are crucial to the finding that economic integration may speed up growth' (p. 548). At the same time they show that in the lab equipment model ideas *per se* have no effect on production and, moreover, extending or permitting international flows of ideas can have no economic effects.

More generally, the macroeconomic theoretical literature has shown that the possibility to re-use existing knowledge may produce increasing returns and long-run welfare effects, which depend on the geographical extension of the knowledge flows. It is worthwhile emphasizing that in both Grossman and Helpman and Rivera-Batiz and Romer knowledge-driven models, endogenous growth is guided by disembodied knowledge spillovers. These knowledge-driven macroeconomic models have brought the attention to the different effects on growth rates of the different mechanisms through which knowledge flows – or spills over – at the international level. These models were able to push the empirical research to enquire whether the accumulation of foreign R&D stock affects domestic productivity and to raise questions on the different channels along which ideas may be transferred.

A first generation of empirical work, in line with the macroeconomic modelling, has been performed at the aggregate level (Coe and Helpman, 1995; Eaton and Kortum, 1996, 1999; Keller, 1998). Evidence points to the existence of international knowledge spillovers but the interpretation that should be given to these results is somewhat controversial. Coe and Helpman (1995) use country-level data and assume that productivity is a function of domestic and foreign R&D stocks. Foreign R&D capital stock is defined as the import-share-weighted average of the domestic R&D capital stocks of trade partners, interacted with the fraction of imports on GDP of the country that receives the spillovers.[7] Their (highly cited) results show that international spillovers from foreign R&D stocks affect positively domestic productivity growth and that this effect is larger for small countries. However, it is not clear which is the exact channel of knowledge transmission and whether pure knowledge spillovers effectively occur. In their empirical framework, country a increases its productivity if country b increases its R&D expenditures (other things – like import shares – being equal). On the one hand, knowledge might be embedded in a new – more R&D intensive – intermediate good that is imported and adopted – in this case we should talk of a rent spillover – on the other hand a knowledge spillover might occur and country a increases its productivity using the increased knowledge stock produced by country b.

Keller's (1998) econometric exercise and Eaton and Kortum (1996) cast doubts on the possibility to use flows of goods to measure rent or knowledge spillovers. Keller performs a Monte-Carlo-based robustness test with randomly created trade patterns and finds positive evidence of international R&D spillovers. In a quality-ladders model of innovation Eaton and Kortum (1996) show that a country's relative productivity is determined by its ability to make use of innovations. In this framework, international technological diffusion is very important because 50% of the total growth in 19 OECD countries depends upon innovations in the US, Germany, and Japan and because obstacles to diffusion generate large cross-country differences in productivity. Moreover, when they estimate the determinants of the number of patent applications (per worker) from country i for protection in country n, they show that this is affected by a technological diffusion parameter: the probability that an invention from country i is adopted in country n.

However, they find that this parameter is affected by geographical distance and years of schooling of the adopting country but that imports are not an important channel of technological diffusion.

This literature provides some evidence on the effect of international knowledge transmission on productivity growth. Evidence that trade is important as a vehicle of knowledge transmission is stronger for smaller countries accessing foreign stock of knowledge. But once again it is not clear whether trade promotes knowledge spillovers by circulating goods that can be imitated or reverse engineered, or whether trade is just an indirect measure of knowledge transmission, one that is correlated with 'real' transmission channels such as FDIs, M&A, joint ventures, user–supplier interactions, labor mobility, patenting licensing, and others.

Therefore, the literature has shifted towards empirical studies that use firm-level data to examine directly the microeconomic determinants of learning. However, many of the logical shortcomings and empirical traps outlined above have not been resolved. In particular, in this survey we review two possible channels of spillovers: foreign direct investments (FDIs) from multinational enterprises (MNEs) and trade. We first mention, only briefly, some relevant issues in relation to spillovers through international trade. A complete analysis of this topic would extend this survey well beyond its boundaries. Then we analyse how the production-function approach has been used to look for knowledge spillovers from FDIs.

In order to have a more precise grasp on the role of learning at the international level, the analysis has then shifted from the Coe–Helpman type of aggregate analysis to firm-level econometric studies, which enquire whether international trade and, in particular, exports are conducive to higher productivity levels. It is worthwhile noting that these efforts still represent an indirect way of analysing spillovers from trade. In this respect a consensus has been reached that exporters are larger and more efficient than non-exporters. At the same time, these studies have failed to single out the direction of the causal nexus between export and productivity. In particular, Clerides *et al.* (1998) and Bernard and Jensen (1999) do not find a causal nexus between export and productivity in plants in Mexico, Colombia, and Morocco, and in the United States, respectively. Self-selection seems a more plausible explanation and therefore they do not find empirical support for the learning by exporting hypothesis. This remains a highly debated issue and the empirical evidence may vary according to the specific characteristics of countries and sectors considered.[8]

This controversial evidence suggests looking for different approaches and asking different questions. In particular, the most recent literature aims at measuring directly the knowledge flows and to enquire which are the precise mechanisms through firms learn about foreign technology (MacGarvie, 2003*a*). A promising trajectory of research uses patent citations and will be analysed in the following section of this chapter.

A more widely studied issue concerns the impact of FDIs on domestic firms' productivity and the search for knowledge spillovers from multi-national corporations.[9] The most reliable results come from firm-level panel data analysis.[10] The key results are: (1) knowledge is mostly transferred within firms and foreign-owned firms are, in general, more productive, (2) spillovers to domestic firms depend upon the absorptive capacity of the host countries, (3) there is no robust statistical evidence of local spillover from FDIs, in particular for the developing countries, (4) evidence of positive spillover effects of FDIs on domestic productivity is found mostly for UK manufacturing.

The empirical work in this field uses mostly a production function approach and estimates knowledge spillovers indirectly regressing firm-level total factor productivity (TFP) on a variable measuring the presence of multinational enterprises in the same industry. As an example of the methods used by this type of literature consider the influential work of Aitken and Harrison (1999) and Haskel *et al.* (2002).

Aitken and Harrison (1999) use a large panel of more than 10 000 plants and test whether *foreign ownership* affects the productivity of domestically owned firms in the same industry (ISIC four digit). In particular, their indicator of spillover is the 'foreign equity participation averaged over all plant in the sector weighted by each plant's share in sectoral employment' (p. 608). They find a significant and negative impact of this variable on the productivity of domestic firms. They control also for local spillovers arguing that the benefit from the mobility of skilled workers or from product demonstrations might be grasped only locally. Controlling with a variety of alternative specifications that include the foreign share of employment in a specific location, they conclude that there is no supporting evidence that technology is transferred locally to domestic firms.[11]

Haskel *et al.* (2002) also use a large plant-level panel in UK manufacturing in the period 1973–1992. They use two different variables to measure the spillovers: the *regional* share of total employment accounted for by foreign-owned plants and, analogously, the *industry* share of employment accounted for by foreign-owned plants. They use the standard 11 regions in UK and two-digit UK SIC sectors. They justify the use of employment data to calculate shares claiming that 'many spillover theories involve personal contacts' (p. 10). Across a wide range of specifications, they find a significantly positive correlation between a domestic plant's TFP and the industry-level indicator.[12] They do not find significant evidence by region.

We might wonder whether in these papers there are the appropriate sectoral aggregates and regional borders. Probably, two-digit SIC sectors or four-digit ISIC sectors are still too broad and encompass such a wide range of specific technological fields that seem unlikely that people active in these might really catch spillovers as such from FDIs. However, since this type of econometric works use an indirect measure of knowledge spillovers, inferring their presence from their effects on local productivity, it remains impossible to know which type of spillover they are looking for. These authors in their interpretation of the results tend to use the term spillover referring in particular to pecuniary or rent externalities. However, we are not able to distinguish among alternative mechanisms. Therefore, we do not know whether the firm-level analysis for Venezuela and Morocco does not find significant results because there are no pure spillovers or rather because there is a lack of formal exchanges between MNE and local firms. The same type of question could be asked regarding the opposite evidence for firms in UK manufacturing.

Moreover, in Aitken and Harrison (1999) words, 'there are benefits from foreign investment, but such benefits appear to be internalized by joint ventures' (p. 617). Thus, the idea is to move the analysis towards a direct estimation of the mechanism that might help transferring knowledge. Veugeler and Cassiman (2004) use the Belgian subsample of the Community Innovation Survey and identify the following mechanisms of technological transfer: licensing, R&D contracting, consulting advice, acquiring and selling companies, and personnel mobility. They show that foreign subsidiaries acquire more technology internationally and therefore might be an important channel for technology diffusion. At the same time, these subsidiaries have a lower probability of transferring know-how locally. The authors interpret this result as a higher appropriation of know-how within MNEs. MNEs might strategically minimize the knowledge spillovers, preferring FDI over licensing and/or constraining the mobility of personnel. Interestingly, Veugelers and Cassiman point to the technological transfer process as a co-operative effort and 'since cooperation typically involves a reciprocal relationship, one cannot ignore the simultaneity of acquiring and transferring know-how within such cooperative agreements' (p. 472).

Javorcik (2004) also notes the sobering evidence on positive externalities from FDIs and claims that MNEs have incentives to prevent horizontal spillovers to local competitors and that spillovers are most likely to occur through vertical linkages. She uses a panel of Lithuanian firms between 1996 and 2000. The spillover variables are calculated similarly to those of Aitken and Harrison (1999): Javorcik first calculates the average (using output as weights) foreign equity participation for all sectors. These variables represent the horizontal spillovers potential. Then, she uses the input-output matrix at the two-digit NACE level to weight the average foreign-equity participation in downstream sectors. She shows that the productivity of the domestic firms is positively correlated with the extent of potential contacts with multi-national customer. At the same time, she does not find a correlation between TFP and the presence of MNEs in the same industry or the existence of multinational suppliers of intermediate inputs.

It is worthwhile noting that Javorcik (2004) also infers spillovers from their impact on upstream domestic firms' TFP. These spillovers can hardly be interpreted as evidence on pure knowledge spillovers. Actually, she claims that: 'These spillovers may take place through (i) direct knowledge transfer from foreign customers to local suppliers; (ii) higher requirements for product quality and on-time delivery introduced by multinationals, which provide incentives to domestic suppliers to upgrade their production management or technology; and (iii) multinational entry increasing demand for intermediate products, which allows local suppliers to reap the benefits of scale economies' (p. 608). Again one can hardly avoid commenting that (i) and (ii) probably entail specific market transactions and consultancy relationship with MNEs and (iii) cannot be interpreted as a pure knowledge spillover.[13]

13.2.3   Summing Up

As a matter of fact, within the knowledge production function literature, the term spillover has by now become a synonym for knowledge flows and transfers of any kind: licenses, labor mobility, and entrepreneurship are all mentioned as channels through which knowledge spills over. But this makes it harder and harder to understand what types of knowledge flows are indeed localized, whether pure spillovers are among those, and why it should be so. Evidence also suggests that MNEs prefer internal transfer and protect their knowledge through a wide array of appropriability means including complexity, lead time, secrecy, and controls over mobility of personnel. Knowledge appears as a crucial strategic asset with limited leaking out.

The review of this literature suggests that it is necessary to reconsider the concept of knowledge spillovers and to re-examine the ways in which it has been used. On the one hand, it becomes relevant to understand under which conditions knowledge becomes an excludable good (Section 13.3). On the other hand, the empirical literature is moving towards the estimation of the most important market or formal mechanisms that allow knowledge transfer and diffusion. This evidence, taken together, suggests that knowledge does not spill over indiscriminately and also when it leaks out it follows specific firm-level, geographical, and technological trajectories that might leave a paper trail (Section 13.4).

13.3   Tacitness Reconsidered: How Knowledge may Flow, and yet not Spill Over

The notion of knowledge tacitness was first popularized in economics by heterodox students of technical change, who suggested that *technological* (and organizational) knowledge is highly contextual, hardly codified via general theories, and not fully articulated through language. Its transmission is disjoint by its use, and may be costly. As a consequence, cross-firm imitation of innovations is not as easy as a standard microeconomics textbook may suggest: technology is not a public good.[14] Recent extensions of the concept of tacitness to the realm of *scientific* knowledge, or science-based additions to technology, suggest that even codification and articulation through language may not be enough to eliminate tacitness.

Cowan *et al.* (2000) suggest that both technical and scientific knowledge are indeed often codified and articulated via an appropriate vocabulary. At the same time, though, the language used for exchanging technical or scientific messages is highly idiosyncratic, as it is the language of a very much closed and restricted community, a so-called *epistemic community*, whose vocabulary the members learn through prolonged studies and, possibly, a few common, hands-on experiences (Steinmueller, 2000).[15] As long as the members of the epistemic community do not disclose their common codebook (e.g. by teaching and translating it into common language, and many examples), the latter may act as a powerful exclusionary device, even for actors who live and work side by side to the epistemic community members. At the same time, since tacitness (in this new definition) and codification are mutually compatible, tacit messages can be sent even over long distances by means of a variety of communication media (both written and oral). It is up to the epistemic community members to follow some rules for retaining or selling or sharing the knowledge they master, especially when it comes to the codebook. These rules may leave it to individual members who achieve a breakthrough (a scientific discovery, or a technological invention) to decide to what extent their results ought to be diffused outside the epistemic community; and what portions of knowledge ought to be freely shared, and/or sold on a for-profit basis (Dasgupta and David, 1994). Hicks (1995) describes convincingly how scientific publications may serve not the purpose of full knowledge disclosure, but that of conveying (to whatever distance) tacit messages concerning the authors' knowledge assets, in order to increase the interest of potential research partners. Similarly, the emerging literature on the markets for technologies suggests that strategic (selective) codification is essential for those markets to survive and grow (Arora *et al.*, 2001). When it comes to university patents, licensing contracts may be extremely sophisticated in specifying what portions of scientists' knowledge should be fully disclosed, and what kept for consultancy (Thursby *et al.*, 2004).

These observations are consistent with definitions of externalities, which see the latter as the outcome of specific institutional arrangements, rather than the consequence of some natural properties of specific goods or services. As Cornes and Sandler (1996) observe:

[t]he literature often treats certain types of physical goods or services as inherently possessing rivalry or non-rivalry, excludability or non-excludability. However, this can sometimes be dangerous. For one thing, the economically relevant characteristics of a good or service derive from the structure of incentives provided for its production and/or consumption. A loaf of bread typically may be thought of as a private good, but a collective enterprise that bakes loaves and distributes its output equally among its workers creates an incentive structure that is similar to that encountered in the context of public good provision. [...] In many contexts there

are *alternative ways of providing and distributing consumption services to individuals [with] varying degrees of excludability and [...] nonrivalry.* (Cornes and Sandler, 1996, pp. 9–10, italics added)

That is, the sharing rules of the epistemic community may encompass both the extremes of pure private and pure public goods (epitomized by private consultancy as opposed to scientific divulgation), and a large number of intermediate cases between the two, such as price-excludable public goods, common property, and club goods.[16]

13.3.1   Knowledge as a Club Good, and the Geography of Membership

An increasingly rich case-study literature on sharing arrangements within communities of scientists and engineers has emerged in the past few years (von Hippel, 1987; Kreiner and Schultz, 1990; see also the studies quoted by Cowan and Jonard, 2000). It shows how knowledge is shared 'on request', i.e. members of the community are bound to help other members to solve well-defined technical problems, even if those other members work for rival firms. Reciprocity obligations within the epistemic community members complement the codebook disclosure rules as a powerful exclusionary device; on top of this, physical distance may, or may not, affect the ease of communicating.[17] Even when distance matters, reciprocity obligations may exclude many non-member neighbors from the knowledge flow. At the same time, such obligations may force the epistemic community members to refuse contacts outside their inner circle, and forgo their chances to access externalities generated outside it, even if at a short distance.

It is possible to object that, although physical proximity *per se* does not imply any epistemic proximity, the former may be needed to create the latter. First, during the early stages of some research projects, or the pioneering of some technology, much of the relevant knowledge still has to be codified, so that it can only be transmitted by continuous interaction, practical demonstrations, and so forth. Secondly, when frequent meetings are needed co-localization may be a necessary requirement for belonging to an epistemic community. However, epistemic communities may well survive the end of co-localization among their members. Even when dispersed in space, these communities will share more jargon and trust among each other than with any outsider within their present local communities. Besides, the extent and speed of the codification process will depend, once again, on economic calculus: codification costs entail some fixed costs, but help saving upon relocation and travel costs, by enabling some long-distance communications (von Hippel, 1994). As a consequence, even the length of time during which the community members will be co-located (or the time spent by a new member in close contact with some fellow ones) is not entirely dependent upon some exogenous characteristics of the knowledge base.

13.3.2   Markets for Technology, and their Geographical Reach

US universities' patenting activity has greatly increased over the past 25 years (Henderson *et al.*, 1998; Hicks *et al.*, 2001). Although only a few patents end up earning significant licensing fees, licensing is the main mechanism through which those patents are exploited. The licensing terms may be extremely complex, and very often involve the inventors themselves as one of the licensees, or as one of the shareholders of the licensee firm. This is because most university patents protect early prototypes and 'proofs of concept' that need much further development, which in turn call for the direct involvement of the inventors (Jensen and Thursby, 2001; Colyvas *et al.*, 2002). In all of these cases, we may expect to observe a good deal of knowledge being transferred from academic inventors to industrial researchers within companies, which we can hardly classify as a spillover. At the same time, as long as the inventor retains his position within the university, but is needed frequently inside the licensee company, these knowledge flows will remain highly bounded in space.

On a similar line, Zucker *et al.* (1998*a*) argue that the notion of spillover does not apply to the biotechnology industry, at least in the phase of its emergence. While the contents of new discoveries are extensively codified, the *techniques* for their experimental replication are not. Thus new knowledge turns out to be characterized by high degrees of *excludability*: anyone wishing to build upon recently generated knowledge must gain access to the research teams and lab settings that generated that knowledge. Under these circumstances, the scientists who make key discoveries ('superstars') tend to enter into contractual arrangements with some existing firms or start up their own firm, in order to extract the supranormal returns from the fruits of their intellectual capital. Quite naturally, when doing so, these scientists tend to prefer jobs or start-up locations within commuting distance from their home or university (where they tend to retain affiliation, also for reputation purposes and as a source of young assistants), thus creating localized effects of university research. Such localization, however, is not the necessary consequence of any intrinsic characteristic of knowledge, but of the need to access an immobile factor of production such as a star scientist.[18]

Outside the realm of academic spillovers (with their problems of inventors' double affiliation), the existence of 'markets for technologies' may not act as an agglomeration force, but rather the opposite. Using historical patent data for the US, Lamoreaux and Sokoloff (1997, 1999) keep track of the career patterns of a number of inventors, to relate the production of inventions to regional manufacturing activities. The main results emerging from their analysis are:

(a) Although there was some clustering in both production and patenting activities, the geographic patterns were quite different. Some production centers did not have any inventive activity, while areas with very little production had very high rates of innovation.

(b) Firms in clusters of production were using obsolete technologies and their location choices reflected the search for cheap material inputs. Firms using newer technologies were thus more spatially dispersed than those using older methods.

(c) Patenting activity tended to be higher in regions where patenting rates *had long been high* and where a *market for technology* (as measured by the sales of patents) had evolved more fully, irrespective of the share of industry production. In regions with such well-developed markets inventors tended to be more specialized, numerous and productive in terms of the number of patents per inventor.

Markets for technologies may call both for an increase of knowledge codification (patents) *and* for an increase of personal interaction between the patent holder, or the inventor, and the customers. This is the case with contracts that bundle together the provision of complementary tacit and codified knowledge, as when technical assistance and training are provided along with a license for exploiting a patent, or using a piece of (patented) machinery or software. Patents here play the ancillary role of 'credible hostages' in the hands of the licensing parties, who threaten to withdraw the license if their customers try to walk away with the tacit knowledge acquired through less accountable, face-to-face contacts (Arora, 1996).[19] In this case, codification makes the transfer of tacit knowledge feasible through enforceable contracts, and promotes both personal interaction and, if needed, co-location.

13.3.3   *Localized Labor Markets for Scientists and Engineers*

An important knowledge-diffusion mechanism often cited as a case of localized knowledge spillovers is the *localized mobility* of individual (skilled) workers. As far as very advanced knowledge is concerned (inventions, new experimental techniques, scientific novelties...) labor mobility generates pure spillovers if and only if workers moving from one firm to another help to create a common pool of knowledge from which *both the former and the new employer* are capable of drawing. That is, one needs to presume that labor mobility helps in spreading knowledge, instead of merely shifting it from one place to another.

Two conditions are necessary for this non-appropriation hypothesis to hold. First, some sharing-inducing incentive mechanism must be in place, which forces a firm's scientists and engineers to make a codification effort to the benefit of their colleagues or employers. Secondly, new employees' knowledge should not be entirely patentable and the protection of trade secrets should not be too strong.

In this respect, Fosfuri and Ronde (2004) examine how different trade secrets law regimes affect the probability that two firms will co-locate, in order to have a chance to recruit each other's engineers. For spillovers to appear along with co-location, the trade secret law must punish illicit behaviors only by awarding damages to former employers, and not by forbidding new employers from producing the copied good at all. Fosfuri and Ronde also find that dropping the 'non-appropriation' hypothesis makes their model unable to explain both the existence of spillovers and any tendency to agglomeration.

On the empirical side, a few findings by Almeida and Kogut (1999) raise doubts on the pervasiveness of labor mobility as a diffusion driver for advanced knowledge. Using a sample of semiconductors-related highly cited patents, these authors find evidence of some agglomeration of inventive activity in a few, important metropolitan areas of the US.[20] They then focus on the mobility patterns of individual inventors (engineers) within the various areas, and find them to be high and highly localized only in Silicon Valley, which also is the only area where mobility affects positively the innovation rate of local firms. In other words, labor mobility may explain localized knowledge spillovers in some cases, but not in others.

We also observe that the loss of experienced workers to the advantage of competitors can have damaging effects for those firms that are engaged in ambitious innovation projects. Those firms may either shy away from co-location or choose to co-locate only after reaching some agreements with other local companies either to limit the mobility of knowledge workers, or to reciprocate any knowledge exchange. Aharonson *et al.* (2004) explore these issues by studying the behavior of entrants in the Canadian biotech industry.[21]

13.4   Direct Measurement of Knowledge Flows

The knowledge production function approach to the study of knowledge spillovers suggests a positive impact of academic research on local innovative activities and a mixed evidence on knowledge spillovers from trade and FDIs. As pointed out above, however, this literature has not yet been able to disentangle pure disembodied spillovers from more market-mediated knowledge flows. In the previous section, we have discussed how the notion of knowledge tacitness is not sufficient to guarantee the localization of both spillovers and technology markets. We have also shown that there is a wide array of mechanisms that individuals and firms may use to make knowledge an excludable good. In addition to more theoretical work and case studies, direct measurement of knowledge flows could help clarifying these matters.

Some of the researchers who first popularized the knowledge production function approach have also contributed in this direction, by pioneering the use of patent citations as 'paper trails' left by knowledge flowing between different companies and inventors. A rough analogy is drawn with a similar use of paper citations in the scientific literature, which sociologists of science have often used to track the intellectual debts within and across various epistemic communities. Later contributions have both questioned the validity of this interpretation of patent citations, and extended their use in the direction of a neater distinction of spillovers from market-mediated diffusion channels.

13.4.1   Great Expectations: The Use of Patent Citations

Patent citations can be found on the 'search reports' produced by the examiners working for national and international patent offices. These reports list what is called the relevant prior art, namely any older patent or piece of scientific and technical literature that can either put in doubt the novelty of the claimed invention, or help understanding better the application contents. Some of the citations come with patent applications, and one can presume it was the inventor who added them to the invention description; others are added by the examiners, who search a number of patent and bibliographic datasets to make sure all the relevant prior art has been cited.[22]

13.4.1.2   Patent Citations: The First Round. The Geographic Localization of Knowledge Spillovers.

The case for using citations as paper trails left from knowledge exchanges was first made by Jaffe et al. (1993; hereafter JTH). In a seminal paper aimed at finding more evidence of the localization of academic spillovers, the three considered a set of university patents, along with two samples of other patents, all of them *cited* by more recent patent documents (*citing* patents, with the exclusion of *self-citing* ones[23]). A *control* sample was also built, by matching each citing patent to a non-citing one, from the same technological class and a similar application date. By checking the inventors' address, all patents could be assigned a geographical spot, both at the national, state, and metropolitan level.[24] As long as the citing and the control patents come from the same technology, and that to some extent the industries using that technology are concentrated in space, they should have a similar geographical distribution. However, JTH found that cited patents were much more likely to be co-located along with the cited ones, and interpreted the result as evidence of the existence of localized knowledge spillovers (however, both the academic and the non-academic patents led to the same result).[25]

Two recent qualifications of this interpretation go in the direction of telling spillovers apart from market-mediated knowledge flows, and explore separately the localization propensity of each kind of flow. Mowery and Ziedonis (2001) observe that the JTH experiment did not control for the possibility that many cited–citing patent couples hide a licensing link, as when a licensee builds upon (and cites) the licensed patent to produce an invention of his own.[26] They examine over 14 000 patents granted over many years to

Columbia University, University of California, and Stanford University, for which they calculate both the number of licenses granted to companies from 50 large metropolitan areas and the number of citations coming from the same areas (excluding citations from the licensees). Separate regressions of the two dependent variables over the distance between universities and metropolitan areas, plus a wide range of controls. They find that distance takes a higher toll on licenses than citations, and conclude that spillovers are less localized than knowledge flows mediated by licenses. The rationale for this conclusion is found in the work by Zucker and co-authors we discussed in Section 13.3.2: technologies licensed by universities require much further development, and call for frequent personal contacts between the licensee and the inventors, the latter providing the necessary complementary know-how. Albeit also affected by distance, pure spillovers travel longer distances than paid-for transfer of 'proofs-of-concept' and prototype inventions.

Agrawal *et al.* (2003) explore the role of social ties between inventors by running a modified JTH experiment, which focus on cited patents by 'mobile' inventors, that is inventors who have moved at least once across different metropolitan areas (as derived from their addresses on patent documents). The units of observations are inventors rather than patents, and the co-location rates of cited–citing inventor couples are compared to the same rates for the cited–control inventor couples. The authors first confirm the JTH results and then move on to examine the matching rates between the cited inventors' early locations and the location of both the citing and the control inventors, again finding JTH-like results: knowledge generated by mobile inventors is more likely to spill over both into their current *and past* locations than anywhere else. Agrawal and his co-authors suggest that mobile inventors may have maintained some social ties with colleagues in their former locations, and that knowledge moves along those ties. As suggested in Section 13.3.1, members of epistemic communities may communicate even at some distance, once they have had a chance to build a common understanding through co-location at an earlier point in time.

Breschi and Lissoni (2005) make an even more direct attempt to test for the importance of social ties. They compiled a dataset of over 30 000 EPO patent applications by Italian inventors as a source of relational data, assuming that a social tie exists between two inventors as long as they are found to be listed together on at least one application. They then build the entire 'social network' of inventors and calculate both the connectedness and the geodesic distance between each pair of inventors.[27] Running once again the JTH experiment, they find that the original results hold only for patents whose inventors are socially connected, and that short social distances greatly enhances the probability to observe co-location between cited and citing patents. This is taken as evidence that geographical proximity is not a sufficient condition for accessing spillovers, as long as these circulate only within tightly knitted social networks.

Thompson and Fox-Kean (2005) have criticized the original JTH paper, suggesting that the technology-matching criteria followed to build the control sample may be faulty, and induce a co-location bias in favor of citing patents. The technological classes used by JTH would be too broad to ensure that control patents mimic closely the contents of the citing ones. As a consequence, the probability for a control patent to be co-located with a cited one would be diluted by the less-than-one probability of any technology relationship with the same patent. When more accurate matching criteria are followed, the co-location premium of citing patents disappears, but for the international level. Thompson and Fox-Kean go on criticizing the whole JTH methodology, by suggesting that even a finer matching may not provide a good enough guide to matching control patents with citing ones, as the USPTO classification system is meant to ease the examiners' search procedures, but bear little relationship with the industrial activities upon which one should judge the closeness of contents between two patents. Albeit strong, this criticism may not apply to the IPC classification system, which is much more detailed and technology-oriented than the one followed by the USPTO.

The prior art cited by patent applications and search reports comprise both older patents and the so-called 'non-patent literature' (NPL). Scientific articles published in major peer-reviewed journals are an important part of NPL, and one to which academic scientists contribute greatly. Quite a few contributions have already exploited NPL citations to prove the growing influence of academic research on a number of science-based technologies (Branstetter, 2001*b*, 2003; INCENTIM, 2003). Much more remains to be done to track the geographic and social ties between the authors of the cited publications and the patent inventors.

13.4.1.2 *Patent Citations: The Second Round. International knowledge spillovers.*

For what concerns international knowledge spillovers the point of departure is the Coe–Helpman approach that is criticized on the following grounds: (i) conceptual problems estimating a production function at the aggregate country level, (ii) no control for heterogeneity in terms of firms, sectors, and regions, (iii) no measure of technological proximity, and (iv) trade is assumed as the only vehicle for spillovers (without having further subsequent support from firm-level panel data econometrics). On this basis, patent citations turn out to be an extremely appealing tool to estimate international spillovers and also to compare them with national and local ones.

Branstetter (2001*a*) uses a patent function to estimate firm-level spillover effects. Based on a panel of 205 firms in five high R&D/sales ratio industries in the period 1985–1989, he provides strong evidence for intranational knowledge spillovers and limited evidence that Japanese firms benefit from knowledge produced by American firms. As it happens, with the results from microeconometric studies surveyed in Section 13.2, Branstetter (2000*a*, 2001*a*) shows that – also using patent citations – the size of international knowledge spillovers could be much smaller than what regressions on aggregate data predict.

Moreover, a set of recent studies using data from both the European Patent Office and the US Patent and Trademark Office cover a large number of countries and analyse the geographical extension of the citing behavior of firms. These studies do not use a knowledge production function approach but rather estimate directly how the probability to cite is affected by geography. These results seem to confirm that there are barriers to knowledge flows. Moreover, an important result of this literature is that knowledge flows are technology specific and this specificity should be grasped within narrowly defined technological classes (Malerba and Montobbio, 2003; Malerba *et al.*, 2003).[28] Maurseth and Verspagen (2002) show that EPO patent citations occur more frequently between close regions and between regions with specific technological linkages. Peri (2003) finds that geographical distance affects more trade flows than knowledge flows. However, he finds that the probability to cite decreases with the geographical distance. In their book, Jaffe and Trajtenberg (2002) collect some of their highly influential and cited works showing that USPTO patent citations display a significant localization of knowledge flows.

Patent citations have also been used to understand and directly test the presence of knowledge flows from FDIs. In particular, Branstetter (2000*b*) and Singh (2004*b*) consider FDIs as one of the possible channels that overcome the geographic localization of knowledge. Branstetter (2000*b*) analyses the impact of FDIs by 187 Japanese firms and shows that knowledge flows occur in both directions. Using USPTO patents and citations, he estimates directly the probability that Japanese firms cite the stock of patents of US firms and the probability that US firms cite the stock of US Patents of Japanese firms, controlling for an extremely wide set of factors including technological proximity. He finds that the variable measuring FDIs by Japanese firms has a significantly positive impact on both probabilities. These results are important because they are a direct estimation of the knowledge flows and because they highlight that spillovers are bidirectional.

Similarly, for a wider set of countries and firms, Singh (2004*b*) observes that the evidence about horizontal knowledge spillovers is controversial and puts forward the hypothesis that the flow of knowledge is bidirectional. Knowledge leaks out from FDIs and, at the same time, MNEs are able to access local knowledge stocks. He follows the matching methodology of JTH (1993) and Thompson and Fox-Kean (2005) and compares patent citations from domestic firms to MNEs subsidiaries with patent citations from MNEs subsidiaries to domestic firms. He finds that 'MNEs subsidiaries are better at gaining knowledge from domestic organizations than the latter are at gaining knowledge from the former' (p. 12).

Finally, a recent paper by MacGarvie (2003*b*) uses patent citations to test whether French exporters and importers receive more spillovers than matched firms not involved in international trade. She finds that there is robust evidence the importers cite more foreign invented patents than non-importers. The evidence for the exporters is weaker. For the exporters then it appears confirmed that association with higher efficiency is mainly due to a self-selection effect. However, it seems that importers have relatively higher access to technology overseas than non-importers.

The availability of large datasets of patent citations has provided a great opportunity to qualify previous results on knowledge spillovers because they are an extremely detailed source of information at the individual and technological level. This has been done in parallel with a departure from the traditional knowledge production function approach and in the direction of testing directly the determinants of the flows of knowledge (i.e. the determinants of patent citations). The main results from this buoyant stream of research are that international knowledge flows are important, in particular along specific technological trajectories. At the same time, there is robust evidence that geography constitutes a significant barrier to knowledge transmission. Moreover, as shown above, the use of patent citations helps having a better understanding about the way knowledge is transferred via FDIs and trade.

While enthusiasm for these results and for the richness of the data sources is legitimate, some of the empirical traps and conceptual problems remain very open. Actually, even if we can measure directly the direction of spillover and take into account sectoral and individual heterogeneity, it is still not possible to know whether these are externalities or simply a proxy for technological transfers. Moreover, the more patent citations have been used, the more doubts have been raised, both by academic discussants and patent experts (such as examiners and intellectual property managers), on whether interpreting citations as inventor-to-inventor knowledge flows is both legitimate and useful. This issue is addressed in the next section.

13.4.2 Afterthoughts: How do Patents Get Cited?

Exploring the intricate details of the examination procedure, and what they imply for the meaning of patent citations, goes beyond the scope of this survey. A few warnings are, however, due. Many authors suggest that citations coming from the patent examiners, as opposed to those disclosed by applicants, cannot be interpreted as paper trails of any communication between inventors, since they were added from a third party. When included in the analysis, they may lead to overestimating the intensity of knowledge spillovers. They also lead to underestimating the importance of geographical proximity, since patent examiners pick their citations from their own patent databases, as opposed to applicants who are supposed to rely on local word-of-mouth information.[29] Moreover, it has been observed that even citations coming from the applicants may have nothing to do with word-of-mouth information: many citations do not come from the inventors' technical reports, but are added by the applicants' lawyers in order to influence the patent-examination process.[30]

First, Jaffe *et al.* (2000*a,b*) indeed find that most inventors, when asked to check the patent applications concerning their own invention, admit they do not know either the patents cited or their inventors. Breschi and Lissoni (2004) however, suggest that knowledge may flow between two inventors not just directly (direct contact between the two), but also indirectly, along longer social chains or echoed by many ties within the social clique the two inventors belong to. It may well be the case that two inventors linked by a citation do not know each other, or are unaware of the intellectual debt one owes to the other, and yet some knowledge mastered by the cited inventor's has reached the citing one. In fact, Breschi and Lissoni find that the probability to observe a citation link between two patents increases with the social proximity of the inventors. Singh (2004*a*) finds similar results.

Alcacer and Gittelman (2004) also find that the geographical pattern of the examiners' citations does not differ widely from the pattern of the applicants' citations.[31] They also find that the examiners' citations provide more accurate information on the technologies to which each patent is most indebted (possibly because, while applicants act under the pressure of disclosing *any* information that can be useful, examiners are required to be highly selective in choosing their citations).

Patent examiners are also responsible for a higher share of self-citations at the inventor level, as if they contribute to disclose intellectual debt that the applicant would like to hide, or is unaware of. On the one hand, these results suggest that the examiners do not add as much noise as feared to citations, and indeed may even correct for some deficiencies of the applicants' citations. On the other hand, they suggest that the same applicants' citations may provide a very biased account of the inventors' prior knowledge.

13.5   Conclusions

This chapter has provided a critical reassessment of the recent literature on the geography of knowledge spillovers. Knowledge spillovers may be an extremely important agglomeration force, but indirect attempts to measure them have largely abused the notion of spillover, thereby generating great conceptual confusion. What might appear, at first, as pure knowledge externalities may be either the result of market transactions, labor-market externalities, or sharing agreements within epistemic communities. For each of these diffusion mechanisms to generate localized, as opposed to far-reaching, knowledge flows, different conditions have to be met. Market for technologies generate localized flows as long as the prevailing contracts combine both explicit messages and tacit ones, and the latter are as frequent as to call for the co-localization of senders and receivers; spillovers from labor mobility appear only insofar former employers may retain some of their lost employees' knowledge, and the gains to be reaped from recruiting the rival firms' employees offset the losses from losing one's own; epistemic communities may form inside specific location (as when a university or a company pioneers a new research field), but thereafter disperse and still exchange tacit messages.

The market origin of many knowledge exchanges makes it also hard to tell pure spillovers apart from rent externalities, such as those generated by thick labor markets and markets for technologies. Telling the various diffusion mechanisms apart requires direct measurement of knowledge flows. Patent citations looks like an indicator that may well serve this purpose. A number of contributions have both confirmed that citations tend to cluster in space and refined the use of citations to track both market transactions and social ties. Some evidence suggests that markets for university technologies may be more localized than pure spillovers from academic research; and that social networks of inventors, as measured by co-authorship data, may influence the likelihood of knowledge exchanges as much as geographical distance does.

Patent citations have also been used to test the presence of international knowledge spillover. Results show that international knowledge flows are important, in particular along specific technological trajectories. At the same time there is strong evidence that geography constitutes a significant barrier to knowledge transmission. Moreover, the use of patent citations contributes to a better understanding about the way knowledge is transferred via FDIs and trade. It seems that knowledge transfer via FDIs is bilateral or vertical to MNEs suppliers. Even if the measurement of spillovers using patent citations allows a more detailed analysis at the sectoral and individual level, it is still not possible to clearly discriminate between externalities and market-mediated technological transfers. However, conjectures from this survey would opt for a prevalence of the latter.

Knowledge-driven models of endogenous growth have singled out knowledge externalities at national and international levels as the main engine of growth. However, these results cast doubt on the presence of these pure knowledge externalities and suggest that knowledge flows through market transactions and, if spillovers occur, they are of a pecuniary kind.

Notes

1. The distinction between the two kinds of knowledge externalities is also extremely important for policy purposes. Whereas the existence of pure knowledge spillovers is an unambiguous signal of a market failure (i.e. investments in R&D lower than the socially efficient level) that calls for public support to R&D, the presence of pecuniary externalities is not necessarily associated to suboptimal market outcomes.

2. A more comprehensive review of the econometric literature on localized knowledge spillovers can be found in Breschi and Lissoni (2001*a,b*).
3. Varga provides a similar explanation of his findings, although one that again mixes pure spillovers (as when he suggests that local high-tech industries allow for the appearance of 'personal networks of researchers in academia and in industrial laboratories'; p. 301) with rent externalities (on the role of business services in promoting academic start-ups; p. 301).
4. On the concept of absorptive capacity, see Cohen and Levinthal (1989). Agrawal and Cockburn (2002) consider such capacity to be in place when the company has at least one patent in the considered field.
5. The recent literature on this issue is rather voluminous. We try to pick out the most relevant works and refer to available surveys. Blomström and Kokko (1998), Cincera and van Pottelsberghe de la Potterie (2001), and Mohnen (2001) provide extensive surveys of the empirical literature on international knowledge spillovers.
6. We do not survey these models here, see Grossman and Helpman (1995) and Barba Navaretti and Tarr (2000) for a link to the empirical literature. See also Eaton and Kortum (1996) for similar implications on the relationship between technology diffusion and productivity growth.
7. See Lichtenberg and van Pottelsberghe de la Potterie (1998) for a comment.
8. Van Biesebroeck (2003) and Aw *et al.* (2000) find mixed evidence from sub-Saharan Africa and Taiwan. In their analysis both self-selection and learning by exporting are important determinants of productivity growth. In a sample of Slovenian firms, De Loecker (2004) finds evidence supporting the learning by exporting hypothesis controlling for the self-selection. For a theoretical treatment of the issue see Helpman *et al.* (2003).
9. There are many surveys on the empirical work on knowledge spillovers created by FDIs. (Blomström and Kokko, 1998; Branstetter, 2000*a*; Görg and Greenaway, 2001, 2004; Görg and Strobl, 2001; Lipsey, 2001; Mohnen, 2001; Haskel *et al.*, 2002; Barbara Navaretti and Venables, 2004).
10. Görg and Strobl (2001) in their meta-analysis of the empirical literature on MNEs and productivity spillover demonstrate that the results are affected by whether the studies use cross-sectional or panel data. Cross-sectional studies overstate the spillovers effect due to endogeneity. Moreover, they show the presence of a publication bias: 'studies of productivity spillovers are more likely to be published if they find statistically significant results for the presence of either positive or negative results' (p. 738).
11. Similar results are found by Haddad and Harrison (1993) for a panel of firms in Morocco and Kathuria (2000) for India, which uses a stochastic production frontier technique.
12. Görg and Strobl (2004) also infer the presence of technological spillovers form a life-enhancing effect on Irish plants of MNEs presence.
13. Görg and Strobl (2004) show that pecuniary externalities from MNEs can affect plant start-up and post-entry performance in terms of survival and growth of firms in the host country. Alfaro and Rodriguez-Clare (2004) note that 'the existence of positive externalities benefiting upstream industries should somehow have a ripple effect and benefit local firms using the same inputs as multinationals' (p. 33).

14. One classic reference on knowledge tacitness and its consequences for the theory of the firm is Nelson and Winter (1982).

15. Steinmueller also observes that technical knowledge, far from being static, is highly dynamic. Incremental technical change takes place in all sectors of activity, and brings about new codes of communications as well as new artifacts, which change the practitioners' vocabulary incessantly: outsiders, however close, may learn nothing of it.

16. Price-excludable public goods occur when the producer can sell simultaneously to many consumers, and it is possible for individual consumers to consume any amount up to the total provision, and also for different consumers to face different prices. With common property goods, access to the good itself is typically restricted to members of a certain community. In addition, there are restrictions on individual members' input levels and implications for the way in which total output is to be shared among the members. For example, in the case of fishing, instead of each taking home his or her own catch, there may be a strongly established tradition whereby the day's aggregate catch is divided up equally among the fishers. Club goods generalize the public-good concept to situations in which the community size is endogenous. Any additional member of the club generates benefits to fellow members by reducing the per capita cost of a given quantity of public good, but contributes to a congestion phenomenon, which in the end places bounds on the desirable size of the club. Both for local public goods share and club goods community size is endogenous, due to the existence of congestion effects. However, physical distance is the only exclusionary mechanism: all the people in the same area have access to the public good, but individuals are free to move around and finally choose the local community, or country, in which to contribute and consume public goods. All these definitions summarize those provided by Cornes and Sandler (1996).

17. For a recent study on a sharing arrangement totally independent from physical distance, see Lakhani and von Hippel (2000).

18. Zucker et al. (1998a) show that the innovative performance of biotechnology firms is positively associated with the *total* number of articles published by the local university 'star' (i.e. highly productive) scientists. However, when a distinction is made between the articles written by the star scientist in collaboration with the *firms'* scientists ('linked') and those co-authored only by other *academic* scientists ('untied'), the explanatory power of the former remains high, while that of the latter nearly vanishes. In this case we are not facing indiscriminate localized knowledge spillovers (a local public good), but tight contract arrangements linking *individual scientists* to *local firms*. For a study reaching similar conclusions outside the field of biotechnology, see Agrawal (2000).

19. Conversely, the licensee may terminate the contract if not provided with as much assistance as needed.

20. This evidence is obtained by replicating, on a smaller scale, the experiment proposed by Jaffe et al. (1993), which we describe extensively in Section 13.4.

21. See also interviews to northern Italy textile machine designers in Lissoni (2000); and Saxenian's (1994) remarks on the labor market in Route 128.

22. This definition of the functions performed by patent citations holds better for the USPTO (the US patent office) than for the EPO (European patent office). On the key differences between the citation rules of the two offices, and their

consequences for the analysis of knowledge flows, see Breschi and Lissoni (2004), which also provide a non-technical introduction to the relevant patent jargon.

23. A self-citation occurs when the cited and the citing patents belong to the same company or group. A proper screening of self-citations requires accurate information on each patent applicant's ownership structure at the time of the application. On the unreliability of self-citation 'cleaning exercises' for large data samples, see Thompson (2003, footnote 6).

24. Jaffe *et al.*'s rules on this point are quite complicated. Two full paragraphs of their article are devoted to their explanation (see page 585 of their paper).

25. Similar experiments on patent citations yield similar results. Maurseth and Verspagen (2002) and Verspagen and Schoenmakers (2000) conduct two studies based upon counting the number of patent citations between pairs of regions, and then estimating a model where these counts are related to the geographical distance between pairs of regions; their estimates show that the number of cross-citations significantly drop as the distance increases. See also Almeida and Kogut (1997, 1999).

26. As a matter of fact, JTH discuss this possibility (pp. 583–584, and footnote 11), but conclude that: 'we expect that, in general, the contract between the two parties [from which the citations arise] will be quite incomplete, making it more likely than not that the citing organization could [...] benefit from at least a partial spillover'. JTH add that the co-localization bias caused by such 'internalized spillovers', may be offset by the opposite bias introduced by the 'noisy' citations added by patent examiners; we come back to examiners' citations in Section 13.4.2.

27. For a definition of connectedness and geodesic distance, see Wasserman and Faust (1994).

28. Malerba and Montobbio (2003) show that international technological specialization is significantly persistent and is affected by the direction of cross-sectoral knowledge spillovers within countries. Malerba *et al.* (2003) analyse the relative effects of national, international, sectoral, and intersectoral spillovers on innovative activity in six large, industrialized countries (France, Germany, Italy, Japan, UK, and US) over the period 1981–1995 and use patent applications at the European Patent Office to measure innovation and their citations to trace knowledge flows within and across 135 narrowly defined technological classes. They find that international spillovers are an important determinant of innovation and mostly occur within narrowly defined technological classes.

29. This observation was originally made by JTH, and is exploited by Thompson (2003) to compare the localization of examiners' citation as opposed to applicants' citations. From 2001, in fact, USPTO data disclose the origin of each citation. Cockburn *et al.* (2004) also observe that patent examiners vary greatly in their ability to assess accurately the extent of the prior art, which implies that the number and the appropriateness of the citations differ widely from patent to patent.

30. According to the USPTO rules, applicants must disclose all the information they have at the time of filing a patent application, which may be useful to assess the novelty step ('duty of candor' rule). As a consequence, lawyers in charge of drafting the application browse a number of datasets (often with the help of

technical experts who are not the same persons as the inventors) to chase for useful references. Even in the EPO system, where the 'duty of candor' rule does not apply, lawyers may try to steer the examiners' attention away from some prior art threatening the novelty step of the patent, by adding a few citations pointing to another direction. In this respect, a warning flag is presented by Bacchiocchi and Montobbio (2004). They test whether the observed processes of knowledge diffusion and obsolescence reflect the specific institutional mechanism generating them. Results show that at the USPTO there are more citations per patent due to the different rules governing citation practices and that their median lag is twice as large relative to the citations at the EPO. They also find that the relative properties of the citation frequencies in different technological fields change according to the patent office considered.

31. In the patent jargon, especially in the US, what we call here 'applicants' citations' are usually referred to as 'inventors' citations'. This follows the legal presumption that inventors are responsible for drafting all of the patent application. As a matter of fact, large parts of the application, especially those requiring a tedious search of the prior art, are trusted to legal experts and consultants. As such, they reflect much more the applicant company's routine procedures, than the inventors' knowledge.

References

Acs, Z. J., Audretsch, D. B., and Feldman, M. P. (1994), 'R&D spillovers and recipient firm size', *Review of Economics and Statistics*, **76**(2): 336–340.

Agrawal, A. (2000), 'Economic issues concerning the mobility of scientific inventions and implications for firm strategy', Unpublished Ph.D. Dissertation, University of British Columbia.

Agrawal, A. and Cockburn, I. (2002), 'University research, industrial R&D, and the anchor tenant hypothesis', *NBER Working Paper* 9212.

Agrawal, A. K., Cockburn, I. M., and McHale, J. (2003), 'Gone but not forgotten: labor flows, knowledge spillovers, and enduring social capital', *NBER Working Paper* 9950.

Aharonson, B. S., Baum, J. A. C., and Feldman, M. P. (2004), 'Desperately seeking spillovers? Increasing returns, social cohesion and the location of new entrants in geographic and technological space', mimeo.

Aitken, B. and Harrison, A. (1999), 'Do domestic firms benefit from foreign investment? Evidence from Venezuela', *American Economic Review*, **89**: 605–618.

Alcacer, J. and Gittelman, M. (2004), 'How do I know what I know? Patent examiners and the generation of patent citations', mimeo.

Alfaro, L. and Rodriguez-Clare, A. (2004), 'Multinationals and linkages: an empirical investigation', 2004 Meeting Papers 145, Society for Economic Dynamics. ⟨http://www.people.hbs.edu/lalfaro/Multinationals%20and%20Linkages.pdf⟩.

Almeida, P. and Kogut, B. (1997), 'The exploration of technological diversity and the geographic localisation of innovation', *Small Business Economics*, **9**: 21–31.

Almeida, P. and Kogut, B. (1999), 'Localisation of knowledge and the mobility of engineers in regional networks', *Management Science*, **45**(7): 905–917.

Anselin, L., Varga, A., and Acs, Z. J. (1997), 'Local geographic spillovers between university research and high technology innovation', *Journal of Urban Economics*, **42**: 422–448.

Arora, A. (1996), 'Contracting for tacit knowledge: the provision of technical services in technology licensing contracts', *Journal of Development Economics*, **50**: 233–256.

Arora, A., Fosfuri, A., and Gambardella, A. (2001), *Markets for technology: the economics of innovation and corporate strategy*, MIT Press.

Arrow, K. (1962), 'Economic welfare and the allocation of resources for inventions', in R. Nelson (ed.), *The rate and direction of innovative activity*, Princeton University Press.

Audretsch, D. B. (1998), 'Agglomeration and the location of innovative activity', *Oxford Review of Economic Policy*, **14**(2): 18–29.

Audretsch, D. B. and Feldman, M. P. (1996), 'R&D spillovers and the geography of innovation and production', *American Economic Review*, **86**(3): 630–640.

Aw, B., Chung, S., and Roberts, M. (2000), 'Productivity and turnover in the export market: micro evidence from Taiwan and South Korea', *The World Bank Economic Review*, January.

Bacchiocchi, E. and Montobbio, F. (2004), 'Patent citation lag distribution: EPO vs. USPTO. Which consequences for the measurement of patent values and knowledge flows?' *Working paper CESPRI*, no. 161.

Barba Navaretti, G. and Venables, A. J. (2004), *Multinational firms in the world economy*. Forthcoming: Princeton University Press.

Barba Navaretti, G. and Tarr, D. G. (2000), 'International knowledge flows and economic performance: a review of the evidence', *The World Bank Economic Review*, 14.

Beaudry, C. and Breschi, S. (2003), 'Are firms in clusters really more innovative?', *Economics of Innovation and New Technology*, **12**(4): 325–341.

Bernard, A. and Jensen, J. B. (1999), 'Exceptional exporter performance: cause, effect or both?', *Journal of International Economics*, **47**: 1–25.

Blomström, M. and Kokko, A. (1998), 'Multinational corporations and spillovers', *Journal of Economic Surveys*, **12**(3) (August 1998), 247–277.

Branstetter, L (2000*a*), 'Looking for international knowledge spillovers. A review of the literature with suggestions for new approaches', in D. Encaoua *et al.* (eds), *The economics and econometrics of innovation*, Kluwer Acadamic Publishers, pp. 495–518.

Branstetter, L. (2000*b*), 'Is foreign direct investment a channel of knowledge spillovers? Evidence from Japan's FDI in the United States.' *NBER Working Paper* no. 8015, November.

Branstetter, L. (2001*a*), 'Are knowledge spillovers international or intranational in scope? Microeconometric evidence from Japan and the United States', *Journal of International Economics*, **53**: 53–79.

Branstetter, L. (2001*b*), 'Exploring the link between academic science and industrial innovation: the case of California's research universities', mimeo (http://www.gsb.columbia.edu/faculty/lbranstetter/research.html).

Branstetter, L. (2003), 'Is academic science driving a surge in industrial innovation? Evidence from patent citations', seminar paper, Center for Economic Institutions, Hitotsubashi University (http://cei.ier.hit-u.ac.jp/activities/seminars/papers/Lee.pdf).

Breschi, S. and Lissoni, F. (2001*a*), 'Knowledge spillovers and local innovation systems: a critical survey', *Industrial and corporate change*, **10**(4): 975–1005.

Breschi, S. and Lissoni, F. (2001*b*), 'Localised knowledge spillovers vs. innovative milieux: Knowledge "tacitness" reconsidered', *Papers in regional science*, **80**(3): 255–273.

Breschi, S. and Lissoni, F. (2004), 'Knowledge networks from patent data: methodological issues and research targets', in W. Glänzel, H. Moed, and U. Schmoch (eds), *Handbook of quantitative S&T research*, Kluwer Academic Publishers.

Breschi, S. and Lissoni, F. (2005), 'Mobility and social networks: localised knowledge spillovers revisited', *Annales d'Economie et de Statistique* (forthcoming).

Camagni, R. (1991), 'Local milieu, uncertainty and innovation networks: towards a new dynamic theory of economic space' in R. Camagni (ed.), *Innovation networks: Spatial perspectives*, London-New York: Belhaven Press.

Camagni, R. (1995), 'Global network and local milieu: towards a theory of economic space', in G. Conti, E. Malecki, and P. Oinas (eds), *The industrial entreprise and its environment: spatial perspectives*, Aldershot: Avebury.

Cincera, M. and van Pottelsberghe de la Potterie, B. (2001), 'International R&D spillovers: A survey'. *Cahiers Economiques de Bruxelles*, **169**: 3–32.

Clerides, S., Lach, S., and Tybout, J. R. (1998), 'Is learning by exporting important? Micro-dynamic evidence from Colombia, Mexico and Morocco', *Quarterly Journal of Economics*, **113**(3), 903–947.

Cockburn, I., Kortum, S., and Stern, S. (2004), 'Are all patent examiners equal? Examiners, patent characteristics, and patent outcomes', in W. M. Cohen and S. Merrill (eds), *Patents in the knowledge-based economy*, Washington: National Academy Press.

Coe, D. and Helpman, E. (1995), 'International R&D spillovers', *European Economic Review*, **39**(5).

Cohen, W. S. and Levinthal, D. A. (1989), 'Innovation and learning: the two faces of R & D', *Economic Journal*, **99**: 569–596.

Colyvas, J., Crow, M., Gelijns, A., Mazzoleni, R., Nelson, R. R., Rosenberg, N., and Sampat, B. N. (2002), 'How do university inventions get into practice?', *Management Science*, **48**:61–67.

Cornes, R. and Sandler, T. (1996), *The theory of externalities, public goods and club goods*, Cambridge: Cambridge University Press.

Cossentino, F., Pyke, F., and Sengenberger, W. (1996), *Local and regional response to global pressure: the case of Italy and its industrial districts*, Geneva: ILO-International Institute for Labour Studies.

Cowan, R., David, P. A., and Foray, D. (2000), 'The explicit economics of knowledge codification and tacitness', *Industrial and Corporate Change*, 9: 211–254.

Cowan, R. and Jonard, N. (2000), 'The dynamics of collective invention', Maastricht Economic Research Institute on Innovation and Technology WP no. 00–018.

Dasgupta, P. and David, P. A. (1994), 'Toward a new economics of science', *Research Policy*, **23**: 487–521.

David, P. A. (1999), 'Krugman's economic geography of development. NEGs, POGs and naked models in space', *International Regional Science Review*, **22**: 162–172.

David, P. A., Hall, B. H., and Toole A. A. (2000), 'Is public R&D a complement or substitute for private R&D? A review of the econometric evidence', *Research Policy*, **29**(4–5): 497–529.

De Loecker, J. (2004), 'Do exports generate higher productivity? Evidence from Slovenia', LICOS Discussion Papers 15104, LICOS – Leuven: Centre for Transition Economics, K.U.

Eaton, J. and Kortum, S. (1996), 'Trade in ideas patenting and productivity in the OECD', *Journal of International Economics*, Elsevier, **40**(3): 251–278.

Eaton, J. and Kortum, S. (1999), 'International technology diffusion: theory and measurement', *International Economic Review*, **40**(3): 537–570.

Ellison, G. and Glaeser, E. L. (1997), 'Geographic concentration in U.S. manufacturing industries: a dartboard approach', *Journal of Political Economy*, **105**(5): 889–927.

Ellison, G. and Glaeser, E. L. (1999), 'The geographic concentration of industry: does natural advantage explain agglomeration?', *American Economic Review*, **89**(2): 311–316.

Feldman, M. P. (1994), *The geography of innovation*, Boston: Kluwer Academic Publisher.

Feldman, M. P. (1999), 'The new economics of innovation, spillovers and agglomeration: a review of empirical studies', *Economics of Innovation and New Technology*, **8**: 5–25.

Feldman, M. P. and Audretsch, D. B. (1999), 'Innovation in cities: science-based diversity, specialisation and localised competition', *European Economic Review*, **43**(2): 409–429.

Feldman, M. P. and Florida, R. (1994), 'The geographic sources of innovation: technological infrastructure and product innovation in the United States', *Annals of the Association of American Geographers*, **84**(2): 210–229.

Foray, D. (2004), *Economics of knowledge*, Cambridge, MA: MIT Press.

Fosfuri, A. and Ronde, T. (2004), 'High-tech clusters, technology spillovers, and trade secret laws', *International Journal of Industrial Organization*, **22**: 45–65.

Geroski, P. (1995), 'Markets for technology: knowledge, innovation and appropriability', in: P. Stoneman (ed.), *Handbook of the economics of innovation and technological change*, Oxford: Blackwell, 90–131.

Glaeser, E. L., Kallal, H. D., Scheinknam, J. S., and Shleifer, A. (1992), 'Growth in cities', *Journal of Political Economy*, **100**: 1126–1152.

Görg, H. and Strobl, E. (2004), 'Foreign direct investment and local economic development: beyond productivity spillovers' in M. Blomström, E. Graham, and T. Moran (eds), *The impact of foreign direct investment on development: new measurements, new outcomes, new policy approaches*, Washington DC: Institute for International Economics, forthcoming.

Görg, H. and Strobl, E. (2001), 'Multinational companies and productivity spillovers: a meta-analysis', *Economic Journal*, **111**: F723–F739.

Görg, H. and Strobl, E. (2003), 'Multinational companies, technology spillovers and plant survival', *Scandinavian Journal of Economics*, **105**(4): 581–595.

Görg, H. and Greenaway, D. (2001), 'Foreign direct investment and intra-industry spillovers: a review of the literature,' GEP Research Paper 2001/37, Globalisation and Labour Markets Programme, Nottingham, Leverhulme Centre for Research on Globalisation and Economic Policy.

Görg, H. and Greenaway, D. (2004), 'Much ado about nothing? Do domestic firms really benefit from foreign direct investment?' *World Bank Research Observer*, **19**: 171–197.

Griffith, R., Redding, S. J., and Simpson, H. (2003), 'Productivity convergence and foreign ownership at the establishment level', *CEPR Discussion Paper* 3765.

Griliches, Z. (1979), 'Issues in assessing the contribution of research and development to productivity growth', *Bell Journal of Economics*, **10**: 92–116.

Griliches, Z. (1992), 'The Search for R&D spillovers', *Scandinavian Journal of Economics*, **94**: Supplement: 29–47.

Grossman, G. and Helpman, E. (1995), 'Technology and trade', in G. Grossman and K. Rogoff (eds), *Handbook of international economics*, **3**: New York: Elsevier.

Grossman, G. and Helpman, E. (1991), *Innovation and growth in the global economy*, Cambridge, MA: MIT Press.

Haddad, M. and Harrison, A. (1993), 'Are there positive spillovers from direct foreign investment? Evidence from panel data for Morocco', *Journal of Development Economics*, **42**: 51–74.

Hanson, G. (2001), 'Should countries promote foreign direct investment?', *UNCTAD G-24 Discussion Paper 9*, February 2001.

Harrison, B., Kelley, M. R., and Grant, J. (1996), 'Innovative firm behaviour and local milieu: exploring the intersection of agglomeration, firm effects, and technological change', *Economic Geography*, **72**: 233–258.

Haskel, J., Pereira, S., and Slaughter, M. (2002), 'Does inward foreign direct investment boost the productivity of domestic firms?', *NBER Working Paper* 8724.

Head, K., Ries, J., and Swenson, D. (1995), 'Agglomeration benefits and location choice: evidence from Japanese manufacturing investrments in the United States', *Journal of International Economics*, **38**: 223–247.

Helpman, E., Melitz, M. J., and Yeaple, S. R. (2003), 'Export versus FDI', *NBER Working Paper* 9439, January.

Henderson, R., Jaffe, A. B., and Trajtenberg, M. (1998), 'Universities as a source of commercial technology: a detailed analysis of university patenting 1965–1988', *Review of Economics and Statistics*, **80**(1): pp. 119–127.

Henderson, V. (1999), 'Marshall's scale economies', *NBER Working Paper* 7358.

Hicks, D. (1995), 'Published papers, tacit competencies and corporate management of the public/private character of knowledge', *Industrial and corporate change*, **4**: 401–424.

Hicks, D., Breitzman, T., Olivastro, D., and Hamilton, K. (2001), 'The changing composition of innovative activity in the US – a portrait based on patent analysis', *Research Policy*, **30**: 681–703.

INCENTIM (2003), *Linking science to technology – bibliographic references in patents*, Research Report to the European Commission (http://www.cordis.lu/indicators/kul_report.htm).

Jaffe, A. B. (1989), 'Real effects of academic research', *American Economic Review*, **79**(5): 957–970.

Jaffe, A. B. and Trajtenberg, M. (2002), *Patents, citations & innovations: a window on the knowledge economy*. Cambridge, M A: MIT Press.

Jaffe, A. B., Trajtenberg M., and Fogarty, M. S. (2000*a*), 'The meaning of patent citations: Report on the NBER/Case-Western Reserve Survey of Patentees', *NBER Working Paper* 7631.

Jaffe, A. B., Trajtenberg, M., and Fogarty, M. S. (2000*b*), 'Knowledge spillovers and patent citations: evidence form a survey of inventors', *American Economic Review*, **90**(2): 215–218.

Jaffe, A. B., Trajtenberg, M., and Henderson, R. (1993), 'Geographic localisation of knowledge spillovers as evidenced by patent citations', *Quarterly Journal of Economics*, **108**: 577–598.

Javorcik, B. S. (2004), 'Does foreign direct investment increase the productivity of domestic firms? In search of spillovers through backward linkages', *American Economic Review*, **94**(3): 605–627.

Jensen, R. and Thursby, M. C. (2001), 'Proofs and prototypes for sale: the tale of university licensing', *American Economic Review*, **91**: 240–259.

Kathuria, V. (2000), 'Productivity spillovers from technology transfer to Indian manufacturing firms', *Journal of International Development*, **12**: 343–369.

Keller, W. (1998), 'Are international R&D spillovers trade related? Analyzing spillovers among randomly matched trade partners', *European Economic Review*, **42**:(8) 1469–1481.

Klette, T. J., Møen, J., and Griliches, Z. (1999), 'Do subsidies to commercial R&D reduce market failures? Microeconomic evaluation studies', *Research Policy*, **29**: 471–495.

Kreiner, K. and Schultz, M. (1990), 'Crossing the institutional divide: networking in biotechnology', paper presented at the *10th International Conference of the Strategic Management Society*, Stockholm.

Krugman, P. (1991), *Geography and trade*, Cambridge, MA: MIT Press.

Krugman, P. (1995), *Development, geography and economic theory*, Cambridge, MA: MIT Press.

Krugman, P. (1998), 'What's new about economic geography', *Oxford review of Economic Policy*, **14**(2): 7–17.

Krugman, P. (1999), 'The role of geography in development', *International regional science review*, **22**: 142–161.

Lakhani, K. and von Hippel, E. (2000), 'How open source software works: 'free' user-to-user assistance', *MIT Sloan School of Management working paper* 4117.

Lamoreaux, N. R. and Sokoloff, K. L. (1997), 'Location and technological change in the American glass industry during the late nineteenth and early twentieth centuries', *NBER Working Paper* 5938, February.

Lamoreaux, N. R. and Sokoloff, K. L. (1999), 'Inventors, firms, and the market for technology in the late nineneteenth and early twentieth centuries', in N. R. Lamoreaux, D. M. Raff, and P. Temin (eds) *Learning by doing in markets, firms, and countries*, Chicago: The University of Chicago Press.

Lichtenberg, F. R. and van Pottelsberghe de la Potterie, B. (1998), 'International R&D spillover: a comment', *European Economic Review*, **48**(8): 1483–1491.

Lipsey, R. E. (2001), 'Foreign direct investment and the operations of multinational firms: concepts, history and data', *NBER Working Paper* 8665.

Lissoni, F. (2000), 'Knowledge codification and the geography of innovation: the case of Brescia mechanical cluster', *TIPIK paper*, Targeted Socio-Economic Research (TSER), European Commission DG XII.

MacGarvie, M. (2003*a*), 'International trade and knowldge diffusion. a survey of the recent evidence'. mimeo.

MacGarvie, M. (2003*b*), 'Do firms learn from international trade?' mimeo (http://people.bu.edu/mmacgarv/papers.html).

Malerba, F., Mancusi, M., and Montobbio, F. (2003), 'Innovation and knowledge spillovers: evidence from European data'. Working Paper no. 39. University of Insubria (prepared for the American Economic Association meeting, San Diego 5 Gennaio 2003) (http://eco.uninsubria.it/dipeco/Quaderni/files/QF2003_39.pdf).

Malerba, F. and Montobbio, F. (2003), 'Exploring factors affecting international technological specialization: the role of knowledge flows and the structure of innovative activity', *Journal of Evolutionary Economics*, **13**(4): 411–434.

Martin, R. (1999), 'The new "geographical turn" in economics: some critical reflections', *Cambridge Journal of Economics*, **23**: 65–91.

Maurseth, P. B. and Verspagen, B. (2002), 'Knowledge spillovers in Europe. A patent citation analysis', *Scandinavian Journal of Economics*, **104**(4): 531–543.

Moen, J. (2001), 'Is mobility of technical personnel a source of R&D spillovers?', *NBER Working Paper* 7834.

Mohnen, P. (1996), 'R&D externalities and productivity growth', *OECD STI Review*, **18**: 39–66.

Mohnen, P. (2001), 'International R&D spillovers and economic growth', in M. Pohjola (eds), *Information, technology, productivity, and economic growth: international evidence and implications for economic development*, Oxford: Oxford University Press, 50–71.

Mowery, D. and Ziedonis, A. (2001), 'The geographic reach of market and non-market channels of technology transfer: comparing citations and licenses of university patents', *NBER Working Paper* 8568.

Nelson, R. (1959), 'The simple economics of basic scientific research', *Journal of Political Economy*, **67**: 297–306.

Nelson, R. and Winter, S. G. (1982), *An evolutionary theory of economic change*, Cambridge, MA: Harvard University Press.

Ottaviano, G. and Thisse, J. F. (2000), 'On economic geography in economic theory: increasing returns and pecuniary externalities', mimeo.

Pakes, A. and Nitzan, S. (1983), 'Optimum contracts for research personnel, research employment and the establishment of rival enterprises', *Journal of Labor Economics*, **1**: 345–365.

Peri, G. (2003), 'Knowledge flows, R&D externalities and innovation', *ZEW Discussion Paper N. 40 /03*, June.

Phelps, N. (1992), 'External economies, agglomeration and flexible accumulation', *Transactions of the Institute of British Geographers*, **17**: 35–46.

Rivera-Batiz, L. A. and and Romer, P. M. (1991), 'Economic integration and endogenous growth', *The Quarterly Journal of Economics*, MIT Press, **106**(2): 531–555.

Romer, P. M. (1990), 'Endogenous technological change', *Journal of Political Economy*, **98**: 71–102.

Saxenian, A. (1994), *Regional advantage. Culture and competition in Silicon Valley and route 128*, Cambridge, M A: Harvard University Press.

Scitovsky, T. (1954), 'Two concepts of external economies', *Journal of Political Economy*, **62**: 143–151.

Singh, J. (2004*a*), 'Inventor mobility and social networks as drivers of knowledge diffusion', mimeo, Harvard Business School (http://www.people.hbs.edu/ jsingh/academic/papers.html).

Singh, J. (2004*b*), 'Multinational firms and knowledge diffusion: evidence using patent citation data', mimeo (http://faculty.insead.edu/singhj/academic/jasjit_-spillovers.pdf).

Steinmueller, E. (2000), 'Does information and communication technology facilitate "codification" of knowledge?', *Industrial and Corporate Change*, pp. 361–376.

Stuart, T. and Sorenson, O. (2003), 'The geography of opportunity: spatial heterogeneity in founding rates and the performance of biotechnology firms', *Research Policy*, **32**: 229–253.

Thompson, P. (2003), 'Patent citations and the geography of knowledge spillovers: what do patent examiners know?', mimeo, Carnegie Mellon University.

Thompson, P. and Fox-Kean, M. (2005), 'Patent citations and the geography of knowledge spillovers: a reassessment', *American Economic Review* (forthcoming).

Thompson, W. T. (1962), 'Locational differences in inventive efforts and their determinants', in R. R. Nelson (ed.), *The rate and direction of inventive activity: economic and social factors*, Princeton, N J: Princeton University Press.

Thursby, M., Thursby, J., and Dechenaux, E. (2004), 'Shirking, shelving, and sharing risk: the role of university license contracts', TOM Seminar paper, Harvard Business School (http://www.hbs.edu/units/tom /research-seminars-03–04.html).

Van Biesebroeck, J. (2003), 'Exporting raises productivity in Sub-Saharan African manufacturing plants', *NBER Working Paper* 10020.

Varga, A. (2000), 'Local academic knowledge transfers and the concentration of economic activity', *Journal of Regional Science*, **40**(2): 289–309.

Varga, A. (2002), 'Knowledge transfers from universities and the regional economy: Mimeo: a review of the literature', mimeo.

Verspagen, B. and Schoenmakers, W. (2000), 'The spatial dimension of knowledge spillovers in Europe: evidence from patenting data', Paper presented at the AEA Conference on Intellectual Property Econometrics, Alicante, April 19–20.

Veugelers, R. and Cassiman, B. (2004), 'Foreign subsidiaries as a channel of international technology diffusion: some direct firm level evidence from Belgium'. *European Economic Review*, **48**: 455–476.

Von Hippel, E. (1987), 'Cooperation between rivals: informal know-how trading', *Research Policy*, **16**: 291–302.

Von Hippel, E. (1994), '"Sticky" information and the locus of problem solving: implications for innovation', *Management Science*, **40**: 429–439.

Wasserman, S. and Faust, C. (1994), *Social network analysis: methods and applications*, Cambridge: Cambridge University Press.

Zucker, L. G., Darby, M. R., and Armstrong, J. (1998*a*), 'Geographically localised knowledge: spillovers or markets?', *Economic Inquiry*, **36** (January): 65–86.

Zucker, L. G., Darby, M. R., and Brewer, M. (1998*b*), 'Intellectual human capital and the birth of US biotechnology enterprises', *American Economic Review*, **88**(1): 290–306.

14

Comparative Localization of Academic and Industrial Spillovers

JAMES D. ADAMS

14.1 Introduction

An expanding literature in economic geography studies the spatial concentration of production and innovation and the role that geographic clustering plays in urban and regional growth. Geographic limits on knowledge spillovers, where spillovers are defined as flows of ideas between agents at less than the original cost (Griliches, 1992), are one factor that may cause geographic localization of innovation and output. According to this hypothesis, knowledge spillovers are an externality that is at least temporarily bounded by geography. As a result, the spillovers confer disproportionate benefits on nearby firms. This, in turn, contributes to regional scale economies and growth (Feldman, 1999). As with more general agglomeration economies (Jacobs, 1969; Mills, 1972), geographic limits on knowledge spillovers become a policy issue. If the limits matter then growth depends on aspects of region building that exceed the decision-making abilities of individual firms and industries.

This chapter characterizes the geographic localization of spillovers. It does so by describing the spatial dimension of firms' learning activities, which include consultation, travel to conferences, expenditures on books and journals, and the like; and by describing the location of closely affiliated universities and firms compared with the firm in question. Electronic communication is not the equal of contact with industrial inventors and university scientists. But travelling further to consult, collaborate, or outsource is costly, so that geographic limits to learning and spillovers are flexible and respond to incentives, and localization is endogenous to the firm (Adams, 2005, forthcoming).

The empirical results are based on new evidence from a sample of research and development (R&D) laboratories owned by US firms.[1] R&D laboratories engage in learning and innovation and are an interface between firms and external R&D performers. An advantage of the data is that localization of learning and spillovers from universities and firms can be compared net of treatment effects for the same laboratories.

Findings from the investigation are the following. University spillovers and learning about universities are geographically more localized than are industrial spillovers and learning about industry.[2] Moreover, R&D of closely affiliated universities is significantly more concentrated in the vicinity of the laboratory than other university R&D. Finally, distances between closely affiliated universities and R&D laboratories are less than distances to closely affiliated firms. The lone exception is that laboratories travel a considerable distance to work with top private universities, suggesting the rarity of cutting-edge science and its economic value. Nevertheless, the findings imply that on the whole, firms go to nearby universities for advice, research, and students. In contrast, industrial interactions take place over a greater distance and occur selectively, as a result of specific personnel movements and collaborative ventures. Since academic research is usually regarded as more of a public good than firm research, this finding poses something of a puzzle. The solution requires one to see that geographic localization of university spillovers reflect ease of dissemination of normal science, which takes place through nearby institutions.

A final set of findings relates to the determinants of learning, patents, and new products in the R&D laboratories. I find that the stock of federal R&D within 200 miles of the laboratory drives geographic localization of academic spillovers. Similarly, for industrial spillovers I find that the stock of company-financed R&D within 200 miles drives geographic localization of industrial spillovers. In addition, evidence on patents suggests localization of spillovers as indicated by learning expenditures, with university spillovers again more localized than industrial spillovers. Likewise, I find that spillovers are weaker and even more localized for new products than patents. Overall, the findings suggest that spillovers occur early on in research. During subsequent product development internal research dominates, consistent with the rising value of secrecy as commercialization draws near.

The rest of the chapter consists of five parts. Section 14.2 reviews the literature on localized production, innovation, and knowledge spillovers. Section 14.3 describes new data on industrial R&D laboratories, whose tasks include learning from academia and industry. Section 14.4 presents descriptive findings on geographic localization. Section 14.5 reports regression-style findings on localization of laboratory learning from academia and industry, as well as localization effects on laboratory patents and innovations. Section 14.6 draws conclusions, offers explanations for the patterns of localization that we observe, and concludes the chapter.

14.2   Review of the Localization Literature

The localization literature is partly concerned with the causes behind growth of firms, cities, and regions. A second part focuses on regional innovation as a function of regional knowledge-based inputs. A final strand of the literature searches for evidence of knowledge spillovers in the form of patent citations, movements of scientists and engineers, and R&D expenditures. Below is a partial review of findings in these areas.

Zucker *et al.* (1998) study firm formation in biotechnology, an industry that is closely linked to fundamental molecular biology. Their analysis of biotechnology start-ups in 183 regions shows that top university researchers in a region contribute to firm formation even after controlling for regional factors such as skill intensity, supply of venture capital, and growth. Using data on US regions, Swann and Prevezer (1996) compare firm formation and growth in computing and biotechnology. They find that feedback across sectors of computing (such as hardware, software, and peripherals) contributes to entry in any one sector. This feedback pattern is absent from biotechnology. While computing includes complementary sectors, biotechnology consists of distinct applications. Unlike computing, however, Swann and Prevezer find that entry in biotechnology relies on regional universities, consistent with the findings of Zucker *et al.* (1998). The results of Swann and Prevezer imply that knowledge spillovers are localized, but have contrasting origins: industrial for computing, academic for biotechnology. Harhoff (1999) analyses firm formation in West Germany. His study contrasts entry into high-technology industries with other industries, finding that regional diversity of industries and scientific personnel are important mainly for high-technology entry. Coupled with his finding that regional specialization matters less in high technology, the Harhoff study finds that localized cross-industry spillovers drive high-technology growth.

Glaeser *et al.* (1992) study growth in cities. Their results are based on a cross section of 1000 US city-industries whose wage and employment growth is measured between 1956 and 1987. The heart of their work compares the effects of industrial specialization and diversity on city growth. While diversity (Jacobs Externalities) contributes to growth, specialization (Marshall–Arrow–Romer, or MAR Externalities) does not. As in Harhoff (1999) this suggests that local cross-industry spillovers are the key to growth. Glaeser *et al.* argue that regions specialize for other reasons: labor-market pooling of specialized skills and the reduced expense of specialized inputs, as pointed out by Marshall (1920) and recently re-emphasized by Krugman (1991).

Henderson *et al.* (1995) take issue with the findings of Glaeser *et al.* (1992). Henderson *et al.* use the share of an industry in city employment as their measure of specialization. Unlike Glaeser *et al.* this measure is not divided or normalized by the industry's national share in employment, a somewhat different set of controls is included, and a distinction is made between mature and high-tech industries. Henderson *et al.* find that specialization (MAR Externalities) matters for both types of industries, but that diversity (Jacobs Externalities) matters only for high-tech industries, similar to Harhoff (1999). Thus, to an extent they challenge the emphasis of Glaeser *et al.* (1992) on diversity of industry as the principal engine of urban growth.

Dumais *et al.* (1997) examine the location of new plants in the light of various theories of geographic concentration. They find that the most important factor behind this decision is suitability of the local labor market, especially in more volatile industries, consistent with Marshall (1920). In contrast, localized intellectual spillovers and savings on transport costs are of secondary importance.

A second strand of literature explains the workings of regional innovation. Jaffe (1989) examines the interaction between corporate patenting and R&D and university R&D in a panel of US states. His main findings are that geographic coincidence between universities and industrial laboratories contributes to corporate patents, in addition to the main effect of university research. Perhaps more important, university R&D stimulates corporate R&D and indirectly corporate patents. Audretsch and Feldman (1996) explore the determinants of regional concentration of innovation in 163 manufacturing industries. Using a cross section of US innovation counts in 1982 classified by location and industry, they find that Gini coefficients for the 163 industries, a measure of concentration, increase as a function of skilled-labor requirements and university research that are relevant to firms, where relevance is based on the Yale Survey of R&D Managers. Both Jaffe and Audretsch and Feldman suggest the importance of local university research to industrial innovation in a region.

Finally, the literature seeks to measure localized spillovers. Jaffe et al. (1993) examine patent citations to nearby and distant firms. Their measure of localization is the excess frequency of citations to patents of nearby firms over and above a sample of control patents in the same patent class and year of issue. They find that the excess frequency of localized citation is significant. They also find that the excess frequency tends to disappear as patents age, implying that localization of knowledge spillovers in industrial patents fades over time with the diffusion of ideas. This finding is consistent with Mansfield et al. (1981) and Mansfield (1985) on the importance of imitation and the rate at which industrial technology leaks out.

Audretsch and Stephan (1996) explore localized employment of university scientists working for biotechnology firms that were Initial Public Offerings (IPOs) in the early 1990s. Their data are unusually precise, in that the linkages of firms with scientists, locations of the firms and scientists, and the roles served by scientists (as founder, scientific advisor, or consultant) are all known. Audretsch and Stephan find that scientists are more likely to be from the same region as firms if they are founders, chairs of scientific advisory boards, or Nobel Prize winners. But older scientists are not as localized and are probably consultants. These results suggest that *time-intensity* of university-firm relations is a determinant of localization of university spillovers.

Adams and Jaffe (1996) explore localization of the effects of R&D within the firm on total factor productivity of the firm's manufacturing plants. They find that R&D in the same state or within radii of 100 to 400 miles is more potent than distant R&D of the same firm. They also find that R&D in the same general product area as the plant has a stronger effect on productivity than R&D in other product areas. Thus, the effects of R&D do not flow unimpeded through the firm, but are hampered by geographic and technological distance, just as spillovers seem to be hampered by geography and technological dissimilarity.

Mansfield and Lee (1996) follow R&D expenditure trails from firms to universities. Their principal finding is that firms prefer to work with local university researchers, formalized as a distance within 100 miles of the firm's R&D laboratories. However, this fadeout in firm support of universities, as one might expect, is less for basic research than applied research. Another finding is that firms support applied research of less-distinguished faculties nearly as much as faculty in top schools, though basic research supported by firms takes place mostly at top schools.

In summary, a variety of studies suggest that localization of knowledge spillovers contributes to firm formation, growth, and innovation. The contribution of this chapter lies in comparing localization of spillovers from academic and industrial sources at the regional level and in interpreting this comparison. By this means, further insight may be gained into the determinants of geographic localization.

14.3   Description of the Data

14.3.1   Survey of R&D Laboratories

The empirical work is based on a 1997 survey of R&D laboratories. The survey quantifies learning activities of the laboratories as well as the identities of closely affiliated universities and firms.[3] Learning expenditures include meeting with university scientists, joint research, travel to conferences and meetings, and so on. Learning entails an important element of search and exploration rather than commercialized invention. It should come as no surprise that managers regard learning expenditures as a modest component of budget, on the order of 5 per cent. But in characterizing the expenditures by source and distance from the laboratory, information on localization comes to light that would otherwise remain hidden. I exploit this information below.

I selected 600 laboratories owned by 200 firms as subjects for analysis. Parent firms were a random sample from the Compustat database of publicly traded firms. Laboratory addresses within the firms were drawn from the *Directory of American Research and Technology* (1997). The firms were performers of R&D and manufacturers of chemicals, machinery, electrical goods, or transportation equipment. Firms had to report R&D and sales in Compustat and had to be patent assignees in the US Patent and Trademark Office (USPTO) database. These criteria allow for validation of the survey data on R&D, sales, and employment from the years 1991 and 1996.

Responses include 220 laboratories owned by 116 firms, yielding a response rate of 37 per cent (220/600). However, three firms aggregated their responses to the firm level, resulting in 208 observations. Twenty-nine of the 116 firms were publicly traded for under 16 years in 1996, so that young companies form a large part of the sample. Nevertheless, respondents were experienced R&D managers who had been with their firms for roughly 15 years.

Table 14.1 shows the distribution of firms and laboratories by industry of the parent firm. The distribution is uniform except for a smaller number of firms and laboratories in transportation equipment. This pattern is to be expected given the greater concentration of transportation equipment compared with other industries. The number of responses by industry is roughly proportional to the number of laboratories surveyed.[4]

Table 14.2 reports characteristics of the laboratories averaged over 1991 and 1996. Consider R&D inputs first. The average laboratory employed 157 scientists and engineers, of which 23 held a PhD (or MD) degree. Average R&D was 14 million dollars of 1987.[5] The large standard deviations suggest a positive skew of laboratory R&D, perhaps because of processes favoring large programs (Cohen and Klepper, 1992). The large variation makes it clear that the laboratories have different functions. Some are small testing facilities in manufacturing plants, while others are stand-alone centers engaged in research that ranges broadly from basic science to development.

Now turn to R&D outputs. Table 14.2 reports two measures of patents. The first line shows patents granted as reported in the survey. These average 8.3 per laboratory. Some of the laboratories, especially several larger ones, did not report their patents. The second line replaces missing patents with an estimate based on US-issued patents for the firm, laboratory location, and year. The data were downloaded from the *US Patents Database* (1999). Patents including imputes average 12.6 per laboratory.

The method for imputing patents is this. I match two-digit zip codes to addresses of all inventors in the US patent data for a given company using the Zip Code database of the post office. Next, I match patents of the parent

TABLE **14.1** *Distribution of firms and R&D laboratories by industry*

Industry	SIC code	No. of firms	No. of laboratories
Chemicals	28	32	59
Machinery	35	37	58
Electrical equipment	36	33	57
Transportation equipment	37	14	34
All industries	—	116	208[a]

Source: *Survey of Industrial Laboratory Technologies 1996.* [a]The 208 observations represent 220 laboratories because of the aggregation of laboratories under a single response by several firms.

TABLE 14.2 *Size characteristics of the R&D laboratories (standard deviations in parentheses)*

Variable	Mean (S.D.)
R&D Inputs	
Number of scientists and engineers	157.3
	(442.7)
Number of PhD (or MD) scientists and engineers	22.9
	(113.8)
Laboratory R&D budget (in millions of 1987 $)	14.0
	(41.7)
R&D outputs	
Patents granted from the survey	8.3
	(23.3)
Patents granted from the survey, supplemented by	12.6
USPTO patents for firm and laboratory locations	(40.2)
Number of new products from the survey	6.6
	(17.9)

Source: *Survey of Industrial Laboratory Technologies 1996*. The data are averages across 1991 and 1996.

firm by two-digit zip code of the laboratory. Finally, I assign imputed patents to the years in the survey (1991 and 1996) according to their issue dates.[6]

Choosing more detailed zip codes runs the risk of losing patents issued by inventors who live farther away from the laboratories. Choosing one-digit zip codes includes many more inventors who belong elsewhere in the firm. Thus, the present method occupies a middle ground on the breadth of imputation. And yet it is imperfect, as is shown by laboratories on the boundaries of states. Often, their inventors live in different states and two-digit zip codes from the laboratory and the method fails to pick up these patents.

Moreover, patents can be co-assigned to different locations in the firm, and different laboratories may cluster in the same zip code, leading to over-counts of the patents. I handle the first problem by multiplying imputed patents by the fraction of the top four inventors on the patent who reside in the same two-digit zip code as the laboratory. I handle the second problem by recording the laboratories that are in the same firm and zip code and apportioning patents to the laboratories by shares of scientists employed. In any event, leaving out the imputed cases has little impact on the results (Adams, 2005, forthcoming).

The sample of laboratories accounts for 2000–4000 patents in a year. This is a 5–10 per cent sample of US industrial patents in the mid-1990s. The laboratories produce one patent for every 12 scientists and engineers. Based on National Science Board (1998), Appendix Tables 3–15 and 4–4, the industry average is one patent for every 19 scientists and engineers. Thus, the laboratories produce more patents than average. But R&D elsewhere in the firm contributes to laboratory patents and this 'virtual' R&D brings the patent/R&D ratio closer to the average.

The survey yielded counts of new products as well as patents. While not all R&D managers could estimate new product counts, since some laboratories are not engaged in commercialization, for those responding the average number of new products was 6.6 per laboratory (compared with 12.6 for patents). This agrees with British data used in Van Reenan (1996), where innovation counts are also fewer than patents, not all of which become products. Finally, we would like indicators of the value of patents and new products, but these data are not available.

14.3.2   Construction of the Variables

The empirical work focuses on learning, spillover sources, localization, and their effects on innovation. To undertake this analysis I designed a questionnaire that would measure expenditures on learning and identify spillover sources and their location relative to the laboratory. A discussion of the variables follows.

14.3.2.1   Measurement of Laboratory Learning and its Localization. Besides laboratory R&D budget the survey asked for percentages of budget earmarked for various purposes. Specifically, the questionnaire asked respondents to check the percentage of budget devoted to learning about academic R&D, and to learning about academic R&D within 200 miles of the laboratory. Likewise, the questionnaire asked respondents to check the percentage of budget devoted to learning about industrial R&D and to learning about industrial R&D within 200 miles of the laboratory.[7] Estimated laboratory learning expenditures are the fraction of budget times R&D budget. Learning accounts for about 5 per cent of budget.

I measure regional localization of learning expenditures as the log difference: the logarithm of learning about research within 200 miles minus the logarithm of learning about research beyond 200 miles of the laboratory. I carry out this calculation for learning about both academic and industrial sources. The log difference rises as more learning is targeted on sources that lie within 200 miles and falls as more is targeted on sources beyond 200 miles, so that this is indeed a measure of localized learning. The choice of the 200-mile radius is motivated by this chapter's interest in regional (rather than urban) localization, as well as Adams and Jaffe (1996). Their findings reveal a sharply higher impact of R&D within 100 or 200 miles on plant productivity than more distant R&D, and a rapidly declining sharpness as larger circles are constructed. Finally, the logarithmic transformation reduces the skew of the ratio of nearby and distant learning effort and produces a distribution that lies somewhat closer to the normal.

14.3.2.2   Measurement of Distances to Closely Affiliated Universities and Firms.   The questionnaire asked R&D managers to cite up to five universities and up to five firms, along with their city and state locations, which were influential for the laboratory's R&D.[8] We refer to these as closely affiliated universities and firms. But here an asymmetry arises. Respondents name closely affiliated universities more often than firms. And besides, R&D expenditures of universities by field of science are available through NSF's CASPAR database and can be assigned to specific locations. In contrast, data on firm R&D by location is difficult to obtain. For both reasons, the data on cited universities are more complete and more useful than the data on firms. But the firm data are still of interest because with nearly every citation the laboratories give precise city and state locations of the divisions of firms that they work with; so that distances can be accurately measured even if firm R&D by location is not available. Another concern is that relationships with closely affiliated firms and universities differ. R&D laboratories go to universities for students, faculty consultants, and access to findings (Adams *et al.*, 2001), but are linked to other firms in a complicated web of product competition, temporary collaborations, and migration of scientists and engineers. I concur, but this is all the more reason why the effect of firm–firm spillovers should be weaker per dollar than university–firm spillovers.

   If the laboratory cites particular universities and firms I calculate distances from the laboratory as follows. First, I assign zip codes to citing R&D laboratories and to cited US universities and firms, though I exclude foreign universities and firms from these calculations because their R&D data are missing. Next, I assign latitudes and longitudes to zip codes using the Places file of the US Census Bureau. At this stage I have reasonable data on the locations of citing and cited parties. Finally, I use the locations to compute distances between the laboratories and cited universities and firms.[9] Later, I compare distances from citing laboratories to cited universities and firms and I use these distances to construct nearby and distant spillovers as a means of assessing localization.

14.3.2.3   Measurement of Academic and Industrial Spillovers.   I construct the academic spillover as follows. Respondents identify up to five of 18 science and engineering fields that they regard as most relevant to their laboratory.[10] Matching R&D expenditures by field of science are taken from NSF's CASPAR database for the closely affiliated universities that the laboratories indicate are most important for their research. The CASPAR data cover the period 1973–1995.[11]

   The academic spillover is the sum of federally funded academic R&D accumulated into stocks over a period of 17 years for up to five sciences and universities cited by the R&D managers. Thus, the measure of the relevant stock of academic R&D is:

$$\text{Academic R\&D} = \sum_{j=1}^{18} \delta_j K_j. \tag{14.1}$$

Here, K_j is the stock of federally funded R&D in field j summed over the cited universities. The term δ_j equals one if the laboratory rates a field as important and zero otherwise. Thus eqn (14.1) is the sum of the R&D stocks weighted by the laboratory-specific δ_j weights for the 18 sciences. Federally funded R&D is chosen to avoid double counting and has the effect of separating university R&D from company R&D. This is an important distinction to make since US universities rely on industry for about 7 per cent of their research support (Mansfield, 1995).

In addition to eqn (14.1) I construct the local academic spillover as the sum over the relevant stocks of R&D for closely affiliated universities that are within 200 miles of the laboratory. This distance matches that of localized learning expenditures and may drive these expenditures. Likewise, I construct the distant academic spillover as the sum over the relevant stocks of R&D for closely affiliated universities that lie beyond 200 miles of the laboratory. This variable serves as a likely driver of distant-learning expenditures.

Corresponding data on closely affiliated firm R&D by location does not exist. Instead I rely on the Census-NSF R&D survey to construct an estimate of the industry R&D spillover by location. At the first step, the estimated spillover is the weighted sum of company R&D stocks over the 35 product groups that are included in the US SIC system of classification, where the weights capture the importance of each product group to the laboratory.[12] Thus:

$$\text{R\&D in the Rest of Industry} = \sum_{j=1}^{35} \gamma_j \tilde{R}_j. \tag{14.2}$$

Here, $\tilde{R}_j$ is the stock of R&D over a period of 13 years in product j (net of parent firm R&D). The γ_j weights are fractions of technologies in an SIC group that are relevant to each laboratory.[13] The survey technologies have been mapped into SIC codes by Corporate Technology Information Services (1994). Therefore, the technology codes can be aggregated to the SIC groups used in the Census-NSF R&D data.

At the second stage I estimate the amount of industrial R&D within and outside 200 miles of the laboratory. In order to do this I construct the fraction of state-level industrial R&D within 200 miles and the fraction outside 200 miles. Industrial R&D by state is contained in Research and Development in Industry (National Science Foundation, various years).[14] I assign a center that is near the largest city in each state.[15]

Next, I assign latitude and longitude co-ordinates to the state centers and as above, compute distances from the laboratories to these centers. If any distance is less than or equal to 200 miles, then all the R&D data for that state is brought inside the circle 200 miles around the laboratory. The R&D data for the different nearby states are then summed to create state-level industry R&D within 200 miles of the laboratory.

One problem is that state-level R&D includes all the different areas of technology carried on in a given state.[16] Only some are relevant to the laboratory, as the discussion of eqn (14.2) points out. To handle this problem I estimate Industry R&D within 200 miles of each R&D laboratory as the product of the share of state level R&D within 200 miles of the laboratory times eqn (14.2), R&D in the rest of industry:

$$\text{Industry R\&D within 200 miles}$$
$$= \frac{\text{State-Level Industry R\&D within 200 miles}}{\text{State-Level Industry R\&D}} \qquad (14.3)$$
$$\times \text{ R\&D in the Rest of Industry.}$$

R&D in the Rest of Industry differs by laboratory as noted in eqn (14.2), because the γ_j weights are specific to the laboratories. This estimate of industry R&D within 200 miles of the laboratory exploits information on relevance contained in the γ_j weights and on proximity contained in the laboratory location. While eqn (14.3) contains errors, it is the best measure that I have. Finally, Industry R&D beyond 200 miles of the laboratory is eqn (14.2) minus eqn (14.3).

14.4 Descriptive Findings on Localization

Tables 14.3 to 14.8 describe localization of laboratory linkages to universities and firms. Table 14.3 records mean expenditures on learning from universities and firms by 200-mile radius from the laboratory. As pointed out above these expenditures amount to 5 per cent of laboratory budget or about $600 000 (of 1987) per year. Their distribution by distance depends on the spillover source. Lines 1 and 2, column (A), show that university learning is concentrated within 200 miles of the laboratory, while the reverse is true of industrial learning in column (B). Line 3 is the 'localization ratio' or ratio of nearby learning to distant learning, while line 4 is its logarithm. If we treat the logarithm as normally distributed we can apply a paired t-test to the difference in localization ratios in columns (A) and (B).[17] The statistic is $t = 3.35$, significant at more than the 1 per cent level.

Earlier I remarked that laboratories cite up to five closely affiliated universities that they consider most influential for their R&D. How localized is the R&D of these universities? To answer this question I accumulate the R&D of universities that are cited and not cited by the laboratories within and outside circles that are 200 miles from the laboratory. In this comparison, the set of relevant sciences is the same for closely affiliated and all other

TABLE 14.3 *Localization of learning expenditures on industrial and academic research (in millions of 1987 $) (standard deviations in parentheses)*

Variable	Mean expenditures on learning about academic research (A)	Mean expenditures on learning about industrial research (B)
(1) Learning expenditures within 200 miles of the laboratory	0.169 (0.630)	0.126 (0.490)
(2) Learning expenditures beyond 200 miles of the laboratory	0.109 (0.637)	0.224 (1.129)
(3) Nearby learning/distant learning, (1) ÷ (2)	1.551	0.563
(4) Log (nearby learning/distant learning), Log [(1) ÷ (2)]	0.925*	0.102*

Source: *Survey of Industrial Laboratory Technologies 1996.* *t-test for the difference in means between (A) and (B) is $t = 3.35$ ($N = 293$), significant at greater than the 1 per cent level. The dataset is a panel of laboratories covering the years 1991 and 1996.

universities, as indicated in each case by the R&D managers. Table 14.4 displays R&D by distance from the laboratory for closely affiliated universities in column (A) and for other universities in column (B). The first three lines show the amounts within 200 miles of the laboratory, outside 200 miles, and their ratio. Clearly the R&D of closely affiliated universities is closer to the laboratory than university R&D taken at random. I take the logarithm of these 'localization ratios' on line 4. If I treat this log difference as approximately normally distributed and take the difference of the log differences in (A) and (B), the paired *t*-statistic for the difference in means is $t = 7.67$. Thus, the R&D of closely affiliated universities is significantly more localized than university R&D taken at random.

Table 14.5 characterizes the distance to closely affiliated universities by laboratory characteristics. Panel (A) computes distances to cited universities for the subsample of 32 laboratories that work with at least one of a set of top private universities that consists of Harvard, Yale, Columbia, Princeton, Chicago, Stanford, MIT, Cal Tech, Cornell, and Johns Hopkins. The most striking result is that the laboratories are almost 900 miles from these schools on average and about 700 miles from other institutions. Almost surely this pattern reflects a demand for cutting-edge science by the laboratories, where the economic value and rarity of the research makes the journey worthwhile. In the 85 laboratories that do not have a top private university connection, the distance to cited universities drops to 400 miles. A two-sample *t*-test of the difference in mean distances yields a value of $t = 2.12$ with approximate degrees of freedom of $f = 69$, significant at greater than the 2 per cent level.[18]

TABLE 14.4 *Localization of federal R&D in closely affiliated universities (in millions of 1987 $) (standard deviations in parentheses)*

Variable	Mean federal R&D in closely affiliated universities (A)	Mean federal R&D in all other universities (B)
(1) Federally funded academic R&D within 200 miles of the laboratory	229.3 (409.7)	972.9 (1435.1)
(2) Federally funded academic R&D beyond 200 miles of the laboratory	246.5 (461.2)	9395.3 (6245.1)
(3) Nearby federal R&D/distant federal R&D, (1) ÷ (2)	0.93	0.10
(4) Log (nearby federal R&D/distant federal R&D), Log [(1) ÷ (2)]	1.10*	− 3.22*

Source: *Survey of Industrial Laboratory Technologies 1996.* *Approximate t-test for the difference in means between (A) and (B) is $t = 7.67$ ($N = 203$), significant at greater than the 1 per cent level. The dataset is a panel of laboratories covering the years 1991 and 1996.

I conclude that collaboration with universities of more average rank is more localized, consistent with the findings of Mansfield and Lee (1996). But there is an important aspect of this comparison that should not go unnoticed. While top universities exert influence over a greater distance than most others, this does not preclude their having a larger local influence as well. A top university like MIT has greater influence at every distance, but this influence fades out more slowly with distance.

Panel (B) looks at the effect of size of R&D budget on distances to universities. Laboratories with a budget under $1 million travel 250 miles to universities, while laboratories with budgets greater than $20 million travel 550 miles, suggesting the greater importance of new research to larger laboratories. A two-sample t-test of the difference in means yields a value of $t = 2.98$ with approximate degrees of freedom of $f = 32$, significant at more than the 1 per cent level. Panel (C) looks at the effect of PhD share in employment on distance to closely affiliated universities. The relationship is monotonically increasing, consistent with the view that the PhD share again captures a demand for cutting-edge academic research, though the t-statistic is not significant at conventional levels.

Table 14.6 reports mean distances from the laboratories to closely affiliated universities and firms. All US universities and firms that could be identified are included in the tabulations.[19] However, the table excludes citations to other divisions in the same firm and citations to foreign universities and firms so as to concentrate on distances to US spillover sources, for which data are available. Despite the small sample these data allow us to

TABLE 14.5 *Distances between R&D laboratories and closely affiliated universities, by laboratory characteristics (number of observations in brackets)*

Sample	Variable	Distance to cited universities in miles
(a) Effect of linkage to 10 leading private universities on distance to cited universities		
Subsample of laboratories that cite one or more of the 10 leading private universities*	Distance to 10 leading private universities	884.7[a] [$N = 32$]
Subsample of laboratories that do not cite the 10 leading private universities	Distance to all other cited universities	724.8 [$N = 32$]
	Distance to cited universities	405.9[a] [$N = 85$]
(b) Effect of size of laboratory R&D budget on distance to cited universities		
Budget less than $1 million	Distance to cited universities	259.8[b] [$N = 25$]
Budget between $1 and $4 million		559.2 [$N = 35$]
Budget between $4 and $20 million		482.8 [$N = 26$]
Budget greater than $20 million		559.9[b] [$N = 19$]
(c) Effect of PhD share in laboratory employment on distance to cited universities**		
PhD Share between 0 and 0.05	Distance to cited universities	411.2[c] [$N = 41$]
PhD Share between 0.05 and 0.2		480.4 [$N = 31$]
PhD Share greater than 0.2		578.6[c] [$N = 42$]

Source: *Survey of Industrial Laboratory Technologies 1996*. *Note*: *N* is the number of laboratories meeting the sample criteria. *The top 10 private universities are Harvard, Yale, Columbia, Princeton, Chicago, Stanford, MIT, Cal Tech, Cornell, and Johns Hopkins. **The PhD share is the number of PhDs in the laboratory divided by the number of scientists and engineers. [a]Two sample *t*-test for the difference in log (means) is $t = 2.12$ with approximate degrees of freedom of $f = 69$, significant at greater than the 2 per cent level. [b]Two sample *t*-test for the difference in log (means) is $t = 2.98$ with approximate degrees of freedom of $f = 32$, significant at greater than the 1 per cent level. [c]Two sample *t*-test for the difference in log (means) is $t = 0.87$ with approximate degrees of freedom of $f = 92$ and is insignificant at conventional levels.

compare distances to universities and firms. The result again suggests that university spillovers are more localized.

Line 1 of Table 14.6 reports distances to US universities and firms separately. Mean distances to universities and firms are respectively 493 and 851 miles. The second line compares university and firm distances for a sample of 48 observations from the same laboratories. Mean distances to universities and firms are 478 and 827 miles, about the same as above.

Table **14.6** *Comparative distances between R&D laboratories and closely affiliated universities and firms (number of observations in brackets)*

Sample	Variable	Distance to cited universities in miles (A)	Distance to cited firms in miles (B)
(1) Unpaired data, self and international citations excluded	Distance	492.5 [N = 117]	851.2 [N = 66]
(2) Paired data, self and international citations excluded	Distance	477.8 [N = 48]	826.5 [N = 48]
(3) Paired data, self and international citations excluded	Log (distance)	5.35* [N = 48]	6.49* [N = 48]

*Source: Survey of Industrial Laboratory Technologies 1996. Note: N is the number of laboratories meeting the sample criteria. *t-test for the difference in means between the logarithm of columns (A) and (B) is $t = -3.16$ (N = 48), significant at greater than the 1 per cent level.*

Line three calculates means of the logarithm of distances to universities and firms in the paired data and performs a paired *t*-test on the mean difference. The result is $t = -3.16$, indicating a significantly shorter distance to universities than to firms. From a number of perspectives Tables 14.3 to 14.6 imply that academic spillovers are more localized than industrial spillovers.

Tables 14.7 and 14.8 conclude the presentation of descriptive statistics. The tables report correlation coefficients between localized learning and indicators of university and firm influence. Localization is measured by the logarithm of learning expenditures within 200 miles of the laboratory minus the logarithm of learning expenditures beyond 200 miles. These indicators of university and firm influence are derived from Likert-scale indicators of the importance of each channel.[20] If respondents indicated a score of three or more out of five then a value of one was assigned to the channel to indicate its importance, and zero otherwise. The tables list four interactions between the laboratory and universities: engineering graduates, patent licensing, outsourcing of R&D to universities, and faculty consulting. Likewise, technical publications, patents, joint research with other firms, and outsourcing of R&D to other firms are four interactions between the laboratory and other firms.

Table 14.7 reports correlations between localization of learning about university research and the four channels of university influence. Nearly all the channels increase localization. Table 14.8 reports correlations between localization of learning about firm research and the four channels of firm influence. Unlike Table 14.7 some firm–firm channels (technical papers and patents) reduce localization. Tables 14.7 and 14.8 suggest in yet another way that linkages between laboratories and universities are more localized than linkages with firms.

TABLE 14.7 *Correlations between localization of laboratory learning about academic research and channels of interaction with universities*

Measure of localization of learning about academic research	Channel of interaction with universities	Correlation (*P*-value)
Log (learning expenditures within 200 miles)/(learning expenditures beyond 200 miles)	Outsourcing of R&D to universities important (1 if yes, 0 if no)	0.229 (0.001)
	Faculty consulting important (1 if yes, 0 if no)	0.157 (0.007)
	Licensing of university patents important (1 if yes, 0 if no)	0.096 (0.098)
	Engineering graduates important (1 if yes, 0 if no)	0.169 (0.004)

Source: *Survey of Industrial Laboratory Technologies 1996. Note:* channels are dummy variables coded as 1 if a respondent indicates that a particular interaction is important and 0 otherwise. See the text for a discussion.

TABLE 14.8 *Correlations between localization of laboratory learning about industrial research and channels of interaction with other firms*

Measure of localization of learning about industrial research	Channel of interaction with other firms	Correlation (*P*-value)
Log (learning expenditures within 200 miles)/(learning expenditures beyond 200 miles)	Outsourcing of R&D to other firms important (1 if yes, 0 if no)	0.060 (0.304)
	Joint research with other firms important (1 if yes, 0 if no)	0.073 (0.335)
	Other firms' technical publications important (1 if yes, 0 if no)	−0.153 (0.009)
	Other firms' patents important (1 if yes, 0 if no)	−0.097 (0.096)

Source: *Survey of Industrial Laboratory Technologies 1996.*
Note: Channels are dummy variables coded as 1 if a respondent indicates that a particular interaction is important and 0 otherwise. See text for a discussion.

14.5   Localized Learning and Innovation

Tables 14.9 to 14.11 study the determinants of localized learning and innovation. Tables 14.9 and 14.10 explain localization of learning about academic and industrial research. Table 14.11 explains numbers of patents and new

TABLE 14.9 *Localization of learning about academic research*
(asymptotic normal statistics in parentheses)

Variable or statistic	Log (learning about academic R&D within 200 miles) (9.1)	Log (learning about academic R&D beyond 200 miles) (9.2)
Estimation method	Tobit	
Year and time dummies	Yes	Yes
Outsourcing of R&D to universities important (1 if yes, 0 if no)	1.43 (2.1)	0.41 (0.3)
Faculty consulting important (1 if yes, 0 if no)	2.46 (2.7)	2.74 (1.6)
Licensing of university patents important (1 if yes, 0 if no)	2.02 (3.0)	0.80 (0.6)
Engineering graduates important (1 if yes, 0 if no)	−1.27 (−1.5)	−4.81 (−3.0)
Log (non-PhD laboratory scientists and engineers)	1.17* (5.4)	−0.42* (−1.1)
Log (PhD laboratory scientists and engineers)	0.46 (4.3)	0.56 (2.8)
Firm owns other R&D laboratories (1 if yes, 0 if no)	−0.51 (−0.9)	2.68 (2.1)
Log (closely affiliated university R&D within 200 miles of the laboratory)	0.16* (2.8)	−0.18* (−1.5)
Log (closely affiliated university R&D beyond 200 miles of the laboratory)	0.03 (0.6)	0.43 (3.6)
Fraction of left censored observations	0.64	0.83
Log likelihood	−323.9	−206.2
χ^2	175.3	58.0
Root MSE	3.52	5.84

Source: *Survey of Industrial Laboratory Technologies 1996*, the Census-NSF survey, and the NSF-CASPAR database of universities. The number of observations is $N = 269$. *Estimated coefficients in eqns (9.1) and (9.2) differ at greater than the 1 per cent level of significance. The dataset is a panel of laboratories covering the years 1991 and 1996.

TABLE 14.10 *Localization of learning about industrial research*
(asymptotic normal statistics in parentheses)

Variable or statistic	Log (learning about industrial R&D within 200 miles) (10.1)	Log (learning about industrial R&D beyond 200 miles) (10.2)
Estimation method	Tobit	
Year and time dummies	Yes	Yes
Outsourcing of R&D to other firms important (1 if yes, 0 if no)	1.33* (2.9)	−0.60* (−0.9)
Joint research with other firms important (1 if yes, 0 if no)	−0.05 (−0.1)	−1.41 (−1.9)
Other firm's technical publications important (1 if yes, 0 if no)	−0.36** (−0.5)	3.25** (3.0)
Other firm's patents important (1 if yes, 0 if no)	0.44 (0.7)	0.93 (1.1)
Log (non-PhD laboratory scientists and engineers)	0.83 (4.7)	0.84 (3.4)
Log (PhD laboratory scientists and engineers)	0.31 (4.4)	0.27 (2.6)
Firm owns other R&D laboratories (1 if yes, 0 if no)	−0.54* (−1.0)	3.03* (3.6)
Laboratory meets at least weekly with other laboratories in the firm (1 if yes, 0 if no)	0.71** (1.2)	−2.19** (−2.5)
Log (industry R&D within 200 miles of the laboratory)	0.40** (2.5)	−0.06** (−0.3)
Log (industry R&D beyond 200 miles of the laboratory)	−0.23 (−1.6)	0.16 (0.8)
Fraction of left censored observations	0.50	0.59
Log likelihood	−430.1	−407.3
χ^2	108.2	66.6
Root MSE	3.20	4.45

Source: Survey of Industrial Laboratory Technologies 1996, the Census-NSF R&D survey, and the NSF-CASPAR database of universities. The number of observations is $N = 269$. *Estimated coefficients in eqns (10.1) and (10.2) differ at greater than the 1 per cent level of significance. **Estimated coefficients in eqns (10.1) and (10.2) differ at greater than the 5 per cent level of significance. The dataset is a panel of laboratories covering the years 1991 and 1996.

TABLE 14.11 *Laboratory innovation and localized learning (asymptotic normal statistics in parentheses)*

Variable or statistic	Patents granted		Number of new products	
	(11.1)	(11.2)	(11.3)	(11.4)
Estimation method	Negative binomial regression			
Year and time dummies	Yes	Yes	Yes	Yes
Patent imputation dummy (1 if yes, 0 if no)	0.87 (3.5)	0.89 (3.5)		
Log (learning about academic R&D within 200 miles)	0.07 (1.8)		0.08 (2.1)	
Log (learning about academic R&D beyond 200 miles)	0.06 (1.4)		−0.12 (−3.3)	
Log ('composite' learning about academic R&D)^b		0.09 (2.6)		0.08 (2.1)
Log (learning about industrial R&D within 200 miles)	0.12 (3.1)		0.05 (1.5)	
Log (learning about industrial R&D beyond 200 miles)	0.09 (2.8)		0.01 (0.2)	
Log ('composite' learning about industrial R&D)^a		0.19 (5.0)		0.07 (2.0)
Log (internal research of the laboratory)	0.44 (6.3)	0.38 (5.4)	0.39 (5.6)	0.36 (5.0)
Log (stock of R&D in the rest of the firm)	0.09 (4.7)	0.09 (4.8)	−0.00 (−0.1)	−0.00 (−0.2)
N	262	262	202	202
Log (likelihood)	−630.0	−626.5	−511.7	−511.6
χ^2	212.3	219.5	144.0	144.3

Sources: *Survey of Industrial Laboratory Technologies 1996*, Standard and Poor's Compustat, and the NSF-CASPAR database of universities. ^{a}In eqns (11.2) and (11.4) 'Composite learning about industrial R&D' is simply the sum of learning about industrial R&D within 200 miles of the laboratory, plus learning about industrial R&D beyond 200 miles. ^{b}In eqn (11.2) 'Composite learning about academic R&D' is the sum of learning about academic R&D within 200 miles of the laboratory, plus 0.6 times learning about academic R&D beyond 200 miles. See the text for a discussion. In eqn (11.4) 'Composite learning about academic R&D' is the sum of learning about academic R&D within 200 miles of the laboratory, minus 0.2 times learning about academic research beyond 200 miles. See the text for a further discussion. The dataset is a panel of laboratories covering the years 1991 and 1996.

products as functions of nearby and distant learning about academic and industrial R&D and other variables.

Table 14.9 reports findings for learning about academic R&D. Explanatory variables include industry and time dummy variables and the logarithms of non-PhD and PhD laboratory scientists, which together control for laboratory size and research intensiveness. In addition, I include the four channels of university influence already discussed: outsourcing of R&D to universities, faculty consulting, licensing of university patents, and engineering graduates.

The dependent variables of eqns (9.1) and (9.2) are the logarithms of learning about academic R&D within and beyond 200 miles of the laboratory. The estimation method is Tobit analysis, since over half of the observations are left censored. The higher proportion of censoring in eqn (9.2) indicates localization of laboratory linkages to universities, given that many of the laboratories do not find it worthwhile to learn about university research at a distance.

According to eqns (9.1) and (9.2) most of the channels of university influence contribute to localization. Outsourcing to universities, licensing of university patents and engineering graduates all seem to contribute more to nearby learning, though the coefficients are not significantly different.[21] The number of non-PhD scientists, however, does contribute to localization, while PhD researchers have no effect. Combining these results, laboratories that are less PhD intensive learn more locally from university research, consistent with Table 14.5. Presumably such laboratories seek advice on normal, widely available science and engineering. In addition, the equations include a dummy variable for whether the firm owns other laboratories. This variable diminishes localization, perhaps because larger firms are geographically dispersed in both research and production.

Finally, I include the logarithms of nearby and distant R&D in closely affiliated universities as determinants of benefits of learning from nearby and distant universities. As one might expect, R&D in nearby universities increases localization while distant R&D decreases localization.

Table 14.10 presents parallel findings on learning about industrial research. As before, logarithms of learning about nearby and distant industrial research are the dependent variables. The equations include year and time dummies and channels of interaction with other firms, the logarithms of non-PhD and PhD scientists, and the dummy, as above, for whether the firm owns other laboratories. I also include nearby and distant industrial R&D, although, as pointed out in the discussion of eqns (14.2) and (14.3), this evidence on industrial spillovers is not as specific as that on university spillovers. R&D of closely affiliated firms, unlike closely affiliated universities, cannot be assigned to a location. Table 14.10 also includes two dummy variables, one for other laboratories in the firm, and another that equals one if the laboratory meets at least monthly with other R&D units in the firm, and zero otherwise. These variables control for firm size and focus of the laboratory on its locality.

Equations (10.1) and (10.2) are Tobit estimates of the logarithms of nearby and distant learning about industrial R&D. Tobit is the preferred method since half or more of industrial learning expenditures are left censored.[22] Outsourcing of R&D to other firms and joint research contribute to localization. The importance of other firm's technical papers on the other hand diminishes localization, perhaps because it indicates interest in joint or external research in industry. Both non-PhD and PhD scientists increase learning expenditures, consistent with their interpretation as measures of laboratory size, but neither contributes to localization. As expected, nearby and distant industrial R&D, respectively, increase and decrease localization, though only the former is significant across equations.

Consistent with its interpretation as a measure of the parent firm's size and geographic dispersion, ownership of other laboratories diminishes localization in eqns (10.1) and (10.2). Consistent with its interpretation of the time-intensity of intrafirm interactions, frequency of meeting increases localization.

Table 14.11 concludes the empirical work. In this table, I explore the implications of localized learning for laboratory patents and number of new products. The dependent variables are counts of patents and new products. These are non-negative, include many zeroes and are positively skewed. The Poisson family of distributions fits this class of variable well. But the Poisson assumes that the mean equals the variance and ignores the fact that the variance exceeds the mean in most microdata. The Negative Binomial distribution handles this 'overdispersion' problem and is the method used in Table 14.11.[23] The dependent variable in eqns (11.1) and (11.2) is patents granted. The dependent variable in eqns (11.3) and (11.4) is the number of new products originating in the laboratory.

The idea behind this table is that in order to innovate the laboratory must first learn from the outside and engage in internal research.[24] Seen in this light, academic and industrial learning as well as internal laboratory and parent-firm research should intermediate the effects of spillovers. Consistent with this approach the spillover variables that I have are generally insignificant while the learning variables are significant. Thus, Table 14.11 concentrates on learning and internal research, as well as localization in learning, on patents and new products.

The explanatory variables are nearly the same in the two pairs of equations, the only difference being the patent imputation dummy in eqns (11.1) and (11.2). The imputation dummy is associated with more patents because imputation occurs in several of the larger laboratories and because the procedure tends to include research conducted elsewhere in the firm.

Otherwise independent variables are the same in the patents and new products equations. The explanatory variables include learning about industrial and academic R&D differentiated by distance from the laboratory.

Equations (11.1) and (11.2) follow two approaches to differentiation by distance. In eqn (11.1) I enter the logarithms of nearby and distant learning as separate variables. In eqn (11.2) I construct 'composites' of academic and industrial learning expenditures $\log (l_n + \beta l_d)$ that are of the form $l(n =$ nearby, $d =$ distant). To pin down β, I perform a grid search over values of β ranging over 0.0, 0.2 ... 1.4 in the case of academic and industrial research. This procedure allows for non-linear effects of learning in Negative Binomial regression and compares the effects of nearby and distant R&D.

Using separate variables does not work well for academic research in eqn (11.1): both nearby and distant R&D are insignificant and their effects are not estimated very precisely. The results for industrial R&D suggest some fade-out with distance, but this fadeout is not significant. The grid search in eqn (11.2) turns up a best-fitting combination of $\beta = 1.0$ for distant learning about industrial research, and $\beta = 0.6$ for distant learning about academic research. This suggests that learning is more localized in the case of academic research, though the sample is small and the estimates are imprecise.

Equations (11.3) and (11.4) explain the number of new products. I enter separate variables in eqn (11.3) for nearby and distant learning about academic and industrial research. It seems clear that localization of learning is greater for new products than patents. Indeed, distant learning about academic research has a negative effect on patents, the interpretation being that laboratories that work with distant universities are occupied with more basic research that precedes new products. This result is consistent with the nature of university–firm collaborations in biotechnology as documented by Arora and Gambardella (1990), which also occur in the early stages of innovation. A fadeout of industrial learning with distance is again apparent, though the estimates are again imprecise.

Equation (11.4) applies the grid-search methodology to new products. Again, I construct 'composites' of academic and industrial learning expenditures l that are of the form $\log (l_n + \beta l_d)$ ($n =$ nearby, $d =$ distant), for which I perform a grid search over values of β ranging over $-0.4, -0.2, \ldots 1.4$ for academic learning (given the negative sign in 10.3) and over β ranging over $-0.4, -0.2, \ldots 1.4$ for industrial learning. The best-fitting equation indicates $\beta = -0.2$ for distant academic learning and $\beta = 0$, or no effect of distant learning about industrial research.[25]

These results indicate greater localization at the commercialization stage than the invention stage. As the firm approaches commercialization and secrecy becomes more valuable, it seems plausible that most of the research in the laboratory would be internal development work.

14.6   Discussion and Conclusion

The results of previous sections support the notion that academic knowledge spillovers are geographically localized. The spillovers are more localized than one would expect on the basis of the geographic distribution of university R&D, and they are more localized than industrial knowledge spillovers. This judgement is based on the behavior of laboratory learning effort differentiated by distance and on the distance of closely affiliated universities and firms from the laboratories.

The patterns in geographic localization that we observe are related to differences in the characteristics of academic and industrial spillover sources, to differences in the characteristics of the R&D laboratories, and to differences in the productive functions of universities. Let us work through these relationships in order.

The differences in characteristics of academic and industrial spillover sources that seem most salient are the system of open science for academic spillovers and the system of proprietary information and intellectual property for industrial spillovers. Open science makes it possible for firms to go to local universities to obtain information that is reasonably current and not proprietary, or in other words to gain access to normal science. This increases the localization of academic spillovers. Despite a limited degree of participation in open science in order to attract able scientists and maintain their edge (Hicks, 1995), firms are primarily interested in defending proprietary technologies, which are a key to profitability. Contractual arrangements are needed to gain access to proprietary information in industry, often at a considerable distance, since information about industrial technologies does not circulate with the same freedom as in the university system.

Characteristics of the laboratories also determine the extent of localization. In Table 14.5 laboratories that work with top private universities search over longer distances, not merely with these top institutions, but also with other universities. Larger and more PhD-intensive laboratories also search over longer distances to work with universities. I conclude that size and sophistication of the laboratories diminish the geographic localization of academic spillovers.

The above discussion points out that universities differ in their functions. Top private universities concentrate more than others on basic research. Spillovers from these institutions are not especially localized as Table 14.5 has demonstrated. The situation is otherwise for the public universities that comprise most of the remaining schools. I shall argue that public universities are constrained by policies that are conducive to localization. While these ideas contain an element of speculation, I set them down in the interest of further research.

The industry-university co-operative movement has very likely contributed to geographic localization of academic spillovers. This movement began formally in the United States with the Morrill Act (1862), which granted land for the establishment of one college in a state with its primary objective the teaching of courses in the agricultural and mechanical arts.[26] Later, the Hatch Act (1887) established the state agricultural experiment stations on the campuses of Land Grant colleges. The Hatch Act contributed to a joining together of teaching and research functions within the same institution, increasing the diffusion of research results to the states. The Land Grant colleges were to serve agriculture and industry by providing practical education and research. As employment shifted away from agriculture, training in Land Grant universities shifted with it but maintained an applied focus in research and teaching, in keeping with ongoing funding pressures by state government. The industry–university co-operative movement seems from the first to have been an expression of state interests' demands for jointly exercised, practical training and research. These developments laid the foundations for the close industry–public university ties that we observe in the present data. It seems plausible that these ties would be much weaker in countries that lack such policies.

World War II changed this setting by increasing federal support for university research. The National Science Foundation, the National Institutes of Health, and other programs were the result of success in harnessing university research to wartime needs.[27] But by 1980 complaints began to mount that federal funding, which led universities in a more basic direction, also weakened university–firm linkages.[28] In 1980, Congress passed the Bayh–Dole Act, which allowed universities to patent inventions from federal research. At the same time NSF and other agencies began to found Industry–University Cooperative Research Centers (IUCRCs). The IUCRCs compensated faculty for working with firms. By these means, the federal government has bolstered the co-operative movement in relation to industry.[29] In conclusion, it would seem that the US has successfully pursued a long-run policy that has coupled scientific training and research with state and national interests. It would also appear that by strengthening the ties between universities and firms this policy has proven to be a strong complement to the institution of open science.

This chapter has presented evidence on the localization of knowledge spillovers using data from a sample of R&D laboratories. I have examined forces that determine concentration of learning effort in the vicinity of the research group, as opposed to more distant locations. Perhaps the most important of this chapter's findings are that university spillovers are more localized than firm spillovers and more localized than the general distribution of university R&D. The paradox is that a form of knowledge that is more of a public good than almost any other should be so localized. The resolution is that localization of university research represents dissemination of knowledge that, if not free, is certainly cheaper than doing the research over again.

This evidence raises additional policy issues. Perhaps the main one is, how local should the university–firm connection be? University research that is primarily supported by the state internalizes benefits to that state. Clearly, research that has a wider scope than this, including much basic research, is better funded at the national or international levels, where more benefits can be internalized. This way of putting it explains the trend away from state funding of research and suggests limits to the arguments underlying the industry–university co-operative movement.[30] Perhaps the best combination is that of universities serving state and local interests through training and dissemination, coupled with national and international funding of more wide-ranging research that almost without notice crosses political boundaries.

Acknowledgements

This research was supported by NSF grant SBR-9502968. I thank Eleanora Voelkel and Richard Anderson for collection of the underlying survey data, as well as Meg Fernando and Janet Galvez for programming and database management. Comments by two referees and an editor (Richard Arnott) significantly improved the style and substance of the chapter. Needless to say, any remaining errors are my responsibility.

Notes

1. Throughout this chapter the term 'R&D laboratory' refers to any research group in a firm and not necessarily to a separate, formally dedicated research establishment.
2. Although I find that university spillovers are geographically *more* localized, this statement should not be read as denying the productive functions of localized industries as discussed in Marshall (1920), Krugman (1991), Glaeser *et al.* (1992), Henderson *et al.* (1995), Dumais *et al.* (1997), and many others.
3. The survey instrument was refined in three stages. A former R&D manager critiqued the initial draft. Afterwards, the survey team tested a beta version of the instrument on 10 laboratories. Using these comments the team produced a third and final version of the survey instrument. We then contacted the laboratories by phone. A mass mailing was then made to all laboratories that granted permission to send the instrument. The resulting data are confidential and cannot be released except in aggregate form.
4. The exception is the lower response rate of pharmaceutical laboratories, due to the large volume of surveys that they receive and the cross-industry nature of this survey, not exclusively focused on ethical drugs.
5. This figure, which follows NSF definitions, represents R&D purged of all overhead or non-research charges. It is a lower bound on omnibus figures for total R&D appropriations that are reported in Compustat. The survey figures on R&D place less emphasis on production engineering and more on applied research.
6. I thank Meg Fernando for downloading the patent data and Janet Galvez for translating them into SAS[TM] format.
7. An example is: 'Check the per cent of your laboratory's R&D budget for 1991 and 1996 that was spent on learning about research *in firms within 200 miles of your lab*. Fill in "Other" if the per cent exceeds those listed.

Budget per cent	1991	1996
1. None	—	—
2. 0.1–1 percent	—	—
3. 2–3 percent	—	—
4. 4–5 percent	—	—
5. 6–7 percent	—	—
6. Other percent	—	—

,

8. An excerpt from this type of question is: 'List as many as five firms and locations whose research was most important for the conduct of your laboratory's R&D over the past five years. *Please print.*
Firm # 1 _____
City, State, Country _____ .

9. The appendix to Adams (2001) explains the distance calculations in detail.

10. Science disciplines include astronomy, chemistry, physics, other physical sciences; computer science, mathematics and statistics; atmospheric sciences, earth sciences, and oceanography; and agriculture, biology, and medicine. Engineering disciplines include aeronautical, chemical, civil, electrical, mechanical, and other engineering.

11. For more details on the university data, see Adams and Griliches (1998).

12. The 35 industries include agricultural chemicals; aircraft; communications equipment; construction and materials-handling equipment; drugs; electrical components; electrical industrial apparatus; engines and turbines; electrical transmission and distribution equipment; fabricated metals; farm and garden equipment; primary ferrous metals; food and kindred products; inorganic and organic chemicals; missiles and space vehicles; motor vehicles; metalworking equipment; soap, paint, and miscellaneous chemicals; other electrical equipment, including appliances and wiring; computers and office equipment; optical, surgical, and photographic instruments; ordnance; special and general industry machinery; ships, railroads, and other transportation equipment; petroleum refining; plastics, resins, and fibers; primary non-ferrous metals; audio, video, and radio equipment; rubber and plastics; search and detection equipment and lab apparatus; stone, clay, and glass; textiles; pre-packaged software; computer services; and telecommunications services. The first 32 industries are the Census applied product fields in manufacturing. The last three industries, taken from Compustat, are R&D-intensive sectors outside manufacturing. Each of the 35 groups can be assigned to a two- or three-digit SIC major industry group.

13. To clarify the meaning of the γ_j weights, consider SIC 357, Office Machines and Computing, one of the applied product groups in the Census-NSF R&D data. The following 10 technologies in the survey fall within SIC 357: business equipment, computer accessories/components, computer memory systems, central processing units, computer monitors and input devices, microcomputers/minicomputers, mainframes/semiconductors, peripheral controllers and output devices, computer-related services, and terminals. If an R&D manager indicates that three of the above sectors are important, then $\gamma_j = 0.3$. If the manager indicates seven, then $\gamma_j = 0.7$. Thus the γ_j weights are laboratory

specific. Similar calculations apply to other technologies that form technologies within the Census-NSF product groups described in note 12, above.

14. The state is the most detailed level of geographic detail in the NSF data on industrial R&D. This creates some errors in the measure of localized R&D, defined as within 200 miles of the laboratory, but nothing can be done about the problem.

15. For example, the R&D center in Pennsylvania is Harrisburg, in New York, Binghamton, in Illinois, Chicago, and so on.

16. R&D by state and by applied product are collected independently of one another in the Census-NSF survey of industrial R&D that yields state-level industry R&D.

17. This test is approximate at best, because the logarithm of the localization ratio is essentially the difference in the logarithms of two budget proportions.

18. See Brownlee (1965), pp. 299–303, or another text. The test assumes unequal variances and was developed by Welch and for this reason is sometimes called the Welch test.

19. Privately held companies, many of them start-ups, are difficult to identify in standard business directories.

20. An excerpt from the question about university channels is, 'Below are some firm–university interactions. *Circle the number to indicate the importance of each to your lab.*'

Firm–university interaction	Not applicable	Unimportant	Important	Very important
Engineering graduates	1	2	3	4	5

The question for firm–firm interactions is worded similarly.

21. Tables 14.9 and 14.10 do not include equations where the difference in the logarithms of nearby and distant learning is the dependent variable. The reason is that distribution of the dependent variable is difficult to specify. In essence, it is the distribution of the difference in the logarithms of two budget proportions. For this reason I use two equation Tobit to conduct cross-equation tests between eqns (9.1) and (9.2) and (10.1) and (10.2).

22. The increase in left censoring from 50 to 59 percent as learning changes from nearby to distant indicates some degree of localization.

23. The Negative Binomial is derived by assuming that the Poisson parameter is Gamma distributed. Integrating over the Gamma error term, the marginal distribution is found to be Negative Binomial (Johnson and Kotz, 1969). For references see Maddala (1983) or Greene (2000). For applications of random effects Poisson (Negative Binomial) and fixed effects Poisson (Conditional Logit) regression to patents, see Hausman *et al.* (1984).

24. Cohen and Levinthal (1989) and Adams (2001*b*) pursue this approach further.

25. I impose an additional constraint, that $Spillover = \max(0, l_n + \beta l_d)$ in order to take the logarithm of $l_n + \beta l_d$.

26. Chapter 1 of Huffman and Evenson (1993) documents earlier initiatives that were precursors of the Land Grant Act. The agricultural division of the US Patent Office almost from the start undertook seed collection, experimentation, and diffusion–activities that were later included in the research of agricultural

colleges. Early agricultural colleges allowed for institutional experimentation that contributed to the Land Grant colleges.
27. For a discussion, see Mowery and Rosenberg (1998).
28. See Dertouzos *et al.* (1989).
29. See Adams *et al.* (2001) for an analysis of contributions of IUCRCs to firm R&D.
30. National Science Board (1998), Appendix Table 5-2 shows that the share of academic research accounted for by states fell from 13.2 percent in 1960 to 7.6 percent by 1997.

References

Adams, J. D. (2001), 'Comparative localization of academic and industrial spillovers'. NBER Working Paper no. 8292, Cambridge, MA.

Adams, J. D. (2005, forthcoming), 'Learning, internal research, and spillovers: evidence from a sample of R & D laboratories'. *Economics of Innovation and New Technology.*

Adams, J. D. and Jaffe, A. B. (1996), 'Bounding the effects of R&D: an investigation using matched firm and establishment data'. *RAND Journal of Economics,* **27**: 700–721.

Adams, J. D., Chiang, E. P., and Starkey, K. (2001), 'Industry–university cooperative research centers'. *Journal of Technology Transfer,* **26**: 73–86.

Adams, J. D. and Griliches, Z. (1998), 'Research productivity in a system of universities'. *Annals of INSEE,* **49/50**: 127–162.

Arora, A. and Gambardella, A. (1990), 'Complementarity and external linkages: the strategies of the large firms in biotechnology'. *Journal of Industrial Economics,* **38**: 361–379.

Audretsch, D. A. and Feldman, M. P. (1996), 'R&D spillovers and the geography of innovation and production'. *American Economic Review,* **86**: 640–650.

Audretsch, D. A. and Stephan, P. E. (1996), 'Company–scientist locational links: the case of biotechnology'. *American Economic Review,* **86**: 641–652.

Brownlee, K. A. (1965), *Statistical theory and methodology in science and engineering,* 2nd edn. New York: John Wiley and Sons.

Cohen, W. M. and Levinthal, D. A. (1989), 'Innovation and learning: the two faces of R&D'. *Economic Journal,* **99**: 569–596.

Cohen, W. M. and Klepper, S. (1992), 'The anatomy of industry R&D distributions'. *American Economic Review,* **82**: 773–799.

CorpTech: Corporate Technology Database (1994), Woburn, M A: Corporate Technology Information Services, Inc.

Dertouzos, M. L., Lester, R. K., Solow, R., and the MIT Commission on Industrial Productivity (1989), *Made in America: Regaining the productive edge.* Cambridge, MA: MIT Press.

Directory of American research and technology (1997), 31st edn. New Providence. NJ: R. R. Bowker, Inc.

Dumais, G., Ellison, G., and Glaeser, E. L. (1997), 'Geographic concentration as a dynamic process'. NBER Working Paper no. 6270, November. Cambridge, MA.

Feldman, M. P. (1999), 'The new economics of innovation, spillovers and agglomeration: a review of empirical studies'. *Economics of Innovation and New Technology,* **8**: 5–25.

Glaeser, E. L., Kallal, H. D., Scheinkman, J., and Shleifer, A. (1992), 'Growth in cities'. *Journal of Political Economy*, **100**: 1126–1152.

Greene, W. H. (2000), *Econometric analysis*, 4th edn. Upper Saddle River, NJ: Prentice-Hall.

Griliches, Z. (1992), 'The search for R&D spillovers'. *Scandinavian Journal of Economics*, **94**: S29–47.

Harhoff, D. (1999), 'Firm formation and regional spillovers'. *The Economics of Innovation and New Technology*, **8**: 27–55.

Hausman, J., Hall, B., and Griliches, Z. (1984), 'Econometric models for count data with an application to the patents–R&D relationship'. *Econometrica*, **52**: 909–938.

Henderson, V., Kuncoro, A., and Turner, M. (1995), 'Industrial development in cities'. *Journal of Political Economy*, **103**: 1067–1090.

Hicks, D. (1995), 'Published papers, tacit competencies and corporate management of the public/private character of knowledge'. *Industrial and Corporate Change*, **4**: 401–424.

Huffman, W. E. and Evenson, R. E. (1993), *Science for agriculture: a long-term perspective*. Ames, IA: Iowa State University Press.

Jacobs, J. (1969), *The economy of cities*. New York: Random House.

Jaffe, A. B. (1989), 'Real effects of academic research'. *The American Economic Review*, **88**: 957–970.

Jaffe, A. B., Trajtenberg, M., and Henderson, R. (1993), 'Geographic localization of knowledge spillovers as evidenced by patent citations'. *The Quarterly Journal of Economics*, **108**: 577–598.

Johnson, N. L. and Kotz, S. (1969), *Distributions in statistics: discrete distributions*. Boston: Houghton-Mifflin.

Krugman, P. (1991), *Geography and trade*. Cambridge, MA: MIT Press.

Maddala, G. S. (1983), *Limited-dependent and qualitative variables in econometrics*. Cambridge: Cambridge University Press.

Mansfield, E. (1985), 'How rapidly does new industrial technology leak out?' *The Journal of Industrial Economics*, **34**: 217–223.

Mansfield, E. (1995), 'Academic research underlying industrial innovations: sources, characteristics, and financing'. *The Review of Economics and Statistics*, **77**: 55–65.

Mansfield, E. and Lee, J.-Y. (1996), 'The modern university: contributor to industrial innovation and recipient of industrial support'. *Research Policy*, **25**: 1047–1058.

Mansfield, E., Schwartz, M., and Wagner, S. (1981), 'Imitation costs and patents: an empirical study'. *Economic Journal*, **91**: 907–918.

Marshall, A. (1920), *Principles of economics*, 8th edn. London: Macmillan.

Mills, E. S. (1972), *Urban economics*. Glenview, IL: Scott, Foresman, and Company.

Mowery, D. C. and Rosenberg, N. (1998), *Paths of innovation: technological change in 20th century America*. Cambridge: Cambridge University Press.

National Science Board, Science and Engineering Indicators (1998), Washington, DC: US Government Printing Office.

National Science Foundation (various years), *Research and development in industry*. Washington, DC: Government Printing Office.

Swann, P. and Prevezer, M. (1996), 'A comparison of the dynamics of industrial clustering in computing and biotechnology'. *Research Policy*, **25**: 1139–1157.

US Patents Database (1999), Baltimore, MD: Community of Science, Inc.

Van Reenan, J. (1996), 'The creation and capture of rents: wages and innovation in a panel of UK companies'. *Quarterly Journal of Economics,* **111**: 195–226.

Zucker, L. G., Darby, M. R., and Brewer, M. B. (1998), 'Intellectual human capital and the birth of US biotechnology enterprises'. *American Economic Review,* **88**: 290–306.

PART V

15

Towards a Knowledge-Based Theory of the Geographical Cluster[1]

PETER MASKELL

15.1 Introduction

One of the most significant consequences of the present process of globalization is the way in which it continues to turn inputs, previously crucial to the competitiveness of firms, into ubiquities. Ubiquities are inputs equally available to all firms at more or less the same cost almost regardless of location (Weber, 1909). A large domestic market is, for instance, no longer an unquestioned advantage when global transport costs are becoming negligible; when the loyalty of customers toward national suppliers is dwindling; and when most trade barriers have eroded. Domestic suppliers of the most efficient production machinery are, similarly, no longer a solid competitive advantage, when the sales and marketing strategies of the suppliers reach across borders, and their equipment becomes available world-wide at essentially the same cost. The omnipresence of organizational designs of proven value makes, furthermore, a long industrial track record less valuable. So when input becomes ubiquitous, all competing firms are, in a sense, placed on an equal footing. What everyone has cannot constitute a competitive advantage.[2]

Firms cope with this situation in various ways. Some invest heavily in order to increase productivity, while others outsource, leaving the old industrial areas in a slowly more and more desolate and jobless state. 'Automate, emigrate or evaporate', as the saying goes. Other firms, in contrast, confront the new competitive situation by sharpening their abilities to learn and create knowledge a little faster than their competitors.

The creation of knowledge is usually seen as a process requiring dedicated investments either as pre-competitive research and education through universities, etc., or at the level of the individual firm through R&D activities. At least as important is, however, the investment in incremental 'low-tech' learning and innovation (Laestadius, 1996; Maskell, 1998) that takes place when firms, also in fairly traditional industries, create strongly corroborated knowledge while handling and developing mundane day-to-day operations like resource management, logistics, production organization, personnel, marketing, sales, distribution, industrial relations, etc. (Malerba, 1992). The possessors might know little or nothing of the origin of the knowledge they utilize or how they have come to know it, but 'it's here' and 'it works' (Baumard 1996; Spender 1996).

However, scholars and policy makers have increasingly come to suspect that the specific spatial arrangement of economic activities might also *in itself* somehow influence the creation of knowledge and, consequentially, economic growth (OECD, 1999).

Broadly, we may recognize two major categories of agglomeration economies (Estall and Buchanan, 1961). First are those that accrue from the geographical propinquity of industries and services in general, usually referred to as 'urbanization economies' (Hoover, 1970). The second category is usually referred to as 'locational economies' and embraces those economies that arise from the geographical agglomeration of related economic activities. It is the second category of geographical agglomerations or 'clusters' that in particular have been selected in recent years by scholars from a number of different disciplines as *the* territorial configuration most likely of enhancing learning processes.[3]

Some justification for this choice has been found in empirical studies showing, for instance, how 'innovative activity, as measured by patent data, and the location of high-tech industries is...highly concentrated' (Breschi, 1995), and how the agglomeration of firms within one or a few interrelated industries in the Italian industrial districts gave rise to superior performance and some of the highest regional income levels in Europe (Bellandi, 1989). Today, Silicon Valley and Hollywood are probably the world's best-known examples of successful non-random market-led clusters.[4]

Presumably, clusters of related firms have been contributing to economic growth for quite a while but the contemporary turn towards a knowledge-based economy (Carter, 1994) in many parts of the world has certainly sharpened our interest in understanding the nature of this process.[5]

The existing literature provides two types of understanding of the phenomenon. One source of insight is to be found in ideographic, historical work on how clusters have originated and developed into fruition, occasionally accompanied by accounts of subsequent descents (Malmberg and Maskell, 2002). Another attempts to specify conceptually the mechanisms that provide advantages to be reaped by firms located in a cluster. The present chapter is concerned with the latter aspect. It suggests a way of structuring our perception regarding how the cluster might partake in knowledge creation. In dealing with this issue, it is moves mainly within the world of concepts, raising a set of questions regarding the way in which economic performance is related to space in general, and to the role of localized learning in particular.

The aim of the chapter is thus to investigate the nature of the cluster when knowledge creation becomes key. It does not necessarily assert that learning and innovations take place in the cluster only or deny that a good portion of all firms is happily located outside the cluster. Neither does the focus on the cluster exclude the fact that circumstances, events, and decisions in distant parts of the world heavily influence many firms today. It merely presupposes that the cluster plays a role in knowledge creation that is by and large sufficiently important to affect what is going on in the world to warrant analysis.

The chapter is structured along the following lines. Section 15.2 looks briefly into previous cost-based accounts of how firms might benefit when being part of a cluster. It is suggested that such approaches often fall short when addressing the more fundamental question of the cluster: the existence of many co-localized firms in related industries rather than a single, but larger entity, carrying the same tasks. It is proposed that the reason for the existence of the cluster can be found in the enhanced knowledge creation that takes place along its horizontal and vertical dimensions. In section 15.3, the learning advantages stemming from the intrinsic variation between co-localized firms with similar capabilities is discussed, while Section 15.4 deals with the division of labor and the interaction taking place among firms along the cluster's vertical dimension. The various factors contributing to the growth of the cluster are sketched out in Section 15.5 before moving to the more detailed discussion on the boundaries of the cluster. In Section 15.6 it is suggested that the boundaries can be defined by the interdependence between certain kinds of economic activities on the one hand and their appropriate institutional framework on the other. An institutional endow-ment favorable towards one kind of economic activity can be hostile to others. The very reasons for why cognitive distance might be small within the cluster will, it is asserted, make the cognitive distance very great between clusters. When access to dissimilar bodies of knowledge is required in product innovation, too much clustering becomes perhaps a burden and further clustering ceases. Section 15.7 considers the policy challenges and options relevant in three different stages of the cluster's proposed life cycle. The final section points to areas where future research is needed to expand and elaborate on the theory of the cluster.

15.2 The Existence of the Cluster

At least since Alfred Marshall's initial reflections on localized industries and the industrial district were published in his 'Principles of Economics' in 1890 scholars from a range of different fields have regularly concerned themselves with the issue.[6] The bulk of the studies in most of the next century were, however, mainly ideographic and the reasons why firms cluster were assumed or implied rather than carefully investigated and specified. It was almost as if the benefits associated with the cluster were considered self-evident enough to require little discussion (Feser, 1999). When an explanation was offered it was usually based on a model where the balance between centripetal and centrifugal forces determined the locational pattern of firms. The dispersing forces normally included the costs of congestion, or the bidding-up of prices for land and labor. The concentrating forces were, in contrast, often identified as the cost advantages in transportation or when sharing an environment made particularly agreeable by, for instance, a dedicated infrastructure, a pool of notably skilled labor, an educational systems of distinctive relevance, etc.

This model largely disappeared as the swelling interest in the clusters towards the end of the twentieth century occasioned a number of novel research propositions to unfold.[7] Instead, the main emphasis shifted towards explanations more or less explicitly based on transactions costs including search and information costs, bargaining and decision costs, as well as policing and enforcement costs (Babbage 1832; Dahlman, 1979).[8] As Coase pointed out:

> In order to carry out a market transaction, it is necessary to discover who it is that one wishes to deal with, to inform people that one wishes to deal and on what terms, to conduct negotiations leading up to a bargain, to draw up a contract, to undertake the inspection needed to make sure that the terms of the contract are being observed, and so on. These operations are often extremely costly, sufficiently costly at any rate to prevent many transactions that would be carried out in a world in which the pricing system worked without cost. (Coase, 1960, p. 15)

Much in this spirit, some of the recent cluster studies have emphasized how the local activity will rise and the economic growth rate increase when the co-localization of firms benefit from the information easily available on potential partners in the vicinity and, perhaps more importantly, by the ease to conduct business with such local firms. The reason for the latter is found in the behavioral constraint imposed on co-localized firms by the knowledge of the unattractive consequences of misbehaving. In a cluster, it will immediately be noticed if a firm attempts to overutilize asymmetrical information; or pass defective or substandard goods as first class; or create hold-ups in order to benefit at the expense of others in the local milieu. The information of such misbehavior will be passed on to everyone, who in the future will tend to take their business elsewhere. Worse still, by becoming a local outcast the firm is deprived of the flow of knowledge, including its tacit parts, which can prove very difficult to substitute. Co-localized firms will therefore, it is asserted, often benefit from the emergence of a general climate of understanding and trust[9] that help reduce malfeasance, induce reliable information to be volunteered, cause agreements to be honored, place negotiators on the same wavelength, and ease the sharing of tacit knowledge.

The cluster thus exists, it is often implied, because the co-location of firms cuts the expenses of identifying, accessing, or exchanging products, services or, not least, knowledge between firms.

However, it is not always realized that such costs might be eliminated altogether by joining the different activities and placing them under one common authority or ownership. When it comes to reducing transaction costs only, the single firm is superior to all market configurations imaginable – even to the high-trust cluster. The benefits of substituting interfirm interaction with the managerial authority of a single firm is, incidentally, one of the most significant reasons identified in the management literature for the birth and rise of the successful multinational enterprise as Teece, among others, has observed:

Internal trading changes the incentives of the parties and enables the firm to bring managerial control devices to bear on the transaction, thereby attenuating costly haggling and disruptions and other manifestations of non-co-operative behavior. Exchange can then proceed at lower cost and with higher returns to the participants. (Teece, 1980, p. 232)

The joining together of co-localized firms in related industries under one common ownership will, in addition to possible scale economies,[10] both help to align incentives and to diminish transaction costs.[11] It seems to follow that no theory attempting to explain the existence of the cluster can be based on the advantages of scale or the advantages of curtailed information, transaction, or transport costs only.[12]

In order to get a grip on the problem at hand we need to start by recognizing how the continued formation and survival of the cluster attest that the total economic effect of curtailed transport, information, and transaction costs as well as of scale advantages are *inferior* to the locational economies available when *being separate firms*.

The advantages of proximate specialized suppliers and customers in the cluster is in principle equally available to one big firm as to, say, 20 smaller firms doing similar things. Similarly, the advantages related to skill formation at the local labor market are not likely to be greater for 20 co-localized firms of a given size as for a single firm, 20 times as big.

But what then *are* the advantages of N co-localized firms of size S undertaking related activities that are not transferable to a single firm of size $S \times N$ doing the same? This is arguably the single most important question for understanding the existence of the cluster, yet largely ignored in the conversation on the subject.

In order to structure the discussion that follows I find Richardson's (1972) now classical dichotomy helpful when distinguishing between the horizontal dimension of the cluster, consisting of firms with similar capabilities that carry out similar activities, and the vertical dimension composed of firms with dissimilar but complementary capabilities that carry out complementary activities.[13] Richardson explains:

Now it is quite clear that similarity and complementarity . . . are quite distinct; clutch linings are complementary to clutches and to cars but, in that they are best made by firms with a capability in asbestos fabrication, they are similar to drain-pipes and heat-proof suits. Similarly, the production of porcelain insulators is complementary to that of electrical switchgear but similar to other ceramic manufacture. And while the activity of retailing toothbrushes is complementary to their manufacture, it is similar to the activity of retailing soap. (Richardson, 1972, p. 889)

Complementarity between firms signals scope for fruitful exchange, while similarity in capabilities among and between firms spells contest and market encounter. The firms in the vertical dimension of the cluster will, accordingly, often be business partners and collaborators. The horizontal dimension will, on the contrary, consist mainly of rivals and competitors. Both dimensions contain features that might contribute in explaining the existence of the cluster and both will in turn be looked into below.

15.3 The Horizontal Dimension of the Cluster

Alfred Marshall (1890) long ago hinted at an explanation for the existence of the cluster along the horizontal dimension of the cluster. Marshall's reflection concerns the advantages of variation that are caused by the parallel performance of similar tasks. It is based on the conjecture that firms (i.e. owners, managers, and employees) have different perceptive powers, divergent insights, and unlike attitudes. Their different valuation of the information at hand result from an idiosyncratic and at least partly tacit way by which the information is initially assembled and interpreted (Casson, 1982). Consequently, firms develop a variety of solutions as an intricate part of their daily operations when holding dissimilar beliefs about their chances of success if using one of several possible approaches to similar problems (von Hayek, 1937).

Even when trying hard it would be extremely difficult and often impossible for a single, multidivisional firm to replicate internally the process of parallel experimentation and testing of a variety of approaches that take place among a group of independent firms doing similar things in the cluster. For, as Loasby points out:

Competing visions between firms are necessary features of an evolutionary or experimental economy. But competing visions within firms, unless very carefully managed, and limited in scope, cause trouble. (Loasby, 2000, p. 11)

Co-localized firms undertaking similar activities find themselves in a situation where every difference in the solutions chosen, however small, can be observed and compared. While it might be easy for firms to blame the inadequate local factor market when confronted with the superior performance of competitors located far away, it is less convincing when the premium producer is located down the street. The sharing of common conditions, opportunities, and threats make the strength and weaknesses of each individual firm apparent to the management, the owners, the employees, and everyone else in the cluster who cares to take an interest. Co-location, furthermore, provide firms with an arsenal of instruments to obtain and understand even the most subtle, elusive, and complex information of possible relevance developed along the horizontal dimension of the cluster.

It is by watching, discussing, and comparing dissimilar solutions often emerging from the everyday practices that firms along the horizontal dimension of the cluster become increasingly engaged in the process of learning and continuous improvement, on which their survival depends. Harrison C. White saw this very clearly in his account for the essence of competition:[14]

Markets are self-reproducing social structures among specific cliques of firms and other's actors who evolve roles from observing each other's behavior. I argue that the key fact is that producers watch each within a market. Within weeks after Roger Bannister broke the four-minute mile, others were doing so because they defined realities and rewards by watching what other 'producers' did, not by guessing and speculating on what the crowds wanted or the judges said. Markets are not defined by a set of buyers, as some of our habits of speech suggest, nor are the producers obsessed with speculations on an amorphous demand. I insist that what a firm does in a market is to watch the competition in terms of observables. (White, 1981, p. 518)

If the firms operating along the horizontal dimension of the cluster were to be spread thinly throughout a large city among many unrelated businesses their ability to monitor and subsequently learn from each other's mistakes and successes would be severely restricted. In the focused and transparent environment of the cluster, successful experiments can more easily be distinguished from the less successful by the knowledgeable local observers. Sharing a communal social culture including collective beliefs, values, conventions, and language often significantly assists them in this process. Promising avenues identified by one firm become available to others. Even when carefully guarded or protected by a patent, enough information often leaks out to set local competitors on the track and enable them to 'invent around' the protection (Mansfield et al., 1981; Mansfield, 1985). Firms along the horizontal dimension of the cluster are constantly given the opportunity to imitate the proven or foreseeable success of others while adding some ideas of their own.

The resulting enhanced knowledge creation following from the ongoing sequence of variation, monitoring, comparison, selection, and imitation of identified superior solutions is in essence why N similar firms of size S is not equal to one firm of size $N \times S$ doing the same.

The advantages suggested stem from the specific forms of knowledge creation available to the individual firm when pursuing self-defined objectives, but not to the division of a larger entity where instructions are received and actions restrained by some procedure or limitation imposed from above.

It might be worth emphasizing an essentially Darwinian feature of the process of variation; as long as the firms share a common language and certain codes that ease their interpretation of local events no trust is required as a prerequisite for learning. The sequence of variation, monitoring, comparison, selection, and imitation can take place without any close contact or even an arms-length interaction between the firms. While suppliers and customers on the other hand simply *need* to interact with each other in order to do business, competitors don't. Most relationships in the cluster will therefore be along the vertical dimension.[15] This is not the same as implying that the firms in the horizontal dimension of the cluster never co-operate by helping each other in overcoming technical problems, by lending materials and swapping surplus capacity or by exchanging information. In fact, they may interact regularly, even intimately so, in order to forward some particular scheme (Allen, 1983). On the other hand, they might just as well hate each other intensely, never exchanging anything useful but still be able to benefit from their proximity by the mechanisms outline above.

The proposition put forward here simply suggests that the cluster exists because of locational economies *that are largely independent of the internal degree of interaction*. The sole requirement is that *many firms undertaking similar activities* are placed in circumstances by co-locating where they can monitor each other constantly, closely, and almost without effort or costs.

Other arguments for the existence of the cluster can be found along the vertical dimension of the cluster and we shall turn to these next.

15.4 The Vertical Dimension of the Cluster

The vertical dimension of the cluster consists of firms linked through input–output relations.[16] Specialized suppliers and critical customers become attracted to the cluster, once established, by the particular opportunities available. The vertical dimension of the cluster might, however, also be developed by task partitioning, which tend to evolve spontaneously when economic agents are free to pursue their own advantage, as pointed out by Adam Smith more than 250 years ago:

In a tribe of hunters and shepherds a particular person makes bows and arrows, with more readiness and dexterity than any other. He frequently exchanges them for cattle or for venison with his companions; and he finds at last that he can in this manner get more cattle and venison than if he himself went to the field to catch them. From a regard to his own interest therefore, the making of bows and arrows grows to be his chief business, and he becomes a sort of armourer. (Smith 1776, p. 119)

Some firms will thus gradually move from the horizontal to the vertical dimension of the cluster by concentrating on some particular process, where they believe they possess or might develop certain lucrative capabilities, dissimilar to others. Such distinct capabilities, once developed, will gradually be improved through a continuing process of learning-by-doing. As the cluster's vertical dimension develops and firms become more specialized they often find solutions to problems otherwise overlooked and bypassed, even when specializing in performing some particularly trivial tasks. An extended division of labor is therefore often closely associated with an acceleration of the growth of knowledge in the cluster.

The steady deepening of the division of labor is limited not only by the extent of the market,[17] but also by information asymmetries and the costs of co-ordination. Knowledge dispersed needs to be reassembled in order to be useful and firms need to co-operate in matching their related plans in advance since '... the one that make the heads of the pins must be certain of the cooperation of the one who makes the points if he does not want to run the risk of producing pin heads in vain' (List, 1841, p. 150).

In addition, firms hold asymmetrical knowledge about products and market opportunities. These asymmetries arise as an unavoidable consequence of the way in which knowledge is produced. Interfirm learning is therefore always subject to both thresholds, before the knowledge bases of firms divided have grown sufficiently apart for interacting to imply learning, and ceilings, after which the cognitive distance become too great for firms to bridge, and where learning, consequentially, will cease.

Firms in the cluster might have some advantages on both accounts compared to outsiders. The spatially defined community that often emerges when related firms co-locate makes it easier for them to co-ordinate and to bridge communication gaps resulting from heterogeneous knowledge endowments (Eliasson, 1996) and understand motives and desires that in other circumstances would remain opaque. By reducing the costs of co-ordination and by overcoming problems of asymmetrical information the process of clustering tilts the balance in favor of further specialization so that a higher level of knowledge creation might be obtained. The main advantages are not the ease of intracluster interaction as such, as our manner of speech sometimes seems to suggest, but the deepening of the knowledge base that it enables.

The analysis thus so far suggests a reason for the existence of the cluster along the vertical dimension supplementing the one offered in the previous section on the horizontal dimension. When creating an appropriate vertical differentiation new economic activities become possible, knowledge creation is forwarded, and the resulting extension of the internal market help make the process self-reinforcing (Young, 1928).

There is, however, an upper limit to the benefits that might arise from this process. If all firms in the cluster hold complementary capabilities while no two firms hold similar capabilities, then all learning through variation and monitoring must necessarily cease. A continued division of labor among firms in the cluster might thus only be expedient for the overall knowledge creation up to a certain point. Beyond that, the benefits might be offset by the corresponding reduction in knowledge creation as variation is diminished and fewer possible avenues of progress are tried out in parallel. Only by a steady increase in the number of firms in the cluster would it be possible to create knowledge simultaneously by variation and by the division of labor.

15.5   The Boundaries of the Cluster

The processes of knowledge creation along the horizontal and vertical dimensions of the cluster are rooted in the day-to-day operations of the firms but influenced by a complex set of institutions developed over time.[18] Some of these institutions are of a general nature, equally applicable and useful for promoting the economic activity in all clusters, or at least in a large number of clusters, almost regardless of the particular activities carried out by the firms located there. The emergence of general formal constraints, communal regimes of appropriation and a common climate of understanding and trust, discussed above, belongs to this category.[19]

Other institutions have, however, a definite scope and will differ from one cluster to the next.[20] It is reasonable to assume that the cluster's particular set of institutions has emerged as a response to the special requirements of the activities performed in the cluster.[21] There is thus a fundamental *interdependence* between the economic structure and the institutions of the cluster as they have developed over time.[22]

At a more operational level the interdependence is often even more pronounced. Infrastructure[23] becomes dedicated to the tasks at hand as does the routines that emerge when certain kinds of activities geared towards certain purposes or markets come to dominate the local economy. It has been suggested that while the cluster's particular set of activities affects what is done within and among the firms in the cluster and therefore *what is learnt*, it is the institutions and practices in the cluster that define how things are done and consequently *how learning takes place* (Lundvall and Maskell, 2000).

Just as the set of firms undertaking similar and complementary activities differ between clusters, so do institutions and related operational practices. Different activities each have their own mode of learning that gives rise to different practices that in turn assist the firms of the cluster when facing the challenges and opportunities presented by changes in the outside world.

The significance of an appropriate *fit* between industry and institution also suggest why certain types of activity are never found in the same cluster. A cluster producing fashion wear or financial services will simultaneously develop (dissimilar) institutions that most likely will turn out to be alien to the production of ships, coal, or cars.

The restrained ability to 'stretch' an institutional endowment to serve different kinds of economic activities equally well might also partake in explaining why new clusters emerge; when knowledge grows and the economic activity begins to differentiate, requirements start to depart and new clusters are likely to be established with institutions of their own.

The boundaries of the cluster might therefore be defined by the *fit* between the economic activities carried out by the related firms of the cluster on the one hand and the particular institutional endowment developed over time to assist these activities on the other.[24] The expansion into new activities along the vertical dimension of the cluster ceases to be feasible when the fit begins to weaken.

This framework might also account for the dispersing forces at work when the additional value created from spanning across distant bodies of knowledge must justify the additional transaction costs involved. Firms heavily engaged in interfirm innovation across usually unrelated activities and bodies of knowledge might, perhaps, be better off if not being *too* embedded in a particular cluster and, as an unavoidable consequence, be facing an even greater cognitive distance to potential partners when interaction is required.

Furthermore, the framework might provide an explanation for the demise of clusters as existing value chains at some point become fragile and new ones are being molded. As the new vertical dimension is gradually developed, the needed institutional adjustments will almost inevitably meet resistance from old incumbents struggling to survive. If some compromise is not found the resulting tension can easily lead to steady decline.

15.6 Public Policy Options

If, for the sake of brevity, we allow ourselves to assume that clusters follow a life cycle model, with stages of infancy followed by increasing maturity and subsequent stagnation or decline, the framework developed in the previous sections may be taken to suggest how each such stage can merit a set of specific public policies distinctively different from what will be generally beneficial at the other stages.

At the infant stage, when firms with complementary or similar capabilities by experimentation or conjecture have started to reap some of the benefits of co-location, the relevant public policy options are mainly *market conformist* by supporting what is already in the making and by helping to provide inputs in short supply. *Targeted* labor mobility-improving measures, *specific* educational efforts and vocational training programs, *dedicated* initiatives to enhance creativity and collaboration, physical infrastructure improvements, actions to develop *competent* seed and venture capital *sensitive to the particular requirements and structure* of the local firms through taxation relief or by redirecting public funds all belong to this set of infant-stage policies.

Most of the abundant policy ambitions and initiatives to support and develop clusters in recent years has been concerned with the next, mature, stage of cluster development. The arguments put forward in this chapter question the value of these initiatives and view them as being at least partly misdirected. Without denying that the crucial local buzz (Bathelt *et al.*, 2004) and other forms of local learning along the horizontal and vertical dimensions of the cluster is highly dependent on particular local institutional preconditions the important point is that such local learning largely takes care of itself. In contrast, it is not inward- but outward-looking measures that sometimes requires specific policy support. While co-localized firms usually have a good sense for and understanding of the relevant global technological frontiers they are less well equipped to monitor and grasp categorically new knowledge especially if differently organized. The reason is that the clustered firm's international network of contacts to suppliers, customers, and immediate competitors does not automatically include novel developments along parallel technological or commercial trajectories even when pertinent for future competitive positions. Rather than making extensive efforts in generating and promoting local buzz through various forms of social engineering the main emphasis should therefore be placed on external, translocal communication policies directed towards widening the horizon and extending the reach of the local actors by confronting them with other equally competitive or superior ways of how to organize and develop the cluster's specific products or services.[25]

Finally, when clusters for one reason or another become stagnant, or start to decline, the policy challenge shifts from being supportive to becoming creatively destructive by actively disjoining present means-ends designates and by dismantling institutions molded to accommodate and support yesterday's economic structures. By assisting communities when faced with the need to unlearn previously successful routines such policies provide cognitive and economic space for new waves of entrepreneurial activity that might subsequently help put the cluster on a new and promising track.

Interestingly, there appears to be a great local variation in the ability to unlearn. Some clusters can inaugurate novel institutions and simultaneously dissolve the obsolete, while similar or stronger efforts in other clusters are unsuccessful. In the volatile environment of the current globalizing exchange economy such 'unlearning' capabilities might turn out to be of paramount significance for the ability of clusters (as well as the larger entities of regions or even nations) to attract firms and participate in sustaining their competitiveness in an already established industry, or to build competitiveness afresh by developing new industries. In areas less fortunately equipped, the appropriate policy response is all the more formidable. In such difficult circumstances, a successful outcome of even the most energetically pursued and cleverly designed policies may appear so late that little remains to be saved. More than one initially enthusiastic development agency have, over the years, come to a complete standstill by the numerous and complex difficulties that emerge when renewal implies jeopardizing the interests of individuals or larger groups with the incentive and power to prevent or impede the process in spite of the cost of their actions to the overall society.[26] Openness, and competition among different political entities, provides the arguable best check. While local co-ordinated action is usually a blessing, too tightly knit local power groups is thus an unquestioned evil when uncomfortable decisions have to be made.

In spite of the difficulties of deliberately transforming and refurbishing stagnant or declining clusters the main target in the restructuring process is to create room for novel private-sector initiatives as swiftly and effectively as possible rather that to pursue some governmental strategy of picking the winner by applying a range of top-down measures. Countless well-meant but ineffectual cluster policies from all parts of the world seem to highlight the limits of the nation state, or whatever political authority, in creating economically sustainable competitive advantages by design from above. No kind of vogue phrasings or remolded instrument packages can apparently alter the fact that the role of policy in the development of cluster advantage can only be marginal, indirect, and long-term. Results, if any, are measured not in years but in decades.

15.7   Final Comments

The core of the argument presented in this chapter is that any economic theory of the cluster must address certain basic questions in order to be satisfactory.

First, such a theory must at the very least contain an explanation for the *existence of the cluster*. The theory must specify the process or processes that impel related firms to assemble and stay together at one place and – by doing so – make them thrive. More specifically, the theory must provide an explanation for the advantages that *many* related and co-localized firms might accrue but that are not available to a hypothetical *single* firm carrying out precisely the same activities, even if at the same location, using the same suppliers, customers, and workforce.

In the preceding sections, I have argued that the cluster exists because of the enhanced knowledge creation stemming from the variation developed along the horizontal dimension of the cluster, supported by the reduced costs of co-ordinating dispersed knowledge, of overcoming problems of asymmetrical information and aligning incentive, as well as of easing the actual transactions taking place along the vertical dimension.

Secondly, a theory of the cluster must include an explanation for the *growth of the cluster*. It must identify how new firms emerge and add to the strength of the cluster.

I have argued that the cluster, once established, acts as a selection device, attracting particular kinds of economic activity comparable with the incumbents and reducing the ambiguity and costs facing local entrepreneurs when keeping close to the activities already present.

This selection device carries with it a set of constraints that might hamper future prosperity when external changes make readjustments necessary.

Thirdly, the theory of the cluster must be able to identify *the boundaries of the cluster* by specifying why the clustering of some economic activities preclude the integration of others.

The reason forwarded in this chapter is based on the idea of a close interdependence or *fit* between the specific economic activity of a cluster and the particular institutional endowment developed. A dawning mismatch leads to decreasing returns. Negative feedback loops start to develop. Policy remedies may threaten vested interest. Local losers, keenly aware of their possible loss, often try to direct the political process so as to foil the changes that adversely affect them.

There are other important aspects that require further consideration in subsequent research: The question of the *internal organization* will, for instance, be concerned with the ways that different configurations within the cluster might influence its knowledge-creating abilities. The theory of the cluster might also be asked to further specify the reasons for the decline of the formerly successful cluster.

Maybe, over time, new research will also make us able to tell whether the possible mismatch between a slowly adjusting institutional endowment and the highly dynamic requirements of many contemporary industries is the primary reason why innovative firms also survive and prosper without being supported by the many proposed advantages of the cluster. The theory of the cluster will not be complete until we more fully understand the successful solitarian.

Notes

1. This chapter is a modified version of a paper I initially published in *Industrial and Corporate Change* (2001) vol. 10, no. 4, pp. 921–944 under the title 'Towards a knowledge-based theory of the geographical cluster'.
2. The role of ubiquities in changing the competitive environment is discussed in more detail in Maskell *et al.* (1998) and in Maskell and Malmberg (1999).
3. The terms 'geographical agglomeration' or 'cluster' are used almost synonymously in the literature together with 'industrial agglomeration' or 'localization', while the term 'industrial district' initially used by Marshall (1890) for the result of locational economies is now often applied when wishing explicitly to emphasize the values and norms shared by co-localized firms (see, for instance, Brusco, 1982).
4. In order to exclude 'random' agglomerations the number of co-localized firms must be larger than if no locational economies are present (Ellison and Glaeser, 1994; Malmberg and Maskell, 1997).
5. The swelling interest has occasioned a number of distinct schools of thought to develop including the GREMI approach (Maillat, 1991, 1998; Camagni, 1995; Ratti *et al.*, 1998), the many largely Marshallian studies of the Italian industrial districts (Brusco 1986, 1999; Brusco and Righi 1989; Beccatini, 1990; Garofoli 1992*a*, 1992*b*, 1993; Dei Ottati, 1994*a*, 1994*b*, 1996; Bellandi, 1996; Gottardi, 1996; Belussi, 1999*a*, 1999*b*), the French 'proximité' tradition (Blanc and Sierra, 1999; Kirat and Lung, 1999), an econometric type of cluster analysis (Swann *et al.*, 1998), different 'systemic' analysis (Markusen *et al.*, 1986; Saxenian, 1994; Malecki, 1991) some of which have focused explicitly on the geography of innovation (Feldman, 1994; Stenberg, 1999; Breschi, 2000), as well as the cherished approach applied by Porter (1990). Most recently has a broader 'knowledge school' emerged (see Loasby, 1999 and Malmberg, 1996, 1997 for an overview).

6. Since the outstanding contributions by Marshall (1890, 1919), major works have been published by Weber (1909), Hoover (1948), Perroux (1950), Hirschman (1958), Ullman (1958), Jacobs (1961), Chinitz (1961), Greenhut (1970), and Pred (1976, 1977).

7. Accounts of this literature can be found in Harrison (1992), Norton (1992), Baptista (1998), Storper (1995), Bianchi (1998), and Yeung (2000).

8. Other costs of using the market include the cost of establishing the appropriate incentive arrangements (Foss, 1993).

9. Trust is, in most of this literature, defined along the lines suggested by Glaeser *et al.* (1999) as the commitment of resources to an activity where the outcome depends upon the co-operative behavior of others.

10. Economies of scale might be defined as those that result when the increased size of a single operating unit reduces the unit cost of production or distribution.

11. Babbage (1832), for instance, observed how flour could be purchased cheaper on the market than if the government produced it themselves. Nevertheless, the latter course of action was preferred rather than to carry the costs of verifying each sack of flour purchased. Information asymmetries give rise to monitoring costs that make authority more efficient than market governance.

12. Historically, the agglomeration literature has been abundant with case studies showing how transport and time economics can be important elements in propelling individual firms to co-locate. Recently, some more rigorous work has been conducted in this area (e.g. Harrigan and Venables, 2004). The point I wish to make in this section is at a more fundamental level by addressing the reason for the continued existence of individual firms even when mergers, acquisitions, or outright selection appears to be even more advantageous than mere co-localization.

13. Activities are defined broadly by Richardson (1972, p. 888) as 'related to the discovery and estimation of future wants, to research, development and design, to the execution and co-ordination of processes of physical transformation, the marketing of goods and so on'.

14. White's proposition can be found in several later works and his idea is at the core of Porter's (1990) concept of rivalry.

15. This theoretical point has been supported by empirical findings (Håkanson, 1987).

16. The product innovation literature has firmly established that firms learn from each other when interacting. See, for instance, Rosenberg (1972), Freeman (1982, 1991), Håkansson (1987), Kline and Rosenberg (1986), Hagedoorn and Schakenraad (1992), and OECD (1992).

17. See Smith (1776), Young (1928), and Stigler (1951).

18. See Cannan (1912). We might here follow North (1994, p. 360) in defining institutions as 'humanly devised constraints that structure human interaction. They are made up of formal constraints (e.g. rules, laws constitutions), informal constraints (e.g. norms of behavior, conventions, self-imposed codes of conduct), and their enforcement characteristics ... '

19. It might be argued that the specific way by which trust is obtained will make it differ from cluster to cluster and that very few 'general institutions' can therefore be expected to be found in practice.

20. This emphasis on the difference of institutional endowments across space is in line with much of the innovation systems literature (Lundvall, 1992; Nelson,

1993) and with recent work on knowledge architectures (Amin and Cohendet, 2004).

21. On the national level, recent research has shown the existence of such a correlation between patterns of specialization in production and trade, on the one hand, and the knowledge base on the other (Archibugi and Pianta, 1992).

22. Some argue that the differences emanate mainly from structural characteristics (Breschi and Malerba, 1997) while others look at how institutional specificities affect the location of certain industries (Guerrieri and Tylecote, 1997). See also Gertler (1995, 1996, 1998), Maskell and Törnqvist (1999), Maskell (2000), and Maskell *et al.* (1998).

23. In addition to the physical infrastructure, we might add Smith's (1997) economic (knowledge) infrastructures that result from conscious policy decisions and investment programs and include special programs in local schools and universities, government-supported technical institutions and training centers, specialized apprenticeship programs, etc.

24. If no such mechanism restricted the cluster's institutional endowment to a *certain kind of related industries only*, we would ultimately expect to end up with a single and rather large cluster containing all the economic activity now residing anywhere in the global economy.

25. This is, of course, but a modern interpretation of John Stuart Mill's initial reflection that '... the economical advantages of commerce are surpassed in importance by those of its effects which are intellectual and moral. It is hardly possible to overrate the value ... of placing human beings in contact with persons dissimilar to themselves, and with modes of thought and action unlike those with which they are familiar.... Such communication has always been ... one of the primary sources of progress' (Mill, 1848/1987, p. 581).

26. Friedrichs (1993), in proposing a theory of urban decline, gives several examples of how local élites, made up by corporate management, trade unions, and urban/regional managers or politicians, when trying to protect their vested interests, tend to form alliances that act to prevent structural change in periods when previously dominating local industries are fading or dying away. In the steel industry, for instance, the 'Ruhr patriarchate' in Germany or the 'steel aristocrats' in Pittsburgh have played such roles during an extended period.

References

Allen, R. C. (1983), 'Collective invention'. *Journal of Economic Behaviour and Organization*, **4**: 1–24.

Amin, A. and Cohendet, P. (2004), *Architectures of knowledge. Firms, capabilities and communities*, Oxford: Oxford University Press.

Archibugi, D. and Pianta, M. (1992), *The technological specialization of advanced countries*, Dordrecht: Kluwer.

Babbage, C. (1832), *On the economy of machinery and manufactures*, London: Charles Knight.

Baptista, R. (1998), 'Clusters, innovation and growth: A survey of the literature', in P. G. M. Swann, M. Prevezer, and D. Stout (eds), *The dynamics of industrial clustering.*

International comparisons in computing and biotechnology. Oxford: Oxford University Press, pp. 13–51.

Bathelt, H., Malmberg, A., and Maskell, P. (2004), 'Clusters and knowledge: local buzz, global pipelines and the process of knowledge creation'. *Progress in Human Geography*, **28**(1): 31–56.

Baumard, P. (1996), 'Organizations in the fog: an investigation into the dynamics of knowledge', in B. Moingeon and A. Edmondson (eds), *Organizational learning and competitive advantage.* London: Sage.

Becattini, G. (1990), 'The Marshallian industrial districts as a socio-economic notion', in F. Pyke, G. Becattini, and W. Sengenberger (eds), *Industrial districts and inter-firm co-operation in Italy.* Geneva: International Institute for Labour Studies, pp. 37–51.

Bellandi, M. (1989), 'The industrial district in Marshall', in E. Goodman and J. Bamford (eds), *Small firms & industrial districts in Italy.* Routledge: London.

Bellandi, M. (1996), 'Innovation and change in the Marshallian industrial district.' *European Planning Studies*, **4**(3): 357–368.

Belussi, F. (1999*a*), 'Path-Dependency vs. industrial dynamics: an analysis of two heterogeneous districts'. *Human Systems Management*, **18**: 161–174.

Belussi, F. (1999*b*), 'Policies for the development of knowledge-intensive local production systems'. *Cambridge Journal of Economics*, **23**: 729–747.

Bianchi, G. (1998), 'Requiem for the Third Italy? rise and fall of a too successful concept'. *Entrepreneurship and Regional Development*, **10**: 93–116.

Blanc, H. and Sierra, C. (1999), 'The internationalisation of R&D by multinationals: a trade-off between external and internal proximity'. *Cambridge Journal of Economics*, **23**(2): 187–206.

Breschi, S. (1995), *Identifying regional patterns of innovation using patent data.* Paper presented at the workshop on 'Regional Innovation Systems, Regional Networks and Regional Policy', Organized by the STEP group at Lysebu Conference Centre (Oslo), Norway, October 27–29.

Breschi, S. (2000), 'The geography of innovation: a cross-sector analysis'. *Regional Studies*, **34**(3): 213–230.

Breschi, S. and Malerba, F. (1997), 'Sectoral innovation systems', in C. Edquist (eds), *Systems of innovation: technologies, institutions and organizations,* London: Pinter Publishers.

Brusco, S. (1982), 'The Emilian model: productive decentralisation and social integration'. *Cambridge Journal of Economics*, **6**(2): 167–184.

Brusco, S. (1986), 'Small firms and industrial districts: the experience of Italy', in D. Keeble and E. Wever. (eds), *New firms and regional development in Europe. London: Croom Helm*, pp. 184–202.

Brusco, S. (1999), 'The rules of the game in industrial districts', in A. Grandori (eds), *Interfirm networks. Organization and industrial competitiveness.* London: Routledge, pp. 17–40.

Brusco, S. and Righi, E. (1989), 'Local government, industrial policy and social consensus: The case of Modena'. *Economy and Society*, **18**(4): 405–424.

Camagni, R. P. (1995), 'The concept of innovative milieu and its relevance for public policies in European lagging regions', *Papers in Regional Science*, **74**(4): 317–340.

Cannan, E. (1912), *The history of local rates in England in relation to the propor distribution of the burden of taxation,* London: P. S. King & Son, Orchard House.

Carter, A. P. (1994), *Measuring the Performance of a Knowledge-based Economy*. Working Paper no. 337, Brandeis: Brandeis University, Departments of Economics.

Casson, M. (1982), *The entrepreneur. An economic theory*, Oxford: Martin Robertson.

Chinitz, B. (1961), 'Contrasts in agglomeration: New York and Pittsburgh'. *American Economic Review*, **LI**(2): 279–289.

Coase, R. H. (1960), 'The Problem of social cost'. *Journal of Law and Economics*, **3**: 1–44.

Dahlman, C. J. (1979), 'The problem of externality'. *Journal of Law and Economics*, **22**(1): 141–162.

Dei Ottati, G. (1994a), 'Co-operation and competition in the industrial district as an organisational model'. *European Planning Studies*, **2**: 463–483.

Dei Ottati, G. (1994b), 'Case study I: Prato and its evolution in a European context', in R. Leonardi, and R. Y. Nanetti (eds), *Regional development in a modern European economy: The case of Tuscany*. London: Pinter Publishers, pp. 116–144.

Dei Ottati, G. (1996), 'Trust, interlinking transactions and credit in the industrial districts'. *Cambridge Journal of Economics*, **18**: 529–546.

Eliasson, G. (1996), *Firm objectives, controls and organization. The use of information and the transfer of knowledge within the firm*, Dordrecht: Kluwer Academic Publishers.

Ellison, G. and Glaeser, E. L. (1994), *Geographical concentration in the US manufacturing industries. A dartboard approach*. Working Paper no. 4840, Cambridge, MA: National Bureau of Economic Research (NBER).

Estall, R. C. and Buchanan, R. O. (1961), *Industrial activity and economic geography*, London: Hutchinson.

Feser, E. J. (1999), 'Old and new theories of industrial clusters', in M. Steiner (eds), *Clusters and regional specialisation. On geography, technology and networks*. London: Pion, pp. 19–40.

Feldmann, M. P. (1994), *The geography of innovation*, Dordrecht: Kluwer.

Foss, N. J. (1993), 'More on Knight and the theory of the firm'. *Managerial and Decision Economics*, **14**: 269–276.

Freeman, C. (1982), *The economics of industrial innovation*, London: Pinter Publishers.

Freeman, C. (1991), 'Networks of innovators: A synthesis of research issues'. *Research Policy*, **20**(5): 5–24.

Friedrichs, J. (1993), 'A theory of urban decline. Economy, democracy and political elites', *Urban Studies*, **30**(6): 907–917.

Garofoli, G. (1992a), 'Industrial districts: Structure and transformation', in G. Garofoli, (eds), *Endogenous development and Southern Europe*. Aldershot: Avebury, pp. 49–60.

Garofoli, G. (1992b), 'The Italian model of spatial development in the 1970s and 1980s', in G. Benko and M. Dunford (eds), *Industrial change and regional development*. London: Bellhaven Press, pp. 85–101.

Garofoli, G. (1993), 'Economic Development, Organization of Production and Territory'. *Revue d'Économie Industrielle*, **64** (2e trimestre 1993): 22–37.

Gertler, M. S. (1995), '"Being there": proximity, organization, and culture in the development and adaptation of advanced manufacturing techologies'. *Economic Geography*, **71**: 1–26.

Gertler, M. S. (1996), 'Worlds apart: the changing market geography of German machinery industry'. *Small Business Economics*, **8**: 87–106.

Gertler, M. S. (1998), 'The Invention of Regional Culture', in R. Lee and J. Wills (eds), *Geographies of economies*. London–New York–Sydney–Auckland: Hodder Headline Group, pp. 47–58.

Glaeser, E. L., Laibson, C. L., Scheinkman, J. A., and Soutter, C. L. (1999), *What is social capital? The determinants of trust and trustworthiness.* Working paper no. 7216, Cambridge, MA: NBER.

Gottardi, G. (1996), 'Technology strategies, innovation without R&D and the creation of knowledge within industrial districts'. *Journal of Industry Studies*, **3**(2): 119–134.

Greenhut, M. L. (1970), *A theory of the firm in economic space*, New York: Appleton-Century-Crofts.

Guerrieri, P. and Tylecote, A. (1997), 'Interindustry differences in technical change and national patterns of technological accumulation', in C. Edquist (ed.), *Systems of innovation: technologies, institutions and organizations*, London: Pinter Publishers.

Hagedoorn, J. and Schakenraad, J. (1992), 'Leading companies and networks of strategic alliances in information technologies'. *Research Policy*, **21**: 163–181.

Håkansson, H. (ed.) (1987), *Industrial technology development – a network approach.* London: Croom Helm.

Harrigan, J. and Venables, A. J. (2004), *Timeliness, Trade and Agglomeration.* Working Paper no. 10404, Cambridge, MA: National Bureau of Economic Research (NBER).

Harrison, B. (1992), 'Industrial districts. Old wine in new bottles?' *Regional Studies*, **26**: 469–483.

Hirschman, A. O. (1958), *The strategy of economic development*, Clinton MA: Yale University Press.

Hoover, E. M. (1948), *The location of economic activity*, New York: McGraw-Hill Book Company.

Hoover, E. M. (1970), *An introduction to regional economics*, New York: Alfred A. Knopf.

Jacobs, J. (1961), *The death and life of great American cities*, New York: Random House.

Kirat, T. and Lung, Y. (1999), 'Innovation and proximity: territories as loci of collective learning processes'. *European Urban and Regional Studies*, **6**(1): 27–38.

Kline, S. J. and Rosenberg, N. (1986), 'An overview of innovation', in: R. Landau, and N. Rosenberg (eds), *The positive sum games*, Washington, D.C.: National Academy Press.

Laestadius, S. (1996), *Technology level, knowledge formation, and industrial competence within paper manufacturing.* Working paper: Kungliga Tekniska Högskolan, Department of Industrial Economics and Management.

List, F. (1841), *The national system of political economy*, London: Longmans, Green and Co.

Loasby, B. J. (1999), 'Industrial districts as knowledge communities', in M. Bellet and C. L'Harmet, C. (eds), *Industry, space and competition. The contribution of economistc of the past.* Cheltenham: Edward Elgar, pp. 70–85.

Loasby, B. J. (2000) *Organisations as interpretative systems.* Paper presented at the DRUID Summer Conference, Rebild, Denmark (www.business.auc.dk/DRUID).

Lundvall, B.-Å. (eds) (1992), *National systems of innovation: towards a theory of innovation and interactive learning.* London: Pinter.

Lundvall, B.-Å. and Maskell, P. (2000), 'Nation states and economic development – From national systems of production to national systems of knowledge creation and learning', in G. L. Clark, M. P. Feldmann, and M. S. Gertler (eds), *The Oxford handbook of economic geography.* Oxford: Oxford University Press, pp. 353–372.

Maillat, D. (1991), 'Local dynamism, milieu and innovative enterprises', in: J. Brotchie, M. Batty, P. Hall, and P. Newton (eds), *Cities of the 21st century*. London: Longman.

Maillat, D. (1998), 'Innovative milieux and new generations of regional policies'. *Entrepreneurship and Regional Development*, **10**: 1–16.

Malecki, E. J. (1991), *Technology and economic development: the dynamics of local, regional and national change*, Harlow: Longman.

Malerba, F. (1992), 'Learning by firms and incremental technical change'. *Economic Journal*, **102**(413): 845–860.

Malmberg, A. (1996), 'Industrial geography. Agglomerations and local milieu'. *Progress in Human Geography*, **20**: 392–403.

Malmberg, A. (1997), 'Industrial geography: location and learning'. *Progress in Human Geography*, **21**: 573–582.

Malmberg, A. and Maskell, P. (1997), 'Towards an explanation of industry agglomeration and regional specialization'. *European Planning Studies*, **5**(1): 25–41.

Malmberg, A. and Maskell, P. (2002), 'The elusive concept of localization economies: towards a knowledge-based theory of spatial clustering'. *Environment and Planning A*, **34**(3): 429–449.

Mansfield, E., Wagner, S., and Schwartz, M. (1981), 'Imitation costs and patents: an empirical study'. *Economic Journal*, **91**: 907–918.

Mansfield, E. (1985), 'How rapidly does new technology leak out?' *Journal of Industrial Economics*, **34**: 217–223.

Markusen, A., Hall, P., and Glasmeier, A. K. (1986), *High tech America*, Boston: Allen and Unwin.

Marshall, A. (1890), *Principles of economics*, London: Macmillan.

Marshall, A. (1919), *Industry and trade. A study of industrial technique and business organization, and of their influences on the condition of various classes and nations*, London: Macmillan.

Maskell, P. (1998), 'Successful low-tech industries in high-cost environments: the case of the Danish furniture industry'. *European Urban and Regional Studies*, **5** (2): 99–118.

Maskell, P. (2001), 'Towards a knowledge-based theory of the geographical cluster'. *Industrial and Corporate Change*, **10**(4): 919–941.

Maskell, P. and Malmberg, A. (1999), 'Localised learning and industrial competitiveness'. *Cambridge Journal of Economics*, **23**(2): 167–186.

Maskell, P. and Törnqvist, G. (1999), *Building a cross-border learning region. The emergence of the Northern European Øresund region*, Copenhagen: Copenhagen Business School Press.

Maskell, P., Eskelinen, H., Hannibalsson, I., Malmberg, A., and Vatne, E. (1998), *Competitiveness, localised learning and regional development. Specialisation and prosperity in small open economies*, London: Routledge.

Mill, J. S. (1848/1987), *Principles of political economy*, 7th edn (1871) reprinted 1987 and published by Augustus M. Kelley: Fairfield.

Nelson, R. R. (ed.) (1993), *National innovation systems. A comparative analysis*. New York: Oxford University Press.

North, D. C. (1994), 'Economic performance through time'. *American Economic Review*, **84**(3): 359–368.

Norton, R. D. (1992), 'Agglomeration and competitiveness: from Marshall to Chinitz'. *Urban Studies*, **29**(2): 155–170.

OECD (1992), *Industrial policy in the OECD countries*. Annual Review Paris: The Organisation for Economic Co-operation and Development.

OECD (1999), *Boosting innovation: the cluster approach*. OECD Proceedings. Paris: The Organisation for Economic Co-operation and Development.

Perroux, F. (1950), 'Economic space, theory and applications'. *Quarterly Journal of Economics*, **LXIV**: 89–104.

Porter, M. E. (1990), *The competitive advantages of nations*, London: Macmillan.

Pred, A. (1976), 'The interurban transmission of growth in advanced economies: empirical findings versus regional-planning assumptions'. *Regional Studies*, **10**: 151–171.

Pred, A. (1977), *City systems in advanced economies. Past growth, present processes and future development options*, London: Hutchinson.

Ratti, R., Bramanti, A., and Gordon, R. (eds) (1998), *The dynamics of innovative regions. The GREMI approach*. Aldershot: Ashgate.

Richardson, G.B. (1972), 'The organisation of industry'. *Economic Journal*, **82**: 883–896.

Rosenberg, N. (1972), *Technology and American economic growth*, White Plains, NY: Sharpe.

Saxenian, A. (1994), *Regional advantage. Culture and competition in Silicon Valley and route 128*, Cambridge, MA: Harvard University Press.

Smith, A. (1776), *An inquiry into the nature and causes of the wealth of nations*, London: W. Strahan and T. Cadell.

Smith, K. (1997), 'Economic infrastructures and innovation systems', in C. Edquist (eds) *Systems of innovation: institutions, organisations and dynamics*, London: Pinter.

Spender, J.-C. (1996), 'Competitive advantage from tacit knowledge? Unpacking the concept and its strategic implications', in B. Moingeon and A. Edmondson (eds), *Organizational learning and competitive advantage*, London: Sage.

Stenberg, R. (1999), 'Innovative linkages and proximity: empirical results from recent surveys of small and medium sized firms in German regions'. *Regional Studies*, **33**: 529–540.

Stigler, G. J. (1951), 'The division of labor is limited by the extent of the market'. *Journal of Political Economy*, **LIX**(3): 185–193.

Storper, M. (1995), 'The resurgence of regional economies, ten years later: the region as a nexus of untraded interdependencies'. *European Urban and Regional Studies*, **3**(2): 191–221.

Swann, P. G. M., Prevezer, M., and Stout, D. (1998), *The dynamics of industrial clustering. International comparisons in computing and biotechnology*, Oxford: Oxford University Press.

Teece, D. J. (1980), 'Economies of scope and the scope of the enterprise'. *Journal of Economic Behavior and Organization*, **3**(1): 223–247.

Ullman, E. L. (1958), 'Regional development and the geography of concentration'. *Papers of the Regional Science Association*, **IV**: 179–198.

von Hayek, F. A. (1937), 'Economics and knowledge'. *Economica*, **IV** (New series) (13): 33–54.

Weber, A. (1909), *Über den standort der industrien*, Tübingen: J. C. B. Mohr.

White, H. C. (1981), 'Where do markets come from?' *American Journal of Sociology*, **87**(3): 517–547.

Yeung, H. W. (2000), 'Organising "the firm" in industrial geography I: networks, institutions and regional development'. *Progress in Human Geography*, 24.

Young, A. (1928), 'Increasing returns and economic progress'. *Economic Journal*, **38**: 527–542.

16

Deconstructing Clusters: Chaotic Concept or Policy Panacea?

RON MARTIN AND PETER SUNLEY

'When I use a word', Humpty Dumpty said in a rather scornful tone, 'it means just what I choose it to mean – neither more nor less' (Lewis Carroll, *Through the Looking Glass*, 1872).

For an idea ever to be fashionable is ominous, since it must afterwards be always old-fashioned (George Santayana, *Winds of Doctrine*, 1913).

16.1   Introduction: Clusters and the Reassertion of Location

In recent years, there has been a growing interest in the role of location in the global economy. Some have argued that globalization is rendering the significance of location for economic activity increasingly irrelevant (O'Brien, 1992; Cairncross, 1997; Gray, 1998). Others, however, espouse the opposite view, that globalization is actually increasing rather than reducing the importance of location, that it is promoting greater regional economic distinctiveness, and that regional economies rather than national economies are now the salient foci of wealth creation and world trade (Ohmae, 1995; Coyle, 1997, 2001; Krugman, 1997; Storper, 1997; Porter, 1998a; Scott, 1998, 2001; Fujita *et al.*, 2000). Thus, as the business economist Michael Porter puts it:

In a global economy – which boasts rapid transportation, high speed communications and accessible markets – one would expect location to diminish in importance. But the opposite is true. The enduring competitive advantages in a global economy are often heavily localised, arising from concentrations of highly specialised skills and knowledge, institutions, rivalry, related businesses, and sophisticated customers. (Porter, 1998*c*, p. 90)

At the same time, it is alleged, increasing global economic integration itself leads to heightened regional and local specialization, as falling transport costs and trade barriers allow firms to agglomerate with other similar firms in order to benefit from local external economies of scale (Krugman, 1991; Fujita *et al.*, 2000), which in their turn are thought to raise local endogenous innovation and productivity growth (see Martin and Sunley, 1998). For these and other related reasons, it has become fashionable within certain academic and policy circles to talk of the 're-emergence of regional economies' (Sabel,

1989), the 'localization of the world economy' (Krugman, 1997), and the rise of a 'global mosaic of regional economies' (Scott, 1998).

One of the most influential – indeed, the most influential – exponent of this emphasis on economic localization is Michael Porter, whose notion of industrial or business 'clusters' has rapidly become the standard concept in the field. Moreover, Porter has not only promoted the idea of 'clusters' as an analytical concept, but also as a key policy tool. As the celebrated architect and promoter of the idea, Porter himself has been consulted by policy makers the world over to help them identify their nation's or region's key business clusters or to receive his advice on how to promote them. From the OECD and the World Bank, to national governments (such as the UK, France, Germany, the Netherlands, Portugal, and New Zealand), to regional development agencies (such as the new Regional Development Agencies in the UK), to local and city governments (including various US states), policy makers at all levels have become eager to promote local business clusters. Nor has this policy interest been confined to the advanced economies: cluster policies are also being adopted enthusiastically in an expanding array of developing countries (see Doeringer and Terka, 1996; Schmitz, 2000; World Bank, 2000). Clusters, it seems, have become a world-wide fad, a sort of academic and policy fashion item.

The more so because the concept has become increasingly associated with the so-called 'knowledge economy', or what some have labeled the 'New Economy'. Norton (2001), for example, argues that the global leadership of the US in the New Economy derives precisely from the growth there of a number of large, dynamic clusters of innovative entrepreneurialism. In the US, Porter is himself leading a major policy-driven research program to 'develop a definitive framework to evaluate cluster development and innovative performance at the regional level' in order to identify the 'best practices' that can then be used 'to foster clusters of innovation in regions across the country' (Porter and Solvell, 1998; Council on Competitiveness, 2001; Porter and Ackerman, 2001; Porter and van Opstal, 2001). Likewise, the OECD (1999, 2001) sees innovative clusters as the drivers of national economic growth, and as a key policy tool for boosting national competitiveness.

But the mere popularity of a construct is by no means a guarantee of its profundity. Our argument here is that seductive though the concept is, there is much about it that is problematic, in that the rush to employ 'cluster ideas' has run ahead of many fundamental conceptual, theoretical, and empirical questions (Held, 1996; Steiner, 1998). While it is not our intention to debunk the cluster idea outright, we do argue for a much more cautious and circumspect use of the notion, especially within a policy context. We begin by asking why it is that Porter's notion of 'clusters' has gate-crashed the economic policy arena when the work of economic geographers on industrial localization, spatial agglomeration of economic activity, and the growing salience of regions in the global economy, has been largely ignored (Martin, 2001).

16.2   Why 'Clusters'?

As Porter admits, the idea of specialized industrial localization is hardly new. As is well known, Alfred Marshall, writing at the end of the nineteenth century, included a chapter in his *Principles of Economics* (1890) on 'the concentration of specialised industries in particular localities'. His characterization of these local concentrations of specialized activity was cast in terms of a simple triad of external economies: the ready availability of skilled labor, the growth of supporting and ancillary trades, and the specialization of different firms in different stages and branches of production.

A century later and Porter's neo-Marshallian cluster concept has burst on the scene. Its origins can be traced to his earlier work in the late 1980s and early 1990s on national competitive advantage and international competitiveness, in which he argued that the success of a nation's export firms depends on a favorable national 'competitive diamond' of four sets of factors: firm strategy, structure, and rivalry; factor input conditions; demand conditions; and related and supporting industries. The more developed and intense the interactions between these four sets of factors, the greater will be the productivity of the firms concerned (Porter, 1990).

Porter then argued, and this has since become his key theme, that the intensity of interaction within the 'competitive diamond' is enhanced if the firms concerned are also 'geographically localized' or 'clustered'. In his view, the geographic concentration of firms in the same industry is 'strikingly common around the world' (1990, p. 120). More specifically, he suggests that a nation's most globally competitive industries are also likely to be 'geographically clustered' within that nation. Hence, what originally started out as a way of decomposing a national economy, the competitive diamond as a group of interlinked industries and associated activities, has become a spatial metaphor, the cluster as a geographically localized grouping of interlinked businesses. The competitive diamond is the driving force making for cluster development, and simultaneously the cluster is the spatial manifestation of the competitive diamond (Fig. 16.1). The systemic nature of the diamond produces local concentration of the leading rival firms, which in its turn magnifies and intensifies the interactions between the factors. Hence, according to Porter (1990, p. 157), 'The process of clustering, and the intense interchange among industries in the cluster, also works best where the industries involved are *geographically concentrated*' (emphasis added). There is then an obvious affinity between Porter's schematic 'competitive diamond' of local business clustering and Marshall's 'triad' of external economies of industrial localization.

But Porter's cluster notion is not the only rediscovery and reinvention of Marshall's ideas to have taken place in recent years. For the past two decades or more, economic geographers have devoted considerable effort to studying

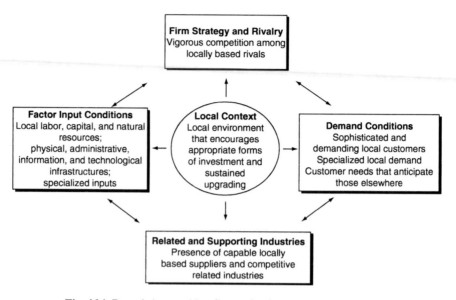

Fig. 16.1 Porter's 'competitive diamond' of local industrial clustering
(based on Porter, 1998a, Ch. 10).

local industrial specialization, spatial economic agglomeration, and regional development, and to identifying the economic, social, and institutional processes involved. They too have invented a whole series of neologisms to capture and represent the spatial form and nature of local business concentrations, including: 'industrial districts', 'new industrial spaces', 'territorial production complexes', 'neo-Marshallian nodes', 'regional innovation milieux', 'network regions', and 'learning regions' (see, for example, Scott, 1988, 1998; Amin and Thrift, 1992; Harrison, 1992; Harrison *et al.*, 1996; Markusen, 1996; Asheim, 2000). Not only is this corpus of work by economic geographers largely ignored by Porter (and by other economists who have recently discovered geography, such as Paul Krugman), in total contrast to his cluster concept their ideas have singularly failed to have any major impact on policy makers. Why then has his work proved so fashionable and influential while that of economic geographers has not? Why have some economic geographers themselves started to use cluster terminology in preference to their own (for example, Pinch and Henry, 1999; Keeble and Wilkinson, 2000; May *et al.*, 2001; Scott, 2001; Keeble and Nachum, 2002)?

One possible reason is that, from the beginning, Porter has rooted and promoted his cluster concept within an overarching focus on the determinants of 'competitiveness' (of firms, industries, nations, and now locations). This resonates closely with the growing emphasis given by politicians and policy makers to the importance of competitiveness for succeeding in today's global economy. Porter's avowed aim is to inform companies, cities, regions, and nations how to compete on the world stage, and the undoubted lure of his cluster concept is that it sits well with the current preoccupation with microeconomic supply-side intervention, and especially with the policy imperatives of raising productivity and innovation (Porter, 1996, 1998*b*, *c*, 2000*a–c*). As an alleged key determinant of competitiveness, Porter's clusters have inevitably attracted considerable interest, particularly given the emphasis he is currently assigning to geographical industrial clusters in promoting the competitive advantage of the US economy (Porter and van Opstal, 2001). Economic geographers' work on industrial localization and regional agglomeration, on the other hand, has tended to be more diffuse in its aims, and much less concerned with core issues such as the performance, productivity, and competitiveness of firms.

A second, and related, reason could be the way in which Porter has conveyed his ideas on clusters. His discussion is framed directly in terms of the economics of 'business strategy', and not in terms of the sorts of more general theoretical debates and concepts – such as 'post-Fordism', 'flexible specialization', 'modes of regulation', and so on – found in economic geography. The latter do not chime easily with, or translate readily into, practical business and policy strategy. In contrast, Porter's explicit goal 'is to develop both rigorous and useful frameworks for understanding competition that effectively bridge the gap between theory and practice' (1998*a*, p. 2). Cluster theory, he argues, is 'not only a tool for managers, but also a microeconomic-based approach to economic development for governments that is closely tied to actual competition' (1998*a*, p. 7).

At the same time, in line with this goal, his easy 'business- and policy-friendly' writing style, at once both accessible and commonsense, is undeniably seductive, and is quite different from the more 'academic' discursive approach that characterizes much economic geography writing. Reinforcing this, there can be little doubt that the popularity of Porter's cluster concept, compared to economic geographers' work on similar notions, derives in large part from his celebrated international profile as a business economist. This reputation, combined with his self-confident, authoritative, and proselytizing style, lends his cluster concept an apparent authenticity and legitimacy that policy makers have found difficult to resist. In contrast, economic geographers have had much less influence on business policy: indeed the shaping of public policy has, unfortunately, taken something of a back seat in the discipline's research agenda (Markusen, 1999; Martin, 2001).

But a third, and equally important reason for its rapturous reception is the very nature of the 'cluster concept' itself. Porter's cluster metaphor is highly generic in character, being deliberately vague and sufficiently indeterminate as to admit a very wide spectrum of industrial groupings and specializations (from footwear clusters to wine clusters to biotechnology clusters), demand-supply linkages, factor conditions, institutional set-ups, and so on, while at the same time claiming to be based on what are argued to be fundamental

processes of business strategy, industrial organization, and economic interaction. Rather than being a model or theory to be rigorously tested and
evaluated, the cluster idea has instead become accepted largely on faith as
a valid and meaningful 'way of thinking' about the national economy, as a
template or procedure with which to decompose the economy into distinct
industrial-geographic groupings for the purposes of understanding and promoting competitiveness and innovation. The very definitional incomplete-
ness of the cluster concept has been an important reason for its popularity
(Perry, 1999): clusters have 'the discreet charm of obscure objects of desire'
(Steiner, 1998, p. 1). However, although the definitional and conceptual
elasticity of the cluster concept can be seen as a positive strength, in that it
permits a wide range of cases and interpretations to be included, we consider
it to be problematic. The concept has acquired such a variety of uses,
connotations, and meanings that it has, in many respects, become a 'chaotic
concept', in the sense of conflating and equating quite different types,
processes, and spatial scales of economic localization under a single, all-
embracing universalistic notion.

16.3   A Chaotic Concept?

A major source of ambiguity is that of definition. Because Porter's definitions
are so vague, in terms of geographical scale and internal socio-economic
dynamics, this has allowed different analysts to use the idea in different ways
to suit their own purposes (see, for example, the multiplicity of interpretations used in the World Congress on Local Clusters, OECD-DATAR,
2001). The result is conceptual and empirical confusion.

The dramatist Alan Bennett tells the story of how his aged mother once
looked at sheep and said 'I know what they are, but I don't know what they're
called' (Bennett, 1994, p. 127). The situation in the cluster literature seems to
be the reverse: we know what they're called, but defining precisely what they
are is much more difficult. In his own work, Porter has defined clusters as:

Geographic concentrations of interconnected companies, specialised suppliers, service providers, firms in related industries, and associated institutions (for example,
universities, standards agencies, and trade associations) in particular fields that
compete but also co-operate. (Porter, 1998a, p. 197)

Thus, there are two core elements in Porter's definition. First, the firms in
a cluster must be linked in some way. Clusters are constituted by interconnected companies and associated institutions linked by commonalities and
complementarities. The links are both vertical (buying and selling chains),
and horizontal (complementary products and services, the use of similar
specialized inputs, technologies or institutions, and other linkages). Moreover, most of these linkages, he argues, involve social relationships or
networks that produce benefits for the firms involved. Hence,

A cluster is a form of network that occurs within a geographic location, in which the proximity of firms and institutions ensures certain forms of commonality and increases the frequency and impact of interactions (Porter, 1998a, p. 226).

The second fundamental characteristic, therefore, is that clusters are geographically proximate groups of interlinked companies. Co-location encourages the formation of, and enhances the value-creating benefits arising from, networks of interaction between firms.

The obvious problem raised by these cluster definitions is the lack of clear boundaries, both industrial and geographical. At what level of industrial aggregation should a cluster be defined, and what range of related or associated industries and activities should be included? How strong do the linkages between firms have to be? How economically specialized does a local concentration of firms have to be to constitute a cluster? There is no explicit reference in Porter's definitions that clusters are economically specialized entities in the Marshallian sense, yet all of his examples are, often very narrowly so. In addition, at what spatial scale, and over what geographical range, do clustering processes (interfirm linkages, knowledge spillovers, rivalry, business and social networks, and so on) operate? What spatial density of such firms and their interactions defines a cluster? The difficulty is not just that the boundaries of clusters, as Porter admits, are 'continuously evolving', as new firms and industries emerge and established ones shrink or decline. More fundamentally, the definition itself seems intentionally opaque and fuzzy.

Cluster boundaries, according to Porter (1998a, p. 204), 'rarely conform to standard industrial classification systems, which fail to capture many important actors in competition as well as linkages across industries.... Because parts of a cluster often fall within different traditional industrial or service categories, significant clusters may be obscured or even go unrecognised'. He refers to the 400-firm medical devices cluster in Massachusetts, which he says has long remained all but invisible, buried within larger and overlapping standard industry categories. In part then, defining the boundaries of clusters appears to be about deriving a detailed reclassification of industries that more accurately reflects the range of specialized economic activity. But then a cluster is also about linkages within and between such specialized activities, about tracing the supply chains supporting what is seen as the 'core' activity of the cluster. So as Porter admits,

Drawing cluster boundaries is often a matter of degree, and *involves a creative process* informed by understanding the most important linkages and complementarities across industries and institutions to competition. (1998a, p. 202; emphasis added)

He suggests that 'the strength of "spillovers", and their importance to productivity and innovation determine the ultimate boundaries'; that 'cluster boundaries should encompass all firms, industries and institutions with strong linkages', whereas 'those with weak and non-existent linkages can safely be left out' (1998a, p. 202). Exactly how the 'strength' of different sorts of linkages and spillovers should be measured, and where the cutoff between 'strong' and 'weak' ties falls, are, however, issues that are left unspecified. The existence of clusters, appears then, in part at least, to be in the eye of the beholder – or should we say, creator.

And how does the requirement of 'geographical proximity' enter into the equation? Although throughout his work on clusters Porter emphasizes the critical role of 'geographical proximity' in the formation, performance, and identification of clusters, the term is never defined with any precision. Indeed, it appears to be highly and ridiculously elastic, for he suggests in fact that clusters can be found at almost any level of spatial aggregation: 'They are present in large and small economies, in rural and urban areas, and at several geographic levels (for example nations, states, metropolitan regions, and cities)' (1998a, p. 204); their geographical scope can even encompass 'a network of neighbouring countries' (1998a, p. 199). To make matters worse, 'the appropriate definition of a cluster can differ in different locations, depending on the segments in which the member companies compete and the strategies they employ' (1998a, p. 205). Such geographical license has given authors unlimited scope in their definition and application of the concept (see Table 16.1).

At one extreme, the term has been used to refer to national groups of industries and firms that are strongly linked (in terms of traded interdependencies), but dispersed over several different locations within a country, with no obvious major geographical concentrations (this was, in fact, Porter's original use of the 'competitive diamond'). At the other extreme, the term is used to refer to a local grouping of similar firms in related industries within a highly spatially circumscribed area – such as the media cluster in Lower Manhattan, New York (Porter, 1998a, p. 205), or the film and media cluster in Soho, London (Nachum and Keeble, 1999). In between, Porter refers to 'regional clusters', such as the California agribusiness cluster, and the Massachusetts medical devices cluster. He lists some 60 of these in the US (Porter, 1998a, p. 229), although in most cases the clusters are far from being state-wide. Elsewhere, the terms 'clusters' and 'regions' are used interchangeably (Enright, 1996, 2001; Baptista and Swann, 1998). Thus Enright (2001, p. 2) claims that 'Regional clustering is found in virtually every advanced economy and increasingly in developing countries as well'. The confusion is further heightened by other studies that equate clusters and 'cities' (see, for example, Swann, 1998, p. 63). Still others suggest, more specifically, that the proximity inherent in a cluster extends up to a 'range of fifty miles' (May et al., 2001), but such demarcations are obviously quite arbitrary.

The problem is that geographical terminology is used in a quite cavalier manner, depending it seems, as Porter himself admits, on what the aim of the exercise is, or the client or policy maker for whom the analysis is intended.

TABLE 16.1. *Clusters: the confusion of definitions*

Porter (1998a, p. 199) 'A cluster is a geographically proximate group of interconnected companies and associated institutions in a particular field, linked by commonalities and complementarities.'

Crouch and Farrell (2001, p. 163) 'The more general concept of "cluster" suggests something looser: a tendency for firms in similar types of business to locate close together, though without having a particularly important presence in an area.'

Rosenfeld (1997, p. 4) 'A cluster is very simply used to represent concentrations of firms that are able to produce synergy because of their geographical proximity and interdependence, even though their scale of employment may not be pronounced or prominent.'

Feser (1998, p. 26) 'Economic clusters are not just related and supporting industries and institutions, but rather related and supporting institutions that are more competitive by virtue of their relationships.'

Swann and Prevezer (1996, p. 139) 'Clusters are here defined as groups of firms within one industry based in one geographical area.'

Swann *et al.* (1998, p. 1) 'A cluster means a large group of firms in related industries at a particular location.'

Simmie and Sennett (1999a, p. 51) 'We define an innovative cluster as a large number of interconnected industrial and/or service companies having a high degree of collaboration, typically through a supply chain, and operating under the same market conditions.'

Roelandt and den Hertog (1999, p. 9) 'Clusters can be characterised as networks of producers of strongly interdependent firms (including specialised suppliers) linked each other in a value-adding production chain.'

Van den Berg *et al.* (2001, p. 187) 'The popular term cluster is most closely related to this local or regional dimension of networks ... Most definitions share the notion of clusters as localised networks of specialised organisations, whose production processes are closely linked through the exchange of goods, services and/or knowledge.'

Enright (1996, p. 191) 'A regional cluster is an industrial cluster in which member firms are in close proximity to each other.'

The key weakness is that there is nothing inherent in the concept itself to indicate its spatial range or limits, or whether and in what ways different clustering processes operate at different geographical scales. We are not suggesting that the cluster concept should refer to a particular pre-specified geographical size or scale; but to use the term to refer to any spatial scale is stretching the concept to the limits of credulity, and assumes that 'clustering processes' are scale independent. If the same externalities and networks that typify clusters do indeed operate at a whole variety of spatial scales, this surely weakens the empirical and analytical significance of the cluster concept.

This lack of geographical precision and consensus is further compounded by the vague typologies of cluster types and evolutionary paths that have been proposed. Porter suggests that clusters 'vary in size, breadth, and state of development' (1998a, p. 204). Some clusters consist primarily of small and medium-sized firms (he cites the Italian footwear and North Carolina home furniture clusters). Other clusters contain both small and large firms (he gives the German chemical cluster as an example). There are university-centered clusters and clusters with no university connections; clusters of traditional industries and clusters of high-technology industries. There are nascent clusters, new clusters, established clusters, and declining clusters. Other authors have sought to construct typologies based on the evolution of clustering processes. Rosenfeld (1997), for example, distinguishes three types. 'Working' or 'overachieving' clusters are 'self-aware' and produce more than the sum of their parts. Latent or 'underachieving' clusters present opportunities that have not yet been fully exploited. 'Potential' clusters have some of the key conditions but lack some inputs and critical mass. This latter type is particularly problematic, since it becomes difficult to exclude almost any firm from a 'potential' cluster, especially when policy makers are eager not to be left out of the cluster-promotion game (indeed, many supposed clusters are 'aspirational' or the product of 'wishful thinking'). In practice, there are probably very few firms that do not have horizontal or vertical links (co-operative or competitive) of some sort with other loosely defined 'geographically proximate' firms. Does this mean that virtually every firm could be considered part of a 'potential' cluster? Typologies that employ categories such as 'embryonic', 'latent', and 'potential', come close to incorporating almost all firms in clusters of one type or another, and as such become virtually meaningless. Equally problematic is the tendency to devise typologies that relate specifically and only to the particular set of clusters being studied, with little or no intention to discern elements or features that might be of wider relevance.

The proliferation of cluster typologies may well be a genuine attempt to recognize the diversity of cluster forms and cluster development. But appeals to such diverse forms, sizes, stages of development, emergence, depth, breadth, level of aggregation, and the like, is equally an indication that the cluster concept is something of a chaotic one. Porter sees the Italian industrial districts as one form of cluster just as high-technology areas such as Silicon Valley are another. What he calls clusters, French analysts refer to as 'local production systems' (see OECD-DATAR, 2001). Recently, drawing on a survey of European examples, Crouch et al. (2001) see 'empirical clusters' as one of three types of local production system, distinct from industrial districts on the one hand and what they refer to as the 'networked firm' on the other. In contrast, in his discussion of the role of regions in the recent competitive resurgence of the US economy, Best (2001) uses the terms industrial districts and clusters interchangeably. And so the confusion goes on. Classification is of course an important stage of theorizing and analysis. But to be meaningful and useful, typologies need to be based on in-depth comparative analyses of cluster profiles and processes [Markusen's (1996) typology of industrial districts provides some pointers in this regard]. Despite the vast and still expanding literature on clusters, however, there has been little detailed work of this kind.

16.4   What Sort of Theory for What Sort of Cluster?

All of which begs the issue of the status of 'cluster theory'. Porter's 'clusters' are constructs. They are as much analytical creations as they are objectively real phenomena. They have no essential self-defining boundaries, whether in terms of intersectoral or interfirm linkages, information networks, or geographical reach. The notion is so generic that it is used as a sort of cover term to refer to a whole assortment of types and degrees of specialized industrial localization (for example, see Porter, 2001). Little wonder, then, that cluster theory is in a similar state of confusion.

According to Porter:

A variety of bodies of literature have in some respects recognized and shed light on the phenomenon of clusters, including those on growth poles and backward and forward linkages, agglomeration economies, economic geography, urban and regional economics, national innovation systems, regional science, industrial districts and social networks.... Overall, most past theories address aspects of clusters or clusters of a particular type. (1998a, p. 207)

While eclecticism can be a virtue under certain circumstances, forging a theoretical synthesis out of this list of perspectives would seem a dubious endeavor. Yet this is what Porter tries to do. He sees his task as 'embedding clusters in a broader and dynamic theory of competition that encompasses both cost and differentiation and both static efficiency and continuous improvement and innovation, and that recognizes a world of global factor and product markets' (1998a, p. 208). Porter's theory of competition is not simply about cost advantages and factor inputs, but also about 'strategic positioning' by companies, that is choosing activities that are different from and superior to those of rivals. Essentially, Porter sees a cluster as a self-reinforcing system that stimulates the competitive strategies of the firms in the cluster and hence the 'competitiveness' of the cluster itself. He then argues that these processes depend in part on personal relationships, face-to-face communication and social networks (social capital) so that 'cluster theory bridges network theory and competition' (Porter, 1998a, p. 226). He goes even further: 'Clusters offer a new way of exploring the mechanisms by which networks, social capital and civic engagement affect competition' (1998a, p. 227). What is being proposed here, therefore, is nothing less than a general theory of clusters and their socio-economy.

Yet three questions immediately arise. First, just how far can the full complexity of economic, social, and institutional factors and processes alleged to underpin cluster formation, development, and success, be reduced to or subsumed within an overarching concept of 'competitiveness'? Secondly, to what extent is it possible to construct a universal theory of cluster formation, dynamics, and evolution capable of covering the wide range of cluster types and processes thought or argued to exist, without degenerating into superficial generalities of the sort that have surrounded industrial districts (see Amin, 2000)? And thirdly, just how far does Porter's cluster theory really illuminate the socio-insitutional processes that are alleged to be so important in cluster formation and dynamics?

In Porter's work the notion of 'competitiveness' is used to link a variety of conceptual scales: the individual firm, the industry, the regional or local business cluster, and the nation. For Porter, firms compete, clusters compete, and nations compete. He talks of the 'competitiveness of locations' (see Porter, 1998a). At the heart of Porter's 'theory of competitiveness' is his long-standing idea of 'competitive strategy', which posits three generic strategies that companies must follow to establish a lead in their market: differentiation (of product or service), cost leadership, and focus strategy (focusing activities on the needs of specific segments of the market). The role of clusters in this theory is that through concentrating the interaction between the elements of the 'competitive diamond' they enhance all three aspects of strategy. But while clustering may well enhance the competitiveness of firms, is this the same thing as talking about the 'competitiveness of clusters or locations'? Locations obviously do not develop competitive strategies in this sense (though many policy makers seem to believe they should).

In any case, Porter's approach to competition and competitive strategy are far from universally accepted within the business economics, industrial organization, and management studies fields (Jacobs and De Jong, 1992; O'Malley and Vanegeraat, 2000). Several authors have criticized Porter's three generic competitive strategies as being too superficial, for lacking specificity, for being difficult to measure, and for not being as independent of one another, or as universally applicable, as Porter assumes. As Buckley *et al.* (1988) have shown, the notion of competitiveness is highly complex and varies with the economic scale at which the concept is being used. Indeed, yet other economists view the very notion of 'competitiveness' with extreme skepticism. They argue that while the term may have meaning at the level of the firm, it becomes increasingly more problematic as we move up the scale of economic aggregation (see, for example, Krugman, 1994, 1996; Turner, 2001). According to these authors, nations and regions do not compete with one another in the way that firms do, and the analogy between a company and a nation or region is false.

The problem is reinforced because Porter uses the terms 'competitive advantage', 'competition', and 'productivity' interchangeably. In fact, he has directly equated regional competitiveness with regional productivity (Porter, 2002). Certainly, productivity is a key index of regional and local economic performance, and both the measurement and determinants of regional productivity are important topics of enquiry. However, equating competitiveness with productivity is to invite tautology and ontological confusion: is a region more competitive because it is more productive, or is it more productive because it is more competitive? Furthermore, a simple productivity view of regional competitiveness obscures the complex nature of competition itself. As Klein (2001) convincingly argues, Porter's notion is highly restrictive and fails to recognize the several different modalities that competition can assume.

Yet a further complication is that Porter's 'competitiveness theory' of clusters is founded on the assumption that the important clusters are those orientated to external trade. He estimates that these account for about 32 percent of total US employment (Porter, 2002). This is consistent with the view of other observers (such as Krugman, 1996 and Turner, 2001) that in today's highly urbanized world, the bulk of production serves local demand. Unfortunately, Porter confusingly refers to this non-traded aspect of regional economies, which he estimates makes up 67 percent of US total employment, as 'local clusters' (thereby implying that no less than 99 percent of the US economy is clustered!). Not only is it misleading to use the term 'local clusters' to describe non-tradable local services and activities that are found in every urban area, it is also unclear what is meant by competitiveness in relation to such activities. While the productivity or more accurately the productivity growth, of local non-tradable activities is critical for local wealth and prosperity, as Krugman (1997) argues this has nothing to do with 'competitiveness'.

If there are difficulties with clusters in Porter's theory of competitiveness, the generality of his 'cluster theory' adds to the problem. Clusters vary considerably in type, origin, structure, organization, dynamics, and developmental trajectory, yet Porter's theory is supposedly intended to fit all. It is not clear, however, whether this is because it is assumed that all clusters can be explained in the same way, despite their diversity, or because the highly general nature of the theory is intended to cover all eventualities, allowing analysts to pick and choose different elements to suit different types of cluster. The difficulty is that Porter's cluster model actually combines ideas from quite different perspectives – from agglomeration theory to social network theory – some of which are complementary and others much less so. As a result, empirical observations of clusters and clustering can then be interpreted in quite different ways, thereby buttressing a generalized notion of the benefits of clustering by conflating elements for which there may actually be little evidence with elements to which the evidence more directly relates.

In response to this shortcoming, Gordon and McCann (2000), argue for distinguishing three main cluster models (theories). The first is the 'pure agglomeration economies' model, which they trace from Marshall through to modern urban economic theory, and that emphasizes the external economies of geographical concentration (see also, Bellflame *et al.*, 2000). The second is what they call the 'industrial complex' model, in which clusters are seen primarily as the spatial counterparts of the input–output models of regional economics, as geographical concentrations forged by interfirm trading links and the minimization of transactions costs. And the third is the 'social-network' model, which as the term suggests interprets clusters mainly in terms of strong local networks of interpersonal relations, trust, and institutionalized practices. Gordon and McCann argue that,

Defining analytically which of these types is the dominant structural characteristic of a particular cluster (or set of clusters) is essential, in order to be able to discuss their performance empirically, and to determine what more general lessons may be drawn from that. (2000, p. 515)

However, while helpful, this tripartite theoretical schema is not unproblematic. For one thing it fails to specify the particular circumstances, economic and spatial, under which one theoretical model should be more applicable than another. To be convincing, cluster theory ought to be able to specify *a priori* how different sorts of cluster are likely to develop under different conditions. Otherwise, explanation is reduced to a 'best-fit' exercise on a case-by-case basis. Secondly, as Gordon and McCann themselves acknowledge, these three theoretical models are ideal types. By their very nature, ideal typical models never fit reality exactly, and in this case it is difficult to think of a pure agglomeration economies cluster, a pure industrial complex cluster, or a pure network cluster. While Gordon and McCann admit that a given cluster may contain elements of more than one model, nevertheless they insist that

Contrasts in the policy implications of these three ideal types of cluster make it particularly important to avoid confusing features of one with those of another, even though elements of each may coexist in particular situations. (2000, p. 528)

In reality, such coexistence is likely to be the rule. Indeed, what are social networks in this context, other than a particular form of external economy associated with agglomeration? Porter argues that 'social embeddedness' – the existence of facilitative social networks and social capital – is crucial for the successful functioning and upgrading of clusters. Moreover,

... cluster theory also provides a way to connect theories of networks, social capital and civic engagements more tightly to business competition and economic prosperity ... Cluster theory helps to isolate the most beneficial forms of networks ... [and] may reveal how network relationships form and how social capital is acquired. (Porter, 1998a, p. 227)

Despite this claim, however, the social dimensions of cluster formation and cluster dynamics remain something of a black box in Porter's work. While he stresses, for example, the importance of local social networks for the production and flow of information and knowledge within clusters, these processes are conspicuously under-theorized in his cluster model. And even in his case-study examples, there is little explicit empirical investigation of these social and knowledge networks, which more often than not are simply inferred from the presence of particular formal and informal institutions within a cluster.

The problem of conceptualizing and empirically analysing knowledge networks and other 'soft' socio-cultural-institutional features of clusters and spatial economic agglomerations is not, of course, confined to Porter's work. There is, in fact, an increasing tendency to explain cluster formation and development in terms of local knowledge and 'collective learning' (see, for example, Hassink, 1997; Steiner and Hartmann, 1998, 2001; Pinch and Henry, 1999; Keeble and Wilkinson, 2000; Maskell, 2001). The argument is that in a globalized economy the key resources for competitiveness depend on localized processes of knowledge creation, in which people and firms learn about new technology, learn to trust each other, and share and exchange information (Cohen and Fields, 1999). The emphasis is on the role of 'tacit' as against 'codified' knowledge, in that the former is viewed as being especially dependent on localized face-to-face contacts and spillovers. Indeed, the assumed link between localization and tacit or informal, uncodified knowledge is now almost accepted axiomatically (Breschi and Lissonie, 2001). And according to Leamer and Storper (2001) in the new information economy not only is the role of tacit knowledge increasing, this in turn is accentuating the spatial agglomeration and localized specialization of economic activity.

This local knowledge 'cluster theory' itself faces several difficulties. First, despite the numerous assertions that 'tacit' knowledge is the key to business success, this remains an unsubstantiated and obscure proposition. Not only are the distinctions between different forms of knowledge less clear cut and more fluid than binary divisions such as formal and informal, codified and tacit, suggest (Amin and Cohendetet, 1999; Breschi and Lissonie, 2001; Breschi and Malerba, 2001), it is too simplistic to argue that a given form of knowledge is inevitably linked to one form of geographical socio-economic organization (clusters) or any one scale of social relationships. Secondly, many accounts refer to localized tacit knowledge without making clear precisely what it is, or how it acts as a source of competitive advantage. More helpfully, Lawson and Lorenz (1999) argue that the key form of tacit knowledge may actually be embedded in firm routines, which guide a firm's innovativeness, problem-solving, and adaptability. Ironically, however, the problem here is that the cluster literature, including Porter's own approach, lacks any serious analysis or theory of the internal organization of business enterprise (Best and Forrant, 1996). Instead, it emphasizes the importance of factors external to firms and somehow residing in the local environment. In too many accounts local 'territorial learning' is privileged, yet what this process actually is remains ambiguous and its interactions with firm-based learning are left completely unexamined (Hudson, 1999). Related to this, and as May *et al.* (2001) rightly argue, given the current fashion for non-economic explanations, cluster studies often assume that 'institutional thickness' refers to non-firm institutions rather than examining the key institutions of firms and labor markets.

A further, and in our view fundamental, limitation of the current state of 'cluster theory' is that it abstracts clusters from the rest of the economic landscape, so that they often appear as isolated and self-contained entities (Breschi and Malerba, 2001). Two things are missing. On the one hand, what is needed is a cluster theory that situates cluster development within the dynamics and evolution of industry and innovation more generally. In effect, Porter's approach is to delimit clusters and then to analyse them as if they are isolated islands in the economy. Not all firms in a given sector of activity need be clustered, and we should also consider the evolutionary trajectories and interdependencies of firms outside clusters as well as those inside clusters. In one of the very few attempts to address this issue, Pouder and St John (1996) draw on a range of theoretical ideas (from institutional evolution, organizational ecology, management cognition, as well as standard agglomeration economies) to construct an evolutionary model of the development of clustered and non-clustered firms. They argue that the economies of agglomeration that initially draw firms together into clusters eventually erode. The competitive strategies of firms in clusters, which are initially highly innovative compared to firms outside clusters, tend to converge (for example through mimetic and normative isomorphism) and to be less innovative over time because cluster firms define their field of competition as the cluster to which they belong, rather than as the wider external industry. This restricted collective perspective gives rise to competitive 'blind spots' that limit cluster firms' innovative potential, strategic positioning, and ability to anticipate and react to industry-wide shocks. Non-clustered firms tend to be less constrained and potentially remain more adaptable to sudden system-wide changes. In effect, these authors sketch out a theory of cluster formation, growth, and decline, set against the background of the development of the wider industry as a whole. The very networks of interdependence that were a source of strength in the early phase of cluster formation and growth are hypothesized to become, over time, sources of inertia and inflexibility, relative to the firms outside the clusters. While Porter does refer to potential problems of cluster decline, Pouder and St John's theory assumes that relative if not absolute decline is an inherent systemic feature of cluster dynamics.

By the same token, cluster theory provides a highly partial view of regional development. Not only are clusters one possible form or source of regional economic growth, they tend to be analysed as if they are separate from wider processes of regional development. Yet, while Pouder and St John's cluster theory represents an advance over Porter's in this respect, even their approach fails to consider the dynamics of cluster formation and obsolescence within a more holistic theory of uneven regional development. This is where, potentially, economic geographers could make a significant contribution; but unfortunately they seem to have all but abandoned their former interest in theorizing the development of the economic landscape as a whole in order to focus too on particular types of region economy (invariably successful regional economies) in isolation from the wider interregional system as a whole.

16.5   Selective Empirics and the Cluster-Creation Game

Obviously, a vaguely defined and theorized concept does not lend itself to easy or precise empirical delimitation. In fact, in most applications the geographical mapping of clusters is surprisingly unsophisticated and stylistic. While Porter's diagrammatic 'flow diagrams' of particular clusters of (upstream and downstream) interlinked activities are often detailed, his 'cluster maps' are extraordinarily simplistic and unexplained (for example, see his map of regional clusters of competitive US industries in Porter, 1998*a*, p. 229). There is no agreed method for identifying and mapping clusters, either in terms of the key variables that should be measured or the procedures by which the geographical boundaries of clusters should be determined (a similar problem exists for industrial districts – see Paniccia, 2002). Hence, different authors use different types of data and different methods to identify them empirically, with the result that varying claims are made for how many clusters exist and what their geographies are. For example, while Porter (1998*a*) identifies and maps some 60 significant clusters in the US, according to the Secretary-General of the OECD, the US contains no less than 380, producing some 60 percent of the country's output (Johnston, 2001). Yet again, while Porter identifies a mere handful in the UK, others claim to identify several dozen (see Crouch and Farrell, 2001).

Empirical methodologies and 'mapping' strategies vary considerably (see Table 16.2). At one extreme are the 'top-down' national mapping exercises that utilize selective types of data to identify, on an industry-by-industry basis, particular important localizations of specialized activity or linked activities. At the other extreme are 'bottom-up' approaches that are only concerned with identifying clusters in a particular regional or local area, often in a highly qualitative, impressionistic way. In between are all sorts of combinations. Even top-down studies take different forms. Following Porter's (1990) original major work on national competitiveness, an initial stage in constructing clusters adopted by some authors is to identify first those national 'core' industries that are 'globally competitive', usually defined in terms of each industry's market share of world exports, or of world value added. National input–output tables are then constructed to determine the

TABLE **16.2** *Varieties of cluster and the cluster measurement problem*

Cluster concept	Conceptual/ definitional depth	Empirical methodology	Ease of measurement	Empirical support
Co-location	Shallow	Top-down	Easy to measure (quantitative)	Indirect evidence
Co-location and technological proximity Input–output table and complementarities Co-location and superior performance Marshallian externalities Network firms Explicit collaboration Informal knowledge spillovers	Deep	Bottom-up	Hard to measure (qualitative)	Direct evidence

Adapted from Swann (2002).

nature and extent of the trading linkages based around these 'core', globally competitive industries. Essentially, this approach to defining 'national industry clusters' seeks to subdivide the economy by forming industrial groupings (clusters) linked by particularly strong or distinctive supply–demand transactions. In other accounts, attention is focused on some other subset of activities, whether they are globally competitive or not (e.g. high-tech industries). In yet others, all of a nation's industries are examined (see Crouch *et al.*, 2001; Miller *et al.*, 2001). Since interindustry trade data are rarely available for subnational geographical areas, in most top-down approaches the cluster-mapping exercise itself typically reduces to the mapping of regional or subregional level data on employment and/or number of businesses, or value added, in order to estimate the local significance of the industry clusters being investigated (see Feser and Bergman, 2000).

The drawbacks of such analyses are obvious. Recall Porter's arguments that clusters typically cut across the sort of standard industrial sector classifications used to collect employment, output, and related business data. Yet most top-down (and other) studies have no option but to use data based on such classifications. To compound the problem, census-type geographical data on industrial employment and business populations are collected on the basis of pre-given administrative and political units – such as metropolitan areas and states in the US, and standard regions, local authority areas in the UK, or NUTS regions in the EU – which may bear no close relationship with the geographical boundaries or reach of clusters, however the latter are defined. Moreover, even with a given national context, the size of such regional or local data-collecting units can vary substantially. If the spatial units are too large, they can overbound and obscure local clusters. On the other hand, since the degree of local economic differentiation and special-ization tends to increase as the size of geographical units decreases, the use of small area data may exaggerate the number and significance of clusters.

Given the problem of establishing the precise boundaries and composition of clusters, many studies take an easier route. That is, they take relatively large-scale geographical units, such as states and regions, and make the highly contestable assumption that sectoral employment totals for these units provide a direct measure of the strength of cluster development in each area. For example, Baptista and Swann (1998) examine the introduction of manufacturing innovations across UK regions and conclude that a firm is more likely to innovate if located in a region where the presence of firms in its own industry is strong, as measured by employment, so that clustering furthers innovation (see also Baptista, 2000; Beaudry *et al.*, 2000). But to what extent can the strength of regional employment in a sector be taken as evidence of the existence of a cluster in that region? In response, Baptista and Swann (1998) assert that agglomeration benefits and externalities be-come stronger when the geographical level of analysis is reduced, so that using relatively large-scale regional data biases against the relevance of spillovers and externalities. This may be so, but this surely does not mean that clusters necessarily exist in regions where employment in any one sector is high. A high regional employment total could surely just as easily reflect the presence of several large, dispersed, and unconnected employers within that region. There is also no agreement on what degree of spatial concentration of an industry or industry group constitutes a cluster. Many studies employ location quotients to measure relative spatial concentration, and high values of location quotients are taken to indicate the presence of clusters. But although location quotients make some adjustment for the varying size of areal units, they do not of themselves discriminate between the presence of a large number of small or medium-sized interlinked firms, and a large single firm employing the same overall number of workers. Associated data on the geographical distribution of individual businesses by size and sector are clearly essential. In addition, how much greater than unity does a location quotient have to be to indicate the existence of a cluster (see Miller *et al.*, 2001)? In some studies, the statistical acrobatics employed to map 'signifi-cant' clusters are complex (see, for example, Ellison and Glaeser, 1997). In other studies, the 'rules' used to distinguish clusters are highly arbitrary (for an example, see Crouch and Farrell, 2001).

The extensive methodologies of top-down mapping exercises can at best only suggest the existence and location of possible clusters: they provide a shallow, indirect view of clusters. They cannot provide much if any insight into the nature and strength of local interfirm linkages (traded and untraded), knowledge spillovers, social networks and institutional support structures argued to be the defining and distinctive features of clusters. Thus, a common tendency is to identify clusters in a piecemeal way and then deduce their benefits and effects from the co-variation and co-location of selected variables. As Hanson (2000, p. 481) explains. 'The externalities that contribute to spatial agglomeration, such as spillovers between workers, learning across firms, or cost and demand linkages between local industries, are difficult to observe. We are left to infer their existence from the covariance of observed variables such as wages, employment and output'. This process of inference has produced some very mixed and inconclusive results, and even when covariance is found it is never precisely clear exactly what type of externality is responsible. For example, there has been a long-running and unresolved debate on whether localization economies are conducive to higher productivity and employment growth, firm entry, and innovation; or whether in fact urbanization economies are more important and beneficial (Glaeser *et al.*, 1992; Henderson *et al.*, 1995; Feldman, 2000). Indeed, while Porter believes that urbanization economies are declining in importance, others suggest that innovative clusters are driven by precisely these economies (Simmie and Sennett, 1999*a*, *b*).

In view of these difficulties, it is perhaps not surprising that many studies give up on the idea of identifying clusters directly. Instead, they tend to rely on loose *ad hoc*, 'bottom-up' means of identification (Doeringer and Terka, 1996). Some analysts simply ask local economic agencies to supply lists of 'local clusters' in their area that are then studied in more detail (for example, see Van den Berg *et al.*, 2001). In many of these instances, however, what are claimed to be clusters often turn out, on closer empirical inspection, to be small and only loosely connected collections of similar or related firms, and sometimes have more to do with local policy aspirations than with realities on the ground. Indeed, some cluster enthusiasts appear to eschew any prior empirical identification of clusters at all, on the assumption that latent clusters are out there everywhere if only their constituent businesses, institutions, and agencies realized it. Thus, for example, according to Cluster Navigators Ltd (one of the increasingly numerous cluster consultancies and promotional bodies):

Our experience is that *extensive analysis is not required to identify initial arenas* [i.e. clusters] for collaborative engagement [i.e. between cluster firms and policy makers].... The time for detailed analysis and systematic cluster benchmarking is *after* initial engagement has been obtained, *not before*. (www.clusternavigator.com, emphasis added)

This putting of the promotional cart before the analytic horse is understandably attractive to cluster consultancies and public policy makers eager to enter the cluster promotion game. No doubt many (and perhaps Porter himself) would argue that excessive (academic) analysis only leads to policy paralysis; that the detailed structure and workings of a cluster will become obvious soon enough once we begin to think about an activity in cluster terms. But to our minds, such arguments require an *a priori* faith, and compound the difficulties surrounding the cluster concept.

All of which renders many of the claims about the superior performance of clusters of dubious validity. Clusters, it is argued, raise the productivity, innovativeness, competitiveness, profitability, and job creation of their constituent firms, of the geographical areas in which the clusters are located, and thence of the wider national economy. But what is the evidence for these claims? Some advocates assert that the economic advantages of clusters have already been empirically demonstrated (Baptista, 1998, 2000). Even the Secretary General of the OECD states that it has been shown that being located in a cluster raises the profitability of firms on average 'between two and four per cent' (OECD-DATAR, 2001, p. 8). A more detached review suggests that the evidence is incomplete, and that far more detailed comparative research needs to be carried out. Much of the evidence used in support of the superior performance argument is anecdotal and based on success stories about particular locations (Malmberg, 1996), and there are few extensive studies that document how common and important clustering is within particular industries (Malmberg and Maskell, 1997), or studies that carefully compare similar firms inside and outside of clusters.

The evidence of a positive association between clustering and innovation is not consistent. One of the few detailed studies that exist, of metalworking across the US, by Harrison *et al.* (1996), actually found no evidence that firms in local concentrations adopted new technologies more rapidly than their more geographically dispersed or isolated counterparts. Likewise, in their study of the impact of clusters on firm growth and innovation for a range of industries across Europe, Beaudry *et al.* (2000) found the results to be ambivalent. While firms located in clusters that were strong in their own industry tended to grow faster and have higher propensities to innovate, firms in clusters that were strong in other industries did not have faster growth and innovation rates. Moreover, it has not been conclusively shown that regions based on specialized clusters consistently enjoy a higher rate of innovation and economic growth (Steiner, 1998; Segal Quince Wicksteed, 2001; Rodriguez-Pose, 2001). At the very least, the case that clusters invariably boost business performance and local economic development is not conclusively proven (Best, 2001).

Far from being the general rule and the key missing link in local competitive advantage, the benefits realized from geographical clustering appear to be specific to certain industries at certain stages of development in certain places, and are only realized under particular conditions (Glasmeier, 2000). For example, Audretsch and Feldman (1996) examined the distribution of commercial innovative activity across the US and concluded that the propensity to cluster is itself greatest in industries with a high dependence on new economic knowledge, as captured by industry and university R&D, and skilled labor. Indeed, the dominant view is now that clustering is most significant in sectors that are crucially dependent on tacit or informal knowledge, often in pre-commercialization stages (Audretsch, 1998; Keeble and Wilkinson, 2000). But even within high-technology and knowledge-based activities, the significance of clustering has been found to be variable and produced by different processes. Thus, studies of computing in the US and the UK find that employment growth is promoted by own-sector employment within particular states, and that firm entry is positively associated with regional employment in only a few subsectors, mainly hardware and components (Baptista and Swann, 1999). A similar study of US biotechnology, however, concludes that firm employment growth has been positively associated with own-sector employment but that firm entry in this case is attracted by the strength of the science base more than by own-sector employment with a particular state (Swann and Prevezer, 1996; Prevezer, 1997). The common message from studies of biotechnology and aerospace in the UK is that there are signs of clusters only in certain parts of these industries (Prevezer, 1997; Shohet, 1998; Beaudry, 2000). There is no evidence that firms in some biotechnology sectors (for example, related to food, chemicals, and agriculture) attract each other, possibly because large firms are able to absorb and internalize any knowledge spillovers. To complicate things further, a study of UK financial services, using the same methodology, found that own-sector employment has promoted both employment growth and firm entry, while other-sector employment negatively affects firm growth due to congestion effects (Pandit et al., 1999).

Given that there are so many different ways of identifying clusters, their advocates can always counter any disappointing results or criticism of their findings by insisting that the cluster boundaries or their economic outcomes have been incorrectly and inappropriately specified and measured. Ultimately, it seems that it is impossible to support or reject clusters definitively with empirical evidence, as there are so many ambiguities, identification problems, exceptions, and extraneous factors.

16.6   Cluster Policy: Hard Targets or Fashion Labels?

Despite these weaknesses, few other ideas can begin to rival the current popularity of the clusters notion among local economic practitioners and national and regional policy communities: 'It is difficult to identify another equally obscure concept that appeals to such a broad spectrum of academic disciplines, professions and even lay people' (Bergman, 1998, p. 92). Cluster policies fit in well with a growing trend towards the decentralization of policy responsibility and a focus on the indigenous potential of localities and regions (Temple, 1998). Enright and Ffowcs-Williams (2001) argue that cluster policies should be delivered by the level of government most closely matched to the geographical extent of the cluster (assuming that this can be known). But given that there is so little empirical work that conclusively demonstrates that clustering actually produces increased local economic prosperity, this extraordinary popularity begs explanation. As there is no agreed and shared definition of what a cluster is, it is hardly surprising that there is no one single model for such policy, and cluster labels are often attached to quite different sorts of policies.

In terms of recommendations on best practice, however, there is a consensus that cluster-promotion policies are unlikely to succeed in creating clusters *ab initio* (Schmitz and Nadvi, 1999). Rather, they should somehow attempt to build on the potential already present in a particular economy. While this seems sensible advice, it begs the question of what agencies should do if they lack the basis of embryonic clusters. Such a question is not just hypothetical, since it has particular relevance to debates on cluster promotion in lagging peripheral regions in developed economies as well as to a wide range of developing countries. No convincing answers are given in the cluster literature. A typical response is to argue that there are few if any regions that have no cluster potential, however limited that might be.

The standard rationale for cluster policies is they can help promote the supply of those local and regional public goods that are absent due to market failure (Scott, 1998; OECD, 1999). Four main varieties of such goods are usually identified. First, cluster policy emphasizes the benefits of creating co-operative networks and encouraging dialog between firms and other agencies. In such networks, it is claimed, firms can exchange information, pool resources, design collective solutions to shared problems, and develop a stronger collective identity. Thus, some cluster policies start by appointing brokers and intermediaries to organize these dialogs. This, it is suggested, can also yield a better co-ordination both between public and private agents and between different public agencies (Lagendijk and Charles, 1999). Secondly, and related to this, cluster policies often involve collective marketing of an industrial specialism, based on place marketing and raising awareness of the region's industrial strengths. Cluster policy typically represents a relatively cheap form of regional policy, but it is one that is able to raise the public relations profile of particular economies. Thirdly, it is also argued that cluster policy should aim to provide local services for firms such as financial advice, marketing, and design services. A key recommendation is that local service provision should be targeted on particular industrial specialisms so as to ensure that it meets specific local needs. For instance, a widespread aspiration for some high-tech initiatives is to develop links with relevant university research facilities and further the commercialization of their research. Fourthly, it is argued that cluster policies should identify weaknesses in existing cluster value chains and attract investors and businesses to fill those gaps and strengthen demand and supply links (Brown, 2000). In some cases, marketing strategies should target particular types of investor who will add key pieces to the cluster jigsaw.

It is by no means our intention to argue that all of these measures are, in themselves, misguided and of no benefit to local and regional economies. However, what is dubious is whether setting and attempting to implement such policies within a cluster framework actually improves their effectiveness and outcomes. In many cases it appears that the cluster framework is either unnecessary or even constraining. The decentralized promotion of local indigenous economic potential certainly does not depend on a cluster approach. There are many types of network policy that promote information sharing between firms that do not depend on a cluster framework and remit (see, for example, Cooke and Morgan, 1998). Indeed as Rosenfeld (2001) argues, what has happened in actual fact is that many local authorities have backed into cluster initiatives from pre-existing network support programs.

The first major problem inevitably encountered by such initiatives is how their boundaries should be drawn. Which firms should be left out? How far upstream and downstream of the 'core' cluster activity should policies extend? There is a fundamental tension between the public policy desire to include as many firms as possible and the notion that policy interventions can be more cost effective if they are targeted in some way. But if the policy is too targeted, then it starts to look like old-style industrial policy and too close to the discredited notion of 'picking winners'. The tension is nicely captured in this ambiguous advice by Enright and Ffowcs-Williams (2001, p. 5): 'A policy on clusters should aim to provide services that all firms merit access to, whether they are clustered or not, but in a more targeted fashion'. In the case of generic services, which would benefit all firms, it would seem preferable to drop the cluster framework altogether. Moreover, is it really wise to exclude certain firms from 'institutional dialogs', particularly when the future course of local industrial and technological change is so hard to predict and previously marginal firms can become key nodes in the local economy? Indeed, partly in response to this, Danish industrial policy has shifted to using the less exclusive notion of 'resource areas' (see Drejer et al., 1999). The linkages in wider and more diverse networks may well be weaker but they may provide greater long-run local adaptability (Grabher, 1993).

What is clear is that, strictly speaking, most cluster policies do not identify working clusters, but rely instead on more immediately and statistically visible broad industrial sectors. Policy makers are clearly under pressure to find clusters in as many regions as possible for fear of offending some regional interests. The Sainsbury (1999) report on biotechnology clusters in the UK, for example, finds established biotechnology clusters around Cambridge and Oxford, but also identifies earlier clusters in Surrey, Sussex, Kent, the North East, the North West, North Yorkshire, London, Central Scotland, Wales; that is, in almost all regions of the country, even though in many regions the 'clusters' are small and lack the interfirm linkages and spillovers that are held to be key cluster features. Likewise, in the DTI's more recent general investigation of business clusters across the UK (Miller *et al.*, 2001) there is an obvious political tension between mapping significant industry clusters wherever these happen to be, on the one hand (and many are in South East England), and ensuring an even spread between the various Regional Development Agency areas, on the other.

It is hard to avoid noticing the similarity in the types of clusters distinguished by many cluster-promotion programs (Rosenfeld, 2001). To some extent this no doubt reflects the enormous practical difficulty of identifying working clusters and the inevitable ambiguities and complexities involved. Faced with this difficulty, many public authorities resort to using the same set of cluster consultancy companies (flying 'cluster-makers'), who are commissioned, often at considerable public expense, to rapidly produce a cluster decomposition of the relevant local or regional economy. We are doubtful that such quick diagnoses are able to identify weak links in local value chains, understand the relevant spillovers and knowledge flows, detect how different industries are developing and anticipate the necessary service requirements. More generally, how should public authorities distinguish market failures in service provision? If firms are not paying for particular services, does this indicate a lack of information or a shared fear of free-riders; or is it because the services are not really needed? Another important ambiguity in the literature is whether policy should aim to differentiate between different clusters and, if so, in what ways. On the one hand, Porter (1995, 1996, 1998*a*) recommends that policy makers should not try to discriminate between clusters; rather, he suggests that 'it is not what you do but how you do it' that matters, and favoring some clusters is 'bad economics'. On the other hand, as we have already noted, Porter (1998*a*) argues in a neo-Keynesian manner that it is outward-oriented (export-based) clusters, rather than those supplying local demand, that are the primary long-run source of economic growth and prosperity. Other authors insist that policy makers should distinguish between clusters according to their growth potential (Fisher and Reuben, 2000), so that responses to survival clusters of microscale enterprises with limited competitive potential should be distinctive (Altenburg and Meyer-Stamer, 1999). A related issue is whether interfirm collaboration is appropriate in all industries, and to what extent policies can promote both competition and rivalry, at the same time as furthering firm collaboration (see Enright, 1996). How are public cluster sponsors supposed to know when, and on which issues, to encourage knowledge sharing and exchange, and when to urge knowledge retention and proprietary secrecy in order to sustain innovation incentives?

In the context of these uncertainties and questions, it is increasingly evident that policy makers, seeking safety in numbers perhaps, tend to be drawn to promoting similar varieties of 'high-technology, knowledge-based' clusters. But, even assuming that the new knowledge economy has a coherent meaning, it is unlikely that all regions can rely on the same, high-skill, knowledge-intensive sectors. As Keep and Mayhew (1999, pp. 57–58) have argued:

While it is relatively straightforward to aspire to the high performance vision when it is applied to some sectors of the economy, it becomes a very much greater challenge when the focus shifts to the economy as a whole. Policy-makers need to guard against the dangerous tendency to seize upon leading edge practice located within a particular sector or competitive environment and then to assume that this can be, or indeed is being generalised across the entire range of economic activity.

Nevertheless, such generalization or replication is precisely what Porter appears to be currently advocating. His present cluster-mapping project across the US is expressly aimed at identifying 'best practice' in successful clusters as a 'blueprint' for promoting innovativeness and competitiveness across regional America as a whole. While successful clusters may well hold lessons for policy practice elsewhere, the idea that there are cluster 'blueprints' that can be readily implemented in quite different local economic, social, and institutional contexts is highly debatable. Cluster-policy texts also say little about how interregional distribution issues should be approached. If one region implements a new cluster strategy should this be allowed to undermine established clusters elsewhere or should regional clustering somehow be made complementary (DTI, 2001)? Porter (1996) argues that regional authorities should avoid 'smokestack chasing' as using tax incentives and subsidies to bid against each other to attract key inward investors produces a zero-sum competition. Yet, in practice, cluster policies are surely likely to encourage just such a process.

What is striking is that in much of the literature on cluster policies, there is no real reason why place marketing and the advertising of industrial specialisms really needs to be tied to a 'cluster' label of doubtful relevance and content. There is no reason why co-ordination between different policies and groups should be handicapped with a confusing cluster framework, or why the provision of demand-led, productivity enhancing services to firms would be improved by setting up some imagined cluster boundaries. Moreover, there are also several potential dangers associated with promoting clusters (see Table 16.3). First, cluster policy may sponsor an exaggerated view of the extent to which firm performance is determined by local context. For instance, Porter (1998a) claims, 'The presence of clusters suggests that much of competitive advantage lies outside a given company or even outside its industry, residing instead in the locations of its business units' (p. 198, see also Steiner, 1998, p. 4). Internal and external advantages are clearly not independent, but if a company suffers from poor management, culture, and practices it is hard to believe that it can rely on the competitive advantage of its location. While supporting institutions and a networked semi-public

TABLE 16.3   *Clusters have costs as well as benefits*

Claimed advantages	Potential disadvantages
Higher innovation	Technological isomorphism
Higher growth	Labor-cost inflation
Higher productivity	Inflation of land and housing costs
Increased profitability	Widening of income disparities
Increased competitiveness	Overspecialization
Higher new-firm formation	Institutional and industrial lock-in
High job growth	Local congestion and environmental pressure

sphere may often be necessary for innovative and dynamic firm performance, such factors are unlikely to be sufficient.

Local and regional specialization also represents a risky strategy (Perry, 1999). The risk of decline and profound instability in specialized regional economies is well known and its relevance has been underlined by the recent downturn in Silicon Valley. Economic landscapes are littered with local areas of industrial specialization that were once prosperous and dynamic but have since gone into relative or even absolute decline. Porter himself argues that the causes of decline can be both internal to the cluster and the result of radical changes in external conditions, such as technological discontinuities. Internal decline will be rapid if the cluster suffers from the lock-in of established ways of thinking and doing things, or if technological isomorphism (through the normative or mimetic behavior of firms) occurs. And there are some authors who suggest that a reliance on local face-to-face contact and tacit knowledge does indeed make local networks of industry especially vulnerable to lock-in (Amin and Cohendet, 1999).

Clustered firms may be capable of incremental and continuous improvement within certain parameters, but may be unable to adapt to radical shifts in technology and product (see Pouder and St John, 1996; Loasby, 1998). There is clearly a danger that by encouraging highly specialized localizations of industry, cluster policies may actually reduce innovation rates. The evidence from urban economics suggests that, for many industrial sectors, innovation is associated with location in a diversified urban base. As Duranton and Puga (2000, p. 553) write 'The link between innovation and diversity seems fairly robust, so that highly innovative clusters cannot be bred in previously specialised environments'. None of the swelling ranks of cluster adherents seem to explain how policies should respond to these dangers. Fritz *et al.* (1998) argue that policy makers should see local industrial specialization as having a 'risk-return trade off', plotting the risk of ossification against the higher returns gained from clustering (a point made some time ago by Conroy, 1975, in his study of regional specialization versus regional diversification). In practice, constructing such 'trade-offs' is obviously very far from straightforward.

A further risk related to clusters concerns that of localized inflation and 'overheating'. The cluster literature itself tends to downplay the importance of cost-based competition. To quote Steiner (1998, p. 4): 'The existence of clusters is the decisive element for the competitiveness of regions and nations, not cheap land, labor, or energy, nor even high subsidies and low social costs, nor even high-technology strong and leading industries'. Other more cautious sources express concern about the effects of clusters on local costs. For example, the DETR (2000) notes that the growth of industrial concentrations tightens the labor market, leads to increased congestion, and puts pressure on the housing stock, destroying the features conducive to development. It adds, 'Firms with lower margins may be forced out of the area and workers on lower incomes, perhaps working in essential services or sectors which support the cluster, find it more difficult to find affordable housing' (DETR, 2000).

The question of the impact of cluster growth on other local sectors of activity is unresolved. The cluster orthodoxy would presumably be that as costs rise in the cluster, less-productive firms are either put out of business or move away. In Porter's (1998a, p. 245) view, 'Rising local wages and profits reflect economic success. This means that less-skilled and less-productive activities *should* move to other locations' (his emphasis). However, if these firms are labor intensive this would have a large negative impact on the local labor market. There is no theoretical guarantee that the high-productivity growth firms will be able to absorb the excess labor. Those working within the 'core' cluster firms in a locality may enjoy high living standards and rising wages as a compensation for the growing congestion, while those in non-core activities have to make do with inferior real wages and living standards, or have to move away. It cannot, therefore be assumed that the promotion of one or several clusters within a regional economy leads to balanced economic development, or greater competitiveness, or greater well-being across the entire region. Rather the outcome will depend on how the cluster affects the costs and employment of others sectors and localities (Venables, 1996).

Given these potential disadvantages, it would seem more advisable for local and regional authorities to concentrate on encouraging productivity improvements in all local firms, as well as improving their business environments, without necessarily committing to a cluster mind-set. The danger of a cluster-based approach to policy is that it detracts from the need to take a more holistic view of regional development. It is likely that dynamic regions will produce networks even without government incentives (Rosenfeld, 2001). Furthermore, even cluster enthusiasts find it enormously difficult to point to any examples of deliberate cluster-promotion programs that have been unambiguously successful. Given the consensus that public programs that attempt to directly create and steer clusters are likely to be ineffective, some argue that cluster policies should concentrate on accommodating the formation of new firms and investing in education and support infrastructure (Breschi and Malerba, 2001). But, once again, there are no clear grounds for tying such measures to confusing cluster frameworks. As Porter (1998*a*) himself rightly emphasizes, many of the most significant influences on industrial development stem from the way in which national regulatory frameworks influence the demand for sophisticated products, the course of industrial innovation, and levels of entrepreneurship (see also Miller *et al.*, 2001). Such regulation, along with the quality of the economic and social infrastructure, may well represent a better focus for policy makers' attention. At its best, the current policy preoccupation with cluster strategies looks like a fad for a fairly imprecise and flexible label for differing combinations of measures. Like many fashion labels that are not accompanied by a high-quality product, the cluster approach could go out of fashion as quickly as its popularity has mushroomed.

16.7   Conclusions: The Cluster Brand?

Constructing a critical review of clusters is a difficult task. There are now so many different varieties of clusters and so many confusing claims about their theoretical basis, form, identification, and significance that the concept is peculiarly elusive and hard to pin down (Malmberg, 2002). The feeling that there must be 'more to it than this' is endemic. The cluster literature is a patchy constellation of ideas, some of which are clearly important to contemporary economic development and some of which are either banal or misleading. But there are two key limitations that we wish to emphasize in conclusion. First, a concept so elastic as the cluster cannot provide a universal and deterministic model on how agglomeration is related to regional and local economic growth. At present, the siren of universalism is pulling the cluster concept into shallow waters. It is being applied so widely that its explanation of causality and determination becomes overly stretched, thin, and fractured. Secondly, and related to this, economic geographers and other regional analysts have long been aware that just because there is an association between some high-growth industries and various forms of geographical concentration does not mean that this concentration is the main cause of their economic growth or relative success. The empirical case for clustering remains in its infancy and repeatedly makes the mistake of jumping from particular associations to general causality and applicability.

But this heterogeneity and chaos is only half the story. It would be tempting to conclude that the notion of clusters has no real significance. Yet this is clearly at odds with the enormous policy popularity of the notion and the generous tolerance granted to the idea by a usually critical academic community. The answer to this paradox may lie in the way in which the cluster concept has been marketed by Porter and other enthusiasts as a brand, rather than just another intellectual product. Just as large corporations use branding to distinguish their products from other largely indistinguishable products (for example, see Klein, 2000), so the 'cluster brand' has been much more successful despite the existence of many similar theories and policy recommendations of industrial agglomeration. It has certainly attracted many more 'buyers' in the policy and practitioner markets than its rivals. The reason appears to lie not so much in the theoretical or empirical superiority of the concept, but in the way in which it has been closely tied to a set of positive images and associations. Again, just as branded products are ultimately image based so that consumers come to associate them with rewarding lifestyle experiences, the cluster brand at its core is based on an image of a high-productivity, knowledge-rich, decentralized, entrepreneurial, and socially progressive economy within the reach of local policy makers (a regional version of the American Dream, perhaps?). In this way, it conforms with, and reinforces, the ideological appeal of the 'new regionalism' (see Lovering, 1999). And just as brands are not confined to particular products but can exploit synergies between them, so we should expect the cluster idea to act as an umbrella brand for many different things. The core meaning of clusters lies more in this image than in a coherent and carefully defined set of ideas.

In short, Porter's cluster idea displays all of the key features needed for such a metaphor to assume the power of a successful 'brand' (or even myth – see Harfield, 1998). First, the metaphor must accord with some strong, if not always clearly defined, aspirations – in this case promoting innovation and competitiveness. It must be expressed in language sufficiently flexible as to permit a wide range of interpretations – in this instance, the hybrid nature of the cluster concept. The metaphor must have authority – here Porter's 'expert knowledge' on competition and business strategy. It must be capable of continual and consistent reinvention and reapplication – Porter's cluster concept is itself the latest stage in his evolving theory of competitive advantage, now being actively applied to the latest phase of economic development, the so-called new knowledge economy. And the language of the metaphor must allow the possibility of providing practical action – the cluster as a policy tool.

It is as if, in effect, Porter has applied his theory of competitive strategy – of 'strategic positioning' – to his cluster idea itself. Clever positioning and marketing of the cluster idea have been extremely influential in selling it to policy makers the world over. In adopting the cluster idea, policy makers purchase the 'Porter brand', and in doing so serve to reinforce the brand's prominence. What this implies, of course, is that given the power of the 'cluster brand', academic critiques such as this are unlikely to have much of an impact on the concept's popularity. It is perhaps only as the actual limits to 'brand-based cluster policy making' emerge, along with the marshalling of careful evaluative research, that the grip that Porter's cluster idea currently exerts on analytical and policy circles will lessen. As Santayana reminds us (in the quote at the beginning of this chapter), fashionable ideas tend to share one thing in common: they all eventually become unfashionable.

Acknowledgements

Earlier versions of this chapter were presented at the Regional Studies Association Conference on Regionalising the Knowledge Economy, London, November 21, 2001; at the Cluster Workshop, University of Lund, Sweden, April 5, 2002; at the High Technology Small Firms One-Day Clusters Conference, Manchester Business School, April 18, 2002; and at the Department of Geography, University College London. Many valuable comments were made on those occasions. We are grateful also to two anonymous referees for helpful suggestions.

References

Altenberg, T. and Meyer-Stamer, J. (1999), 'How to promote clusters: policy experiences from Latin America'. *World Development*, **27**(9): 1693–1713.

Amin, A. (2000), 'Industrial districts', in E. Sheppard and T. Barnes (eds), *A companion to economic geography*. Oxford: Blackwell: ch. 10, pp. 149–168.

Amin, A. and Cohendet, P. (1999), 'Learning and adaptation in decentralised business networks'. *Environment and Planning D: Society and Space*, **17**: 87–104.

Amin, A. and Thrift, N. J. (1992), 'Neo-Marshallian nodes in global networks'. *International Journal of Urban and Regional Research*, **16**: 571–587.

Asheim, B. (2000), 'Industrial districts: the contributions of Marshall and beyond', in G. L. Clark, M. Feldman, and M. Gertler (eds), *The Oxford handbook of economic geography*. Oxford: Oxford University Press: ch. 21, pp. 413–431.

Audretsch, D. (1998), 'Agglomeration and the location of innovative activity'. *Oxford Review of Economic Policy*, **14**(2): 18–29.

Audretsch, D. and Feldman, M. (1996), 'R&D spillovers and the geography of innovation and production'. *The American Economic Review*, **86**(3): 630–640.

Baptista, R. (1998), 'Clusters, innovation and growth: a survey of the literature', in G. M. P. Swann, M. Prevezer, and D. Stout (eds), *The dynamics of industrial clustering: international comparisons in computing and biotechnology*. Oxford: Oxford University Press, pp. 13–51.

Baptista, R. (2000), 'Do innovations diffuse faster within geographical clusters?' *International Journal of Industrial Organization*, **18**: 515–535.

Baptista, R. and Swann, P. (1998), 'Do firms in clusters innovate more?' *Research Policy*, **27**: 525–540.

Baptista, R. and Swann, P. (1999), 'A comparison of clustering dynamics in US and UK computer industries'. *Journal of Evolutionary Economics*, **9**: 373–399.

Beaudry, C. (2000), 'Entry, growth and patenting in industrial clusters: a study of the aerospace industry in the UK'. Working paper no. 413, Manchester Business School.

Beaudry, C., Breschi, S., and Swann, P. (2000), 'Clusters, innovation and growth: a comparative study of European countries'. Working Paper, Manchester Business School.

Bellflame, P., Picard, P., and Thisse, J.-F. (2000), 'An economic theory of regional clusters'. *Journal of Urban Economics*, **48**: 158–184.

Bennett, A. (1994), *Writing home*. London: Faber.

Bergman, E. M. (1998), 'Industrial trade clusters in action: seeing regional economies whole', in M. Steiner (eds), *Clusters and regional specialisation: on geography, technology and networks*. London: Pion, pp. 92–110.

Best, M. (2001), *The new competitive advantage: the renewal of American industry*. Oxford: Oxford University Press.

Best, M. and Forrant, R. (1996), 'Creating industrial capacity: Pentagon-led versus production-led industrial policies', in J. Michie and J. Grieve Smith (eds), *Creating industrial capacity: towards full employment*. Oxford: Oxford University Press.

Breschi, S. and Lissonie, F. (2001), 'Localised knowledge spillovers versus innovative milieux: knowledge 'tacitness' reconsidered'. *Papers in Regional Science*, **80**: 255–273.

Breschi, S. and Malerba, F. (2001), 'The geography of innovation and economic clustering: some introductory notes'. *Industrial and Corporate Change*, **10**(4): 817–833.

Brown, R. (2000), 'Clusters, supply chains and local embeddeness in Fyrstad'. *European Urban and Regional Studies*, **7**(4): 291–306.

Buckley, P. J., Pass, C., and Prescott, K. (1988), 'Measures of international competitiveness: a critical survey'. *Journal of Marketing Management*, **4**: 175–200.

Cairncross, F. (1997), *The death of distance*. London: Orion Business Books.

Cohen, S. and Fields, G. (1999), 'Social capital and capital gains in Silicon Valley'. *California Management Review*, **41**(2): 108–130.

Conroy, M. (1975), *Regional economic diversification*. New York: Praeger.

Cooke, P. and Morgan K. (1998), *The associational economy*. Oxford: Oxford University Press.

Council on Competitiveness (2001), 'US competitiveness 2001: strengths, vulnerability and long-term priorities' (www.compete.org).

Coyle, D. (1997), *The weightless world: strategies for managing the digital economy*. London: Capstone.

Coyle, D. (2001), *Paradoxes of prosperity: why the new capitalism benefits all*. London: Texere Publishing.

Crouch, C. and Farrell, H. (2001), 'Great Britain: falling through the holes in the network concept', in C. Crouch, P. Le Galés, C. Trogilia, and H. Voelzkow (eds), *Local production system in Europe: rise or demise?* Oxford: Oxford University Press, pp. 161–211.

Crouch, C. Le Galés, P., Trogilia, C., and Voelzkow, H. (2001), *Local production system in Europe: rise or demise?* Oxford: Oxford University Press.

DETR (2000), *Planning for clusters*. London: HMSO.

Doeringer, P. B. and Terka, D. G. (1996), 'Why do industries cluster?', in U. Staber, N. Schaefer, and B. Sharma (eds), *Business networks: prospects for regional development*. Berlin: Walter de Gruyter, pp. 175–189.

Drejer, I., Kristensen, F. and Laursen, K. (1999), 'Cluster studies as a basis for industrial policy: the case of Denmark'. *Industry and Innovation*, **6**(2): 171–190.

Duranton, G. and Puga, D. (2000), 'Diversity and specialisation in cities: why, where and when does it matter?' *Urban Studies*, **37**(3): 533–555.

Ellison, G. and Glaeser, E. L. (1997),'Geographic concentration in US manufacturing industries: a dartboard approach'. *The Journal of Political Economy*, **105**: 889–927.

Enright, M. (1996), 'Regional clusters and economic development: a research agenda', in U. Staber, N. Schaefer, and B. Sharma (eds), *Business networks: prospects for regional development*. Berlin: Walter de Gruyter, pp. 190–213.

Enright, M. (2001), 'Regional clusters: what we know and what we should know'. Paper presented at the Kiel Institute International Workshop on Innovation Clusters and Interregional Competition, November 12–13 .

Enright, M. and Ffowcs-Williams, I. (2001), 'Local partnership, clusters and SME globalisation'. OECD Workshop paper (www.oecd.org).

Feldman, M. (2000), 'Location and innovation: the new economic geography of innovation, spillovers, and agglomeration', in G. L. Clark, M. Feldman, and M. Gertler (eds), *Oxford handbook of economic geography*. Oxford: Oxford University Press, pp. 373–394.

Feser, E. J. (1998), 'Old and new theories of industry clusters', in M. Steiner (ed.), *Clusters and regional specialisation: on geography, technology and networks*. London: Pion, pp. 18–40.

Feser, E. J. and Bergman, E. M. (2000), 'National industry cluster templates: a framework for regional cluster analysis'. *Regional Studies*, **34**(1): 1–20.

Fisher, E. and Reuben, R. (2000), 'Industrial clusters and SME promotion in developing countries'. Commonwealth Trade Enterprise Paper Number 3, London: Commonwealth Secretariat.

Fritz, O., Mahringer, H., and Valdenama, M. (1998), 'A risk-oriented analysis of regional clusters', in M. Steiner (ed.), *Clusters and regional specialisation: on geography, technology and networks*. London: Pion, pp. 181–191.

Fujita, M., Krugman, P., and Venables, A. (2000), *The spatial economy: cities regions and international trade*. Cambridge, MA: MIT Press.

Glaeser, E., Kallal, H., Scheinkman, J. A., and Shleifer, A. (1992), 'Growth in cities'. *Journal of Political Economy*, **100**(6): 1126–1152.

Glasmeier, A. (2000), 'Economic geography in practice: local economic development policy', in G. L. Clark, M. Feldman, and M. Gertler (eds), *Oxford handbook of economic geography*. Oxford: Oxford University Press, pp. 559–579.

Gordon, I. R. and McCann, P. (2000), 'Industrial clusters: complexes, agglomeration and/or social networks?' *Urban Studies*, **37**(3): 513–532.

Grabher, G. (1993), 'The weakness of strong ties: the lock-in of regional development in the Ruhr area', in *The embedded firm: on the socio-economics of industrial networks*. London: Routledge, pp. 255–277.

Gray, J. (1998), *False dawn: the delusions of global capitalism*. London: Granta Books.

Hanson, G. (2000), 'Firms, workers, and the geographic concentration of economic activity', in G. L. Clark, M. Feldman, and M. Gertler (eds), *Oxford handbook of economic geography*. Oxford: Oxford University Press, pp. 477–494.

Harfield, T. (1998), 'Strategic management and Michael Porter: a postmodern reading'. *Electronic Journal of Radical Organisation*, **4**: 1.

Harrison, B. (1992), 'Industrial districts: old wine in new bottles?' *Regional Studies*, **26**: 469–483.

Harrison, B., Kelley, M., and Gant, J. (1996), 'Innovative firm behaviour and local milieu: exploring the intersection of agglomeration, firm effects, and technological change'. *Economic Geography*, **72**: 233–258.

Hassink, R. (1997), 'Localised industrial learning and innovation policies'. *European Planning Studies*, **5**: 279–282.

Held, J. R. (1996), 'Clusters as an economic development tool: beyond the pitfalls'. *Economic Development Quarterly*, **10**(3): 249–261.

Henderson, V., Kuncoro, A., and Turner, M. (1995), 'Industrial development in cities'. *Journal of Political Economy*, **103**(5): 1067–1090.

Hudson, R. (1999), ' "The learning economy, the learning firm and the learning region' ": a sympathetic critique of the limits to learning'. *European Urban and Regional Studies*, **6**: 59–72.

Jacobs, D. and De Jong, M. (1992), 'Industrial clusters and the competitiveness of the Netherlands'. *De Economist*, **140**(2): 233–252.

Johnston, D. (2001), 'Opening remarks in world congress on local clusters'. Paris: OECD-DATAR: 7–9.

Keeble, D. and Wilkinson, F. (eds) (2000), *High technology clusters, networking and collective learning in Europe*. Aldershot: Ashgate.

Keeble, D. E. and Nachum, L. (2002), 'Why do business service firms cluster? Small consultancies, clustering and decentralisation in London and Southern England'. *Transactions of the Institute of British Geographers* (forthcoming).

Keep, E. and Mayhew, K. (1999), 'Towards the knowledge-driven economy: some policy issues'. *Renewal*, **7**(4): 50–85.

Klein, J. (2001), 'A critique of competitive advantage'. Paper presented at the Critical Management Studies Conference, University of Manchester, July 2001.

Klein, N. (2000), *No logo*. London: Flamingo.

Krugman, P. (1991), *Geography and trade*. Cambridge, MA: MIT Press.

Krugman, P. (1994), 'Productivity and competitiveness', in *Peddling prosperity*. New York: W. W. Norton, pp. 268–280 (Appendix to Chapter 10).

Krugman, P. (1996), 'Competitiveness: a dangerous obsession. Myths and realities of US competitiveness', in *Pop internationalism*. Cambridge, MA: MIT Press, pp. 3–24 and 87–104 (Chs 1 and 6 respectively).

Krugman, P. (1997), *Pop internationalism*. Cambridge, MA: MIT Press.

Lagendijk, A. and Charles, D. (1999), 'Clustering as a new growth strategy for regional economies? A discussion of new forms of regional industrial policy in the UK', in *Boosting innovation: the cluster approach*. Paris: OECD, pp. 127–153.

Lawson, C. and Lorenz, E. (1999), 'Collective learning, tacit knowledge and regional innovative capacity'. *Regional Studies*, **33**(4): 305–317.

Leamer, E. and Storper, M. (2001), 'The economic geography of the internet age'. Working Paper 8450, National Bureau of Economic Research, Washington.

Loasby, B. (1998), 'Industrial districts as knowledge communities', in M. Bellet and C. L'Harmet (eds), *Industry, space and competition: the contributions of economists of the past*. Cheltenham: Edward Elgar, pp. 70–85.

Lovering, J. (1999), 'Theory led by policy? The inadequacies of the "new regionalism" '. *International Journal of Urban and Economic Research*, **23**: 379–395.

Malmberg, A. (1996), 'Industrial geography: agglomeration and local milieu'. *Progress in Human Geography*, **20**(3): 392–403.

Malmberg, A. (2002), 'Why the cluster is causing continuing confusion – despite being potentially a core concept in economic geography'. Paper presented at the Cluster Workshop, University of Lund, Sweden, April 5.

Malmberg, A. and Maskell, P. (1997), 'Toward an explanation of regional specialization and industry agglomeration'. *European Planning Studies*, **5**(1): 25–41.

Markusen, A. (1996), 'Sticky places in slippery space, economic geography'. *Economic Geography*, **72**: 293–313.

Markusen, A. (1999), 'Fuzzy concepts, scanty evidence and policy distance: the case for rigour and policy relevance in critical regional studies'. *Regional Studies*, **33**: 869–886.

Marshall, A. (1890), *Principles of economics*. London: Macmillan.

Martin, R. L. (2001), 'Geography and public policy: the case of the missing agenda'. *Progress in Human Geography*, **25**(2): 189–210.

Martin, R. L. and Sunley, P. (1998), 'Slow convergence? The new endogenous growth theory and regional development'. *Economic Geography*, **74**: 201–227.

Maskell, P. (2001), 'Towards a knowledge-based theory of the geographical cluster'. *Industrial and Corporate Change*, **10**(4): 921–943.

May, W., Mason, C., and Pinch, S. (2001), 'Explaining industrial agglomeration: the case of the British high-fidelity industry'. *Geoforum*, **32**(3): 363–376.

Miller, P., Botham, R., Martin, R. L., and Moore, B. (2001), *Business clusters in the UK: a first assessment*. London: Department of Trade and Industry.

Nachum, L. and Keeble, D. E. (1999), 'Neo-Marshallian nodes, global networks and firm competitiveness: the media cluster of central London'. Working Paper 158, ESRC Centre for Business Research, University of Cambridge.

Norton, R. D. (2001), *Creating the new economy: the entrepreneur and US resurgence*. Cheltenham: Edward Elgar.

O'Brien, R. (1992), *Global financial integration: the end of geography?* London: Pinter.

O'Malley, E. and Vanegeraat, C. (2000), 'Industry clusters and Irish indigenous manufacturing: limits of the Porter view'. *Economic and Social Review*, **31**(4): 55–80.

OECD (1999), *Boosting innovation: the cluster approach*. Paris: OECD.

OECD (2001), *Innovative clusters: drivers of national innovation systems*. Paris: OECD.

OECD-DATAR (2001), *World congress on local clusters*. Paris: OECD.

Ohmae, K. (1995), *The end of the nation state: the rise of regional economies*. London: HarperCollins.

Pandit, N., Cook, G., and Swann, P. (1999), 'The dynamics of industrial clustering in UK financial services'. Working paper no. 399, Manchester Business School.

Paniccia, I. (2002), *Industrial districts: evolution and competition in Italian firms*, Cheltenham: Edward Elgar.

Perry, M. (1999), 'Clusters last stand'. *Planning Practice and Research*, **14**(2): 149–152.

Pinch, S. and Henry, N. (1999), 'Paul Krugman's geographical economics, industrial clustering and the British motor sport industry'. *Regional Studies*, **33**(9): 815–827.

Porter, M. E. (1990), *The competitive advantage of nations*. London: Macmillan.

Porter, M. E. (1995), 'The competitive advantage of the inner city'. *Harvard Business Review*, **74**: 61–78.

Porter, M. E. (1996), 'Competitive advantage, agglomeration economies, and regional policy'. *International Regional Science Review*, **19**(1): 85–94.

Porter, M. E. (1998*a*), *On competition*. Cambridge, M A: Harvard Business School Press.

Porter, M. E. (1998*b*), 'Location, clusters and the "new" microeconomics of competition'. *Business Economics*, **33**(1): 7–17.

Porter, M. E. (1998*c*), 'Clusters and the new economics of competitiveness'. *Harvard Business Review*, December: 77–90.

468   DECONSTRUCTING CLUSTERS

Porter, M. E. (2000*a*), 'Locations, clusters and company strategy', in G. L. Clark, M. Feldman, and M. Gertler (eds), *Oxford handbook of economic geography*. Oxford: Oxford University Press, pp. 253–274.

Porter, M. E. (2000*b*), 'Clusters and government policy'. *Wirtschaftspolitische Blätter*, 47(2): 144–154.

Porter, M. E. (2000*c*), 'Location, competition and economic development: local clusters in the global economy'. *Economic Development Quarterly*, 14(1): 15–31.

Porter, M. E. (2001), 'Regions and the new economics of competition', in A. Scott (eds), *Global city regions*. Oxford: Blackwell, pp. 139–152.

Porter, M. E. (2002), 'Regional foundations of competitiveness and implications for government policy'. Paper presented at the Department of Trade and Industry Workshop on Regional Competitiveness, DTI, London.

Porter, M. E. and Solvell, O. (1998), 'The role of geography in the process of innovation and the sustainable competitive advantage of firms', in A. Chandler, P. Hagstrom, and O. Solvell (eds), *The dynamic firm: the role of technology strategy, organizations and regions*. New York: Oxford University Press, pp. 440–457.

Porter, M. and Ackerman, F. D. (2001), 'Regional clusters of innovation'. Washington: Council on Competitiveness (www.compete.org).

Porter, M. E. and van Opstal, D. (2001), 'US competitiveness 2001: strengths, vulnerability and longterm priorities'. Washington: Council on Competitiveness (www.compete.org).

Pouder, R. and St John, C. H. (1996), 'Hot spots and blind spots: geographical clusters of firms and innovation'. *Academy of Management Review*, 21(4): 1192–1125.

Prevezer, M. (1997), 'The dynamics of industrial clustering in biotechnology'. *Small Business Economics*, 9: 255–271.

Rodriguez-Pose, A. (2001), 'Local production systems and economic performance in France, Germany, Italy and the UK', in C. Crouch, P. Le Galés, C. Trogilia, and H. Voelzkow (eds), *Local production system in Europe: rise or demise?* Oxford: Oxford University Press, pp. 25–45.

Roelandt, T. and den Hertog, P. (1999), 'Cluster analysis and cluster-based policy making in OECD countries: an introduction to the theme', in *Boosting innovation: the cluster approach*. Paris: OECD, ch. 1, pp. 9–23.

Rosenfeld, S. A. (1997), 'Bringing business clusters into the mainstream of economic development'. *European Planning Studies*, 5(1): 3–23.

Rosenfeld, S. (2001), 'Backing into clusters: retrofitting public policies'. Paper available (www.oecd.org).

Sabel. C. (1989), 'Flexible specialisation and the re-emergence of regional economies', in P. Hirst and J. Zeitlin (eds), *Reversing industrial decline: industrial structure and policies in Britain and her competitors*. Oxford: Berg, pp. 17–70.

Sainsbury, D. (1999), 'Biotechnology clusters: report of a team led by Lord Sainsbury, Minister for Science', London: DTI/TSO.

Schmitz, H. (2000), 'Does local co-operation matter? Evidence from industrial clusters in South Asia and Latin America'. *Oxford Development Studies*, 28(3): 323–336.

Schmitz, H. and Nadvi, K. (1999), 'Clustering and industrialization: introduction'. *World Development*, 27(9): 1503–1514.

Scott, A. J. (1988), *New industrial spaces: flexible production organization and regional development in North America and Western Europe*. London: Pion.

Scott, A. J. (1998), *Regions and the world economy*. Oxford: Oxford University Press.

Scott, A. J. (eds) (2001), *Global city regions: trends, theory and policy*. Oxford: Oxford University Press.

Shohet, S. (1998), 'Clustering and UK biotechnology', in G. M. P. Swann, M. Prevezer, and D. Stout (eds), *The dynamics of industrial clustering: international comparisons in computing and biotechnology*. Oxford: Oxford University Press, pp. 194–224.

Simmie, J. and Sennett, J. (1999*a*), 'Innovation in the London metropolitan region', in D. Hart, J. Simmie, P. Wood, and J. Sennett (eds), 'Innovative clusters and competitive cities in the UK and Europe'. Working Paper no. 182, Oxford Brookes School of Planning.

Simmie, J. and Sennett, J. (1999*b*), 'Innovative clusters: global or local linkages?' *National Institute Economic Review*, **170**: 87–98.

Segal Quince Wicksteed (2001), *Study of the information technology, communications and electronics sectors*. Cambridge: SQW Ltd.

Steiner, M. (eds) (1998), *Clusters and regional specialisation: on geography, technology and networks*. London: Pion.

Steiner, M. and Hartmann, C. (1998), 'Learning with clusters: a case study from Upper Styria'. *European Research in Regional Science*, **8**: 211–225.

Steiner, M. and Hartmann, C. (2001), 'Looking for the invisible: material and immaterial dimensions of clusters. Paper presented at the Regional Studies Association Annual Conference on "Regionalising the Knowledge Economy"', November 21, London.

Storper, M. (1997), *The regional world: territorial development in a global economy*. New York: Guilford Press.

Swann, G. M. P. (1998), 'Towards a model of clustering in high technology industries', in G. M. P. Swann, M. Prevezer, and D. Stout (eds), *The dynamics of industrial clustering: international comparisons in computing and biotechnology*. Oxford: Oxford University Press, pp. 52–76.

Swann, G. M. P. (2002), 'The implications of clusters: some reflections'. Paper presented at the Clusters Conference, Manchester Business School, April 18.

Swann, G. M. P. and Prevezer, M. (1996), 'A comparison of the dynamics of industrial clustering in computing and biotechnology'. *Research Policy*, **25**: 139–157.

Swann, G. M. P., Prevezer, M., and Stout, D. (eds) (1998), *The dynamics of industrial clustering: international comparisons in computing and biotechnology*. Oxford: Oxford University Press.

Temple, P. (1998), 'Clusters and competitiveness: a policy perspective', in G. M. P. Swann, M. Prevezer, and D. Stout (eds), *The dynamics of industrial clustering: international comparisons in computing and biotechnology*. Oxford: Oxford University Press, pp. 257–307.

Turner, A. (2001), 'The competitiveness of nations: myths and delusions', in *Just capital: the liberal economy*. London: Macmillan, pp. 23–50.

van den Berg, L., Braun, E., and van Winden, W. (2001), 'Growth clusters in European cities: an integral approach'. *Urban Studies*, **38**(1): 186–206.

venables, A. J. (1996), 'Localization of industry and trade performance'. *Oxford Review of Economic Policy*, **12**(3): 52–60.

World Bank (2000), *Electronic conference on clusters*. Washington, D. C.: World Bank.

Index

Abbate, J 162
Abbott 84
absorptive capacity, and knowledge
    diffusion 38–9, 40, 41, 43
Acer 251
Acer Capital America 253
Ackerman, F D 434
ACMA 177, 178
Acz, Z 335
Adams, J D 379, 382, 385, 386, 387
address models 30
Advanced Magnetics 272, 276
agency theory, and spin-off firms 12,
    201–4, 219–20
agglomeration:
  and categories of 412
  and cross-sectoral differences 7
  and diverse phenomena of 55
  and drivers of 57
  and evolutionary theory 4
  and geographical specificities 55–6
  and innovation 35
    patterns of 54, 68–9
  and intersectoral differences 55,
    56–7
  and intersectoral specificities 54
  and Italian industrial sectors 61–3
    data and methodology 63–4
    quantitative analysis 64–9
  and learning regimes 54, 57, 68–9
  and location-wide drivers 57–8
    model of 58–61
  and measures of 57
  and sectoral specificities 23, 54, 55–6
  and sectoral variability 55
Agrawal, A 349, 362
Agricultural Research Service 140
Aharonson, B 360
Aitken, B 353, 354
Akerloff, G 81, 93, 95, 301
Albert, R 43, 48
Alcacer, J 366
Allayer 253

Allen, B 34
Allen, R 37, 38, 418
alliances, and multiple networks in
    biotechnology 265, 268–71
Almeida, P 261, 360
Altenburg, T 457
AMD 252
American Home Products 263
American Machine and Foundry 177
Amgen 84, 143, 262, 285
Amin, A 177, 179, 436, 444, 447, 459
Amit, R 213
AMS 147
An, M 34
Andersen, E 85, 136–7
Anderson, P 204, 220
Anderson, S P 30
Anderson, T 141
Anselin, L 346
Anton, J J 201, 202, 203, 204,
    210, 219, 220
Antonelli, C 55
Aoki, M 240
AOL 147
Apollo Computer 304
Apple 100
Applied Biotechnology 272
Applied Materials 251–2
Appold, S A 137
Argule 272
Ariad 276
Arora, Ashish 115, 356, 359
ARPANET 152
Arrow, K J 309, 347
Art Cities 102
Arthur, W 59
Asheim, B 140, 436
assymetric knowledge 8, 81, 93
    and Europe-USA innovation
        gap 81, 103–4
    and regional innovation systems 95
AstraZeneca 84
Athreye, Suma 115